An acknowledged authority on the countryside and its history, Dr Oliver Rackham is a Fellow of Corpus Christi College. He has also written *Trees and Woodland in the British Landscape*, *The Last Forest*, *The Illustrated History of the Countryside* (winner of the Sir Peter Kent Conservation Award and the *Natural World* Book of the Year Award), and (with Dr J.A. Moody) *The Making of the Cretan Landscape*, which won the Runciman Prize.

THE
HISTORY
OF THE
COUNTRYSIDE

OLIVER
RACKHAM

PHOENIX
GIANT

A PHOENIX GIANT PAPERBACK

First published in Great Britain by J. M. Dent in 1986
First paperback edition published in 1987
This paperback edition published in 1997
by Phoenix, a division of Orion Books Ltd,
Orion House, 5 Upper St Martin's Lane,
London WC2H 9EA

A CIP catalogue record for this book is available
from the British Library.

ISBN: 0 75380 173 6

Printed and bound in Great Britain by
Butler & Tanner Ltd, Frome and London

CONTENTS

LIST OF PLATES

Between pages 208 and 209

ACKNOWLEDGEMENTS

Topographical history is an interest given me by my father, the late Mr G.H. Rackham. I was fortunate enough to be instructed in the Cambridge ecological tradition of Dr A.S. Watt and his successors. Among these, I am specially grateful to Dr D.E. Coombe for introducing me to historical ecology and to the workings of woods and heaths, and for a quarter of a century of visits to wonderful places – notably to the Lizard Peninsula which has been a resort of Cambridge botanists for 300 years.

Historical ecology sometimes involves the set-piece methods of scientific research: problems defined in advance and information collected wherewith to solve them. But in many areas this will not work because the facts are too thinly scattered to justify a deliberate search. Much of the material for this book has come my way in the course of other researches: facts have turned up and have been filed away until enough has been hoarded to suggest questions and answers. Insights may also come at random from travels made, or documents read, for some quite different purpose. I went to Texas to discuss Cretan archaeology, and what I saw made me revise my views on hedges. Almost everything in this book has come into my mind through some friend or invitation or visit or reading, and I cannot hope to acknowledge them all except in a general way.

For academic and financial help I am indebted to Corpus Christi College, Cambridge, Cambridge University Botany School, the Natural Environment Research Council, and the Nature Conservancy Council. Among individual Cambridge botanists my thanks are due to Dr H.J.B. Birks, Professor C.D. Pigott, the late Dr J. Rishbeth, Mr P.D. Sell, Dr S.M. Walters, Professor R.G. West, and especially my old friend the late Mr W.H. Palmer. Among historians I must mention Mr D.P. Dymond and Mrs C.P. Hall. Those who have helped me in other parts of England include Dr Margaret Atherden, Mr J. Bingley, Mr B. Cave, Mrs V. Chesher, Mr and Mrs J. Hart, Mrs K. Hayward, Mrs H. Heygate, Dr and the late Mrs J. Litchfield, Dr C. Lovatt and Professor and Mrs P.M. Warren. In Wales I have been helped by Professor W. Linnard and by Dr P.F. Williams and his colleagues; in Scotland by Mr R. Callander, Mrs A. McBurney and the late Professor C.B. McBurney, and Dr M.D. Swaine; and in Ireland by Dr R. Bradshaw and his colleagues. In Europe I am grateful to Dr J. Bintliff, Dr D. Moreno, Dr J.A. Moody, Professor A.M. Snodgrass, the late Madame and Monsieur F. Vuillermet, and Professor P.M. Warren. For American parallels I acknowledge the kindness and hospitality of Dr Kathy Biddick, Dr Susan P. Bratton, Dr R. Brewer, Dr D. Houston, Dr J.A. Moody, and Dr P. White.

The work would not have been possible without the friendly cooperation of many landowners and keepers of archives and of the staff of the Map Room, Cambridge University Library.

I thank Merton College, Oxford for permission to reproduce the map of Gamlingay 1601 (Fig. 2.2); the University of Cambridge Committee of Aerial Photography for permission to reproduce the aerial photographs in the plate section; also Christopher Taylor (Fig. 12.1), D.E. Coombe and John Baker, Publishers (Fig. 13.1), Paul Drury (Fig. 8.4), Max Hooper and Ann Hart (Fig.

9.4), the Natural Environment Research Council, Institute of Terrestrial Ecology (Fig. 4.1); also the British Library and the Syndics of the Cambridge University Library.

The text was read by Mrs J. Evans and by Mr and Mrs C.E. Ranson, to whom I am grateful for their encouragement and for many valuable criticisms.

To Susan Ranson
and in memory of Colin Ranson
my trusty friends and helpers

North Rona

ORKNEY

Cape Wrath

Lord Reay's Forest
CAITHNESS
SUTHERLAND

St Kilda

Outer Hebrides

ROSS & CROMARTY
Beinn Eighe
ELGIN
NAIRN
BANFF
Tomatin
ABERDEEN
Abernethy
Bulgownie
Deeside
Maryculter
INVERNESS
KINCARDINE
Skye
ANGUS
Auchattan's
Glen Lyon
PERTHSHIRE
Blairdores
ARGYLL
Loch Lomond
FIFE
Menteith
Isle of May
STIRLING
Loch Leven
BUTE
Bannockburn
Edinburgh
Paisley
Cumbernauld
BERWICK
Yadrow
Lammermuir
Farne Islands
Hills
LANARK
Kelso
Ayr
PEEBLES
Jedburgh
Chillingham
Ettrick
NORTHUMBERLAND
AYRSHIRE
DUMFRIES
Kielder
Newminster Abbey
KIRKCUDBRIGHT
Galloway
Sweetheart
Winddarda
North York Moors
WIGTOWN
Abbey
Inglewood
DURHAM
&
Forest
Weardale
Durham
Pickering Forest
CUMBERLAND
Teesdale
Tees
Lake
WESTMOR-
Julian
DONEGAL
LONDON-
ANTRIM
District
LAND
N. RIDING
Park
Whitby
DERRY
Drapersown
Fawcett Forest
Tabular Hills
TYRONE
DOWN
Furness Abbey
Jervaulx
Rievaulx
FERMANAGH
ARMAGH
Malham
Four-
Geltres Forest
SLIGO
LEITRIM
Craven
tains
Stamford Bridge
MAYO
CAVAN
LOUTH
Kirkstall
York
EAST RIDING
ROSCOMMON
LONGFORD
LANCASHIRE
Selby
Bewerley
Holder-
GALWAY
WESTMEATH
MEATH
Rossen-
Bentley
WEST
ness
Wigan
dale
Grange RIDING
OFFALY
DUBLIN
Manchester
Peak
LINDSEY
Dublin
ANGLESEY
POINT
CHESHIRE
Tideswell
CLARE
LEIX
Glen of the Downs
Vaynol
DENBIGH
Mold
Rudheath
NOTTINGHAM
LINCOLNSHIRE
KILDARE
Snowdon
Ridley
Dieulacres
DERBY
HOLLAND
KILKENNY
Glendalough
CAERNARVON
Llangollen
STAFFARD
Needwood
KESTE-
LIMERICK
CARLOW
WICKLOW
Harlech
SHROPSHIRE
Forest
LEICESTER
VEN
TIPPERARY
WEXFORD
MERIONETH
MONTGOM-
Wellington
RUTLAND
ISLE
KERRY
Enniscorthy
ERY
Stiperstones
Sutton Coldfield
NORFOLK
WATERFORD
Traeth Mawr
Domen
Cleo
Skyre
Arden
HUN-
TING-
Killarney
Strata Florida
Cumhir
Aston
NORCS.
WARWICK
DON
ELY
CORK
RADNOR
NORTHAMPTON
CAMBRIDGE
CARDIGAN
Mac
Malverns
SUFFOLK
CAERMARTHEN
ias
BEDFORD
PEMBROKE
Dynevor
HEREFORD
Tewkesbury
HERTFORD
Great
Rockwood Forest
BUCKS
Skokholm
Forest
Forest
Carmarthen
of Dean
GLOS.
OXFORD
ESSEX
Reose
BERKSHIRE
MIDDLESEX
GLAMORGAN
Braydon Forest
Penarth
Malmesbury
SURREY
KENT
SOMERSET
WILTSHIRE
Great
Urchfont
HAMPSHIRE
Lundy I.
Mendip
WEST
EAST
Braunton
Exmoor
Maure
Grovely
SUSSEX
Bideford
Holland
Sedgly
Porton Down
Queen Dart
Nerroche
Clarendon
Fordingbridge
ISLE OF WIGHT
Crediton
Forest
New
DEVON
Exeter
DORSET
Horton
Forest
Shown at larger scale
CORNWALL
Bodmin
Moretonhamp-
Beall
Piddletown
Moor
Dartmoor
stead
Isle of Portland
Brownsea Island
Totnes
Holne
Helford River
Scilly
Land's End
Mousehole
Hayle
Isles
Goonhilly Down
The Lizard

X

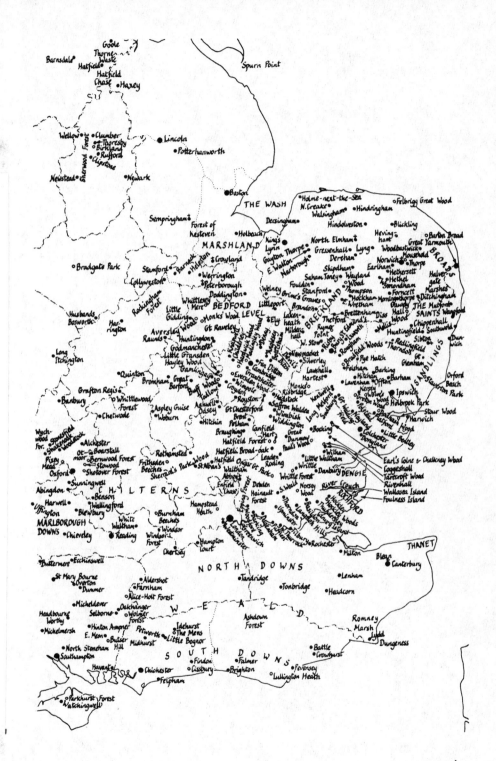

Goole
Barnsdale   Thorne Waste
           Hatfield
           Hatfield
           Chase •Haxey   Spurn Point

                                                            THE WASH

Wellow •Clumber
        •Thoresby
        •Birkland   •Lincoln
        •Rufford
Newstead   •Clipstone
                                  •Potterhanworth
Newstead   •Newark

                                        •Boston

                     Sempringham•   •Holme-next-the-Sea   •Felbrigg Great Wood
                                                   N.Creake
                              Forest of   •Walsingham •Hindringham
                              Kesteven   Dersingham
                                    •Holbeach MARSHLAND   Hindolveston   •Blickling
                                                King's   Heving-   •Barton Broad
•Bradgate Park   •Crowland   Lynn North Elmham Lyng• ham• Woodbastwick Great Yarmouth
                     Stamford• Barnack• Hilgton   Gayton Thorpe Gressenhall• Dereham   Norwich• Moushold BROADS
     •Collyweston   •Werrington   E.Weston   Earlham• Hethersett Halver-
                                  •Peterborough   Welney Narborough Shipdham• Wayland Hethel Shotesham gate
                              Little Doddington   Foulden Stanford   Thompson• Wood• Forncett Marshes
     •Husbands   Rockingham Whittlesey   Grime's Graves Brandon• Wretham• Hockham Morningthorpe• Ditchingham
      Bosworth   Forest   Mere Littleport   Laken-   Thetford Brettenham Diss• Hall• THE
                 Monks Wood BEDFORD •Ely heath   Mildenhall• Rymer• Bridge St Edmund's• Melks Wood SAINTS Wangford
•Harr-   Gidding Wood LEVEL   Witney Mildenhall   •W.Stow Point Bury St Edmund• Chippenhall Southwold
 ington   Aversley Wood Gt Raveley   Newmarket• Bowtham Brasfield Woods Redlingfield Sibton Dun-
Long Raunds Huntingdon• Hayley Wood   Monks• Thornton Rye Hatch Felsham Glenham wich
•Itchington Godmanchester Fen Ditton   Risbridge• Silverley Barking Orford
          Little Gransden Cambridge Newton   Lawshall Lavenham Offton Beach
     •Quinton Bromham Gamlingay Buff Wood   Haverstock Kersey Barham Park
•Grafton Regis Gt   Everden Wood Croydon•   Melford• Offton •Wolves Stour Wood
•Banbury •Whittlewood Barton Napole• Royston   Saffron Walden St Helen's •Ipswich Holbrook Park
           Forest Aspley Guise Hitchin Blackstock   Wimbish Wickham Hood Little Bentley Harwich
     •Chetwode   Woburn   Broad   Widdington Bocking• Colchester Weeley
Wych- Stansfield   Odsey Braughing• Canfield   Great   Paul's Wood   Earl's Colne & Chalkney Wood
wood Shotesham   Alchester Hatfield Forest   Dunmow   •Witham   Coggeshall
For. Woodstock Ot- Boarstall Rothamsted   Leaden Little Waltham Yarcroft Wood
Pixly •moor Bernwood Forest Frithsden   St Alban's Park   Roding   Writtle DENGIE Rivenhall
Mead •Oxford Stowood Shotover Forest Beeches   Waltham Abbey's Norsey River Crouch Wallasea Island
•Abingdon   Sunningwell   Sherwood's Park Wood   Enfield Debden Wood   ROCHFORD Foulness Island
•Harwell •Benson CHILTERNS Chase Hainault   Forest
Uffington Wallingford Burnham   Forest   Hampstead
MARLBOROUGH Blewbury White   Beeches Heath   London
DOWNS •Chieveley Waltham Windsor Windsor Greenwich Lewisham Rochester   THANET
•Buttermere •Ecchinswell •Reading Forest Hampton Milton   Blean• Canterbury
St Mary Bourne• Aldershot• Court NORTH DOWNS   •Lenham
Overton• Farnham• Tandridge•   Canterbury
Dummer• Alice-Holt Forest •Tonbridge •Headcorn
•Micheldever Oakhanger• WEALD
Headbourne Selborne• Wolmer Ashdown   Romney
Worthy Hinton Ampner• Forest Petworth Forest   Marsh
•Michelmersh E.Mean• •Idehurst   •Lydd
North Stoneham• Butser Midhurst •The Mens   Dungeness
•Southampton Hill Little Bognor •Battle
       Hayling• SOUTH Findon• Falmer• Crowhurst
•Chichester •Cissbury DOWNS Pevensey
Parkhurst Forest Felpham• •Brighton •Lullington Heath
•Watchingwell

xi

PREFACE

This book is about the ordinary countryside. In my south Norfolk childhood I wondered why roads had bends, why lanes were sunk into the ground, what dogwood and spindle were doing in hedges, why fields were of odd shapes, why elms stopped abruptly just north of Bungay, and so on. These are difficult questions, and their roots go deep into the past.

The ordinary landscape of Britain has been made both by the natural world and by human activities, interacting with each other over many centuries. This is not an easy idea to grasp. In the last century people (that is, writers) often thought of the country as the world of Nature in contrast to the town. The opposite exaggeration now prevails: that the rural landscape, no less than Trafalgar Square, is merely the result of human design and ambition. Most articles in such journals as *Landscape History* deal with the landscape as artefact, and hardly mention the other player in the game. In popular belief this view is simplified into the 'Enclosure-Act Myth', the notion that the countryside is not merely an artefact but a very recent one. This notion is quite prevalent even among Ministers of Agriculture, and exerts its defeatist influence against the conservation of the landscape.

In reality the countryside records human default as well as design, and much of it has a life of its own independent of human activity. Trees are not just things that people plant, like gateposts: a friend of mine has cut a good crop of ash trees which have arisen where his predecessor planted pines. The landscape ranges from the almost wholly artificial, like the middle of a barley field, to the almost wholly natural, like the moors of Caithness. Most of this book is about 'semi-natural' areas – those that are neither virgin vegetation nor planted crops. With many features, such as ponds and hedges, it is still not possible to say where Nature stops and human activity begins.

The topics of this book bring together the inanimate world of climate, soil, and landforms; the world of plants and animals; the world of archaeology; and the world of historical documents. I have no chapter on barrows, for these are well described in archaeological books; but I am concerned with the less familiar questions of what the landscape around barrows looked like when they were made, and whether any of it still exists. Nor am I concerned with villas and other recognized archaeological 'sites' – villages and hamlets, deserted villages, garden remains, standing buildings, etc. – except when these have a biological dimension or tell us about the landscape at large. Nor shall I discuss the details of vegetation (eg. the different kinds of salt-marsh) unless they have a known historical dimension. Natural landforms are also excluded, except where they can be confused with artefacts.

The core of the book is woodland and wood-pasture. This does not only reflect my own interests; woods are indeed at the heart of historical ecology. They are inherently stable and long-lasting, and have outlived many changes in human affairs. They take us straight back to the Middle Ages and, with imagination and further knowledge, conjure up before us the wholly natural landscape into which civilization was first introduced. They contain in themselves evidence of at least a thousand years of care and use. Many of them happen to preserve evidence of the non-woodland landscape as well.

I have concentrated on particular regions and places – Eastern England, the Lizard Peninsula, Little Gransden, etc. This partly results from my own interests and those of my colleagues; but it is also more instructive to consider and connect the woods, meadows, moors, etc. of the same area than to draw examples of these from unrelated areas. Also the areas chosen are where the four worlds of this book are all well represented. In South Wales, in contrast, surprisingly much of the ancient landscape has survived industrialization, but there are few pollen diagrams, few medieval documents, few maps earlier than 1750, few timber buildings, few ancient woods in good condition – a historical ecology can be written, but it is hard work. But let me not be discouraging; the reader who thinks I have been unfair to his part of the country will find the most satisfying rejoinder in writing his own book.

My time-span is the *post-glacial* (or *present interglacial*) period – the 12,000 years of temperate climate since the end of the last Ice Age. There have been at least five previous interglacials, spaced out between Ice Ages over the last million years. In the first half of the present interglacial the vegetation was almost wholly natural – largely wildwood peopled by Mesolithic men. Civilization began quite suddenly with the arrival of Neolithic men in about 4000 BC. The second half of the post-glacial is concerned with the development of the cultural landscape.

This book deals particularly with the Middle Ages and earlier. I do not disparage eighteenth- and nineteenth-century contributions to the landscape, but they are well known and easily over-emphasized. The outstanding mystery is what happened to the English landscape in the Dark Ages between the Romans and the literate Anglo-Saxons (AD 410–700). Most of us were taught that the Angles and Saxons moved as pioneer settlers into an abandoned land, whose previous inhabitants had fled or been slain. Many recent excavations reveal a gradual changeover with little apparent effect on the landscape; sometimes, as at Rivenhall (Essex),[1] it is not easy to tell at what point the Romano-Britons turned into Anglo-Saxons. The ecological evidence strongly favours continuity. When the curtain is raised by Anglo-Saxon documents, much of what we now regard as the 'classic' English landscape was already there, had already acquired its regional differences, and as far as we can tell was not new. It increasingly seems likely that, at least since the Iron Age, every inch of the British Isles has either belonged to somebody or has been expressly set aside for communal use. Not just main roads but wide areas of fields and lanes are Roman (or earlier) antiquities, and survived the Dark Ages almost intact.

Conventions

The counties in this book are geographical, not administrative, and are as shown on pp.x–xi.

Where a map bears two dates, I quote the date of survey, not of publication. 'Woodland' does not normally include wood-pasture or plantation.

Prehistoric dates are quoted in actual calendar years BC. Most of them have been adjusted from radiocarbon years bc and depend ultimately on the annual rings of very long-lived American trees.

Regions into which Anglo-Saxon charters are classified (Fig. 2.1) are named with capitals: e.g. North-East England, Mid Hampshire.

English Measures

1 inch		= 25 mm
1 foot	= 12 in.	= 0.30 m
1 yard	= 3 ft	= 0.91 m
1 modern perch	= 16½ ft	= 5.0 m
1 mile	= 1760 yards	= 1.6 km
1 modern acre	= 4840 square yards	= 0.40 ha
1000 modern acres		= 4.0 km²

(The acre is a rectangle measuring 40 × 4 perches. The historic perch could vary from 15½ ft, as at Little Gransden, Cambs (Ely Coucher Book[19]), to 30 ft, as at Rufford, Notts.[613] Local historic acres could therefore vary from 0.88 to 3.30 modern acres.)

1 cubic foot		= 0.028 m³
1 ton		= 1.0 t
1 *d*		= £0.0042
1 *s*	= 12*d*	= ¹⁄₂₀ £

Fig. 0.1 shows the value of money at different periods.

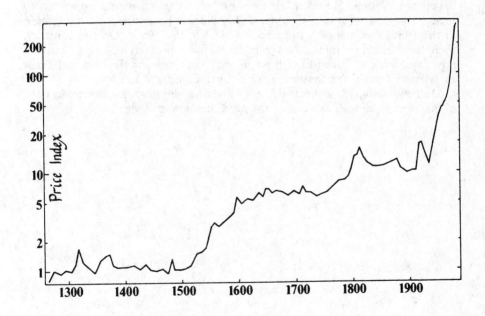

Fig. 0.1 Index of retail prices for middle and south England, 1264–1984. Logarithmic scale. The base year (index = 1.00) is 1450. Mainly after E. H. Brown and S. V. Hopkins.[89] The medieval penny must be thought of as something like sixpence in the money of the seventeenth century, a shilling in the mid-nineteenth, and well over £1 today.

Periods

Pleistocene	*c.* 2,000,000 BC onwards
Last interglacial (Ipswichian)	*c.* 130,000–100,000 BC
Last glaciation (Weichselian)	*c.* 100,000–12,000 BC
Post-glacial *alias* present interglacial	*c.* 12,000 BC onwards
Palaeolithic	to *c.* 10,000 BC
Mesolithic	*c.* 10,000–4500 BC
Neolithic	4500–2000 BC
Bronze Age	2400–750 BC
Iron Age (in England)	750 BC–AD 40
Roman (in England)	AD 40–410
Dark Ages (in England)	AD 410–700
Anglo-Saxon (in England)	AD 410–1066
Middle Ages	AD 1066–1536
Post-medieval	AD 1536 onwards

Note to the 1997 issue

This book has now been in print for eleven years, during which the study of historical ecology has made many advances and whole shelves of new books have been written. However, there is not much that I would now wish to unsay, and most of it is in Chapter 3. My gloomy prognosis for conservation in the 1980s has, happily, not been fulfilled in the 1990s. On the contrary, there has been a dramatic change in favour of conservation. In particular, I now pay tribute to Forest Enterprise, Forest Authority and the National Trust as defenders and rehabilitators of ancient woodland and heath.

My 1994 book, *The Illustrated History of the Countryside*, includes an account of this change, as well as some of the advances in knowledge since 1986.

CHAPTER 1

Regions

We are not entitled to make for ourselves any one typical picture of the English vill . . . in all probability we must keep at least two types before our minds. On the one hand, there is what we might call the true village . . . In the purest form of this type there is one and only one cluster of houses. It is a fairly large cluster; it stands in the midst of its fields, of its territory, and until lately a considerable part of its territory will probably have consisted of spacious 'common fields' . . . . the parish boundaries seem almost to draw themselves. On the other hand, we may easily find a country in which there are few villages of this character. The houses . . . are scattered about in small clusters; here two or three, there three or four. These clusters often have names of their own, and it seems a mere chance that the name borne by one of them should be also the name of the whole parish . . . We see no traces of very large fields. On the face of the map there is no reason why a particular group of cottages should be reckoned to belong to this parish rather than to the next . . .

Two little fragments of 'the original one-inch ordnance map' will be more eloquent than would be many paragraphs of written discourse. The one pictures a district on the border between Oxfordshire and Berkshire cut by the Thames and the main line of the Great Western Railway [Fig. 1.1]; the other a district on the border between Devon and Somerset, north of Collumpton and south of Wiveliscombe [Fig. 1.2].

F.W. Maitland, 1897[2]

Why is Herefordshire more like rural Essex than either of them is like Cambridgeshire? Textbooks try to present regional differences as being forced upon us by the natural world of hills, soils, and rainfall. Sometimes they are; but there are also instances where men have made different landscapes out of apparently similar natural environments, or the same landscape out of different environments. Even where there is a natural explanation for two regions, the boundary is often unexpectedly sharp; we suspect that human endeavour has removed what would naturally have been a transition zone.

It is part of the business of this book to investigate what men, and when, were responsible for the human element in regional differences. It is not a simple matter, as Maitland conjectured it to be, of Celt *versus* Saxon. Regions are of great antiquity, for county and parish boundaries determined a thousand years ago completely ignore them. The north-west corner of Essex has a Cambridgeshire-type landscape, and the south-east corner of Cambridgeshire is like Essex.

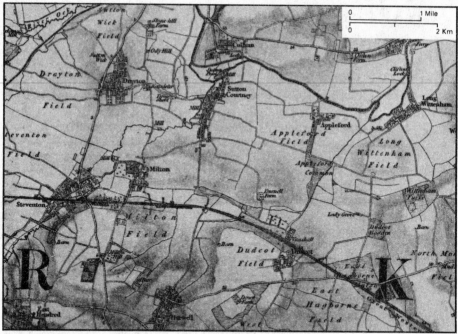

Fig. 1.1. Planned Countryside just after parliamentary enclosure. The 'Field' belonging to each village is a recently abolished, or sometimes still existing, open-field. Berkshire–Oxfordshire border, Ordnance Survey, 1830 (Great Western railway added later).

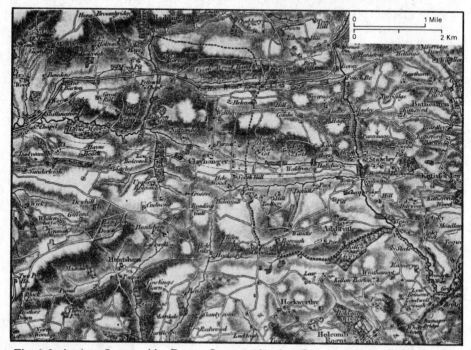

Fig. 1.2. Ancient Countryside. Devon–Somerset border, Ordnance Survey, 1809.

2

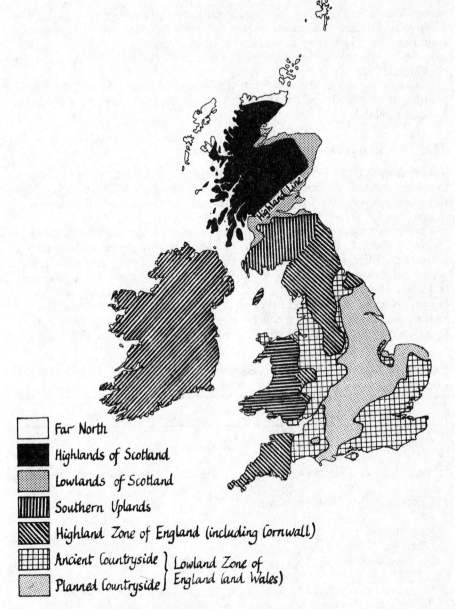

Fig. 1.3. Regions of the British Isles.

Scotland (Fig. 1.3)

The great division in the Scottish landscape is the Highland Line. It is sharper than the gradual rising of the mountains. In one mile we are in a neat land of wide hedged fields, thickly scattered farmsteads, conifer plantations, and Anglo-Danish place-names. The next mile we are in a wild country of moors, ancient pinewoods, small farms set precariously among bogs, and Gaelic place-names. This frontier, though nowhere a county boundary, cuts deep in Scottish history: the Highlands differ more from the rest of Scotland than the latter does from England. The history of the Scots Highland landscape is still little known. Written records are very scarce, for kings and monks took little interest in their own Highlands.

Within Scotland I shall also separate the far north, beyond the natural limit of continuous woodland, and the Southern Uplands* which continue the Highland Zone of England.

The Two Landscapes of Lowland England

Within England it is usual to separate the Highland Zone, running discontinuously from the Scots to the Cornish border. Although not all of high elevation, this is a land of moors, dales, ancient oakwoods, and a mountain way of life.

The rest of England – the Lowland Zone – is divided by a remarkable contrast (Figs. 1.1 and 1.2, Table 1.1). On the one hand, as in Essex or Herefordshire, we have the England of hamlets, medieval farms in hollows of the hills, lonely moats and great barns in the clay-lands, pollards and ancient trees, cavernous holloways and many footpaths, fords, irregularly-shaped groves with thick hedges colourful with maple, dogwood, and spindle – an intricate land of mystery and surprise. On the other hand there is the Cambridgeshire type of landscape, the England of big villages, few, busy roads, thin hawthorn hedges,

Table 1.1 Modern differences between Ancient Countryside and Planned Countryside

Ancient Countryside	Planned Countryside
Hamlets and small towns	Villages
Ancient isolated farms	Eighteenth- and nineteenth-century isolated farms
Hedges mainly mixed, not straight	Hedges mainly hawthorn, straight
Roads many, not straight, often sunken	Roads few, straight, on the surface
Many public footpaths	Few footpaths
Woods many, often small	Woods absent or few and large
Pollard trees, if present, away from habitations	Pollard trees (except riverside willows) absent or only in villages
Many antiquities of all periods	Antiquities few, usually prehistoric

* With this exception, I use the term *upland* to mean 'that which is not fen', not as a synonym for the Highland Zone.

windswept brick farms, and ivied clumps of trees in corners of fields; a predict-able land of wide views, sweeping sameness, and straight lines. These I call Ancient Countryside and Planned Countryside. As slight research will show, the one is the product of at least a thousand years of continuity and most of it has altered little since 1700 (though, as we shall see, some areas have signs of deliberate planning in remote antiquity). The other is, in the main, a mass-produced, drawing-board landscape, hurriedly laid out parish by parish under Enclosure Acts in the eighteenth and nineteenth centuries; but occasionally there survive features, notably woods, that the enclosure commissioners failed to destroy. The distinction between the two landscapes is often very sharp: it bisects each of a dozen parishes on the Cambridgeshire—Suffolk border.

The distinction between the Two Landscapes fascinated Maitland; he saw it mainly in terms of villages *versus* hamlets, but that may not be its oldest manifestation. It becomes even more evident as we go back in history (Table 1.2). In the sixteenth century Thomas Tusser contrasted the 'seuerall' and 'champion'; as an Essex man, he favoured the former.[3] (Many early writers call the several, or Ancient Countryside, the Woodland, meaning not 'woodland' in the ordinary sense but land that yielded wood from hedges.)

This contrast runs all through Europe. The difference in Wiltshire between the south-west corner – the intimate, complex Semley country – and the rest of the county is like that between the *bocage* and the wide-open *champagne* parts of France (p.181). The same difference appears in Tirol, between the big villages and open-fields of the large valleys and the tangled lanes and farmsteads of the mountains, and I have found it even in Greece.[4] In Crete, that island of supreme diversity, there is a mysterious difference between the east, with its few, large, villages, and the intricate pattern of hamlets (there is not room on the map to print all their long names) crammed into the west.

Table 1.2 Historic differences between Ancient Countryside and Planned Countryside

Ancient Countryside	Planned Countryside
Open-field either absent or of modest extent and abolished before *c.* 1700	Strong tradition of open-field beginning early and lasting into Enclosure Act period
Most hedges ancient	Most hedges modern
Many, though often small, woods	Woods absent or few and large
Much heathland	Heaths rare; little bracken or broom
Non-woodland trees oak, ash, alder, birch	Non-woodland thorns and elders
Many ponds	Few ponds

CHAPTER 2

Historical methods and the use of evidence

He that should deeply consider the prodigious *waste* which these voracious *Iron*, and *Glass-works* have formerly made but in *one County* alone, the *County* of Sussex, for 120 miles in length and thirty in breadth (for so wide, and spacious was the antient *Andradswald*, of old one intire *Wood*, but of which there remains now little, or no sign) would be touch'd with no mean *Indignation*.

John Evelyn, 1664[5]

The great Foundaries, or Iron-Works, which are in this County [Sussex], and where they are carry'd on at such a prodigious Expence of Wood, that even in a Country almost all over-run with Timber, they begin to complain of the consuming it for those Furnaces, and leaving the next Age to want Timber for building their Navies: . . . I found that Complaint perfectly groundless, the Three Counties of *Kent*, *Sussex*, and *Hampshire*, . . . being one inexhaustible Store-House of Timber never to be destroy'd, but by a general Conflagration, and able at this time to supply Timber to rebuild all the Royal Navies in Europe.

Daniel Defoe, 1724[6]

The historian has to combine the several types of evidence at his disposal. A story based on one kind of evidence is never so complete or secure as one that is corroborated from some quite different direction. Unfortunately, many historians confine themselves to the written word or, worse still, to the literary word; they are reluctant to put on their boots and to see what the land itself, and the things that grow on it, have to say. At best this shortens perspectives and over-emphasizes the achievement of people who had much to say for themselves. At worst it manufactures false conclusions. For example, writers still attribute the draining and farming of the Fens to the Dutch engineers and their English patrons, skilled controversialists, of the seventeenth century. The draining and farming of the Fens in Norman times are underestimated because the men of that age were inarticulate and have left few and obscure records. The draining and farming of the Fens in Roman times, an equal achievement, has left not a single written word and is known only from archaeology.

Archaeological evidence is all that we have for prehistory and down to the early Anglo-Saxon period. In historic times it complements the written word. Documents are precise as to date but (apart from maps) usually vague as to place; the reverse is true of field evidence. Archaeology does not lose its importance as time goes on. Verbal evidence is rarely complete or wholly trustworthy, and is not necessarily fuller for later than for earlier periods. For instance, stories that woods were felled during World War II need to be confirmed – or disproved – by looking for the stumps.

The written (and some of the other) sources used by the landscape historian are described in two well-known books by Professor W.G. Hoskins (1959, 1967). For the documentation of historical ecology see Sheail (1980) and Rackham (1979). I shall not repeat all that has been said, but shall dwell on some of the difficult sources and those on which this book offers new interpretations.

Pollen Analysis

Historical evidence lies in plant debris, ranging from tree-trunks to bud-scales. By far the most abundant are the pollen grains of trees and other plants, preserved in vast numbers in peat-bogs, lake muds, some archaeological deposits, and occasionally in acid soils. Different plants produce pollens which can be identified under the microscope. In a peat-bog or lake a stratified deposit has been laid down year by year. The pollen analyst takes a core, identifies the pollen grains centimetre by centimetre through the deposit, and reconstructs the vegetation that produced the pollen in the centuries while the deposit was building up. The method goes back to an idea of the German botanist C.A. Weber in 1893; it was introduced to Scotland by G. Erdtman in 1924;[7] and it has now, through the fifty years' labour of Professor Sir Harry Godwin and his colleagues, become a substantial science (Godwin 1975).

Pollen analysis tells us nearly all we know about wildwood – the natural vegetation of early prehistory – and about the impact of prehistoric men. It has limitations: one can (just) identify the two species of lime tree, but the two oaks produce indistinguishable pollens; hazel and bog-myrtle, by unlucky chance, are very difficult to distinguish; and among grasses all that can be done is to separate the pollens of reed and of cereals from others. Many plants, especially those pollinated by insects, shed little pollen and are difficult to detect. Early agriculture is recognized more from the pollens of weeds (eg. plantains) than of crops. Pollen analysts have recently begun to allow for the fact that the pollen of some trees is shed more abundantly, or scattered more widely, than that of others.

Pollen evidence has so far been less used for the historical period. Many deposits have lost their top layers by erosion or peat-digging. Methods of dating, such as by carbon-14, may not be precise enough. In the fragmented structure of the historic landscape it is often difficult to sort out pollen coming from the immediate surroundings of a deposit from that contributed by crops, woods, hedges, etc. at varying distances away.

Archaeology

Landscape archaeology is the study of features visible on the surface. It is to be recommended to the amateur, especially as (unlike excavation) it leaves the site as found; the evidence remains intact to be re-observed or re-interpreted later. In this book I particularly use soil-marks and crop-marks, woodbanks and hedgebanks, ridge-and-furrow, and differences of level.

Evidence comes from other kinds of archaeology. An important technique is field-walking to look for scatters of potsherds. This, and the detailed surveys and excavations in advance of motorway building, have discovered many hundreds of settlement sites, and have filled the landscape with habitation and agriculture many centuries earlier than was previously thought possible. The

7

study of standing timber buildings and the excavation of ancient waterfronts and of prehistoric trackways tell us much about tree management and what ancient woods looked like.

Written Records

The documentation of England is much more copious than of Wales, Scotland, or Ireland. It is true that in Wales the *Book of Llandaff*[8] preserves a few details from the Dark Ages when England has almost nothing. Scotland has the *Statistical Accounts* of 1791–9 and 1845,[9] which are more systematic, if perhaps less reliable, than anything in England. Ireland has the *Civil Survey* of the 1650s[10] – a greater and more detailed Domesday Book – and anticipated England in large-scale Ordnance maps (Chapter 5). These apart, almost all classes of record are more abundant in England, and many are confined to it.

Place-names The earliest records of extensive value are names of rivers, towns, villages, hamlets, some farms, woods, roads, prehistoric earthworks, and a few fields. In England many of these go back well before the Norman Conquest, and have been studied by generations of scholars. Being in dead languages – Old English or Anglo-Saxon, Old Norse, Cornish – they can be roughly dated on linguistic grounds even if not named in surviving early documents. The English Place-name Society has produced a long, though still incomplete, series of county volumes. Place-names in Wales, Scotland, and Ireland have been less studied. Some are just as ancient as English names; but many are in living (and very conservative) Celtic languages and cannot be dated on internal evidence.

Many place-names tell us something by their mere existence: a wood which has an Old Norse wood-name (Chapter 5) must go back to Viking times. But most place-name research deals with meanings. There are three difficulties:
(i)   Knowing what exactly the ancient words mean: for instance, are the two Anglo-Saxon words for elm synonymous, or do they mean different kinds of elm (Chapter 5)?
(ii)   The development of place-names independently of the rest of the language, often in ways that suggest false derivations. *Hather*leigh (now often misspelt Heatherleigh) refers to hawthorn, not heather; Firs Wood is often a corruption of Furze Wood.
(iii) The tradition among place-name scholars of not admitting ignorance, clutching at straws, and reading into place-names more than they say. Allusions to trees, eg. *Elm*ham, have wrongly been taken to imply woodland. Staveley, 'stave-clearing', has been misinterpreted as 'clearing whence staves were cut'; but there is nothing to suggest 'whence' or 'were cut', and we shall never know the relation between the stave and the clearing. Scholars assume that 'cat' in place-names means wildcat and compound this error by assuming that wildcats imply woodland.

A single place-name is weak evidence. Even the earliest surviving spelling – often in Domesday Book or an Anglo-Saxon charter – may already be corrupted. Places may often be named after unusual, rather than commonplace, features: 'Birch Wood' may have been a hornbeam wood with just one conspicuous birch tree. Place-names are difficult to date; specialists are now less confident than they used to be about Anglo-Saxon names of early and late forms.[11] A chance mention by the Venerable Bede may back-date to the seventh century a place-name which would otherwise be guessed to be of the eleventh or even twelfth. Northern England is difficult because of the lack of Anglo-Saxon charters and (for four counties) of Domesday Book. Place-names are best handled in the form of distribution maps (eg. Fig. 5.7), which give a general picture for about the middle Anglo-Saxon period, in which occasional errors for particular points do not matter much.

Anglo-Saxon charters In England, as probably nowhere else at so early a date, we have a large set of documents which clothe the archaeological record with vivid detail and tell us what specific pieces of country looked like.

An Anglo-Saxon charter is the conveyance of a piece of land, drawn up in proper legal form. The text, usually in Latin, included a sermon, the name of the premises, the nature of the transaction, a list of witnesses, and a terrible curse on him who should subvert the title. It may contain details of land management and common-rights. I am chiefly concerned with those charters to which are appended a *perambulation* defining the piece of land by describing its boundaries, usually in Old English, sometimes in Latin. It proceeds from point to point in a sunwise direction:

> First up from the Thames along the *merflēot* [= boundary creek]; to the pollard stump; so to *Bulung* fen; from the fen along the old ditch to Cowford; from Cowford up along *teobern* [the river Tyburn] to the wide army-road; from the army-road to the old post-built St Andrew's church; so into London fen; along the fen south to the Thames to mid-stream; along the stream by land & shore back to the *merflēot*.
>
> *Bounds of Westminster, dated 959*[12]

There are about 840 perambulations, attached to charters bearing dates from about AD 600 to 1080. Early ones, most frequent in Kent, are usually laconic, though the foundation charter of Crediton Abbey, dated 739, has almost the longest of all, with 82 landmarks enclosing much of Devon. More than half the dated bounds are between 930 and 980 – there was a vintage year in 956. After the Norman Conquest the *genre* fades away, though there are occasional perambulations (eg. of legal Forests) as late as the seventeenth century.* Bounds may be earlier or later than the dates of their charters. Many charters (despite the cursing clause) are forgeries, but these either incorporate genuine pre-Conquest bounds or betray the imposture by their ignorance of Old English grammar. Conversely, successive conveyances of the same land often copied the bounds unaltered. Uncertainties of date are not of great importance in this book: I am much concerned with regional differences but say little about changes with time. Charters on average portray the England of some 100–200 years before Domesday Book. I leave to more learned scholars the question of whether there is any difference between the Englands portrayed by eighth- and eleventh-century charters.

The charter just quoted covers the West End of London. This has changed since 959! It is not immediately obvious that the 'wide army-road' is High Holborn or that 'London Fen' is around Fleet Street. There were then cows,

---

* In the poorly-mapped United States, auctioneers' advertisements to this day include perambulations.

pollards, and creeks between London and Westminster, and Tyburn was no more than an innocent stream. But this is an exceptional amount of change. Most charters show that England has altered surprisingly little in the last thousand years. They conduct us through a familiar world of rivers, mill-streams, ditches, hedges and hedgerow trees, roads, lanes, paths, bridges, heaths, thorns, small named woods, stumps, pits, and old posts. It was already a world of antiquity, with barrows, hillforts, 'heathen burials', 'ancient cities', and Roman roads. Little is said about villages, partly because perambulations deal more with the edges than the centres of habitation, but also because there really were fewer villages than after the Conquest.[13] Only rarely do the charters mention something, such as a wayside crucifix or a dragon's hoard, which has disappeared from the modern scene.

Some charters are preserved as original documents, others as medieval copies. Most were printed by J.M. Kemble[14] or by W. de G. Birch,[15] but others are scattered in obscure publications and a few probably remain to be discovered. There are commentaries by C.R. Hart[16] and a list by P.H. Sawyer.[17]

What do we do with the information? Perhaps the most exciting of all the historian's tasks is to go back with the text into the field and to trace the boundary of a thousand years ago. Surprisingly often, one can still find the same woods, roads, hedges, heathen burials, and even ditches, pits, and stones.* Many charters have been solved by G.B. Grundy[18] or by Dr Hart, but there are plenty left for the amateur. It is usually necessary to follow the bounds on the ground and to consider how far one point is visible from the next (p.310). The task is often helped by the Anglo-Saxon boundary following a modern parish boundary.

English charters mention a total of 14,342 objects. Some are point features such as trees, others linear such as hedges.† Dr Della Hooke (1981), analyzing the perambulations of the West Midlands, has produced distribution maps for some features. To do this on a national scale is complicated by the uneven distribution of the charters. They are thick on the ground in west Berkshire, south Worcestershire, and south Wiltshire, but few in the East Midlands and almost none in East Anglia and the north. Danes and charters did not get on well together. (In Cornwall some of the features are named in Old Cornish. In South Wales there are charters in Welsh,[8] but I shall use these less because they are short and deal in features such as streams and mountains.)

In this book I try to make the charters tell us whether there existed in Anglo-Saxon times the regional differences of Chapter 1. I have divided the charters of England into 31 regions (Fig. 2.1). They are chosen so that each region is, as far as possible, homogeneous – in terms both of the modern landscape and of Domesday Book – while having enough points to provide a statistically valid sample (where possible between 400 and 700 points). For

---

* But beware! I know one manifestly modern hedge on the approximate line of a hedge mentioned in a charter.
† For statistical purposes the following rules are necessary:
    1. Where a perambulation mentions the same object twice (eg. by leaving a road and returning later to what is apparently the same road) it is counted twice.
    2. The same object mentioned in two different perambulations (eg. two adjacent estates whose bounds, where they coincide, mention apparently the same pit) is counted twice.
    3. Where two successive charters of the same land have different perambulations, both are counted, even though some of the objects appear to be the same.
    4. Where the bounds of one charter are repeated identically, or with only minor alterations, in another charter, only one is counted.

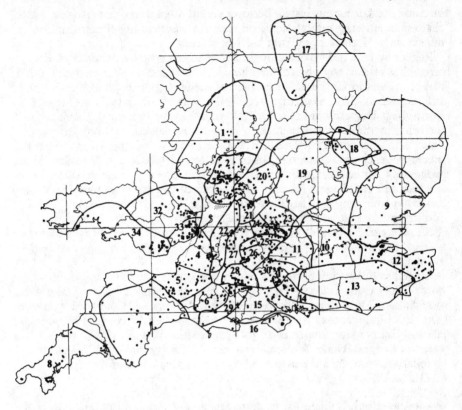

Fig. 2.1. Perambulations in the Anglo-Saxon and early Welsh charters. Each dot (or circle for places with Welsh charters) is a piece of land for which a boundary clause survives. The perambulations are grouped thus:

Regions later to be Ancient Countryside (including Highland Zone)

1 N.W. Midlands
2 N. Worcestershire
3 S. Worcestershire
4 Mendips
5 Mid Somerset
6 N.W. Dorset
7 Devon
8 Cornwall

9 Essex and Suffolk
10 London Basin
11 Reading Basin
12 Kent
13 Weald
14 Hampshire-Sussex Downs
15 Hampshire Basin
16 Isle of Wight and Purbeck

Regions later to be Planned Countryside

17 N.E. England
18 Fens
19 E. Midlands
20 Vale of Evesham
21 Woodless Cotswolds
22 Wooded Cotswolds
23 Oxfordshire
24 Berkshire Claylands

25 Uffington Scarp
26 Marlborough Downs
27 Wiltshire Claylands
28 S. Wiltshire Downs
29 Dorset Chalklands
30 N. Hampshire
31 Mid Hampshire

Wales

32 Wye Basin
33 S. Monmouthshire

34 Glamorgan

instance the Uffington Scarp (Berkshire), although a very small area, has 22
charters mentioning a total of 591 objects; the whole of north-east England can
muster only 11 charters mentioning 139 objects.

Region by region, I have counted references to particular types of object as a
percentage of the total objects mentioned by the charters. For example, out of
14,342 objects in all the English charters, hedges are mentioned (under eight
different terms) 378 times; that is, 2.64 per cent of the features are hedges. In
North-West Dorset, words for 'hedge' occur 33 times among 526 objects, or 6
per cent; in the Dorset Chalklands, hedges are named six times among 531
objects, or 1 per cent. The charters of all England can be divided into what was
later to be Ancient Countryside, 16 regions, total 7562 objects, of which 253 are
hedges (3.4 per cent); and Planned Countryside, 15 regions, total 6664 objects,
of which 119 are hedges (1.8 per cent).* Ancient Countryside therefore already
had, as in later centuries, an above-average percentage of hedges, and Planned
Countryside a below-average percentage. North-West Dorset was specially
above average, as it still is in ancient hedges; mid Dorset was well below
average. Fig. 9.1 is a complete map of above-average and below-average regions
for hedges.

As well as linguistic problems – which words mean 'hedge', and do the eight
words imply eight kinds of hedge? – there is the question of how landmarks
were chosen. The difference between Ancient and Planned Countryside, though
certain, is less great than we might expect from medieval records of hedges. Did
Planned Countryside lose some of its hedges after the date of the charters – or
were its hedges, being few and conspicuous, more likely to be chosen as
boundary features than the many and commonplace hedges of Ancient Countryside?

Domesday Book William the Conqueror's great survey of 1086 still astonishes
us. What modern census-taker would contemplate getting such a project commissioned, planned, surveyed, sorted, and published, all within a year? It can
hardly have been the first such census, nor was it quite the last. The Hundred
Rolls of 1279 were an even more detailed survey, giving the names of most of the
adult population, but the rats have eaten most of them. Domesday was commissioned and used as a record of land tenure, the work of an efficient conqueror
wanting to know, when the dust had settled, who owned what in his new
kingdom. It is not a mere fiscal survey: it omits many things, such as shipyards,
that were taxable assets, but includes others, such as woods, that were not.

The questions on the forms from which Domesday Book was compiled were
changed several times in the course of the survey. Here are three typical returns:

> Harold held Hadfeld in the time of King Edward for 1 manor and for 20 hides.
> Then 51 villeins, now 60. Then 19 bordars, now 30. Then 20 slaves, now 22. Then
> 9 ploughs in demesne, now 8, & 3 rounceys & 40 animals & 195 swine & 192
> sheep. Then 40 men's ploughs, now 31½ – this loss was in the time of all the
> sheriffs and through the death of the beasts. Wood for 800 swine, 120 acres of
> meadow. Pasture whose rent is 19 wethers in the manor & 41 acres of
> ploughing . . .
>
> *Hatfield Broad-oak, Essex*

---

* The figures do not add up because a few charters are of unknown places.

GRATEDENE is assessed for 5 hides. There is land for 9 ploughs. In demesne 2½ hides. & there is 1 plough and 2 could be made. There 8 villeins & 3 bordars with 6 ploughs. There 4 slaves. Meadow for 3 ploughs. Pasture for the cattle of the settlement. Wood for 60 swine & 2 shillings from the custom of the wood. In all it is worth in value 8 pounds. When received 9 pounds. In the time of King Edward 15 pounds. This manor lies & has always lain in the possession of the church of Ely.

Little Gransden, Cambs

[Richard] holds THERSENT [from Count Mortain]. Alwin held it in the time of King Edward & paid geld for 1 hide. But there are 2 hides there. There is land for 12 ploughs. In demesne are 2 ploughs & 6 slaves & 5 villeins & 11 bordars with 5 ploughs. There is pasture 3 leagues long & 2 leagues wide. Wood 1 league long and ½ league wide.

Trezance, that is Cardinham, Cornwall

The returns enumerate the ploughs on the demesne – the land which the lord of the manor farmed himself – separately from those of the 'men', the villeins, bordars, and other inhabitants. They try to record changes since before the Conquest ('in the time of King Edward'). The more detailed record, including 'rounceys', 'animals', and other demesne livestock, is typical of Norfolk, Suffolk, and Essex. These counties may have been taken first and found to be producing more information than could be handled, hence the less detail for the other counties. Recording woodland in terms of swine is probably an archaism, abandoned when it was found that people no longer thought of woods in this way.

The unit of recording is the *estate*, the land of a particular owner in a particular place. The unit of location is the *settlement* (*uilla*); it could be a city, a town, a village (Little Gransden), a cluster of hamlets (Hatfield Broad-oak), a scatter of farms (Cardinham), or a single hamlet or farm. Most estates consisted each of one *manor* (*manerium*), but some were too small to be proper manors, and some were *giant manors*, estates extending over many settlements and administered as a unit. Amesbury (Wiltshire) included places 15 miles away. In the Midlands each *uilla* was often in a single ownership, forming one manor and one estate and later one parish and one modern village. This simple arrangement was not at all universal: it is common for a dispersed township, or even a village, to be divided among several manors.

As with modern surveys, the form did not always prove adequate, and kinds of information not anticipated in advance were somewhat neglected. As well as the standard particulars, Domesday sometimes records pasture, underwood, mills, saltpans, churches, etc. These records are more or less casual: there are many Anglo-Saxon churches still standing which are not in Domesday. In south-west England there is an approach to a systematic record of pasture (Chapter 15), and in a few counties underwood is consistently separated from other wood (Chapter 5).

In some south-western counties the information is complete enough to be checked against the actual area of land (p.311). Usually there is a shortfall, although in Dorset this amounts to only 14 per cent, which is probably within the limits of uncertainty of the calculation (p.335). Domesday appears to omit 29 per cent of the area of Devon and 32 per cent of Cornwall. These shortfalls are due mainly to the omission or under-recording of large common pastures and moors, especially those such as Dartmoor which did not belong to any one settlement.

Domesday has nothing to say of Northumberland and Durham and very little of Cumberland and Westmorland. It is poor for Lancashire and the Welsh parts of Herefordshire, although it does include parts of north-east Wales.

Domesday is a record of land, and is poor at recording towns or any activity

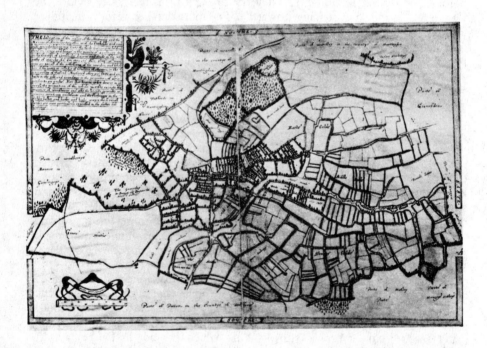

Fig. 2.2a. Gamlingay (Cambridgeshire) in 1601 and 1900; typical of Planned Country-side. In 1601 open-field cultivation covered more than half the parish, but there were also many hedges and hedgerow trees, especially around the little town. The many woods were somewhat unusual. Most of the landscape was transformed by Enclosure Acts in 1808 and 1841; strip-cultivation was replaced by a network of straight hedges, and the Great Heath was destroyed (with the loss of many rare plants, for which the more recent Great Heath Wood is no compensation). The pre-1601 hedged fields largely escaped

involving little or no land. It says little of roads, hedges, or trees. It is not a record of sea-fishing, mining, shipping, wheelwrighting, smithing, stone-masonry, bell-founding, or many other activities of which there is independent evidence.

Domesday Book has been the subject of two centuries of research. The great controversies about population, the meaning of the hide, etc. are only marginal to this book. I am indebted to my predecessors who published the text,

these changes. So did the woods: Avenelles, Mertonage, White, Potton, and Cockayne Hatley Woods have altered little since 1601 (the last is omitted from this map but is shown on one of its companion maps). Waresley Wood existed in 1601 but was smaller and did not reach the area of the map. Lambcott Wood was destroyed after 1601 and the Park Plantations which now stand on its site have no connection with it.

(The 1601 map[617] is reproduced by permission of the Warden & Scholars of Merton College, Oxford.)

identified the places, determined the units of measurement, and mapped the data: notably to F.W. Maitland[2] and, more recently, to Professor H.C. Darby and his colleagues for their regional and national volumes (Darby 1971; Darby and Versey 1975).

Within its limitations, Domesday is surprisingly accurate, and statistical conclusions can be drawn from it. It records an England that was about 35 per cent arable land (derived from a total of 81,000 ploughs at the rough-and-ready rate of 120 acres per plough), 15 per cent woodland and wood-pasture, and 1 per cent meadow. Pasture may reasonably be estimated at 30 per cent of the country. This leaves us one-fifth of England to be taken up with mountains, heaths, moorland, and fen (where not recorded as pasture), houses and gardens, and lands wasted by the Conqueror's wrath.

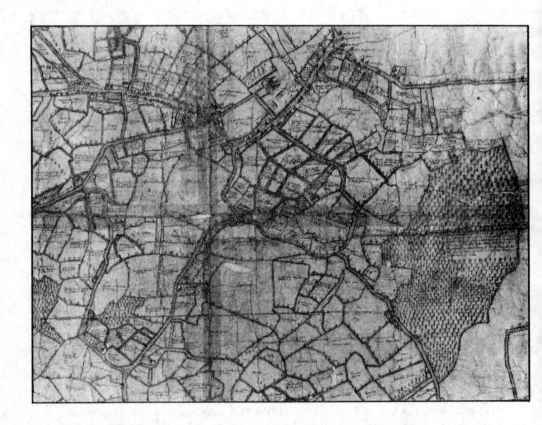

Fig. 2.2b. Earl's Colne (Essex) in 1598 and 1896; typical of Ancient Countryside. There was no strip-cultivation and no Enclosure Act. Almost everything in the modern landscape was already there in 1598, but it has been somewhat thinned out by the removal of

Medieval records Record-keeping is not a story of continuous progress. After Domesday Book a dark age sets in until the mid-thirteenth century. Many types of record then become abundant, of which four particularly concern us. The fourteenth century is well documented in England; records then gradually fade away, and there is another dark age from about 1450 until record-keeping was again revived at the dissolution of the monasteries.

Surveys (alias *extents*), beginning with the Ely Coucher Book commissioned by Bishop Hugo de Northwold in 1251 (p.62),[19] are detailed verbal descriptions of

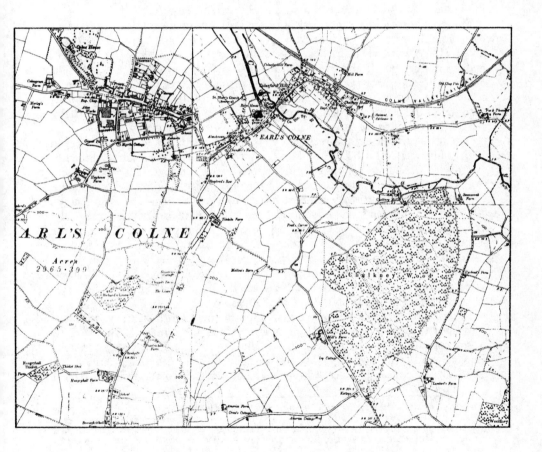

occasional hedges, roads and cottages here and there. The wood outline is exactly the same as in 1598. For a detail see Fig. 12.9.

(1598 map[50] reproduced by permission of Essex Record Office.)

landed estates, listing the types of land, names of fields, woods, and meadows, and often the labour services which tenants could be called upon to do by way of rent. *Accounts* (Latin *compoti*) give the year-by-year income and expenditure of an estate, including sales of produce, purchase of materials, hire of craftsmen, and transport of produce from one estate to another. *Court rolls* deal mainly with banalities such as petty assault and inheritance, but reward the searcher with occasional pearls of information about such things as highways, hedges, pits, and watercourses (p.181). The king's correspondence, enrolled in the *Close, Patent,* and *Liberate Rolls*, tells us about Forests, feasts, royal gifts, and materials and transport for the king's building works.

Maps The better-known early county maps, such as those of Saxton, Norden, and Speed, are of little use to us. They are at small scales (except for the tiny counties of Rutland and Middlesex) and make no claim to accuracy: trees, for instance, are usually decoration, not topography. Useful early maps are those of individual estates at scales of 6 inches to the mile or larger.

Mapping does not have a history of progressive improvement; it runs in cycles of technical perfection and decline. Accurate mapmaking appears suddenly about 1580.* Some of the earliest large-scale maps (Fig. 2.2) show every hedge, hedgerow tree, pond, and even identifiable buildings. In the seventeenth and eighteenth centuries large-scale maps, though more numerous, are not necessarily more accurate. For about half the parishes in England there is an Enclosure Act of the eighteenth or nineteenth century; its accompanying map usually covers the whole parish, though in less detail than earlier maps.

The art of accurate small-scale mapmaking (1 or 2 inches to the mile) began with John Rocque in the 1750s. Most English counties have a late eighteenth-century map, such as Chapman and André's Essex surveyed in 1772–4. These are of varying quality, for instance good for Forests (and common-land generally) and poor for woods; they can be arbitrary in what they omit, and can include fictitious information (e.g. conventionalized field boundaries). The same shortcomings occur in the earlier manuscript drawings and published sheets of the 1-inch Ordnance Survey. The methods of the Ordnance Survey were tightened in about 1830. Sheets published subsequently are as accurate as any later edition, but those already published – about a third of England and Wales – were usually allowed to stand. Occasionally (eg. in south Essex) there are separate pre-1830 and post-1830 published editions.†

Large-scale mapmaking was revived in the nineteenth century with the published Ordnance Survey of Ireland at 6 inches to the mile (1834–44). This was accompanied by the making of a manuscript Tithe Award map for most English and Welsh townships that had not had an Enclosure Act. From 1853 to 1893 all England and Wales was surveyed at 6 inches to the mile. For most

---

* There may have been an earlier cycle of mapmaking. Professional surveyors existed in the Middle Ages, and a few fourteenth- and fifteenth-century surveys give areas of irregular fields and even woods down to ¹⁄₆₄₀ acre. As far as I can tell, they are accurate to a fraction of an acre.[20] This implies the ability to make an accurate map. But I know of no surviving medieval large-scale map that is better than the roughest sketch.[21]

† There are two modern reprints. That published by Harry Margary reproduces the Ordnance Survey sheets as originally surveyed and published. The reprint by David and Charles is from the first edition as issued in the late nineteenth century, by which time many original details had become illegible through the plates wearing, and railways and other alterations had been added; it is of less value as a historical record.

places there are also 25-inch editions which give almost the same information but add the acreages of fields. The beautiful maps of the 1860s and 1870s, which attempt to record every hedgerow tree and the details of every building, are the zenith of rural mapmaking in Britain and perhaps in the world.

Boundaries

England and Wales are traditionally divided into *parishes*, anciently called *townships*, *towns*, or *vills*; these are grouped into *hundreds* or *wapentakes* and these into counties. Large townships sometimes have subdivisions such as the *turns* of St Keverne (Cornwall). Irish parishes are regularly divided into *townlands*, and grouped into *baronies* and these into counties.

The English system was already old by Domesday Book and changed little until recent decades (Beresford 1957, chapter 2). Boundaries are very conservative and were preserved by memorable customs: for instance, at Great Gransden (Huntingdonshire), when 'cessioning' the bounds they used to dig a hole at a certain spot and hold the Vicar's head in it.[22] Many a parish boundary on the modern map exactly corresponds to an Anglo-Saxon perambulation, which in turn may be interpreted as the boundary of a Roman or Iron Age estate. Until the early Norman period, minor changes were possible in order to keep lands in one ownership within the same administration. Hence some of the detached portions of parishes and counties – such as the complications where Worcestershire, Warwickshire, and Gloucestershire meet – or the parish boundaries altered to go round early parks (Fig. 6.2). In about 1180 the system froze and could no longer be altered when land changed hands.

Parishes are full of curiosities. There are huge ones like Writtle (Essex), 13,568 acres, and tiny ones like its neighbours Shellow Bowells, 469 acres, and Chignall Smealy, 476 acres. There are parishes with two or more villages, and villages divided among two or more parishes. There are extra-territorial places like Monks' Risbridge (Suffolk), the assembly-place of Risbridge Hundred. Sometimes we suspect deliberate planning in the blocks of long narrow parishes, set out at right angles to some natural feature, as if designed to give each community a share in all the types of land. This is usual in the chalklands of Wiltshire, Dorset, Berkshire, and Cambridgeshire (Fig. 2.3).

Where possible boundaries usually follow streams, roads, hedges, woodbanks, etc.; they are valuable evidence as to whether such features existed in 1180. Zigzags are clear evidence that the land had already long been parcelled out into fields or furlongs (Fig. 2.4). In Planned Countryside, parish boundaries are among the most likely places for ancient hedges. Boundaries may follow the ghosts of forgotten Roman roads or of tidied-up rivers. A pair of curious irregularities in a Somerset boundary (Fig. 2.5) turns out to be due to two otherwise undetected prehistoric ring-earthworks. In moorland or heath, parish boundaries often run unmarked from point to point. The point landmarks are often of interest, especially those at which many parishes meet (Fig. 16.5).

In woodland, most parish boundaries are marked by banks; in effect they create two separate woods. But there are several ancient woods divided by well-documented boundaries of which I can find no trace on the ground.

There are some pitfalls. Especially in woodland, boundaries are occasionally forgotten, and even Tithe Maps may disagree. It has long been the custom of officialdom to while away idle hours by tidying boundaries and removing enclaves, meanders, etc. These tinkerings, though seldom of practical advantage, destroy some of the meaning, which has to be recovered from nineteenth-century maps. Even the first edition 25-inch Ordnance Survey does not always show the true course of boundaries.

Plants

Plants sometimes furnish primary information. Annual rings of trees are a dated record not only of the age of the tree but of the circumstances in which it grew when young, and of pollarding, Elm Disease, drainage, and other things that have affected its growth. Many trees, such as the pollards of deserted villages (p.233) and the giant coppice stools of ancient woods (p.102), are historical monuments themselves. Some plants, such as fairy-ring fungi (p.343) and lichens on stones and walls (p.203–4), go on growing in ever-widening circles at a rate which can be measured.

It is also observed that areas of vegetation of recent origin differ from those of the same kind which are ancient. One does not find oxlip in a wood, spindle in a hedge, or pasque-flower in grassland that is less than a century old. These differences can go back many centuries and can be used to resolve questions of date. They also provide a record of management such as grazing. The reasons are discussed in the chapters on woods, hedges, and grassland.

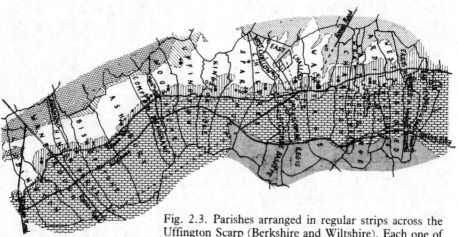

Fig. 2.3. Parishes arranged in regular strips across the Uffington Scarp (Berkshire and Wiltshire). Each one of more than twenty townships shares in all the successive geological formations; but there is no attempt either at equal slices or at an exact correspondence between villages and parishes. Many of the boundaries are described in Anglo-Saxon charters, but the system is probably much older: the boundaries ignore not only railways and canals but also Roman roads and even the prehistoric Ridgeway, 'Roman Way', and Grim's Ditch. The one exception, in the Letcombes and Challows, is in an area of complication, evidently the result of rearrangement to fit the landownerships of a later age. The Letcombes prove that it is not strictly necessary for a community to have shares in all the types of land. (Earlscourt is regarded as part of Wanborough, Hardwell of Uffington, and West Ginge of Ardington.)

20

Aerial Photographs

Air photography is a well-established archaeological science. It reveals traces of earthworks and buildings, and also natural features such as pingos (Chapter 16), in various ways (St Joseph 1977). Slight 'humps and bumps' cast shadows early and late in the day. Differences in vegetation show up especially on infra-red false-colour film. Ploughed-out features may produce *soil-marks*, patterns of different soil colour. Buried foundations and ditches often create *crop-marks*, differences in the height, colour, or ripening of crops, especially cereals, growing over them.

Air photographs are also historical documents themselves. There exists a large mosaic of the district around Cambridge, assembled from hundreds of

Fig. 2.4. Open-field strips in Widdington and Newport, north-west Essex, surviving in the form of parish-boundary anomalies. The two townships, unusually, had strips intermingled in a shared open-field. By the eighteenth century the open-field had been abolished and a great park, unrelated to the previous landscape, was made over the site; but the strips remain as enclaves of one parish within the other. Ordnance Survey, 1877.

exposures taken in 1922.[23] The Cambridge University Collection, begun in 1950, already records many features now vanished. Perhaps the most valuable of all historic photography is the great survey of much of Britain, especially the east and south, flown by the Germans in August and September 1940 when contemplating an invasion. These magnificent photographs, which record almost every tree, hedge, bush, pingo, and pond in several counties, were captured by the Americans and are now in the National Archives in Washington. The fortunes of war have preserved a convincing record of what was still, in many places, a medieval landscape, much of it since damaged or effaced (Plates III, VIc, XIII, XXII).

Testimony and Tradition

G.E. Evans has reminded us of the importance of the testimony of aged men.[24] Folk who actually did things, or whose grandfathers did them, can tell us many details which were never thought worth writing down. This is most useful for some activities, such as ploughing or anything to do with horses, which were familiar to everyone. It is more difficult to find out about specialized crafts such as woodmanship: once the crafts have died the traditions about them soon disappear.

Testimony should seldom be used on its own and probably never for more than three generations back. In Britain we do not have the African and Polynesian skills in the accurate oral transmission of detail. Aged countrymen, like the rest of us, enjoy telling and embroidering a good story; they do not always separate what they have read from what they have seen; and, like scholars, they are tempted to guess at explanations of what they do not know. More than once I have been told by someone familiar with a wood that 'nothing had been done to it in his time'; yet the tree-rings have shown indisputably that it must have been felled well within his recollection!

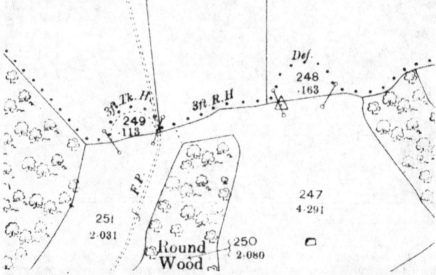

Fig. 2.5. Parish boundary between Butcombe and Wrington, Somerset. The two semi-circular deviations each represent half of a circular prehistoric enclosure. Ordnance Survey, 1902.

With testimonies written down in earlier centuries there is often the difficulty of not knowing the status of the story. Tales told as fiction are re-told as if they were fact. Tap-room gossip achieves semi-respectability as 'tradition', passes into print, and acquires a date from which even the *circa* is dropped in re-printing. The scientist is easily deceived: for instance most books quote the slaying of the last wolf in Scotland in 1743 as if this were known to be fact (p.36).

The Critical Use of Historical Sources

Translations Beware of other people's translations from Latin, Old English, or Norman-French. Translators (besides misreading their texts) guess at the meanings of unknown technical terms or fail to uphold distinctions of meaning. For instance, 'meadow' and 'pasture' may not be differentiated (Chapter 15), nor 'timber' and 'wood'; 'copse' is confused with 'spinney' and also with 'grove' (Chapter 5); and 'Forest' – a Norman invention – may be introduced by mistranslation into pre-Conquest documents.

General and specific sources Throughout this book I try to argue from the particular to the general: from workaday records of what particular people did in specific places and with what result. I have avoided, or used with great caution, much of the stuff of traditional 'histories' of the landscape – the contemporary generalizations and abstractions embodied in theories, textbooks, complaints, legislation, and literary works. These can be used to write a history of what people – that is, articulate people – *thought* about the landscape. Professor K. Thomas has done so in a scholarly book.[25] Let us not confuse this with the history of what people *did* with the landscape, still less with the history of the landscape itself or of what the landscape did with people.

Generalized evidence, uncritically used, easily creates false conclusions. With woodland there has grown up a 'pseudo-history' more widely read than the real history. Authors still relate that woods ceased to exist because people used up the trees; that there was a national shortage of timber as early as the sixteenth century; and that the history of woodland has been dominated by naval ship-building. These statements have been copied from author to author for centuries; but it is difficult to sustain them from the records of a single actual wood (see Chapter 5).

The quotations at the head of this chapter cannot both be right: matters had got worse in the sixty years between Evelyn and Defoe. Evelyn was the greater man, and it is his thesis that has been plagiarized and is the stuff of pseudo-history. But there can be no doubt that he was wrong and Defoe was right. Evelyn was a polemic writer: he does not mention that his statement about Andradswald was lifted from the *Anglo-Saxon Chronicle* for AD 892. The Chronicle slightly exaggerates: the Weald is nearer 80 miles by 30, and even then was hardly 'one intire Wood'. The fragmentation of the Wealden woods was due to medieval agriculture (p.88) long before Evelyn's ironworks and glassworks became big industries. It ceased with the Black Death. Great remnants of Andradswald survived in 1350, were still there in Evelyn's time, and were still there in 1945. The furnaces used mainly underwood, not timber, and with rare exceptions care was taken that the trees grew again (Rackham 1976).

On the other hand, Defoe's words about rebuilding all the navies of Europe were almost literally to be fulfilled. Between 1724 and 1774 the British navy roughly doubled in size. Including the replacement of ships and the much larger growth of the merchant fleet,[26] this involved building at least the equivalent of all the warships in Europe in 1724. There was not the slightest real difficulty in producing the oak, for the price paid by naval dockyards did not even keep up with inflation, and both the Navy and the merchant fleet more than doubled again in the forty years after 1774.

This is not the only myth in woodland history to have drawn strength from the great authority of Evelyn. But I have not discussed it to show that he is specially unreliable. On the contrary, Evelyn was one of the most learned men of his day, and had family connections with iron-smelting. He, more than anyone, should have known what he was talking about; if he did not, all kinds of contemporary generalization are brought into discredit.

Kinds of things recorded Records are usually made for a specific purpose, not to tell a complete story. For example, the Forestry Commission's 'Censuses of Woodlands' are chiefly concerned with timber trees, and underrecord non-timber species such as lime and hawthorn.[27] Nevertheless, they have been accepted as definitive for other purposes, and posterity may not realize that they tell a one-sided story.

Many classes of records are from monasteries and other large and well-organized landowners. Are they typical of the whole landscape? It is difficult to get a balanced story of complex multiple land-uses, such as the Crown's, landowners', and commoners' interests in Forests (Chapter 5).

Most records were written by unobservant people. They noticed oak because it is easily identified, valuable, belongs to landowners, and has many uses for which other trees will not do; thorn because it hurts; birch because it is conspicuous; service because it is rare and curious. They did not often notice hornbeam, which is not distinctive and has no specific uses. One record of hornbeam must therefore be given the weight of many records of oak.

People record sudden changes, especially those which advance civilization, more often than they record stability, gradual change, or decline. The felling of trees or their death through disease attracts attention; the growth of new trees from year to year is seldom recorded except by the camera. Grubbing out a wood to create a field is an event and an investment; an abandoned field turning into a wood is a symptom of decline and is not noticed (p.68). Many kinds of record over-represent the unusual; if something is not put on record, it may merely have been too commonplace to be worth mentioning.

CHAPTER 3

Conservation

Neither war nor earthquake is so destructive of historic amenities as too much money.

An Austrian architect friend, on beholding an Aegean island city

We have 250 acres and make a perfectly good living; our neighbour has 300 acres; why does he want to grub out that wood?

An Essex farmer friend

Any fool can break eggs without making an omelette.

A proverb

This is not a book of conservation; that book has already been written, with more literary skill than mine, by Richard Mabey (1980). But I cannot analyze the historic landscape without noticing how much of almost every aspect of it has been lost since 1945. When large, obvious, and even legally protected ancient monuments – barrows, camps, deserted villages – are destroyed weekly for the gain of trivial areas of land, the unscheduled historic countryside naturally fares even worse. The commonest cause has been destruction by modern agriculture; the second, destruction by modern forestry. Urban development comes a long way behind; roads, quarrying, and so on are only locally important. There is also loss through neglect of traditional land-uses and consequent natural changes, especially trees growing where they do not belong.

The nature and extent of the destruction, and whether it was necessary, have been fully set out by Marion Shoard (1980). Her book has been noisily denounced, but its central arguments have not been controverted, and are confirmed by the economic arguments of Richard Body (1982). In adding to these polemics I am not attacking farmers in general; the severest critics of recent practices are themselves farmers. The trouble lies with that powerful lobby which insists that farming is an industry (by which is meant *merely* an industry) and yet requires it to be subsidized, and allowed to do anti-social things, to a degree which no other industries enjoy. The Common Market has made matters worse, but is not chiefly to blame: most of the destruction took place before Britain joined.

It is not just through the rosy spectacles of childhood that we remember the landscape of the 1940s to have been richer in beauty, wildlife, and meaning than that of the 1980s. It was, and the Luftwaffe aerial photographs prove it. The landscape of the 1800s was richer still, as we learn from the writings of Professor Babington (p.328). There are four kinds of loss. There is the loss of beauty, especially that exquisite beauty of the small and complex and unexpected, of

25

frog-orchids or sundews or dragonflies. There is the loss of freedom, of highways and open spaces, which results from the English attitude to landownership; the Englishman enjoys more freedom in Austria, Ireland or Greece
than in his own country. There is the loss of historic vegetation and wildlife,
most of which once lost is gone for ever: to re-create an ancient wood is beyond
human knowledge, though we might re-create a historic grassland if we were to
live to the age of 200 (cf. Chapter 15). In this book I am specially concerned with
the loss of meaning. The landscape is a record of our roots and the growth of
civilization. Each individual historic wood, heath, etc. is uniquely different
from every other, and each has something to tell us.

Polemicists tell us not to oppose the destruction of the historic countryside on
three main grounds, all of them fallacious. The first is that it is not really
historic. The 'Enclosure-Act Myth', that the English landscape is almost wholly
the artificial creation of the last 250 years, is a long time dying. When a very
distinguished scientist opposes the conservation of hedges, on the grounds that
the majority of them were planted since 1782,[28] we begin to despair that the
truth will ever prevail. The second fallacy is that the destruction is necessary.
People still rehearse the arguments, some of them quite good ones (bigger fields,
more land needed, etc.), on which woods, hedges, and fens were destroyed in
the 1950s, without realizing that times have changed and that these are no
longer good arguments for destroying such woods, hedges, and fens as remain in
the 1980s.

Unreason still triumphs in a third fallacy, the 'Kaleidoscope Myth': the belief
that the countryside has always been changing; that its features were made by
farmers and are no more than the passing product of agricultural fashions; that
new habitats are created as well as old ones destroyed; and that a bit of
(unspecified) extra change matters little. The nature of the evidence and the
inclinations of scholars both tend to make the most of change, which is easier to
establish than stability and makes a more exciting story. In reality, changes have
happened at some times and in some places but not in others. Except for town
expansion, almost every hedge, wood, heath, fen, etc. on the Ordnance Survey
large-scale maps of 1870 is still there on the air photographs of 1940. The
seventy eventful years between, and even World War II itself, were less destructive than any five years since. Much of England in 1945 would have been
instantly recognizable by Sir Thomas More, and some areas would have been
recognized by the Emperor Claudius.

Changes in the eighteenth and nineteenth centuries were not so commendable
that they should be quoted as precedents to be followed in the twentieth. Most
good farmland had been made centuries earlier, and there were few genuine
opportunities for creating more. 1851 was a black year: the year we lost the
unique Whittlesey Mere (Huntingdonshire) and Hainault Forest (Essex) for
merely a few more farms, some of which proved to be temporary. Protests at the
destruction of Hainault were the foundation of the modern conservation movement, but the short-sighted Victorians acquiesced in the destruction of Whittlesey Mere. Since 1945 there have been some twenty-five years each as bad as
1851.

The argument that changes create new habitats has something to be said for it
as regards towns and industry: suburban gardens and disused quarries are well
worth having. It is seldom true of modern farming or forestry. Almost every
rural change since 1945 has extended what is already commonplace at the

expense of what is wonderful or rare or has meaning. Skylarks are not a substitute for bitterns, nor pines or oaks for the native lime tree: there are plenty of skylarks and oaks already. Nor is even the planting of native lime (which has recently become quite a fashionable tree) a substitute for preserving native woodland.

Is it really necessary to sacrifice the landscape in order to grow every possible ounce of food? If we managed without growing corn on the Halvergate Marshes in the dark and hungry days of World War II, what pressing need can there be to do so in the 1980s? Why do we devote so many acres not to human nutrition but to animal foodstuffs, or to sugar, or to food that is wasted? How is it that other Common Market countries (eg. France) have destroyed so little of their historic landscapes? How is it that in Britain some individual estates, many small farms, and occasionally much of a county (eg. Cornwall, except for its woods) have avoided the general destruction? All these show that the cause is not real necessity. So it has been before:

> The grubbing up of Hedge Rows is become general, and the Growth of Timber in them is thereby totally destroyed, owing to the great Price given for Corn since the Bounty took place for exporting of Corn and Beer, which gives every Farmer encouragement to grub Hedge Rows up, and convert them into Corn Land.
> *House of Commons Journal, 1792*, p.318

The recent arguments of Mr Body represent a particular, anti-Corn-Law philosophy which not all readers will support; but there can be no arguing with his conclusion that present agricultural politics, especially regarding cereals, are not good value. We contrive at the same time to subsidize agriculture much more than any industry, *and* to have expensive food, *and* a ravaged countryside. Our overproduction, alas, is of no benefit to the hungry in distant countries. Nor does it benefit farmers as a whole, nearly half of whom have given up farming. The beneficiaries are some of the big farmers, and the makers of chemicals, fertilizers, and machinery.

Agricultural improvement and 'reclamation' is a noble philosophy, but already in the seventeenth century it was reaching the limits of the worth-while, and was encouraged by hopes and policies rather than by practicalities. Since 1945 the improver has not known when to stop, and has not realized that in Britain the need for more land has been undercut by plant breeding. In 1945 the (official) average yield of wheat was 0.95 ton per acre; in 1982 it was 2.44 tons per acre. The wheat that we grew in 1945 can now be grown on well under half the acres. Most of the credit is due, not to farmers, but to plant breeders, and there is no reason to suppose that they are near the end of their ability to grow more crops on the same land. Plant breeding has far outweighed the loss of farmland to development (which, anyway, has been exactly balanced by the loss of roughland to farmland). The practical pressure on land is now less than it has been within living memory, and is likely to diminish. This is not an argument for wasting land: it is a pity, for instance, to use so much on motorway verges. But it does release us from any further need to destroy roughland. From now on, every acre of moorland ploughed, of marsh drained, of downland made to grow wheat (all at the public expense) will have one of two results. Either an acre goes out of production somewhere else – to the detriment, maybe, of another country's historic landscape – or an acre's-worth is added to the surplus production of the existing farmland. We Cambridge dons already grunt over our Intervention Butter; there is a limit to what can be eaten.

The argument against more forestry is different. Britain is dependent on imported timber and wood to an extent which cannot be appreciably reduced by sacrificing wild vegetation to grow more at home. There is not the space. If all our woods and heaths were to be transformed overnight into the most productive plantations, this would not be noticed by the user of timber: the extra amount grown would be less than is now wasted in sawdust. There is a weak case for afforesting moorland (p.326).

The 'economics' of modern forestry were never convincing (p.93); they have been pulled to pieces by fashion, recession, and politics. The Forestry Commission changes its mind over which species are 'best'; at times there is no market for timber (eg. poplars) which was fashionable when planted. In 1984 the Commission is being forced to sell hundreds of plantations. To create them, ancient woods and heaths were sacrificed. Some were successful as plantations and are now being sold at prices which do not repay the public money spent on them; others were less successful and, once ruined, have been rejected and sold off. Many of the lesser plantings date from the 1960s, only just before the value and variety of ancient woods and heaths became fully known. The Commission would probably not now be allowed to do to East Anglia what it did twenty years ago, but the waste and most of the damage are irretrievable.

The Wildlife and Countryside Act, 1981, has made matters worse. It has neutralized the Nature Conservancy Council by bogging it down in the paperwork of administration. Its provisions for compensation are scandalously open to abuse. One man, refused permission to drain a marsh, is able *in perpetuo* to draw public money to match both the hypothetical produce and the subsidies foregone; while another, forbidden (under a different statute) to build a factory in his garden, gets nothing.

It is not my business to lay down details of what should be done. Conservationists should not usually seek the restitution of features already destroyed, which is rarely worth-while. They should seldom seek to remove land from production: long-standing land-uses should be maintained or restored. But they should resolutely oppose any further advance of the commonplace or loss of meaning. Historic landscapes and historic buildings are similar in many ways, and both should have the same kind of legal protection. The case for conservation is weakened by lack of coordination between those concerned with scenery, wildlife, antiquities, and freedom. The arguments, naturally, differ, but the objectives are often the same. One proponent often accepts compromises which weaken the case of the others.

More intractable than destruction in pursuit of a purpose, albeit a dead purpose, is the blight of tidiness which every year sweeps away something of beauty or meaning. In the past we were content to cut down trees. In 1984 we must needs grind away the stumps with a special machine, as though ashamed to admit that the trees ever existed. Tidiness is worst in arable country. Cereals do not need attention all the year, and leave men and machines long weeks looking for something to do. That something often takes the form of destroying ivy-tods and 'misshapen' trees, cutting hedges to the ground every year, devouring saplings, levelling churchyards, filling ponds, pottering with paraquat – all the little, often unconscious vandalisms that hate what is tangled and unpredictable but create nothing.

Education in the knowledge and care of the countryside has far to go and has yet to reach many important people. No art gallery's conservation department would think of burning a picture by Constable, however badly decayed, and substituting a picture in the style of Constable by Tom Keating. Yet this kind of pastiche is daily perpetrated in the guise of the 'conservation' of the landscape.

It is painful to record that the National Trust's management of historic landscapes had not always matched its well-informed care of historic buildings and gardens. The Trust has indeed cared admirably for Wicken Fen over the last thirty years and for Hatfield Forest over the last ten. Against these must be set a sad tale of woods arbitrarily replanted (eg. Frithsden Great Copse, Herts) and other solecisms. The Wimpole Estate (Cambs) was left to the Trust in 1976. The splendid scene shown in Plate XIX, with the great south avenue of 1718 cutting diagonally across the hedges and fields of an earlier landscape, was then still recognizable. Two-thirds of the elms had recently died, but the landscape was well within the Trust's powers of restoration. Instead, since 1976, the dead elms, disease-resistant elms, the boundary hedges of the avenue, and almost every hedge and tree within half a mile of its northern half have been annihilated. The old grasslands and their faint earthworks have been destroyed, and the avenue is now (1984) merely a ploughed strip across prairie-farming. There are plans to replant it; if they succeed (one attempt has failed) the new avenue will be a mere decoration, with nothing to show that there had been an avenue before. Never again can it have the meaning which the old one had. There was not the excuse of ignorance, for Plate XIX is a famous picture. This is a local tragedy and sets a deplorable example.

Too much attention, and too much money, goes into the automatic and unintelligent planting of trees. Tree-planting is not synonymous with conservation; it is an admission that conservation has failed. The land is full of young trees which would grow into big trees if tidy-minded people did not cut them down. There seems to be no rational way of deciding what species to plant: advice on the subject usually consists of a poorly-argued claim that native trees are good and exotics are bad, coupled with an inaccurate list of native species. People plant trees, and get grants for doing so, without even looking to see whether there are trees on the spot already. Round the corner from my house, the local authority has planted ashes where there are already perfectly good ash saplings.

Planting trees, except in replacement for trees known themselves to have been planted, erodes the historic landscape. It diverts funds and attention away from real conservation, and encourages people to go on destroying wild trees. It may damage existing meadows, ancient woods, and other places where the planted trees are to grow. Tree-planters seldom understand, still less respect, the meaning of trees. The countryside is urbanized no less by introducing trees with urban associations – horsechestnut, weeping willow, Norway maple, etc. – than by erecting urban buildings. Every oak or alder planted in Cambridge (traditionally a city of willows, ashes, elms, and cherry-plums) erodes the difference between Cambridge and other places. Part of the value of the native lime tree lies in the meaning embodied in its mysterious natural distribution; it is devalued by being made into a universal tree.

The landscape is like a historic library of 50,000 books. Many were written in remote antiquity in languages which have only lately been deciphered; some of the languages are still unknown. Every year fifty volumes are unavoidably eaten

Conservation

by bookworms. Every year a thousand volumes are taken at random by people who cannot read them, and sold for the value of the parchment. A thousand more are restored by amateur bookbinders who discard the ancient bindings, trim off the margins, and throw away leaves that they consider damaged or indecent. The gaps in the shelves are filled either with bad paperback novels or with handsomely-printed pamphlets containing meaningless jumbles of letters. The library trustees, reproached with neglecting their heritage, reply that Conservation doesn't mean Preservation, that they wrote the books in the first place, and that none of them are older than the eighteenth century; concluding with a plea for more funds to buy two thousand novels next year.

CHAPTER 4

Animals and plants:
Extinctions and new arrivals

> During a visit to Cornwall Mr Borrer stayed some time with the Vicar of Sancreed, an old friend of his, although no botanist. In the course of his rambles [*c.* 1840] Borrer alighted upon the beautiful moss *Hookeria* [now *Cyclodictyon*] *laetevirens* in a cave at Mousehole; and after his return home wrote to his clerical friend requesting him to gather a few additional specimens of this moss, as it was new to England and not known in any other habitat. The clergyman found the cave, and had no difficulty in distinguishing the desired plant . . . But just here his zeal outran his discretion, for he calmly set to work to strip the walls bare, lest, as he explained, any other person but Mr Borrer should possess even a scrap of such a prize! Borrer's feelings may be imagined.
>
> *E.D. Marquand, 1890*[29]

Animal and plant species reflect millennia of interactions between nature and human activities. If mankind had originated in South America, Britain would still have elephants, rhinoceroses, and probably lions, but no rabbits, no sycamore trees, no house-mice, and almost no conifers.

There is usually a hard-and-fast distinction between wildlife and domesticated animals or cultivated plants. The latter – dogs, sheep, tame pigs, wheat, sugar-beet, Corsican pine, planted oak trees – exist because somebody has put them there and tends them. Most have either been imported from overseas or bred *de novo* by farmers and gardeners. Those which have not, such as the oaks of plantations, are often genetically different from wild individuals of the same species. Although there are some border-line cases there is rarely any doubt as to whether an animal or plant is wild. When we snare rabbits, cut ash poles in a coppice, exercise grazing rights on Dartmoor, or cut reeds in a Norfolk Broad we are using wildlife – even though the wood, moor, and Broad may all be the result of past human activity and neglect, and the wild rabbits are descended from semi-domestic rabbits. It is cultivation, not exploitation nor the original introduction, that makes animals and plants domestic.

The history of cultivated plants and domestic animals is generally well known* and is beyond the scope of this book. Many were introduced, already in a domestic state, in the Neolithic period, and others in historic times.

Native, Naturalized, and Exotic Species

Some species of wildlife, such as the fox and oak tree, are *native*: they arrived here by natural processes in prehistoric times.

---

* But not to producers of historical films: they do not allow Charles I to fly in a plane, but they do let him ride among Corsican pine plantations or Frisian cattle!

Other plants and animals were originally introduced by human agency from overseas, but now maintain themselves without further intervention. These are termed *naturalized*, in contrast to *exotic* species which are dependent on domestication. The rabbit, pheasant, sweet-chestnut, and Oxford ragwort are naturalized; guinea-pig, peafowl, walnut, and *Cannabis*, although of respectable antiquity as introductions, show no sign of becoming wildlife and remain exotics. Doubtful cases may arise, as we shall see with collared dove, rosebay, and *Bromus interruptus*. Even within the brief time-span of human history, plant and animal species are not quite static: once in a while a new species arises or an existing one spreads to new territories of its own accord.

I illustrate the many changes in the fauna and flora of the British Isles by examples of species which are either of special interest to the historian or are examples of general processes. Changes of the last hundred years are well covered in other books; I shall not re-tell the effects of pesticides on birds of prey, the decline of the otter, the loss of the Large Copper and Large Blue butterflies, nor the effect of anglers on fish.

Extinct Animals

In prehistoric times Britain was full of great beasts. Some, like the lion, leopard, and hyaena, were almost identical to species still living in Africa. Others, like two species of elephant, two rhinoceroses, the cave bear, and the Irish elk, were related to (though often bigger than) extant species; and there were a few, such as the sabre-toothed cat, which the layman cannot easily imagine. Giant mammals were not creatures of remote geological epochs, like dinosaurs; some of them lived at a period only three times as distant from us as the Pyramids.

Why did the great beasts die out? Not through changes of climate. There was, it is true, one creature now of southern Europe, the pond tortoise, which briefly inhabited England in the early post-glacial, when summers were apparently warmer than they are now. Giant mammals were not so dependent on particular climates. They had survived previous glaciations and deglaciations: the temperate species had moved south during cold periods and had been replaced by arctic species coming from the north. The woolly rhinoceros could certainly live in the present tundras of Canada or Siberia. There can be little doubt that the cause was human activity. Palaeolithic men preyed on giant mammals, which they slew by driving over cliffs or otherwise. All the other continents had their great beasts, which disappeared very soon after their human inhabitants acquired the means of hunting them.[30] Giant mammals would be specially vulnerable, being long-lived, slow-breeding, and not easily hidden. The prospect of killing so much meat at once was specially attractive in glacial times when the frozen subsoil was a ready-made deep-freeze.

The spectacular extinctions resulted from Palaeolithic greed and technology. This was followed in later prehistory by the destruction of wildwood, and in historic times by that of fens and heathland. This affected large, rather than giant, mammals – bear, wild swine, etc. – and big birds such as the crane and bustard. It is doubtful whether any species was directly exterminated by loss of habitat (some, such as wolves, live in moorland as well as wildwood); but numbers were reduced to the point at which greedy or fearful men could finish off the survivors. The British Isles, being for millennia relatively densely populated and sparsely wooded, have lost all the large mammals except red deer and possibly native cattle. Nearly all of them survive, usually in small numbers, elsewhere in Europe.

The nineteenth century was a period of gamekeeping, highland sheep-farming, and the collecting of birds' skins and eggshells. These activities were not new, but they became universal, professional, and single-minded as never before. Almost the commonest word in any nineteenth-century county bird book is 'shot'. The age of greedy keepers, sheep-owners, and ornithologists coincides with the sudden decline of what had been common beasts and birds of prey. Usually these were declines rather than extinctions, and hence will be dealt with later. Among British birds, the osprey became temporarily (and the sea-eagle so far permanently) extinct.

Where an animal survived late enough to have a written record, this is often liable to misinterpretation. There are not only actual beasts but beasts heraldic and metaphorical: anyone wishing to infer bears from the place-name *Bar*ham (Kent) should ask himself whether he would likewise infer lions from *Lyon*shall (Herefordshire). Even when the animals are real, they die out in remote places: the last survivors are not closely observed and may be misidentified (how many readers can swear to the difference between a wolf and an Alsatian dog?). Animals on the verge of extinction become the theme of romance and song in which fact is confused with fiction.

Aurochs This, the wild ancestor of European domestic cattle, is one of the few modern examples of an animal now extinct both in Britain and throughout the world. The aurochs is familiar in European Palaeolithic art. Archaeological evidence proves that it inhabited England and Ireland in this interglacial, but it is unlikely to have survived beyond the Bronze Age.[31] The Anglo-Saxons knew about it, and called the runic letter *ur*, equivalent to U, after it, but there is no reason to suppose that they were more directly familiar with it than they were with lions.

In the Middle Ages the aurochs was still a continental animal. In Corpus Christi College, Cambridge we treasure a great horn, given to us at our foundation in 1352, almost certainly of this extinct animal; I have often drunk from it. The workmanship of the silver-gilt mounts strongly indicates that it came from Germany. The last aurochsen were carefully observed in Jaktorowa Forest, Poland, where they died out in 1627.[32]

How the aurochs became extinct will never be known with certainty, but it seems always to have been a woodland animal, and destruction of wildwood probably reduced its habitat to a point at which the survivors could easily be caught.

Bear The bear in Britain is a shadowy beast lurking on the borders of prehistory. Remains of him are scanty indeed compared to those of wolves; but scattered finds of bones from England, Ireland, and Wales attest that he was here in this interglacial.[33] He died out too early to give rise to the place-names which one would expect of such a formidable and unmistakable creature. Bear place-names[34] are very few and uncertain; such references to bears – if that is what they are – could have been heraldic or divine rather than zoological.

Literary references to bears in Britain are vague and doubtful. The first-century poetaster Martial refers to a 'Caledonian bear' that executed a criminal in the amphitheatre,[35] but this is hardly evidence: where would showmanship be without a little exaggeration? The undated Welsh *Y Naw Helwriaeth* (The Nine Huntings) tells us how to hunt the bear, but tracts on hunting often refer to foreign beasts, and the bear may merely have been added to make up the magic 3 × 3 structure which literary convention demanded. There have, indeed, been tame bears, the star performers at baitings and circuses down the centuries; but they are no more likely to be indigenous than were the medieval lions in the Tower.

In much of Europe the bear was abundant well into historic times; in the Alps it outlived the wolf and (just) still exists. This was apparently not true of Britain. With us, bears were never common; they are unlikely to have survived the Roman period and may have died out much earlier.

Beaver The beaver was once common throughout Europe and has given rise to many place-names, especially in the Alps. It survives in Scandinavia and in two small parts of East Germany and south-east France.

In Britain, beaver remains are fairly widespread in prehistory, but by the historic period the animal was almost extinct. It survived into Anglo-Saxon times in east Yorkshire and gave its name to a number of places, including *Beverley*. (Welsh and Gaelic beaver place-names cannot certainly be distinguished from those involving otter.)

The late twelfth-century writer Giraldus Cambrensis gives an account of the beaver and of its habits of felling trees and making lodges. He says that England and Ireland had none but that they existed on the Teifi in Wales and on an unnamed river in Scotland.[36] His account has the ring of truth. Beavers seem not to be mentioned again except by authors copying Giraldus, and they probably became extinct soon after. In the later Middle Ages the beaver was a semi-fabulous beast; everybody knew that his fur was imported to make the best hats, and that when pursued he abandoned his testicles (the other commercial part of him) and so escaped.

The beaver is a rather strictly woodland animal of commercial value which draws attention to itself by building dams. It is surprising that it should have survived so long in a land which had lost all its flood-plain wildwood (p.98). The late survival in east Yorkshire is unexpected, although even in the eleventh century there was a concentration of woodland around Beverley (Fig. 5.4).

There have been several introductions of American beavers but these have proved to be a nuisance and have been successfully exterminated.[37]

Wolf The wolf is our best-recorded extinct beast. His bones have been widely reported in excavations, but his very familiarity makes the written record unsatisfactory. There are two-legged wolves, symbolic wolves, and wolves spiritual. In Anglo-Saxon times, unpersons and men on the run were declared *wulveshēafod* (wolf's-head) and if caught ended on a wolf's-head-tree. Despite this connotation, 'wolf' in various combinations (Ethel*wulf*, Beo*wulf*, etc.) was a favourite personal name. A 'wolf-tree' is what modern foresters call a tree that grows inordinately fast to the detriment of its neighbours; who can tell which of the wolf-springs, wolf-hedges, wolf-leaps, etc. in Anglo-Saxon charters have some such metaphorical meaning and which are connected with actual wolves?

We do not know how widespread wolves were in Anglo-Saxon times. They are not specially woodland beasts; they are threatened by extermination campaigns rather than by loss of habitat. They thrive on war and social upheaval and may have waxed and waned with political instability. The charters mention many 'wolf-pits', one of which gave rise to the Anglo-Saxon village-name Woolpit (Suffolk), *Wlfpeta* in Domesday Book. This, however, was identified in the twelfth century with what were already 'very ancient ditches', and is not evidence for wolves in Anglo-Saxon Suffolk, any more than 'Giant's Grave' is evidence for giants.

Records of wolves in medieval England seem to be confined to the Welsh Border counties and the north. The one exception is a bounty of 5s. paid for a wolf caught at Freemantle (Surrey) in 1212;[38] this quite large sum cannot often have been paid out. Evidence of wolves continues up to 1281, when Edward I exterminated them. He employed Peter Corbet 'to take and destroy all the wolves he can find in . . . Gloucestershire, Worcestershire, Herefordshire,* Shropshire, and Staffordshire'. Coppicing was encouraged in the Forest of Dean to deny cover to 'wolves and malefactors'.[37] This campaign was largely success- ful: apart from one allegation in 1290 that they had destroyed the deer in a park at Farley (county unknown),[37] wolves disappear from the records of most of England. In 1300 the Rev. William, a bogus doctor, needing four putrid wolves for a medical purpose, imported them from abroad, which got him into trouble with Customs.[39] People continued to hold lands in many places by serjeanty of killing wolves and keeping wolfhounds, but this merely illustrates the medieval love of sinecures. Do we not still keep wolfhounds? Are not the Lieutenants de Louveterie still a respected body in France, though they have had no wolves to slay for a century and a half?

The final and mysterious record in England is in 1394–6, when the monks of Whitby paid 10s. 9d. 'for tawing 14 wolfskins'.[37] There are many intriguing wolf place-names and legends in north-east Yorkshire, but apparently no other datable evidence.[41] Nevertheless, the most plausible interpretation of the Whit- by record is that wolves held out in the North York Moors for a century after they had become extinct elsewhere.

Wolves may have been exterminated earlier in Wales. According to William of Malmesbury, King Edgar of England arranged for King Idwal of Wales in *c.* 985 to render 300 wolfskins annually in lieu of a tribute which he owed. The Welsh ran out of wolves within three years.[42] This may be thought a far-fetched story (it was written 140 years later) but I do not know of any later records in Wales, apart from a mad wolf (which could have been misidentified or have escaped from England) which killed twenty-two people in Caermarthen in 1166.[37]

Wolves lasted much longer in warlike and sparsely-populated Scotland. Even in the Lowlands, a bounty was paid for two wolves in 1491 in Linlithgow.[43] Records from the Highlands are frequent in the sixteenth century, although by 1570 difficulty was reported in getting wolfskins.[44] There are 'legends', none of them substantiated, of woods being burnt to deny cover to wolves. The last positive record is of the very large, and therefore exceptional, bounty of £6 13s. 4d. paid for a wolf in Sutherland in 1621.[43] A number of less specific but not implausible stories of 'last wolves' follow up to 1682. In 1769 the naturalist Thomas Pennant,[45] after extensive inquiries, concluded that the wolf was by

* The campaign is allegedly commemorated by an iron wolf's-head on a contemporary door at Abbey Dore.[40]

then extinct; a conclusion with which I see no reason to disagree.

The last word on wolves in Scotland is the famous story, to which the date 1743 has been assigned, of the slaying of a 'large black beast', identified as a wolf, below Tomatin in the Findhorn Valley (Nairnshire). The tale was not published until 87 years later;[46] we shall never know whether its hero Mac-Queen, who told it as an old man, meant it as fact. It is a fine bloody Homeric narration; but I am reluctant to believe it. Apart from the suspiciously long interval since the last previous mention of wolves, there is the circumstance that the victim had just killed two children; such behaviour is a mark of the fictional rather than the zoological wolf.

In Ireland wolves were still sufficiently evident for legislation to be passed against them by the English government in 1652, 1653, and 1662.[47] Specific reports for killing wolves continue in County Cork until 1709–10.[37] Thus the wolf became extinct in the British Isles.

Wild swine The wild pig still flourishes in many parts of Europe, albeit often encouraged as a beast of the chase. He used to be found in Wales, where a specific hunting season was specified in the possibly tenth-century Laws of Hywel Dda, and in Scotland, where he gives rise to Gaelic place-names involving *fiadh-thorc* (wild boar) or *fiadh mhuc* (wild sow).[37] In Ireland, although some zoologists have denied that he ever existed, Giraldus Cambrensis says that there was a small variety of wild swine in the twelfth century;[48] and there are said to be *torc fiadhain* place-names.[37] Wild swine presumably disappeared from these countries early; only in England is there any considerable record.

Many writers claim that the medieval tame pig was very similar to the wild pig and often cross-bred with it. This may be so as concerning bone remains, but medieval records are never in any doubt as to which is meant; *aper* and *laya*, the normal Latin words for a wild boar and wild sow, are contrasted with the tame *porci*, *porculi* and *porcelli*. It is less clear whether place-name evidence is specific. The Anglo-Saxon *eofor* is often supposed to mean a wild boar and *bār* a tame boar. If this is so, *eofor* place-names such as *Evers*den (Cambs) and *Evers*ley (Hants) indicate a much wider distribution of wild pig than in later centuries, but we have no confirmatory evidence.

By the Middle Ages wild swine were very rare. I have records only from the Forests of Pickering (north-east Yorks) and Dean. Wild boars and sows were official beasts of the king's Forest; his hunters regularly visited Dean and occasionally Pickering and took specified numbers for the table royal. After the great Christmas dinner of 1251 (p. 119) at which Henry III had 200 wild swine from Dean and 100 from Pickering, they disappear rapidly from the record. Queen Eleanor ate 50 sows and 20 boars at her Christmas feast in 1253, and the king consumed 80 at Christmas in 1257.[49] Small numbers were given to the king's friends. Unless later records turn up for some private Forest, the dozen which Henry III ordered killed for a friend in the Forest of Dean in 1260 were the last free-living wild swine in England.

Wild swine lived on in heraldry and romance. Englishmen knew the courtly science of pig-sticking from visits to France, and represented its weapons and ceremonial in art (eg. the stone tympanum which remains from the Norman church of Little Langford, Wilts) and literature (eg. the splendid boar-hunt in *Sir Gawain and the Green Knight*, written in the fourteenth century but set in a romantic England of long before).

The animals themselves continued to be kept in semi-captivity in parks (see Chapter 6). Swine-parks are known in all centuries from the thirteenth to the twentieth, though it is most unlikely that there has been enough continuity to preserve any genes from the English wild pig. Pig are devilish animals to fence in, and swine-parks were rare and often short-lived status symbols. For example, in 1223 Henry III ordered Thomas de Langley to take two of the king's wild swine in his custody and put them into the royal park of Havering (Essex); their descendants remained there for at least 37 years (Rackham 1978). In 1263 the Sheriff of Forfar fed 4½ chalders of corn to the King of Scotland's *porci silvestres*.[43] Around 1500, the De Veres, Earls of Oxford, used Chalkney Wood (Earl's Colne, Essex, Fig. 2.2b) as a swine-park:

> This wood in tymes paste was empaled: And the Erles of Oxenforde in former tymes (for their pleasure) bredd and maintayned wilde Swyne in the same untill the Reigne of King Hary the Eight. About wch tyme they were destroied by John (then Erle of Oxenford) for yt he understode, that the Inhabitaunts thereabouts sustained by them very greate losse and damage.[50]

The great park of Chartley (Staffs) had wild swine as well as wild cattle in the sixteenth and seventeenth centuries. In 1617 Charles I arranged a boar-hunt at Windsor.[37]

The wild pig was a very noble beast. The De Veres were particularly attached to him, imagining their family name to be derived from *verres*, a swine. Tudor and Stuart monarchs liked to be given 'wild-boar pye'.

This does not entirely exhaust the records of wild swine in England. Around 1540 some were taken alive in Savernake Forest (Wilts); the expenses included 4*d*. 'for 8 hempen halters to bynd their legs' and 4*d*. 'for drink for them that helped to take them'.[37] They could not have been a surviving wild population: neither the many letters of Henry III concerning the beasts of Savernake nor the medieval poaching cases abundantly chronicled by Lord Ailesbury[51] make any mention of pig. These, and a few other wild swine reported from areas where there was no tradition of them, presumably escaped from parks.

Wild swine, next to beaver, are most likely to have been affected by destruction of wildwood. The European countries in which they survive have at least 20 per cent of woodland. The wooded area of England fell below this figure in Anglo-Saxon times (Chapter 5) and the survival of wild swine then became precarious. They lingered in the Forest of Dean, one of the largest wooded areas in Britain. Henry III exterminated them, not so much by the excesses of his table (which a large French or German Forest could have supported to this day) as by encouraging industry in Dean and destroying their solitude.

Crane The crane is a great bird which breeds in the fens of Northern Europe and migrates to Africa in winter. It figured largely in Henry III's feasts (p.119). Cranes were a luxury article of diet, along with teal, snipe, curlews, fieldfares, and even the occasional thrush, hoopoe, bittern, and coot.[52] In 1534 many edible birds were protected by statute; cranes' eggs carried the heaviest penalty, 20*d*. per egg, which suggests rarity.[53] The crane is said to have ceased breeding shortly after, and is now a rare vagrant. Its extinction as a breeding bird is usually blamed on fen drainage; this is unlikely, for the sixteenth century was not a time of advancing drainage.

Garefowl The great auk, penguin, or garefowl is another species extinct all over the world. Its story has often been told, eg. by J. Fisher and R.M. Lockley.[54] It was a remarkable sea-bird, incapable of flying, and similar (though unrelated) to the penguins of the southern hemisphere to which it gave its name. It was an arctic bird, much eaten by Palaeolithic men during the last glaciation. It remained common until the Iron Age, its bones having been found all over Europe. Like other flightless birds, it was easy to catch, but its vast numbers long resisted predation.

By the historic period the garefowl was reduced to about six regular breeding colonies on very remote islets ranging from St Kilda to Canada. One by one they succumbed to raids for eggs, meat, and feathers. The St Kilda colony was apparently only a memory when Martin Martin went there in 1697. A stray pair bred and was killed in Orkney in 1612. When one last garefowl visited St Kilda in 1840 it was slain by the superstitious natives. The last pair of all was killed in Iceland in 1844.

Animals Which Have Declined

Wild cattle A mysterious survival from the Middle Ages are the fierce shy white cattle of a few very grand parks. Since the twelfth century wild bulls (*tauri sylvestres*) have been distinguished from domestic oxen. Four herds are still extant, in parks at Chillingham (Northumberland), Woburn (transferred from Chartley, Staffordshire), Dynevor (Carmarthenshire), and Cadzow (Lanarkshire). Similar herds have been established in other places by cattle-breeders, most successfully from 1872 onwards at Vaynol (Caernarvonshire). Details have been collected by G.K. Whitehead.[32]

These cattle, although always called wild, are known chiefly as beasts of the park. There are records of about twenty park herds having existed. Apart from the relatively domesticated cattle of Dynevor, the authentic records appear to be from northern England or south or middle Scotland. Records are few in the Middle Ages but more numerous in the seventeenth century.[37] Wild cattle were treated as a kind of super-deer eaten on festive occasions and possibly the object of specially thrilling hunts. The Archbishop of York ate six 'wylde bulls' at his installation feast in 1466.[37] Like deer, cattle were transferred from park to park. In recent times they have been cross-bred with domestic cattle to form a number of new herds.

It is usually supposed that park cattle are descended from wild cattle which roamed the wilder parts of England and Scotland near which the parks are located. Much lore about free-living wild cattle was collected by John Storer a century ago,[55] but is contaminated by pseudo-legends and by bulls invented to explain surnames such as Turnbull. Evidence definitely relating to the bulls of this world is fragmentary. The twelfth-century writer Fitzstephen includes bulls among the wild beasts of the woods on the Chiltern plateau.[56] In 1277 Edward I specifically ordered wild bulls and cows to be taken in Windsor Forest.[49] Hector Boece, the sixteenth-century writer, refers to wild white cattle in woods and Forests in and around Stirlingshire. He claims that they had been survivors of those that had inhabited a former 'great wood of Calidonia' once covering most of Perthshire as well. The Calidonian Wood is probably enlarged in Boece's romantic exaggeration, but his account of the 'quhyt ky and bullis' and their extreme shyness carries conviction and is corroborated by others. They were apparently all slain as one of the 'gryt enormities perpetuat' by a wicked war-lord Earl of Lennox.[57]

White cattle are still mysterious and controversial. The medieval records are not from parts of the country where park herds were later prevalent. The surviving park herds differ from each other and may not have a common origin; none of them is documented earlier than 1600; there is no evidence as to whether the park herds were derived from the free-living or *vice versa*. A study of the Chillingham cattle shows that their skull anatomy resembles that of domestic cattle and rebuts the oft-repeated theory that they are more directly related to the aurochs.[58]

Wild cattle are probably the longest-running example in Europe of the conservation in semi-captivity of an otherwise extinct subspecies. They owe their survival to being a medieval status symbol; how they came to be such is unknown.

Native deer In this interglacial there have been four native deer in the British Isles. The reindeer died out soon after the last glaciation: the belief that it survived into historic times rests on a single, mistaken, mention by an Icelandic saga-writer ignorant of deer.[41, 59] The elk* was the second most important food animal at the Mesolithic site of Star Carr (north-east Yorks) but died out soon after.[60]

Red deer were one of the most important animals in the prehistoric economy. They were almost ubiquitous in woodland, moorland, and even tundra. They provided meat, skins, and antlers and bones used as tools. They are the most abundant of all mammals excavated at Star Carr. The Neolithic flint-miners of Grime's Graves (Norfolk) used over 50,000 antlers as picks.[61]

As farmland advanced deer declined. By the Middle Ages red deer were no longer common in England, though still found in most areas except East Anglia and the north-east Midlands. With the institution of parks and Forests (Chapter 6), red deer were given the status of semi-domestic animals, although they were soon outnumbered by fallow deer which were more suitable for systematic management. I have evidence of red deer for about thirty of the eighty or so royal Forests. By the thirteenth century the largest numbers were in the moorland Forests of the Pennines and Exmoor; they also lived in wooded Forests (eg. Grovely, Wilts; Bernwood, Bucks) and heathland Forests (Sherwood, Notts; Wolmer, Hants).[62] Red deer, then as now, were abundant in the Scottish Highlands.

With the decline of the Forest system red deer almost died out in England. By the late nineteenth century they survived, outside a few parks, only in the north and in Exmoor.

Roe deer were also a major food in prehistory. By the Middle Ages they had declined to a greater extent than red deer. The medievals did not, as often stated, despise roe deer (p.119), but, being nocturnal and difficult to confine, roe were not suitable for systematic management. I have records of them for eleven Forests and a few parks. They were not then exclusively woodland deer: they are recorded in the fens of Huntingdonshire (p.389) and south-east Yorkshire and probably in the Pennine moorlands (Rackham 1980). By 1800 roe are

---

* The red deer is closely related to the animal that Americans call elk or wapiti. The elk is equivalent to the North American moose.

supposed to have died out in England and Wales, except in the extreme north.

Red and roe deer have recovered in the last hundred years and are now more abundant in Great Britain than they were in the heyday of the Forest system. (Red deer are still scarce in Ireland and roe were never native there.) The reasons for this are discussed under fallow deer (p.49). Red deer in Scotland have long been the subject of systematic gamekeeping. Roe in England result in part from deliberate reintroduction, although they are so secretive that survival is difficult to disprove.

Polecat, marten, and wildcat These three beasts declined quite recently. They have been studied by P.J.W. Langley and D.W. Yalden.[63]

The foulmart or polecat was once widespread throughout Great Britain (never Ireland). I have encountered it in medieval (and even eighteenth-century)[64] Norfolk:

> *Young peafowl* . . . .4, of which 2 devoured by *le fulmerd*
> *Hindolveston 1309–10*[65]

Bounties were paid on its head, as on those of other 'vermin', and appear in seventeenth- and eighteenth-century churchwardens' accounts. Despite substantial numbers killed, the polecat was found in every county (except islands) until 1850. It then rapidly declined, beginning in east Scotland and south-east England, and by 1915 had become extinct everywhere except mid Wales and the Lake District. It has since slowly increased.

The marten, like the polecat, appears at prehistoric sites. It is documented as a fur animal. Until 1800 it occurred throughout the British Isles, except for some islands, but was rare in southern England. It was not limited to remote or well-wooded areas, nor to pine trees (despite the name 'pine marten' bestowed on it by modern academics). It declined a little earlier than the polecat. By 1915 it was limited to the remote moorland of Snowdon, the Lake District, and the north-west Highlands. The decline was less severe in Ireland. It has recently increased in Scotland but remains rare in England and Wales.

The wildcat is less well known because of confusion with the domestic cat. 'Cat' appears in Anglo-Saxon place-names (eg. Catshaw), and the medieval foxhunter did not disdain the hare and cat which, like the fox, were regarded as 'beasts of the warren'. Scholars usually assume that these were the wildcat rather than the mere wandering pussy, but I can find no evidence to support this contention. A usual word for the cat as a huntable beast is *murilegus*, 'mouse-taker', which indicates the ex-domestic cat. Discounting these ambiguous allusions, the wildcat was native in Scotland (except the Lowlands and islands), northern England, and Wales; it was a creature of moorland and not of the farmed countryside. Its decline began soon after 1800; by 1880 it was limited to the Scottish Highlands, in which it has slowly expanded since 1900.

As Langley and Yalden point out, the decline and partial recovery of these beasts of prey (and of birds of prey such as the buzzard and the two species of eagle) coincide with the rise and partial decline of professional gamekeeping. Other causes, such as destruction of woodland, are most unlikely. The physical countryside of 1900 was not conspicuously less favourable to beasts and birds of prey than that of 1800. Woods had been grubbed up and there was some urbanization; but these changes (offset by some increase in plantations and hedges) are not sufficient to account for such a general decline. Gamekeepers – by 1850 armed with breech-loading shotguns – would be more efficient as predators than churchwardens. The geography of the patterns of survival of animals of prey is to some extent related to differences in gamekeeping: for instance, the polecat is less of a moorland animal and survived not in Scotland but in Wales, where gamekeeping on low ground may have been less intensive. Gamekeeping declined during the World Wars and was restored in a somewhat less single-minded and predatory form. The recovery of birds of prey, which are protected by law, has been more complete than that of beasts which are not.

Some details remain to be cleared up. How did gamekeepers manage to exterminate martens and wildcats, which are nocturnal, but not stoats and weasels, which are almost equally invisible but easy to trap? The nineteenth-century fashion for gamekeeping, like the twentieth-century fashion for hedge-grubbing, was not universal; what happened on the lands of people who disapproved of it?

Kite The kite was once one of our commonest birds of prey. In the fifteenth and sixteenth centuries it was common in towns: travellers such as Václav Šašek from Bohemia in 1465 and Andrea Trevisan from Venice in 1500 were specially impressed by the kites of London,[66] which were so tame as to snatch bread-and-butter out of the hands of children. They were told that to kill a kite was an offence punishable by death etc., but this I cannot confirm. Modern writers usually claim that kites were protected because they ate up carrion lying in the street; this assumption seems to be based on the kites in Shakespeare, which proverbially consume fallen warriors. The black kite, *Milvus migrans*, is indeed a scavenger in oriental cities to this day, but not so the red kite, *M. milvus*; and contemporary observers (corroborated by some archaeological evidence) agree that the London kites were red.[67] There is still some mystery as to what they were doing in sixteenth-century London and why they were no longer doing it in the seventeenth century. Possibly, like their successors in Wales,[68] they lived on mice as well as carrion.

Rural kites persisted throughout Great Britain (never Ireland) until the early nineteenth century. Place-names involving *puttock* usually refer to the kite, although it was sometimes confused with the buzzard. The bird then rapidly declined and before the end of the century was extinct in England and Scotland. It just lived on in Wales and is now gradually expanding under the most strenuous protection. This decline is usually, and probably rightly, attributed to the rise of gamekeeping. Keepers were not specially ill-disposed to the kite, but not being shy it was more easily exterminated than other birds of prey.

Extinct and Declining Plants

The early and systematic extermination of a whole group of fauna has no parallel among plants. We shall never see the elephants and rhinoceroses of prehistoric Britain, but we still have the limewoods which were their habitat, albeit reduced to a ten-thousandth of their original extent. Plants arouse less greed and fear than animals; they can survive in smaller numbers and on smaller areas of land. Lime trees hide from mankind more effectively than elephants and rhinos.

We may have lost some plants that were never common and have left no fossil record; but known extinctions are confined to the last 300 years, while botanists have been keeping watch. In that time the British Isles have lost 15 species of flowering-plants and ferns (about 1 per cent of the total of native species), 20 mosses and liverworts (2 per cent of the total), and about 40 lichens (3 per cent).[69] Most of the recorded extinctions are among bryophytes and lichens, even though these are less completely known, and also much less attractive to collectors, than flowering-plants. Many more species have reached the verge of extinction. In 1900 about 3 per cent of the flowering-plants of the British Isles were limited to one or two 10-km squares of the National Grid; by 1970 this figure had more than doubled through the decline of plants formerly more widespread.[69] The rise of nature conservation came too late to save many of our animals; it could yet save many plants, insofar as human endeavour or forbearance can do so.

Destruction and alteration of habitat Causes of decline or extinction can sometimes be inferred with reasonable certainty. Destruction of habitat affects certain groups of plants, to be mentioned in detail in later chapters. The fritillary and pasque-flower are destroyed by even a single ploughing of the grasslands in which they grow; they never return, nor do they colonize new grassland. The mania for drainage has drastically reduced many species on fens and bogs and even on roads (p.280). Other declines can be traced to neglect or changes of management. Increasing heath fires are a likely cause of the decline in the clubmoss *Lycopodium selago* and juniper. Allowing heath, grassland, or fen to become overgrown with trees does more damage than burning and is almost as destructive as ploughing. Many woodland plants are affected by the decline in woodland management. For instance, all the four species of wood-spurge have declined, and one has become apparently extinct, through not periodically felling the woods in which they grow. The most severe declines in all wild plants are among the weeds (p.53)

Collecting and eradication Gathering of plants for food can seldom be proved to have diminished their abundance. Two relatively rare plants have been regularly eaten, Bath asparagus (*Ornithogalum pyrenaicum*) and seakale (*Crambe maritima*), the former being sold in Bath market; yet both still exist in easily-accessible places. When a certain wood was declared a nature reserve I was sorry to see that a local inhabitant, who had for many years collected oxlip flowers to make oxlip wine, was warned to stop. The plant is abundant here and the extra flowering resulting from resumed woodland management (Chapter 5) should have more than made up for this degree of predation. (These remarks should not be made a precedent for collecting uncommon plants in places where there is not already a tradition of using them.)

People have occasionally objected to plants as being poisonous or harbouring pests. In the Age of Reason moralists were wont to quote, as an example of 'superstition', the prejudice of farmers against the barberry:

> This Tree has an ill Name . . . . for attracting Blights to the Corn that grows near it; insomuch that an ignorant malicious Farmer of *Frethesden*, by *Gaddesden* [Herts], about the Year 1720, conceived such a Hatred against a large one, that grew in his Neighbour's Ground, very near him, that, for this very Reason, he poured several Pails of scalding Water on its Roots, in the Night-season, at different Times, 'till he killed it.[70]

As everyone now knows, barberry is indeed the alternate host of *Puccinia graminis*, the fungus that causes black stem rust of wheat. After this was discovered in 1865, eradication campaigns were held against barberry in Denmark and North America with, it was claimed, some success in preventing the disease.[71] In England barberry is not necessary to the life-cycle of the fungus, and although farmers from time to time have dug up the bushes, it is unlikely that barberry was ever common or has been much diminished. More recently there has been a similar disapproval of spindle, as a host of the agriculturally important aphid *Myzus persicae*, but spindle remains common in ancient hedges and woods.

The collecting mania of the nineteenth century extended to plants. People picked flowers, which usually did little harm, but also used to dig up ferns, orchids, and other rare plants. It is often alleged that picking flowers, or more plausibly, digging up roots for sale, has locally exterminated even such a relatively common plant as the primrose. This example has never been documented in detail and is hard to accept: I do not find that primroses are systematically more abundant in private woods than in those accessible to the public.[72] Collecting may mask the less obvious ill-effects of a change in habitat. Primroses declined in woods and wood-pastures around London at a time when shade was increasing owing to lack of woodcutting (p.93). The last few primroses in Epping Forest may have been taken by visitors, but it is unlikely that they would have survived the shade much longer had there been no visitors; had woodcutting continued the primroses would have remained in good health and might have withstood the depredation.

Collecting is still a threat to rare and spectacular plants such as the lady's-slipper orchid, but it is unfortunate that preventing it should be so much emphasized in recent legislation rather than more fundamental kinds of protection. The Wildlife and Countryside Act (1981) protects some rare plants against depredation by collectors and scientists, but not against the mass destruction which so often results from 'good agricultural and forestry practice'.

Air and rain pollution Possibly the most pervasive change which someone returning from the Middle Ages would notice in the modern countryside is the appearance of tree-trunks. Trunks everywhere used to be covered with a patchwork of grey, brown, white, green, and yellow lichens, with occasional mosses. This normal aspect of a tree-trunk is still to be seen in the remoter parts of western England, Wales, Scotland, and Ireland. To most English countrymen now, tree-trunks are grey-green with a thin layer of a single lichen, *Lecanora conizaeoides*. In suburbs tree-trunks are bright green with the alga *Pleurococcus*. In cities and downwind of industry trunks have a clean dark-brown appearance, sterilized by acid rain.

The cause is air and rain pollution, chiefly by sulphur dioxide, to which nearly all lichens except *Lecanora conizaeoides* are very sensitive.[73] *Pleurococcus* is more resistant than any lichen but even it has a limit. Eighteenth- and nineteenth-century records show that places like Epping and Hatfield Forests (Essex) were once rich in lichens,[74] and I have recently found proof of this in the wattle-and-daub of medieval buildings at Hadleigh and Hartest (Suffolk). The wattle rods (p.87) have their original bark on which are preserved medieval lichens. The rods are of only seven years' growth and establish that all trees, even of that age, were as fully covered with lichens in Suffolk as they are now in the clean rain of Devon.

Not all extinctions of lichens can be attributed to rain pollution, but this is certainly why lichens have declined catastrophically in the eastern half of England, in lowland Scotland, and near all large towns. A given amount of sulphur dioxide does less damage in areas of high rainfall: Plymouth has had little effect on the lichens of Dartmoor, whereas Cambridge has devastated those of Suffolk. The decline of lichens is more severe than distribution maps such as Fig. 4.1 would indicate: lichenologists are skilled in recording wretched remnants of once thriving populations, which often hang on to the bases of ancient trees when they have long disappeared elsewhere.

Mosses in general are less affected than lichens by air pollution, but some species that grow on trees are sensitive.[75] The trees themselves, like most flowering-plants, are almost unaffected in Britain.

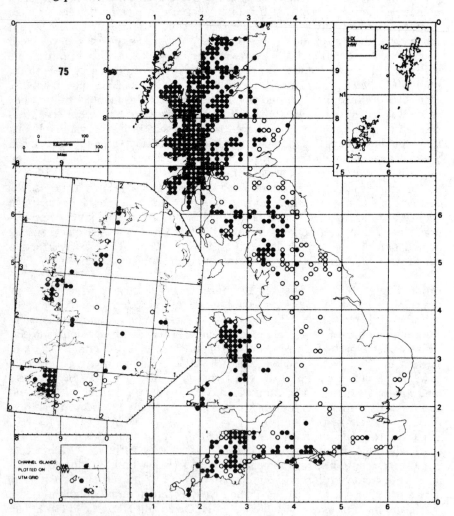

Fig. 4.1. Decline of the very pollution-sensitive lichen *Lobaria pulmonaria*. Open circles: not seen since 1960. (Map by Dr M. Seaward, reproduced by his kind permission.)[618]

Inexplicable declines This is a field in which scholars are reluctant to admit ignorance; but there are many declines for which no convincing explanation can be given.

The name broomrape was originally applied to *Orobanche rapum-genistae*,* a remarkable and conspicuous leafless parasite on the roots of broom. It used to occur wherever there was broom or furze: Anne Pratt in 1854 called it 'by no means infrequent on gravelly heaths',[76] and even the *British Flora* (compiled 1948) says it can be found 'throughout England and Wales'.[77] From 1930 onwards it suddenly disappeared, and nobody knows why. Despite the destruction of heathland, broom and furze are not uncommon. In recent years this broomrape has been seen in only two or three places. I know one such place in Suffolk, a little heath, with nothing special to explain why *Orobanche* should choose to survive there; the broomrape, like the broom itself, comes and goes cyclically over the years.

Many seaside plants have declined, often too early or in the wrong places to be explained by coastal urbanization. The sand-dune spurge *Euphorbia peplis* is extinct in the British Isles; the sand-dune plant *Otanthus maritimus*, once quite widespread, is reduced to one Irish locality; and the stock *Matthiola sinuata* is reduced to five localities. These three and several others are Mediterranean plants here at their northern limit, and some have supposed that an unspecified change of climate has driven them southwards; a conjecture rendered unlikely by the fact that *Mertensia maritima*, here at its southern limit, has retreated northwards.

The two fen ragworts, *Senecio paludosus* and *Senecio palustris*, became extinct in the nineteenth century.[78] Both had occurred in many places in the Fens, and *S. palustris* in the Norfolk Broads also. Because of the fenland habitat it is customary to ascribe their loss to drainage, but this hardly bears examination. Many records are from ditches, which were not destroyed by drainage. Neither the habitat of *S. paludosus* in Wicken Fen nor that of *palustris* in the Broads was in fact appreciably altered by drainage at this time, so the complete loss of these plants must remain a mystery. In 1972 the mystery deepened when T.W.J.D. Dupree found three plants of *paludosus* in a fenland ditch which had been newly dug in 1968; they had lain dormant or escaped detection for at least 115 years since the previous definite record.[79]

Naturalized Animals

The establishment of foreign animals began in prehistory. The less highly domesticated livestock can escape and become wild: we thus have the wild sheep of St Kilda, the wild goats of North Wales and elsewhere, the Dartmoor ponies whose predecessors are recorded in Domesday Book, and formerly 'wild' cattle in various places. Rats and clothes-moths follow the camp of civilization. In recent years animals like budgerigars and muntjac deer have escaped and become naturalized.

In the nineteenth century there was a curious fashion for deliberately releasing exotic beasts and birds with the thought that they would 'enrich' a supposedly unsatisfactory native fauna. In the United States societies were formed and subscriptions paid in order to naturalize European birds, beginning with

---

* Named after Latin *rapum*, 'turnip', from its tuberous base.

the sparrow and starling, as though God had not already given America birds enough.[80] People insisted on learning the hard way what are the ill-effects of importing creatures. Britain has suffered less from this strange folly, but the grey squirrel is an example which shows how foreign species displace the native fauna (instead of merely being added to it) and can menace the native plant life. Rabbits and fallow deer illustrate how an exotic animal may not get out of hand until centuries after its introduction.

Rats and mice The common house-mouse is a prehistoric introduction; it has followed civilization around the world. In Britain the first reliable identification is from the Iron Age in Dorset.[81]

The coming of rats was until recently a mystery. The medieval species was the 'black' rat, *Rattus rattus*. Rats, ratcatchers, and ratsbane have certainly been commonplace at least since the 1290s,[52] but there is a curious lack of earlier evidence. Giraldus Cambrensis refers twice to 'greater mice which are commonly called rats' (*majores mures qui vulgariter rati vocantur*) in terms which imply that by the late twelfth century they were familiar in Great Britain and Ireland and were not remembered as recent arrivals.[82] There is an apocryphal story that rats were brought by Crusaders from the Holy Land. But if their coming was as late as the Crusades, why did no chronicler notice what must have been an impressive and fearsome event? Why did no moralist denounce this new, gigantic, and terrible mouse as a divine judgement on a sinful nation, as on the Philistines in the days of Samuel? Such silence implies that rats came in an earlier and dark age when there were no chroniclers or preachers.

The matter is resolved by archaeology. Finds of rat (and rabbit) bones are often worthless because they may be of animals that burrowed into earlier strata and died there. Recently in several excavations, for instance of wells at York and London, the remains of rats have been found in Roman or Anglo-Saxon deposits sealed in such a way that they could not have got in later. There can be no doubt that the black rat was present in several towns by the third century AD and persisted through the Anglo-Saxon period.[607]

The black rat is now thought to be a native of south India. It was not known to such Classical naturalists as Theophrastus and Pliny. In late Classical times it spread into Mediterranean lands and Germany and reached Britain. We do not yet know how abundant it was, how quickly it adapted itself to our climate, or whether it was confined to towns.

Does the coming of the rat, thus back-dated, explain the mystery of the Dark Ages? As we all know, the black rat carries bubonic plague. It now becomes plausible, as has long been conjectured, that the 'Justinian' pestilence which ravaged Europe in the 540s, and the epidemics which followed it, were this disease.[83] A new disease, striking for the first time at a nation already disrupted by war, could easily have had effects more calamitous still than the Black Death of 1349. It is notoriously difficult to diagnose historic diseases: there are a few historians who do not accept that even the 1349 pestilence, well documented though it is, was bubonic plague. But the plague hypothesis covers the known facts and peculiarities of the Dark Ages. In particular it allows us to accept that country life and the landscape should have been much less disrupted than town life.

The modern rat of Britain is the 'brown' rat, *R. norvegicus*, which came from Eastern Europe – not Norway, despite the Latin name. It is so like the black rat that the difference was not noticed at first. Had it arrived before 1704 it would probably have been recorded by John Ray, the naturalist. The first definite record appears to be by Robert Smith, ratcatcher to Princess Amelia, who distinguished the two rats in 1768 (Lever 1977). The introduction lies somewhere between those dates; the date 1728–9, quoted by many authors, is unwarrantably precise. The brown rat quickly spread throughout the British Isles at the expense of the black, which now survives only in some seaports and small islands.

Rabbit The rabbit in this interglacial is a western Mediterranean animal; Roman authors thought of it as characteristic of Spain and the Balearic Islands. John Sheail (1971) has written a book on its history in Britain.

The rabbit appears in England at the beginning of the twelfth century. The circumstances strongly indicate deliberate introduction. It is delicious, and by the next century had become an important commercial animal; but it is not mentioned nor implied in Anglo-Saxon documents or Domesday Book. The earliest secure archaeological finds – discounting rabbits that may have burrowed into earlier strata – are of *c*. 1100 at Ipswich and at Hadleigh (Essex).[84] The first written record is for the Scilly Islands in 1176 (Sheail 1971). The earliest representation that I have seen is of a dog and rabbit on a corbel of Kilpeck church (Herefordshire), ascribed to the 1150s or 1160s.

The word 'warren', originally referring to hunting rights in general, soon came to imply rabbits much as 'Forest' (Chapter 6) implied deer. Early warrens were set up on small islands: Scilly, Lundy, Skokholm (Pembrokeshire), the Farne Islands, Isle of May (Fife), etc.* This solved the problem of fencing, for rabbits hate to swim. By the thirteenth century warrens were being established inland and in Scotland[85] and Wales. The bigger ones, often owned by monks, were on heathland; others were in parks and later in Forests. Sheail gives a map of hundreds of Warren place-names all over England except for mountains, fenland, and the most intensive agriculture. Coney, the old name for rabbit, gives rise to place-names such as Conygre, Conyfare, and Conifer Wood.

The medieval rabbit was not like ours. It was delicate and needed cherishing in this climate. At first it could not dig its own burrow; Sheail records among the tools used in Henry VIII's warren a great auger 'to make and bore cony holes'. Earthworks were made to encourage burrowing. These are clusters of rectangular flat-topped mounds, a few feet high and of very variable sizes; archaeologists call them *pillow-mounds* and sometimes find stone-built burrows inside them.[86] In the 1640s Lord Morley, the downtrodden landowner of Hatfield Forest (Essex), was repeatedly fined before his own manorial court 'for making Coney Burroughs';[87] a score of pillow-mounds are still to be seen in the part of the Forest called The Warren; they appear to have been adapted from some prehistoric earthwork.

Already in the Middle Ages rabbits proved impossible to confine and did some damage. The lord of Petworth (Sussex) in 1347–8, when establishing an orchard, bought '2½ gallons of tar . . . . for greasing the . . . . young trees to protect them from rabbits'.[88] Sheail quotes other claims of damage, usually by

---

* They appear also to have been put on small Mediterranean islands, such as Delos and Antiparos in Greece.

neighbours of warrens, but concludes that rabbits were not widely regarded as a pest until the late eighteenth century.

Rabbits were kept all over Great Britain until the late nineteenth century. Sheail estimates that warrens covered 11 per cent of the Breckland in the early nineteenth century. (The history of a big commercial warren is given on p.292). It was stated that 2.3 million rabbit carcases were sold in eight markets in the 1872–3 winter. The fur continued to be used in clothing; the loose hair, stuck together with shellac, constituted felt hats. The faded lettering 'HATTERS' FURRIERS' can still be read on the wall of a Breckland factory in Brandon. Many landowners kept rabbits as a deliberate alternative to cattle and sheep; others encouraged them as sporting beasts.

From the mid-eighteenth century onwards a more narrow-minded attitude to the rabbit developed. It conflicted with the ploughing-up of heaths and commons (Chapter 13). People who kept rabbits were unpopular with their neighbours and attacked in anti-rabbit propaganda. Rabbit products were imported from Australia as if there were no rabbits at home. By World War II rabbits had almost ceased to be commercial animals, but were more numerous than ever in the wild; strenuous attempts were made to exterminate them, although many farmers still appreciated rabbit meat.

As rabbits became more abundant and better adapted to the English countryside they descended the human social scale. In the thirteenth century the market price of the carcase averaged $3\frac{1}{2}d.$, plus a further $1d.$ for the skin.[52] It was therefore a luxury, worth rather more than a craftsman's daily wage.[89] In the fifteenth century an average rabbit was worth $2\frac{1}{4}d.$ and was a possible Sunday dinner for a craftsman, who worked less than half a day to earn its price. During the sixteenth century the price of rabbit meat fell behind the general rate of inflation, but this was more than offset by a fall in the standard of living; by 1600 a rabbit was worth about $7d.$, more than half the daily wage. The seventeenth century was a time of steady prices, including that of rabbits, and slightly rising wages. By 1760 the price of rabbits had fallen to about $5d.$, about a fifth of a craftsman's wage, and in the nineteenth century they became cheaper still and a staple food of the relatively poor.

In 1953 someone, disapproving of rabbits, introduced the South American myxomatosis virus via France, and promptly killed at least 99 per cent of the rabbits in Britain. For many years the animal remained uncommon, but it is now slowly increasing; the disease is still present but the rabbits will eventually win. Wild rabbits are still perfectly eatable: the virus attacks no other British animal, not even hares.

The rabbit was one of the most successful farming innovations; its commercial decline is part of the modern fashion for concentrating on only a few crops. Its history illustrates Darwinian evolution. The changes from the tender, expensive animal of the twelfth century to the self-reliant rabbit of the eighteenth and the ubiquitous pest of the nineteenth are almost certainly due to genetic change and adaptation to our climate. Since 1953, the terrible selection imposed by disease has produced a different rabbit again, a tough and unsociable animal which lives on the surface and so does not infect its colleagues. The rabbits outside my college windows are solitary and survive the Cambridge winter without burrows.

The disappearance of rabbits has had disastrous consequences for the kinds of grassland and heath which they used to maintain (Chapters 13 and 15). Wire-netting now makes it possible to keep a rabbit-warren without upsetting one's neighbours, and in two Breckland nature reserves this is now being done in order to preserve plants which depend on grazing and disturbance by rabbits.

Fallow deer The prehistory of fallow deer has been described by D. and N. Chapman (1975). They existed in Britain in previous interglacials but did not return after the last glaciation; their homeland is now the Levant or Near East. Prehistoric deposits in Britain are full of red and roe deer but have no remains of fallow.

The belief that fallow deer in Britain date from a Roman introduction has been repeated by author after author, but is almost certainly untrue. The Romans kept fallow deer in parks in Italy. Whether they did so in Britain is not quite certain; archaeologists have found bones but cannot swear simultaneously to both their identity and their stratigraphy. If fallow were then introduced they did not persist. The Anglo-Saxons and their Welsh contemporaries[90] knew the high or red deer and the roe but not the fallow. (Ælfric mentions the animal in his *Colloquies* (*c.* 1000), but this is a school textbook of Latin, and is not evidence that the beasts which it mentions were English.) Nor have authentic fallow remains been found in Anglo-Saxon contexts.

The evidence points to the Normans as having introduced fallow deer, probably at the same time as rabbits. The *Anglo-Saxon Chronicle*'s obituary of William the Conqueror (1087) says that he loved high-deer and boars; it mentions Forests as his innovation (p.130), and could hardly have missed the introduction of a new deer had he been responsible. The early twelfth century would have been an appropriate time for the Normans of England to have acquired fallow deer from their colleagues, the Normans of Sicily, who had inherited Classical and Islamic traditions of keeping oriental beasts in parks. By the thirteenth century the fashion for fallow had spread to Wales, Scotland, and Ireland.

For many centuries fallow deer were semi-agricultural animals, not roaming the countryside but enclosed in parks or protected in Forests (Chapter 6). In the nineteenth century their numbers probably reached a low ebb, as many Forests were destroyed and attempts were made to remove the deer from others (eg. the New Forest, Dean, Whittlewood).

Since the 1920s there has been a remarkable change. Fallow deer, escaped from parks, have established themselves in the countryside at large. The Chapmans report them from every county of England, much of Ireland and Wales, and the southern half of Scotland. Although fallow are specially characteristic of the British Isles they are increasing in Europe also. There has been an equally spectacular increase of native deer and of muntjac and Chinese water deer, both introduced from China about 1900. All five species are now within 20 miles of Cambridge, one of the least suitable parts of England for deer.

Deer are now more numerous and more easily seen than at any time for a thousand years. Why is this so? It is often assumed that it comes from making plantations, but deer are not concentrated in big twentieth-century plantations; many woods which have acquired them are no larger than they were a century ago. The most likely explanation is that fewer people work on the land, and deer can more easily avoid human contact. Before 1920 every field was visited by somebody – usually armed – at least once a week, and a deer which left the protection of park or Forest did not live long. Deer damage crops, but their

49

effects are less concentrated and less noticeable than those of rabbits and many farmers tolerate them. They do much more damage to woodland (p.118).

Fallow deer and rabbits were introduced, within a decade or two of each other, for the same purpose of producing meat from poor-quality land. Both were kept for centuries, and when eventually they became unfashionable they escaped from captivity and made a nuisance of themselves in the countryside at large. This change in fallow deer does not seem to involve the genetic changes that we have invoked for rabbits.

Deer are the nearest that we have to the great beasts of prehistory; few of us can resist the wonder and adventure of seeing them. Nor should we: the Common Market can spare them a little corn. But as with other good things, enough is enough, and the proliferation of deer is the most serious of all natural threats to the future of woodland. Where fallow deer are abundant, coppicing can only be done inside an expensive deer-fence. The medieval arts of living with deer need to be revived. Their numbers at present are limited often by starvation and poaching; it is hardly even good for the deer themselves that so much excellent meat should be running round the countryside not properly used.

Pheasant The pheasant is an oriental bird thought to be native in Central Asia and south-east Russia.[91] It was well known to the Romans and is often alleged, though not on good evidence, to have been kept by them in Britain.[92] Roman introductions, if any, did not survive: no Anglo-Saxon writer mentions pheasants, and such a striking and edible bird could not have escaped record had it been present.

Early records of pheasant in England are unsatisfactory. It is said to be mentioned as a huntable bird in monastic charters of Rochester in 1098 and of Amesbury and Malmesbury (Wilts) in 1100;[93] but I cannot find these documents in Dugdale's *Monasticon*. The canons of Waltham Abbey (Essex), writing in c. 1170, included pheasant among the birds which, they said, King Harold had ordered for their diet in 1060;[94] but we cannot assume that the menu had really not changed in 110 years, and all we can safely infer is that there was a tradition of pheasants by 1170. The pheasant, therefore, was certainly here by the mid-twelfth century and may have come in the late eleventh. The Normans possibly got it via Sicily, where I have seen it depicted in the mosaics of Monreale Cathedral.

Pheasants rapidly became widespread in England. They are fairly frequent in medieval poaching cases, eg. in Essex[95] and Staffordshire.[96] They were regarded as creatures of the warren, but seem not to have been the object of systematic management as were rabbits. They were sometimes the object of hawking for sport.[93]

Pheasants are often heard of at royal, noble, or occasionally academic feasts (p.119). Unlike deer, they were bought and sold and had a monetary value. The medieval and Tudor value of a pheasant was about four times that of a rabbit,[52] which makes it a very delicate bird indeed, roughly as costly, weight for weight, as swan.

The pheasant was apparently slow to spread into Scotland, Wales and Ireland; it remained uncommon until the rise of modern gamekeeping.[97]

As a serious land-use, gamekeeping for pheasants dates from the late eighteenth century. Artificial pheasant-rearing grew into a virtual industry with professional keepers, buildings, and equipment for feeding birds and keeping down predators. Gamekeeping carried to excess had a deplorable effect on beasts and birds thought to be carnivorous; also, more than any other activity up to that time, it corrupted country life and produced ill-feeling between land-owners and other folk. Nevertheless, the pheasant filled a vacuum which the decline of woodmanship (p.93) was leaving. Pheasant-keeping is now less often carried to excess and is useful in maintaining the fabric of the countryside: by providing a rival crop it limits the excesses of prairie-farming.

Gamekeeping is not responsible for the survival of pheasants, which kept themselves in England for centuries before the modern keeper. Even now twice as many wild as artificially-reared pheasants are shot.[98]

Squirrels The grey squirrel comes from North America, and was deliberately released on at least thirty-one occasions between 1876 and 1929.[99] Why this was done, and why it was *Sciurus carolinensis* rather than the various other American squirrels, is not recorded: our grandfathers were as whimsical about introducing foreign animals as we are about planting foreign trees. Most of the introductions were along a line from Chester to Folkestone. The grey squirrel spread at about one mile a year and by 1940 had occupied most of the Midlands, south-east England, Cheshire, Yorkshire, and small areas in Scotland and Ireland. It now inhabits almost the whole of England and Wales, central Scotland, and a large part of central Ireland.[59]

As is well known, the grey squirrel has largely replaced the red squirrel, *Sciurus sciurus*. However the red squirrel has a history of wide fluctuations, independently of the grey, and is itself not wholly indigenous.

Red squirrels are fairly well recorded in the Middle Ages, partly in the form of fur. They inhabited southern and midland England and possibly Wales and north Scotland.[99] Fur records for Ireland do not quite prove that they were native there,[100] and cease around 1500. The squirrels of Scotland, although recorded all over the Highlands in the eighteenth century, are thought to have become extinct by 1840.[99] Squirrels were deliberately reintroduced into Scotland from 1772 onwards and into Ireland from 1815. These introductions (mostly of unknown provenance) spread and multiplied, and during the nineteenth century red squirrels increased all over the British Isles; they were killed in tens of thousands as pests. Between 1900 and 1920 there was a catastrophic decline, followed by recovery in areas which the grey squirrel had not reached.

The red squirrel is now largely a creature of conifer plantations, but this cannot have been its habitat in earlier centuries when conifers were rare. The population explosion in the nineteenth century has been plausibly attributed to the growing fashion for planting conifers. Less reasonable is the conjecture that the red squirrel's earlier fluctuations, its extinction in Scotland and Ireland (if it occurred there) were due to the destruction of woodland.[99] There is no evidence that woodland disappeared at the particular places and times when squirrels became extinct. The woods of, for instance, Argyll or Killarney, even at their least extent, covered many square miles and ought to have been amply sufficient. The 1900–1920 decline was attributed to epidemic disease (coccidiosis); although the evidence was not very extensive, the explanation is plausible and is a possible cause for the earlier declines also.

Various links between the rise of the grey squirrel and the decline of the red have been suggested, but are difficult to prove. The killing of red squirrels by grey is rare and can hardly be decisive. The two squirrels compete for food and habitat, but not severely, as the grey prefers deciduous trees. It has been alleged that greys carry parasites which are transmitted to reds and kill them, but detailed evidence is lacking, and the decline of 1900–1920 was not linked to the presence of greys. Nevertheless, the circumstantial evidence of a link is very strong. The two species rarely coexist for long; the red usually disappears a few years after the arrival of the grey. The red still exists on islands (Wight, Brownsea (Dorset), Anglesey which the grey cannot reach.

In North America the grey squirrel is regarded as harmless. In Britain it is treated as a serious pest because it damages trees, especially beech and syca-more, by gnawing the bark. This is not always regrettable, for beech and sycamore can be pests themselves, but greys also take eggs and young birds. Red squirrels do some of these things, but only in the late nineteenth century do they appear to have been abundant enough to be a significant pest. The most serious ecological effect of greys is probably on hazel. They pluck off the entire crop of hazel-nuts in September; they may not eat them all, but those that they bury are too unripe to grow. Where nutting was an important social occasion a century ago, it is now impossible to find a single ripe nut. In grey-squirrel territory I rarely see a young hazel except in the Bradfield Woods (where squirrels are persecuted) or in the gardens of friends who keep airguns. Hazel, which has shaped our civilization from prehistoric times, is the most seriously threatened British tree except elms.

Collared dove This bird reminds us that spectacular changes in the distribution of animals can sometimes be a complete mystery.

The collared dove used to be an obscure creature of Asia and south-east Europe.[98] After 1930 it spread north-westward across Europe at about 50 miles a year, reaching France in 1950 and Norfolk in 1955. It is now throughout the British Isles, except where there is much moorland, and is one of our most familiar birds in village and suburb.

Collared doves are birds of houses and gardens and especially of spilt corn; they are roughly the bird equivalent of the rat. Why did they not get here centuries ago? The bird has spread progressively on its own wings and has not been suddenly transported to a distant land. There has been no change in human habits or in climate commensurate with so great an expansion. We cannot suppose that almost the whole of Europe, with all its variety of habitats, has suddenly ceased to be unsuitable for collared doves. We have to conjecture that the collared dove of 1980 is not the same as its ancestor of 1920; that some genetic change has created a new variety with different ecological behaviour.

New and Naturalized Plants

The limits of the native British flora are not easy to define. Pollen analysis proves many plants native, in that they are known to have been here since before civilized men, but the converse is more difficult to prove. Plants that produce little pollen or grow in dry places are unlikely to have a pollen record even if they were present.

Many forms of wild vegetation – meadows, chalk downland, hedges, and even moorland and felled woodland – depend to some extent on past or present human activity. Some of their plants originally lived in different habitats: the flora of moorland is partly derived from tundra. A few are known to have been brought, usually by accident, from overseas; the willowherb *Epilobium adeno-caulon* was introduced from North America *c.* 1890 and is now widespread in woodland after felling. New arrivals may not always be the work of mankind; for instance, the rare cress *Rorippa islandica* grows only on the winter feeding grounds of geese and may have been brought on their muddy feet as they migrate from Iceland.[69]

As well as redistributing existing plants, human activity creates new species. Animals evolve chiefly by the classic Darwinian process of small genetic changes which, under the selective influence of the environment, gradually produce a new species over many generations. The modern rabbit is an example. Plants are less reluctant than animals to form hybrids between species; they also have mechanisms whereby new species are formed suddenly in one or two genera-tions. *Spartina anglica* is a recent, well-documented example of how this pro-cess, which is widespread in our flora, is often linked to some human activity. Elms (Chapter 11) are another, more problematic group of plants in which rapid evolution is closely connected with human affairs.

Plant evolution and distribution are full of romantic mysteries, of which *Bromus interruptus* is given as an example in the following pages. How did a single tree of the Whitty Pear (*Sorbus domestica*) get into a remote spot in Wyre Forest (Worcs) at some time before 1600,[101] its nearest locality being Brittany? What of the moss *Tortula stanfordensis*, whose known distribution in 1961 was a certain footpath at the Lizard plus the campus of Stanford University, Califor-nia? (It has since been found elsewhere in England, and a close relative grows in Australia.) And how does the rush *Juncus planifolius* come to be known from the South Pacific, Hawaii, and one particular remote lough in western Ireland?[102]

Weeds Weeds are very specialized plants, intimately linked to farming. Many of them could not survive in the wild: they cannot withstand shade and have little power of competition. Although traditionally listed as 'native', they go with the introduction of agriculture in Neolithic times. Our ancestors were less certain than we about which were weeds and which were crops. Ground-elder (*Aegopodium podagraria*) was introduced by the Romans and grown in gardens until recently (Godwin 1975). Tollund Man, of the Danish Iron Age, had porridge containing goosefoot (*Chenopodium album*) and persicaria (*Polygonum lapathifolium*) for his execution breakfast.

Many weeds, such as plantains, mugwort, and shepherd's purse, were orig-inally arctic plants living in the tundra of late-glacial Britain; they somehow survived the millennia of wildwood, and in Neolithic times found a new lease of life as weeds. Other weeds, such as poppies and corn-cockle, came from the oriental homeland of agriculture. In the Akrotiri Mountains of Crete I have found what may be one of their original natural habitats. On a south-facing limestone cliff, too hot and dry for trees, there are little pockets of soil in which grow chickweed, shepherd's needle, annual dog's mercury, and other winter annuals. Brought from such a ferocious environment to lush and gloomy Bri-tain, they attached themselves to farming and found a new function.

The modern decline of weeds began with the shrinking variety of crops. Vastly less flax and *Cannabis* are grown than in past centuries, and we have lost

53

the special weeds that go with these crops, such as gold-of-pleasure *Camelina sativa* (itself once a crop) and the hemp broomrape *Orobanche ramosa*. Other weeds have declined through seed-cleaning. A book last reprinted ten years ago says of corn-cockle 'one is almost sure to find this beautiful flower'; it is now probably extinct except where deliberately preserved. Since the large-scale use of weedkillers in farming, arable weeds have become the most severely threatened part of the British flora.

A decrease in weeds is doubtless to be welcomed, but even here it is arguable that enough is enough. Mediterranean peoples live with weeds, enjoy them, and eat some of them. Weedkillers seem to have killed the wrong weeds: they have almost exterminated Venus's looking-glass, shepherd's needle, and many other beautiful and harmless plants, but have left us with the prosaic and pernicious blackgrass and wild oats. Weeds are part of the historic flora and should be protected from dying out altogether.

Chestnut The chestnut of England is the sweet chestnut, *Castanea sativa*. It is a historic, but not a native, member of our flora. Until the invention of pollen analysis we did not know that it was not native.*

Early writers such as Evelyn treated chestnut as indigenous: only in the eighteenth century did doubts arise. In 1769 there was controversy in the Royal Society over whether chestnut was native. This debate began the science of historical ecology and anticipated many of the methods later to be used in woodland history.

Daines Barrington, the correspondent of Gilbert White, claimed that a native tree ought to satisfy four conditions, and that chestnut did not fulfil them:

1. They must grow in large masses, and cover considerable tracts of ground, nor must such woods end abruptly, by a sudden change to other trees, except the situation and strata become totally different.
2. If the tree grows kindly [ie. naturally] in copses, and shoots from the stool it must for ever continue in such a wood, unless grubbed up with the greatest care . . .
3. The seed of such tree must ripen kindly: nature never plants but where a succession may be easily continued, and in the greatest profusion.
4. Lastly; Many places . . . must receive their appellation from indigenous trees which grow there . . .[103]

A reply was made by the Kentish antiquary E. Hasted and two of his colleagues.[104] They demonstrated, with examples, that chestnut did sometimes fulfil Barrington's four postulates: they stated that it grew freely from seed and was not, as Barrington had claimed, usually to be found in regular rows where it had been planted; woods contained a succession of different ages of trees; and chestnut sometimes grew intermixed with other trees. They argued against postulates 1, 2, and 3 on the grounds that some undoubtedly indigenous trees failed to meet them. (The reader should re-examine these postulates after reading Chapter 5.)

---

* The horse-chestnut, *Aesculus hippocastanum*, is a quite unrelated (and poisonous) tree introduced in the sixteenth century from Albania. It is still unmistakably exotic and has not become wild. It is a sad example of a once glamorous species, associated with oriental romance and spectacle, being deprived of its meaning through being made the universal tree of bus-stations.

Hasted produced positive evidence of the antiquity of chestnut in England: quotations from ancient documents; place-names supposed to be derived from it; ancient buildings in which its timber had supposedly been identified; and ancient trees still alive in 1769 or mentioned in earlier works. For instance, in Milton near Sittingbourne (Kent) the lessees of the manorial mills had been required to gather 'nine bushels of chestenottes, in Chestnott wood' as a labour service. In the twelfth century Henry II had given the tithe of chestnuts in a remote part of the Forest of Dean to the monks of Flaxley Abbey. In Hasted's time the Milton woods still contained chestnuts

> many of them, by their appearance, of great age . . . now seem almost worn out and perishing, being made use of as *the termini* or *boundaries*, as well of private property as of parishes . . . first pitched upon, in preference to others, for that purpose, as being the largest and most antient ones of any then existing . . . they must have stood sacred to this use from the first introduction of private property into this kingdom, and the first division of it into parishes.

Not all Hasted's 'chestnut' place-names were genuine. The 'Chestnott wood' in Milton is so recorded back to the thirteenth century, but earlier names are often uncertain because of confusion between the Old English for chestnut, *cyst* or *cisten*, and other Anglo-Saxon words. And the timbers in buildings such as the roofs of Westminster Hall and King's College Chapel, Cambridge turn out on re-examination to be oak. There are medieval records of chestnut as a building timber, but as with the legendary 'old ships' timbers' and 'Irish bog oak' it has yet to be confirmed by actual finds.

Despite these imperfections, the logic of Hasted's arguments is overwhelming: he was justified in concluding that 'These chestnuts are undoubtedly the indigenous growth of Britain, planted by the hand of nature'. But unreason commonly triumphs in arguments about trees. Barrington was the more famous man, and his views, despite the lack of good evidence, gradually gained credence. At one time it was believed that chestnut was not indigenous anywhere in Europe, and some books still repeat the story that the nuts are not produced in England. It is easier to copy previous authors than to look for nuts oneself.

Barrington was eventually to be vindicated, though not in the sense of modern introduction in which he wrote, by the evidence of pollen analysis. Prehistoric chestnut pollen is known in southern Europe but has not been found in Britain. For various technical reasons this is not quite conclusive, but it is as certain as negative evidence can be that the tree is not native.

Chestnut is now known to be indigenous in the Balkans, Italy, and probably Spain.[105]★ The nuts are an important foodstuff, especially in Italy where flour is made from them,[106] and the tree has been widely spread in consequence. The Romans introduced it to England: there are six reports of its wood and charcoal from Roman excavations, discounting finds of nuts which could have been imported (Godwin 1975).

The Romans brought many plants to England: nearly all, including the walnut, either died out in the Dark Ages or were maintained only in gardens. Chestnut survived, acquired an Anglo-Saxon name, and became naturalized. When next heard of, in the Middle Ages, it was no longer a tree of inhabited

---

★ 'Spanish chestnut' is an academic name referring to the importation of the nuts.

places but of woodland, sometimes of remote woodland (as in the Forest of Dean). It had acquired a definite ecological context: medieval records associate it with oak and beech, then the typical trees of very acid soils. Walnut, in contrast, has never had an ecology of its own but has been planted at random on all soils at the whim of growers.

Early records are supplemented by ancient trees, such as the famous chestnut of Tortworth, Gloucestershire (Plate I, p.231); ancient coppice stools in woods, as in Stour Wood and Holbrook Park near Ipswich; and archaeological finds. Most are in Kent and Essex, but a few are scattered as far west as Worcestershire, Gloucestershire, and Dorset.

Why the Romans introduced chestnut is not known. The English tree is not one of the special nut varieties developed by Italian growers. The medievals nevertheless valued it for its nuts and seem to have been unaware of the excellence of its wood, which is more rot-resistant in the ground than any other historic tree except yew. Nuts were later imported – size being valued more than flavour – and the local nuts were neglected and forgotten. From the late seventeenth century onwards, and especially in the nineteenth century, chestnut-woods were planted in south-east England as a source of underwood poles, especially of the large poles used by growers of hops.

Although far north of their homeland, English chestnuts have prospered. On acid soils the tree slowly spreads at the expense of native species: nuts grow more easily into trees than do those of hazel, beech, or oak; when coppiced, chestnut's fast regrowth gives it an advantage over its competitors. Ancient chestnut-woods can be recognized by their coppice stools of all sizes and ages, up to 10 feet or more across, intermingled. Recent plantings, which are probably much commoner, have small stools of even spacing and uniform size; they are not confined to acid soils.

Chestnuts are not naturalized elsewhere in north-west Europe, and our woods are almost unique to England. A comparable place is western Crete, where the chestnut is also an ancient introduction, and where there are venerable pollards in immense coppice stools; chestnuts have become part of society and are honoured with festivals. English chestnut-woods are specially valuable for having escaped the ravages of *Endothia parasitica* (p.246) in France and Italy.

Sycamore Sycamore, *Acer pseudoplatanus*, is a native of central Europe. With us it is an aggressive tree, successfully forming secondary woodland and invading native woods. In its homeland it is rather local and lives peaceably with its neighbours in native vegetation. The romantic *Ahornböden*, Sycamore Flats, lie in recesses of the Karwendel mountains behind Innsbruck; they are not unlike English parks, grasslands grazed by cattle and scattered with ancient mossy lichen-hung trees; but the great trees here are sycamores, and (instead of a park pale) 3000-foot precipices of grey dolomite soar into the snow.

The oft-repeated statement that the Romans introduced sycamore is based on no evidence. It is first definitely mentioned in Lyte's *Herball* (1578) but only as a garden tree; in 1635 a garden in St Keyne (south-east Cornwall) had 'fourteen sickumers in the herb garden'.[107] Evelyn in 1679 advised that it 'be banish'd from all curious *Gardens* and *Avenues*' on account of its honeydew,[108] but in spite of the great man's disapproval it grew in popularity and began to be planted away from houses. In the 1670s William Windham I set it in a plantation at Felbrigg (Norfolk);[109] and two sycamores are mentioned among hedgerow trees at Bardwell (West Suffolk) in 1730.[110] In Cornwall, a survey in 1727–9 of trees in churchyards and glebe-land names sycamore as the third commonest species, half the sycamores being recorded as newly planted.[107]

Sycamore is difficult to destroy, and most of the trees ever successfully planted must still be alive, at least as coppice stools. Although the tree did not become universally fashionable until the late eighteenth century, earlier introductions would account for the big stools, up to 6 feet across, occasionally to be found in woods. Once put in a wood sycamore multiplies and spreads at the expense of native trees; its saplings can live for many years in shade – which few indigenous trees can do – and then take over the wood at the next felling. It also easily forms secondary woodland, especially on the sites of industries. Its two enemies, the grey squirrel and sooty bark disease (caused by the fungus *Cryptostroma corticale*), spoil the tree as timber without exterminating it. Most conservationists disapprove of sycamore, which is supposed to be a poor habitat for wildlife and has a heavy shade and dense leaf-litter, and spend much time trying to kill it. Although it is chiefly a menace in Wales and western England, it is a tree which no responsible person should plant without carefully considering the long-term consequences.

Other naturalized trees and shrubs Britain is remarkable for how many exotic trees and shrubs have been introduced and how few are naturalized. *Rhododendron ponticum* was in Ireland in previous interglacials but is now confined as a native to south-west Spain and Portugal, south-east Europe, and the Levant. It was introduced to the British Isles and became abundant in the nineteenth century.[111] It is now widely naturalized on acid soils, chiefly in woods but also on heaths, bogs, and even sand-dunes. Its inhospitable evergreen shade and extreme tenacity of life make it a menace to conservation.

Trees widely planted and occasionally naturalized include Turkey-oak, Corsican pine, and Douglas fir. Scots pine is a tree native in the Scottish Highlands but naturalized in parts of England (p.297); conversely beech, native only in the south-east half of England and Wales, is naturalized and spreading well outside this range.

Rosebay Willowherb An amazing change in the ecological behaviour of a supposedly native plant is that of rosebay, *Epilobium (Chamaenerion) angustifolium*. This plant is large and arrestingly beautiful, and even the dullest passer-by notices it. Its rise from rarity to abundance within 150 years is documented in scores of Floras but remain a mystery, the subject of unlikely conjecture. The most popular 'explanation' is the felling of woodland during World War I, as if woods had never been felled in previous centuries!

Rosebay is a perennial plant, dispersed by its light wind-blown seeds, and rather intolerant of shade. Its habitats fall into two groups. 'Highland' habitats, in northern England and Scotland, are streamsides, cliffs, screes, etc. which are stable and relatively natural. 'Lowland' habitats, which now cover much of the British Isles, include felled plantations, railway yards, industrially derelict land, roadsides, and ruinous (especially bombed) buildings; they all involve human activity, especially disturbance of the soil or burning. In ancient woodland rosebay appears for a few years after coppicing and dies as the wood grows again; it is not usually abundant and is often confined to bonfire sites.

The first record of rosebay in Britain is in Gerard's *Herball* (1597); the locality, in the Yorkshire fens near Goole, suggests an outlier of the highland type of habitat. The second record is in 1666 for 'Greenwich in the place where Balast is taken up'[112] – precisely the industrially-disturbed land in which rosebay is common now. There were two more records (Sussex, Lincs) in the seventeenth century and a dozen in the eighteenth.

A study of the Floras of lowland counties shows that rosebay spread sporadically over many decades. For the Isle of Wight there were 12 localities as early as 1856. In Herts there are 37 records by 1887, and in Wiltshire 33 records by 1888. On the other hand, the Suffolk Flora of 1889 gives only 7 records, and the Bedfordshire Flora of 1911 gives only 5. In Nottinghamshire the plant is not recorded at all until 1880, and in Anglesey there was only one record by 1895. Nineteenth-century records often mention railways and occasionally canals, but this is not the whole story; the Essex Flora of 1862 gives 11 records, five of them for ancient woods.

The earliest definite record in a highland habitat is for Perthshire in 1778. This is rather late, but botanists were slow to investigate highland areas and there is no strong evidence of actual expansion comparable to what we have seen in the lowlands. The Northumberland Flora of 1868, for instance, gives rosebay only on the 'banks of nearly all the hill streams'; it had not yet begun to appear in industrial habitats.

Rosebay is widespread in the Northern Hemisphere. In North America it has always been associated with clearings, burnt areas, and beaver activity; it is one of the plants there called Fireweed. In Europe it now has much the same range of habitats as in Britain, and botanists seem not to have noticed any recent change in its behaviour; it may, however, have expanded in France, where in 1805 its habitat is given only as 'mountain woods'.[113]

The highland populations of rosebay in Britain are probably indigenous: there is some pollen evidence that the plant occurred in prehistory (Godwin 1975). The lowland populations are independent of these; they began in southern England and expanded north, west, and east over many decades. Lowland and highland populations first met in northern England in the late nineteenth century. In much of northern Scotland rosebay was still confined to highland habitats until well into the twentieth century. It is even now uncommon in the corners of Great Britain – Land's End, Anglesey, north-west Scotland, the Hebrides, Shetland – and is thinly scattered in Ireland. This invasive history is highly characteristic of an introduced plant. Lowland and highland rosebays are indistinguishable in outward appearance, and attempts to find differences between them have so far proved inconclusive;[114] but circumstantial evidence leaves little room for doubt that they differ in their genetic make-up as well as in their ecological behaviour.

Lowland rosebay was probably introduced into England from America or central Europe in the seventeenth century. Why did it not then spread? In the ensuing 180 years, woods were cut down, towns were burnt, industry despoiled the countryside, and canals were made; but rosebay spread only slowly. By 1840 lowland rosebay had got into at least half the counties of England, but usually to only one or two places in each. Its opportunity came with the railways, which provided habitats, especially the raw surfaces of newly-made earthworks, and transported the seed. The plant soon spread into other places and took advantage of many modern habitats. Nineteenth-century railways – not twentieth-century wars and dereliction – are the cause of its present abundance. The felling of woods in the 1914–18 War merely encouraged a spread that had already advanced far in the previous half-century, a time of abnormally *little* felling of woodland. A minor factor which may have aided the early spread into woodland (as in Essex) was the practice of burning lop-and-top when a wood was felled. This custom was itself an indirect product of railways – for previously, before coal became cheap, branches of trees had been used as fuel – and made woodland a more suitable habitat for rosebay than it would otherwise have been.

Oxford ragwort A close parallel is the spread of Oxford ragwort, *Senecio squalidus*. This is unquestionably of exotic origin: it is a plant of central and southern Europe. The plant, originally brought from Mount Etna, was grown in Oxford Botanic Garden from about 1690. Like lowland rosebay it spread slowly at first, being recorded in six places before 1840.[115]

Oxford ragwort is a more urban plant than rosebay and has not advanced quite so fast. It too is strongly associated with railways: the light fluffy fruits have been observed to travel in carriages and to get off at stations.[115] Like rosebay, Oxford ragwort flourished in World War II, and the two grew together on almost all the bombed buildings of London and Norwich. It has now reached roughly the position that rosebay had by 1900.

Oak mildew Naturalization is not limited to flowering-plants. The Southern Hemisphere moss *Orthodontium lineare* was introduced in the 1910s, probably on timber imported via Birkenhead; it has prospered much better than the native *O. gracile* and is now the commonest moss on old oak stumps in England and Wales. Several seaweeds have been brought from distant oceans, one of which, *Sargassum muticum*, introduced to France with Japanese oysters, has crossed the Channel and may well become a menace to British shore life.[116]

Among fungi, the best-known new species are those which draw attention to themselves by causing plant disease. Often the belief that they are introduced is merely a guess hiding the failure of botanists to notice the disease earlier; an example is Dutch Elm Disease (Chapter 11).

Oak mildew is a disease whose spread round the world is well documented. The leaves of oak-trees are often covered with a white film looking like a thin coat of whitewash. This is the fungus *Microsphaera alphitoides*, one of many species of mildew each of which attacks some particular wild or cultivated plant. Mildew affects almost every oak in Britain except perhaps where severe air pollution acts as a fungicide. It is very conspicuous and could not have been overlooked by the great mycologists of the nineteenth century had it been present. Up to 1908, plant pathology textbooks describe many obscure species of *Microsphaera* but regard oak mildew as peculiar to North America. Editions after 1908 record it throughout Europe as well. The change was remarked on at the time and there can be no doubt that the fungus crossed the Atlantic and spread like lightning through Europe.

Oak mildew may not be the trivial disease which it seems. Oaks have mysteriously lost the ability, which they had until the nineteenth century, to grow easily from seed in existing woods. It is still extremely easy to grow an oak from an acorn in one's garden or in an abandoned field, but it has become very difficult to do so in most woods. Several changes unfavourable to oak have occurred: for instance most woods are no longer coppiced, which deprives the young oak of light. The critical change could well be the introduction of mildew, which may have deprived oak of the power of surviving in shade. An oakling, partially shaded by tall trees, may succumb if it has to contend with mildew as well as shade.[117]

Cord-grass (*Spartina anglica*) The south-west European grass *Spartina maritima* extends north to southern England, where it is a well-known but uncommon native salt-marsh plant. In the nineteenth century its harmless North American relative, *S. alterniflora*, was accidentally introduced to Southampton Water but has not spread. The two species crossed to produce a hybrid, *S.* × *townsendii*, which was sterile (like a mule) and also has not spread naturally.

At some time in the late nineteenth century something went wrong with the division of a certain cell in a plant of *S.* × *townsendii*. The nucleus divided but the cell itself failed to split. The resulting cell had 124 chromosomes instead of the normal 62. From it grew a plant which was fertile and by all the usual criteria counts as a new species, to which the name *S. anglica* has been given. This plant was aggressive, unlike its three ancestors. It has spread throughout Britain, assisted by people who, unwisely, have planted it as a sea-defence. It has already proved catastrophic to the ecology of many salt-marshes by crowding out other plants.

This process, known as allopolyploidization, is repeatable and is presumed to have happened many times in history and prehistory. The two original species have to be closely related enough to hybridize, but are not usually so closely related that the hybrid is fertile. Primrose and cowslip, for instance, which form a fertile hybrid, have not produced a polyploid. Accidental doubling of the chromosomes restores fertility to the hybrid and creates a new species of different ecological behaviour from its parents.

There is strong circumstantial evidence that many British plants have arisen in this way. Sometimes, by way of experiment, it has been possible to re-make a polyploid species from its parents.[118] Although a natural process, polyploidization is partly linked to human affairs. As with *Spartina*, plants are brought together which would not otherwise have had a chance to hybridize. Polyploids tend to do well in the kinds of habitat which human activity provides. Many crop plants, such as wheat and apples, have been created in this way by the unconscious plant-breeding of prehistoric men. Polyploids are specially frequent among the 'common-or-garden' wild plants of hedgerows and meadows and around habitations. Examples are *Poa annua*, probably the commonest garden weed grass, possibly derived in antiquity from the sand dune *P. infirma* and the alpine *P. supina*; white clover, hemp-nettle (*Galeopsis tetrahit*); and wall-rocket (*Diplotaxis muralis*).

The grass *Bromus interruptus* The extraordinary story of this plant has been told by F.H. Perring and D. Donald.[119] It lives in arable land, especially sainfoin fields. It was discovered as a new species at Odsey in Ashwell (Bedfordshire) in 1849. Further finds rapidly followed and by 1920 the grass was widely scattered over the southern third of England. Supposing this to be a real spread, and not merely the effect of increasing interest among botanists, it would be the classic invasion pattern of an introduced species, especially as the plant is confined to a very artificial habitat. Nevertheless, diligent search has failed to find it in any other country except Holland, whither it was probably introduced from England.

The disappearance of *Bromus interruptus* was equally remarkable. It slipped away unnoticed in the 1930s, well before the invention of weedkillers capable of selecting against grasses. In the summer of 1963, along with many Cambridge botanists, I searched for it; but only once was it found, at Pampisford, a few miles from Odsey. Attempts were made to keep it alive, both on the spot and in cultivation, but it died out by 1972; in *Flora Europaea* (1980) it has the unique designation of an extinct plant endemic to Britain (ie. found nowhere else).

This, however, was wrong. Unknown to his colleagues, an Edinburgh botanist, Dr Philip Smith, had been keeping *Bromus interruptus* alive among a collection of experimental plants. It was 'rediscovered' in 1979 and has now been distributed among several growers.

Although *Bromus interruptus* is very different from others of its genus, there can be little doubt that it arose in the nineteenth century as a new species through some big and sudden genetic change.

CHAPTER 5

Woodland

The Wood. There is one wood which is called Heyle which contains fourscore acres. Item, there is one other wood which is called Litlelund, which contains thirty-two acres. . . .

William Clark holds one virgate of arable . . . he has to cut one cartload of underwood for one work, but not to cart it. And he has to cut rods and collect them and make from them two fold-hurdles for one work, or three hurdles if he finds the rods ready . . .

> *Hayley Wood, Cambridgeshire, in the Ely Coucher Book, 1251.*[19] (A 'work' is a unit of labour-service, to be done by way of rent.)

A certain Wood called Heylewode which contains 80 acres by estimate. Of the underwood of which there can be sold every year, without causing waste or destruction, 11 acres of underwood which are worth 55s. at 5s. an acre . . . A certain other Wood called Litlelond which contains 26 acres by estimate. Whose underwood can be sold as a whole every seventh year. And it is then worth in all £6.10s. at 5s. an acre.

> *Survey of the Bishop of Ely's estates, 1356.*[120]

The Queen . . . to Our dear John Spurlinge . . . We have granted and leased . . . All that wood and underwood . . . called by the name . . . of Haly wood . . . Except . . . all the great trees of oak and all the Timber trees and all . . . the fair saplings of oak (*pulchris lez Saplings quercuu'*) . . . And at every felling sufficient Staddells in every acre . . . John Spurling shall cause the woods and under-woods . . . to be felled only twice . . . in the term of the present lease [21 years] . . . and after each felling . . . shall well and sufficiently enclose and encoppice it with . . . fences . . . and shall guard and protect it from the bite Trampling and damage of animals . . . which may be able to hurt the shoots and regrowth (*virgult et lez Springs*) . . .

> *Queen Elizabeth's lease of Hayley Wood, 1584.*[121] (Saplings and staddells are different sizes of young timber tree.)

Haley Wood Acording to the Best inteligence I can gett of it Contains one hundred & Five Acres which Will fall seven Acrs and a half every year at fourteen years Growth wich will make Fifty four pounds per Anum Besides paying of the Tythe . . . Alowing five Acres for fencing.

> *Valuation of Hayley Wood, 1765.*[122] (This does not include timber or bark, which were valued at a further £18. 15s. per year.)

I have a fine wood of 120 acres, which formerly was a never-failing resource in all times of emergency, as I could sell any quantity of oak timber at 4*s*. 9*d*. per [cubic] foot, and I now cannot find a purchaser at 2*s*. 4*d*. for the fall of that spring . . . with the greatest ease I would sell a hundred pounds' worth of underwood annually; this winter my woodman has effected the sale of about thirty pounds' worth with much difficulty; this I attribute solely to the want of money, which is experienced in this neighbourhood to a ruinous degree.

Hayley Wood, 1816.[123] (From an inquiry into the economic recession of those days.)

Among the treasures of the Suffolk Trust for Nature Conservation, in the Bradfields near Bury St Edmund's, are two adjacent woods called Felsham Hall Wood and Monks' Park. Almost all our native trees are there: ash, maple, hazel, lime, several different elms, two birches, alder, two species of sallow, oak, two hawthorns, etc. Every year part of the wood is cut down, leaving the oaks standing, but the wood grows again and is not diminished; nor, with trifling exceptions, have trees ever been planted in the Bradfield Woods. The produce consists of poles, part of which are used by a factory making rakes, scythe-sticks, etc. or by other woodworking concerns, while the surplus supplies the neighbourhood with stakes and firewood. Every spring, in areas felled the last winter but one, there is the astonishing brilliance of countless oxlips, anemones, violets, water-avens, and wood-spurge. Different stages of regrowth are full of nightingales and other birds, of summer flowers, of bush-crickets and other insects. The Bradfield Woods are a place of colour and song, of gnarled tree-stools and mysterious ponds, and of rare and difficult fungi. They are a Grade I* Potential National Nature Reserve (Ratcliffe 1977). In the 1960s we nearly lost them; they were saved (in part) from destruction by the energetic opposition not of the scientific world, for the Bradfield Woods were then almost unknown, but of local people who loved them.

The Bradfield Woods were owned by the great Abbey of Bury St Edmund's before the Dissolution. They are well documented back to 1252 and would still instantly be recognized by Abbot Symon of that year. The outline of the woods was virtually unaltered until the 1960s, and is demarcated by a mighty bank which may already have been old in Abbot Symon's time. The woodland is managed almost exactly as it was then, and some of the very trees may still be alive and productive. The soils and plants are all indicative of a wood that has developed over many centuries. The Bradfield Woods are a living example of medieval England, as important an antiquity as the Abbey ruins themselves.

These woods have doubtless always been specially beautiful and rich in plants and animals, but until recently there was nothing unusual about their survival. In 1910 there were thousands of woods which had changed only in minor detail for at least 650 years. They were part of the England of George Sturt, who wrote of the late-Victorian heyday of woodworking crafts.[615] Sturt's countryside had inherited these woods from the different Englands of William Cobbett, Oliver Goldsmith, Robert Ryece, Shakespeare, Turner the herbalist, Chaucer, and Abbot Symon. Even to Symon such woods were relics of an unwritten past; their names speak of the England of King Alfred and Guthrum the Dane. Felsham Hall Wood was anciently *Ffelshamhalle*, Anglo-Saxon for 'At the Felsham corner'; it goes back to when English words such as *halh*, 'corner', had a dative case like Latin. Some things in woods are inherited from a much more remote past still: Mesolithic men hunted beneath lime trees and drank from the mysterious ponds (see Chapter 16).

Woods, more than most wild vegetation, result from long-running interactions between human activities and natural processes, to both of which the historian has to give due weight. Their history should never be based on written records alone. I have never seen a wood, however well documented, which has not produced some surprises when visited for the first time. Earthworks and surface features, trees, other plants, pollen analysis, and the timber and wattle of ancient buildings all complement the written record.

The history of woods is infiltrated and corrupted by myth and pseudo-history. Trees arouse strong feelings and give rise to complaints, regulations, policy statements, textbooks, laws, and Letters to the Editor. The things that people have *said* about woods have an unreasonable fascination for scholars, who even now retail them at face value without investigating what was happening to the woods themselves. There are even works that try to combine pseudo-history and real history on the assumption that both are true. In one chapter I cannot include everything; if I say little about, for instance, laws relating to woodland, it is because they had little practical effect.

This chapter is based on studies which I have elsewhere published as the greater part of three books, to which I refer the reader for more detailed illustration (Rackham 1975, 1976, 1980).

Men and Trees

In the beginning, and for millennia after the end of the last Ice Age, the British Isles were covered with natural forests collectively known as *wildwood*. On the Continent, wholly natural wildwood survived in places well into historic times, and we have heard of it through European legend. In eastern North America patches of wildwood, with trees closely related to ours, still survive, though most of it was destroyed by the pioneer settlers. In Britain, we have no memory of our pioneering days; our great wildwoods passed away in prehistory and have left neither written record nor legend. They have to be reconstructed from pollen analysis.

Throughout history, trees have been part of our cultural landscape and have been managed and used. There are six traditional ways in which trees interact with human activities:
1. *Woodland.* Woods are land on which trees have arisen naturally. They are managed by the art of *woodmanship* to yield successive crops of produce in a perpetual succession. When cut down the trees replace themselves by natural regrowth.
2. *Wood-pasture.* This land-use involves grazing animals as well as trees. There is a conflict, in that the shade of the trees spoils the pasture and the livestock eat the regrowth of the trees. Various techniques have existed for reconciling the two uses.
3. *Plantation.* Here the trees are not natural vegetation; somebody has planted them. Plantations are usually of just one or two species, often conifers or other exotic trees, and do not maintain themselves. They usually die when felled and are replaced by a new plantation. This is the practice of *forestry* as understood in Great Britain and Ireland.
4. *Non-woodland*: the tradition of trees in hedgerow and field.

5. *Orchards.*

6. *Trees of gardens and streets.*

Five of these traditions go back at least to Anglo-Saxon times and are the background to the whole of our written history. Plantations are relatively recent. Of the six traditions, woodland is the most closely related to the prehistoric wildwood; this chapter traces how the one developed into the other. Other chapters deal with wood-pasture, plantation, and non-woodland trees. Orchards, garden trees, and other formal plantings are outside the scope of this book.

The six categories are distinct, though one may change into another at a particular site, and there are intermediates. Woodmanship is not an early form of forestry but an independent and parallel technique. In the last hundred years plantations have often been confused with woodland, though (surprisingly) not with orchards; a plantation of trees, with only grass beneath them, is included in official statistics of 'woodland' if the trees happen to be poplars, but not if they are apple-trees.

The word 'forest' has been much abused in its history (p.129). In this book I use it only in two distinct senses. A Forest (spelt with a capital F) is land on which the king (or some other magnate) has the right to keep deer. This is the original sense of the word: *to the medievals a Forest was a place of deer, not a place of trees*. If a Forest happened to be wooded it formed part of the wood-pasture tradition (Chapter 6); but there were many woodless Forests which are discussed under moorland, heath, and fen. I also use *forestry* in the modern sense as the art of managing plantations. Historians of modern forestry often fall into the trap of assuming that it is the successor of the medieval Forest system, but the two have little in common but the name.

Woods and their Behaviour

Woodland management Almost all woods in Britain, though of natural origin, have been managed, often intensively, for centuries. (The exceptions are a few very inaccessible groves on cliffs, and some woods of recent origin.) The following is the normal practice of woodmanship over most of England.

Woodmen traditionally make use of the self-renewing power of trees. As all gardeners know, some trees such as pines can be got rid of by cutting them down, but nearly all native species grow again either from the stump or from the root system. Ash and wych-elm, for instance, *coppice*: the stump sends up shoots and becomes a *stool* from which an indefinite succession of crops of poles can be cut at intervals of years (Fig. 5.1). Aspen, cherry, and most elms *sucker*: the stump normally dies but the root system remains alive indefinitely and sends up successive crops of poles, forming a patch of genetically identical trees called a *clone*.

Coppicing and suckering are efficient and reliable ways of getting a new crop. Sallow can grow at 2 inches a day, reaching 11 feet high in the first season after felling; even oak can stand 7 feet high and an inch thick after one summer's growth. Such shoots, though largely immune from rabbits and hares which destroy slower-growing seedlings, are a favourite food of cattle, sheep, and deer; and in places where these animals could not be fenced out it was the practice instead to *pollard* trees in order to get a crop. Pollards are cut at between 6 and 15 feet above ground, leaving a permanent trunk called a *bolling* (to rhyme with

Woodland

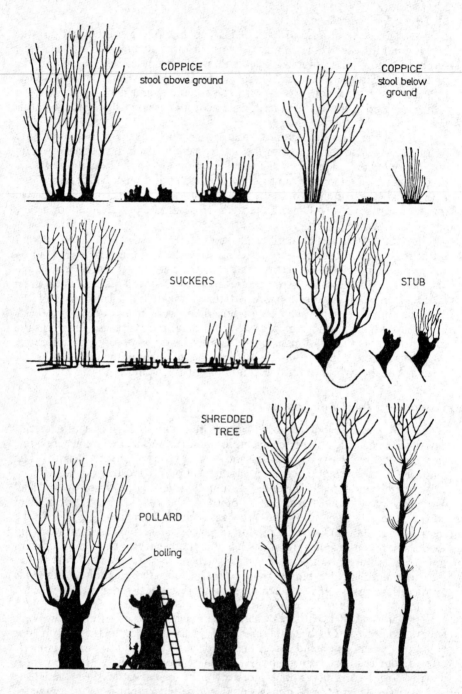

Fig. 5.1. Ways of managing wood-producing trees. For each method the tree, or group of trees, is shown just before cutting, just after cutting, and one year after cutting. All drawn to the same scale.

'rolling'), which sprouts in the same way as a coppice stool but out of reach of livestock. Pollarding is much more laborious than coppicing, and is typical of wood-pasture and some non-woodland trees but not of the interiors of woods.

The trees of a wood are divided into *timber* trees (a minority) and *underwood*. Every so often an area of underwood, called a *panel, cant,* or *hag,* is felled and allowed to grow again by coppicing or suckering. Scattered among the underwood are the timber trees, which are allowed to stand for several cycles of regrowth and are felled when full-grown. Timber trees are usually replaced by seedlings. The whole wood is demarcated from its surroundings by an earthwork called a *woodbank* with a ditch on its outer side, traditionally set with a hedge to keep out livestock and with pollard trees at intervals to define the legal boundary.

The wood therefore yields two products, *timber* from the trunks of the timber trees, and *wood* from coppice stools or suckers (plus the branches of felled timber trees). **Timber and wood had different uses and are not to be confused**; we still talk of 'timber' buildings and 'wood' fires. Wood is rods, poles, and logs, used for fencing, wattlework, and many specialized purposes but in large quantities for fuel. Timber is the stuff of beams and planks and is too valuable (and too big) to burn. Underwood was normally the more important product; woods were traditionally regarded as sources of energy.

Woods do not cease to exist through being felled. Popular writers suppose that a wood gets 'exhausted' as if it were a coal-mine or a pine plantation. Not so: a wood is self-renewing, and is no more destroyed by being cut down than a meadow is destroyed by cutting a crop of hay. The Bradfield Woods have been cut down at least seventy times and show no sign of disappearing. Woods cease to exist through being deliberately destroyed (in order to use the land for something else), through misuse (especially long-continued grazing), or occasionally through natural encroachment of sand-dunes or blanket-peat. When a wood disappears one should not ask 'Why was it cut down?' – for all old woods have been cut down from time to time – but 'Why did it not grow again?'.

Secondary woodland Some woods are believed to be derived from the original wildwood; others (*secondary woods*) have arisen on land that has at some time not been woodland.

Almost all land by nature turns into woodland. Let a field be abandoned – as many fields have been down the centuries – and within a year it will be invaded by oaks springing up from acorns dropped by passing jays, or by birches from wind-blown seed. In ten years it will be difficult to reclaim; in thirty years it will have 'tumbled down to woodland'. The same happens to chalk downs, heaths, fens, and some moorland whenever the grazing and burning cease that had held trees in check.

Secondary woods may be of any age from prehistory onwards.* In general they are not the same as ancient woods; they are composed of those *pioneer* trees – oak, birch, hawthorn, ash – which easily invade vacant ground. Ancient hornbeam-woods have recent oakwoods alongside them; only after a century or more does hornbeam get into a secondary wood, and lime† may never colonize

---

* The term *primary wood* is not a synonym for 'ancient wood' (cf p.74).
† 'Lime' throughout this chapter means the pry tree, *Tilia cordata*, 'small-leaved lime', the lovely and uncommon tree of ancient woodland; not the common lime, *T. vulgaris*, the sticky lime tree of avenues and municipal parks.

at all. Secondary woods also lack many of the herbaceous plants of ancient woodland.

Secondary woodland is familiar on railway land and old quarries; it covers about a sixth of Surrey; its spread is a chief threat to the conservation of heath and old grassland. In the eastern United States an area much greater than the whole British Isles has tumbled down to woodland since 1800. There have been many scientific studies of the subject, including the classic experiment of Broadbalk Wilderness at Rothamsted (Herts), an arable field which was left untouched after 1882 and had become a wood by 1914 (Tansley 1939). Secondary woodland is now curiously unfashionable; recent writers, ignoring all these examples, call for expensive tree-planting as if it were the only way to create new woodland. Like all gradual changes which cost nothing, succession to woodland often goes unnoticed. How many inhabitants of the Mendips have noticed that their local woods have grown bigger since the 1920s?

Wildwood

Woodland history begins for practical purposes about 11,000 BC, when the last glaciation ended and the British Isles became suitable for tree growth. The trees which had retreated to southern latitudes during the Ice Age slowly migrated north again. The first to colonize our tundra were birch, aspen, and sallow. These were followed by pine and hazel; then alder and oak; next lime and elm; then holly, ash, beech, hornbeam, and maple. The process was rather like the making of secondary woodland now; the distances were greater but there was no farmland to stand in the way of the advance, nor at first was there an English Channel or Irish Sea. Birch, aspen, and sallow are relatively arctic trees. The later species were either trees of warmer climates (hornbeam, maple) or bad colonizers (lime). Latecoming species were slow to become abundant, for there was no vacant ground to occupy; they had to wait for existing trees to die.

After the complex changes of the first millennia there came a long period of apparently stable climate, about 6500 to 4000 BC. Tree species fought one another by the natural processes of succession to form a series of 'climax' woodland types, which covered all the British Isles except for small areas of natural moorland and grassland (Chapters 14, 15) on high mountains and in the far north, and for coastal dunes and salt-marshes. Such was the natural wildwood before the beginning of large-scale human activity.

The fully-developed wildwood Pollen analysts used to regard the climax wildwood, as it had developed by 4000 BC, as a rather monotonous 'mixed oak forest' of oak, alder, elm, and a little lime and pine. Research in the last ten years shows the reality to have been much more complex. We now know more about the behaviour of native trees and how much pollen each produces. Lime and ash have been greatly underestimated in the past because they shed less pollen than oak or birch. Hazel has been under-valued because it was thought to be an understorey shrub; it is in fact a canopy tree and produces little or no pollen if shaded by taller neighbours. Alder has been over-estimated because it is a wet-land tree, specially common around the edges of those wet places in which pollen is preserved.

To understand the wildwoods of British prehistory we should look across the Atlantic at the wildwoods encountered by the early American settlers and still surviving in fragments. The pollen evidence for the British Isles shows that they once had a pattern of variation resembling that of the eastern United States.[124] Our wildwoods should be divided into five provinces (Fig. 5.2):

1. The Pine Province of the eastern Scottish Highlands, with outliers on mountains in England and Ireland.
2. The Birch Province of the western Scottish Highlands.
3. The Oak-Hazel Province of southern Scotland, Highland England, most of Wales, and parts of Ireland.
4. The Hazel-Elm Province of most of Ireland and probably of south-west Wales.
5. The Lime Province of Lowland England.

Within each province there were many types of woodland, to some extent reflecting the different soils; these included, in special places, outliers of woodland more typical of other provinces.

In the Lime Province most pollen diagrams show lime (pry) as the commonest tree, hazel as the second commonest, and oak and elm as the next most abundant. This province had a favourable climate and the greatest variety of tree species and of woodland types; it is reminiscent of the western Appalachians, in which an American species of lime is often abundant. Probably there was a patchwork of areas of lime-wood and areas of hazel-wood, for lime, a tall and densely-shading tree, could hardly have coexisted with hazel. Oak and elm may have mingled with the lime and also have formed types of woodland on their own – oak-wood (an outlier of the Oak-Hazel Province) – perhaps on specially infertile soils. Pools and fens were fringed with alder. Other local types included pine-woods (an outlier of the Pine Province) in the eastern Fenland, birch-woods (an outlier of the Birch Province) in the Somerset Levels, and ash-woods in south Norfolk. In the future Epping Forest lime was almost ubiquitous but beech had begun to appear.[125]

In the Oak-Hazel Province there was evidently a general mosaic of these trees with outliers of other woodland types. Surviving fragments suggest hazel-woods on the more fertile and oak-woods on the less fertile soils. In County Durham there were areas of elm-wood and pine-wood;[126] lime-woods grew locally in warmer parts of the Lake District. Similar variation can be shown for other provinces.

Pollen analysis tells us almost nothing about the sizes and ages of wildwood trees. North American wildwoods have an enormous variety of structures. The mighty hemlocks and tulip-trees of damp fertile valleys in Tennessee grow to 180 feet high and 7 feet thick. Some of the 'bog oaks' dug up in our Fens reached almost this size (p.382), but may have been peculiar to this habitat. At the other extreme are the Lilliput-like oak and pine wildwoods of New England mountain-tops; these too probably existed on our windswept coasts. Many American woods have areas of trees all of the same age, the regrowth after great fires or hurricanes. Such catastrophes are unlikely in Britain: native woods (except pine-woods) will not burn, and our storms uproot or break only single trees here and there. Our wildwoods are more likely to have renewed themselves by saplings or suckers growing into gaps left by the death of single trees. American woods, in general, are full of saplings. Ours are not, partly because of our recent management (or neglect) of woods, which has given few opportuni-

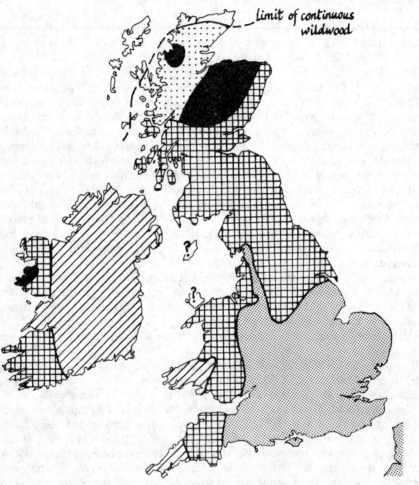

Fig. 5.2. Wildwood provinces in 4500 BC. Small outliers are omitted. Derived from the work of H.J.B. Birks and others.[105, 619]

ties for new saplings to arise; but also because we have few native trees (chiefly beech and yew) that can grow up in the shade of other trees.

The structure of British wildwoods will have depended on how particular trees fell down. A big beech may be uprooted when still alive and crash down on its neighbours, making a wide gap in which other species can grow. A big lime rots at the base and crashes down, leaving a stump which being tenacious of life (like its American sister) sprouts and continues to occupy the spot. An oak usually dies standing and takes about twenty-five years for the roots to rot through, by which time the gap may have been filled by the expansion of neighbouring trees. An elm falls to pieces branch by branch, doing little damage and leaving a small gap which may be filled by its own suckers.

A Mesolithic inhabitant, could he return to the modern British Isles, would first notice that we have got rid of 99 per cent of the original woodland, and even the remaining 1 per cent would no longer be wildwood; for instance, its management history has deprived it of old trees and saplings. But some features of that 1 per cent would still be familiar to him. We still have Scottish pine-woods and birch-woods. Oak-woods are still a speciality of the Highland Zone, even though 6000 years of human intention and default have favoured oak relative to other trees in the Lowland Zone. Our visitor would wonder what had happened to the lime, unless he were in one of the mysterious lime-wood areas (p.102) where it is still the commonest woodland tree. But by careful search he could still find native lime, here and there, within exactly that region – north-ward to the Lake District and the Tyne – in which it grew in 4000 BC. Ash and beech are now much commoner than in his time, though much of the increase of beech is as a planted tree; and very recently birch has also increased. What he would make of our maple-woods and hornbeam-woods I cannot say; their Mesolithic distribution is unknown, for maple sheds very little pollen, and hornbeam is the woodland tree of areas around London and in upland East Anglia in which little pollen analysis has been done.

Destruction of the wildwood It is usually assumed that until men began to till the soil they had no more effect on vegetation than the beasts on which they preyed. Mesolithic and even Palaeolithic men made temporary clearings around their homes; but men were so few that they could have made little impact merely by cutting down trees, even if they had nothing else to do.

Hunting and gathering may possibly not have been simple unorganized activities, but may have involved the definite management of land and vegetation.[127] Some North American Indians, whom we would call 'Mesolithic', produced a kind of wood-pasture by periodic burning (p.120), but this would seldom have been possible in British wildwood. Our only native tree which can be burnt standing is pine, whose early disappearance from most of England has been ascribed to prehistoric men setting fire to it, but this may not be so. Pines are not inflammable by misfortune: many foreign species *need* to be burnt (by lightning) from time to time, otherwise they are infiltrated and replaced by their competitors. Scots pine is not one of these, but it can spring up abundantly from seed after a fire, and occasional burning may not necessarily eliminate it. It has been conjectured that Mesolithic men may somehow be responsible for the great abundance of hazel in pre-history; they are known to have eaten largely of the nuts.

There is no doubt about the sudden impact of Neolithic men. Settlers arrived about 4000 BC and brought with them those crops, animals, and weeds which constitute agriculture. They immediately set about converting Britain to an imitation of the dry open steppes of the Near East, in which agriculture had begun. They attacked elms and caused a sudden drop in elm pollen production, perhaps by letting loose Elm Disease (Chapter 11). This 'Elm Decline' is associated with early pottery and Neolithic tools, with an increase in plants of open land relative to trees, and with crops such as emmer wheat and weeds such as plantains.

Neolithic men spread almost instantly throughout the British Isles, though at first not in large numbers. Within 2000 years they had converted large tracts of country to farmland or heath. In the East Anglian Breckland, where there was a dense, and even an industrial, Neolithic population, the wildwood vanished never to return. The same happened on much of the chalklands, the Somerset Levels, and the coastal Lake District.

During the Bronze Age the inroads of civilization on the wilderness ceased to be merely local. Most wildwood disappeared from high altitudes and river valleys, and inroads were made on some of the heavy soils. It is still controversial how extensive these clearings were, but I shall hazard the guess that half of England had ceased to be wildwood by the early Iron Age (500 BC); some archaeologists would put it earlier.

To convert millions of acres of wildwood into farmland was unquestionably the greatest achievement of any of our ancestors. It belongs to an age far beyond record or memory, and we know little of what men were involved, how they were organized, how much of their time they spent on it, how many man-hours it took to clear an acre, or what they lived on while doing it. There have been many recent experiments on 'clearing' woodland with prehistoric tools,[128] and we now know all too well how to destroy tropical wildwoods (eg. in Brazil); but let these observations not be hastily extrapolated to prehistoric Britain. Compared with the world's trees as a whole, most British species are difficult to kill: they will not burn, and grow again after felling, though this growth is eaten by cattle and sheep. Farmers and foresters who have destroyed historic woods since 1945 have found it no light investment, even with machines and poisons.

British woodlands (except pine) burn like wet asbestos; this was so even when the great drought of 1976 coincided with the height of the fashion for burning stubble. Stone axes are supposed to compare favourably with metal ones (and even with chain-saws!) for cutting down smallish trees, but this only begins the task. Felled trees will not burn where they lie, but have to be cut up and stacked. A log of more than 10 inches diameter is almost fireproof and is a most uncooperative object. There are the bigger problems still of digging up or ploughing round the stumps and preventing regrowth.

In New England a task of similar magnitude was accomplished by European settlers in about 180 years (1650 to 1830). A settler might clear one to three acres a year.[129] Many of the trees were ring-barked, which kills American species, and left standing to reduce the problem of disposing of big logs. The Americans were a large population, continually reinforced from the homeland. Their task was lightened by having metal tools; by coming to woods which were partially combustible and which were in places already periodically burnt by Indians; by meeting conifers which were easy to kill; by living where periodic hurricanes had removed most of the very big trees; and by growing maize, which needed little attention and left them with time to spend on grubbing out trees. On the other hand, they had boulders to remove as well as trees, and regrowth on any land temporarily neglected was more rapid than in Britain. Almost the whole area had become woodland again by 1900 – American agriculture is a story of wasted toil.

Our Neolithic ancestors also wasted much of their effort, for some clearings appear to have reverted to woodland after a few years. These have been compared to the shifting cultivation of the modern tropics, where clearings are easily made and are cultivated for only a few years because the soils become exhausted. In Britain, especially in lowland areas, this analogy is unconvincing: our soils in general are more fertile than those of tropical forests, and experiments at Rothamsted have shown that crops can be grown indefinitely at a primitive level without fertilizer. Even if our ancestors were ignorant of dung, they need not persistently have chosen the most infertile soils. Abandoned clearings may result from social or political rather than ecological troubles.

Cattle, sheep, and goats probably helped the clearance process by browsing the regrowth and eventually killing the stumps. Doubtless they also roamed the wildwood and scratched a living from whatever grew within their reach. Although there are many historic instances of grazing alone destroying woodland (p.301), it takes a great deal of grazing to go on consuming all the tree saplings year by year for centuries. We may doubt whether in prehistory there were enough livestock to do this, except very close to settlements.

Origins of woodmanship It is often assumed that farmland resulted from people felling trees for use. This has rarely happened in history: trees felled to make farmland have normally been wasted. Without iron tools and hard roads it would have been most difficult to find uses for the great trees of wildwood. Woodmanship is part of civilization, and is separate from destroying wildwood. By the earliest Neolithic period, someone had made the discovery that the regrowth shoots from a stump are of more use than the original tree.

The world's earliest evidence of woodmanship comes from the wooden trackways buried in the peat of the Somerset Levels, described on p.382. The earliest, the Sweet Track, was already an elaborate structure of oak timber, large underwood poles of ash, lime, elm, oak, and alder, and small poles of hazel and holly. Many of the poles were undoubtedly grown for the purpose in a mixed coppice-wood very like the still-extant Cheddar Wood nine miles away. Later trackways are made of woven wattle hurdles made of large numbers of hazel rods, grown in an elaborate coppicing system designed to produce rods of exactly the same size (and therefore of different ages), because there were not then metal tools with which to split the thick ones. The rods may have been a by-product of the growing of hazel leaves as a crop (p.243). Such hurdle-ways continue into the Bronze and Iron Ages; the wattle hurdles still made in Somerset are a 6000-year-old industry.

Wattle-work, and the woodmanship needed to produce the materials, were of immense importance up to Anglo-Saxon times and beyond. Remains have been found, though seldom adequately recorded, in innumerable excavations. As the reconstructions at Butser Hill (Hants) show, Iron Age round-houses were no mere 'huts made of branches of trees' (has anyone ever tried to make a hut of *branches* of trees?) but engineered structures – they could be greater in span than a cathedral – made of poles and rods of various sizes for particular functions.

Roman Woodland

It can no longer be maintained, as used to be supposed even twenty years ago, that Roman Britain was a frontier province, with boundless wildwoods surrounding occasional precarious clearings on the best land. On the contrary, even in supposedly backward counties such as Essex, villa abutted on villa for mile after mile, and most of the gaps were filled by small towns and the lands of British farmsteads.[130] More and more settlements are being found by people who look for potsherds now scattered in farmland or for Roman bricks and flue-tiles reused in the walls of churches.

The Romans lived in some places that the medievals thought to be uncultivable, and sometimes their predecessors had done so long before. Their settlements extended deep into what were later to be great woods; for instance Wychwood Forest (Oxon) – which also has Bronze Age and Neolithic sites,[608] – Rockingham Forest (Northants), Grovely (Wilts), and Micheldever Wood (Hants).[13] Roman England can hardly have been a very wooded country, but let us not make the opposite mistake of supposing that there was less woodland then than there is now. Only a minority of ancient woods can be shown both to be medieval and to have Roman remains beneath them, and even where they do the remains seldom prove that the whole wood is post-Roman.

Roman England probably had two types of terrain: regions where there was a patchwork of woodland and farmland (eg. Herts, Essex); and regions where all the woodland had disappeared (the great river-valleys and most of the chalkland). We are beginning to understand the Romans' carpentry[131] but have no direct knowledge of their woodmanship, which presumably had developed into something like its medieval and modern form. Not merely, as in Neolithic times, was it necessary to grow poles and rods of sizes which were difficult to get from wildwood. The Romans needed to conserve a limited resource and to organize supplies to woodless places. They dwelt in cities and had great timber-framed buildings, bridges, and ships; they needed not only timber but also a permanent supply of wood, for they indulged in things like baths, bricks, hypocausts, corn-driers, iron, lead, and glass.

The Romans knew about woodmanship in Italy; they even planted coppices and worked out the yields and the labour required.[132] Columella, in the first century AD, recommended cutting chestnut underwood at five years' growth and oak at seven years':

> Areas of this plantation . . . have 2,800 stools (*capita*) of chestnut, which easily provide twelve thousand poles, per *iugerum*.* The lengths cut nearest the butt are generally split into four, and then the second lengths of the same tree provide rods split into two; this kind of split pale lasts longer than a round stake.[133]

> *4500 stools, yielding 18,750 poles, per English acre.

This is a mere textbook recommendation, inspired by Italian practice, but it may not be irrelevant to England. The Romans certainly introduced chestnut, which has persisted and become wild (Chapter 4). It is just possible that some ancient chestnut woods still extant (eg. Stour Wood near Harwich) may be derived from Roman plantations.

In one place we can estimate the extent of Roman woodmanship. Among their many activities in the Weald the Romans had military ironworks. Their output has ben estimated by Dr Henry Cleere at 550 tons a year for 120 years. From his figures I have calculated that these ironworks could have been sustained permanently by the charcoal produced from 23,000 acres of coppice-wood[134]. There were many other Roman ironworks in the Weald. Roman metallurgy influenced more woodland than medieval, and may not have been much surpassed even in the seventeenth century.

The Dark Ages and Anglo-Saxon Period

If, as we used to suppose, Roman Britain went down in the fifth century in a cataclysm of battle, murder, and sudden death, then within fifty years it should have reverted to woodland. England in the seventh century ought to have looked like New England in the twentieth, with thousands of miles of field-walls lost in the woods, and the cellar-holes where thousands of farmsteads had rotted back into the ground. In America there was merely an economic cataclysm, and only pots lie under the bushes; in England there ought to have been skulls as well. Out of this the Anglo-Saxons (we supposed) laboriously hewed a new landscape, but had not got far by the time of the Norman Conquest.

Is this a true picture? For a beginning, neither pollen analysis nor archaeology give any hint of a massive return of secondary woodland invading even the good land. At Shakenoak (North Leigh, Oxon) the lands of a Roman villa did tumble down to woodland, but not until three centuries after the legions left;[135] its abandonment was not the effect of a national catastrophe but of a local retreat of cultivation in the Wychwood area, which continued for centuries. Other evidence is best approached by working backwards from the end of the Anglo-Saxon period.

Domesday Book The great survey of 1086 makes it perfectly clear that England was not then a very wooded land. Out of 12,580 settlements for which adequate particulars are given, only 6208 possessed woodland. This is not due to random under-recording, for wooded and woodless areas form a definite pattern (Fig.5.3). For thirty-five miles around London everywhere had a wood; there were well-wooded areas in north-west Warwickshire and adjacent Worcestershire, in Derbyshire, east Somerset, etc. Conversely, there was almost no woodland in the Breckland, or the Fens, or in a belt extending from east Yorkshire across the Midlands to Wiltshire. This distribution is entirely supported by documents from later centuries.

For more than half England, the sizes of woods are given, either in terms of length and breadth or as so many acres. They can be converted to modern acres on the basis that a Domesday woodland acre was 1.2 modern acres, and the area of an irregular wood is, on average, 0.7 times its length times breadth. For other counties woods are given either as 'wood for so many swine' or as 'wood rendering so many swine for pannage'. Such entries refer to the ancient practice of driving tame pigs into woods in autumn to fatten on acorns (or beechmast if any) before being slaughtered and salted down (p.122). Unfortunately this is not the down-to-earth method of estimating the area of a wood that it seems to be. The acorn crop is (and was) very undependable. By 1086 the wood-swine had become swine of the imagination; real pigs were counted separately and fed in other ways. We cannot objectively tell whether a wood for only a few swine was a small wood, a hornbeam wood (not yielding acorns), a coppice wood (lacking big oaks), or a wood owned by a pessimist. Nevertheless it is possible, by comparing Domesday with thirteenth-century records of the same woods, to form a rough impression of how much woodland there was.

The results of the calculation are given by counties in Table 5.1 and in the form of a map in Fig. 5.4. Domesday Book covers 27 million acres of land; of these 4.1 million, that is 15 per cent, were woodland (including wood-pasture). Rough though these figures necessarily are, they show that England was not well wooded even by the standards of twentieth-century, let alone eleventh-century, Europe. It had a proportion of woodland between those of modern France (20 per cent of the land) and modern Denmark (9 per cent).

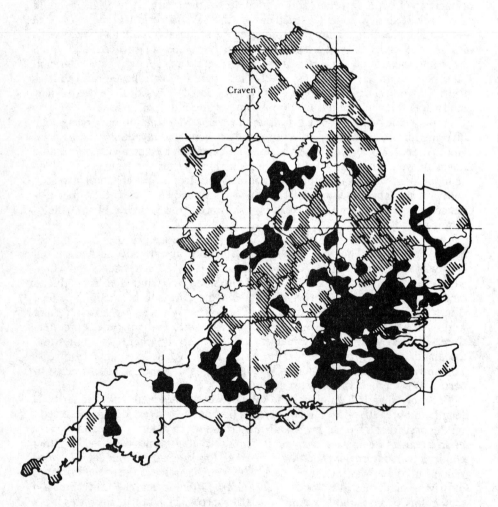

Fig. 5.3. Presence of woodland in Domesday Book England in 1086. Hatched areas: no woodland recorded at all. White areas: some settlements had woodland but not others. Black areas: every settlement had woodland. No account is taken of the amount of woodland. There are no usable returns for five northern counties nor for Craven.

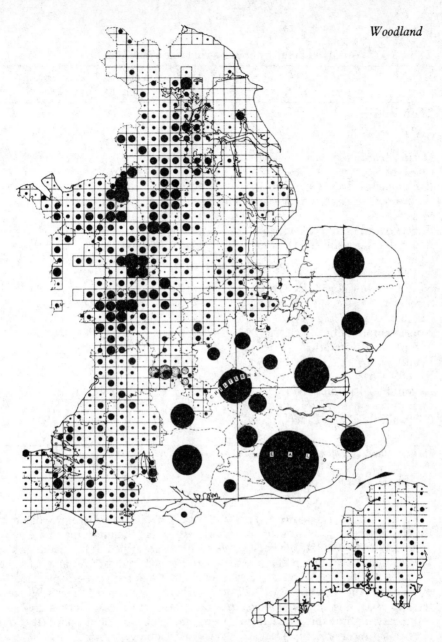

Fig. 5.4. Area of woodland in England in 1086, as recorded by Domesday Book. In counties for which the dimensions of woods are given, areas are mapped by 10-km National Grid squares: each black circle represents, at the scale of the map, the total woodland area possessed by places within the square. (Except for Amesbury (A) in Wiltshire, no attempt has been made to redistribute woodland belonging to places located in a different square.) In eastern and south-eastern counties, for which the returns are in the form of swine or swine-rents, each black circle is an estimate of the woodland area of a whole county (or of the Weald or Chilterns separately). Stippled circles in Oxfordshire represent Forests, of which an unknown proportion was woodland.

Table 5.1 Woodland areas by counties in Domesday Book

	% of woodland (including wood-pasture) in 1086
The Weald??	70
Worcester	40
Stafford	32
Hertford?, Middlesex?	30
Cheshire	27
Buckingham?, Derby	26
Berkshire??, Essex?, non-Wealden Surrey??	20
Warwick	19
Flint, Oxford?, W. Yorkshire	16
Bedford?, Hampshire??	15
Gloucester	14
Dorset, non-Wealden Kent??, Wiltshire	13
Norfolk?, Nottingham, N. Yorkshire	12
Somerset	11
Rutland	10
Northampton, Suffolk?	9
Shropshire?, Hereford??	8
Huntingdon	7
Isle of Wight??, non-Wealden Sussex??	6
Devon, E. Yorkshire	4
Cambridge?	3½
Cornwall, Leicester, Lincoln	3
Isle of Ely	1

? indicates the degree of uncertainty associated with swine records, and ?? that associated with swine-rents.

After Rackham (1980).

Most of England consisted of farmland with islands of wood. But woodland in the eleventh century was much less evenly distributed than its remains are now, and a few areas were still mainly wooded with large islands of farmland. In the Weald, trees were still predominant, though not continuous, over an area some 75 miles by 30. The second largest wooded area was the Chiltern plateau, 40 miles by 25, immediately north of London; there were others in north Worcestershire extending into Warwickshire, in east Cheshire, east Derbyshire, and south-east Staffordshire. Smaller concentrations of woodland included those later called the Forests of Dean, Selwood, and Epping.

Even the bigger wooded areas were not uninhabited wildwood; it was nowhere possible in Norman England to penetrate into woodland further than four miles from some habitation. Conversely, many villages were over four miles from any wood, and a day's journey from any substantial woodland. Single woods ranged in size from over 1000 acres to fractions of an acre. Domesday records 518 separate woods for Somerset, half of them of less than 35 acres, and 767 woods for Devon, half of them smaller than 17 acres.

The landscape of Norman England was not like that of modern Borneo but like that of modern France. France has now rather more woods and fewer villages than England then, but it retains the distinction between wooded and unwooded areas. The modern Vosges, like the Norman Weald, are well over half tree-covered, but penetrated by roads and full of villages and hamlets in clearings. At the other extreme, the vast woodless cornlands of Champagne or around Chartres correspond to the environs of Rugby or Cambridge in 1086.

Anglo-Saxon charters The perambulations tell us of an earlier state of England which we might expect to have been more wooded. In practice this is not obviously so: many of the features (eg. downs) are specifically non-woodland, and others, such as trees, would have been of no value as landmarks within a wood.

The Anglo-Saxon language is rich in words for woodland. Some we still use, such as *wudu* 'wood', *grāf* 'grove', *scaga* 'shaw', *hangr* 'hanger'; others – *bearu*, *holt*, *fyrhþ*, etc. – are forgotten. There is no evidence as to what different kinds of woodland these meant, and etymologists' guesses are not to be believed.

All the words for 'wood' together comprise 384 landmarks in the charters – 471 if we include place-names involving woods – making up about one in thirty of all boundary features. When mapped (Fig.5.5) they agree well with the distribution of woodland in Domesday Book. Many woods are mentioned in the Weald; almost none in those parts of the Midlands that were woodless in 1086. Both in the charters and in Domesday, the almost woodless eastern Cotswolds contrast with the very wooded western Cotswolds; the moderately wooded Marlborough area (Wilts) contrasts with the almost woodless claylands to the north. Only in two districts do the charters place woods where there appear to have been none by 1086. In Mid Hampshire there seems to have been an under-recording of woodland in Domesday; perhaps nobody had heard of swine-rents there. In the Fens, woods are surprisingly frequent in charters; this may be because there were few alternative landmarks, but probably also the charters were just in time to catch almost the last of the Fenland woods before they disappeared.

Woods in the charters have individual names and were permanent; at least one in four of the woods was still there in the twentieth century. A very early perambulation, that of Shottery by Stratford-on-Avon in *c*. 704, mentions a *Westgraf*;[136] the map still shows a Westgrove Wood in Hazelor. Also in Warwickshire, the bounds of Long Itchington, dated 1001, pass through 'a high oak in the middle of Wulluht grove';[137] and there is still – unless some modern evil has befallen it – a 200-acre wood here bisected by the Ufton-Long Itchington parish boundary. Examples from charters and other sources could easily be multiplied. Wayland Wood (Watton, Norfolk), anciently *Wanelund*, is one of the many wood-names based on Old Norse *lúndr*, a grove or sacred grove (Smith 1956), which therefore go back to Viking times. Domesday refers not directly to the wood but to Wayland Hundred, a division of the county named after the wood, where the hundred court was probably held. This was thus a grove of assembly, perhaps even of heathen worship, long before the Conquest. Much later it was to become the Babes-in-the-Wood wood, and by some miracle of continuity it is still intact and now belongs to Norfolk Naturalists' Trust.

Woodland was not always situated in the place to which it belonged. The charter for Benson (Oxfordshire) in 996, having traced the main boundary, then says 'These are the bounds of the wood that belongs to the land', and goes on to perambulate a separate piece of land some miles away in the Chilterns.[138] About twenty such detached 'woods' are described in detail – they were seldom wholly woodland – and many more are named. Others are first recorded in medieval sources, though the arrangements themselves seem always to have been pre-Conquest. For instance, the biggest concentration of woodland in south-west England was of about 15,000 acres south of Taunton, later known as the Forest of Neroche; as Mr Michael Aston has shown, the greater part of this consisted of detached parts of townships lying up to twelve miles away to the east; until recently much of the evidence was preserved by the parish boundaries. Domesday Book records the woodland as part of the parent settlements, and therefore shows too little land-use in the Neroche area itself and too much in the area to the east.

Almost the whole of the Weald was parcelled out into dependencies of places lying outside it. Originally this had been connected with the seasonal pasturing of pigs, much more important in the woodland economy of the Weald than elsewhere. By 1086 the pig economy was being replaced by conventional settlement and agriculture,[139] but most of the settlements were still regarded as part

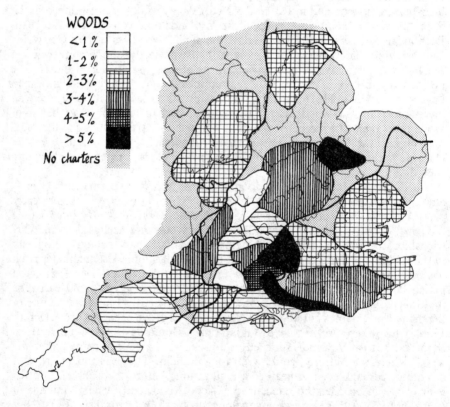

WOODS

< 1 %
1-2 %
2-3%
3-4%
4-5%
> 5 %
No charters

Fig. 5.5. Distribution of woodland in Anglo-Saxon charters. The number of woods mentioned – including all the Old English words for woodland – is mapped as a percentage of the total number of boundary features. The thick lines mark the extent of what is now predominantly Planned Countryside.

of their parent manors. Tonbridge, for instance, though a quite important place, was subsumed in Otford, ten miles away. For this reason the Weald is poorly recorded in Domesday Book, and generations of writers (forgetting its Norman architecture) have misrepresented it as a desert of untrodden wild-wood.

'Neroche anomalies' are widespread in southern England and the south-west Midlands, west to Somerset and north to Worcestershire. Allowing for them, woodland was yet more unevenly distributed than Domesday Book says. The south-east half of Warwickshire and north Oxfordshire were almost totally woodless; the small woods which belonged to places in those areas (Fig.5.4) were really situated at a distance in the wooded halves of both counties.[140]

The charters do not set out to tell us the uses of woodland, but they let slip incidental details which make it clear that woods were not under-used. There are many references to coppicing and the supply and transport of rods, fuel, and other wood; less often to timber. The woodland pig economy and its undependability are mentioned. Wood-pasture is differentiated from other woodland (p.120), and common woods are separated from private woods. Here are some examples.

Pasture for 70 pigs in that wooded common . . . which the country-folk call Wulfferdinleh [Wolverley, Worcs] and 5 wagons full of good rods (*virgis*) and every year one oak for building . . . and wood . . . for the fire as necessary.

Grant by Burgred, king of Mercia, 866[141]

60 fothers of wood . . . in the wood at Horn. And 12 fothers of grove and six fothers of poles.

Annual supply to Sempringham, Lincs, 852[142]

(Horn is in Rutland, 16 miles from Sempringham, and was by no means the nearest wood. A fother is a kind of cartload. I do not know what 'grove' is as a woodland product.)

A place in which salt can be got and with [right of] access for 3 carts into the wood which is called Blean.

Grant at Lenham, Kent, 850[143]

(The Blean is still the second largest wooded area in Kent; it is 15 miles from Lenham.)

The old coal-pit where the three boundaries go together.

Apsley Guise, Beds, 969[144]

(A coal-pit in Bedfordshire has to be a pit for making charcoal.)

I give the lands at Brycandune to St Peter of Westmenstre, except that I will that they fatten two hundred swine for my wife, if there be mast.

Brickendon, Herts, 989[145]

81

Woodland

Woods were valuable private property: a wood near Powick (Worcs) was the subject of a complicated lawsuit in 825.[146] We might expect their boundaries to have been demarcated. There are ninety-three instances in the charters of the mysterious word *wyrtruma* or *wyrtwala*, literally 'plant-strength' or 'plant-wall'. It is a linear feature like a hedge and is usually associated with woodland: at Rimpton (Somerset) one passed along the *wyrtruma* of a wood called Eatan bearu, and at Stoke Bishop (Bristol) there was the *wyrtruma* of Dynninces grove. Although it is not quite certain that a *wyrtruma* was always at the edge of a wood, it is hard to resist the conclusion that this is the Old English technical term for the woodbanks which already demarcated some woods. *Wyrtwalan* are most frequent in areas with only moderate amounts of woodland, such as the east Midlands, north-west Dorset, and south Gloucestershire (Fig. 5.6).

Place-names An earlier stratum of evidence still is that of place-names; not, for this purpose, the names of woods themselves, but of settlements implying substantial woodland. The many hundreds of villages and hamlets named *-ley* and *-hurst* (eg. Bromley, Stoneleigh, Stoneley, Leigh-on-Sea, Hawkhurst) appear to mean an inhabited clearing surrounded by woodland. Names in *-feld*, such as Beaconsfield, appear to mean not a 'field' as we know it but an open space in sight of woodland with which to contrast it.[147] Most, if not all, such

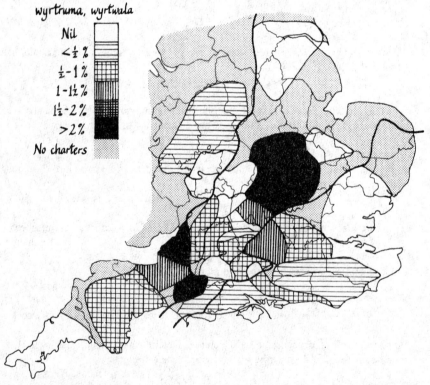

Fig. 5.6. Distribution of *wyrtruma* and *wyrtwala* in Anglo-Saxon charters, as a percentage of all boundary features.

places already existed in Anglo-Saxon times, and many of them early in that period. Do not *Tues*ley, *Wednes*field, and *Thor*ley go back to the twilight of the heathen gods?

These place-names are mapped in Fig. 5.7. They form yet another distribution which is an unexpectedly good fit to that of woodland in Domesday Book. Woodland place-names are thick on the map in the Weald, the Chiltern plateau, north-west Warwickshire and adjacent Worcestershire, east Derbyshire, etc. Areas which were woodless in the eleventh century, such as the Breckland, Fens, Lincolnshire, south-east Warwickshire, north Oxfordshire, and east Gloucestershire have few or no such place-names. (The derivations are not always certain, and a few places named after later meanings of 'ley' and 'hurst' may have slipped in – cf. p.333).

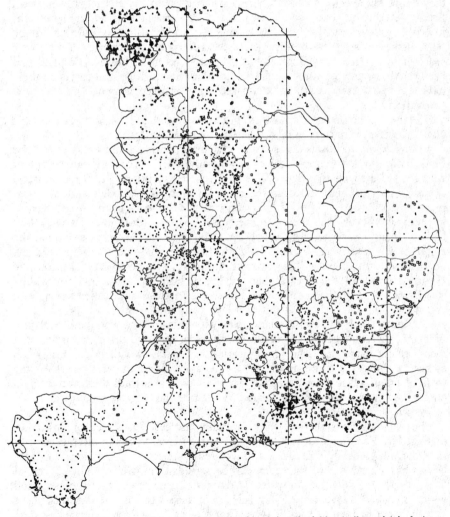

Fig. 5.7. Names of towns, villages, and hamlets involving 'ley' (dots), 'hurst' (circles), or 'thwaite' (triangles), and of towns and villages involving 'field' (squares).

always certain, and a few places named after later meanings of 'ley' and 'hurst' may have slipped in – cf. p.333).

Conclusions There is nothing to suggest that the Anglo-Saxons were pioneers, spending their lives digging up trees among boundless woodland. Such may have been the business of folk in the Weald or around Birmingham, but not of the country as a whole. As far back as records go, most of England had an ordered, stable, and predominantly agricultural countryside. The glimpses that we are given of the Anglo-Saxon way of life show woods having a place in the landscape and in human affairs not very different from that which they were to hold in the Middle Ages.

Allusions to the actual destruction of woodland are remarkably uncommon. The charters rarely mention the word *styficing*, a place of stumps; not once do they expressly specify a place where a wood used to be. Barnet 'burnt area', Brentwood 'burnt wood', and a few other place-names have been interpreted as woods destroyed by fire, but this cannot be done; there is nothing in the place-names to suggest anything more destructive than charcoal-burning or a bracken fire. Domesday Book says that many woods in Eastern England had been rated at a greater number of swine in 1066 than in 1086, but this is unlikely to be due to a decrease in their extent since there is no corresponding increase in cultivation.[148]

Had the Anglo-Saxons started with boundless woodland, we would expect the place-names and charters to record earlier stages in its destruction than Domesday Book. Only locally is this so. The charters mention some woodland in the Fens, and the *-ley* names of west Cambridgeshire record a minor tract of wildwood destroyed by 1086. With such small exceptions the three sources, despite their different dates, agree on what were the wooded and woodless regions. It follows that that distribution was not the work of the Anglo-Saxons but was taken over from their predecessors. If Roman south-east Warwickshire had had plenty of woodland, or had been allowed to revert to woodland at the Anglo-Saxon takeover, *-ley* and *-field* would be as thick on the map as in the north-west of the county. They are not. Roman north-west Warwickshire, like Hertfordshire and the Weald, had evidently been wooded, but not wholly woodland; there had been open areas which the Anglo-Saxons called fields, leys, and hursts, as well as hewing out new leys and hursts for themselves.

Continuity with the Roman landscape accounts for the woodland exclaves. Pioneers, given a free choice, could hardly have imposed upon themselves the inconvenience and the legal complications of siting woodland, from which awkward loads had to be brought, at a distance. Such an arrangement is the work of a new social order having to take the woods as it finds them and to share out, as best it can, a landscape created by the previous regime for a different set of purposes.

The Anglo-Saxons in 600 years probably increased the area of farmland, managed the woodland more intensively, and made many minor alterations. But they did not radically reorganize the wooded landscape. A few names of large woods have come down from even earlier periods than 'Blean'. The charter of West Monkton, Somerset, apparently dated 682, mentions 'that famous wood which is called Cantocwudu';[149] and also in Somerset the historian Asser tells us that the Ancient Britons had the name Coit Maur, 'Great Wood', for Selwood on the Wiltshire border.[150] Quantockwood and Selwood were still great woods in the nineteenth century; they succumbed not to Anglo-Saxon or medieval farming but to modern forestry.

The Middle Ages

A mention of an identifiable wood in an Anglo-Saxon document is somewhat of a rare survival, like an Anglo-Saxon church. This is not so from the thirteenth century onwards, when woods, more than most types of land, benefited from the revolution in land recording. An extract from the *Ely Coucher Book* appears at the head of this chapter. This and other great surveys of the lands of monasteries and bishoprics mention many hundreds of specific woods. Other woods are listed in the surviving part of the Hundred Rolls of 1279 and in innumerable surveys of private estates.

By 1250 woods covered only a few per cent of England. More than half the Bishop of Ely's estates, scattered from Norfolk to the Thames, had none. Woods had definite names, boundaries, and acreages, were private property, were intensively managed, and were permanent. Hayley Wood and the nearby Hardwick Wood (also in the *Ely Coucher Book*) are still with us after 734 years; they are copiously documented for all the intervening centuries, and there can be no question that they are the same woods (Rackham 1975). Hayley is exactly the same apart from minor changes due to the making of a railway; its companion wood, Litlelund, was grubbed out in the 1650s. Hardwick Wood has had a more complex history (it has lost its original name of Bradeleh) and only half the present wood is original. (Both woods are now nature reserves of Cambridgeshire and Isle of Ely Naturalists' Trust.)

These are not exceptional survivals. From other pages of the *Coucher Book*, all the five woods of Barking (Suffolk), in area from 5 to 130 acres, still exist with at least roughly the same areas and four out of the five names; so do Balsham Wood (east Cambridgeshire) and part of Hadstock Wood (north-west Essex). The woods of Dereham and Shipdham (Norfolk) succumbed to seventeenth- and eighteenth-century agriculture; the great wood of Hitcham (Suffolk) was grubbed out in the 1850s (Plate III); Doddington Heute, the last of the Isle of Ely woods, survived until 1942; and the little Oxenholt in Glemsford (Suffolk) was tragically replanted only in 1971. Roughly half the woods named in thirteenth-century surveys were still there in 1945.

Most medieval woods were shared by timber trees and underwood. Both were self-renewing and produced a sustained yield. This was usually taken for granted but occasionally, as in the 1356 survey at the head of this chapter, stated in writing. Underwood was usually the regular and more important product. Most surveys either state a felling rotation or give the annual return expected from underwood. Occasionally there survive estate accounts which show, as practical experience would suggest, that the actual area cut varied from year to year. Hardwick Wood was supposed in the 1356 survey to be felled every five years; the accounts, which survive for most years from 1341 to 1495, show that a five-year cycle was a good average estimate of a practice which could vary from cutting nothing in three years to felling a third of the wood at once (Rackham 1975). Five years, which seems to us a very short interval between fellings, was not unusual; coppice cycles could be of only four years and were not often of more than eight, though some rotations of sixteen to twenty years are known.

Timber trees were felled at irregular intervals as required. In Hardwick Wood there were big fellings of oaks in 1377–86 and again in the 1450s, but such a long interval was unusual.

Boundaries By 1270 woods were valuable property: the return from under-wood alone – leaving out timber, hazel-nuts, and other produce – averaged 6*d* per acre per year, which was more than from arable land. Their boundaries were carefully defined by a great bank and ditch, usually with a hedge or a fence. This prevented encroachment by neighbours and kept out livestock which would eat the young shoots. Most woodbanks appear to have been already in existence – that of Knapwell Wood (west Cambridgeshire), which still exists, is mentioned in the twelfth century [151] – but I have seen the accounts for making three miles of new woodbank round the Norwich Cathedral Priory woods at Hindolveston, Norfolk, in 1297–8. The work was done by five contractors at a cost of £8. 16*s*. 5*d*, financed by selling the 'branches of trees and underwood' growing on the line of the earthwork; items include planting a hedge on the bank and providing bridges, gates, and padlocks at the entrances to the woods. [152]

Timber and underwood in buildings Archaeology tells us all the little we know of woodmanship in prehistory. For the Middle Ages and later, the records are complemented by samples of produce: timber in standing buildings and underwood preserved in wattle-and-daub (Plate II).

Buildings were the biggest single use of timber and tell us much of the management of woods in general, though they can rarely be related to particular woods. Timber is not inherently perishable: many thousands of timber-framed buildings survive from the fifteenth century, and those that have come down to us from the twelfth century, though few, are not in a worse state of decay than those of the eighteenth. Nor was timber a poor man's substitute for stone: the choice of material is quite unrelated to whether or not there was woodland, and evidently depended on local fashions and etiquette which we cannot now explain. Cambridge had abundant easily-worked stone and no local woodland; but apart from colleges it was an almost entirely timber-framed town. Somerset, though well-wooded in parts, has no rural timber-framing at all. Well-wooded north Norfolk had less timber-framing than poorly-wooded Suffolk or even the woodless Breckland. The only generality is that, where a region has not much timber building, it will be urban: for example the timber (or timber-fronted) buildings of towns in Cornwall, Dorset, and Somerset, and of Edinburgh and formerly of Irish cities. Timber was an architectural medium: a 'wealth of exposed beams' looked picturesque and expressed prestige; it was not necessary to hold up the structure.

Over 90 per cent of building timbers are oak. This is not just an accident of survival, for other species are preserved as well. Records show oak to have been the most expensive as well as the commonest timber tree; other species – elm, ash, aspen – are most often found in medieval terrace houses and other homes of the relatively poor.

Most medieval buildings are made from large numbers of small oaks; every timber, large or small, is made from the smallest tree that will serve the purpose. The carpenter chose trees of the sizes required and squared them up, usually leaving the corners rounded ('waney'). Oaks, then as now, were crooked and carpenters made ingenious use of the irregular shapes into which they grow. This was from choice: carpenters could saw big oaks lengthwise into several beams when they had to for a special reason, and often sawed a tree down the middle to make two rafters or a pair of crucks; but lengthwise sawing was expensive and was avoided where possible. (It is often supposed that trees were split lengthwise, but most British oaks are too knotty to split well; most halved timbers in fact bear saw-marks.)

It is possible to count the oaks that went into a building. A typical fifteenth-century Suffolk farmhouse, rather larger than average, turns out to be made of some 330 trees. Only three trees were as much as 18 inches in diameter, a usual size for a 'mature' oak nowadays; half of them were less than 9 inches in diameter, and one in ten was as small as 6 inches. Such sizes are typical of medieval houses, barns, colleges, and the less grand church roofs.[153] They imply a practice of woodmanship with a rapid turnover of small oaks and no difficulty in replacing them. This is just as true of the well-wooded Weald – see the buildings in the Weald and Downland Museum at Singleton (Sussex) – as of East Anglia. Oaks grew among underwood which suppressed their lower boughs, producing a trunk about 20 feet long, above which the crown of the tree branched out. This maximum usable length for an ordinary oak-tree was an important factor in the design of buildings, especially great barns.

The panels between the timbers of framed buildings are usually filled with wattle-and-daub made of interwoven underwood rods. Underwood, where it has not been thrown away by 'restorers', is often excellently preserved, down to the very lichens which grew on the rods when alive (p.43). It is not so informative as timber, for most of it was used for other purposes, and the wattles of buildings are not necessarily a random sample; but it tells us something of species and management. Hazel, in my experience, is the commonest species of wattle, and sallow (much less often mentioned in records) the second commonest. I have encountered elm, aspen, birch, and maple, and once the bast fibre of lime used as string. Rods were commonly cut at five to nine years' growth – the evidence of woodland records is vindicated by the produce itself – and had grown to about 2 inches in diameter at the butt. The rods of medieval wattle-and-daub are evened in thickness by splitting the thicker ones.

Examining the timber and underwood of a medieval building may bring back to life the trees and the men of a long-vanished wood. But let us be cautious. Building materials are not always local; the medievals had good roads and used them on the slightest pretext (Chapter 12). Trees more than about 25 feet in usable length or 18 inches in diameter did not normally grow in the local woods; they were rare and expensive and were brought from a distance. They were used in the king's castles and the great roofs of cathedrals; but nearly every place in England had one outsize timber, namely the post, probably 40 feet long and 2 feet square, on which the windmill stood and was rotated into the wind. Mill-posts were then commonly set in the ground and rotted or worked loose, and accounts are full of the trouble and expense of getting replacements.

Outsize timbers are still to be admired in the twelfth- and thirteenth-century timber church towers of Essex and Herefordshire. By the fourteenth century they were rarer than at any time before or since. The Octagon of Ely Cathedral of *c.* 1330, probably the grandest timber structure ever built in England, shows evidence of having been adapted during construction to use smaller trees than the original design called for. The carpenter evidently expected to be given sixteen oaks, each 40 feet long by 13½ inches square, but had to make do with getting the utmost length out of trees not quite big enough.

Not only outsize trees, but ordinary timber and even underwood was moved about the country. Much timber, especially big trees, came not from woods but from hedgerows, parks, and Forests.

There was a large import trade from Norway, the Baltic, and Central Europe.[154] Pine did not grow in England; so when, as in a building in Ely, we find a thirteenth-century roof largely made of small pine trees, we are reminded of the pine scaffolding-poles which the fabric rolls of Ely Cathedral record as having been brought from Norway.[155] Pine boards survive in several medieval structures, such as the thirteenth-century doors of the Chapter-house in York Minster. The documents speak of a large trade in oak as well as pine boards, and not merely to places without woodland. Hindolveston sent timber and underwood to other Norwich Cathedral estates all over Norfolk; yet wainscots – a kind of foreign oak board – were brought to Hindolveston from the port of King's Lynn in the 1360s merely to make a shed.[156] Boards, especially thin ones, cannot be made and seasoned in small quantities or at short notice; they are best made by specialists who have the skill and equipment (including power saws) and a supply of suitable trees. Imported wainscot boards survive most often in medieval church furniture and doors. They do not carry the stamp NOT MADE IN ENGLAND so obviously as do the pine boards; yet with practice one can distinguish the giant, straight-grained, slow-grown oaks of Central Europe, accurately sawn in a board factory, from the small, crooked, fast-grown local oaks used for the structural frames of the same buildings.

Even wood was occasionally imported into Sussex; Rye Corporation levied a duty on it in 1377.[38]

Woods Down the Centuries

The woods of 1250, as we have seen, were already relics of an Anglo-Saxon and Norse social system. The ill-documented intervening two centuries had been a time of rising population and of such land-hunger as we have never experienced since. Woodland was to shrink from 15 per cent of England in 1086 to perhaps 10 per cent by 1350, an average destruction of 17½ acres a day. In the Weald some 450,000 acres were grubbed out in at most 260 years, about 5 acres a day, 'an achievement without parallel in medieval England',[157] reducing the woods to something like their present extent by 1350. Much the same happened in the Chilterns. Most of the second- and third-rank wooded areas, eg. Arden in Warwickshire, east Derbyshire, and Neroche, became no more wooded than the rest of the country. Where there was less woodland less of it was destroyed, but in almost every county – even Cambridgeshire – some encroachment is known.

This period was suddenly cut short by the Black Death in 1349. The surviving population made less use of the land. Any wood then remaining had a good chance of surviving the next 500 years. Some land probably reverted to woodland. Secondary woodland is seldom recorded in writing; but all over Eastern and Midland England there are woods which show evidence on the ground of having been smaller at some time earlier than the sixteenth century.

Why were woods stable? It is an error to present woodmanship solely in economic terms. Woods have social functions as well, and successive ages have disagreed as to which costs and benefits come within the scope of economics. There is the further difficulty of a long time-scale: to set income from under-wood against the capital accumulation of timber can only be done by guesswork. A landowner may maintain a wood because he thinks it pays better than an alternative use for the land; but also because he has not the labour to grub it out, because he does not want his tenants and neighbours to be cold, because he appreciates it as a pheasant-covert or an antiquity, etc., etc. We can rarely ascertain why one wood has survived and another not; but the prices of wood and timber, averaged over many woods, do provide part of the explanation for why woods have been stable.

A few documents capture an earlier age before woods had had much scarcity value, but even in the eleventh century we find the Bishop of Norwich trying to prevent Thorpe Wood from turning into Mousehold Heath (p.301). At Hindol-veston (Norfolk) we have a rare record of a change to a different regime. In 1272 the revolting citizens of Norwich sacked their Cathedral Priory. The monks, to pay for the repairs, promptly sold £214 worth of produce from their Hindolves-ton woods; this great sum presumably came from timber allowed to grow over many years to insure against just such an emergency. Thereafter they reorgan-ized the woods to produce more income from underwood.[158] Since wood is easy to steal, this involved attention to security, making a new woodbank, and hiring a woodward.

From the latter thirteenth century woods were valuable land, and not just in eastern England. In well-wooded Hampshire the account-book of Beaulieu Abbey in 1269–70 specifies the logs, faggots, stakes, and charcoal to be got from an acre of twenty-year-old underwood – our earliest account of woodmanship in the abstract. It expects a return of 2s. 1½d. per acre per year of growth, much greater than from arable and little less than from meadow.[159]

Woodland provided income and capital, and unlike modern forestry it cost almost nothing. Expenses, chiefly in maintaining boundaries, could be passed on to the purchaser of the wood. For at least 600 years prices of trees, both timber and underwood, either remained steady or rose in real terms. In eastern England, in the later Middle Ages, an acre of underwood at ten years' growth would have cost around 5s., and an oak tree measuring 20 cubic feet would have fetched 2s. By 1830 the underwood would have cost about £4 and the oak £5. Most of the difference was, of course, due to inflation.

The price of underwood, in relation to the value of money, rose only once, by about 75 per cent between 1540 and 1553. This I attribute to colder winters (the 'Little Ice Age'), rising population, and rising standards of domestic heating; people were building chimneys in their halls instead of the previous uncomfort-able but more efficient heating by a bonfire on the floor. (The *retail* price of firewood, especially in cities, was probably increased by greedy wholesalers.) The supply could not be increased, for the area of woodland was stable or declining. Some additional wood was got from hedges (p.189), but the extra demand was eventually met by coal. I can find no further rise, in real terms, in the price of underwood in the seventeenth and eighteenth centuries.

Prices of oak-trees rose more slowly. From 1510 to 1690 there was a rise of about 50 per cent above inflation; a surprisingly modest rise, considering all the building done in this period. However, the fashion for covering up timbers, making them merely structural instead of part of the architecture, would have reduced the amount needed; a seventeenth-century house, made of big oak-trees sawn thin, contains only about a third of the timber of a medieval house. The high price of oak-trees relative to underwood by 1830 is the effect of an accelerating price rise from 1750 onwards, which we shall discuss later.

The economic and social value of woods, plus the capital expense of destroying them, tended to preserve woodland against other land-uses from 1350 to 1850. Occasional woods were grubbed out when individual owners happened not to like woodland. There was some general destruction when farming prospered, and especially when, as from the mid-eighteenth century, it was subsidized by the government (p.27).

Woods and industry Industries follow almost inevitably from the fact that not everywhere possessed a wood. Woods attract specialist craftsmen, and their owners often prefer to sell finished articles rather than trees. Already in the thirteenth century many estates, though having woods, bought in things like wheels and hurdles. In the fourteenth century there appears to have been a hurdle-factory at Hindolveston. These were an earlier state of the woodland crafts later to be described by Sturt and his successors (Fitzrandolph and Hay 1926), which many modern writers have wrongly supposed to be the *raison d'être* of woods and woodmanship. There were also the heavy industries that made iron, glass, leather, and ships.

Economic historians have built an inverted pyramid of argument on the belief that woods were largely destroyed by felling for fuel, especially by the charcoal iron industry between 1550 and 1700. Woods felled are supposed to have ceased to be woodland, leading to a 'timber famine', high prices, restrictive legislation, industries moving further afield, and even the invention of coke as a substitute for charcoal. Finally the ironmasters, having 'used up' the woods of England, are supposed to have committed economic suicide in the flames of the remaining woods of Scotland and Ireland. The argument is stated in general terms: I am not aware that a single named wood has been proved to have disappeared from the map which would still be there had the iron-men not felled it.

This thesis has been overturned by the researches of M.W. Flinn and G. Hammersley;[160] here I can but mention their main arguments and add a few of my own. The tip of the inverted pyramid, on which all else rests, is the notion that *timber* trees were used for fuel and did not grow again. This is not true. Ironworks were not fly-by-night enterprises; they used mainly underwood, often from their own woods, and protected their supplies.[161] The 'timber famine' and high prices are largely the illusion of those economic historians who forget about inflation. The fortunes of the industry were not determined by the relatively small cost of standing trees but by other costs, especially labour, or by foreign competition. Ironmasters who moved into Scotland were expanding their production, not abandoning England. Coal and coke were substituted for wood, in different industries over a long period, not because wood was scarce but because the labour costs of coal were less.

Fuel-using industries lived near large woods because charcoal was difficult to transport. Like all heavy industries, they disrupted local society and were unpopular. Industrialists, who had many bigger bills to pay than that for trees, could afford to buy up woods and to deprive local people of previously cheap fuel. Although they preferred not to waste labour on chopping up timber for fuel, they may have discouraged the growth of timber trees which took up space that might have been growing underwood. It is hardly surprising that politicians and the public should have been angry with industrialists and, in their anger, should have overlooked the distinction between harvesting trees and destroying woodland. The sixteenth-century legislation against industries was no more than a half-hearted attempt to prevent this competition.

The theory that industry destroyed woodland fails to pass a simple test. If it is true, less medieval woodland ought to survive in areas where there was industry than where there was not. Exactly the opposite is the case. The woods did not disappear from the Weald – the chief home of the iron industry – or the industrial Lake District or the Forests of Dean or Wyre. It was non-industrial Norfolk, the land of agricultural innovation and prosperity, that lost three-quarters of its medieval woods, more than any other county, between 1600 and 1790. The evidence supports those seventeenth-century polemical writers, such as Yarranton,[162] who claimed that the iron industry preserved (and even created) woods. The survival of almost any large tract of woodland strongly suggests that there have been industries to protect it against being destroyed for farmland.

Another well-worn belief is that the history of woodland has been everywhere dominated by the influence of the sea. We are told that shipyards were chronically short of timber, and in their search for suitable trees destroyed the ancient forests, or (in another version) maintained the ancient woods. It has even been claimed that coppice-with-standards woodland was invented in order to produce crooked branchy timber trees specially needed for the curved shapes of hulls.

As the Greeks and the Dutch bear witness, it is not necessary for a nation with a proud seafaring tradition to have had much woodland. In Britain shipbuilding was not a steady influence touching every wood in the country; it became a major consumer of timber only through the growth of intercontinental trade and the arms race from the later eighteenth century onwards. The output of timber-built ships between 1800 and 1860 was probably equal to that in all the rest of history put together. Much shipbuilding timber, especially in large sizes and special shapes, came from hedges and parks, not from woodland.

The belief that shipbuilding timber was scarce depends on complaints or forebodings of shortage from the sixteenth century onwards. These concern timber for building warships and are not to be taken at face value: had there been the slightest difficulty in finding timber for the tiny fleet that defeated the Armada, it would have been utterly impossible to build the sixtyfold larger fleet that defeated Napoleon. Civilian dockyards were bigger builders of shipping than the Navy, but bought timber at the market price and did not complain of difficulty in getting it. Naval dockyards were parsimonious and wasteful; they were short of funds, not of trees. The Navy preferred to scrounge timber from the wood-pasture of the Royal Forests, and when forced to buy expected to get the large sizes and special shapes of timber for building warships at no more than the average price for ordinary oak. H.M.S. *Victory*, built 1759–65, is ingeniously put together from great numbers of the smallest, and therefore cheapest, practicable oaks. Each of her lower-deck beams is 17 by 20 inches by up to 50 feet long, and carries six tons of cannon. These timbers, although very large, are well within the size to which oaks then grew; yet each is scarfed together from three lesser oaks, saving about a quarter of the cost of a single great tree.

In medieval and Elizabethan times shipbuilding had been insignificant compared to other uses of timber. Not until about 1780 did its growth begin to catch up with the supply of trees. Rising prices of oak are often quoted as evidence of shortage, but were mainly the effect of inflation. In relation to prices in general, the price of oak-trees rose only slowly during the eighteenth century. During the Napoleonic Wars the price shot up to nearly twice what it had been in 1690, but not until 1809 were the naval dockyards at last constrained to use other materials such as oak from Albania. The price rise cannot, however, be due to naval shipbuilding, for it continued after the wars ended. We might attribute it to merchant shipbuilding, which went on increasing in peacetime; but much of the rise in the price of trees was in the bark, not the timber, and had quite another cause.

Throughout history the bark of oak – other trees will not do – has been used for tanning leather. Medieval accounts record sales of bark as a by-product of felling timber; an unimportant by-product, since the timbers of many pre-1600 buildings still have some of their bark left on. The trade went on quietly until 1780, when there was a sudden boom in leather which followed the same course as the contemporary boom in shipping. From 1780 to 1850 the tanyards were no mere users-up of by-products but a gigantic industry, a much bigger consumer of oak-trees than the naval dockyards and almost certainly a bigger consumer than the merchant shipyards. The supply came mainly from the historic oak-wood regions – Scotland, Wales, Highland England. Thousands of acres were maintained as oak underwood, in which timber production was sacrificed for a greater yield of bark. Even in Lowland England bark, as a by-product of timber trees, came from almost every wood and hedge.

What effects have the industries left? Most of the woods that supplied the iron industry outlived its decline. In oakwood regions, especially the Scottish Highlands, the tanbark trade took over and perpetuated these woods. But in Lowland England, the abnormally high prices for oak bark and timber from 1820 to 1850 disrupted the traditional balance between timber and underwood. Many landowners encouraged the growth of an unreasonable number of oaks. In the 1850s the booms in oak-bark tanning and timber shipbuilding both collapsed; the oaks were not felled in due time but went on growing bigger, spoiling the underwood by their shade and jeopardizing the natural stability of the woods.

Woodland in decline Until the early nineteenth century woods had outlived many changes in rural society and economics. There had been some destruction, but only locally (as in Norfolk) was it extensive. Changes of detail had included lengthening coppice rotations, allowing of timber trees to grow bigger, and such natural processes as the spread of elm.

Since 1800 woodland has become linked, to varying degrees, to the boom-and-bust cycles of the modern economy. Because of the long time-scale, woods tend to perpetuate the economic fashions of at least 50 years earlier. The first major change came with the high prices of oak bark and timber at the same time as the coming of the railways brought cheap coal to the countryside. The habit of mind therefore grew up of regarding woods as sources of timber rather than of energy. Excessive numbers of timber trees were grown, to the detriment of the underwood; and these trees (and the habit of mind) went on growing after the original reasons for them had ceased to exist.

Next there came a short-lived boom in agriculture after 1840. Ancient woods were grubbed out more than ever before (eg. Hitcham Wood, Suffolk and many in Rockingham Forest, Northants). At the same time commons and heaths, where not destroyed, often fell into neglect and became secondary woodland. The agricultural slump which followed after 1880 created yet more secondary woods without, of course, bringing back the ancient woods.

The nineteenth century brought the first large-scale attempts to apply modern forestry to existing woods. The distinction between woods and plantations began to be forgotten, and many landowners planted conifers and other fashionable trees (eg. sycamore, rhododendron, Huntingdon elm, horse-chestnut) in woods. Often these failed, although the underwood, particularly on acid soils, was damaged in the attempt.

There was also the rise of organized gamekeeping. Gamekeepers kept alive (as they still do) many otherwise disused woods that might have been grubbed out; they also kept up the coppicing. But they took it upon themselves to persecute beasts and birds of prey (Chapter 4) and to exclude the public from woods. This need not have been so. France, Germany, and Switzerland are equally good shooting countries, and yet ancient woods are everyone's heritage; in Britain alone have we lost that birthright, and with it our knowledge and love of woods. A generation of people grew up who, except in such fortunate areas as south Essex, had never been in a wood and could easily be persuaded that woods had merely an economic function. People who have been rudely expelled from a lime-wood are unlikely to oppose its destruction.

A great deal of timber was felled to meet the sudden demands of two World Wars. Probably more was felled in the social upheavals between the wars; prices were low, but a quarter of England is said to have changed hands in four years,[163] and capital was often needed in a hurry. It is not true, as many writers tell us, that these fellings destroyed much woodland. Successive Ordnance maps make it quite clear that almost all the ancient woods surviving in 1870 were still there in 1945 (Fig. 5.8). The few woods that disappeared did so for some special reason, such as making an airfield. Ancient woods have great powers of recovery; the 1914–45 fellings did little more than catch up, for some woods, with the neglect of timber felling between 1860 and 1914.

Coppicing retreated from the north. The specialized underwood trades did not become obsolete – their heyday may well have been as late as 1900 – but they suffered from disorganization and lack of capital and machinery. Renewable fuels became forgotten in the successive fashions for coal, atomic energy, and heating oil. The timber trade adapted itself to handling foreign imports. We got paper-pulp and even charcoal from overseas, often grinding up other nations' wildwood while neglecting our own woods. By 1950 it was rare for a wood still to be coppiced outside south-east England and Essex.

The greatest threats to ancient woodland for a thousand years came from the destructive courses which both agriculture and forestry took in Britain after 1945. Many hundreds of woods were grubbed out to make farmland (*after* the wartime need to plough every acre had disappeared), and thousands more were wrecked by replanting.

For its first twenty-five years, the Forestry Commission had little direct impact on woodland; but after 1945 foresters acquired woods and treated them as if they were moorland, trying to poison or otherwise destroy the existing vegetation and to replace it by plantations, usually of conifers. This was justified by a crude kind of cost-benefit analysis, which treated a plantation as if it were an investment like Government stock, and tried to set off hoped-for income against present expenditure by a discounting procedure. The calculation is a

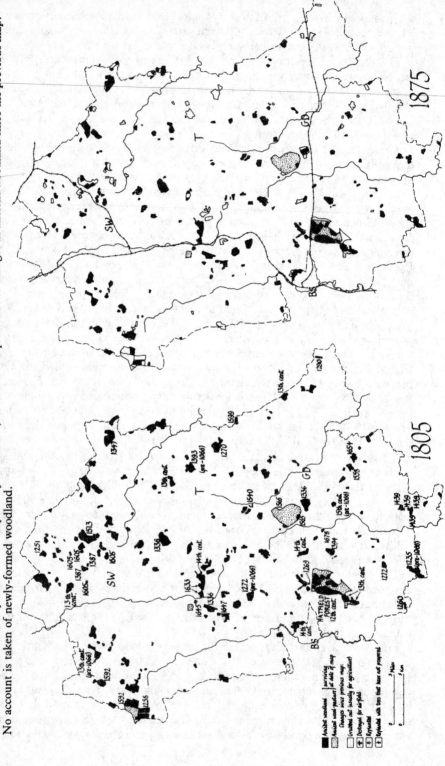

Fig. 5.8. Ancient woodland of north-west Essex (the present Uttlesford District) in 1805, 1875, 1945, and 1980. The woods shown existed in 1805 and appear not to have been recent then: dates of early written records are given for some of them. (Many of the woods have a complex medieval or earlier history and are not all primary woodland.) Each later map shows the changes in ancient woodland since the previous map. No account is taken of newly-formed woodland.

94

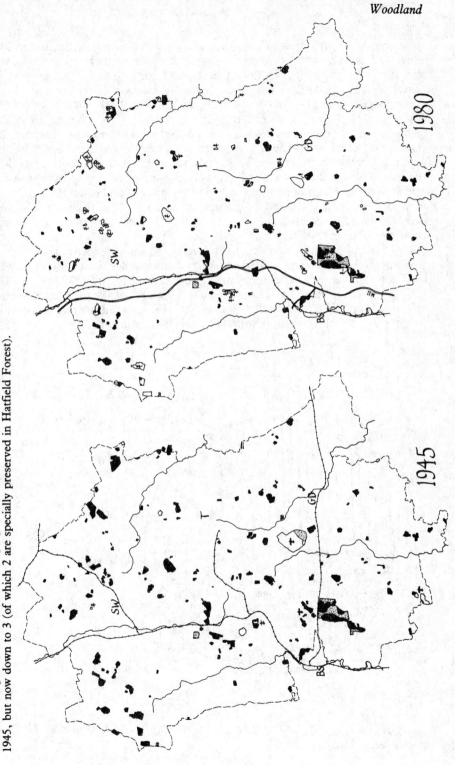

Woodland

SW: Saffron Walden   T: Thaxted   BS: Bishop's Stortford   GD: Great Dunmow
In 1805 there were 286 ancient woods covering 7200 acres (4.5 per cent of the land area); in 1980 there were 165, covering 3100 acres (1.9 per cent). The big woods have suffered disproportionately: in 1805 there were 16 woods of more than 100 acres, reduced to 8 by 1875, still 8 in 1945, but now down to 3 (of which 2 are specially preserved in Hatfield Forest).

fallacy: its outcome depends very sensitively on an arbitrary rate of interest which cannot be arrived at by any process of logic; and foresters themselves, like the rest of us, do not care or even remember what their fathers spent forty years ago. But in the twentieth century any arithmetic carries conviction, and a third of our ancient woods have been the victims of this habit of thought.

Successful replanting destroys not only the trees of a wood but the herbaceous plants as well, which succumb to evergreen shade or are buried by heavy leaf-litter. Like other plantations, those on the sites of woods are meant to be replanted every few decades for ever; after two replantings it is unlikely that anything but the woodbanks will remain to show that there was once a wood on the spot. Not that this is as easy to achieve as was expected. Many ancient woods refuse to die; replanting merely wastes money but has no lasting effect. Or the native trees may be killed and the planted trees also die, and birch or sallow take over the wood. Unfortunately wasted money is soon forgotten and people persevere in trying to plant trees in woods.

Fig. 5.8 and 5.9 show what has happened to the ancient woods of north-west Essex in the last 180 years. About a quarter of the woodland area was destroyed by nineteenth-century agriculture, mainly between 1840 and 1870. From 1870 to 1939 there was almost no change. About 4 per cent of the woodland was the victim of World War II airfields. From 1950 to 1973 agriculture and forestry, in roughly equal shares, ate up a third of the ancient woods remaining in 1945.

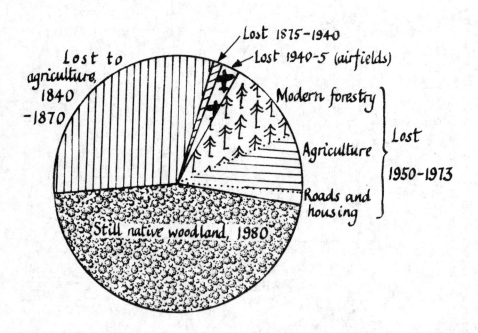

Fig. 5.9. Fate of ancient woodland by area, north-west Essex, 1805 to 1980. Note the long period of stability 1870 to 1945.

This has been repeated almost throughout Britain. North-west Essex has relatively little woodland, and lost an unusually large amount of it in the nineteenth century. Modern forestry operates best on a large scale, and in well-wooded areas has usually taken much more than here. The county of Essex has been vigilant in protecting its woods and is lucky to have lost as little as a third, as anyone can see who visits Dorset, Oxfordshire, or Nottinghamshire. In England as a whole the loss of ancient woodland is nearly one-half.* As much ancient woodland was destroyed in twenty-eight years as in the previous 400 years; the rate of destruction in the 1950s and 1960s was without parallel in history.

North-west Essex is typical in that more of the smaller woods survive. Except in specially-protected Hatfield Forest, only one wood bigger than 100 acres now remains intact of the fourteen in 1805. Woods bigger than 30 acres have been reduced by more than half. Owners of big woods are more likely to grub them out. In small woods, attempts at replanting are less common and are usually cancelled by later neglect. Although 'economic necessity' is pleaded as the excuse for destroying woods, experience shows that they, like other antiquities, survive more often at times and in places where there is too little money than where there is too much.

Woods as they are now

Woods on the map It is typical of England that woods are individual places, like towns and villages. Even the smallest wood has its own name, often of similar antiquity to the names of villages.

We have already mentioned woods that have Viking or Anglo-Saxon names. Way*land*, *Lound*, and *Lownde* Woods are modern spellings of Old Norse names in *lúndr*. A wood now called The Frith or Free Wood or Beare Wood is almost certain to be pre-Conquest, from Old English *fyrhþ* or *bearu*. The Old English *lēah* can mean a wood as well as a clearing and has given rise to some of the many woods called Hayley (hedge *lēah*), Brockley (badger *lēah*), Trundley (circular *lēah*), Littley (little *lēah*), etc.; but let us beware of other woods named after nearby settlements derived from *lēah* meaning 'clearing'. Woods composed of particular trees have names ending in -*ett*, such as Birchet, Haslet, Oket; the only frequent name so derived is Spinney, a wood of thorns (Medieval Latin *spinetum* from *spina* 'thorn').

Wood-names referring to management include Coppice (and its spelling variant Copse), Spring, and the northern Hag; all these mean a wood managed by coppicing but tell us nothing of the date. The Anglo-Saxon equivalent is *hris* 'underwood', which gives rise to names such as Royce Wood; the Norman-French word is *tailz* (Modern French *taillis* 'coppice'), now spelt Tails Wood or Taylor's Wood. Some woods are named after historic persons: Robin's Wood in eighteenth-century Hindolveston commemorated John Robynes, the unfree tenant of Norwich Cathedral Priory who 400 years earlier had leased the wood for a hurdle-making business. The names Park Wood and Out Wood are almost always connected with a medieval deer-park (p.145). There are many unsolved mysteries, such as the wood called Canfield Hart near Great Dunmow, Essex.

* In eleven counties analyzed in detail by the Nature Conservancy Council, 49 per cent of the area of 'ancient woodland' (rather widely defined) in 1930 had been grubbed or replanted by 1983.[164]

Wood-names that indicate recent origin include Plantation, Cover, Jubilee Wood, Furze (or Firs) Wood, Hundred Acre Wood (an ancient wood of that size would have had a more distinctive name), etc. Occasionally these are re-namings of ancient woods.

Woods are not on land that was good for growing trees, but on land that was bad for anything else. The bad lands of the Middle Ages were not quite the same as ours. Fertility mattered much more, for it could not then be bought in a sack, but steep slopes and poor drainage were then less severe obstacles to cultivation. Ancient woods in Lowland England tend to be on high ground, on flat hilltops and plateaux, where there are patches of infertile sands and gravels or specially wet clays. In the Highland Zone they are often on the steepest slopes of valleys. Woods avoid land liable to flooding by rivers, which was the most valuable land of all as grassland, especially meadow (Chapter 15). England lost its big flood-plain woods by the Iron Age, and medieval woods avoid the flood-plains of quite small streams; there are even salients of meadow along streams within woods.

Ancient woods tend to avoid main roads. Where a medieval wood adjoins a road, its woodbank is often set back by 50–100 yards owing to an anti-highwayman clearing called a *trench* (for details see p.270).

Ancient woods have a characteristic sinuous or zigzag outline by which they can usually be picked out on the 2½-inch map. Such outlines appear, exactly as they are now, on the earliest large-scale maps of woods from about 1580 onwards (Fig. 2.2). They date from a period when the landscape was set out on the ground rather than in the draughtsman's office, and when the countryman saw no purpose in straight lines. Sinuous outlines may result from having to take a boundary ditch round individual large trees. Zigzags may represent successive grubbings-out of woodland, an acre one year and an acre the next, until the Danes or the Black Death intervened and no more acres were taken.

Straight edges are usually of the eighteenth century or later (Dodnash Wood in Bentley, Suffolk, is a rare, possibly medieval, exception). When a wood has been either enlarged or partly grubbed out since 1700 the new edges are usually straight or regularly curved. In Planned Countryside the irregular shapes of ancient woods sit awkwardly among the straight hedges laid out around them by Enclosure Act commissioners (Fig. 2.2a). In Ancient Countryside, the ghost of a grubbed-out wood may haunt the map as the irregularly-shaped perimeter of a 'Wood Farm' whose internal hedges are anomalously straight (Plate III).

Earthworks The visitor to an unknown wood should first walk the boundary. A typical medieval wood boundary has a strong bank with an external ditch, 20 to 40 feet in total width, which follows all the sinuosities and zigzags. The profile is usually rounded (Fig. 5.10 and Plate VII) but may be steeper on the outer face. There are often pollard trees halfway down the outer slope. Where the bank turns a sharp corner there is a corner mound.

There are many variations on woodbanks. Banks change with time: the ditch may be cleaned out and the spoil dumped on top of the bank; or sheet erosion may cause several feet of the adjacent field to creep away downhill, effacing the ditch and leaving the bank at the top of a miniature cliff (Fig. 8.3). There are variations of local custom: Canfield Hart (Essex) and its neighbouring woods, though of impeccable written history, have only boundary ditches and not banks. In the Mendips and elsewhere in west England woodbanks are faced, and sometimes replaced, by dry-stone walls; the wall of Cheddar Wood has been

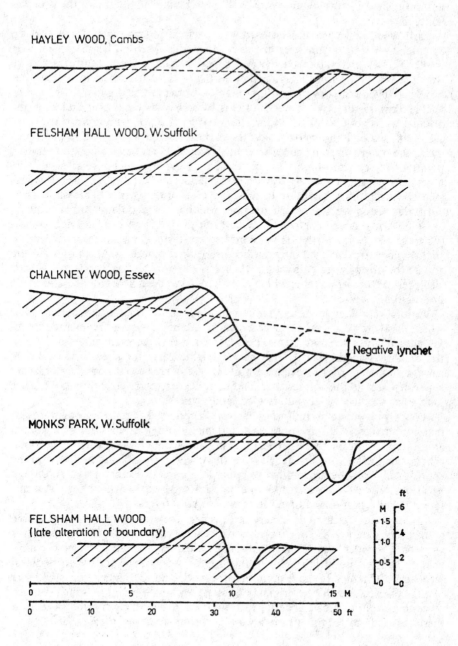

Fig. 5.10. Profiles of woodbanks. The wood side of each boundary is shown on the left. Felsham Hall Wood: medieval or earlier wood-boundary. Chalkney Wood: similar but on a slope. Monks' Park: boundary of early deer-park, with remains of internal (as well as external) ditch. The vertical scale is exaggerated twofold.

left unfinished in a way which proves that the bank came first and the wall was added later.

Early woodbanks are massive earthworks which in small woods may take up as much as a sixth of the area of the entire wood. They go far to explain why wood outlines are stable. New wood edges formed in later centuries can be detected by their successively weaker earthworks. Where part of a wood has been destroyed, the original outline may be preserved as a ghost hedge, or be visible from the air as a soil mark in fields. Where a wood has been added to, the original woodbank is left behind in the interior. If a wood adjoins a road, there are often two or more woodbanks: the earliest and most massive is the innermost, the others marking successive encroachments on the road or the reincorporation of an anti-highwayman trench. New wood boundaries of the nineteenth century are straight, with feeble banks and ditches (or no earthworks at all) bearing flimsy hawthorn hedges, just like contemporary field boundaries.

Inside woods we find some features peculiar to woodland, others known outside woods. Many ancient woods are full of ponds and natural depressions (Chapter 16). Some of the depressions are mysteriously filled up with sand to slightly above the surrounding surface level. Such ponds and 'sand-lenses' are among the obstacles to cultivation which have kept places as woodland. Woods also preserve minor streams which elsewhere have been straightened and made into field ditches.

Within woodland there are banks which separate two contiguous woods or which divide a wood among several owners. Manors became fragmented ('subinfeudated') into separate farms, each of which took and embanked a share of the manorial wood. Usually this happened too early for a detailed record to survive, but the order of events can often be inferred from how the banks are superimposed at their junctions. The complex earthworks of Fig. 5.11 tell a long story of successively subdivided land ownership.

Woods may contain hillforts, barrows, territorial ditches, Roman roads, mounds of debris left by potteries, and many other prehistoric and Roman antiquities. Some of these prove that the site was not woodland at the time; others, such as the pottery debris, that there was a wood-using industry on the spot. It can rarely be proven that woodbanks are not of Roman origin, although occasionally the medieval banks overlie faint earthworks which suggest a different distribution of woodland in the more remote past.

Among medieval non-woodland earthworks, the ridge-and-furrow of arable cultivation (Chapter 8) conclusively proves that many woods in the Midlands were once smaller. Dams and coal-mines (Chapter 16) are often now within woods, but tell us little of the history of the wood. The moats of medieval farmsteads (Chapter 16) have often become woodland, perhaps by the suckering of elms planted around the original house. Many small groves in arable country owe their origin to moats abandoned from the fourteenth century onwards, but there are also moats which have always had woods around them (p.363).

Trees A normal wood consists of underwood and timber trees. The latter are usually oak, whatever the underwood, but that does not make nearly every wood an oak-wood. Timber trees come and go; few woods now have oaks more than 200 years old, and in the past they would have been younger. They are the most artificial part of a wood; they reflect merely the decision of past woodmen to treat oak (or some other species in default) as timber and other trees as

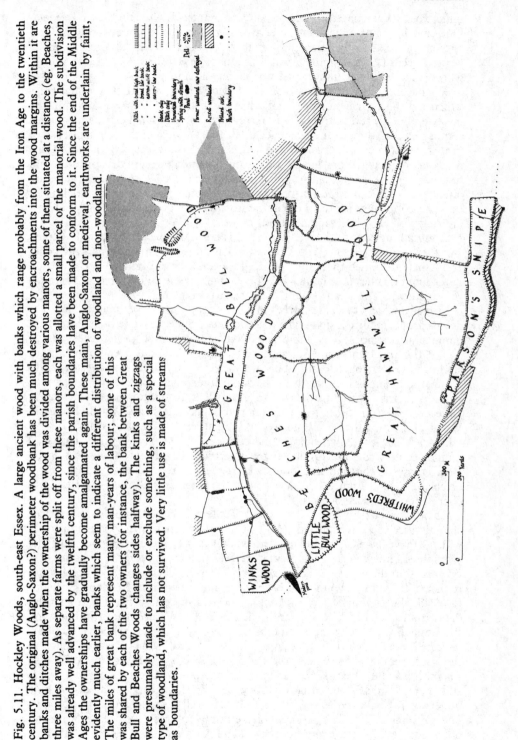

Fig. 5.11. Hockley Woods, south-east Essex. A large ancient wood with banks which range probably from the Iron Age to the twentieth century. The original (Anglo-Saxon?) perimeter woodbank has been much destroyed by encroachments into the wood margins. Within it are banks and ditches made when the ownership of the wood was divided among various manors, some of them situated at a distance (eg. Beaches, three miles away). As separate farms were split off from these manors, each was allotted a small parcel of the manorial wood. The subdivision was already well advanced by the twelfth century, since the parish boundaries have been made to conform to it. Since the end of the Middle Ages the ownerships have gradually become amalgamated again. These main, Anglo-Saxon or medieval, earthworks are underlain by faint, evidently much earlier, banks which seem to indicate a different distribution of woodland and non-woodland.

The miles of great bank represent many man-years of labour; some of this was shared by each of the two owners (for instance, the bank between Great Bull and Beaches Woods changes sides halfway). The kinks and zigzags were presumably made to include or exclude something, such as a special type of woodland, which has not survived. Very little use is made of streams as boundaries.

underwood. The continuity of a wood, its connexion with the natural vegetation, and its distinction from other woods reside in the underwood and herbaceous plants. (Timber trees, especially oaks, are given undue prominence in written records: their felling was infrequent and called for special notice, whereas the felling of underwood was merely an annual routine).

Whenever timber or underwood are felled, we can count the annual rings which are the primary evidence of what has happened in a wood within the lifetime of the present trees. This record may be extended back for about a century by the stumps (and branches if left lying about) of the previous crop of timber trees. For underwood, the annual rings of poles tell us about the previous coppicing. Occasionally we can cut a section through the above-ground base of a coppice stool (Plate V), from which we can with care – for the rings are often microscopic and the centre is hollow – estimate the age of the stool itself. Previous coppicings are recorded in the stool base by cycles of suddenly narrowing rings followed by gradual recovery.

A minimum limit to the age of a wood is normally the age of its oldest trees, but there are exceptions. Secondary woodland may incorporate park or hedge trees that are older than the wood; these may be recognized by their low spreading branches now hemmed in by younger trees. Pollard trees that are not on earthworks arouse suspicions of secondary woodland.

In many woods the oldest trees are the coppice stools. A maple when cut down sprouts to form a stool, which gets bigger on successive fellings. Stools are not men or machines; they do not die of old age or wear out; the process can go on indefinitely. In up-state Massachusetts, where there has been coppicing for about 250 years, I have found stools of American red maple (*Acer rubrum*) up to 2½ feet in diameter; but stools of the English maple in our ancient woods may be 15 feet across. Ancient stools of ash (Plate IV) spread into rings which may be 18 feet across; sometimes these are on waterlogged sites, such as the Bradfield Woods, on which they grow slowly, and are at least a thousand years old. (An ash-tree if not cut down falls to pieces in about 200 years and disappears.) Similar giant stools are produced by lime, oak, hornbeam, and occasionally alder; those of chestnut and non-suckering elms are probably younger for a given size. Giant coppice stools are among the oldest living things in Britain but continue to produce good crops of poles.

Ancient woods are of many kinds. Table 5.2 is a summary of the tree communities so far recognized. Many of these have their own separate histories which I have given in detail in *Ancient Woodland*. Here I can but take the example of lime-woods. Lime (pry) is well-documented; people took notice of it because it produced bast (a low-grade fibre) as well as being a tree of delight and romance. In prehistory lime had been the commonest tree of Lowland England. It is still the commonest tree of *ancient* woods in certain small and sharply-defined areas of Lowland England, such as between Lavenham (Suffolk) and Braintree (Essex). Why this should be so is a mystery, but it is known that lime retreated mostly before the Anglo-Saxon period and has not changed much in the last thousand years. One of the Essex lime-woods was called in Old English *Lindris* (*linde* 'lime tree' + *hris* 'underwood'); a thousand years later, part of it is still there (Paul's Wood, Black Notley) and indeed has great stools of lime underwood. Chalkney Wood, Earl's Colne, is well documented in an account-book of 1603–12.[165] Parts of it consisted entirely of 'prye'; parts were of pry and other trees including ash and hornbeam; and parts contained no pry at all. This is exactly how pry is distributed in Chalkney Wood today; it is a gregarious tree and occurs as patches of pure lime-wood rather than mixed with other species.

The same could be told of many other trees. Maple is less distinctive than pry, but it too is well recorded in medieval and Anglo-Saxon sources. It was specially typical of woods *within Forests* on clay soils (eg. Hatfield Forest (Essex), Rockingham Forest (Northants), Wychwood Forest (Oxon), whose remnants are still notable for maple-woods.

Most ancient woods contain several different types of woodland; for instance Tarecroft Wood (Rivenhall, Essex) has within 16 acres areas of seven kinds of woodland (Fig.5.12). The variation appears to be wholly natural: the boundaries between tree communities, some of which are abrupt and others show gradual transitions, are irregular, eschew straight lines, and disregard rides and management boundaries. Every ancient wood is uniquely different from every other; the natural properties of trees, and their reactions (past and present) to soils, spring-lines, and other aspects of the environment, still shape the character of woods despite the levelling-down effects of centuries of management.

Ancient woods still perpetuate the provinces and some of the variants of the prehistoric wildwoods. The variety of tree communities is greatest in eastern and south-eastern England and decreases north-westward. Lime has greatly diminished, especially south of the Thames, but still extends throughout the prehistoric Lime Province. Oak-woods (woods in which oak is so abundant that it has been treated as underwood as well as timber) are the commonest woodland

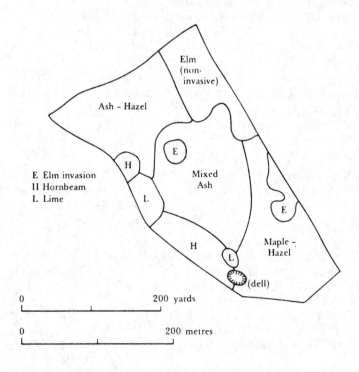

Fig. 5.12. Types of woodland in Tarecroft Wood, Rivenhall (Essex).

Table 5.2 Two classifications of ancient woodland

For Great Britain, after Peterken (1981)	For Eastern England, after Rackham (1980)
Ash – wych-elm woods	
1 Limestone and chalk, southern	NR
2 Limestone, northern	NR
3 Wet clay	
4 Wet sandy	Mixed Ash-wood (part)
5 Limestone, N.E. Midland	
6 Clay on limestone, with sessile oak	NR
7 Western valley	NR?
Ash – maple woods	
	Ash – Hazel wood (part)
8 Ash – maple on wet clay	Mixed Ash-wood (aspen variant)
9 Maple on wet clay	Maple-wood
	Maple – Hazel wood
10 Ash – maple on wet light soils	Ash – Hazel wood (part)
11 Ash – maple on dry light soils	Mixed Ash-wood?
12 Ash – maple on dry heavy soils	Mixed Hazel-wood (part)
Hazel – ash woods	
13 Heavy acid soils, with pedunculate oak	
14 Light acid soils, with pedunculate oak	Variants of Mixed Hazel-wood
15 Limestone, southern	
16 Limestone, northern	
17 Acid soils, with sessile oak	NR
Ash – lime woods	
18 Acid soils, with birch	Lime – Ash wood
19 With maple, eastern	NR?
20 With maple, western	NR?
21 With sessile oak	NR
Oak – lime woods	
22 With pedunculate oak	Pure Lime-wood
23 With sessile oak	Oak – Lime wood
Birch – oak woods	
24 Highland, with sessile oak	NR
25 Highland, with hazel and sessile oak	
26 Highland, with pedunculate oak	NR (and in part not ancient)
27 Highland, with hazel and pedunculate oak	NR
28 Lowland, with sessile oak	
29 Lowland, with hazel and sessile oak	Oak-wood
30 Kentish sessile oak-wood on chalk	NR
31 Lowland, with pedunculate oak	Oak-wood (often not ancient)
32 Lowland, with hazel and pedunculate oak	Oak-wood
	Pure Hazel-wood

Alder-woods

33 Acid valleys	} Valley Alder-wood
34 Calcareous valleys	
35 Peaty depressions	Not regarded as ancient
36 Calcareous springlines	} Valley Alder-wood
37 Acid springlines	
38 Plateaux	Plateau Alder-wood
39 Slopes	NR
40 With bird-cherry, Lowland	Valley or Plateau Alder-wood
41 With bird-cherry, Highland	NR

Beech woods

42 Acid, with sessile oak	NR
43 Acid, with pedunculate oak	Beech wood-pasture
44 Dry calcareous, with pedunculate oak, ash, lime, wych-elm	NR
45 Damp calcareous, with ash and wych-elm	NR
46 Dry calcareous, with ash and maple	NR
47 Acid, with ash and pedunculate oak	NR
48 Acid, with ash and sessile oak	NR
49 Limestone, with ash and sessile oak	NR

Hornbeam-woods

50 With birch, hazel, and pedunculate oak	Pure Hornbeam-wood (and its hazel variant) Maple – Hornbeam wood
51 With ash and maple	Hornbeam – Ash wood
52 With sessile oak, acid	Oak – Hornbeam wood
53 With sessile oak, calcareous	NR

Suckering elm-woods

54 Invasive	} Elm Invasion
55 Valley	

Pine-woods

56 Without oak	NR
57 With oak	NR

Birch-woods

58 Birch only	Birch-wood (mostly not ancient)
59 With hazel	Pure Hazel-wood (birch variant)
	Pure Ash-wood
	Lineage Elm-wood
	Hatfield Forest oak-wood
NR	Chestnut – Lime wood
	Chestnut – Hornbeam wood
	Chestnut – Oak wood
	Aspen-wood
	Holly-wood
	Hawthorn-wood

Notes. NR: not represented. The names of Peterken's woodland types have been simplified.

of the Highland Zone, from Cornwall to the western Scottish Highlands, and correspond exactly to the Oak-Hazel Province. Within Lowland England, oak-woods are either recent or else are on very acid infertile soils. The hazel-woods of the Lime Province survive more extensively than lime-woods themselves; those of the Oak-Hazel Province have largely disappeared, but there are remnants of hazel-wood on pockets of more fertile soil within highland oak-woods.

I have emphasized the continuity of ancient woods, but let us not suppose that they are wholly unchanging. Much happened unrecorded in prehistory and the early historic period. There can be little doubt that much of what is now hornbeam-wood, beech-wood, and chestnut-wood was originally lime-wood. Only one stool of lime (and one place-name) survive in the whole southern half of Essex, where hornbeam is now the commonest woodland tree. One of the best historic chestnut-woods is Stour Wood near Harwich (belonging to the Woodland Trust), yet this still has a few surviving lime stools.

Elms, birch, and ash have increased. Those kinds of elm that sucker tend to spread into existing woods and turn them into elm-woods. The process has been helped by coppicing; circular patches of elm, spreading outwards at about 2 feet a year, are familiar in Midland woods such as Hayley. Sometimes, as in Overhall Grove (Boxworth, Cambs) elms have taken over almost a whole wood, leaving only remnants of what was there before. Birch had its heyday in the early post-glacial period. In later prehistory it was squeezed out by more competitive and longer-lived trees. In the last hundred years it has returned on a large scale. This probably began with secondary woodland on heaths, fens, and derelict land. Birch colonizes such places and produces wind-blown fruits which drift into ancient woods. Traditional woodmanship might not have favoured birch, but it has been helped by the fashions for growing abnormally large numbers of oaks and then felling them, and for planting conifers which often die. Both practices damage the underwood and make room for birch, which is now increasing even on clay soils on which it was once thought incapable of growing. Ash has recently increased in many woods from Shropshire to Somerset and Huntingdonshire. In the Mendip 'ash-woods', for instance, there are some ancient ash stools, but most of the ashes are no older than the last coppicing but one. The woods are really hazel-woods and lime-woods now turning into ash-woods. The change began at different dates and there is no obvious change in management to account for it. Woods have a life of their own, and we should take warning not to guess at facile explanations of similar changes in prehistory.

Floras of woods The pry tree, *Tilia cordata*, is a living link with Mesolithic times. It now grows from seed with difficulty (partly because the climate has turned against it), and until recent years has seldom been planted. It is therefore largely confined to ancient woodland. In south Suffolk it grows, often in abundance, in about thirty woods, all of which are known or suspected on other grounds to be ancient. Some of the woods have increased in size, and lime faithfully picks out the parts of the wood inside the original woodbank. In Groton Wood, for instance, which was enlarged probably in the seventeenth century, pry fills the old wood but is still rare in the new wood (Fig.5.13).

Oxlip, *Primula elatior*, is a plant confined to a well-defined area in Cambridgeshire, Suffolk, and Essex. Here it grows, usually in abundance, in nearly every wood (over 100 woods) known on documentary or topographical grounds to be ancient, but very rarely in secondary woods, even those that are at least

350 years old. When an ancient wood increases in size oxlip spreads slowly into
the addition (at about 4 feet a year); but it is very reluctant to jump across even a
hundred yards of open country to colonize an isolated secondary wood (Rackham 1975).

Other plants strongly and widely associated with ancient woodland include
service, woodland hawthorn (*Crataegus laevigata*), and Herb Paris. Dr George
Peterken has listed fifty indicator species of ancient woodland in Lincolnshire,

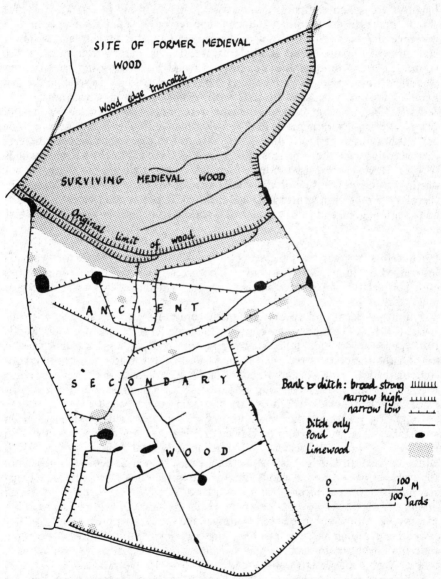

Fig. 5.13. Groton Wood, Suffolk. The northern third of the wood represents about half
of a medieval wood. The remainder is seventeenth-century secondary woodland; it is full
of weak banks and ditches relating to its former use as fields.

including such quite common plants as anemone, wood-sorrel, and barren strawberry.[166]

Recent woods contain plants that have no particular connexion with woodland but are widespread in hedges and other habitats, such as ivy (seldom abundant in ancient woods), cow-parsley (*Anthriscus sylvestris*), hedge-garlic (*Alliaria petiolata*), and lords-and-ladies.

Floras are valuable evidence on woodland history but should be used intelligently. Woodland plants can, on occasion, survive in old grassland. Evidence should be based on a suite of indicator species rather than a single one. The presence of *Tilia cordata* is strong evidence that a wood is ancient, and is almost conclusive if the lime forms giant stools; but lime is missing from much of the country, and its absence does not prove a wood recent. Pry indicates ancient woodland throughout its English range, but not all species do so. Spindle is a plant of ancient woodland in Lincolnshire but is only a weak indicator in Suffolk. The investigator should make a regional list of ancient woodland plants. A good beginning is to find out what plants grow in woods known to be ancient but not in hedges. Lime is very rare in hedges even in limewood areas; the exceptions are those hedges which are the ghost outlines of former woods (p.183). Hayley Wood used to have four million oxlip plants, but there was not one in the hedges abutting on the wood, some of which were already 'antient' in the early seventeenth century. Dog's-mercury is much commoner in hedges, and is a less good indicator of ancient woodland, in Suffolk than in the Midlands.

Herbaceous vegetation The *flora* of a wood – the plant species present – is influenced by the wood's continuity. The *vegetation* – the plant communities and their relationships to each other – is partly determined by the history of management.

The magnificent and spectacular plant communities, the displays of primroses, oxlips, and anemones, are in part the product of coppicing. Most woods have had years of light followed by years of shade, going back in cycles to beyond the memory of records. Their plants, on the whole, do not like continuous shade. Primroses and other spring flowers flourish in the years of light; they also require years of shade to suppress the tall grasses and other non-woodland plants which would overwhelm them outside woods.

Coppicing plants are gloriously unpredictable, and each wood has its own specialities. The wetter parts of Hayley and Hardwick Woods are yellow with countless oxlips in the second and third springs after felling. Norsey Wood (Billericay, south Essex) has one of the greatest concentrations of bluebells in the world. In the Mendip woods there is the miraculously brilliant blue *Lithospermum purpureocaeruleum*. All these plants survive the shade years in an attenuated form but flower in abundance in the years of release. Many other plants come up from buried seed waiting since the last coppicing. In Chalkney Wood red campion and wild raspberry are completely killed by the shade of tall lime and hornbeam but come up in their tens of thousands from seed after each felling. Wood-spurge can wait as seed for at least 125 years.

Stinging-nettle, elderberry, and goosegrass are significant because they live on phosphate, and mankind is a phosphate-accumulating animal. Most ancient woods are short of phosphate, which is one reason why they are still woods, and these plants will not grow in them. Phosphate plants grow where people have lived (and especially where they have died), and where they have thrown bones and the ashes of faggots. The phosphate thus accumulated lasts for centuries in non-acid soils. Little Gidding (Huntingdonshire), the famous deserted village forgotten by 1640, is still marked by an elm-grove full of ear-high nettles. On the Grovely Ridge near Salisbury, patches of phosphate plants in the woods mark where Romano-British villages were abandoned over 1600 years ago.

Woodland rides and the lanes round the edges of ancient woods often have a special suite of plants, such as ragged robin *Lychnis flos-cuculli*, devil's-bit *Succisa pratensis*, and the umbellifer *Pimpinella major*. The 'woodland grassland' which contains these plants is of special interest; in many parts of the country it is almost the only surviving old grassland. At first sight it seems to be a relatively artificial component of a wood; yet it has much in common with natural glades in wildwood, especially in earlier interglacials when they were kept open by the browsing of great beasts (pp.330–1).

Wales

In prehistory most of Wales belonged to the Oak-Hazel Province. There were many outliers of other kinds of woodland; lime and in the south-east beech were native. As in England, most of the wildwood was destroyed in prehistory to make farmland and moorland.

The Welsh charters suggest that, at the time of the Anglo-Saxons in England, south-east Wales was quite wooded. Of the boundary features, 5.9 per cent are words meaning some kind of wood (Latin *silua*, Welsh *coit, luin, gelli*, etc.); this is twice the proportion in the English charters. But the laws attributed to Hywel Dda, king of South Wales, show that woods were valuable property; compensation equivalent to 30 sheep for cutting down somebody's oak and 3¾ sheep for a mere hazel stool does not suggest superabundance. Domesday Book describes woods in north-east Wales which add up to 16 per cent of the land area.

Little topographical detail is known for Welsh woods, but their documentary history has been related in detail by Dr William Linnard (1982). The impression is of a land less wooded as a whole than England; but because half Wales was moorland, woodland was more concentrated and more prominent in the *inhabited* countryside than in England. Many medieval Welsh woods have been identified, though their boundaries are seldom known.

Domesday Book mentions secondary woodland in Radnorshire, springing up on land depopulated by war; but in general the woodland area probably diminished, as in England, up to the Black Death. Giraldus Cambrensis in the twelfth century reproved the greedy monks of Abbey Dore, in the Welsh part of Herefordshire, for making a notable oak-wood into a wheatfield.[167] In the thirteenth century there are many references to grubbing, suggesting demand for land by a growing population. Woods played an important part in the military campaigns of English kings. The armies of Edward I were accompanied by up to 1800 woodmen conscripted from England to cut down woods alongside main roads. Whether these were permanent clearings, in the manner of the trenches of England, is not known. I have found a possible surviving example at Coed Allt-y-rhiw north of Bridgend, Glamorgan.

Linnard gives many scattered references to medieval woodmanship, to systematic coppicing (underwood prices were at least as high as in England), charcoal for industrial fuel, sales of bark, and thefts of timber. Timber is known chiefly from the accounts of royal castles; more timber appears to have been sent; from England to Wales than *vice versa*. Pannage of swine is often referred to, as befits a land of oak-woods, but the custom died out, as in England, in the later Middle Ages.

By 1600 Wales as a whole had less than 10 per cent of woodland. Figures for estates in Monmouthshire, for instance, add up to 10 per cent of the land area; but this was one of the most wooded counties (Linnard 1982), and against it must be set not only the moorland areas but also Anglesey, which by the Middle Ages had virtually no woodland at all.[609] Wales (minus its moorland) would have distinctly been more wooded than England at the time. There was a large charcoal iron industry, including a specialist wire trade in Monmouthshire. Ironmasters litigated over fuel supplies with wire-drawers and with each other, as well as with local inhabitants. Coppicing for industrial fuel and tanbark went on into the later nineteenth century.

What happened to the Welsh woods? There is a map of the southern half of Wales in the fourteenth century, by W. Rees, showing the locations of 41 Welsh woods.[168] Comparing this with the Ordnance Survey of the 1830s, I find that 20 of the woods were apparently still there, and of the remainder 18 sites were farmland. The survival rate, about 50 per cent over 500 years, confirms the impression that the forces of conservation were a little weaker in Wales than in England. The destruction, as in England, was greater in agricultural areas, and popular complaints against industrialists for destroying woodland, though persistent, cannot be substantiated. As early as the sixteenth century a bard had sung against the felling of woods in the industrial valleys of Aberdare and Merthyr Tydfil.[169] His lament is the less convincing for being repeated in the same place 200 years later,[170] and in fact both valleys, well into the nineteenth century, remained among the most wooded in the British Isles. But rustic Montgomeryshire lost nearly all its woods in 200 years.

Woods in the industrial valleys were destroyed late, and not directly by industry. The distinction between woodland and wood-pasture is not as strong in Wales as in England. Some grazing has been allowed in woods for several centuries, though evidently not so continuously as to prevent resistant trees such as oak from maintaining themselves; indeed several South Welsh woods increased in size in the eighteenth and nineteenth centuries. In the late nineteenth century boundary walls were allowed to fall down so that sheep could get in at will and devour the regrowth the next time the wood was felled. Well over half the woods in the Rhondda, Aberdare, Merthyr, and Rhymney Valleys have become bracken with occasional scattered trees, or their remains have been swallowed up in Forestry Commission plantations. Only the remote and beautiful upper Taff Bargoed somehow escaped both industrialization and excessive grazing and is still in something like its medieval state. A well-preserved ancient wood is now a rarity in Wales; most have been badly damaged by grazing or replanting.

At low altitudes and on relatively good soils surviving woods are predominantly hazel, with alders along streams and many other trees including occasional lime. They have sinuous outlines and woodbanks in the English tradition, overlain by a fascinating variety of industrial remains. In the high valleys ancient woods ascend to 1700 feet, perhaps the nearest approach to a natural upper limit of trees in the British Isles. These are mainly of oak, with some beech which appears to be native and (as in places in the Alps) does unexpectedly well at the tree-line. But as we shall see, the apparent poverty of these high woods is due less to the inhospitable climate and soils than to grazing. The tumbled remains of the boundary walls which here replace woodbanks show that our ancestors cared more about the problem than we.

Scotland

Scotland has fewer types of native woodland than England: pine-woods, birch-woods, oak-woods, hazel-woods, and ash-woods. All these except perhaps ash-woods have existed since the wildwood. Only scraps of hazel-wood and ash-wood remain.

Most of the wildwood disappeared in prehistory, partly from natural causes (Chapter 14).

Written evidence for the Middle Ages is scanty, especially for the Highlands where most of the surviving woods are. To judge by vague references,[44] medieval Scotland was in general a not very wooded land, much like medieval England; but it did have woods in parts of the Lowlands and Southern Uplands from which almost all trace has since disappeared. What was done with the woods is hardly known. One or two grants, such as that of 100 loads of hazel rods annually to Lindores Abbey in 1250, imply extensive coppicing. Scotland, like England, imported timber from Norway and Prussia.[171] Medieval wood-manship must remain largely conjectural until archaeological evidence like that for Ireland is forthcoming.

Ancient woodland survives less often in Scotland than in England. In 1845 the *New Statistical Account* records 0.91 per cent of Scotland as 'natural woodland';[172] this area was not so minute as it sounds, for half of Scotland was moorland, but many of the woods have since been lost to plantations.

Oak-woods The oak-woods of the south-west Highlands correspond to the Scottish part of the Oak-Hazel Province (Fig.5.2). From the late seventeenth century they are well documented.[173] They yielded charcoal for ironworks, bark for tanning, and a little timber. The iron industry continued well into the nineteenth century and overlapped with the heyday of the leather industry. The woods were highly organized and were coppiced on an inflexible rotation of twenty-one to thirty years. The longest-lived furnace, at Lorn (Argyll), went on until 1876 and maintained about 10,000 acres of underwood.[161] The woods outlived the decline of the industries, and the ironworks area is still the most wooded in Scotland, despite the inroads of modern plantations.

Birch-woods These have probably been for centuries the commonest native woodland of Scotland. There is some evidence that the Highlands once had a birch economy like that of Norway, everything – even roofs, wheels, and tubs – being made of the tree.[174] It had some industrial uses in the nineteenth century, but the Scots, unlike other northern nations, have latterly neglected their birch-woods.

Birch-woods seldom appear to be ancient. The trees are usually all of one age; the woods have no defined boundaries; and the plants are those of moorland rather than of woodland. Probably a piece of land is invaded by birches when grazing declines for a few years; the trees live out their short lives, die, and are not replaced. After many decades of general decline, the birch-woods are now advancing again, often as an incidental consequence of forestry fences interfering with the grazing habits of sheep and deer.

Pine-woods The famous and distinctive 'Caledonian' pine-woods are of a peculiar subspecies of pine unknown outside Scotland. In places, as at Abernethy,[175] there is a pollen record which goes back unaltered to the early post-glacial.

In early prehistory pine-woods had covered most of the eastern and middle Highlands, but by the time of the earliest documents they were already rare; they had shrunk through prehistoric tillage and pasture or the growth of blanket peat. 'Legends' of great pinewoods being burnt by Vikings and others to consume their enemies, and never recovering, are unlikely to be historical (p.306).

The pine-woods are usually said to have been 'discovered' about 1600, but the less remote ones are recorded in the late Middle Ages. 'Mamlorn Forest', identified with the still-extant woods of Glen Lyon (Perthshire), supplied ships' masts,[44] which normally came from pine-exporting countries. Mr Robin Callander tells me that the pine-woods of Deeside were systematically managed and conserved by the Bishops of Aberdeen. Since the seventeenth century the pines have been heavily exploited. There is some evidence of losses of area, especially in Deeside, though most of the seventeenth-century pine-woods still exist. Like the birch-woods they have no defined boundaries and may not always have been in exactly the same place.

Even now these famous historic woods are not wholly secure. Some are still threatened with too much grazing or with planting of other conifers. In the north-west they are still retreating before the spread of peat (p.307). In Deeside, where there is less peat, the Caledonian pine-woods are now advancing after centuries of shrinkage. Grazing has evidently declined; whole hillsides, moorland on the Ordnance Survey of 1927, are now young secondary woodland of native pine.

Ireland

Much has been written on the history of Irish woodland, but in a vague and general way; except in Killarney[176] there is not one wood whose history over the last 400 years is known. Irish pollen analysts have made good use of the wealth of material in the bogs, which sometimes runs continuously from the early post-glacial to the present.[177] The written evidence is poor for the Middle Ages but good after 1600. Fieldwork in woodland history has hardly begun.

The prehistory of Irish woodland is not very different from that of Great Britain, though with no native lime, hornbeam, maple, or beech fewer types of woodland are possible. The Neolithic revolution spread to Ireland without delay. The dense population and cultivation of Iron Age Ireland are still evident to the most casual observer, for Irish Iron Age farmsteads, unlike English ones, have left massive earthworks called raths. Some 30,000 raths are known[178] – one to 500 acres of land other than bog – so there was no room for great tracts of wildwood; indeed many later well-wooded areas contain raths.

Ireland survived the Dark Ages of the rest of Europe as a civilized and populous land. Some pollen evidence supports the conjecture that the violence and disruption of the Viking and Norman periods allowed some new woodland to appear on deserted farmland. But for the last thousand years Ireland appears to have had even less woodland than England.

The seventeenth century In 1600 Dr Eileen McCracken has estimated that 'forested areas' occupied one-eighth of Ireland.[179] This must *not* be taken as the actual area of woodland, for the estimate is based on maps of too small a scale to show wood boundaries, on verbal descriptions and even legends; all sources which, as English experience shows, exaggerate woodland areas. Dr McCracken rightly points out in an earlier work that her 'forested areas' were not all woodland.[180]

More definite evidence comes from the Civil Survey of 1654–6 and its associated maps. These record several thousand woods by townland (whence they can often be located to within half a mile) with their areas and some indication of their character ('shrubby', 'copps', 'shrubbs and Boggs', 'timber-wood', etc). The surveys have been published for 15¼ of the 31 counties of Ireland,[10] and Dr McCracken has obtained woodland totals for seven more,[179] making up three-quarters of the country.

Adding up the areas of woods in the surveys, and allowing in proportion for counties for which no records survive, I arrive at a total woodland area of 420,000 acres, 2.1 per cent of Ireland. In general the south and west were more wooded than the north and east (Fig.5.14). The most wooded county, Clare, had only 7 per cent of woodland; Roscommon had 6 per cent; five southern counties (and also probably the unrecorded Wicklow) had between 3 per cent and 4 per cent; but at least eight counties had less than 1 per cent of woodland.

Are the figures too small? I have already allowed for the Irish acre then being some 60 per cent larger than we use today, and have been generous with the definition of woodland (eg. 'pasturable wood' counts as woodland; 'woody pasture' counts as half woodland). The Civil Survey often omits moors, bogs, and commons with no identifiable owner, but is meticulous about woods: even one-acre groves were carefully recorded and are often separately indexed. The only possible error is that land areas were often estimated, and may turn out on comparison to be too small. Even allowing for such underestimation, we can hardly make the Ireland of the 1650s more than 3 per cent wooded.

Had much woodland disappeared between 1600 and 1654? Probably not: these were evil years, in which men won lands by the sword and not the mattock. Trees were felled for timber or because they got in the way of fighting, but would have grown again. There are occasional mentions in the Civil Survey of woods disappearing, eg. in Tyrone 'by the frequent Burning of the Wast grasse in late tymes', but these could easily have been outweighed by new woods springing up unnoticed on devastated lands. Most of the activities later blamed for destroying woods had begun only on a small scale by the 1650s. Except possibly in Co. Offaly, where sixteenth-century descriptions seem to require more than the 500 acres of woodland remaining in 1654, the scarcity of wood-land may well have been long standing.

Seventeenth-century Ireland had less than a third as much woodland as England in relation to its area; but the uneven distribution gave many visitors the illusion of a well-wooded country. The woods of south Wicklow, Wexford, Waterford, and around Limerick were in properous and easily-accessible parts of the south. Midland Ireland was entirely farmland and bogs and even a small wood was a rarity.

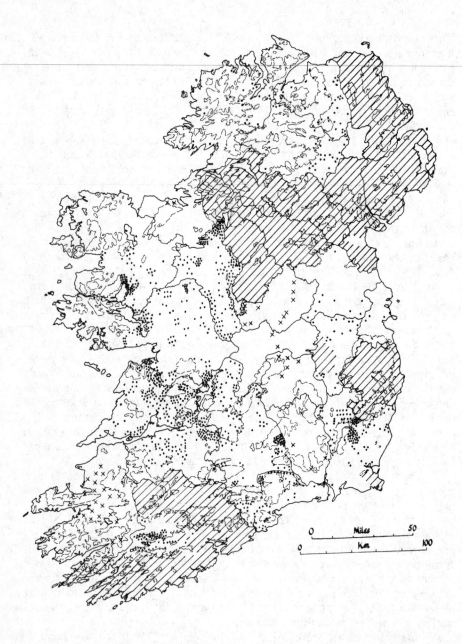

Fig. 5.14. Woodland in Ireland in the 1650s. Each dot represents 250 modern acres (100 ha) of woodland as recorded in the Civil Survey; the size of dot is approximately 250 acres at the scale of the map. The crosses each represent 250 acres in those counties for which the only information is the woodland totals of McCracken.[179] No information survives for hatched areas. The map gives county boundaries and the 500-foot contour.

Where woodland is described the commonest type is 'shrubby', which suggests that there were still extensive survivals of prehistoric hazel-woods, especially on limestone rocks in the west. The prehistoric elm-woods had completely disappeared; presumably they grew on the best land and had been annihilated in prehistory. Oak-woods, which had been less common in prehistory, are abundantly recorded; as in Great Britain, they were the woodland of infertile soils, in glens of acid rocks and on the eskers (hillocks of glacial material) which form islands in bogs. One of the commonest place-names in Ireland is *derry*, equivalent to the rare English *oket*, a wood composed of oak-trees. Several hundred islands in bogs are called Derry, and some of them were still wooded in the seventeenth century. The Survey occasionally mentions alder-woods and ash-woods.

How much of the woodland was ancient we cannot tell. Entries such as 'thick thorny wood with hazell and Elder') (Robin & Any, Co. Roscommon) suggest secondary woodland. There were occasional woods on bog surfaces and probably in river flood-plains of which we can now have little conception.

Uses of woodland Viking and medieval Ireland had a coppicing tradition. Excavations have revealed the immense importance of wattle-work in Cork and Dublin; whole buildings were made of it.[181] It implies the management of woodland on a large scale. Irish cities had timber-framed buildings, but these were an exclusively urban tradition not necessarily related to local woods. The Civil Survey lists many such 'cagework' houses, but they were all demolished in the eighteenth and ninteenth centuries and not a single survivor is known.

Woodmanship continued into the seventeenth century. The Civil Survey very often records 'underwood' and 'copps'; where land values are given, as in Co. Waterford, underwood was worth little less than arable.

Destruction of woodland Much has been said of the destruction of woodland in the seventeenth and eighteenth centuries by the supposed ravages of industry, especially the making of barrels and iron. There can be no doubt of the destruction. Except in Co. Waterford, it is very unusual to find a wood on the 6-inch Ordnance Survey of 1834–44 in a place where there was one in the Civil Survey. In general, at most only a tenth of the Irish woodland of 1655 was still there 180 years later, compared to at least three-quarters in England. Most sites of woods were ordinary farmland by 1835; it is rarely possible to pick out the ghost of a grubbed-out wood among the field boundaries.

The size and destructiveness of the industries have been exaggerated. Irish trees grow again, just as English ones do, but authors have written as if they were non-renewable.

Complaints about the barrel industry found their way into the Civil Survey. In Co. Carlow it was alleged that the woods had been

> very much wasted and spoyld by that plague of all good timber (*to wit*) pipe staves and barrell staves, &c. soe that . . . this county will . . . lament the loss thereof which might be imployed to more honourable uses . . . If not timely prevented, it may be conjectured that the inhabitants of this nation must with Diogines live in tubbs for the choycest timber is imploy'd to that use.

But cooperage is a very specialized craft, using only a minority of high-quality trees; most Irish woodland would have been useless, and it is inconceivable that a whole wood, even an oak-wood, could have been turned into barrels. Nor can the export of a few thousand tons of barrel-staves a year have had any real effect on 420,000 acres of woodland.

The iron industry was larger and less specialized. McCracken lists about 150 rural ironworks, besides others in cities. Most of them were in places where the Civil Survey shows woodland, but there were some in apparently woodless areas, and the woodland was often of small extent and fragmented ownership. The Draperstown ironworks (Co. Londonderry), for instance, had access to at most 1100 acres of woodland, which it shared with two other ironworks and doubtless with other uses as well. Yet it was sustained for at least 150 years, which can only mean a small-scale enterprise using renewable fuel and probably serving a local market. Only in a few places was there any possibility of ironworks as big as those of England. The ironworks of Enniscorthy (Co. Wexford) adjoined 11,000 acres of woodland, much of it in one ownership; the works went on for 232 years and must have come to terms with its fuel supply. Irish ironworks were not an extension of those in England nor an unreasonable use of woodland. Ireland had to get its iron from somewhere.

Did areas with ironworks lose their woodland more completely than those without? In all Ireland there was only one big wooded area which was just as extensive in 1840 as it had been in 1650, namely western Co. Waterford. This had supplied at least five ironworks, two for over a century. Other seats of the iron industry, eg. Wicklow, Wexford, eastern Clare, kept some ancient woodland into the nineteenth century; non-industrial Limerick, Tipperary, and northern Clare lost almost every scrap. The myth of the destructive ironmasters fails the same test as it failed in England, Wales and Scotland.

The real destroyer of the woods was agriculture. From 1700 to 1840 Ireland combined long periods of peace and modest prosperity with a fourfold rise in population. Every inch of possible land (and much that was impossible) was tilled or grazed. With the ironworks in decline, wattle building unfashionable, and plenty of plenty of peat for domestic fuel, there was no obstacle to reducing the whole country to the woodless state of the Irish Midlands. Even the last of the derries, with very rare exceptions, were grubbed out and farmed. The 6-inch Ordnance Survey of Ireland, dating from just before the Great Famine, shows many little farms with 'derry' names in the wilds of Roscommon: the homes of people driven by overpopulation to wrest a living even from morainic islands in bogs.

Some woods may have been preserved for the time being by being incorporated into demesne parks, but here they were jeopardized by the loss of the woodmanship tradition. Anglo-Irish landowners took to forestry plantations earlier and more completely than in England, and the last native woods may have been the victims of replanting. The idea that trees have a life of their own and are not mere artefacts has been forgotten even more thoroughly in Ireland than in England.

Irish woods today Ireland appears at first sight to be almost without ancient woodland. The only well-known examples are the Killarney woods, described by D.L. Kelly and documented back to the sixteenth century. Much of interest remains, despite the ravages of tree-planting, rhododendrons, and deer.[176]

There are some fragmentary survivals. In the Glen of the Downs (Co.

Wicklow) is a steep wood of oak, with hazel-wood on the better soils of the lower slope, which still has a coppice structure. The giant oak stools are evidently several centuries old. The wood is on the Down Map of 1655–7 – the only Irish wood known to me that has both written and field evidence of antiquity.

On an island in a boggy lough in Co. Offaly is an extraordinary wood of great ancient oaks, hung with ancient ivies (one ivy trunk is thicker than a fat man); it has the largest hazel and largest spindle-tree that I have ever seen (Plate VIII). I hesitate to claim it as wildwood, although it is full of fallen giants; but it tells us what the derries may have been like. A nearby, more accessible, derry looks like an ancient wood on the map, has a possible ancient woodland flora, and has a respectable woodbank dividing it from the bog; the trees are oaks but, alas, show every sign of being a plantation.

These are examples of what might be found by the diligent searcher. The task will not be easy, for it is difficult to interpret fragmentary survivals without having a complete ancient wood to tell us what to look for. But other fragments of the historic woods of Ireland may well lurk amidst demesne plantations; they ought to be recognized before the next round of replanting sweeps them away.

Conservation

The prospects for ancient woods are much better than ten years ago. There is less money to spend on destroying them. Owners of woods more often understand them and are proud of them for what they are. Replanting is less often seen as a patriotic duty and more often as a destructive waste of money. Many woods have passed into the hands of local authorities or of semi-public bodies such as the county Naturalists' Trusts or the Woodland Trust; almost all of these (except until recently the National Trust) manage woods conservatively and have no use for modern forestry.

There has been less destruction of ancient woods in the last ten years. Some woodland owners deplore and try to reverse the replanting done by their fathers. Attempts to destroy woods are still made, usually after a change of ownership, but do not go unopposed as they used to.

Uses of woodland have been revived, especially as fuel is no longer cheap. In Essex there are now more than 100 woods actively coppiced for specialized trades, for firewood, as a specific habitat for plants and animals, or as a historic public amenity.

There is no longer any need to reach compromises with farming or modern forestry: both interests have had their fair share of ancient woodland and there is no good reason for them to have any more. Our historic woods are not mere isolated relics of antiquity, but belong to an unbroken tradition extending through the Middle Ages back to the beginnings of civilization and beyond. Nor are they mere outliers of those on the Continent; some parts of England are as rich in variety of ancient woodland as anywhere in Europe, and we have an international duty to preserve hazel-woods, maple-woods, and bluebell-woods. There is still much to be done in identifying and recording our heritage.

I do not indiscriminately recommend preserving every ancient wood. Many are already ill-preserved. A common type of woodland has densely-set oaks, the result of nineteenth-century forestry, beneath which a remnant of hazel underwood struggles to survive. Such a wood is no longer self-renewing and will create an intractable problem when the oaks come to be felled: let it be a warning against too many oaks in an ancient wood. Conversely, many woods (especially small ones) that ten years ago might have been written off as irretrievably damaged by replanting have proved unexpectedly resilient: the plantation has been neglected, the underwood has grown again and is winning the fight with the conifers.

Almost every wood of which the coppice stools still remain is worth preserving. Normally re-coppicing is the best conservation policy, for it brings to life the traditional working of the wood and all its plants and animals. This may be difficult where the tradition of selling underwood has been lost, or where deer have recently proliferated (p.49) and devour the regrowth. If we cannot coppice for the present, let us not be ashamed of doing nothing. It is easy to spend money on spoiling a wood to no purpose by trying to plant trees in it. But every wood, whether coppiced or 'neglected', needs protection from browsing animals. Few woods are now deteriorating through neglect, but all over Wales, Scotland, and Highland England woods have been ravaged for decades by sheep getting in through breaches in the boundaries.[182] The simplest conservation measure of all is three strands of barbed wire.

CHAPTER 6

Wood-pasture –
Wooded commons, parks and
wooded Forests

25 November 1251. Order to G. de Langeley, justiciar of the Forest, that he shall cause 150 hinds to be taken in the king's Forest of Englewod [Inglewood near Carlisle] for the king's use against the imminent feast of Christmas, and . . . shall deliver them to the king's sheriff of Cumberland to be transported to York.

26 November 1251. Order to the seneschal of the Forest of Gautriz [Galtres near York] that he shall cause 50 roe-deer to be taken in the king's aforesaid Forest for the king's use, to be transported to York against the imminent feast of Christmas . . . he shall do his diligence to have them ready there on the third day before the said feast.

12 December 1251. Order to the sheriff of Noting[ham] that he shall receive . . . all the [wild] boars and sows, which the constable of St Briavel shall deliver to him by the king's order, and shall cause them to be transported to York against the imminent feast of Christmas, so that they shall be there at latest on the eve of the same feast . . . And when the king knows the cost, he will cause it to be repaid. [St Briavel's is by the Forest of Dean, 170 miles from York via Nottingham. The king had ordered 200 head of wild swine from this, the last remaining source of them.]

22 December 1251. Order to Picot de Lascelles that he shall come to the king's help with his hounds and nets to take roedeer in the king's Forest of Langwast [Langthwaite, a very long day's ride north-west of York] against the imminent feast of Christmas . . .

Calendar of Close Rolls

(For his Christmas dinner, 1251, Henry III had 430 red deer, 200 fallow deer, 200 roedeer, 200 wild swine, 1300 hares, 450 rabbits, 2100 partridges, 290 pheasants, 395 swans, 115 cranes, 400 tame pigs, 70 pork brawns, 7000 hens, 120 peafowl, 80 salmon, and lampreys without number.)

In many parts of England we find the remains, and occasionally the living practice, of a tradition of using the same land for trees and for grazing animals. Wood-pasture is well documented for the last 1200 years; but it is likely that, as with woodland, written records tell only the last fifth of a story that really began in the Neolithic age if not earlier.

Wood-pasture has a self-contradiction stronger than that which exists between the timber and underwood of woodland. 'Wood' and 'pasture' seem

119

almost mutually exclusive. Livestock are fond of the leaves of most trees but cannot climb for them. Little sustenance is to be got from woodland herbs, many of which are poisonous or distasteful (eg. dog's-mercury, bluebell, anemone). Grasses that grow in shade are so attenuated as to be hardly worth eating. The more trees there are, the less abundant and the worse will be the pasture; and the more animals there are, the less likely saplings or coppice shoots are to survive to produce a new generation of trees. Woods that are pastured therefore have different trees and other plants and a different structure from those that are not, and are managed in ways that separate the grazing from the regrowth of the trees.

Wood-pasture in Prehistory

Wood-pasture, although perhaps uniquely complex in England, has been re-invented many times in different countries. In North America it was practised both by Red Indians and by early settlers. Nineteenth-century explorers in Michigan found a landscape of great oaks set in grassland; Indians had managed the vegetation, mainly by burning, to encourage the native game animals.[183] I have seen a few scraps of this that survive at Kalamazoo: they look very like an English park, though the oaks are of a different species. In the southern Appalachians, settlers of the early nineteenth century pastured livestock on the wooded mountain-tops, which became glades called 'grass-balds' set with beautiful flowering shrubs. Here too the scattered ancient trees, though of unfamiliar species of birch and horse-chestnut, give the air of an English wood-pasture. In both instances, as in England, the vegetation depends on continued grazing; when grazing ceases, trees of different species move in and the land becomes secondary woodland (Chapter 5) in a few decades.[184]

From these and other examples, we can hardly doubt that Neolithic men would have practised wood-pasture as soon as they took domestic livestock into the wildwoods of northern Europe; indeed Mesolithic men could well have practised it before them. There is some more definite evidence. Many of the hazel-rods which form Neolithic trackways in Somerset (p.382) have been cut twice. The top of the living rod was cut off, and a new top allowed to grow, a few years before the rod itself was cut and used in a hurdle.[185] Both cuts were made in summer (as shown by the last annual ring being incomplete), most plausibly in order that the leaves might be used to feed cattle. To use leafy shoots of pollarded trees as fodder would come naturally to anyone trying to herd livestock in wooded terrain. The practice can still be seen in the remoter parts of the Alps and Greece, and on a large scale in Nepal. In the British Isles the best-documented example is the use of pollard holly as fodder (despite the spiny leaves) in many parts of Highland England until recently.[186]

Wooded Commons

Archaeologists can only by rare chance identify the products of wood-pasture; most of the evidence has to come from documents. Several Anglo-Saxon charters refer specifically to wood-pasture commons, for instance:

> And here are the pastures of swine, four *mansiones*: in the place called Boganora, at Hidhurst in the wood, and on the wood-pasture common (*communi silva pascuale*) called Palinga Schittas.

Charter of the exclaves of Felpham, W. Sussex, 953.[187] (*Mansio* is some kind of unit of settlement; Palinga Schittas may be the wood-pasture called The Mens in Kirdford, now the property of Sussex Naturalists' Trust;[188] Idehurst and [Little] Bognor are nearby hamlets.)

Domesday Book often mentions wood-pasture, *silua pastilis*, as distinct from underwood, *silua minuta*. In Derbyshire, Nottinghamshire, and Lincolnshire it systematically records them as separate land-uses. In each county the coppice-woods add up to some 2 per cent of the total land area, but the wood-pasture varies from 24 per cent of Derby to 10½ per cent of Nottingham and 2 per cent of upland Lincolnshire. This suggests that much of the 'woodland' of Norman England was really wood-pasture: the inhabitants coppiced as much of the woods as they needed, but in better-wooded areas there was a surplus of woodland which was used in less intensive ways.

Most Domesday wood-pasture was communal; there is not in England (as there is in Wales and formerly Ireland) a tradition of private pasturing in woods. By 1300 wood-pasture commons had greatly diminished. In some the grazing element had got the upper hand and they had become heaths (p.301) or grassland. Others had been encoppiced and made into private woods. Others had become Forests or parks. Here we are concerned with the minority that remained wood-pasture commons.

Uses of wood-pasture commons Wooded commons are only a small part of the larger subject of commons in general. Like other commons they belonged to a landowner, usually the lord of the manor; but the right to use them belonged to commoners who were the occupiers of particular properties. Usually the grazing belonged to the commoners and the soil (including mineral rights) to the lord. The trees might belong to either: often timber belonged to the lord, and wood – from pollards or underwood – to commoners (not necessarily the same persons as those who had the grazing). Sometimes the lord's tenants had quotas of wood for fuel and fencing (*firebote, hedgebote*) and were allowed timber when needed for buildings and equipment (*housebote, cartbote*, etc.), but botes often applied to hedgerow trees and occasionally to private woodland; they do not imply that there was a common wood.

By the Middle Ages such rights already dated from time immemorial. They were administered, and could be revised, by the manorial courts, which were composed mainly of the commoners themselves and were seldom unduly favourable to the lord's interest. Although the number of livestock allowed to each commoner was limited, extra beasts were grazed on payment of a small 'fine' which was really no more than a grazing rent.

A typical wood-pasture common was grassland or heather with more or less thickly scattered trees and bushes. The grass was grazed by livestock ranging from horses to geese. Trees were cut for firewood and sometimes timber. The normal practice was pollarding, in order to produce repeated crops of wood (or occasionally leaves) without the animals eating the regrowth. Fuel could also come from cutting bushes, even on commons which did not normally have trees. Occasionally, as at Minchinhampton (Gloucestershire),[189] there was coppicing, the regrowth being protected by compartmentation like that to be described for parks and Forests; but such a system was rarely set up in commons, doubtless because it was too favourable to the landowner as owner of the trees.

Manorial courts rarely tried to enforce a *regular* pollarding cycle. Sometimes they understood the ecology of trees remarkably well, as with the sixteenth-century byelaws that preserved the lime trees on Dedham Heath, Essex (p.291).

Pannage A famous though not very important use of wood-pasture, and to a lesser extent of woodland and non-woodland trees, was for the *pannage* of pigs. Tame swine were fed in autumn on the acorns (or beechmast if any) before being slaughtered and salted down. For this common-right the lord received a rent or one pig in ten. Pannage customs were often jocular or fanciful, and sometimes deterrent, as at Hatfield Broad-oak (Essex) in the fourteenth century, where every pig-keeper was supposed to give the lord two swine for 'avesage':

> If he has [only] two pigs he shall give them for Avesage. And if he had [only] one pig he shall buy another identical pig and give both for Avesage. And if he has no pigs he shall give nothing for the same.[190]

How did the idea of pannage compare with reality? The idea is familiar from medieval pictures of the Labours of the Months and has become a commonplace of historical thought;[191] many archaeologists unthinkingly equate pigs with woodland. This may be justified on the Continent (where the Labours of the Months originated) but not with us. In France or Italy, acorns abound in most years and pigs (and occasionally men) may depend on them. In medieval, as in modern, Britain, the oak's bounty was worth something only in about one year in three, 'when it happens' (*cum acciderit*). To breed animals to use so unpredictable a crop was not practical. The chief stronghold of pannage was in the Weald, where the woods were still too vast to exploit more fully, but even there it was in decline by the eleventh century.[139] Elsewhere, the livestock statistics of Domesday and later sources make it quite clear that pig-keeping (eg. in the Cambridge area) was not dependent on woodland. Pannage was written into manorial customs all over England and Wales (rarely Scotland), but was only an occasional bonus to the pig-keeper and brought in an erratic and usually trivial rent to his lord. It lingered in some places until the end of the Middle Ages. In the New Forest it is an active common-right even now.

Continuity Manorial courts did not always successfully preserve trees on commons. If trees disappeared through long-continued severe grazing, the common remained a common and trees could return if grazing diminished (for example Mousehold Heath, p.302). It is more difficult to establish the historical continuity of trees in wood-pasture than in woodland: if a wood loses its trees it ceases to be a wood and disappears from the record.

Parks

A park in this book means a deer-park, a piece of private land surrounded by a deer-proof fence called a *park pale*, which the owner uses for keeping deer.

The making of parks The park tradition goes back to ancient times. Columella in the first century BC gives its essential features: the emparking of existing woods within wooden pales or stone or mud-brick walls; the keeping of beasts, both native (red and roe deer, wild swine) and exotic (fallow deer, gazelles); water supply and winter feeding.[192] He indicates that parks were a familiar luxury in Italy and Gaul. Although utilitarian (the produce was sold) they were placed where the owner could see them, and appear to have continued a tradition of parks as beautiful landscape, derived by scholars from Achaemenid Persia if not from the Garden of Eden itself.

If there were Roman parks in Britain they did not outlast the Empire. Parks are conspicuously absent from Anglo-Saxon, though common in medieval, perambulations. Our park tradition derives from the Normans' interest in deer husbandry. This began before Domesday Book, in which thirty-five parks are recorded. But there is one pre-Conquest reference: at Ongar (Essex) a will dated 1045 mentions 'the wood . . . outside the deerhay'.[145] The Anglo-Saxon word, *derhage*, is ambiguous – it normally means a hedge for keeping deer out or a device for catching them – but Ongar is the site of one of only two Domesday parks in Essex, well known in later centuries as Ongar Great Park. The Norman fashion for parks therefore began to penetrate England just before the Conquest.

Parks multiplied in the twelfth century, doubtless because of the introduction of fallow deer (Chapter 4) which were easier to keep in a confined space than native species. In the thirteenth century we have a systematic record of park-making, because a new or enlarged park required 'planning permission' in the form of a licence to empark. The Close Rolls abound with such licences, often accompanied by gifts of deer from the king's Forests to start new parks.

Many historians have searched for written records of parks. I estimate, from the lists of myself and others in eight well-studied counties, that there were about 3200 parks in England in the heyday of parks around 1300 (Rackham 1980 p.191). Not all the parks of which we have records existed at one time; but this factor would be offset by the existence of many parks of which no record has yet come to light. Professor L.M. Cantor has listed parks all over England and has produced a map of 1800 places (Fig. 6.1). (This smaller number is due partly to some counties being less well documented than others, and partly to different listing conventions, such as counting only one park where there were two or three in the same locality.) If the average area of a park was 200 acres, parks would have covered up to 2 per cent of England.

Whatever the original habitat of the fallow deer may have been, the medievals thought it to be a woodland animal. Many records of parks specify woodland, and their distribution closely reflects that of woodland in Domesday Book (Fig. 5.4). In general parks were thickest on the ground in well-wooded areas such as Worcestershire, Staffordshire, north-west Warwickshire, south-east Berkshire. The most parky county of all appears to have been Hertfordshire, with ninety known parks, one to seven square miles of land.[194] There were few parks where woodland was scarce, as in Lincolnshire, Cambridgeshire, south-east Warwickshire, north-west Berkshire, Devon, and Cornwall. Even small groups of woods, as in west Cambridgeshire and near King's Lynn, generated parks.

For many counties there was something like one medieval park (by Cantor's reckoning) to every 1500 acres of Domesday woodland, but there are some anomalies. The Weald – the biggest wooded area of all – had little above the average density of parks; did it lack gentry to establish them? Why were there many parks in poorly-wooded Leicestershire and the non-Wealden part of Sussex, and a number even in the woodless part of east Gloucestershire? As we

Fig. 6.1 Medieval parks. Each dot represents about 400 acres at the scale of the map; the average size of an English park was about 250 acres. For England (and Ireland) the map is redrawn, by kind permission, from L.M. Cantor[193] and adopts his conventions of ending at the date 1485 and of not counting more than one park in each manor. For Wales most of the information comes from Rees[168] and Linnard (1982), and for Scotland from Gilbert.[85] The boundaries of the Highland Zone and of the Scottish Lowlands are shown.

shall see, although woodland was preferred, parks could at a pinch be made on almost any terrain.

Wales and Scotland were lands of petty Forests; they had but few parks. About fifty medieval parks are known in Wales, mainly near the English border,[193, 195] and about eighty in Scotland.[85] There were a handful in eastern Ireland.

Organization and management Anyone could have a park who could afford it. All respectable English earls, bishops, and monasteries had several parks, but the Crown had relatively few. Like other status symbols, parks descended the social scale and even nunneries, minor gentry, and colleges had them.

It is an error to call parks 'hunting preserves'. They could be the scene of hunts: in 1221 Henry III gave permission to chase the fox in Havering Park (Essex) to the Abbess of Barking, perhaps our earliest known fox-hunting prelate.[196] But a confined space full of trees offers little scope for a good hunt. The real purpose of a park was the prosaic supply of venison, other meat, wood, and timber.

The beasts of nine parks out of ten were fallow deer. We hear of parks for red deer and occasionally roedeer, wild swine, wild bulls (Chapter 4), and hares. It was common practice to graze cattle or sheep, to let grazing to local farmers, and to sell hay. Wood came from pollarded or coppiced trees.

But the function of parks was not just economic. Venison was no ordinary meat: it was a special dish for feasts and the honouring of guests. It was beyond price – I have not a single record of a sale or valuation – and a haunch was a gift that money could not buy. Outsize timber trees (p.87) were a rare resource for which some parks were noted.

Ongar Great Park, Essex (Fig. 6.2), the 'deerhay' of 1045, may well have been the prototype of English parks. It survived largely intact, though disused, until 1945; its subsequent destruction is probably the worst loss of a visible Anglo-Saxon antiquity this century, though much can be reconstructed from maps and surviving remains. Like many early parks it was very large, about 1200 acres, and had the typical shape of a rectangle with rounded corners – a compact shape for economy in fencing. Another early feature is that the parish boundaries are displaced to conform to the shape of the park.

The chief expense of a park was the pale. Fallow deer are as strong as pigs and more agile than goats, and even now it is not easy to fence them in. A medieval pale was made of cleft oak stakes individually set in the ground and nailed to a rail (Plate IX). Repairs as the pales rotted were costly in labour and good timber. Sometimes there was a wall instead. The pale at Ongar was set on a mighty bank with a ditch each side. Later parks tend to be smaller and of awkward shapes. Parish boundaries became fixed and were no longer altered to fit park perimeters.

Parks were of two kinds. *Uncompartmented* parks were accessible to the deer at all times; the trees were pollarded to protect the regrowth, and new trees arose either in periods of slack grazing or in the protection of spiny thickets of thorn or holly. Other parks were *compartmented*, with some separation between trees and grazing. A park would be divided by internal banks into coppices, each of which would be felled like an ordinary wood and then fenced in the early stages to keep deer out until it had grown sufficiently not to be damaged. For instance:

> There is a park . . . divided into 17 quarters in which 10 acres of underwood can
> be sold every year, worth £4 at 8s an acre. The pasture is worth nothing because of
> the multitude of beasts. The nuts . . . when they happen are worth 12d.

Saffron Walden (Essex), 1336[197]

Some compartments might be accessible to the deer all the time; these are called
launds and were typically grassland with pollard trees.

About one park in two had some kind of compartmentation. At Ongar some
fragments of internal coppice-banks survive. In Monks' Park (part of the
Bradfield Woods, West Suffolk), which was founded within seventy years of the
Conquest, a system of four coppices and three launds can be reconstructed from
surviving banks, the soil-marks of destroyed banks, and written records (Fig.
6.3).

Both at Ongar and at Monks' Park there was a park lodge where the parkers
did their business, set characteristically at the highest point and commanding a
view of whatever was not hidden by trees. Both parks had waterholes made by
digging out natural ponds.

Not every park was wooded. In late medieval Hertfordshire the clergy complained of tithes lost through the emparking of arable land.[194] At Great Baddow
(Essex) in 1247 a park was made of sixty acres of heath.[198] At Egton (north-east
Yorkshire) the turf-built dike of Julian Park sweeps for more than a mile across
the High Moor. The Great Park of Abergavenny (Monmouthshire) included
much of the Sugarloaf Mountain.

Parks down the centuries A park was a troublesome and precarious enterprise. It often belonged to an absentee unable to give it the necessary attention.
Some owners tried to keep far too many deer, which died of starvation and of
less tangible causes like 'Garget', 'Wyppys', and 'Rotte'. Henry III had a
well-run park of 1100 acres at Havering (Essex), from which he ordered an
average of 44 fallow deer annually from 1234 to 1263, besides getting oaks and
grazing rents; yet even here in 1251 he ordered the bailiff to remove 'the bodies
of dead beasts and swine which are rotting in the park' and to provide hay for
the deer (Rackham 1978).

Many particularly of the smaller parks were short-lived. Already by the
thirteenth century some had gone out of use:

> Item, there is there one park which contains in itself sixty acres by estimate . . .
> twenty-nine and a half acres of arable land in the launds of the same park which are
> included in the total of arable land, and the pasture is worth ten pence every acre.

Pulham, Norfolk, 1251 (Ely Coucher Book)[19]

In the later Middle Ages and especially in the sixteenth and seventeenth centuries parks went out of use, and new parks were not made in the same numbers.
Even where a place still had a park, the site might be changed: the modern park
of North Elmham (Norfolk) is not on the site of the medieval park but of the
Anglo-Saxon town.

A disused park might revert to being a wood, often permanently acquiring the
name 'Park Wood'. It might become farmland, especially if the deer had

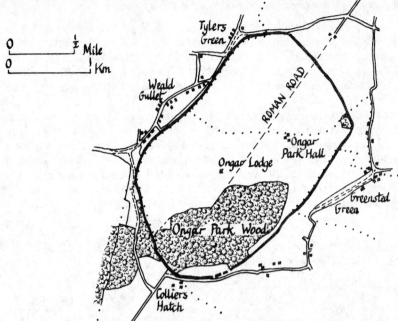

Fig. 6.2. Ongar Great Park, Essex, as it survived until *c.* 1950. The parish boundaries are shown, as is the fragment of park boundary which still exists in the south-west. The rest of the park perimeter survived as a hedge (thick line).

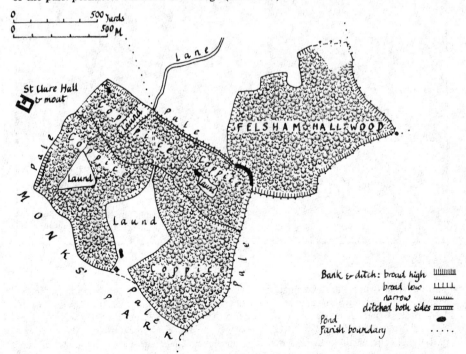

Fig. 6.3. Monks' Park in Bradfield St Clare, Suffolk: reconstruction of the medieval topography with coppices and launds. Felsham Hall was a normal wood excluded from the park.

destroyed the trees. Parks were one of the causes of loss of woodland. The Abbot of Bury St Edmunds's park at Long Melford had been made out of a wood called Elmesete. By 1386, though still called Great Wood, it yielded from its 260 acres £2 per annum in grazing rents but only 8s. worth of wood in the form of faggots.[199] It remained a park until the Dissolution but has now become 'Park Farm'.

Deer as the function of parks gradually declined, although even now there are about a hundred active deer-parks left. They were succeeded by the idea of parks as landscape (Fig. 6.4.) This was not an invention of the eighteenth century. Like other fashions it began at the top of the social scale. The prototypes are the parks that surrounded Henry I's palace of Woodstock (Oxfordshire) and Henry III's palace of Clarendon (Wiltshire). Medieval parks, though usually distant from the owner's house, had their aspects of pleasure and

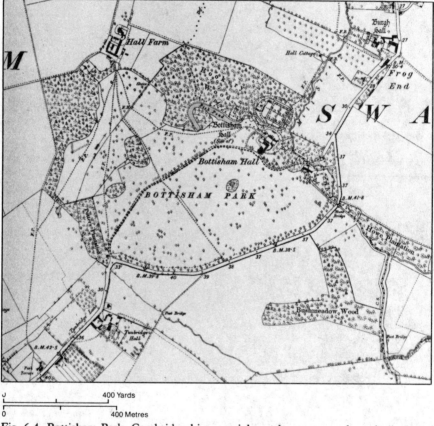

Fig. 6.4. Bottisham Park, Cambridgeshire: an eighteenth-century park made (in stages over half a century) where there had not been a park before. The present Hall was built in 1797 and the road diverted round the edge of the park shortly before. All the woods are derived from plantations; a few trees survive from the previous landscape. Much of the park covers the earthworks of a deserted medieval village, probably called Angerhale, which had eight moats.[550] Most of the moats are now hidden in groves and were overlooked by the mapmakers, except for the 'Fish Pond', really part of the great moat of the former Bottisham Hall. Ordnance Survey, 1886.

romance. Did not the monks of Butley (Suffolk) in 1528 take the Queen of France for 'a picnic under the oaks with fun and games (*joco et ludo*)' in Staverton Park?[200] From the later Middle Ages onwards it became common to re-site a mansion next to a park or *vice versa*.

Some medieval parks were thus given a new lease of life as landscape parks, sometimes in the hands of professional park designers of whom William Kent (1684–1748), Charles Bridgeman (?–1738), Lancelot 'Capability' Brown (1716–1783), and Humphry Repton (1752–1818) are the best known. Writers on these masters often suppose that they 'laid out' landscapes out of nothing and marvel that their patrons were content to plant trees the effect of which would not be seen in their lifetimes. The writings especially of Repton – his famous Red Books with their 'before and after' views – and the evidence of many of the parks themselves tell a different story. Kent and his successors were heirs to an ancient tradition. They did not set out to transform vast tracts of countryside, but to enhance an existing landscape by judicious and often quite small altera-tions. Part of the tradition was that venerable trees should give an air of dignity and continuity to a gentleman's seat. It was not enough to plant trees and wait for them to grow; an 'instant park' was needed, with an appearance of respect-able antiquity from the start, incorporating whatever trees were already there. Hence it comes about that many a Capability Brown park, such as Hevening-ham (Suffolk), contains pollards that were already old in Brown's time; it is a delight of such places to find their surrealist shapes and improbable bulk unexpectedly amid the formality of the eighteenth-century plantings.

Landscape emparking not only preserved and adapted real medieval parks, but also created 'pseudo-medieval' parks by incorporating what had previously been hedgerow and field trees. The two great Suffolk parks of Ickworth (National Trust) and Sotterley (private) each contain mighty pollard oaks and other trees which give, as they were doubtless meant to do, the air of a Plantagenet deer-park. But each park contains a parish church, which no genuine deer-park ever did, and the great trees stand on faint earthworks and around the platforms of vanished cottages. A survey of the parish of Ickworth in 1665 shows no park but hamlets and greens, hedged fields (hence the faint earthworks), groves, and a small open-field.[201] All these were swallowed up when the park was made in 1701. The researches of John Phibbs show that the park itself has a most complex history and contains many trees planted both before and after the time of Capability Brown, to whom popular belief summari-ly ascribes the landscaping.[202] An earlier pseudo-medieval park is the apparent-ly seventeenth-century one of Earlham Hall, Norwich, which inherits the pollard oaks of the deserted village of Earlham. Even the new park of Long Melford Hall, Suffolk, one of the earliest landscape parks of which much now remains, made between 1580 and 1613,[203] includes pre-existing field trees.

Wooded Forests

The mysterious word *forest* may, in its Germanic origin, have meant a tract of trees. In Western Europe it came to mean land on which deer were protected by special byelaws. The laws and the word were introduced to England from the Continent by William the Conqueror. For many centuries *Forest* meant a place of deer. The Authorized Version of the Bible, published in 1611, doubtless encouraged Englishmen to connect *forest* with trees, but the word could still mean 'heath' more than a century later.

A Forest in this book means a Royal Forest or its private equivalent, an unfenced area where deer were kept. Here I deal mainly with those Forests that happened to be wooded, but I re-emphasize that **the word Forest does not imply woodland**; moorland, heath, and fenland Forests are discussed in other chapters.

Forests are a rich field of pseudo-history. Besides the mis-equating of Forests with woodland, there are the notions that they belonged to the Crown, covered a third of England, were set aside for the king's hunting, were guarded by terrible laws, and had a stabilizing influence on the landscape. These old misconceptions have all been given fresh currency (though without fresh evidence) by reputable scholars in the last few years.

How Forests worked in practice differs from how they were supposed to work and also from how in later centuries they were imagined to have worked. This account is concerned with practical aspects, based on documents mainly of the thirteenth century, when Forests were at their heyday. Later writers, romantic such as 'Dame Juliana Berners' in the fifteenth century and scholastic such as Manwood in the sixteenth, set down colourful lore about Forests and hunting. Such tracts are entertaining to read and to plagiarize; but they do not necessarily record how things happened.

It is essential to distinguish between Forests in the *legal* and the *physical* sense. Scholars reconstruct the perambulations by which the legal boundaries of Forests were defined, and imagine that they have ascertained the actual extent of the Forests. They have not. The Forest Laws of all wooded Forests (though not necessarily of other kinds) covered areas much wider than the actual wood-pastures where the deer lived. The legal boundary of Waltham Forest enclosed 60,000 acres, of which the present Epping Forest is 6,000 acres. But Epping Forest is not a fragment of its former extent; it has never been much larger than it is now (Rackham 1978). The difference is due mainly to a change in the meaning of the word, from the legal to the physical Forest. Over three-quarters of the 60,000 acres have always been ordinary Essex countryside – farms, hamlets, ordinary woods, parks, and a town (Waltham Abbey) – in which the deer, should they stray, were still protected by Forest Law. The error of confusing the legal with the physical Forest, multiplied by the error of confusing Forest with woodland, is mainly responsible for the myth that medieval England was very wooded.

Growth of the Forest system The Anglo-Saxons had no Forests nor any word for them. English (and Welsh) kings enjoyed venison and honoured huntsmen, but exercised no more than the sporting rights of any landowner. (Statements to the contrary are based on documents like the 'Laws of Pseudo-Canute', forged in the Middle Ages to give Forest Law an air of respectable antiquity,[204] which even now deceive credulous authors.)

William the Conqueror introduced Forests to England, as his obituary says:

The king W[illiam] set up great protection for deer (*deorfriþ*) and legislated to that intent, that whosoever should slay hart or hind should be blinded . . . he loved the high-deer as if he were their father.

Anglo-Saxon Chronicle, 1087

The word is first mentioned in Domesday Book, which records about twenty-five Forests. There is no foundation for the supposition that all the Forests existed by 1086 but the Commissioners did not trouble to record them systematically. Lands which later became Forests (eg. south-west Essex) are recorded no less fully than the rest of the country; and neglect of Forests would have defeated one of the main objects of Domesday, to define the king's rights where they were liable to conflict with the rights of subjects.

Afforestment was continued by Henry I (1100–35), who may well have introduced fallow deer (p.49); he was probably responsible for declaring Epping Forest (first heard of in the 1130s) and maybe Sherwood (1154). Multiplying the Forests was a way in which the king oppressed the nobility and was curtailed by Magna Carta in 1216. No more Forests were declared in England after this; changes involved merely tinkering with the legal boundaries.

The twelfth century is poorly documented, and no record survives of how a Forest was declared. As with a modern National Park, it would have been necessary to define the boundaries – in effect, to put up notices saying 'This is a Forest' – and to set up a bureaucracy of justiciars, seneschals, wardens, Foresters-of-fee, verderers, riding-Foresters, foot-Foresters, etc. The existing terrain, ownerships, and land-uses would have gone on unaltered. The one practical matter would normally have been introducing some deer. In 1238 Henry III ordered 120 live fallow deer to be caged, carted, and shipped from Havering (Essex) to Flanders, presumably to start a Forest there.[49, 205]

Just before Magna Carta there were at least 143 Forests in England (Rackham 1980) (Fig. 6.5). A Forest was the supreme status symbol of the king and was aspired to by earls and a few princes of the Church. Already in Domesday Book the Earl of Chester had three Forests; but the king always had at least twice as many as all his subjects put together. (The word *Chase* is sometimes, though inconsistently, used to distinguish the Forest of a subject.)

The English Forest system was briefly extended to Ireland. Henry III wrote of his Forests of Obbrun and Slefco, somewhere near Dublin, and Cracelauh (said to be Carlow). In Wales and Scotland Forests developed independently and were more abundant but less well-defined than in England.

The Anglo-Normans set up Forests in Wales. There were well over a hundred; there may have been ninety-four in the southern half of Wales alone.[168] Only a few were royal.[206] Many Forests had a shadowy existence; they were operated by marcher lords out of a taste not so much for venison as for the status symbols of English royalty. I estimate that nearly half the Forests in Wales were associated with woodland; most of the rest were wholly or mainly moorland.

The earliest record for Scotland is of the non-royal Paisley Forest (Renfrewshire) in 1110. Forests multiplied more and flourished later than in England: new ones were declared all through the Middle Ages (eg. Menteith Forest, Perthshire, in 1454). By 1500, according to the lists of M.L. Anderson and J.M. Gilbert,[44, 85] there were or had been about 180 Forests, about half of them royal. Most were either small and wooded or middle-sized and moorland. The earlier Forests were almost confined to the eastern half of Scotland. They later spread into the central Highlands, and after 1600 into the western Highlands, where moorland deer-Forests are operated to this day (Chapter 14).

How a wooded Forest worked This account is of the royal Forests of England, which are much better documented than private Forests or those of other countries.

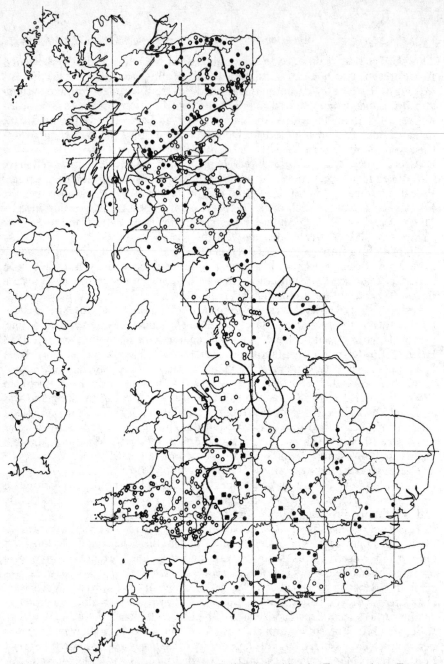

Fig. 6.5. Medieval Forests. Black points: royal Forests (that is, Forests whose Forestal rights belonged to the English or Scottish Crown for all or most of the Middle Ages). White points: private Forests. Squares: Forests mentioned or implied in Domesday Book. The sizes of physical Forests cannot often be ascertained; the circles have an area (at the scale of the map) of 20 square km or 5000 acres, which is something like the average size of an English Forest. In Scotland not all the Forests operated at the same time. The boundaries of the Highland Zone and of the Scottish Lowlands are shown. Principal sources: Anderson,[44] Gilbert,[85] Rees,[168] Linnard (1982), Rackham (1980) and sources mentioned therein.

Forests were not associated with woodland as were parks. The big wooded areas – the Weald, Chilterns, Worcestershire, north-west Warwickshire – had few Forests, and those not royal. Forests were most numerous in moderately-wooded counties such as Wiltshire, Somerset, and Shropshire. Their wild vegetation could as well be moorland, heath, or fen as woodland. The Forests of Cornwall and of Wirral (Cheshire) seem to have been ordinary countryside to which Forest law was applied, probably in order to fine the Bishop or gentry for technical infringements. At a rough estimate about eighty of the 143 Forests contained more woodland than the country at large. Most of the bigger Forests were predominantly moorland (Dartmoor, Pickering) or heath (Sherwood), and several wooded Forests covered less than 1000 acres (Stowood near Oxford). The total area of *physical* Forests was nearly a million acres – 3 per cent of England – but less than half of this was wood-pasture.[207]

The sites of Forests were decided not by the terrain but by where the king had lands or palaces. There were many royal Forests in Somerset, Derbyshire and north-east Yorkshire, where there was much Crown land; even more in the London-Oxfordshire-Dorset triangle, where the king had up to fifteen palaces to be provisioned; but none at all in Hertfordshire, Kent, or Sussex where the king had very little interest (Fig. 6.6). Epping Forest owes its designation to Waltham Abbey, which though not a Crown property was the king's favourite monastery at which he often stayed. In counties such as Somerset there was a Forest to every large royal property. Even in the king's manor of Somerton, where there was no moorland or wood-pasture, a mini-Forest was contrived containing hares, deemed to be mini-deer.

The king owned the deer in his Forests, but not necessarily the land. In some, such as the Forest of Dean, he owned the land and trees if any; in others, such as Epping, somebody else was the landowner. The king's habit of keeping deer on other people's land was why Forests were strongly objected to by earls and barons. Whoever was landowner, most physical Forests were also commons and had common-rights dating from before they had been declared Forests. The parties in a Forest comprised: the king, or in a non-royal Forest the private owner of the Forestal rights (the rights to keep deer, to appoint Forest officials, to hold Forest courts and to pocket the fines levied therein); the landowners; and the various kinds of commoners having rights to pasture or to woodcutting.

Deer in wooded Forests were usually fallow, with small numbers of red and roe; red deer were commoner in moorland. The wild swine, while he lasted (p.36), was an honorary deer, as was the hare in Somerton Forest. These animals were treated with respect, and an inquest was supposed to be held whenever one was found dead. At Somerton in 1256 twelve jurymen duly sat on the body of a hare as if it had been a man.[208]

Forests were not hunting preserves. A few monarchs such as Edward II, the playboy king, may have been 'passionately fond of the chase', but even passion would have been amply satisfied by the twenty-one royal Forests of William the Conqueror. The ordinary working king had no time or opportunity to visit eighty Forests, and records of royal hunts are very few. (Scots kings apparently hunted more.[85]) The king's hunting was done by professionals: the following order is typical of thousands in the correspondence of Henry III.

4 Sept. 1251. Order to William Luvel and Henry de Candour, the king's hunts-men, that when they have taken 60 bucks in the king's Forest of Dean, as the king

ordered, they should go to the king's New Forest and take another 60 bucks there, . . . to be salted and transported to London for the forthcoming feast of St Edward [13 October].

By this time deer were not the everyday diet of the king and the court but were eaten at feasts. Henry III's many feasts at York and Westminster were among

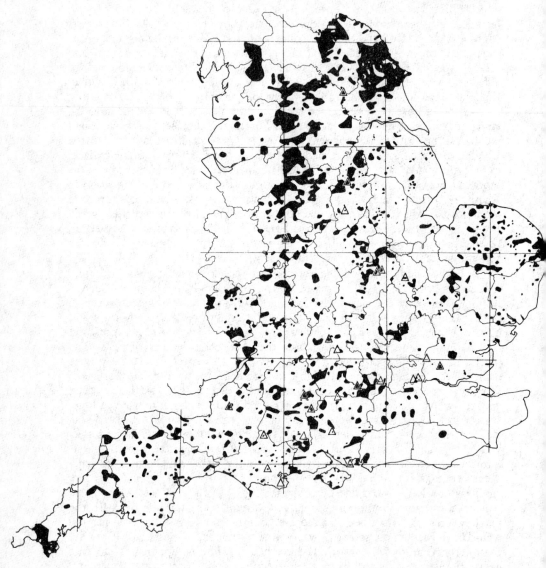

Fig. 6.6. Crown lands and palaces. Black dots and patches are the king's lands as recorded in Domesday Book. Triangles are the places where kings from Henry II to Henry III (1154–1272) had residences or spent much of their time.

the greatest dinners that these islands have known (see quotations at head of chapter). The little Forest of Galtres, crowded in somewhere among the villages north of York, was almost the biggest venison-producing Forest; and the king's lardiner, who stored the carcases, was one of the biggest magnates in York city. The king bestowed deer on favoured subjects, often in honour of their weddings, graduations, consecrations, pregnancies, and other festive occasions.

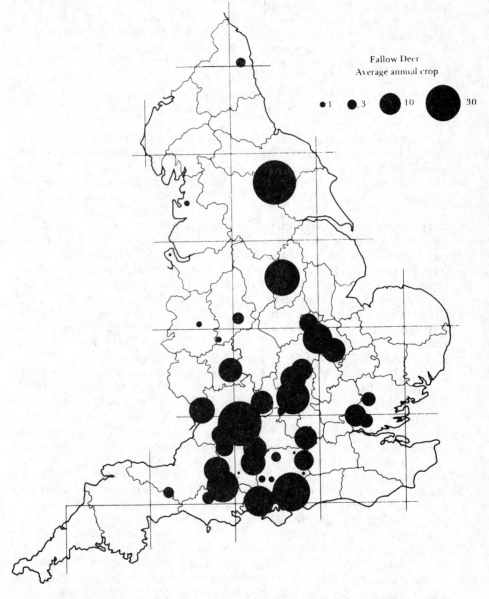

Fig. 6.7. The Forests from which Henry III ordered fallow deer. The size of each spot is proportional to the King's average annual consumption of deer in six sample years of his reign. Parks and private Forests are not included.

135

In an average year Henry III took 607 fallow deer, 159 red, 45 roe, and 88 wild swine (up to 1260).[209] Of the fallow he ate half at his own table, gave a third to the tables of his friends, and gave one-sixth away alive for stocking parks. Seven fallow deer out of eight came from Forests, mostly those close to palaces (Figs. 6.7, 6.6). The numbers bear no relation to the size of the physical Forest: the small Forest of Brayden (Wiltshire) yielded more fallow and more red deer than the vast Forest of Sherwood.

The king owned trees on about half his Forests. By law, every other landowner within a Forest was supposed to get the king's permission for felling trees, but in practice this was done only for unusual fellings; the historian does not, alas, find a file of felling licences for the routine coppicing of every private wood within a legal Forest.

The king took timber from his Forests for works on his castles and palaces, and gave trees to his subjects. He rarely sold timber. For instance:

> 1243. Order to the constable of St Briavel's that he should let the Friars Preachers of Gloucester have 15 oaks for timber in the various bailiwicks of the forest of Dene, with all their by-products (*exkaetis*), for the fabric of their church and the construction of their buildings, where they can most conveniently and closely be taken . . . in the aforesaid Forest.[49]

Such records refer to small numbers of trees (rarely as many as a hundred), which were often transported long distances. They were evidently the rare and specially valuable outsize oaks which we noted on p.87. I have measured the very timbers which the Black Friars of Gloucester made from the oaks which Henry III gave them: the trees, which may have dated from the wildwood days of the Forest of Dean, were about 2 feet 3 inches in diameter at the middle and 50 feet in usable length.[210] Dean was the chief Forest producing timber for the king. Other Forests yielded amounts not in proportion to their size: many oaks came from the little Kingswood Forest near Colchester, and from Sherwood Forest where the king did not have very much woodland.

Wood is recorded in the two forms of *robora* and underwood. *Robora* were used only as fuel; the word probably means a dead pollard (Rackham 1978). Henry III, for instance, remembered his old nurse, Helen of Winchester, and every year sent her two *robora* for her fire. When the king had underwood in a Forest he used small amounts on his works, but most of it was sold. Henry III tried to organize his wood-producing Forests commercially: he had professional sellers of the king's underwood, such as Peter de Neyreford and Nicholas de Rummesye, appointed in 1255 'for the relief of the king's debts'.[49] Sales and grants of wood specifically excluded timber. Newly-felled areas were ordered to be fenced to protect the regrowth, wherever local custom allowed the king to do this. Some Forests were divided into a regular system of compartments corresponding to the coppices and launds of parks, for instance Rockingham Forest (Northamptonshire), Wychwood Forest (Oxfordshire), Hatfield and Writtle Forests (Essex) (Fig. 6.8), Cranborne Chase and Grovely Forest (Wiltshire).

Deer, landowners, and commoners were subject to a special hierarchy of Forest courts. In popular myth these were blood-thirsty courts, cutting off the limbs etc. of even minor offenders against Forest Law, but not a single case has been brought forward as evidence of this having been done. In reality the courts were interested in pence, not limbs, and adjusted the fines so as not to dry up

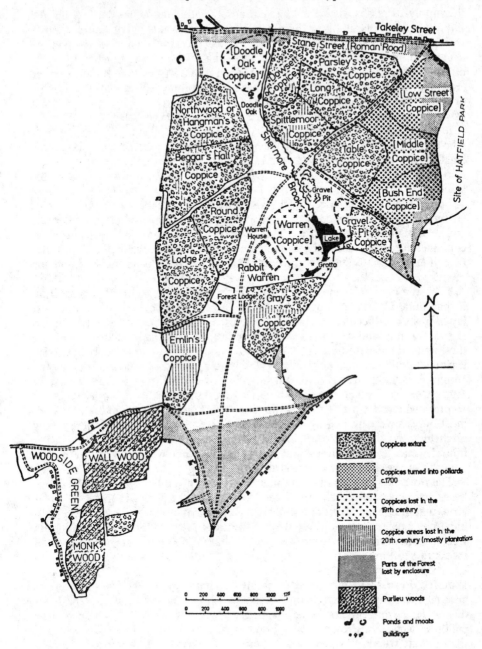

Fig. 6.8. Hatfield Forest, Essex: a small wooded Forest with straggling concave outline, boundary houses, roads, coppices and former coppices. The plains between the coppices are grassland with areas of scrub and with scattered pollard trees. Also shown is Woodside Green, a smallish common with pollards. Wall Wood and Monk Wood are medieval 'purlieu woods' to which some of the Forest Law applied.

the supply. 'Trespasses against the venison' – stealing the king's deer – attracted imprisonment or large fines, though offenders were usually given ample chance to escape or be pardoned. 'Trespasses against the vert' comprised damage to vegetation by 'abuse' of grazing or woodcutting. These were punished by fines, or by confiscating livestock – later redeemed for a fraction of their value (Rackham 1978). Many of the 'fines' are no more than the value of the grazing or wood involved: evidently the courts were being used as a convenient method of collecting revenue from grazing rents or casual woodsales. Some Forest regulations seem to have been purposely designed for collecting fees from those who refused to observe them: for instance, the 'expedition of dogs' living in a legal Forest, in theory the requirement to cut off part of one of the animal's feet lest it run after the deer, was in practice a source of revenue and a negotiable asset.

Forest Law did not succeed in stabilizing the landscape where it operated. Grubbing out private woods or encroaching on commons or on Crown lands within a legal Forest was forbidden, but in practice was either licensed or condoned for a small annual payment. Landscape, and especially woodland, has been if anything less stable within the legal bounds of Forests than just outside them.

What the king got from his Forests varied from one to another. From Dean he had minerals, underwood, timber, red and fallow deer, and wild swine, but few Forests produced more than two of these. From all Forests together he had less than a thousand deer a year, a few hundred big oaks and pollards, and some thousands of acres of underwood; these did not represent an intensive use of at least half a million acres of physical royal Forest. We must not be misled by the emphasis of the written record into supposing that the Crown had a dominating interest in the Forests; it was commoners and landowners, who preserved few records, who did most of the grazing and woodcutting. The king's rights over most Forests were limited by local bylaws; English medieval kings, though they might oppress the nobility, usually respected scrupulously the rights of their humbler subjects. The fines were worth having, but would hardly have paid stipends to the army of Forest bureaucrats.

The Forests were of more than merely economic value to the king. Medieval kings were poor, and their authority depended on the power to make gifts of a kind that money could not buy, such as deer and giant oaks. The Forest hierarchy gave the king unlimited opportunities to reward those who served him well with honorific sinecures. Was not Chaucer, in the middle of a busy life, made under-Forester of an obscure Somerset Forest?

Wooded Forests in later centuries After Henry III the Crown's interests gradually declined, especially in Forests in which someone else was the land-owner. His arrangements for coppicing and selling wood were not kept up; by 1600 the woods in Crown-owned Forests were much less efficiently managed than private woods.[211] There were attempts at revival: the structure in Epping Forest now misnamed 'Queen Elizabeth's Hunting Lodge' is really a 'standing', or observation tower for ceremonial hunts, built by Henry VIII in the 1540s when he tried to make a park in part of the Forest of which he had confiscated the land from Waltham Abbey.[212]

The Crown's loss of interest rarely had much direct effect. A Forest would revert to being an ordinary common, run by landowners and commoners.

Forest courts were often retained to administer the complexities of common-rights, especially where many manors and parishes were involved (as in Epping Forest).

The destruction of wooded Forests was usually the result, not of neglect, over-grazing, or gradual encroachment, but of intervention from outside. Charles I briefly revived the Forest laws in the hope that people would pay to terminate the system.[213] Usually the commoners were too strong for him, but some Forests were sold off and destroyed, such as a third of Neroche (Somerset).

From the later seventeenth century the remaining Crown-owned Forests were encroached upon by modern forestry. Plantations of oak were made, at the expense of wild trees and heath, to save the Navy Board of the future the expense of buying oak for shipbuilding. The early plantations were failures (the Navy of Nelson's time got more timber from Forests such as Hainault (Essex) where it had grown naturally) but were made the precedent for later plantations which in the nineteenth century destroyed the native vegetation of, for instance, Parkhurst Forest (Isle of Wight) and ate up nearly half the New Forest.

Forests were hard hit by Enclosure Acts, which gave landowning parties the power to do what they pleased and expropriated the rights of the commoners and the Crown. The enclosure of Forests was later than that of common fields. Their multiple land-uses, which could not be brought within the scope of cost-benefit analysis, were not understood by eighteenth-century agricultural writers: fashionable philosophy exalted conventional agriculture and despised the king's harts and the widow's geese. Forests were represented as the 'nest and conservatory of sloth, idleness and misery'.[214]

Enfield Chase (Middlesex) suffered an Enclosure Act in 1777, Needwood Forest (Staffordshire) in 1801, Windsor Forest in 1817, and Wychwood Forest in 1857. When a Forest was enclosed its wood-pasture, heath, etc. passed to private owners who, with rare exceptions, instantly destroyed them. This was to little purpose, for the land was mostly bad and attempts at farming it often failed. The destruction of most of Hainault Forest, by specially invented machines, in 1851 was a public scandal; the modern conservation movement began with efforts to avert a like fate for Epping Forest.

Wood-Pastures – Commons, Parks and Forests – As They Are Now

It is a rare coincidence for all the land-uses of a wood-pasture to have survived the centuries; but there are many that survive in disuse, or used for another purpose, or as fragments.

Ancient wood-pastures are among our favourite places of public resort and recreation – for instance Burnham Beeches, Sutton Coldfield Park, Epping Forest – and it is a tragedy that our Victorian predecessors took it upon themselves to destroy so many. Commons, Forests, and some parks have been so used for centuries, and if wooded can withstand quite severe public use; where their fabric has deteriorated this has much less often been through over-use than through neglect of traditional uses. Fortunately many park and common authorities now appreciate that cattle and sheep are a normal part of the scene, and it is to be hoped that they will rediscover the virtues of woodcutting.

Grazing and vegetation The plant life of commons, parks, and Forest differs from that of woods. The difference persists even where the decline of grazing has allowed secondary woodland to spring up between the original pollards. Animals may be affected also; for instance, woods, having low bushes and coppice stools, may have different birds from those that nest in the hollow pollards of wood-pasture.

Cattle, sheep, goats, and deer are not indiscriminate destroyers: they have likes and dislikes. They thus discourage trees and other plants of which they are fond, and by removing competition encourage species that they dislike or cannot easily destroy. They select more effectively than woodmen. We can study these effects by watching the animals feed (although deer rarely let us do this), or by fencing livestock out of particular areas. Long-term effects can be discovered from historical records or fossil pollen of species now vanished; or by comparing a wood-pasture with a wood that has not had a history of grazing (for instance, a Forest with adjacent woods); or by looking at plants which escape grazing by growing on cliffs.

Hayley Wood (p.62) has been inhabited in recent decades by fallow deer; it is, *de facto*, now a Forest. The deer fluctuate in numbers up to a maximum of 72 head on 120 acres. When numerous they devour the regrowth of any coppiced area that is not fenced. In the uncoppiced wood they produce a characteristic *browse-line* by eating the leaves of trees and bushes up to a sharply-defined height; the passer-by, stooping to below the height of a deer's head, can suddenly see a long way through the undergrowth. Ash, elm, hawthorn, and then hazel are their favourite trees; maple and oak are intermediate; aspen, which tastes horrid, is at the bottom of the menu. An ash-dominated part of the wood has, when deer have been active, been transformed into an aspen-dominated area by a single round of coppicing. The trees would now be very different had Hayley Wood been exposed to deer throughout its history.

Other livestock have different likes and dislikes. The muntjac deer which also live in Hayley prefer hazel to ash, but are less destructive than fallow. In general most livestock like ash, elm, and hazel, which are uncommon in wood-pastures unless efficiently compartmented. Oak, beech, hornbeam, and aspen do relatively well when exposed to browsing, either because they are left uneaten, or because they more readily recover. Oak has a big seed, the reserves in which go into making an enormous tap-root; should the top of an oakling be bitten off, there is material in hand with which to replace it. Oak is also a good colonizer of open ground and takes advantage of temporary lulls in the pressure of grazing. It is an ideal wood-pasture tree; the oaks of old England (like the cypresses of old Crete) are in part the result of millennia of cattle, deer and goats eating their more edible competitors.

Maple and hawthorn flourish under an intermediate degree of browsing, as in compartmented wood-pastures. They are the common trees of those compartmented Forests that are not on acid soils (eg. Hatfield, Rockingham, Wychwood). A survey of Rockingham Forest in 1564–5 shows maple and thorn as by far the commonest underwood species in the coppices.[215]

Many wood-pastures are known to have had more tree species in the past: in particular they have lost hazel and lime. Place-names such as *Lynd*hurst attest the former presence of lime in the New Forest, as do La Tillaie and Les Tilles in the Forêt de Fontainebleau near Paris. Pollen analysis shows that Epping Forest was preceded by a wood largely of lime;[125] not a single tree now survives.

Lime-woods still exist all round the Forest of Dean, but there is no native lime within its boundaries. All four places are, significantly, Forests. Lime, though difficult to kill in any other way, is evidently very sensitive to grazing. It was replaced by oak – in Epping Forest the change is dated to the middle Anglo-Saxon period. Later, for less obvious reasons, part of the oak gave way to beech, which in the Middle Ages was a wood-pasture tree quite rare in woodland.

Herbaceous plants are exposed to grazing even more than are trees and shrubs. In Hayley Wood fallow deer (but not muntjac) are very fond of the leaves and flowers of oxlip, and it has become necessary to fence a large part of the wood to protect this rare plant (Rackham 1976). In Wales and the New Forest sheep, cattle, or horse grazing reduces the varied flora of woodland to a monotonous turf of a few grasses.

The supreme example of cliffs as refuges from grazing is the island of Crete, whose hundreds of goat-proof gorges and soaring cliffs are famous for their rich floras. Cliffs do not have to soar to protect their plant life; a precipice 6 feet high is effective. The ancient woods remaining in the upper valleys of South Wales are largely restricted to oak and beech, but not because of their infertile soils. Within and near the woods are cliffs from whose crevices spring many more trees and other plants, for instance wych-elm, lime, holly, aspen (palatable to sheep), and ivy. Any shoot which hangs within a sheep's reach is instantly devoured. The flora of these woods has been impoverished, not only by the recent disrepair of their boundary walls – which has, in effect, turned them into wooded commons – but also by a longer, though less continuous, history of occasional pasturage and shelter. Similarly at Glendalough (Wicklow, Ireland), with a history of severe grazing, I have seen small cliffs with holly, bramble, and the woodrush *Luzula sylvatica*, all of them eaten by sheep, from which – now that grazing has diminished – the surrounding land is being recolonized.

Wood-pasture commons These have the typical shape of commons and not of woods: a straggling shape with concave outlines, funnelling out where they are crossed by roads (Fig. 6.9). This is the shape of a piece of land which it is no one person's duty to fence: there are normally no woodbanks either around the perimeter or along the roads. Lining the perimeter of the common are *boundary houses* facing the common pasture and backing on to their private fields.

Pollard trees, not on boundaries but scattered in the interior, distinguish wood-pasture commons from woods and also from commons that have only recently become wooded. Examples are Burnham Beeches (Buckinghamshire), Frithsden Beeches (the last remnant of the common-wood called Berkhamsted Frith, Hertfordshire), and Felbrigg Beeches (remains of Aylmerton Common, Norfolk, for some 280 years preserved within Felbrigg Park). There are pollard hollies (for fodder) in the Stiperstones (Shropshire).[186]

The different development of a wood-pasture common and a wood are illustrated by Leigh Woods, west of Bristol (Fig. 6.10). The limestone and sandstone cliffs of the Avon Gorge are the best parallel in England to the gorges of Crete: the area has two species of whitebeam found nowhere else in the world and three other whitebeams peculiar to the British Isles, besides many other rare plants. The woodland of the Gorge and the plateau adjoining to the west is of two kinds. The northern part, in the parish of Abbot's Leigh, is a coppice-wood of native lime (pry) with ash, oak, and hazel. It has many characteristics of ancient woodland, including giant stools (p.102) and typical plants such as

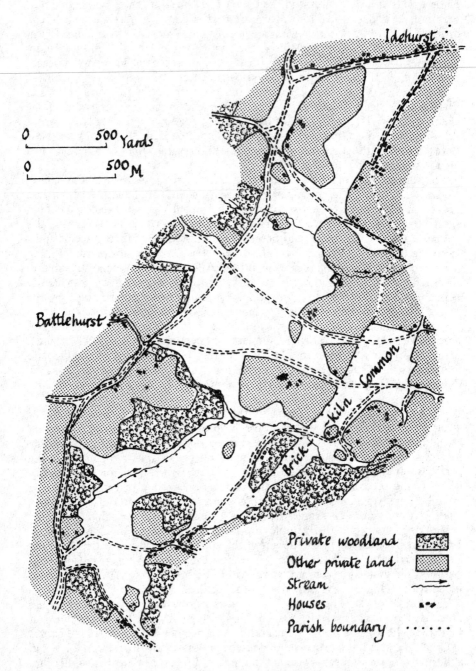

Fig. 6.9. The Mens, Sussex: a wood-pasture common with straggling concave outline, bordered by houses, funnelling into the roads which cross the common, and joining up with another common in the next parish. There are many enclaves of private land including woodland. (Compartment boundaries within the common are omitted.)

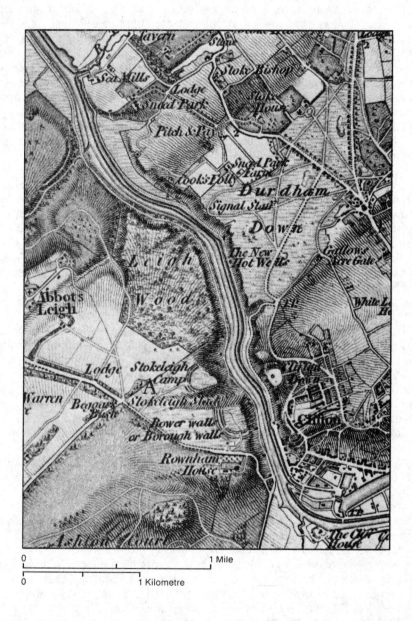

Fig. 6.10. The Avon Gorge and Leigh Woods, Bristol. The line A is a wall marking, approximately, the boundary between Abbot's Leigh and Long Ashton and between 'Leigh Wood' (coppice) and 'Stokeleigh Slade' (wood-pasture). 'Stokeleigh Camp', 'Bower walls', and 'Clifton down' are Iron Age promontory-forts. Durdham Down has the typical shape of a (grassland) common (Chapter 15). Ordnance Survey, 1830 – the Clifton Suspension Bridge does not yet exist.

service-tree, lily-of-the-valley, and lime itself. Although partly destroyed by replanting, it is a good example of the ancient woods of north Somerset.

The southern part of the plateau, around the Iron Age hillfort of Stokeleigh Camp, together with the adjacent lateral gorge of Nightingale Valley, is in Long Ashton parish. The woodland is more complex and has three categories of trees. There are ancient *coppice-stools* of lime here and there on cliff ledges or project-ing outcrops of rock, and other old lime trees on inaccessible cliff faces. On easily-accessible ground there are *pollard* trees of oak (very rarely lime or elm), probably 200 or 400 years old and last pollarded in the mid-nineteenth century. Between the oaks are *unpollarded* trees of ash and wych-elm, none older than the mid-nineteenth century, which now compete with the oaks and have overtopped and killed many of their branches. The boundary between this and the coppice is abrupt.

Records for the Long Ashton part of Leigh Woods go back to *c*. 1260 and for the Abbot's Leigh part to 1331.[216] It appears that the northern plateau has been a normal wood at least as far back as the fourteenth century. The southern plateau was a wooded common, in which the pasturage belonged to commoners and the trees to a private landowner. Both land-uses remained stable into the nineteenth century; the Ordnance Survey of 1817 clearly distinguishes wood-pasture from woodland. Shortly afterwards the grazing rights in Long Ashton were suppressed; there were complaints that the landowner was interfering with public access; and in 1865 the Long Ashton land fell into the hands of devel-opers who built houses on part of it. The remaining part of the former wood-pasture was saved by public protest and eventually given to the National Trust.

The wildwood of north Somerset is likely to have been a mosaic of trees, lime being the commonest. In the coppice-wood of Abbot's Leigh the trees remained roughly in balance, as they do to this day. In Long Ashton, events were different because of grazing rights. Originally the trees were probably coppiced, but the livestock destroyed the lime and other palatable species, except for a few stools surviving out of reach on cliffs and rocks. Such trees as grew up under grazing were oaks, which would not normally be dominant on these limestone soils had not grazing removed their more edible competitors. The owner of the trees abandoned coppicing and took to pollarding instead. (The pollard oaks are of the pedunculate species (*Quercus robur*), which is typical of wood-pastures; the oaks in the coppice are mainly *Q. petraea*, which is not so resistant to browsing.)

When grazing was suppressed in the nineteenth century the wood-pasture reverted to woodland by the growth of young trees. The new wood was not the same as the original wildwood or the coppice-wood, for lime (and *petraea* oak) do not easily return to land made available by the ending of pasturage. Nor were the young trees descendants of the pollards themselves, for oak no longer had grazing to remove competition and encourage it to grow on limestone soils. Instead ash and elm grew up, very palatable trees which, in the absence of livestock, easily form secondary woodland on limestone.

Since 1976 a further chapter in the story has begun with an epidemic of Dutch Elm Disease. Most of the elms have been felled but their roots remain alive. Their places are occupied by elm coppice shoots and saplings of a new genera-tion of ash. Sycamores have begun to invade and may eventually take over the wood.

Parks Ancient parks most often survive as fragments. Place-names such as 'Park Farm', 'Old Park' (close to a New Park), 'Lodge Farm', and 'Park Lane' are significant although not always genuine. At Maryculter near Aberdeen there is a house called 'Templars' Park' – the Knights Templars (who were supposed to be fighting in Palestine, not keeping deer in Scotland) came to a bad end in 1308. A 'Park Wood' may have been either a wood covering the whole area of an ancient park or a wooded compartment within a park. 'Outwood' means a wood excluded from a park.

Of many early parks all that remains is the ghost of the outline, a rectangle with rounded corners, subdivided by later field boundaries. If the park existed before about 1180, the parish boundaries may follow the pale (Figs. 6.2, 6.3). Where the perimeter is intact it is often marked by a bank with an *internal* ditch (Fig. 6.3). A ditch on the inside would come naturally to anyone wanting to fence livestock into a park, but not every medieval park has it: doubtless many were formed out of woods that had already been embanked with external ditches. Actual oaken park pales, in the medieval tradition, can still be seen at Moccas Park, Herefordshire, and Attingham Park, Shropshire (Plate IX). If a park still has woodland it is worth looking for internal woodbanks which may mark a system of compartments (Fig. 6.3).

Sometimes a park still has its original trees. The supreme example is Staverton Park (near Woodbridge, Suffolk) (Plate XII), a famous and awesome place of Tolkienesque wonder and beauty. The mighty and bizarre shapes of oaks of unknown age rise out of a sea of tall bracken, or else are mysteriously surrounded by rings of yet mightier hollies. Some of the birches and rowans, as well as the hollies, are nearly the largest recorded in the kingdom. Over-shadowed giants moulder in the twilit shade or lean half-fallen against other giants. Trees are rooted high in the crotches of other trees.

Staverton is a place of many 'legends' and fancies, and of real mystery; but it is not wildwood, nor a Forest, nor the death-place of the martyred King Edmund. It is a deer-park, well documented back to the 1260s.[217] It has the typical outline (Fig. 6.11), but is not early enough to have displaced the parish boundary. There are some 4,000 great oaks, many of them well over 400 years old; all are pollards last cut in the eighteenth century. There is an unexplained history of pollarding at different heights, involving also the hollies. Much of the 'wildwood' atmosphere of the Park results from the trees having fought each other since woodcutting (and for a time grazing) ceased. Staverton Park may well have been made out of an existing wood – there is one mentioned in Domesday Book – but its history is not simple; it is divided between two parishes, and by careful search I have found several faint banks which appear to result from whatever was there before it became a park.

Staverton is private. Other medieval parks with ancient trees, which are accessible to the public, include Bradgate Park (Leicestershire) and South Weald Park (Essex). The royal park of Henry II at Woodstock, near Oxford, is hidden within the vast eighteenth-century park of Blenheim Palace. Sutton Coldfield Park near Birmingham is a large and well-preserved medieval park of the compartmented type, lacking pollards but divided into coppices (the Seven Hays) and launds.[218]

Parks with ancient trees are just as likely to be pseudo-medieval, but these are no less important. An Ickworth or a Sotterley, or – less obviously – a Wimpole (p.238) gives us a window on to the ordinary countryside of the seventeenth or sixteenth century.

Forests Only the New Forest survives in something like its original form as an institution, with Forest courts and officials (although the Verderers now uphold, not the rights of the Crown, which devolve on the Forestry Commission, but those of the commoners). A shadow of the ancient administration lingers in Dean and Epping. Common-rights are still exercised in these and a few other Forests.

Many historians have written about Forests, but it has occurred to few of them to go and look for Forests on the ground. Fragments of many wooded Forests have escaped the depredations of the last two centuries. Their names often appear on the map, but should not always be trusted: the Ordnance Survey is prone to error on this matter and the Forestry Commission to

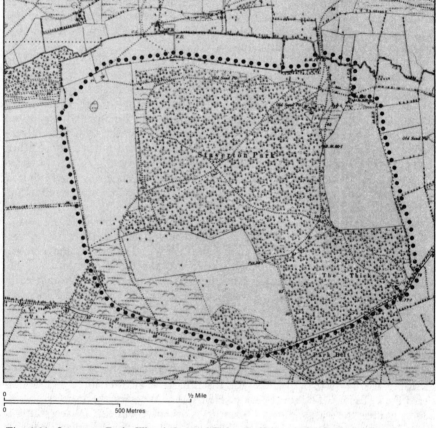

Fig. 6.11. Staverton Park, Wantisden and Eyke, Suffolk: a thirteenth-century deer-park as it appears on the Ordnance Survey of 1881. The original park boundary has been added as a dotted line. Within it are three areas mapped as woodland – 'Staverton Park', 'The Thicks', and Little Staverton (unnamed). They consist mainly of ancient oak pollards; The Thicks is also full of great hollies, rowans, and birches. The park pale also included heaths with only scattered trees, most of which had been ploughed up by 1881.

antiquarian sentiment. Specific features are shown by such place-names as 'Forest Lodge', 'Standing', 'Lawn', or 'Hermitage' (no Forest was complete without a resident hermit).

Wooded Forests cannot easily be preserved in a fragmentary state: even if they are not ruined by tree-planting, the balance between their land-uses is difficult to maintain on a fraction of the area. On paper, a large fragment of Wychwood Forest (Oxfordshire) survives, but most of its historic features have gone. The distinction between Copses and Lights (wooded and grassy compartments) is now invisible, and plantations and sycamore invasion have replaced most of the native woodland. Only the abundance of maple, and the copse boundary-banks snaking through woods and plantations, remind us of the medieval Wychwood.

An even sadder story is that of the Forest of Dean, which has a rich history of pastures, coppices, and outsize timber trees, of deer and wild swine, roadside trenches, and industries going back to the Romans: a history all the more valuable for the lifelong research and learned books of Dr Cyril Hart.[219] Nearly all this heritage has been effaced. Dean is now blanketed with plantations of uniform, poorly-grown oaks whose later replacement, in part, by conifers is hardly to be regretted. The 'greens' or roadside plains have been planted over and the bogs drained. There are still chestnuts in the place called Chestnuts, where there was a famous sweet-chestnut grove in the twelfth century (p.55), but there is nothing to suggest that they are of antiquity; nor do the beeches of medieval Dean appear to have left descendants. This is largely the result of modern forestry: not of the Forestry Commission, though they did destroy the last of the greens and bogs, but of their nineteenth-century predecessors. The foresters of the day, thinking (as foresters do) that they could improve the stock of oaks, exterminated the indigenous oaks and replaced them, all too successfully, with 'superior' *Quercus robur* from outside which has not prospered. Where are the specially large oaks that Henry III sent from Dean for cathedral and castle roofs all over England? Only in one minute patch by the Speech House do mighty oaks and ancient hollies still remind us of what has been lost.

Among the large wooded Forests, Epping Forest still preserves a semblance, though rapidly fading, of its appearance in Plantagenet times (Rackham 1978). It survived almost unchanged from the twelfth to the eighteenth century (Figs. 6.12, 6.13) and still has, in the northern half, a 'common-shaped' outline, a concave straggling shape surrounded by boundary houses and funnelling out into roads: the shapes of Forests are indistinguishable from those of other commons. Epping, anciently Waltham Forest, was uncompartmented, full of pollard trees, and had several hundred acres of heath and grassland. The heath dated from before it was declared a Forest (p.289). As we have seen, the rise of the wood-pasture system was accompanied by changes in the trees. By the Middle Ages the Forest appears to have had beech on the upper slopes, hornbeam on the lower ground, and a narrow zone of oak between; there were also hollies, crab-trees, services, and so on. Beech, oak, and hornbeam were pollarded. The Forest had many landowners and several hundred commoners. The king had the deer and the fines in the Forest courts; the commoners had the grazing and cut many of the pollards; the landowners had the rest of the woodcutting and any timber. The area of the Forest, the balance between trees, grass, and heath, and the composition of the trees were remarkably stable for at least 700 years.

Fig. 6.12. 'Waltham' and 'Henhault', ie. Epping and Hainault, Forests as surveyed in 1772–4 by Chapman and André. Woodland is carefully distinguished from wood-pasture even where a wood adjoins a Forest. The Forests, like all commons (Figs. 6.8, 6.9, 6.10, 13.5, 15.2), had straggling concave perimeters with boundary-houses and road-funnels. These Forests were not compartmented into coppices; the treeless plains had no formal boundaries. Some of the roads are shown as bordered by *trenches*, narrow clearings made in the Middle Ages to protect travellers from highwaymen (Chapter 12). Epping Forest, except in the south, is almost unchanged in outline today, but only fragments of Hainault survive.

Fig.6.13. A detail of Epping Forest from the Ordnance Survey of 1871. What is mapped as woodland was mostly ancient wood-pasture, merging gradually with the heaths and bogs of which much then remained. Some of the heaths had existed since Anglo-Saxon times. The ancient road ABC was still bordered by its anti-highwayman clearings. (The other main roads are nineteenth century, and their clearings merely resulted from embankments and cuttings.) Parish boundaries are defined by 'B[oundary] M[arks] on Pollards'. The boggy pool D contains pollen from the limewood that stood on the site of the Forest until the Anglo-Saxon period.

In the nineteenth century the landowners tried to take over and destroy the Forest. This usurpation was resisted, more strenuously after the loss of Hainault Forest, by the commoners and by those who valued Epping as an open space. In 1878 the landowning rights were transferred to the City of London by the Epping Forest Act. The Act is admirably specific: it requires the Conservators of the Forest to 'protect the timber and other trees, pollards, shrubs, under-wood, heather, gorse, turf, and herbage growing on the Forest'. Had the Act been read, all would have been well. Unfortunately the early Conservators pursued their duty of protecting timber trees with more enthusiasm than their equal duty of protecting the other, more historic and more precarious, features of the Forest. They took a dislike to pollards, thought to be 'the maimed relics of neglect', and promptly terminated the woodcutting rights. They disapproved of hornbeams and bogs, did nothing to prevent trees from overrunning the heather and gorse, and demolished the medieval New Lodge to save the cost of repair. They thought they were promoting the 'natural aspect of the Forest', which we now know to be an illusion, for its natural aspect was a lime-wood which cannot be recreated. The changes incurred controversy, but neither the early Conservators nor their opponents seem to have read the Epping Forest Act; both sides supposed that the management of the Forest was a matter of taste, not law.

A hundred years on, much has been lost. There are still many thousands of pollards, but they are overgrown and cast a shade beneath which nothing will grow. Primroses and polypody have disappeared, crab-trees and services are rare, and even hornbeams and oaks have declined; only holly and birch have prospered. The roadside trenches (Fig. 6.13) and most of the plains are over-grown, and heather is reduced to a fraction of an acre. Although the present Conservators are much more appreciative of the Forest as an antiquity, the decline is now far advanced.[610] In 1878 Epping Forest was a complex and balanced system, every acre the product of centuries of peculiar land-uses, and a thing of distinction and beauty; with its combination of pollards and heather, there was probably nothing quite like it in the world. Now it is well on the way to becoming just another Chiltern-type beech-wood.

The best-preserved of all Forests is Hatfield, Essex (Fig. 6.8). There are still deer, cattle, coppice-woods, seven species of pollards, scrub, timber trees, grassland, fen, and a seventeenth-century lodge and rabbit warren. It is a unique survival in England and possibly in the world: here alone (and in the twin Forest of Writtle, which has lost its plains but still has a hermitage site) one can step back into the Middle Ages to see what a Forest looked like in use. The Crown gave up the landowning and trees in 1241 and the deer in 1446. The Forest had a chequered history in private hands – conflicts between owners and commoners were sometimes settled with sword and pistol – but its physical history has been remarkably stable. It even survived an Enclosure Act in 1851, though with the loss of its original common-shaped boundary. It was preserved as a deer-park by the sympathetic Houblon family, and in 1924 was given to the National Trust.

Hatfield is a small Forest, which is why it survives. It preserves the complex-ity that Wychwood and other compartmented Forests used to have on a larger scale. There were anciently seventeen coppices (now reduced to twelve) around a central plain. These are normal woods, with banks round them; they were supposed to be felled on an 18-year cycle and fenced to protect the regrowth against livestock for the first nine years. The plains, open to grazing at all times, have great oaks, maples, and other pollards; even some of the ancient hawthorns are pollarded. New generations of trees in the plains arise in the protection of tracts of thorny scrub. This Forest, like Epping, Wychwood, and others, was not just formed out of wildwood, for it contains the Portingbury Rings, a supposedly Iron Age set of earthen enclosures.

The recent history of Hatfield Forest is happier than that of Epping. It bears some witness to the nineteenth-century love of horsechestnuts and Austrian pines, and to the twentieth-century love of bulldozers and plantations, but all its essentials survive. Recently the National Trust has revived the coppicing on a large scale and has even cut many of the pollards.

Ancient Wood-pasture Trees

Old trees, though uncommon, are a speciality of England. Europe is a continent of young or youngish trees, like a human population with compulsory euthanasia at age thirty; one can go from Boulogne to Athens without seeing a tree more than 200 years old. Old trees are almost as rare in the United States.

Oaks, limes, and other trees live to at least three times the age, about 150 years, at which they are customarily felled as being 'mature'. If pollarded they live longer still, as do ashes, beeches, and other ordinarily less long-lived trees. Such ancient trees, other than coppice stools, are rare in woods (and have been rare for centuries) and uncommon in hedges; but there are still many in parks, Forests, and a few commons. There are also the ancient planted trees of early avenues and landscape parks, such as the seventeenth-century limes of Hampton Court and of Kentwell (Long Melford, Suffolk).

At least since Shakespeare, the English have loved the beauty and mystery of ancient trees. We have written books and recited verses in their honour; have painted and engraved their portraits;[611] have invested them with railings and plaques and supported them with props and iron fixtures; and have preserved them to give dignity to new parks. Most of our best-loved old trees are in villages and farmland, and more is said of them in Chapter 10. Those of parks and Forests include Shakespeare's Herne's Oak, the Major Oak still extant in Sherwood Forest, and the trees of Windsor Forest which were the subject of magnificent early photographs.[220]

Ancient wood-pasture trees should also be appreciated for the creatures that live on them. In wildwood, presumably, trees in the second half of their life-spans were nearly as common as those in the first half. Old trees, especially pollards, are the home of innumerable special plants and animals: hole-nesting birds and the bats that roost in their hollow interiors; the peculiar lichens of old dry bark and overhangs; and a host of beetles, spiders, and other invertebrates.[221] Much of the well-known value of oak as a home for wildlife depends on *old* oaks.

Every landscape of old trees has its own *genius loci*. In Birkland, the last remaining wooded part of Sherwood Forest, there are several hundred late-medieval oaks, of each its 'high top bald with drie antiquitie'[222] having died back in some forgotten catastrophe. Their curved and sharp-pointed dead limbs form a glamorous and bizarre skyline typical of this area at least since the eighteenth century.[611] Different are the spreading gnarled pollards of Windsor Forest, some of which were calculated to be 800 years old in 1864[220] and have

151

changed little since. Different again are the massive trunks and small crowns of the ancient oaks of Staverton; and the 'grey, gnarled, low-browed, knock-kneed, bowed, bent, huge, strange, long-armed, deformed, hunchbacked, mis-shapen oak men' of Moccas Park (as they were described by Francis Kilvert in 1876).[223] All four places are famous for their insects or lichens or both. In the New Forest, although the old oaks and beeches are seldom of exceptional size, they are very many and are the successors of generations of previous ancient trees; its relative freedom from rain pollution makes the Forest the supreme place in Europe for the special lichens of old trees.[224]

England has been given the special duty of preserving old trees. Natural death is seldom the most urgent threat: most of those named have changed little for at least a hundred years. Sometimes they need protection, as do the oaks of Epping Forest, from being overtopped and shaded by younger trees. More often they are threatened by misunderstanding: people regard trees anthropomorphically as 'senile' or 'dying of old age', as if they had a fixed life-span, and do not realize that hollow trunks and dead boughs are a normal part of a tree's development. Changes of ownership are bad for old trees: new owners too often think in terms of replacement rather than conservation. Ancient wood-pastures sometimes appear to lack a new generation of trees, but remedies should not be attempted without a slow and careful study of what is happening to the old trees and how fast. Ten thousand oaks of 100 years old are not a substitute for one 500-year-old oak.

CHAPTER 7

Plantations

> In the eastern part of Cranemor [in Eye], from arable land he planted a wood, and it is called Childholm. At Witheringtone [Werrington] he planted a wood where a wood had never been before, and surrounded it with a willow ditch.
>
> *Walter de Whittlesey's biography of Abbot Godfrey of Peterborough*[225]
> (The dates are 1304 and 1311; the places are on the Fen edge near Peterborough)

It is not in the nature of tree plantations to become material for historical research. Either a plantation is felled on reaching commercial maturity, and replaced by a new plantation or some other crop; or it is neglected, is invaded by native trees, and joins the history of secondary woodland. Only a few kinds of plantation can have an indefinite existence; for instance the sweet-chestnut coppices – those that are not quasi-natural woodland – of south-east England.*

Modern plantations of conifers, having no relation to woodland, can be traced back to the time of Evelyn. But there is an earlier practice of sowing acorns and other seeds to make an imitation of woodland, apparently meant to be permanent. Felbrigg Great 'Wood', Norfolk, is largely the accumulated plantations of the Windham family from 1676 onwards.[226] It includes chestnut underwood; many of the stools, up to 7 feet across, are likely to be original. Even from the nineteenth century I have found plantations with underwood as well as timber trees. They are recognizable by the small stools and inappropriate species, eg. pure hazel at Ickworth (Suffolk), or hornbeam in areas where it is not native. Censuses, such as the *New Statistical Account* of Scotland in 1845, distinguish between 'plantations' and 'natural woods'.[44]

Before the seventeenth century plantations were rare and small. A famous, but not now certainly identifiable, example is that of oaks in Windsor Great Park, attributed to Lord Burghley in 1580.[220]

There are a few medieval examples. A 'planting' in West Carr, Gressenhall (Norfolk) apparently dated from c.1490.[227] I am indebted to Dr John Harvey for drawing my attention to the plantations of Abbot Godfrey, and the similar acts at the same time by Abbot John de Rutherwyk at Chertsey (Surrey).[228] These few instances are the product of much searching, and are much outnumbered by records of planting trees in hedges and other non-woodland sites. Planting a wood was a rarity, to be recorded among the memorable deeds of a great abbot.

---

* Osiers – willows coppiced at one year's growth to make baskets – may be an ancient cultivated crop. They may either be of low-growing species (*Salix viminalis* and *S. purpurea*) or of tree willows grown as osiers. Some riverside willow-woods have grown out of neglected osier plantations.

Such a plantation may have come down to us. Soane or Bullock Wood, Colchester (now 60 acres) is a fragment of a much larger wood documented back to 1312, when it belonged to the Abbey of St John. There is some evidence that around 1242 the site had been enclosed and sown with trees by the monks. The argument rests partly on a dispute over common-rights, but chiefly on the name, Sowenewode (Latin *boscus seminatus*). Other explanations are possible – something other than trees might have been sown in or near the wood, or the derivation might be false – but a plantation is perhaps the most likely interpretation.[229]

Soane Wood is not immediately recognizable as a plantation. Its boundary banks are straight, but are mainly not original. It has several different types of woodland, including chestnut and oak coppice. Some of the chestnut stools are 7 feet across. The most persuasive field evidence is in the flora, which is specially poor in plants typical of ancient woodland. After 750 years Soane Wood still lacks lime, lily-of-the-valley, and many other species which grow in the other Colchester woods.

CHAPTER 8

Fields

And this field wherein now we are, may be an instance: for you see by the ancient ridges or lands, though now ouergrowne with bushes, it hath beene arable land, and now become fit for no vse, unlesse it be reformed.

I. N[orden], *The Svrveiors dialogue, 1610*

Scholars have studied fields for a century, beginning with F. Seebohm[230] and F.W. Maitland.[2] Shelves of books have been written on land tenure, cultivation, and the theory and philosophy of fields, but less often on actual remains. Even so, the wealth of material defies abridgement: a book larger than this has been published on regional variations alone (Baker and Butlin 1973). Within one chapter I can do no more than exemplify some kinds of field-system and some of the questions which they raise. For a fuller treatment I refer the reader to C.C. Taylor's books (1974, 1975).

Fields are known largely from their boundaries; in Welsh the word *cae* does duty for both 'hedge' and field'. In this chapter I deal with the shapes of fields and the earthworks which they generate.

Fields are subject to fashion; but until recently changing them has involved hard work and often trouble with neighbours and the law. Each successive age has updated some of its predecessors' fields, has left others as it found them, and has made new fields where there were not fields before. Just as we have examples still lived in of fashions in houses since the Norman Conquest, so there are examples in use of nearly all field-systems since the Bronze Age. More can be learnt from fields now disused, but let us remember that their being disused may mean that they were not typical of their age.

Enclosed Fields

Fields demarcated by hedges, walls, ditches, or banks have been typical of the British landscape since civilization began. Books have been written on prehistoric field-systems (Bowen and Fowler 1978). Aerial photographs all over the country display networks and tangles of old field boundaries now visible only as crop- and soil-marks; for instance south of Great Yarmouth the present hedges overlie two earlier sets of field boundaries, all three unrelated to each other.[231] As I know from excavation, not all the ancient ditches which exist have yet been detected from the air. Prehistoric fields which still form part of the above-ground landscape are only a small fraction of those that have existed.

I classify field-systems as *regular* (set out in straight lines according to a preconceived geometry), *semi-regular* (in which the geometry is more complex or less exactly followed), and *irregular* (with no attempt at geometry). Some field

155

systems are *mindless* – they carry on regardless of terrain; others take advantage of streams, slopes, and earlier boundaries. For example, thousands of miles of the American Mid-West are regular and mindless, a grid of straight roads and hedges exactly one mile apart, marching regardless over canyons and rivers.

Reaves and the like All over southern Dartmoor, between 1000 and 1400 feet altitude, the moors are dissected by a pattern of low stony banks called *reaves*.[232] (They are best seen by looking north from Combestone Tor on the road between Holne and Hexworthy.) Reaves are semi-regular and mindless. They consist of parallel main axes, which may run across country for miles, typically about 100 yards apart. The spaces between these main reaves are divided by cross-reaves at irregular intervals (Fig. 8.1). Main reaves have a general sense of direction, but wobble and wander unpredictably; these wobbles are not accidental, for they are accurately repeated in all the reaves of a parallel bundle. The reaves that reach the formidable valley of the Dart peter out towards the wooded lower slopes and reappear on the same alignment on the other side.

Reaves tell a story of country planning on a gigantic scale: of an organization able to parcel out tens of square miles as it pleased, and which set its rules of geometry above the practicalities of dealing with gorges and bogs. England has known nothing like this in the last 1500 years; for a modern parallel we have to go to the land-allotments of Minnesota or Michigan. Reaves are largely ignored by the present, chiefly medieval, land divisions; but an occasional reave still does duty as a parish or intake boundary.

Reaves have been dated chiefly by the enclosures and ruined buildings attached to them. They were in full use in the Bronze Age as the boundaries of arable and pasture fields (see p.308). Even high on Dartmoor, land was already fully used and parcelled out by rules whose purpose we can only conjecture. Presumably reaves extended to lower altitudes but have there been effaced by millennia of later fields.

Many years ago I was mystified by the landscape of The Saints, north-east Suffolk: an area of about 25 square miles divided into little fields by cross-hedges between bundles of parallel, not quite straight, main axes (Fig. 8.2). There is no history of woodland or open-field; the medieval greens and meadows intrude into the semi-regularity. Stone Street, a 'Roman' road, has been insinuated along one of the main axes. This is an exact reproduction, in hedges, of the Dartmoor reaves. The inference that this is a Bronze Age field-system still in use is not so unlikely as it once seemed. Remains of reave-type systems have recently been found in many parts of Lowland England, including Nottinghamshire and Berkshire.[233]*

Reaves were not invented in the Bronze Age. In Ireland the cutting-away of bogs reveals sets of field-walls that date from before the bog grew. Sets of walls with reave geometry in County Mayo have been dated to the Neolithic.[234]

Fig. 8.1. A small part of the Bronze Age reaves of Dartmoor. Prehistoric earthworks and associated cairns and hut-circles are shown in bold lines; thin lines indicate later (presumed medieval) field walls. The reaves, when jumping the gorge of the River Dart, come to a definite end considerably above the present (undemarcated and slowly advancing) edge of the woodland. After Gawne and Cox[232] by kind permission, and with extra details, from Mrs E. Gawne.

* I have found a reave-like hedge-system in Greece.[4]

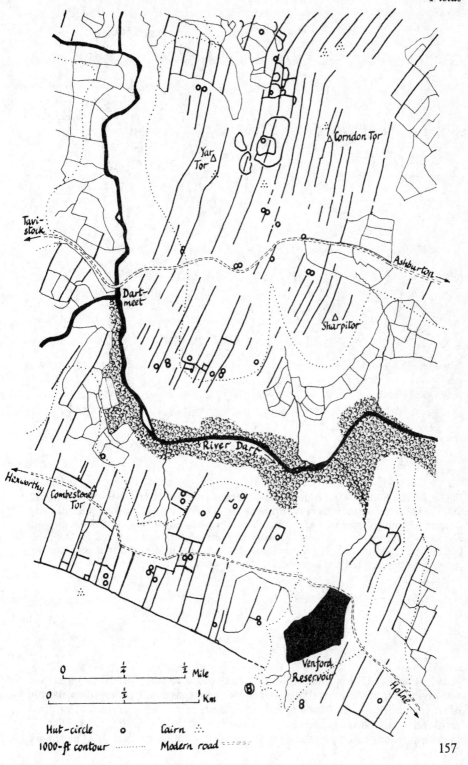

△ Corndon Tor

Yar
Tor △

Tavi-
stock ←

Ashburton →

Dart-
meet

△
Sharpitor

River Dart

Hexworthy ←
Combestone
Tor △

Venford
Reservoir

H pine →

| 0 | ¼ | ½ Mile |
| 0 | ½ | 1 Km |

Ⓑ

8

Hut-circle   o   Cairn   ∴
1000-ft contour ⋯⋯   Modern road ‐‐‐‐‐

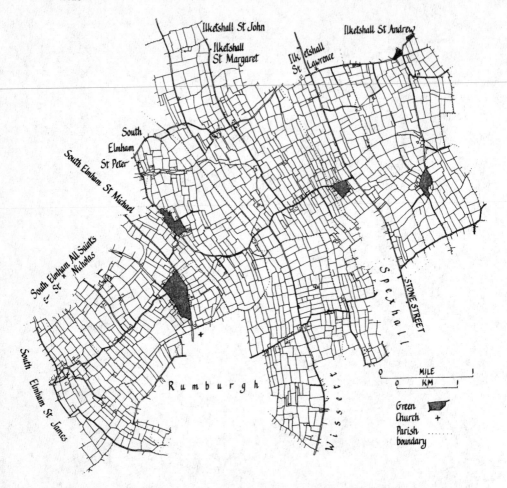

Fig. 8.2. 'The Saints' – the eight South Elmhams and four Ilketshalls – near Bungay, Suffolk. The semi-regular geometry resembles the Bronze Age reaves of Dartmoor. Despite millennia of use and alterations, the framework of sinuous, parallel main axes and irregular cross-hedges was still discernible until recent years (this map is from the Ordnance Survey of 1882–3). Inserted into it is the usual medieval furniture of greens, parish boundaries, scattered farmsteads, churches, and at least 23 moats.

'Celtic Fields' This is the traditional name for the small, squarish, irregular or semi-regular fields whose remains, until modern destruction, covered thousands of square miles on chalk downland, moorland, and other terrain that escaped medieval cultivation (Taylor 1975). Although often of less than an acre, they may be surrounded by great banks, the product of immense labour. The square

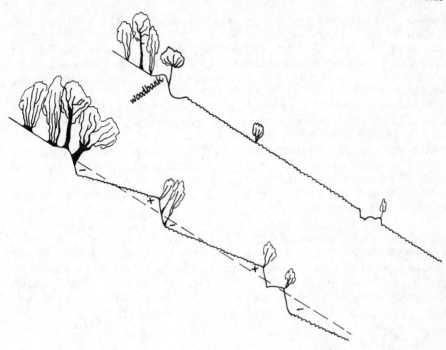

Fig. 8.3. 'Before' and 'after' sketches showing how soil creep in ploughland forms positive lynchets (+) and negative lynchets (−) at field boundaries and the edges of roads and woods. On most British soils some hundreds of years would separate the two sketches.

shape expresses the custom of ploughing in two directions at right angles. Some Celtic Fields seem to be fitted into what had originally been reave systems.

On slopes the action of the plough tends to move earth downhill and to pile it against the lower field boundary to form a terrace called a *lynchet* (Fig. 8.3). The steeper Celtic Fields tend to be narrow and to follow the contours to form the flights of terraces marked as 'Strip Lynchets' on maps. Lynchets, positive or negative,[235] can occur against any ancient cross-slope ploughing boundary, including roads and woodbanks; they are not necessarily prehistoric.*

Celtic Fields and strip-lynchets can be dated from the pottery in their banks (the remains of ploughmen's lunches) and their relation to barrows. Most of them are earlier than the Celtic (that is, Iron Age) period. Some appear to be of Neolithic origin; they were in use throughout the Bronze Age.

Iron Age and Roman fields In Italy, Yugoslavia, and North Africa the Romans indulged in *centuriation*, the planning of land in exact squares of 775 modern yards, oriented exactly north and south (occasionally at 45°), marching mindlessly across mountain and gorge. Centuriation has been claimed in various places in southern England, but the claims are disputed and therefore in my

---

* Prehistoric lynchets can be confused with, if not re-used as, the terraces of medieval strip-cultivation on slopes.

Fields

opinion mistaken: real centuriation is unmistakable.[236] The Romans found Britain already parcelled into ownerships; there was little room for creating a new landscape. They did have an opportunity in the Fens, which had become cultivable through rising land-level; but the 'Celtic Fields' of Roman date whose remains, in the form of soil-marks, are widespread in the Fens show no planning whatever.

But there is plenty of semi-regular field layout. South-east Essex (about a quarter of the entire county) is covered with an unmistakably planned grid of roads and hedges (Plate XIII). Much of this still survives; there was more in the nineteenth century; and yet more has been discovered by air photography. The axes are not perfectly straight; some of their sinuosities are original, others the effect of centuries of use and accident. They differ from reaves in that the north-south and east-west axes are equally strong; nor is a wobble in one axis repeated in its neighbours.

These miles of grid represent planning on an even larger scale than reaves, and are wholly at variance with the chaotic land-use history of south Essex. Nobody for at least a thousand years has been in a position to organize the landscape on this immense scale. (South Essex has no history of open-field; the grid usually avoids woodland.) Mr Paul Drury has neatly proved that parts of the system are Roman or earlier by showing that they are cut across by Roman

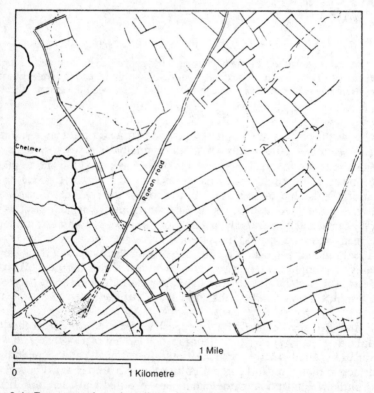

0 — 1 Mile
0 — 1 Kilometre

Fig. 8.4. Roman road cutting diagonally across an earlier semi-regular field system. Little Waltham, Essex. Mapped by P.J. Drury[620] and reproduced by permission of Chelmsford Archaeological Trust.

160

roads (eg. around Braintree) as well as by railways and motorways (Fig. 8.4). Several variants are recognized, some attributed to the Iron Age, others to early Roman times.[130] The modern development of south Essex – the roads (p.262), the plotland towns (now largely turned into secondary woodland) around Basildon and Thundersley, the suburbs of Southend – has all been inserted into a grid laid out nearly 2000 years ago.

As we shall see, surviving fragments indicate that semi-regular field-systems may have been widespread in England by the Roman period.

Anglo-Saxon and medieval fields As will be shown, the tradition of enclosed fields persisted until well into the Anglo-Saxon period. In what is now Planned Countryside, much of the enclosed landscape was effaced when medieval open-fields developed. In Ancient Countryside the tradition of enclosed fields still goes on. Such fields, where still in use, can often be shown from early maps and surveys to go back with minor alterations to the late Middle Ages (cf Figs. 2.2b, 9.2). When they originated can rarely be ascertained. We have so far recognized prehistoric fields by their semi-regularity. But many, perhaps most, prehistoric fields were irregular. If they still remain in use, we cannot normally tell them apart from fields made by the Anglo-Saxons or medievals. With few exceptions, it is not until after the Middle Ages that straight lines were devised to give an air of modernity to new boundaries.

The later study of fields becomes largely that of hedges and is dealt with under that head. The study and classification, and attempts at dating, of field-systems are perhaps best developed in Ireland (Bowen and Fowler 1978). Here I mention the Lizard and Land's End[237] Peninsulas, which are museums of field-systems of different dates, still distinguishable as those of more prosperous parts of the Ancient Countryside often are not.

The oldest datable are the small irregular fields, with their mighty Bronze Age stone banks, still partly in use, in the north-western Land's End (p.183). South of St Keverne church-town on the Lizard, on rather easier terrain, is a reave-like system of semi-regular fields and lanes, possibly of similar antiquity (Fig. 8.5a). Many prehistoric boundaries cross the present moors of both peninsulas (p.323).

The pattern of farms and hamlets in the Lizard (Fig. 14.1), and probably Land's End, was largely complete by the fourteenth century.[238] Many field systems are irregular and undatable, but some definite types can be recognized (Figs. 8.5b, c, d). There are the spiral farms, with successively larger fields taken in from the moor like the chambered shell of a nautilus. These suggest increasing prosperity, probably in the early Middle Ages; one of them, Kestlemerris on the Lizard, is mentioned in a charter of 967[239] but was not yet a farm. There are examples of *infield* and *outfield*, such as the thousand-acre estate of Erisey (Lizard): Erisey hamlet and its daughters Trenoon (=Hamlet-on-Moor) and Trewithno each have their small, highly-cultivated fields surrounded by the moorland of the whole manor, the whole separated by a great outer wall from the common moor. The parish of Mullion once had a small extent of strip-cultivation.

When straight lines were introduced there were still a few places where little farms could be made on cultivable patches in the midst of the moors (Fig. 14.2). These can hardly be later than the sixteenth century: they have names in the extinct Cornish language (eg. Croft Noweth, New Croft); they are early enough

Fields

(a) Moorland ....

Parish boundary ....

0 .... ½ Mile

0 .... 1 Km

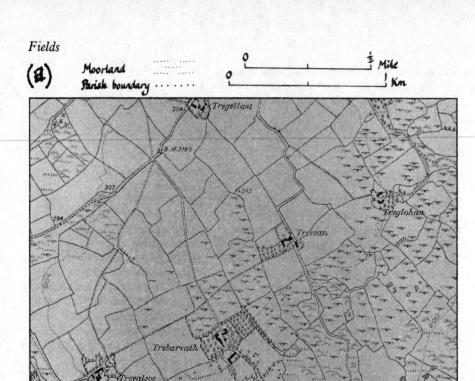

Fig. 8.5. Field systems on the Lizard Peninsula.
(a) Reave-like fields in St Keverne, from the Ordnance Survey of 1877.
(b) The complex system of Erisey in Ruan Major, with its outer perimeter and funnels (F) leading on to the moorland. Half the farm of Trenoon is in a detached part of Grade parish; it is surprisingly common for medieval farmsteads to straddle parish boundaries.
(c) Spiral and egg-shaped farms: Trewillis, Kestlemerris, and Little Kistles in St Keverne.
(d) The Age of Straight Lines: Grochall (? sixteenth-century), St Elena (despite its name, known to be earlier than the exile of Bonaparte in 1815).

162

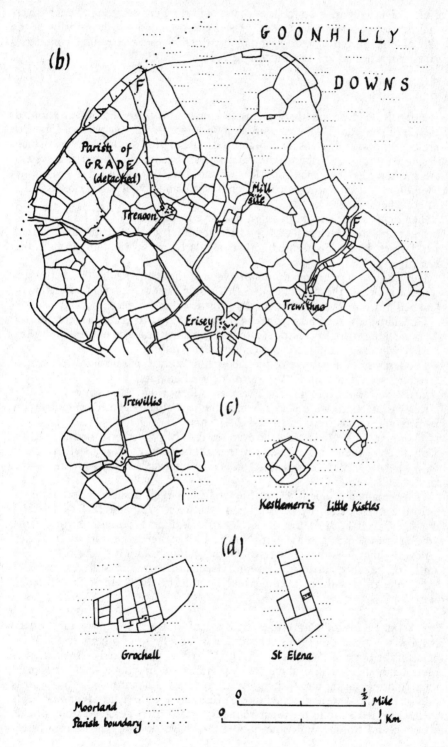

(b)

GOONHILLY

DOWNS

F

Parish of
GRADE
(detached)

Mill
site

Trenoon

F

F

Trewithno

Erisey

Trewillis

(c)

F

Kestlemerris   Little Kistles

(d)

Grochall

St Elena

Moorland ....
Parish boundary ......

0 _____ ½ Mile
0 _____ Km

to have diverted parish boundaries that would have crossed them, which diversions appear on a map of *c*.1690.[240] Later encroachments still, probably of the early nineteenth century, on to the moors themselves have straight boundaries walled not with stone but with turf (p.203).

Open-Fields

After the Roman period there seems to come a break in the organization of fields. By Domesday Book, as we used to be taught, the arable parts of England were covered with immensely complex systems of cultivation in strips, which were to last until the Parliamentary Enclosures. I shall describe one such system in its medieval heyday, shall consider how far open-field extended in geography and in time, and shall speculate on when it began and how it was related to what had gone before.

Open-field, *alias* strip-cultivation, had seven cardinal features:
1. The arable of a township was divided into a multitude of strips, the strips of each farmer being distributed either regularly or at random around the township.
2. The strips were aggregated into *furlongs* and these into *fields*. The same crop was grown by all the farmers on each furlong. Each field was left fallow – ploughed but not sown – every second, third, or fourth year.
3. The animals of the participants were turned loose, to graze the stubble and weeds of all the strips in common, after every harvest and also in the fallow year. (This economized on pasture and conserved fertility.)
4. The farmers shared some of the labours of cultivating one another's strips.
5. Hedges were few and did not form enclosed circuits.
6. Strips were ploughed in such a way as to form ridge-and-furrow.
7. Regular meetings were held at which the participants agreed on cultivation practices and regulations, and fined dissidents.

In not many open-fields can all seven features be proved. Historians of fields spend much of their time arguing whether all the features arose together, and if not in what order. The term *common arable* is often used for field-systems having features 2, 3, and 7.

What remained of open-field in England was largely abolished by a series of Enclosure Acts, parish by parish, mainly between 1720 and 1840. There is a famous survival both of the physical fabric and (in a reduced form) of the working arrangements at Laxton (Notts). Cultivation strips survive in Haxey (Lincs), Soham (Cambs), Portland (Dorset), and Braunton (Devon). On the Continent, notably Austria and south Germany, there are still vast areas of strips, though usually in a straightened-out form and lacking the cropping rotations.

The West Fields of Cambridge In the mid-fourteenth century my College compiled a Terrier describing its own lands, and those of others, in the West Fields of the town of Cambridge.[241] The West Fields consisted of 1480 acres of arable land, divided into about 3350 *selions*, each nominally half an acre in extent and measuring one furlong by two perches (220 yards long by 11 yards wide). The selions were grouped into 68 furlongs and these into four vast fields which extended away to the town boundary, where they adjoined similar fields in Girton and Coton. Cultivation appears to have been organized in a three-course rotation. Each year an approximate third of the land – one field or the two smaller fields – lay fallow and the remainder was sown.

Corpus Christi College, and dozens of other landowners, had lands scattered in *strips*, not quite at random, throughout the West Fields. A strip might be a single selion, or two or three, or occasionally a block of up to forty selions. One-tenth of the crop on each strip was due as tithe to the tithe-owner of one of the dozen ecclesiastical parishes into which Cambridge was divided; tithe-ownerships were scattered through the West Fields almost independently of landownerships. Few owners tilled their strips themselves; between landowners and the land there intervened yet another, largely unrecorded, world of agents, tenants, and subtenants. We know little of how selions were grouped by those who actually cultivated them.

In practice the topography was not so simple. Selions varied from ¼ to ¾ acre. A furlong (Latin *quarentena*) might comprise a dozen strips or more than 150, some of them in blocks at right angles to the others. There were triangular bits of land called *gores* and *butts*, divided into short or tapering selions (Fig. 8.6).

Between and sometimes through the furlongs there ran roads and paths. About one boundary in four between selions was marked by a *baulk*, a narrow uncultivated strip. Baulks were permanent and were carefully noted in the Terrier. They were scattered at random between selions and were not related to ownership or tithe-ownership. As well as these minor baulks, there were occasional major baulks running through furlongs for a mile or so. Baulks were strips of long grass; a few of those in the Cambridge open-fields (and more in nearby Grantchester, p.199) developed into hedges or rows of trees.

The spot on which I now sit and write these words was in the first selion in the west part of furlong no. 7 in Carm Field, described thus:

Furlong abutting at its south end on Cotenpath

.   .   .   .

1 selion of the said Hospital immediately next to the said Custisbalke, and it is longer than the other aforesaid selions at its north end

3 rods Rad[egund]

This was a big selion of ¾ acre; it belonged to the Hospital of St John, predecessor of St John's College, and paid tithe to the nuns of St Radegund as appropriators of St Giles's or St Clement's parishes. Out of my window I can see a slight holloway where Coton Path used to run; in the shrubbery at right angles a weak bank marks the course of the major baulk called Cust's. The next minor baulk was two selions away.

The system had grown up when men ploughed with oxen, although horses were commoner at the time of the Terrier. The selions had the curving shapes characteristic of ox-ploughing, which we shall discuss later. There was always provision for turning a long and awkward team of oxen at the end of the selion. Roads and paths provided turning-space as well as access. Where this was lacking, some furlongs had *headlands* at their ends for turning the plough; these were often shared with the next furlong where its selions ran in the same direction.

Many selions could be reached only across somebody else's land, and on some it was necessary to trespass in order to turn the plough. Where two furlongs adjoined end-to-side, the owners of selions in one furlong were sometimes entitled to use the first selion in the next for turning; such a selion was called in Latin a *forera*. These rights of access were part of the reason for the communal cropping arrangements. The turning of ploughs prevented hedges from growing on headlands and some baulks.

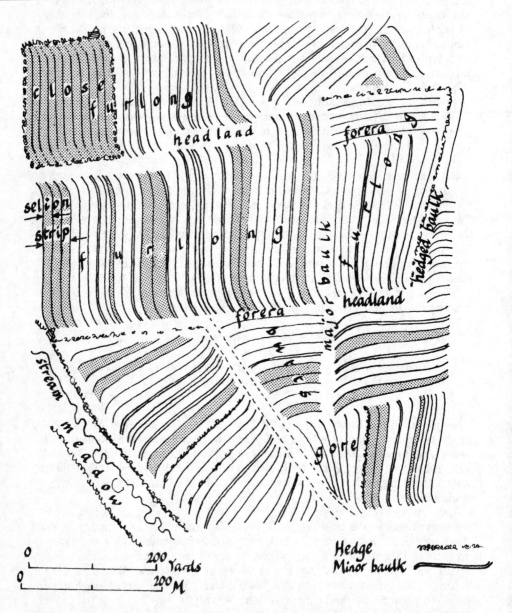

Fig. 8.6. Small part of an imaginary but typical open-field, illustrating the technical terms. The lands of one individual participant are shaded.

Cambridge West Fields were evidently the ramshackle growth of centuries. Some of the gores and long or short selions were dictated by the lie of the land or by watercourses or Roman roads, but others seem to be mindless. Arrangements for access were erratic: Endlesse Weye was a road leading from nowhere to nowhere. Only in Carm Field do Cust's Baulk, Coton Path, and other semi-regularities suggest the remains of a pre-open-field planned landscape. There are signs that the system had reached its full development not long before the Terrier. It then remained without major change for nearly 500 years, until abolished by Enclosure Act in 1802.

The West Fields, although not typical in all respects, exemplify what seems to us the rococo complexity of a classic Midland open-field system. The simplest, but not very usual, form was when one village, one parish, and one manor coincided to form one estate (eg. Little Gransden, Cambridgeshire). Among the few thousand selions, the lord of the manor's own strips would be intermingled with those of the villagers. Cambridge was a town; it had two other independent field-systems besides the West Fields; and it contrived to function without having a lord of the manor. Its tithe complexity was unusual. In many villages there was instead the complication of two or more – occasionally a dozen – manors intermingled with each other, in which the same villager might hold strips of more than one lord. Cambridge was unusual also in that as much as nine-tenths of the available land was open-field. Nearly all open-field townships had more pasture than Cambridge, and most had more private arable; some had woodland.

Open-fields varied. Often, as at Hinderclay (Suffolk),[242] furlongs were grouped into *precincts* and these into fields. There were many names for different kinds of headlands and paths. 'Headland' is sometimes called *haveden* and may appear on the modern map as 'haven'. Baulks were not always present – indeed C.S. and C.S. Orwin, scholars of open-field, denied the existence of minor baulks[243] – but separated *all* the selions in, for instance, Ashmore (Dorset).[244]

We know little of how an elaborate open-field system worked in practice. Survivals, though valuable, are incomplete or atypically simple. For example, how did people identify their strips? It is all very well to assert that peasants know their own land, but many landholders were not peasants. No doubt it was for this purpose that the Cambridge terriers were compiled; did everywhere have such a field-book? I cannot say how the lord of one manor arranged for somebody to find and cultivate the odd strip or two which he might possess in another manor. Why were manorial courts not overwhelmed with disputed identifications?

Ridge-and-furrow In midland and northern England there are, even now, great areas of what has long been pasture which shows wave-like undulations, every 11 yards or so. For centuries it has been appreciated that these result from ancient ploughing practices (p.155). The medieval word *selion* itself, derived from the French for a furrow (Modern French *sillon*), implies a connection between ridge-and-furrow and strip-cultivation.

Ridge-and-furrow comes naturally from driving an asymmetrical mouldboard plough, drawn by eight oxen, within the narrow limits of a half-acre strip. The principles seem to be clear, although the details have yet to be tested by experiment. A selion's length of about 220 yards is supposed to be as far as the

Fields

ox can pull before he needs a rest. With such an unhandy outfit it is difficult to plough in straight lines: it is better to begin the turn well before reaching the headland. Hence the double curve ('reversed-S') of medieval ploughland, familiar in ridge-and-furrow and early maps all over England (Plate XIV). The ploughman has to go round and round a reversed-S selion always in the same direction. At every ploughing a plough's depth of soil is shifted one plough's width towards the middle of the selion (Fig. 8.7). Hence a ridge is formed.

Plough-horses came in gradually from the thirteenth century; for instance, at Barking (Suffolk) in 1251 the plough-team was of four oxen and four horses.[245] The change was slow and was not always one-way. The horse is not better than the ox in all respects. Having no horns to serve as towbars, he needs an elaborate collar and harness;* and he is not edible on retirement. In many places oxen were still used, or re-used, into the nineteenth or even the twentieth century.

Ridge-and-furrow is not confined to the Middle Ages nor to strip-cultivation. For centuries afterwards it was the practice to divide private fields into strips called *stetches* and to form embryonic ridge-and-furrow on them. I have a handbook which told the Land-Girls of World War II how to do this.[246] There was once a debate between E. Kerridge, who claimed that most ridge-and-furrow was thus formed after Enclosure, and M.W. Beresford, who contended that the ridges were the fossilized pattern of open-field strips, abandoned at or before Enclosure and never ploughed since.[247] We now know that both were right.

Ridge-and-furrow of the medieval type consists of blocks of ridges corresponding to selions arranged in furlongs. They are of the appropriate size and shape, varying around 220 by 11 yards; their curves, especially the reversed-S curve, indicate that when first set out they were ploughed with oxen. They display all the little irregularities written in field-books: odd ridges of double or half width, gores and butts, headlands and *forerae*. Many ridges cannot be post-Enclosure, for they are bisected by Enclosure-Act hedges (also by canals and railways). Occasionally they were abandoned much earlier, being overlain by sixteenth-century gardens,[249] old woodland, or old trees.

Although detailed maps of open-field strips are relatively rare documents, it has been possible in at least seventeen places (mainly in Northants)[250] to compare maps with existing ridge-and-furrow or with the soil-marks left by destroyed ridgework. In every instance there is an exact correspondence, save for such changes of detail as took place between the date of the map and the death of the open-field (Beresford 1957). It can hardly be doubted that broad, high, curving ridge-and-furrow represents strip-cultivation as used in the Middle Ages and continued until either abandoned or enclosed.

Late ridge-and-furrow is typically narrower (5 yards or less) and often longer, set out in straight lines, and often weak or inconspicuous. It occurs not in the main arable areas but on moors and downs and sometimes in parks. Much of it is traditionally ascribed to the great ploughing-up of the Napoleonic Wars, though some is earlier. Ridge-and-furrow can also be produced by cart-ruts (p.279), irrigation (p.339), peat-digging (p.323), and coprolite-digging (p.372).

Medieval ridge-and-furrow expresses headlands as well as selions. Ploughing

---

* In Ireland in the 1620s Sir William Uvedale made a nice living out of fining people for 'ploughing by the horses' tails', which was prohibited because it was cruel.[248]

168

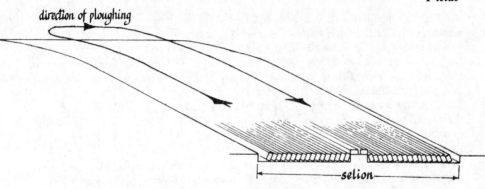

direction of ploughing

selion

Fig. 8.7. How ridge-and-furrow was made. The plough turns the soil to the right. The selion, because of its curved shape, can be ploughed around only in the direction of the arrow. Therefore, at every ploughing, a plough's depth of soil is shifted one furrow's width towards the middle of the selion.

not only shifts earth sideways but also nudges it towards the ends of the furlong, where in time it builds up into a massive ridge, sometimes with a little mound where each selion meets the headland. These ridges can be the only remains of destroyed ridge-and-furrow. Carm Field, Cambridge was once covered with ridgework, of which a patch now remains in Trinity College Fellows' Garden; elsewhere it has been levelled, but the headlands can still be traced along Coton Way.

Ridges are usually arranged up and down slope, making drainage easier. They respond to changes of slope and thus cause some of the changes of direction, gores, taperings, and curves. On very steep slopes, ridge-and-furrow turns into strip-lynchets, following the contours.

Medieval ridge-and-furrow does not occur wherever there was open-field. In the east and south-east Midlands it follows closely the distribution of Planned Countryside; often it covers (or covered) more than half the land area.[251] It extends as far east as Cambridge and the Fenland islands, but then abruptly stops.[252] Ridge-and-furrow, unless late, is remarkably rare in East Anglia, even though there was much open-field and though headland ridges are not uncommon. This is not because it has been destroyed: I have failed to find it even in secondary woodland where it ought to have been preserved.

Ridge-and-furrow can reveal open-field where no written evidence is known. It also shows the changes in an open-field in the eight centuries or so of its existence: for instance, a selion split and made into two; two furlongs ploughed end-to-end as one, eliminating the headland; or a furlong lengthened or shortened or invaded by a landslip. Where there has been a change, the original ridgework has seldom been effaced completely; this indicates that ridges were permanent and were not, as has been suggested, the work of only a few seasons' ploughing capable of being unmade at will.

Ridge-and-furrow is valuable for dating hedges, woods, roads, ponds, etc., according to whether these conform to the ridgework or not. (We must allow space for the plough to turn.) When ridge-and-furrow abuts on an ancient wood there is a headland ridge, and sometimes also a lane, intervening between the ridges and the woodbank. On the north side of Madingley Wood (Cambridgeshire), complex earthworks result from the wood having expanded to cut off first the headland of the adjacent furlong, which for a time served as the woodbank, and then the ends of the selion ridges (Fig. 8.8).

The reasons for ridge-and-furrow are obscure and controversial; many guesses have been made but have not been tested by experiment or surviving usage. It is not an inevitable product of the equipment. The men of east Cambridgeshire avoided making it: either they had straight strips which could be ploughed either way, or they had both left-handed and right-handed ploughs, or they had turn-wrest ploughs which could be used both ways. I leave this question to the experts, as also the mystery of how the Midland ploughman stopped adding to his ridges when they were high enough.

In later centuries there was a notion that ridging increased the land area. More plausibly, it promoted drainage: the crop in the furrows was sacrificed for a better yield on the ridges. This is not the whole answer: ridge-and-furrow is less common on soils which need no drainage, but the relationship is not sensitive. We do not find ridge-and-furrow on patches of clay in areas which otherwise lack it. People made ridge-and-furrow, like many other things, largely because their neighbours did so.

Open-field in space and time Common arable has had a bad press: we learn of it chiefly from records made in its last two centuries, or from writers, such as Tusser (p.189) and Arthur Young, who disapproved of it without having lived with it. From at least the thirteenth century, and widely from the fifteenth, farmers had been exchanging strips so as to form contiguous blocks which could be hedged. It is easy to interpret strip-cultivation as a relic of pristine barbarism, once universal, surviving in places by force of habit until the Age of Enlightenment swept it away.

Enclosure Acts for open-field covered about 4½ million acres, one-seventh of England.[253] This was not all the open-field that there had been: it had already disappeared from County Durham and the Sussex coastal plain, where it had once been widespread. The Orwins found some evidence of open-field in every county of England.[243] Many early maps tell us of rudimentary strip-cultivation, such as small groups of strips in hedged fields (eg. Weston Colville, Cambs, in 1612).[254] But let us not make too much of this evidence: open-field has not been universal, and rudiments of it can be embryonic rather than vestigial.

Open-field does not have a record only of decline and inertia. For at least 500 years men were making strips, at the expense of private land or of commons, as well as abolishing them. In several places in Yorkshire, fields which in the twelfth century were in one ownership were later incorporated into common arable.[255] At Grafton Regis (Northants) open-field strips were made over the site of a building deserted as late as *c.*1500.[256] Even in the sixteenth century, large additions were made to open-fields in Cumberland.[257] There were also reorganizations, occasionally even in the seventeenth century, in which the participants got together and regularized an open-field system; the option of abolishing it was evidently considered and rejected, though – alas – by people who did not write books to tell us what the virtues of open-field were.

Open-field was even introduced to America. In the late seventeenth century – after Sudbury (Suffolk) had abolished its open-fields – Sudbury (Massachusetts) was given an open-field system.[258] It did not last long, but that the attempt was made proves that open-field was by no means obsolete.

The high-water-mark of open-field was at about the time of the Black Death,

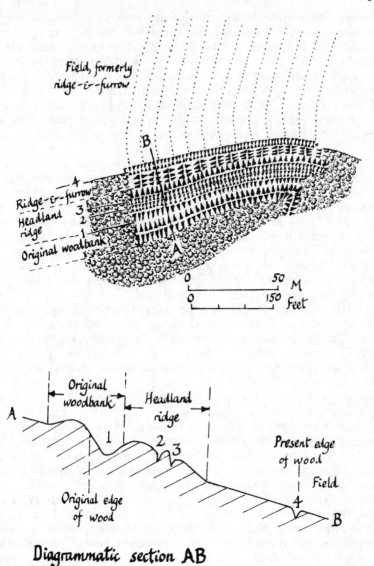

Field, formerly
ridge-&-furrow

B

Ridge-&-furrow
Headland
ridge

4
3
2
1

Original woodbank

A

0 ___ 50 M
0 ___ 150 Feet

A

Original
woodbank

Headland
ridge

1

2 3

Present edge
of wood

Field

Original edge
of wood

4

B

Diagrammatic section AB

Fig. 8.8. Earthworks along part of the north side of Madingley Wood, near Cambridge. The ditches that have successively marked the wood edge are numbered 1 to 4. In the Middle Ages the wood ended in a normal woodbank with Ditch 1. Adjacent was an open-field whose selion ridges ended in a headland ridge against the wood boundary. Centuries ago, this land went to pasture and was encroached upon by the wood. The headland ridge became the woodbank, and Ditches 2 and later 3 were cut into it. In recent decades, after a further expansion of the wood, Ditch 4 was dug through the ridge-and-furrow to define the present edge. The field has since been levelled and the ridges survive only within the wood.

when it covered probably between a third and a quarter of England. There were whole landscapes of strips throughout what is now Planned Countryside. Even here they were not universal; in Cambridge itself about 8 per cent of the farmland was in *crofts* never brought within the common arable. Strip-cultivation had penetrated to many parts of Ancient Countryside, but did not there dominate the landscape; there were patches of it in some townships and some fields. Often, as at Walsham-le-Willows (Suffolk), there were areas of strips but not an organized common-arable system.[259] Some regions, such as the south-east half of Essex, seem never to have had open-field at all.

Open-field in the early Middle Ages Medieval evidence is rarely as detailed as at Cambridge, but H.S.A. Fox has found enough of it to conclude that classic open-field was 'widespread and in perfect working order' by 1300.[260]. In the previous two centuries, from such records as survive, the system appears to have been not quite fully developed. In Dry Drayton (Cambs) there is a remarkable account of a redistribution in *c*.1155: the lords of the five intermingled manors negotiated to simplify the common fields, and got the king to ratify their agreement.[260] I note that among the Bishop of Ely's estates in 1251, on some manors the furlongs had been grouped into fields, but on others (eg. Little Gransden) the furlong was still the biggest unit.[245]

Open-field on a regular plan, with the strips of each participant spaced evenly instead of haphazardly, is attributed to the period before 1250 in northern England; possibly it represents the return of arable farming to lands which had felt the Conqueror's wrath in 1069 (p.313). With the strong Scandinavian culture of the region, historians have seen a resemblance to the Swedish type of regular open-field called *solskifte*.[261]

Another special kind of strip-cultivation showing evidence of planning, indeed of bureaucracy, are the 'giant selions' of the East Riding and the northern Fens. They were sometimes over a mile long, straight, and often mindless. These, too, were probably a twelfth- or thirteenth-century expansion of open-field.[262] At Raunds (Northants) similar 'giant strips' were later chopped up into normal selions and acquired the double curves of ox-ploughing.[256]

Early dating for ridge-and-furrow is less copious than we might hope for. At Bentley Grange, near Huddersfield, twelfth-century coalmines cut into pre-existing ridgework.[263] Other ridge-and-furrow of early medieval or Anglo-Saxon date is known at Hen Domen (Montgomeryshire), Gwithian (Cornwall), and West Stow (Suffolk) (Taylor 1975). All of these examples are outliers from the heartland of open-field, if indeed the ridge-and-furrow proves its existence at all.

Open-field in Anglo-Saxon times As far as I know there is not the slightest evidence that open-fields existed in the Roman period. It used to be thought that the earliest Anglo-Saxon settlers introduced the system from their home-land; but German scholars do not now claim that it developed there any earlier than in England.[264] The present balance of opinion is that common arable developed, in the main, from reorganizing fields that previously had been otherwise arranged; some scholars would date this reorganization after the Norman Conquest.

I am not aware of any certain reference to open-field in Domesday Book. References to arable in the Anglo-Saxon charters are sometimes consistent with open-field. As Dr Della Hooke points out, several charters contain phrases like 'every third acre' which definitely imply strip-cultivation;[265] and there are two more explicit passages:

> The said country is not surrounded by fixed limits, but the acres (*jugera*) lie next to acres.
>
> *Charlton (Berks), 956*[266]
>
> Mixed in common by single acres dispersed hither and thither.
>
> *Avon (Wilts), 963*[267]

Let us study the occurrence in the charters of those words which are associated with open-field in *medieval* documents. If they occur more often in areas which, in later centuries, had a strong open-field tradition – the present Planned Countryside – we may infer that that tradition had already begun in Anglo-Saxon times. The occurrence of nine possible words in charters of what is now Ancient Countryside (weak or no open-field tradition) *versus* Planned Countryside (strong open-field) is shown in Table 8.1.

'Field' itself, Latin *campus*, is often (though erroneously) claimed to imply *open*-field in medieval documents. Anglo-Saxon *feld* had no such implication: it is twice as common in Ancient Countryside charters as in Planned Countryside. In charters it evidently has its original meaning of 'non-woodland', as implied by such combinations as 'heathfield' (p.287). In detail, the word *feld* is an index of the occurrence of woodland: it is less common in Planned Countryside regions because these more often lacked woodland with which a *feld* might be contrasted (p.83). Its connexion with arable land is medieval.

'Gore', Old English *gāra*, is mentioned five times as often in Planned Countryside charters as in Ancient Countryside. It is true that a gore could be any sort of triangle, but there is no particular reason why triangular fields should be commoner in one landscape than another; the discrepancy strongly suggests that *gāra* already had the special meaning of a triangle in open-field. Similarly *furh*, 'furrow', appears eight times as often in what was to be Planned Countryside; this suggests that boundaries already passed through tracts of open-field in which so slight a landmark as a furrow was sufficient definition. We cannot say whether it was a furrow or ridge-and-furrow or a special boundary-furrow.

'Acre' and 'furlong' can either be units of measurement or units of open-field. The charters sometimes refer to so many acres of meadow or woodland; they measure distances by the furlong or the acre (the latter being an acre's *breadth*, 4 perches, about 22 yards (p.xv)). But they also mention acres and furlongs as boundary features. Both are much more abundant in Planned Countryside. This seems to back-date to Anglo-Saxon times the custom of naming specific acres and furlongs in an open-field.

Hēafod means literally 'head', and can be used for the end or top of almost anything. But its greater abundance in Planned Countryside suggests that it had already the additional meaning of 'headland'; indeed *hēafodlond* is a frequent combination. (The discrepancy would be five to one were it not for South Worcestershire, which has half the Ancient Countryside occurrences of *hēafod*.) We sometimes, in Planned Countryside charters, find such explicit combinations as 'the head of three acres' (Wylye, Wilts) or 'the west furrow of the end acre' (Uffington, Berks). Yet more characteristic of Planned Countryside is the combination *hēafod stoccas*, 'head stumps', reminding us of the stakes with

Table 8.1 Frequency in Anglo-Saxon charters of words related to open-field

	Ancient Countryside		Planned Countryside	
	Number of occurrences	Region where specially abundant	Number of occurrences	Regions where specially abundant
feld	64 (0.85%)	Weald (2.5%)	28 (0.42%)	
gāra	16 (0.21%)		53 (0.80%)	Dorset Chalklands (1.7%), Uffington Scarp (1.4%)
furh	11 (0.15%)		77 (1.16%)	Uffington Scarp (2.5%), Vale of Evesham (1.8%)
æcer	36 (0.48%)		80 (1.20%)	East Midlands (2.3%), Oxfordshire (2.2%)
furlang	5 (0.07%)		28 (0.42%)	Wiltshire Claylands (1.1%), Uffington Scarp (0.8%)
hēafod	38 (0.50%)	South Worcs (2.8%)	115 (1.72%)	Uffington Scarp (4.1%), Vale of Evesham (3.8%)
hēafod stoccas	3 (0.04%)		13 (0.19%)	Dorset Chalklands (0.8%)
foryrþ	2 (0.03%)		8 (0.12%)	Uffington Scarp (0.5%)
hlinc	51 (0.66%)	Hants-Sussex (4.2%)	93 (1.40%)	South Wilts (4.1%), Dorset Chalklands (3.2%), Uffington Scarp (2.9%), Marlborough Downs (2.8%)

Figures are of the number of times the object is mentioned; they take no account of its occurrences as a place-name element. Percentages are based on the total number of boundary features in each group of charters.

which Austrian farmers still label the corners of their open-field strips.* *Foryrþ*, 'fore-earth', is reminiscent of the Medieval Latin *forera* of the Cambridge open-fields.

Hlinc, said to mean 'baulk' and also 'ridge', is also more frequent in Planned Countryside. It does not occur everywhere, and is mostly in chalkland (including Hampshire–Sussex among Ancient Countryside). Although a baulk, as such, almost inevitably implies open-field, it is just possible that the word already had the meaning 'lynchet' and could mean the banks of prehistoric fields.

Taking all these features except *feld* together, the supreme concentration is in the Uffington Scarp, where 'open-field' objects form 14 per cent of all landmarks (Fig. 8.9). The charters of this region also mention an exceptional

---

* Dr Hooke offers a far-fetched explanation of stakes for exhibiting the detached heads of criminals.

number of thorns but very few other trees (p.212); very little woodland; and almost no hedges (p.185). They give a very clear picture of that combination of open-field and chalk downland which was to be typical of the Wessex chalk country for nine centuries. The Dorset Chalklands, Berkshire Claylands, and Vale of Evesham also have at least 8 per cent of 'open-field' landmarks, not all together; for instance *hlinc* is common in Dorset but rare in the Claylands. All of these had strong open-field in the Middle Ages and later. All other Planned Countryside regions (except the Fens) have at least two 'open-field' features well represented; these are weakest (3½ per cent to 5 per cent) where there was woodland (Wooded Cotswolds, West Hampshire, North-East).

In Ancient Countryside, every region except four has below 3 per cent of 'open-field' features. The exceptions are Hampshire–Sussex, with its abnormal concentration of *hlinc*; South Worcestershire, with seventeen instances of *hēafod*; the Reading Basin, also with *hlinc*; and the Mendips with unusually frequent *æcer*.

No one of these terms gives conclusive evidence by itself, but with eight independent terms corroboration is multiplied into near-certainty. The distinc-

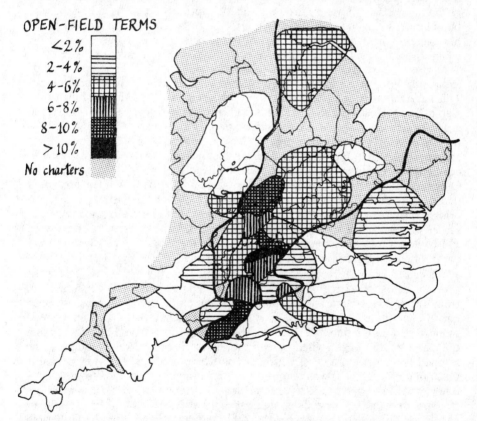

OPEN-FIELD TERMS
<2%
2-4%
4-6%
6-8%
8-10%
>10%
No charters

Fig. 8.9. Distribution of the 'open-field' terms *gāra, furh, æcer, furlang, hēafod, hēafod stoccas, foryrþ,* and *hlinc* in Anglo-Saxon charters as a percentage of all boundary features. The thick lines mark the extent of what is now predominantly Planned Countryside, with a strong open-field tradition.

tion between Ancient Countryside and future Planned Countryside already exists in the charters: every one of the terms later used to refer to open-field is more abundant in the latter. The matter is put beyond doubt by the almost exactly inverse distribution of references to hedges (Fig.9.1).

Open-field, and its technical terms, had spread by late Anglo-Saxon times to those regions that were later to have a *strong* tradition of it. As far as our documents can tell us, west Berkshire was the seat of its development. In the other such regions it was still incomplete, and in some that were more wooded it did not often as yet reach the boundaries of estates.

Was there as yet any open-field in regions that were later to have a *weak* tradition? This is not clear: words such as *æcer* and *hēafod* appear to be used in non-technical senses. For the present I suppose that such open-fields as there were in Ancient Countryside were a post-Conquest development.

Survivals of earlier field-systems Most open-field was not created on virgin land. Whether the strips appeared suddenly or gradually, we should expect them often to have been fitted into existing fields: why should their makers have given themselves the extra trouble and disruption of erasing all the earlier boundaries? Planned Countryside is not the best place to look for Roman fields, but there ought to be some remains of them in furlong boundaries, especially where these have again been re-used as the boundaries of modern fields.

At Holme-next-the-Sea (Norfolk) there is a well-known Roman semi-regular rectangular grid of roads and fields, aligned on Peddar's Way, a Roman road. This survived at least a short period as a two-field strip system, as shown by a map of 1609 (Hoskins 1967). At Tadlow (Cambs) the whole parish – fields, the nearly-deserted village, even the orientation of the church – obeys a semi-regular grid of either Bronze Age or Iron Age type (Fig.8.10). This grid is certainly older than the parish and county boundaries, both of which zigzag in obedience to it; its extensions into neighbouring parishes did not survive the unmaking of their open-fields. The open-fields of Saffron Walden preserved traces of a similar, probably Iron Age, grid.[268] Even in Carm Field, Cambridge, the ways and major baulks were the remains of a planned grid, evidently earlier than a Roman main road which sliced across them. Some of these ways and baulks were used as post-Enclosure roads; the modern street grid of west Cambridge is the shadow of the ghost of the fields of Iron Age Cambridge.

We can thus detect remains of earlier semi-regular field patterns. Where the previous fields were irregular there is normally no means of distinguishing them from furlongs created *de novo*. A possible exception lies in the zigzag or stepped parish boundaries, as at Tadlow. Zigzag boundaries have long been understood to mean that cultivation had reached the township limits from both sides before the early Middle Ages, when parish boundaries became fixed – indeed some stepped boundaries are described in Anglo-Saxon charters. But they probably mean more than this. Two communities, pushing out open-fields towards each other, would be expected to have some demarcation line in advance of meeting. If there were no existing field boundaries, that line ought to be straight or curved. A zigzag demarcation indicates that the two communities had inherited and shared out a pre-existing field network into which open-fields were inserted afterwards.

Open-field outside England Common arable is well known in Wales, Scotland, and Ireland; in each it was both an English introduction and a native Celtic development.

In Wales there were already open-fields at the time of the English conquest in the thirteenth century. Open-field was one among several kinds of Welsh land-tenure; there were small patches of it, not thousands of acres. Selions (Welsh *gerddi*, English 'quillets') were crooked and tapering in shape. A few still exist in Llanynys (Denbigh).[269] In the Englishries of South Wales open-field was probably an introduction, albeit with some Welsh field-names; it was a smaller edition of that in England. Many South Welsh open-fields survived into

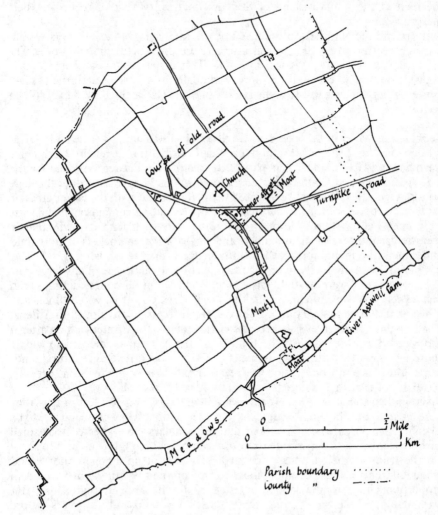

Fig. 8.10. The semi-regular grid of fields of Tadlow (Cambs) as it existed in 1886. An ancient field design – which survived both the making and the unmaking of the open-fields – evidently determined the parish and county boundaries, the course of the old Oxford–Cambridge road, the plan of the (now much shrunken) village, and the orientation of moats and even of the church.[273] The turnpike road, of late eighteenth-century date, is an intrusion.

177

Fields

the nineteenth century, and that of Rhosili (Gower) has still escaped enclosure.[270]

In Scotland open-field, known as 'runrig', was once quite extensive, though abolished earlier than in England. Its details and origin are not well known. Typically the strips lay on the better land, and were surrounded by an outfield, a common pasture, parts of which were ploughed up for short periods. Runrig is a Scots(-English) word, but there was also a Gaelic form of the system in which the lands were redistributed among the participants annually or every third year.[271] This was not just a memory of rude antiquity: almost into my lifetime the men of the remote island of St Kilda met every year to reallocate their meagre ridges.

In Ireland the Normans introduced open-field; it survived in a few places into the eighteenth century. There was also a Celtic open-field, probably of earlier origin, known by the Gaelic word *rundale*. This is not well documented, but is known from many coastal districts. New rundales may have been formed as late as the eighteenth century. In some remote hamlets Gaelic open-field may still be active.[272]

Conclusions Open-field occurs in English, Scandinavian, Welsh, and Gaelic cultures in the British Isles, and on the Continent in French, Germanic, Slavonic, and Greek lands. It is part of the distinction between Ancient Countryside and Planned Countryside that runs through Europe as it does through Britain. Open-field is widely associated with villages and with the larger areas of flat land. In the eastern Alps, for instance, a parish often contains a village with a big open-field system; one or two large hamlets each with its own smaller open-fields; and several small hamlets and single farms, in pockets of cultivable land among the mountains, each with its hedged, private fields.

Open-fields are unlikely to be the pristine cultural landscape of any large part of Europe. They were made by an agricultural revolution no less definite than that which abolished them. From the Dark Ages onwards, a 'De-Enclosure Movement' flooded like a tide, reaching Ireland, Russia, and almost to Athens. The tide did not reach everywhere; its last ripple touched America long after it had receded in other places. The English Midlands were submerged so widely and for so long that little now remains of the pre-open-field agricultural landscape. Our Ancient Countryside was reached only locally and for short periods, and parts of it such as south Essex were not reached at all.

We know little of why open-fields were maintained and still less of why they were created, but there has been no lack of speculation. They came too late to be an inherent consequence of human nature. Scholars have guessed that small farmers combined to contribute oxen to a communal plough-team and to share out the fruits of their labours; or that land was split up among children and grandchildren; or that peasants ploughed up common pasture and shared it in proportion either to the labour invested or to the grazing rights lost. But presumably people were doing these things for thousands of years before strip-cultivation appeared. Open-field, with its rapid spread, has all the marks of a Dark Age invention. Its practical purposes may have been connected with making the best use of arable grazing and not having to maintain fences. But it appears also to have been part of a social revolution, in which people took to living in villages instead of the earlier hamlets and farmsteads. Such a collectivization of agriculture may have been promoted by lords with the power to

178

enforce their theories on their inferiors, although in lordless Cambridge it presumably happened by agreement.

The relation between open-field and writing deserves to be explored. It is hard to imagine that the West Fields of Cambridge could have been operated in their full complexity without field-books to which disputes could be referred.

The distribution of open-field, as we know it in England, is related to the extent of agriculture at the end of the Roman period (p.84). Historians have made much of the bringing of newly-won lands into strip-cultivation, but this, as we know it from post-Conquest documents, is not typical: it was a late addition when there was already an established tradition of open-field to be imitated. Open-field was most successful in reorganizing farmland that had already been made by someone else. Where men had to make their fields before they could till them, they usually remained individualists with scattered dwellings and private fields. Open-field was strongest in districts with little or no woodland; a motive may well have been to make the most of existing farmland where there was no room for expansion.

Post-Enclosure Fields

The distinction between fields formed out of open-field arable and those that have never been open-field is not always sharp, for some strip-cultivation already had hedges. Post-enclosure fields are of four kinds: those that conform to individual strips; those that conform to furlong boundaries; those that disregard the open-field layout; and those that subdivide former woodland, wood-pasture, grassland, heath, moor, and fen.

In many parts of the country there are small fields which preserve the shape, including the double curve, of individual strips consisting of one or more selions (Fig.8.11). At Caxton (Cambs) even houses in the village obey the selion curve.[273] These fields can date from well before the Enclosure Acts; open-fields had hardly been completed before some participants began to fence their strips and to remove them from the system.

When hedges follow furlong boundaries they form a sinuous or curving network, often of mixed hedges (p.194). These are typical of medieval or Tudor enclosures of open-field. In the east Midlands there was much enclosure in the Stuart period, often with elm hedges. Some of the earlier parliamentary enclosures follow furlong boundaries. Sometimes the hedges already existed before enclosure, although this can often be ruled out because the ridges abut directly on the hedge leaving no turning space.

Later parliamentary enclosures are characterized by flimsy hawthorn hedges running in straight lines and disregarding the open-field system. Although they smell of the drawing office, they are seldom quite regular, except in featureless terrain, nor mindless: they take some account of drainage considerations.

The same applies to modern fields formed by reorganizing ancient enclosed fields or where there had not been fields before. When Littlehound Wood (Cambs) was grubbed out *c.* 1650 (p.85), it was divided into three fields with early examples of straight hedges within the original sinuous boundary. Any patch of straight hedges in otherwise irregular terrain is suspicious: it may be the whim of some nineteenth-century farmer with money to spend on rearranging his fields, but it may also mark the site of a vanished wood or green (Plate III). Great expanses of straight, often mindless, banking or walling mark nineteenth-century attempts to farm moorland.

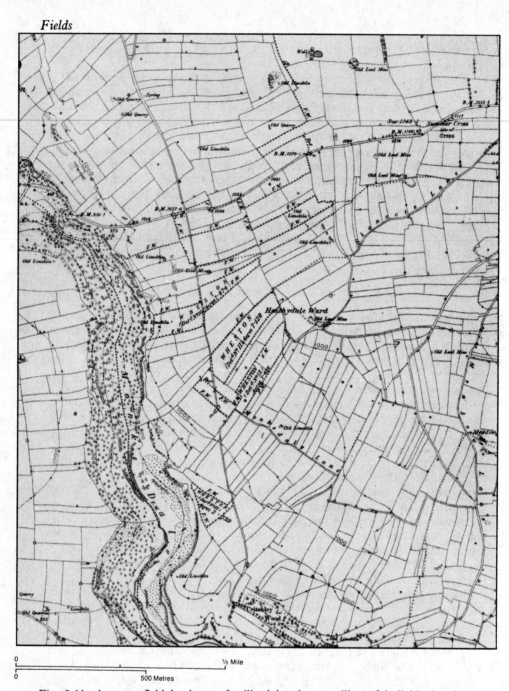

Fig. 8.11. An open-field landscape fossilized by the enwalling of individual strips: Tideswell and Wheston, Derbyshire. Many strips have the reversed-S curve, proving that despite the altitude (over 1000 feet) they were designed for the plough. The open-field was shared between two parishes, giving rise to boundary anomalies (cf. Fig. 2.4). The relation of the north-south road to the strips and parish boundaries is a chronological puzzle. Ordnance Survey, 1879.

CHAPTER 9

Hedges and field-walls

> James Mede complains that John Palmer senior in the month of March [1443] cut down to the ground, took and carried away divers Trees . . . viz. oak, ash, Maples, white thorn & black, lately growing in a certain hedge of the said James between heighfeld and hegfeld, and had been repeating this trespass from time to time for 7 years [previously] . . . by which the said James has been wronged and has suffered damage to the value of 20s.
>
> *Court roll, Hatfield Broad-oak (Essex), 1443*[274]

There are three well-known myths about hedges. People suppose that they are specially English, or British; that they are very artificial, the mere result of somebody planting a hedge, and do not have a life of their own like woods or heaths; and that they are all, or nearly all, a mere 200 years or so old.

The first myth is soon disposed of. Western Normandy is *bocage* country, the tangle of intricately and massively hedged fields that complicated the fighting of World War II. In sudden contrast are the wide-open hedgeless plains of east Normandy. Most of France is a patchwork of hedged *bocage* areas and hedgeless *champagne* areas. The distinction continues far into Europe. There are hedged areas in northern Italy, the Austrian Alps, and around Mount Helicon in Greece;[4] even Crete has one or two hedged parishes. In America I have seen thousands of miles of hedge in a dozen States from Vermont to Texas; there are hedged fields in the Peruvian Andes. Regions with and without hedges are to be found over much of the world. In general, traditions of hedgeless open-field or prairie-farming belong in great plains or broad valleys. Where the whole of a region is not hedged, hedges tend to go either with hilly terrain or with the neighbourhood of woods.

Hedges are of many kinds. In Cornwall a hedge is an earth or stone bank, which may be – but often is not – topped with bushes or trees. In Michigan a 'fence-row' consists of biggish trees closely set on a low bank of loose stones. Neither of these needs to be kept in being by regular cutting or plashing* as does the classic English Midland hedge. Historical documents are sometimes vague about the distinction between hedges and fences: 'fence' in Enclosure Acts can mean any field boundary. Hedgerows are occasionally confused with narrow woods: a map and survey of Plumberow in Hockley (south-east Essex) in 1579 shows a curious network of fields separated by 'hedgerowes' some of which were 100 yards thick.[275]

---

* Called by books 'laying', sometimes misspelt 'layering'.

Where Hedges Come From

In Britain, hedge-planting is familiar and well documented; nearly all more recent hedges have certainly been planted. Let us not slip into the generalization that all hedges have been planted: there are two other ways to get a hedge.

North America lacks this hedge-planting tradition: settlers fenced their fields with wood or wire. Yet the United States now has more miles of hedge than Great Britain. Americans believe that nearly all their hedges arose by default. Tree saplings sprang up alongside the fences and eventually replaced them. I have studied stages of the process. The prairies of middle Texas, near Waco, originally maintained by wild animals (p.329), were parcelled out into farms and fields by barbed-wire fences in the 1880s. Seedlings of Texas elm, black oak, Texas ash, prairie sumach, poison-ivy, and many other trees and shrubs have sprung up at the bases of the fences, which have sheltered them from browsing and cultivation. The hedges have advanced gradually: aerial photographs prove that many of them were discontinuous, or not there at all, twenty years ago. There can be no question of any planting – this has been a time of declining prosperity. Tree seeds have arrived naturally from the wooded canyons nearby. People have failed to prevent the trees from growing, and doubtless have found them a useful relief from replacing rotten fence-posts.

Later stages can be seen in other States. Michigan is parcelled out by nineteenth-century fence-rows. In Massachusetts the seventeenth-century fences were replaced by eighteenth-century hedges, which now take the form of rows of old trees through the nineteenth-century secondary woods which have engulfed the fields. American hedges are usually within three miles of woodland. They are seldom managed except by casual woodcutting. They are nearly always mixed, of at least five species, whatever their age.

Has this happened in Britain? Our tree species have much the same colonizing powers as their American sisters. Close to Hayley Wood (Cambridgeshire) there was a railway from 1862 to 1969, separated from the adjoining field by the usual wire fence and shallow ditch. Since the railway has been disused, trees and shrubs rooted at the base of the fence have grown into an almost continuous row which it will be possible to maintain as a hedge. It is a mixed hedge of hazel, hawthorn, ash, briar, blackthorn, maple, etc., and differs from the oak, birch, and sallow which have sprung up on the disused railway itself. By the usual criterion of hedge-dating (see later) it ought to be 700–800 years old. It cannot be older than 1862; the abundant hazel suggests that it began to develop before 1930, when grey squirrels arrived in the area (Chapter 4). Probably the railwaymen who mowed the grass verges were unable to reach a narrow strip at the base of the fence.

That this has not happened more often in the last 200 years is because farmers and labourers have had time on their hands in slack periods and have chosen to spend it in tidying, 'brushing', and suppressing young trees. This may not always have been so. The American parallel suggests that hedges arise wherever men are few and acres many, and especially in times of moderate agricultural depression. Whenever a ditch, bank, lynchet, or earthen wall is neglected for a few years not too far from a source of tree seed a hedge will result. Fences turn into hedges by birds sitting and dropping seeds; the fence protects the incipient hedge. When prosperity returns the young trees will be managed as a hedge and their origin will be forgotten.

Hedges arise in a third way as the *ghosts* of woods that have been grubbed out leaving their edges as field boundaries. The marginal trees, often already forming a hedge to protect the wood's interior, may be left as a hedge having woodland, rather than hedgerow, characteristics. At Shelley (Suffolk), I have been shown a remarkable roadside hedge (Plate XV) 600 yards long composed almost entirely of the pry tree (small-leaved lime) with occasional service. Pry and service (p.106) are woodland, not hedgerow trees; pry is the commonest tree of ancient woods in the area but is unheard-of growing by hundreds in a hedge. The mystery is resolved by an eighteenth-century map which shows 'Withers Wood' adjoining just that length of road where the pry hedge now stands.[276] Judith's Hedge, said to have been made round Monks' Wood (Huntingdonshire) in *c.* 1080 by one Countess Judith (Pollard and others 1974), is now in part detached from the wood owing to grubbing in the seventeenth century.

History of Hedges and Walls

Prehistoric In the Land's End Peninsula there is one of the most impressively ancient farmland landscapes in Europe. The Peninsula is a miniature Dartmoor, a moorland-covered granite dome surrounded by a belt of farmland, with a strip of rough 'morrop' bordering the cliffs of the coast. The farmland is of tiny irregular pastures separated by great banks, each formed of a row of 'grounders' – huge granite boulders – topped off level with lesser boulders and earth. Their function is to dispose of the boulders which in periglacial times (p.350) had slid down from the moorland on to the fertile land. The banks zigzag and deviate in order to incorporate immovably large boulders or small outcrops. Banks now disused wander down into the morrop or up on to the moor. The area is full of prehistoric settlements ('British Villages')[237] and others may lie unrecognized under the present, medieval, hamlets. Deep lanes meander between the banks and cross streams by clapper-bridges. Within the thickness of one mighty wall is hidden an Iron Age *fogou*, a row of half-underground chambers lighted by 'architectural rabbit-holes' among the grass.

This is a famous example where the whole system is of a piece. The banks, from their construction, are contemporary with the fields; once formed they are difficult to alter and cannot be added to. They can be roughly dated by the Bronze Age objects which were buried in the banks.[277] These banks, indeed, are among the world's oldest artefacts still in use. There may be many other prehistoric walls and hedges still extant, but it is not usually so clear that the present boundaries of early fields are the original ones. The Iron Age fields of Essex (p.160) are now defined by hedges mainly of elm, but the hedges could have been added later to fields originally bounded in some other way. Most study of prehistoric fields has been on disused examples; disuse, while it can prove the antiquity of the fields, destroys most of the evidence for hedges.

Roman The Romans in Italy had a long and elaborate tradition of hedging. The Classical Latin *vepris* means a hedge or bush. Columella, the first century BC agricultural writer, says:

> The most ancient authors preferred a living hedge to a constructed fence, because it not only called for less expense, but was more permanent and lasted for an indefinite time.

> The place which you intend to hedge . . . should be banked around with two
> ditches three feet apart. It is quite enough to make them two feet deep. We let
> them remain empty over the winter while the seeds are being got ready to sow in
> them.[278]

Columella then gives a choice of hedging plants appropriate to southern Europe.
These are to be grown from seed by an elaborate technique summed up four
centuries later by Palladius Rutilius in another textbook:

> It is best . . . to gather the seeds when ripe and to mix them with ground-up grass
> which has been soaked in water, and then to coat old esparto ropes with this kind
> of mixture, so that the seeds stuck on the ropes can be stored until the beginning of
> springtime. Then . . . we lay the ropes with the seeds in the two ditches and cover
> them lightly with earth. In thirty days the thorns come up. When they are young
> we have to support them with small stakes . . .[279]

To return to Columella:

> Obviously this hedge cannot be destroyed, unless you want to dig it up by the
> roots. There is no doubt that after fire damage it grows again better than before.

Siculus Flaccus, a first century AD writer on surveying, says in a section on
boundary-marks:

> If [bushes or] hedges (*vepres*) form the boundary, record their species; whether
> they are only on the extreme edge [of the property], because there are often bushes
> in the middle of fields owing to farmers' neglect; and whether they are artificially
> planted. For if a region does not have shrubs which can form a protection for
> vineyards or gardens, they are imported from distant regions and planted. And
> trees are often to be found put in hedges.[280]

The Romans knew about plashing a hedge, but it was evidently a wonder of
far-off lands and was not familiar in the Italian countryside. Julius Caesar
encountered the practice only just outside Britian in *c.* 55 BC. The Nervii, a tribe
living in Flanders, he says, had an ancient practice

> by which they more easily obstructed their neighbours' cavalry coming at them for
> raiding. They cut into slender trees and bent them over so that many branches
> came out along their length; they finished these off by inserting brambles and
> briars, so that these hedges formed a defence like a wall, which could not only not
> be penetrated but not even be seen through.[281]

A similar kind of hedge, also presented as being a military obstacle, was met
with by Alexander the Great in what is now Persia, according to the history-
book of Quintus Curtius Rufus.

There is some evidence for hedges from excavation. At Farmoor (Oxfordshire) a Roman system of small fields bounded by ditches had been waterlogged
in such a way as to preserve twigs, pollen, etc. of hawthorn, blackthorn, and
briar. Some of the remains were of seeds and bud-scales which had almost
certainly been shed by trees or bushes growing on the spot. This strongly
suggests that the field boundaries had been hedged with thorn.[282]

Part of an actual hedge may have been excavated at Bar Hill (Dunbarton-
shire). Beneath a Roman fort were found hawthorn stems showing the characteristic distortions, cuts, and calluses produced by hedge management. It
appears that there had been fields divided by plashed hawthorn hedges and

ditches. When the fort was made in AD *c*. 142, the hedges were levelled and the remains buried in the ditches.[612]

Anglo-Saxon Old English has several words for hedges and the like: *hege* (our 'hedge'), *haga*, *hegeræwe* ('hedgerow'), *ræw*, etc. Usually these appear to mean hedges in the modern sense. This is most explicit with *ræw* 'row' and its compounds; as well as hedgerows, the charters mention hazel-rows, thorn-rows, willow-rows (and occasionally also rush-rows and stone-rows). *Haga* and *hege* give rise to the compounds *hagaþorn* 'hawthorn' and *hegesugge* 'hedge-sparrow'. An eighth-century charter of Beasfield (Kent) specifies a live hedge (*cwichege*).[283] The permanence of hedges is attested by the twenty-four occurrences of 'old hedge' in the charters; at North Wootton (Somerset) there was an already old hedge in 816.[284] Many charters refer to trees standing in hedges.

The commonest word for hedge, *haga*, can have several meanings. It is the 'haw' or 'haugh' of place-names such as Northaw and Thornhaugh. In Domesday Book *haya* is a device for catching roedeer, mainly in Cheshire and Shropshire outside the area covered by the charters. I can find no topographical distinction between *hege* and *haga* – both of which are linear features and are not necessarily closed circuits – and I agree with most commentators who regard them as mere variants of the same word; *haga* is mainly southern and *hege* western.

The charters mention a total of 378 hedges, hedgerows, haws, and rows, 2.45 per cent of all English boundary features. (There are no such landmarks in the Welsh charters.) The distribution is very uneven (Fig. 9.1): in the London Basin and North-West Dorset one in fifteen of the boundary points mentions a hedge, whereas almost no hedges are mentioned in the Berkshire Claylands, Uffington Scarp, or Vale of Evesham.

At Kington Langley (Wiltshire) in 940 there was 'the hedge row that Ælfric made', probably the earliest record of anyone planting a hedge.[285] At Grimley (Worcestershire) in *c*.966 there was an 'old hedge-place' (*ealdan hegestowe*), which may be the earliest record of a destroyed hedge.[286] Occasional hedges are named after beasts, which perhaps they kept in or out: I have found six roe[deer]-hedges (but does the hedge exist that will confine roe-deer?), six swine-hedges, two wolf-hedges, and a hart-hedge.

Anglo-Saxon hedges were not related to particular soil types, but were quite closely correlated with woodland (Fig. 5.5). They were not necessarily the boundaries of woods, although some were: hedges are mentioned with about 1½ times their usual frequency in those charters that describe the boundaries of woodland exclaves. Hedges existed mainly in regions that also had woodland: they were not, as a rationalizer might guess, a substitute for woods.

To a large extent, the distribution of hedges in the charters corresponds to the distinction in later centuries between Ancient and Planned Countryside. It is the inverse of the distribution of open-field features (Chapter 8). Already it was the custom to have hedges in most of Worcestershire but not in the south-east corner of the county, and in North-West Dorset but not in South Wiltshire. However, the most-wooded of the regions later to be Planned Countryside – West Hampshire, Wiltshire Claylands, Oxfordshire – did have many hedges in Anglo-Saxon times. Conversely, unexpectedly few hedges are recorded in the Weald, Devon, and Cornwall: possibly in those regions hedges were already too numerous to be of use in identifying boundaries.

By the ninth century at latest, regional traditions of having or not having hedges had been established that were to endure for a thousand years. Later centuries were to add many more hedges to regions that already had some, but the general distribution was not radically altered until the Enclosure Acts. Hedges persisted (eg. in Worcestershire) long after the woodland associated with their formation had disappeared.

Field-walls are poorly documented. There are only thirty-two mentions of walls or stonerows, and the only districts where they often occur are the Mendips and Isle of Wight. No wall is mentioned in Devon or Northamptonshire, and only one in the Cotswolds. The other main stone-wall regions of England have no charters.

Medieval Old overgrown hedges, full of blossom in spring and set with hollow ivy-tods and other reminders of antiquity, are part of the romance of the English landscape. We remember them from our childhood and see them in the pictures of Constable and Arthur Rackham and the verses of John Clare; we see them still in places that have escaped the Vandal hand of tidiness. Nearly 800 years ago, such a hedge – it was probably in north-west Dorset, that land of Anglo-

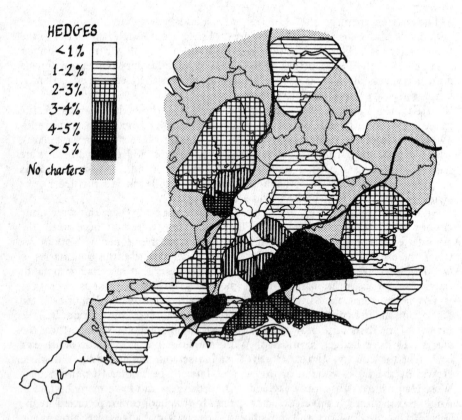

Fig. 9.1. Distribution of hedges in Anglo-Saxon charters, as a percentage of all features mentioned on boundaries.

Saxon hedges – was the setting for the Middle English poem *The Owl and the Nightingale*:

> In a corner of a roughland
> . . . upon a fair bough
> that was well covered in blossom
> In a thick neglected hedge
> mixed with reed and green sedge
>
> . . . . . .
>
> There stood an old stock nearby
> where the Owl sang in her turn.
> It was all overgrown with ivy;
> it was the Owl's dwelling-place.

A third character, the Wren, sits in a lime tree.

Medieval documents abound with more prosaic references. Hedges were planted; were maintained (sometimes by a lord's tenants as a labour service, as on the manors of Ramsey Abbey, Huntingdonshire); they were felled; were stolen; were disputed between neighbours; overgrew the highway; and were used as sources of thorns to repair other hedges. The following are typical examples.

> Expenses . . .
> One man making a certain ditch and planting a live hedge . . . 18 perches [99 yards] long and 7ft wide . . . 6s. at 4d. the perch.
> *Estate accounts, Gamlingay (Cambs), 1330*[287]

> John Sparrow made a trespass . . . cutting underwood on a certain earthwork, *viz.* elm, maple, and bushes.
> *Court roll, Great Canfield (Essex), 1420*[288]

> Richard Benhall has 7 perches of hedge overhanging the King's highway with branches and thorns in the lane called Wodnenlane . . . penalty 40d.
> *Great Canfield, 1512*[288]

> Ralph Cheseman cut down and took away thorns growing in the plaintiff's hedges to the value of ½ mark [£0.33, quite a large sum].
> *Court roll, Newton Longville (Bucks), 1283*[289]

These records and many others (eg. the quotation at the head of this chapter) refer unambiguously to living hedges in the modern sense. There were also 'dead hedges' for temporary fencing, especially in connexion with open-fields. A common type consisted of stakes set about two feet apart and interwoven with long flexible rods called *ethers*,* like a wattle hurdle made on the spot. Such fences often appear in pictures and are sometimes heard of as late as the seventeenth century; I have seen modern examples at Chadacre Agricultural College, West Suffolk. The fencing material produced by coppice-woods (p.67)

---

* The form 'heathers' is a Cockney misspelling.

was probably used for dead hedges. They presumably had a short life and were costly in labour and in top-quality underwood.

Other medieval allusions involve cutting thorns to form the material called *trouse*; this may be why spinneys – woods of thorns – were quite highly valued.[290] We are enlightened by a thirteenth-century poem, *The Man in the Moon*, as interpreted by R.J. Menner.[291] The medievals thought of the Man in the Moon as a stupid hedger (like Shakespeare's Moonshine, 'with lanthorn, dog, and bush of thorn'). In the poem he is bent under a fork-load of thorns. 'He hath hewn somewhere a burden of briar', for which he has been in trouble with the hayward, ie. the hedge-ward who policed such matters. 'Where he might be in the field driving stakes getting ready for his thorns to close his gaps (*dutten is doren*), he must make more trouse with his twybill* or else all his day's work will be lost.' The allusion is to mending a gappy hedge with stakes interlaced with thorns or briars. (Experiment will show that trouse and briars without stakes do not long remain a barrier.)

Hedge management is discussed academically by John Fitzherbert. After dealing with dead hedges he says: 'And lay thy small trouse or thornes, that thou hedgeste withall, ouer thy quicksettes, that shepe do not eate the sprynge nor buddes of thy settes.' (*Book of Husbandry*, 1523)

This suggests two other uses of thorns: to protect the 'quicksets' of a newly-planted hedge, or to protect the 'spring' or regrowth of a hedge newly cut to the ground for underwood.

During the Middle Ages new hedges were added to those inherited from Anglo-Saxon times. Some were planted; others, we may infer, were of the 'American' kind. Temporary dead hedges would tend to become permanent and would be invaded by trees and bushes, a process to be encouraged because every bush would strengthen the fence and reduce the annual chore of remaking it. A fence would develop into the kind of gappy hedge mended by the Man in the Moon, and then into a continuous hedge.

By the fifteenth century hedges in some Ancient Countryside areas were as numerous as they have ever been. A survey of Leaden Roding (Essex) in 1439, for instance, shows every field 'enclosed by hedges and ditches'.[292] Hedges of the Planned Countryside type were beginning to be planted in some ex-open-field townships, especially in Leicestershire. Hedges were frequent in open-field systems themselves, as at Gamlingay (see above); many are recorded in the open-field part of Saffron Walden (Essex) in 1400.[293]

Less is known about field-walls than hedges; such evidence as there is suggests that the medievals were not great builders of them. R. Newton, for instance, after noting some medieval examples, ascribes most of the stone walls of Northumberland to the eighteenth century.[294] Many field-walls in south-west Yorkshire replace medieval hedges.[295]

Sixteenth and seventeenth centuries Early maps (Fig. 2.3) often carefully distinguish hedges from fences, walls, park pales, etc. and from unmarked boundaries. They show beyond argument that almost every parish in England had at least a few hedges; that most of the Ancient Countryside was already fully hedged; and that the majority of the hedges then existing were still there in the twentieth century. This is easily seen in the published selection from the early maps of Essex.[296]

---

* A tool having one axe-edge and one adze-edge.

Enclosures of open-field continued, especially in coastal Sussex,[157] but here and there almost throughout England. Most of this gave rise to hedges, but sometimes walls were used, as at Grassington (West Riding).[297]

Hedges were also occasionally destroyed. Most of the Essex maps show one or two examples of a row of trees across a field, evidently the hedgerow trees remaining from a grubbed-out hedge.

Writers begin to draw attention to the difference between fully-hedged counties and those still relatively unhedged. Thomas Tusser, being an Essex man, preferred the former:

> A comparison betweene Champion countrie and seuerall.
>
> The countrie enclosed I praise,
>> the tother delighteth not me,
> For nothing the wealth it doth raise,
>> to such as inferior be.
> There swineherd that keepeth the hog,
>
> • • • •
>
> there neatherd [ie. cowboy], with cur and his horne,   [Champion]
> There shepherd with whistle and dog,
> be fence to the medowe and corne.
> There horse being tide on a balke,
>> is readie with theefe for to walke.
>
> • • • •
>
> Example (if doubt ye doo make):
>> by Suffolke and Essex go take
>>> [in contrast to Norfolk, Cambridgeshire, and Leicestershire]
>
> • • • •
>
> T'one laieth for turfe and for sedge,   Champion
>> and hath it with woonderfull suit:
> When tother in euerie hedge   Seuerall.
>> hath plentie of fewell and fruit.
>
> *Fiue hundred pointes of good Husbandrie, as well for the Champion or open countrie, as also for the woodland, or Seuerall* (1573 edition)

Tusser means that among the many disadvantages of living in champion country is the lack of firewood and the trouble, or 'suit', of fetching other fuels from a distance. Hence the term 'woodland', used by writers at this time not for woodland in the normal sense, but for land possessing hedgerows which produced wood.

Evidence of the value of hedges as sources of wood does not depend on generalized writers alone. In south Essex, surveys often treat hedges as woods, giving areas and years' growth since last felling. In 1566, for instance, the Belhus (Aveley) estate had 176 acres of wood of which 144 acres were 'severall' (ie. actual woodland) and 28 'in hedgerowes'.[298] At Newhall in Boreham in 1565 a ½-acre hedgerow had been 'fallen about 6 years last past and the spring not preserved', ie. not protected after felling as Fitzherbert recommended.[299]

The Elizabethan age was a time of rising demand for fuel (p.89), some of which came from hedges. The 1590s and 1600s were terrible years of cold and poverty. Courts took an increasingly severe attitude to hedge-stealing, for instance:

Any persons breaking any hedge or stealing wood be put next Sunday or holyday in the stocks for 2 hours at the least, and the wood be placed before them, signifying the cause of the punishment.

Felsted (Essex) 1567[300]

By 1600 at Ingatestone (Essex) hedgebreakers were being whipped until they 'bleed well' and receivers of stolen wood were spending all Sunday in the stocks.[300]

William Turner, the father of English botany, studied hedgerow ecology:

Arum . . . Cuckoopintell . . . groweth in euery hedge almost in England about townes.

Myrrhis [cow-parsley, kex *Anthriscus sylvestris*] is called in Cambrygeshire cas-shes . . . it groweth in hedges in euery countrey.

Vitis sylvestris [wild clematis] . . . groweth plentuously betwene ware and Barck-way [Herts] in the hedges, whiche in summer are in many places al whyte wyth the downe of thys vine.

Alliaria . . . Iacke of the hedges . . . groweth in hedges and diches.

The names of herbes (1548)

Eighteenth and nineteenth centuries The Great Enclosures, though not a universal transformation, were a time of more new hedging than ever before or since. The hedges planted between 1750 and 1850, probably about 200,000 miles, were at least equal to all those planted in the previous 500 years. The same applies to stone walls, in moorland country as well as on former open-field.

Early enclosure hedges could be quite elaborate. The Earl of Orford in 1718 spent the following on a hedge on the straight parish boundary between Snailwell and Chippenham (Cambridgeshire):[301]

Wood for (protective) fence	£15
280 elm and 36,000 'quick' (ie. hawthorn plants)	£5 18s 8d
5000 'crabb setts' (ie. crab-apple)	£1
Labour in planting	£3 4s

Enclosure Act hedging became commercialized. There had been nurserymen at least since the fourteenth century (p.224) and Tusser tells us to:

Buie quickset at market, new gatherd and small,
buie bushes and willow, to fence it withall.[3]

But the thousand million or more hedging plants needed to make 200,000 miles of hedge were big business, and founded the fortunes of several Midland nursery firms.

As time went on hedging became perfunctory. Much of Leicestershire – Quorn and Fitzwilliam fox-hunting country – has strong hedges with plenty of trees, though their straight drawing-board lines cannot be confused with medieval hedges. These mainly Georgian enclosures contrast with the Victorian enclosures of many Cambridgeshire parishes, with their flimsy single rows of hawthorn only. At the last Cambridgeshire Enclosure Act, Hildersham in 1883, few hedges were planted at all.

We should not regard the Georgians solely as creators of hedges. They saw themselves as destroyers of hedges, owing to agricultural subsidies (Chapter 3).

Even in Ancient Countryside, the pattern of hedges in 1900 was not exactly the same as in 1600, but the changes should not be exaggerated. It is sometimes said that early fields were large and that most of the present hedges result from subdividing them. This can seldom be literally true, for halving the average size of a set of fields requires only 40 per cent more length of hedge. And the converse happened at least as often: for instance, at Lawshall (Suffolk) the field size averages 3.9 acres in 1612[302] and 8.6 acres in 1922; at Earl's Colne (Essex) fields averaging 5.4 acres in 1598[50] had been enlarged to 8.2 acres by 1922. Big fields have been subdivided and small fields laid together, but the framework as a whole has often changed little (Fig. 9.2). Hedges added in an early alteration are usually the first to be removed in later alterations. The network remains mainly medieval, but contains many single hedges of all subsequent periods.

New hedging and walling in this period also transformed many Scottish, Welsh, and Irish landscapes; but we cannot yet say how much of these countries was affected. In Aberdeenshire, a study by Robin Callander shows that the present walls ('stane dykes'), which run in straight lines, are the result of a reorganization between 1770 and 1870 more thorough than any known in England. There had previously been walls, but almost every single one was demolished and its stones reused. A stane-dyke earlier than 1730 is now a rarity, except in remote places where the older fabric was preserved by the retreat of agriculture.[303] It is not known whether this is typical of Scotland.

In Ireland it has been supposed that almost all the present hedged and walled countryside results from an enclosure movement beginning in the mid-seventeenth century.[178] This claim seems to be based on the impressionistic kinds of evidence that have proved so unreliable for the history of the English landscape. Hedge systems in Ireland are just as diverse as in England; it is unreasonable that all the different kinds should have arisen within 200 years. 'Quickset hedges' are quite often mentioned in Civil Survey boundary perambulations of 1654.[10]

Recording and Dating Hedges

From 1870 until 1945 there was very little change in hedges. A few were grubbed out (Fig. 9.2); but air photographs of 1940 show a still almost complete network of hedges, even in arable areas (Plates III, XIII). The loss of hedges began after World War II and is now the most familiar aspect of the destruction of the English countryside. It has affected mainly the eastern counties, where some areas once richly hedged (eg. much of Ixworth, Suffolk) are now as featureless as any desert; but the west, and even Cornwall, has not entirely escaped.

In the twentieth century hedges were taken for granted and thought to be uninteresting. The different kinds of hedge were not noticed. Although their complex true history was never quite forgotten,[244] people preferred to believe that hedges were all recent and very artificial. The scientific study of hedges began with the book on the subject by Dr Max Hooper and his colleagues (Pollard and others 1974); it is now an active field of research, extending also to France.[304]

191

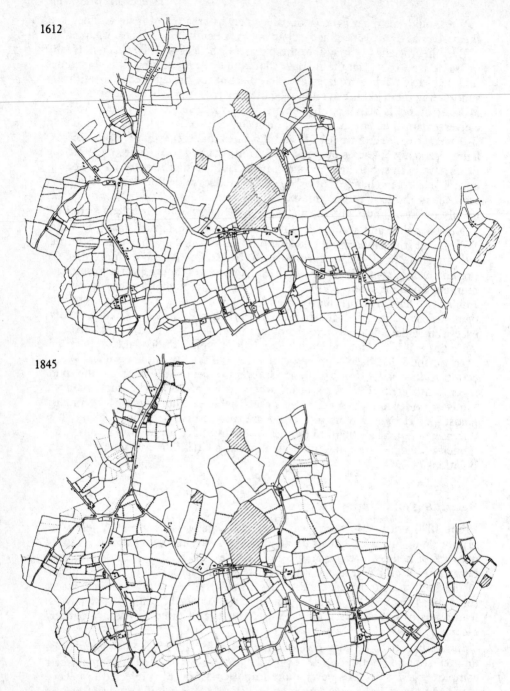

Fig. 9.2. The hedges of Lawshall, Suffolk, in 1612,[302] 1845, 1884, 1924, and c. 1980. Lawshall is a typical Ancient Countryside parish with no sign of open-field or of a semi-regular field layout. Despite many piecemeal alterations, about five-sixths of the hedges now surviving are older than 1612.

1884

1924

c. 1980

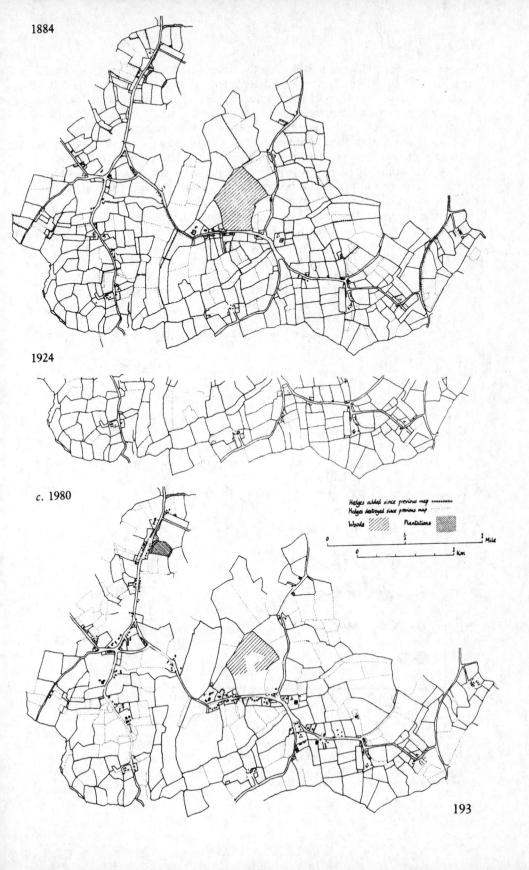

Hedges added since previous map
Hedges destroyed since previous map
Woods   Plantations

0   ½   1 Mile
0   1 Km

Species and age: Hooper's Rule In the time of ignorance we supposed that the trees and shrubs in a hedge were determined, in some vague way, by soil, climate, or management, or by the whims of those who planted the hedge. Dr Hooper noticed that all these were less important than the age of the hedge. He counted the tree and shrub species in 227 hedges whose age, varying from 75 to 1100 years, was known from written records, and found an unexpected degree of correlation between species and age (Fig. 9.3). The number of species, counted in a standardized way, is approximately equal to the age of the hedge in centuries. This rule of thumb has become famous under the misname 'Hooper's Hypothesis' (it is not in fact a hypothesis).

To make Hooper's Rule work, certain conditions have to be observed. It is customary to take a sample length of 30 yards, in which the species of trees and shrubs are listed. Unfortunately there is no standard definition of what is a species and what is a tree or shrub; hedge-daters generally agree not to count undershrubs (eg. brambles) and woody climbers (eg. ivy), nor to observe the finer distinctions of taxonomy (eg. between the different East Anglian elms). In Table 9.1 I suggest a list of recognized species.

Many regional and local studies of hedges have been done. In most of them the proportion of few-species and many-species hedges agrees well with what we

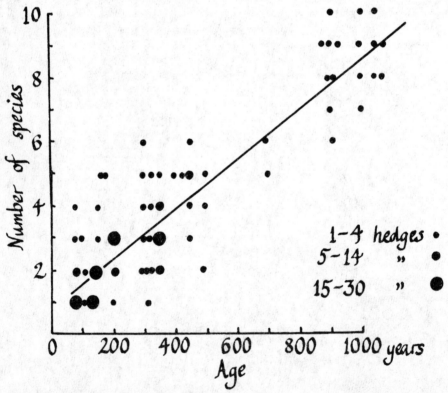

Fig. 9.3. Relation between the number of tree and shrub species in a 30-yard length of hedge and the age of the hedge. Counted on 227 hedges of known date by Dr Max Hooper (Pollard and others 1974) and reproduced by his kind permission.

Table 9.1   List of trees and shrubs for the purpose of hedge-dating

Alder	*Alnus glutinosa*
Apple (including crab)	*Malus sylvestris*
Ash	*Fraxinus excelsior*
Beech	*Fagus sylvatica*
Blackthorn	*Prunus spinosa*
Briar	*Rosa arvensis*
	R. canina
	R. rubiginosa
Broom	*Sarothamnus scoparius*
Buckthorn	*Rhamnus cathartica*
Cherry	*Prunus avium*
Cherry-plum	*P. cerasifera*
Dogwood	*Cornus sanguinea*
Elder	*Sambucus nigra*
Elm: wych	*Ulmus glabra*
English	*U. procera*
East Anglian	*U. minor*
Cornish etc.	*U. stricta*
Dutch, Huntingdon, etc.	*U. × hollandica*
Furze	*Ulex europaeus*
Guelder-rose	*Viburnum opulus*
Hawthorn: hedgerow	*Crataegus monogyna*
woodland (including hybrids)	*C. laevigata*
Hazel	*Corylus avellana*
Holly	*Ilex aquifolium*
Hornbeam	*Carpinus betulus*
Lime: ordinary	*Tilia × vulgaris*
pry	*T. cordata*
Maple	*Acer campestre*
Oak: pedunculate	*Quercus robur*
sessile (including hybrids)	*Q. petraea*
Pine	*Pinus sylvestris*
Plum (including bullace)	*Prunus domestica*
Poplar: aspen	*Populus tremula*
black	*P. nigra*
white	*P. alba*
Privet (wild)	*Ligustrum vulgare*
Rowan	*Sorbus aucuparia*
Sallow	*Salix caprea*
	S. cinerea
Service	*Sorbus torminalis*
Spindle	*Euonymus europaeus*
Sycamore	*Acer pseudoplatanus*
Wayfaring-tree	*Viburnum lantana*
Whitebeam	*Sorbus aria*
Willow: crack	*Salix fragilis*
white	*S. alba*
Yew	*Taxus baccata*

Some trees and shrubs which, though significant, are rare in hedges are omitted.

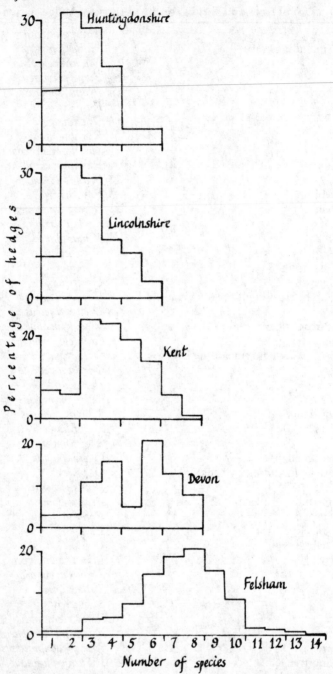

Fig. 9.4. Hedges having different numbers of species (trees and shrubs in a 30-yard sample) in four counties and in the parish of Felsham, Suffolk. The county surveys are by Max Hooper;[621] the 304 hedges of Felsham were recorded by Ann Hart (unpublished). By kind permission of Dr Hooper and Mrs Hart.

know of the history of an area. In Huntingdonshire and Lincolnshire hedges are predominantly *simple*, of 1, 2, or 3 species, but a minority are *mixed*, of 4, 5, or 6 species (Fig. 9.4). These counties have much Enclosure Act country but inherit a few hedges from before 1700. Devon and Kent are Ancient Countryside; although they were well hedged by the late Middle Ages (5 species and upwards), they also have many 3- or 4-species hedges, the result – we may guess – of post-medieval expansion into moor and heath, rearrangement of existing fields, and a small amount of typical enclosure. The oldest hedges of all were discovered by Mrs Ann Hart in Felsham (Suffolk), a parish of ancient scattered farms with remains of a semi-regular field system of the Iron Age or Roman type: hedges of 7 or more species predominate and three hedges have no fewer than 13 species.

The hedges of Rougham, Suffolk, have been studied by Mr David Dymond and Mr Colin Ranson. The parish is of a common East Anglian type with a central, solitary church from which church-paths radiate to six ancient hamlets and four ancient farms (Fig. 9.5). It lies just south of the champion country of the Breckland. The youngest hedges, of 1 to 4 species, are in the middle and north of the parish on the site of open-field and common-land formally enclosed in the late eighteenth century. Mixed hedges, of 5 to 10 species, are in the neighbourhood of the settlements and throughout the south of the parish. Medieval Rougham evidently had a central open-field bounded by heathland on the north and surrounded on the other side by settlements each with its own hedged fields. In the south there may have been substantial woodland in the early Middle Ages, later reduced to the small ancient woods which still survive.

Hooper's Rule can distinguish hedges of the Enclosure Act period from those of Stuart or Tudor times or of the Middle Ages. We cannot expect it to date hedges more precisely, especially as many of the documents which form the primary evidence record the existence rather than the date of origin of a hedge. At present the rule seems not to extend back more than 1100 years; it does not differentiate Anglo-Saxon from Roman hedges.

Why does Hooper's Rule work?
There are three hypotheses to account for the observation that older hedges have more species:
1. A hedge acquires further species as it gets older. Tree and shrub seeds are constantly being brought by chance and birds. They germinate and occasionally get established.
2. In earlier times it was the custom to plant hedges with more species than later. Enclosure Act hedges were generally planted with one species only, usually hawthorn (*Crataegus monogyna*). As with other fashions, it is not easy to determine why, but the large scale and commercial character of the operation encouraged simplicity. Georgian enclosers usually planted hedgerow trees; after the felling of the original trees the regrowth of the stumps gives the hedge a second species. Victorian enclosers often omitted the trees. Pre-Georgian hedges were often planted with two or more species. Lord Orford planted a mixed hedge from choice, but his predecessors often had to use whatever saplings they could dig up in woods or existing hedges:

> Item, in pulling plants of thorns and ashes to put along 1 ditch on the east of the manor-house to the churchyard.

> *Forncett (Norfolk), 1376–8*[305]

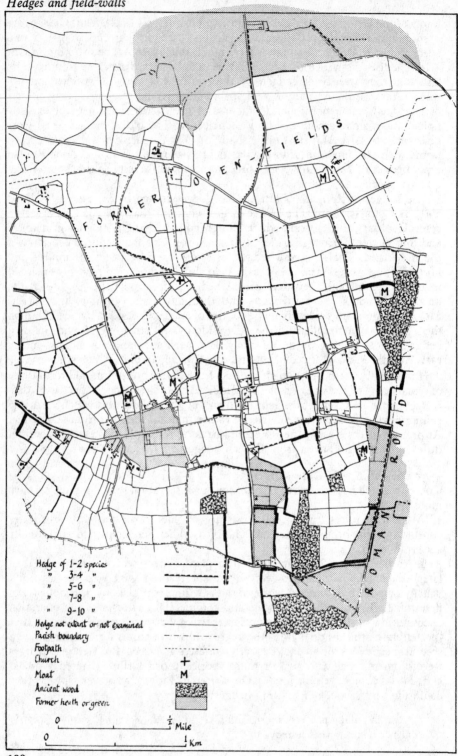

FORMER OPEN-FIELDS

ROMAN ROAD

Hedge of 1-2 species
    "   3-4   "
    "   5-6   "
    "   7-8   "
    "   9-10   "
Hedge not extant or not examined
Parish boundary
Footpath
Church   +
Moat   M
Ancient wood
Former heath or green

0   ½ Mile
0   1 Km

Gette thy quickesettes in the woodecountreye, and let theym be of whytethorne
and crab-tree . . . holye and hassell be goode.

Fitzherbert's Book of Husbandry, 1523

3. The older a hedge, the more likely it is to be natural rather than planted, and
therefore to be mixed from the start. Both kinds of natural hedge – ghosts on the
Shelley model, and accidental hedges on the Texas or Hayley Wood Railway
model – are unlikely to be specifically documented; but conditions for them to
arise have probably been much less rare in the past, especially in the distant
past, than they are now.

The elm exception Elm hedges sometimes have too few species for their age.
Some kinds of suckering elm, whether English or East Anglian (Chapter 11), are
highly competitive: they invade a mixed hedge, suppress the existing species (as
they do in a wood), and turn it into an elm hedge. The ancient field systems of
south-east Essex, for instance, have mainly pure elm hedges. The elms are of
distinctive kinds and evidently an early, possibly original, part of the system,[306]
but they make bad neighbours to other trees. Only here and there, in short
lengths which elms have not reached, do we find the expected mixed hedges.

The Grantchester exception I used to cycle daily along the Cambridge to
Grantchester road, and noticed that the hedge on the east side of the road had
consistently more species than its fellow on the west side. The explanation
illustrates several of the complexities of hedge-dating.

Grantchester was a typical woodless open-field parish, except that it had
unusually many hedges. Some of these lined the roads; others, as a pre-
enclosure map shows,[307] consisted of odd lengths of hedge lying haphazardly
among the strips. Whether these had once formed a more organized system is
not known. The 'Broad Way' leading to Cambridge was hedged on both sides
and varied in width from 40 to 80 feet. The parish was enclosed in 1802 and
some of the old hedges were taken into the new system. The opportunity was
taken to narrow the road to a width of 35 feet. The eastern hedge of the road was
preserved and the western hedge destroyed; it was not completely replaced by a
new hedge until after 1830.[308]

Each of the present hedges of the Grantchester road can be divided into about
fifty 30-yard lengths. The pre-1802 hedge has from 3 to 7, occasionally to 9,

Fig. 9.5. Numbers of species (trees and shrubs in a 30-yard sample) in the hedges of
Rougham, Suffolk. Rougham crosses the boundary between Ancient and Planned
Countryside. There is no village. From a central isolated church footpaths radiate to the
hamlets, greens, and farms. Settlements are thickly scattered in the south and around the
edges of the parish; here the hedges are strongly mixed, especially near the hamlets and
woods, and suggest a landscape mainly of the Middle Ages or earlier. In the north and
middle is an Enclosure Act landscape of big fields, straight simple hedges, and sparse
population. There are some anomalies. Some of the hedges on the sites of greens in the
south have too many species for their age: either they sprang up naturally along fences
(the Hayley Wood Railway exception to Hooper's Rule) or were planted with wild plants
dug up at random (the Neroche exception). Some roadside hedges near hamlets have too
few species, which suggests road-narrowing (the Grantchester exception). From observation kindly supplied by D.P. Dymond and C.E. Ranson.

species per length; the average is 5.2 species (Fig. 9.6). Allowing for a few garden plants like Japanese privet (*Ligustrum ovalifolium*), introduced at the Cambridge end, this indicates that the hedge grew up gradually and piecemeal between the thirteenth and seventeenth centuries, which is consistent with what we know of the history of the area. The post-1802 hedge has from 1 to 4, occasionally to 6, species per length; the average is 2.8 species, which is about one species too many for its age.

The two hedges are readily distinguishable: in all but five places, a 30-yard length of the older hedge has more species than its neighbour across the road. The commonest woody species in the old hedge is blackthorn, followed by hawthorn, elm, maple, dogwood, ash, briar, elder, wild privet, and hazel (Table 9.2), which form an almost random mixture. The new hedge has hawthorn in every length; the next commonest species are elm, blackthorn, ash, briar, maple, and elder. Most of the elm in the new hedge is a gardeners' elm of the *hollandica* group (Chapter 11). East Anglian elms predominate in the old hedge. The distribution of elm and blackthorn strongly indicates that the new hedge, which was in a number of ownerships, was planted partly as pure hawthorn and partly as hawthorn mixed with blackthorn or *hollandica* elm. It has been invaded haphazardly by species from the old hedge – ash, East Anglian elm (suckering beneath the road), briar, and less often maple and elder. Dogwood has only once got into the new hedge and hazel not at all.

The extra species in the post-1802 hedge therefore arise from (i) the tendency of some Grantchester landowners, contrary to the then fashion, to plant two-species hedges; (ii) the unusual opportunity for colonization given by a mixed hedge only a road's width away. The same causes can be seen in other Grant-chester post-1802 hedges, which commonly have 3 or 4 species in a 30-yard length. They are usually dominated by hawthorn or blackthorn, but also have English elm (foreign to this area, and can only have been planted) and various

Table 9.2 Occurrence of trees and shrubs in 30-yard lengths of the hedges of the Cambridge – Grantchester road, 1972

	Pre-1802 hedge	Post-1802 hedge
Total number of lengths	51	46
Total number of species	23	14
Average number of species per length	5.2	2.8
Number of lengths with:		
Blackthorn	45	19
Hawthorn (hedgerow)	39	46
Elm (East Anglian)	32	8
Maple	31	5
Dogwood	21	1
Ash	16	10
Briar (*Rosa canina*)	12	6
Elder	12	4
Privet (wild)	11	–
Hawthorn (woodland and hybrid)	10	1
Elm (*hollandica*)	4	18
Hazel	3	–

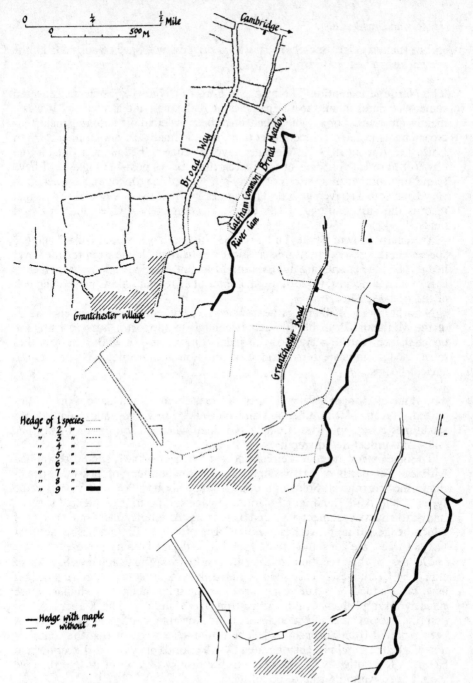

Fig. 9.6. (a) Part of the parish of Grantchester (Cambs), showing the hedges of the unenclosed open-field. From a map made in 1795.[622]
(b) The same area in the 1970s, showing the number of tree and shrub species in every 30-yard length of hedge (whether pre- or post-enclosure) then surviving.
(c) The same area, showing the distribution of maple in hedges. In this instance, the presence of maple is a better indicator of which hedges are pre-enclosure than is the number of species.

shrubs such as elder, buckthorn, and wild privet which have colonized from the pre-enclosure hedges nearby.

The Neroche exception The medieval Forest of Neroche, Somerset, covered some 4000 acres mainly in the parishes of Bickenhall and Broadway. It was a mainly grassland Forest which had once been wooded. It suffered major encroachments in the seventeenth century and was finally carved into fields by an Enclosure Act in 1833.[309] We thus have (a) ancient hedges just outside the physical Forest; (b) hedges of the encroachments; (c) post-1833 hedges. I have found the number of species in twenty-six 30-yard lengths of ancient hedge to vary from 3 to 11, average 6.0. This agrees well with a survey of 1567, which records the surroundings of the Forest as completely divided into enclosed fields.[310]

The encroachment hedges and post-1833 hedges have averages of 6.7 and 6.3 species; in this respect they are statistically indistinguishable from the medieval hedges. But the species are not the same. Elm and hazel are specially characteristic of the old hedges; furze of those of intermediate age; sallow, privet, and oak of the post-1833 hedges.

Neroche was a small area of new enclosure remote from the great enclosures of the Midlands. Probably it was not enough to support a nursery firm; the hedge-makers had to make do with plants dug up in the wild. The resulting mixed hedges indicate some degree of selection and are not the same as the ancient hedges.

The value of Hooper's Rule Hooper's Rule has told us much about the history of hedges from Northumberland and Norfolk[311] to Devon and Kent. It has sometimes been applied uncritically and then, when exceptions are found, has fallen into unjustified disrepute.

To some extent the rule is circumscribed by geography. It should be applied with caution north of Derbyshire, because the number of possible species diminishes northward. Some of the species may not be able to grow on extreme types of soil. After the original planting, hedge composition is affected surprisingly little by management and even by grazing. Attempts to 'cut out' species of which hedgers disapprove have seldom been effective. Elm and ash, the most tasty of trees, are constantly to be found in hedges adjoining pasture.

The first of the exceptions to the rule results from the peculiar behaviour of elm. The Grantchester exception is most likely to arise where recent hedges have been added to a landscape already containing hedges; a similar, more extensive example has been described from Derbyshire.[312] The Neroche exception results from an island of enclosure amid Ancient Countryside; a parallel has been reported from Shropshire.[313] These anomalies warn us that the composition of a hedge should be corroborated by other kinds of evidence. Exceptions to Hooper's Rule often tell us more about the history of a set of hedges than we should learn were the rule to be fulfilled.

Archaeological features Since 1700 most new hedges have run in exactly straight lines, in contrast to the irregular or only approximately straight hedges of earlier periods. This is a fashion which only some strong pre-existing feature (eg. a large stream) can overcome. The post-1833 hedges of Neroche are instantly distinguishable by straightness from the medieval hedges. A sinuous length in an otherwise straight hedge may indicate that part of a pre-existing hedge has been retained in a reorganization of fields.

Hedges are associated with many kinds of earthwork. Some have an immediately obvious meaning: a hedge that cuts across ridge-and-furrow cannot have existed while the ridge-and-furrow was in use, nor can a hedge that follows a headland but leaves no room for turning the plough. Others have a significance which can only be interpreted when sufficient records have been amassed: these include the many kinds of banks, walls, revetments, and lynchets that accompany hedges.

The structure of a hedge may tell us about its history. A post-1800 hedge usually has its original row of hawthorns still discernible; an ancient hedge often has giant coppice stools or pollard trees.

Particular plants are often more informative than the mere number of species. Two-species hedges commonly consist of hedgerow hawthorn with either ash, oak, briar, or blackthorn. Maple and dogwood, which are less good colonizers and are rarely planted, may be the fourth or fifth species in hedges of Tudor age, but are seldom found in recent hedges even if mixed (eg. post-1802 Grantchester and post-1833 Neroche). Hazel and spindle, less good natural colonizers still, are characteristic of hedges which are both pre-Tudor and have at least six other species. Hawthorn grows in nearly all non-elm hedges, except for some of the most ancient mixed hedges which lack it. Elder, a good colonizer but short-lived, occurs at random regardless of the age of the hedge.

Trees and herbs that are normally plants of woodland, not of hedges, may be very significant when they do occur in a hedge.[314] We have considered pry (*Tilia cordata*) as an indicator of a woodland-ghost hedge. The umbellifer *Pimpinella major*, characteristic of the borders of ancient woods adjoining lanes, still flourishes along exactly that length of road in Weston Colville (Cambridgeshire) which once adjoined Moyns Wood, last recorded on a map of 1612.[254] Wood-anemone and primrose may also have this property. In the east Midlands dog's-mercury is a plant of ancient woods, from which it spreads out into adjoining hedges at about 9 inches a year (Pollard and others 1974). This is not necessarily true of counties like Suffolk, where mercury grows in many ancient hedges remote from woods. The woodland species of hawthorn (*Crataegus laevigata*) occurs in a few very ancient hedges.

Dating of field-walls appears to be more difficult to systematize than that of hedges. The megalithic walls of the Land's End Peninsula depend on the abundance of a particular kind of boulder; others, equally ancient but differently constructed, doubtless remain to be recognized elsewhere. At the other extreme, the last (probably early nineteenth century) intakes from the moors in the Lizard Peninsula have very distinctive straight walls made of sods; the grass has disappeared but the alternating topsoils and subsoils of the turves are visible where the wall has been eroded. The wall was a means of disposing of some of the turf which agriculturalists were in the habit of paring off.

Stone surfaces may be datable by their lichen vegetation. At Stonehenge, the upper parts of the standing-stones are completely covered with many species of lichens which have grown over the centuries. Surfaces of stones that have recently been re-erected after being buried in the ground, or from which graffiti have been erased, are barren and take many years to recover their lichens. This has been studied by J.R. Laundon on walls of known date in Bradgate Park (Leicestershire).[315] The species present at different stages of colonization can enable a lichen expert to give the approximate date of the wall. At Bradgate he was unable to infer dates from the rate at which individual lichen plants expand to cover the surface, although this should be tried as a dating method elsewhere;[316] it too can be studied at Stonehenge or more conveniently on tombstones in churchyards. Lichens are much affected by the rock they are growing on as well as by the age of the surface.

Conclusions

The study of hedges has suffered from the belief that they are merely artificial. From the American parallel I hazard the conjecture that perhaps one-quarter of those in England have arisen naturally along fences and boundaries, chiefly at times of recession and neglect. Already in Anglo-Saxon times there were newly-planted hedges and hedges inherited from the Roman landscape; but many hedges had probably arisen by default in the Dark Ages. This explains why there should have been more hedges in the vicinity of woodland: as in America, default more easily produces a hedge where there is a wood to provide the seed.

Hedges are more complex, more difficult to record, and less easily replaceable than is often supposed. We are sometimes persuaded to acquiesce in their destruction on the grounds that a record of them might be preserved. As with historic buildings, this is true only of the more recent and less complex ones. There is little to be said for trying to preserve the typical Enclosure Act hedge; ancient hedges are of much more value both as habitats and as antiquities. No record of an ancient hedge can be complete; recording is not an adequate substitute for protection.

CHAPTER 10

Trees of hedgerow and farmland

. . . To the two oaks that stand into the road; then along the hedge to the east of Lamhyrst; . . . to the ivy-tod (*ifihtan stoc*); . . . to the stock that the swing-gate used to hang on; from the stock out through the middle of Hill-lea to the old ash; from the ash south over the road to the apple-tree; from the apple-tree to the white hazel; . . . along the hedgerow out to the Limburn . . .

Boundary of Havant (Hants), dated 980[317]
(A typical Ancient Countryside charter)

. . .Along the stoneway to the long crucifix at Hawk-thorn; then from Hawk-thorn to the long thorn at Icknield way; so to the third thorn at *Wirhangra*; from the thorn to the fourth thorn standing forth on Wrong Hill; so on to the fifth thorn; to the elder-tree (*elebeame*); then west along the little way up to the thorn . . . along the old ditch to the place of Æþelstan's tree . . . to the red-leaf maple tree . . .

Boundary of Blewbury (Berks), dated 944[318]
(A typical charter of downland and open-field)

This chapter is about the pollards and timber trees of hedges, trees standing in fields (Plate XVI) and around farmsteads, by watercourses, on downland, etc.

Hedgerow trees are poorly understood. Naturalists and writers associate trees with woodland; trees that do not fit that preconception are often misinterpreted as being an extension into the countryside at large of the eighteenth-century ideal of romantic landscape. Yet hedgerow trees are a distinctive and historic feature of England and probably Wales; they used to go far to make up for our relative lack of woodland. They are doubtfully historic in Scotland and Ireland. Most other countries that have hedges do not make our distinction between hedgerow trees and the rest of the hedge.

How Many Farmland Trees Are There?

Nobody knows. There are too many trees to count them all, and they are so unevenly distributed as to be difficult to sample: sampling can easily over- or under-represent the small areas in which most of the trees occur. How big does a young tree have to be before it is counted? How wide does a hedge have to be before it becomes a narrow wood? Such definitions have to be arbitrary, and yet changes of definition can have a large effect on the answer.

In 1951 the Forestry Commission, from a sample survey, estimated that England contained 56 million hedgerow and park trees more than 12 inches in girth, Wales (including Monmouthshire) 11 million, and Scotland 7 million.[319] Since England was about three-quarters farmland this comes to about 2.3 trees

205

per acre of farmland, including park trees. Another sample survey in 1980 estimated 62 million non-woodland trees more than 7 centimetres in diameter (8½ inches girth) in England.[320] Unfortunately the Commission went out of its way, by altering several of the definitions, to make the surveys difficult to compare. In 1980 it included, but did not separately record, trees of girths between 8½ and 12 inches; the omission of these would bring the total down to between 55 and 60 million.

Clearly the two Forestry Commission estimates cannot both be right. Between 1951 and 1980 a great many hedges, with their trees, were grubbed out; we cannot believe that these losses were balanced, let alone exceeded, by the growth of new trees in the remaining hedges. Additionally, about a quarter of the farmland trees in England have been lost to Elm Disease. If there were really 55 million non-woodland trees in 1980 there could not have been fewer than 75 million, at the very least, in 1951. The inconsistency of 40 per cent casts doubt on both surveys. This doubt is strengthened by the figures for regions of England, which vary in no consistent way: for instance, a large decrease was noted in north-east England (where Elm Disease had little effect) and a large increase in south-east England (where very many elms had died).

A survey of elms in 1971 reported 8.9 million elms more than 6 metres high in the south-eastern half of England, excluding woods and towns.[321] This comes to 0.7 elm per acre of farmland. Since elms would have been about a third of non-woodland trees, the total would have been roughly 2 trees per acre. A study by the Countryside Commission in 1974 of seven sample areas in England found between 0.05 and 0.8, average 0.28, tree per acre.[322] Norfolk County Council in 1978 reported 0.53 tree per acre of farmland.

No estimate of farmland trees can be better than an informed guess. The 1980 estimate was based on more samples than the others, and is thus less liable to statistical error; but it is so much higher than any of the other estimates (allowing for changes) that I suspect its definitions of being too wide and of including trees that the other surveys would have excluded. The 1974 estimate seems impossibly low, perhaps because with only seven samples well-tree'd areas were missed; but other, unpublished, surveys suggest that the Norfolk estimate is too high.

Compromising between the surveys, the number of hedgerow and field trees in England in 1980 was somewhere between 20 and 50 million. For purposes of comparison I shall settle for 35 million, 1½ trees per acre of farmland. In 1971 there would have been 2 trees per acre; in 1951 probably 2½ trees per acre, 60 million in all. Eastern England, from which most of my historical evidence comes, had fewer trees than the rest of the country, perhaps 1.5 per acre in 1951, 1.0 in 1971, and 0.6 in 1980. Norfolk had fewer still.

The farmland trees of 1951 would have been very roughly the equivalent in extent of 2½ per cent of woodland. At times they have probably been slightly more numerous. Since the actual woodland and plantation of England at one time declined to less than 5 per cent of the land area, non-woodland trees have, on occasion, amounted to at least a third of the total tree-covered area of England.

Species of Tree

Traditions of hedgerow trees differ from those of the nearby woodland. Oak is not the universal timber tree in hedges that it is in woods; hornbeam and lime (pry) are very rare as hedgerow trees. Among the peculiar trees of hedges, black and white poplars, though not now common, are of such historic importance as to deserve detailed mention. Elms have a separate chapter.

Three poplars are native or ancient introductions to Britain. Aspen, now mainly a woodland tree, used to be quite common in hedges. Black and white poplars are meadow and hedgerow trees and have never been recorded in ancient woods.

Black poplar *Populus nigra* is now one of our rarest and most distinctive trees. No other native tree can compare with it in rugged grandeur. Its massive straight but leaning trunk often reaches 100 feet high and 6 feet thick, with heavy branches which arch and sweep downwards (Plate XVII). The trunk and boughs are covered with great bosses; the bark is very deeply ridged and appears jet-black at a distance. Black poplar is one of the few trees that can often be recognized in drawings and paintings, although artists, even Constable, falsely depict it as upright. Like all poplars it has separate male and female trees. There are at least fifty males (with scarlet catkins in spring) to every female (with green catkins). Seedlings are therefore extremely rare. It normally reproduces by falling down and rooting from the prostrate trunk.

Black poplar is a tree of flood-plains and meadows, less often of hedges; I have only once seen it in a wood, and that wood is younger than the poplar. It is scattered over much of England, perhaps most abundant in fenny valleys in the Breckland and in the Hadleigh area of Suffolk. It has often been over-recorded through confusion with hybrid poplars. Despite its size it is easily overlooked and is still being discovered. Only a few thousand trees are known.[323]

Poplar is richly recorded in medieval documents. The word *popel* or *popular* is systematically distinguished from aspen (*aspe*) and white poplar (*abel*) and must denote black poplar. The diagnosis is confirmed by evidence of its immense size – eg. the sum of 12*d*. paid for the branches alone of one felled at Writtle (Essex) in 1399[324] – and by examples of the timber. Black poplar grows naturally into the great arching curves of cruck buildings. Poplar crucks are too perishable often to survive, but have been found in two barns in Herefordshire and two in Worcestershire.[325] They have the characteristic bosses and rugged bark of *P. nigra*. A massive half-log forms the lid of a medieval chest in East Bergholt church (Suffolk). The place Poplar in east London is first heard of in 1327.[326] Nearby, in the midst of railway dereliction, a single black poplar even now struggles for life.

Black poplar is quite frequent in sixteenth- and seventeenth-century records, although Evelyn thought it was rare. Since 1800 it has steadily declined. Most surviving trees are old.

A few black poplars are famous trees, like the two at Fen Ditton familiar to all Cambridge oarsmen. Mr Tom Beardsley tells me of the ancient Arbor Tree at Aston-by-Clun (Shropshire), in whose honour verses are sung and fertility rites celebrated.

Black poplar is one of the most specially English trees. It is even rarer on the Continent. To explain its occurrence we must go to the American prairies, where a very close relative, cottonwood (*Populus deltoides*), the *alamo* of Spanish-American place-names, still grows in natural woodland. I have seen a wood of poplar and elm, 300 miles long and ½ mile wide, fringing the South Platte River through Colorado and Nebraska. The giant trees have much of the grandeur of our black poplar.* They grow on unstable river-gravels, and it is their business to be uprooted by spates and to root again from the fallen trunks. Our black poplars (and some elms) are evidently the last shadow of the vanished flood-plain wildwood. At Icklingham in the Breckland there is still a combination of poplar meadows and arid sandhills which, multiplied 10,000 times, evokes the landscape of the Cheyenne Indians.

More than almost any other tree, black poplar reminds us of the splendour of the medieval countryside. For centuries it has been largely dependent on people propagating it from cuttings. When cuttings became commercialized and other poplars became fashionable it declined. But it is a very effective (and fast-growing) shade and timber tree; and it does not have a meaning which would be lost (p.29) were it to be more widely grown. Anyone with plenty of space on a suitable site should be encouraged to grow it.

White poplar White poplar, *Populus alba*, is commonly but wrongly supposed to have been introduced, along with its name *abele*, from Holland in the seventeenth century. Evelyn records such an introduction, but makes it clear that white poplar was already in England. In many medieval Suffolk records I have found *abel* as a non-woodland tree connected with, but distinct from, *popeler*: for example see p.337. Gerard's *Herball* (1597) claims the tree as a contraceptive: 'the same bark is also reputed to make a woman barren, if it be drunke with the kidney of a Mule'.

Only in the late seventeenth century was abele fashionable; it is now unpopular but is self-propagating (by suckers) and is not threatened. Many clones result from later planting but some, particularly in west Suffolk, could be ancient. Its origin is doubtful. *Flora Europaea* regards it as southern European, native in France and Germany but not Belgium or Holland. In England it is at least an ancient introduction and could be native.

Hybrid and exotic poplars Grey poplar, *Populus canescens*, is a hybrid between abele and aspen.[327] It could in principle be ancient but in all the clones I know I suspect recent planting.

The familiar Lombardy poplar is said to have been introduced in the mid-eighteenth century. It immediately became fashionable and big ones appear in Constable's paintings from 1805 onwards. It is a planter's tree, always male and incapable of looking after itself.

Since this time fashions in hybrid poplars have come in quick succession. The commonest, though now *démodé*, poplar is the 'Black Italian', a big leaning tree which looks like a factory-made poplar lacking all its rugged distinctiveness (although the French Impressionist painters, having no real black poplars, contrived to see beauty in it).

The Anglo-Saxon Period

The origin of hedgerow, field, and settlement trees is lost in antiquity. The first detailed records show that they were already commonplace by the eighth century AD. There were non-woodland trees in Classical as in modern Italy, but

---

* The tree should not be judged by the miserable variety of it grown by foresters in this country.

Plate I. The Tortworth Chestnut, Gloucestershire, a famous ancient tree (p.56)
April 1977

Plate II. A timber-framed house, probably of the fifteenth century, in Kersey, Suffolk. It consists of a great central hall (now subdivided) with two cross-wings (one shown). The spaces between the timbers are filled with wattle-and-daub containing underwood. Part of the house was later plastered over when exposed timbers became unfashionable.
May 1979

0   1 Mile

0   1 Kilometre

Plate III. Pye-Hatch Wood, Buxhall, Suffolk and its surroundings as photographed by a German pilot of World War II. The wood adjoins Pye Street, a fragmentary Roman road preserved to the north only as a hedge. The narrow clearing (arrowed; since overgrown) between the wood and road is an anti-highwayman trench and proves the wood to be medieval. Until the nineteenth century there were three medieval woods, of which (as often) only the smallest survives. Hitcham Great Wood (H) and Micklewood in Rattlesden (M) are both discernible as 'ghosts' – sinuous outlines enclosing unusual patches of straight parallel hedges.   *August 1940*[626]

Plate IV. A giant coppice stool of ash, the result of many successive cycles of felling and regrowth. About 5 feet in diameter and at least 400 years old. Hayley Wood, Cambridgeshire.   *May 1966*

Plate V. Section through a giant ash stool. It is hollow; the outer shell of wood contains about 150 annual rings, from which the dates of the last five coppicings can be ascertained and the age of the stool estimated. Silk Wood, Westonbirt, Wiltshire.
February 1980

Plate VIa. An area of the Bradfield Woods, Suffolk, in which the underwood was felled last winter and is beginning to grow again. Some of the poles and logs are still waiting to be taken away. The timber trees (oaks) which have been left standing are all young.

July 1977

Plate VIb. Coppice-wood newly felled in the foreground, with underwood of one year's growth behind and old underwood in the background. Bradfield Woods, Suffolk.

April 1972

Plate VIc. A Hitler's-eye view of the Bradfield Woods, Suffolk. Felsham Hall Wood lies to the north-east and Monks' Park (then intact) to the south-west. Both are a patchwork of areas of different years' growth since last coppicing, with a thin scatter of standard trees. A field at the north tip of Felsham Hall Wood has turned into woodland since the date of the photograph. *Luftwaffe photograph, August 1940*[627]

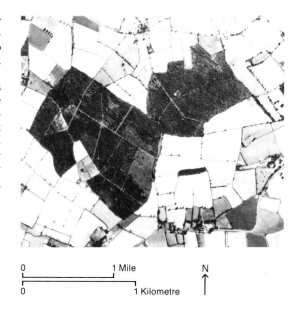

0		1 Mile	N
0		1 Kilometre	↑

Plate VII. A medieval or Anglo-Saxon woodbank, with a pollard oak on it. The underwood on and behind the bank has just been felled to produce the stacks of poles. There are young as well as older timber trees. Bradfield Woods, Suffolk. *April 1981*

Plate VIII. An Irish derry: a wood of ancient oaks and ivies on an island in a lough. Tullamore, Co. Offaly. *February 1983*

Plate IX. A park pale of cleft oak stakes: a slightly modernized version of the medieval park pale, which apparently had only one rail. Moccas, Herefordshire. *August 1974*

Plate X. A 'pseudo-medieval' park: ancient pollard oaks, originally farmland trees, now incorporated in a later park. Whepstead, Suffolk.
January 1982

Plate XI. A wood attacked by fallow deer. The tree foliage ends abruptly at a browse-line 4ft 1in. (1.22 m) above ground. An overgrown ash-maple-hazel wood; the ground is covered with bluebells, which the deer will not eat. Hayley Wood, Cambridgeshire.   *May 1981*

Plate XII. Staverton Park, Suffolk: a medieval deer-park still with its original pollard oaks.
May 1979

0 ————————————————————————————— 1 Mile

0 ————————————————————————————— 1 Kilometre

N

Plate XIII. The Iron Age or Roman field grid of the Dengie Peninsula, Essex. Elm and mixed hedges. *Luftwaffe photograph, September 1940*[628]

Plate XIV. Ridge-and-furrow at Husbands Bosworth, Leicestershire. The ridges represent selions in the open-field and should be studied together with Fig. 8.6. Most of the hedges are unquestionably later than the making of the ridges, but a few, near the village, follow headlands and could be contemporary.   *Cambridge University, May 1962*

Plate XV. The ghost of a former wood: a hedge composed of small-leaved lime, a strictly woodland tree which does not ordinarily get into hedges. Shelley, Suffolk.

October 1978

Plate XVI. Ancient pollard oaks in a field at Risby, Suffolk. Fields with many trees are a speciality of the Breckland edge; those at Risby are recorded (and distinguished from woodland) on a sixteenth-century map. *April 1980*

Plate XVII. A black poplar. Fen Ditton, Cambridge. *July 1971*

Plate XVIII. The 500-year-old oaks of Birkland in Sherwood Forest, Nottinghamshire: a magnificent example of the ancient oaks in which England excels. They prove that stag-headed trees (Fig. 10.2) are not necessarily dying. The dead boughs produce the unique beauty of Birkland as a landscape and its high repute for the special insect life of ancient trees. *November 1977*

Plate XIX. Wimpole Hall, Cambridgeshire: a landscape of many periods, seen in its heyday after World War II. The park was the work of many eighteenth- and nineteenth-century landscape designers, but incorporated earlier features such as the hamlet elms of medieval Wimpole (seventeenth-century examples of which are arrowed). The great south avenue of *c*.1718 cut motorway-like across the hedged fields of the previous landscape. The park also preserved extensive open-field and village earthworks. All these antiquities have since suffered from a combination of Elm Disease, tidiness, and improvement. *Cambridge University, July 1949*

Plate XX. Grime's Graves, Norfolk. The striped foreground is a wholly natural relic of an Ice Age: stripes of heather on deep sand alternate with chalk grassland. In the background are the 'hills and holes' of Neolithic flint-mines.

Cambridge University, January 1975

Plate XXIa. Wych-elm *Ulmus glabra*. Old Byland, N.E. Yorkshire. *March 1983*

Plate XXIb. English Elm, *Ulmus procera*. The newly-fallen bough is characteristic. Falmer, Sussex. *August 1980*

Plate XXIc. Boxworth Elm, one of the East Anglian elms (*Ulmus minor*). Knapwell, Cambridgeshire. *June 1979*

Plate XXId. Pollard elms of the East Anglian group along a deserted lane in a shrunken village. Longstowe, Cambridgeshire. *April 1971*

Plate XXIe. A pendulous kind of East Anglian elm. Felsham, Suffolk.

September 1975

Plate XXIf. 'Lizard Elm', one of the Cornish group of elms (*Ulmus stricta*). Like all suckering elms, it invades hedges and converts them into rows of genetically-identical elm trees. Trelanvean in St Keverne, Cornwall. *May 1980*

Plate XXIg. Intermediate between wych and East Anglian elms. An extreme example of the pendulous habit common in this group. Great Waldingfield, Suffolk.

August 1973

Plate XXIh. The great elms of Long Melford green, Suffolk, intermediate between East Anglian and English. *March 1974*

Plate XXII. Mellis Green, Suffolk: a large green of typical straggling shape, traversed by roads and with houses round its boundary. The straight line is the Ipswich-Norwich railway.   *Luftwaffe photograph, August 1940*[629]

Plate XXIII. Barton Broad, Norfolk. The chains of islands mark the otherwise submerged baulks which subdivide the basin of the Broad and prove it to be a medieval peat-pit. It originally measured about $1 \times \frac{1}{2}$ mile. Nearly half the water area has filled itself in and has become woodland.

Cambridge University, June 1952

0   ½ Mile   N

0   1 Kilometre   ↑

Plate XXIV. The river that turned into a village: Welney, Norfolk. The old course of the River Cam through the Fens is marked as a belt of three parallel curves meandering across the photograph. In its natural course the river built up huge levées of silt on which, already in Roman times, people were living. The Romans diverted it upstream, and it turned into a ridge of silt – a roddon – which has become ever more prominent as the surrounding peat has shrunk. In the Middle Ages villages grew up along the roddon. The middle of the three parallel curves, with houses strung out along it, is a road or a ditch marking the middle, and now the highest part, of the roddon; the flanking curves are ditches at the edges of the roddon. In the south-east corner the roddon acts as a causeway across the Ouse Washes, between the straight, seventeenth-century Old and New Bedford Rivers. This is the greatest of the Fenland roddons. The rest of the photograph is full of lesser roddons, the ghosts of minor pre-drainage creeks, on which are superimposed the geometrical ditches of the Third Draining.

Cambridge University, April 1978

0   ¼ Mile   N

0   500 Metres

Plate XXV. A shoal of pingos. The pastures in the middle of the picture are full of ponds and little bogs surrounded by grassy banks. A similar area to the east is overgrown with trees. Soil-marks to the north and west are shallow pingos now ploughed out. Gayton Thorpe Common, Norfolk.   *Cambridge University, October 1982*

we are not told whether the Romans had them in Britain. The mysterious pit-alignments of Iron Age England – single rows of regularly-spaced soil-marks running sometimes for miles across country[616] – have been proposed as rows of pits in which trees were planted to mark boundaries, but there is no means of confirming this conjecture.

Place-names Old English names of settlements that refer to trees, eg. Thornham, Aston, Sevenoaks, Maplestead, Birch, are common throughout England. Usually they have no woodland association and evidently refer to farmstead or village trees. For instance, in the middle of Ashwell (Herts) the river Cam still bursts from the ground in a great spring, to the Anglo-Saxons a 'well', beneath the roots of an ancient ash, successor to the original tree.

Thorn and ash are the commonest trees named, and with willow and oak make up nearly two-thirds of the total (Table 10.1). Others include hazel, alder, elm, birch, holly, and lime. As we might expect, trees strongly associated with woodland – beech, lime, service – are uncommon. Lime place-names, in the main, are clustered around those districts that still have native lime; but others such as *Lynd*hurst in the New Forest and *Bast*wick (from *bæst*, the fibre of the lime-tree) in the Norfolk Broads show that in early or middle Anglo-Saxon times the tree survived in a few areas from which it has since disappeared (p.102). Birch and alder place-names are commoner in northern England; maple is confined to its present southerly distribution.

Hornbeam is not known in pre-Conquest place-names but is unsuitable, being a woodland tree and difficult to identify. It is less easy to explain the rarity of elder (a tree of habitations, albeit sometimes thought unlucky) or the apparent absence of yew (with its ancient churchyard tradition) and poplar (a very distinctive non-woodland tree).

Some place-names, such as Coven*try*, Brain*tree*, and Ain*tree* (= one tree), are of unspecified trees. Names of hundreds, such as Thedwas*try* (Suffolk), indicate a special tree at which the hundred assembly met. At least twelve hundreds are named after thorns, such as Spelthorne (Middlesex).

Cornish place-names tell a somewhat different story: elder (*scawen*) is frequent, as in Boscawen 'house of elder', but oak (*dar*) is surprisingly rare, and elms, now so typical of Cornwall, are apparently absent from its place-names. Tree-names are also common in Welsh (eg. Llangollen and Derwen, equivalent to English Hazlestow and Oak) but are usually difficult to date. The same applies to Gaelic (eg. *giubhas*, pine; *fearn*, alder).

Charters Anglo-Saxon charters mention 766 trees, 639 being of named species. With 21 trees from the Welsh charters this makes a total of 787, or 5.1 per cent of the boundary features. If we include minor place-names (eg. Ashford), trees are involved in a grand total of 7.2 per cent of all the boundary points.

With rare exceptions these trees were in hedges or free-standing. Often this is clearly stated, as in the quotations at the head of this chapter. Only very rarely does the context imply woodland, in which trees would be of little value as landmarks. In those charters which describe woodland exclaves trees appear no more frequently than in other charters.

There is less evidence for non-woodland trees in Wales than in England, although Welsh laws imply them: anyone felling a tree on to the highway was fined six cows and forfeited both the tree and the cost of removing it.[90]

The trees identified (Table 10.1) differ from those in place-names. Thorn is much more predominant in the charters: although very distinctive, its small stature and commonness perhaps made it less suitable for naming places than as a landmark. Oak replaces ash in second place. The third commonest tree in charters is apple: the context usually implies a wild crab-apple, sometimes distinguished as 'sour appletree'. Other frequent trees in charters are willows and sallows, elder, and alder.*

Pear is the tenth commonest tree. Most of the pear-trees were in remote places and were evidently not orchard trees. These are the earliest written evidence for what is now one of our rarest trees, so rare that few Floras recognize it as native. Pear charcoal is widely recorded from the Neolithic onwards. Wild pear is occasionally mentioned in medieval documents and in 1597 is described in Gerard's *Herball*. It has steadily declined and I have seen only five solitary trees, of which the great pear tree of Hayley Wood (Rackham 1975) is the best known.

Other rare and interesting trees are service (Stoke Prior, Worcs; White Waltham and Chieveley, Berks) and box (Ecchinswell and East Meon, Hants). The one mention of *popul* at Michelmarsh (Hants) may refer to black poplar, which would otherwise be unaccountably absent from the Anglo-Saxon evidence.

Beech, birch, and aspen are uncommon in charters; this is perhaps because they tend to be woodland trees and are gregarious, so that individuals are seldom isolated enough to be used as landmarks. The infrequency of elm is unexpected.

Individual trees are often distinguished, either by somebody's name or by some peculiarity. Many trees were *hār*, 'hoar', an adjective which survives in 'hoar-frost' and is often used of old men's beards. A hoar tree was probably grown with beard-like lichens such as *Usnea* and *Ramalina* species. Surprisingly few trees were 'old'. They were sometimes 'crooked' (*wōh*), and at Abbot's Wootton (west Dorset) there was a 'prostrate oak'. The 'red-leaved oak' at Overton (Hants), 'red-leaved beech' at East Meon (Hants), and others are a record of those rare and striking trees that produce bright scarlet leaves every year: there is just such an oak in Hayley Wood. The 'footy oak' (*fohtyhtan æc*) at North Stoneham (Hants) may have been another genetic variant, one of those oaks with a swollen 'elephant's-foot' base. Trees are occasionally identified by associated plants, such as the 'pignut thorn' (*eorþnutena þorn*) at Overbury (Worcs), the 'ivied alder' at Stoke St Mary (Somerset), and the 'bramble-thorns' at Christian Malford (Wilts) and elsewhere. A curiosity at Bishop's Cleeve (Worcs) was 'appletree and mapletree grown together'.

Sacred trees are few. There was a holy oak at Chetwood (Bucks), and in the Latin bounds of Taunton is 'an ash which the inexperienced call sacred'. 'Crucifix oaks' at Stoke Prior and Tardebigge (Worcs) are reminiscent of the crucifixes set on wayside trees in Austria today. If, as often supposed, a Gospel Oak is where the Gospel of the day was read at a liturgical beating of the parish bounds, it ought to occur in the charters, but does not, although there was an Epistle Oak on the boundary of Ringwood (Hants). (The Gospel Oak at Pol-

---

* The mysterious *elebeam*, mentioned six times, is counted as a spelling variant of *ellerbeam*, 'eldertree'. Anglo-Saxon translators of Scripture used it to render 'olive', but that is impossible in our climate.

stead, Suffolk, still standing in the nineteenth century, was not on the parish boundary.)

Not many pollard trees are mentioned. A pollard oak (*coppedan āc*) is recorded at St Mary Bourne (Hants), and there are several pollard thorns, nowadays rarely met with. What were the 'clipped trees' at Watchingwell (Isle of Wight) and elsewhere? Some trees were 'marked': at Ecchinswell (Hants) there was a marked aspen and a marked oak; at Horton (Dorset), not now lime country, there was a marked lime.

Table 10.1   Occurrence of tree species in English place-names and in Anglo-Saxon and Welsh charters

	Names of towns, villages, and hamlets†	Trees in charters	Trees and tree place-names in charters
Total number of occurrences	812	658	966
Percentage frequency of:			
Thorn	18.0	38.7	29.7
Ash	17.7	7.0	9.9
Sallow, willow, or withy	15.5	7.6	10.9
Oak	11.8	13.1	11.7
Alder	6.9	4.1	5.4
Hazel or nut	7.5	1.1	4.1
Apple or crab	0.5*	9.7	7.0
Elder or *elebeme*	1.4	7.0	5.8
Elm or wych	4.9	2.0	1.6
Birch	3.6	0.8	1.6
Lime	3.1	1.2	2.1
Maple	1.8	2.4	2.5
Holly	3.1	0.9	1.1
Aspen	1.6	0.5	1.0
Beech	1.8	0.2	0.2
Pear	—*	1.7	2.0
Blackthorn or sloethorn	0	0.6	0.8
Yew	0	0.2	1.2
Lusporn (unidentified)	0	0.6	0.4
Chestnut	0.4	0	0
Service	0	0.5	0.3
Box	0	0.3	0.2
Cherry	0.1	0	0
Rowan	0.1	0	0
Plum	0	0	0.2
Poplar	0	0	0.1
	100	100	100

*'Apple' and 'pear' are not counted because some place-names may allude to orchard trees.
†Mainly derived from Ekwall (1960) and Smith (1956).

About fifty of the trees are described as a 'stub' (*styb*), probably meaning a coppice stool. About half the stubs are of elder, a third of thorn, and the rest of eight other trees including sallow and pear. Surprisingly little account was taken of landmark trees that had disappeared, although we occasionally meet 'site of a tree' (*trēowstede*), as at Queen Dart (Devon) or 'site of an ash', as at Hinton Ampner (Hants). At Wood Eaton (Oxon) there was a 'thorn west of where the great thorn stood'.

Geographical distribution of trees in the charters Trees as a whole are relatively evenly distributed (Fig. 10.1a). They are deficient in Cornwall and the Fens; the Reading and London Basins and Wiltshire Claylands have a slight excess. (Most Welsh and Kentish perambulations are sketchy and for this reason show few trees.) In general trees show no correlation with either woodland or hedges. In future Ancient Countryside they are no more often named (5.1 per cent of boundary features) than in open-field districts (5.5 per cent).

Particular trees have very uneven distributions. Oak is by far the commonest tree named in North Worcestershire and forms 3 per cent of all the boundary features there, but no oaks are named in South Wiltshire, the Uffington Scarp, the Woodless Cotswolds, Mid Hampshire, the Isle of Wight, the Fens, or Cornwall. Thorn, in contrast, forms 4½ per cent of all boundary features on the Uffington Scarp but is rarely named in North Worcestershire.

Tree species in charters, like non-woodland trees today, vary with different land-use traditions rather than with particular soil types. The quotations at the head of the chapter contrast the thorns of the Berkshire Downs with the oaks and other trees of South Hampshire. Trees can be divided into three groups, of which oak, thorn, and willow are typical. Trees of the oak group, including also lime, birch, pear, service, and beech, are specially associated with well-wooded regions (Fig.10.1b). Although the actual trees of the charters were not normally in woods, they grew in places where woodland was not far distant. Trees of this group are mentioned nearly three times as often in what was to be Ancient Countryside as in open-field areas, which often lacked woodland (p.179).

Thorn, blackthorn, apple, and elder are especially associated with lack of woodland (Fig.10.1c). They were most abundant on downland and among open-fields. Trees of this group are mentioned twice as often in open-field areas as in Ancient Countryside.

The other trees – willow (including withy and sallow), ash, alder, maple, elm, hazel, holly, aspen, yew, etc. – are not associated either with the presence or absence of woodland but were evidently the general trees of farmland, hedges, and watercourses. Their distribution follows no very specific pattern (Fig.10.1d). They are the commonest trees mentioned in charters of the Fens, Devon, the Mendip area, and Wales. They are about 1½ times as common in charters of Ancient Countryside as of open-field districts: presumably in the latter they were mainly confined to watercourses but in the former occurred in hedgerows as well.

To some extent trees in the charters reflect the behaviour of non-woodland trees to this day. Trees of the oak group, except for oak itself, are still strongly associated with woodland; trees of the thorn group, except perhaps for crab-apple, still occur in downland and among arable well away from woodland; ash, willow, and alder are still the common trees of watercourses independently of woodland. But there have been some changes. Oak has lost the association with woodland which it had a thousand years ago. Maple, holly, and especially hazel are now trees of ancient hedges and are more strongly associated with Ancient Countryside than they were at the time of the charters.

Middle Ages

No trees are directly mentioned in Domesday Book. In the following century *The Owl and the Nightingale* (p.187) mentions the earliest hedgerow trees in English literature, an ivy-tod and a lime.

With the revival of record-keeping in the thirteenth century, evidence for non-woodland trees is resumed. They are usually beneath the notice of surveys, but are mentioned in almost any long run of estate accounts or of court rolls. There were hedgerow trees and trees sheltering buildings, around ponds, lining river-banks, and standing in fields. They gave rise to income, disputes between neighbours or between landlord and tenant, obstructions of the highway, and petty offences:

> From willows round the pond 19*d*. From willows at Fokewic 18*d*.
>
> *Hindolveston (Norfolk) estate accounts 1265–6*[328]

> 1 dry [ie. dead] ash sold on the manor-house moat (*super foueam manerii*) 6*s*. 4*d*. [A gigantic tree: woodland oaks seldom cost as much as 2*s*. each.]
>
> *Hindolveston 1312–3*[329]

> John House complains that William Bene . . . [in 1435] cut off the branches of certain trees of the said John, namely poplars and maples, growing in a certain hedge of his belonging to three rods of arable land of the said John's . . .; and the said William took and carried away the underwood of the branches which he had cut off; and . . . the said William again [this year] in the same way cut off the branches of the said trees and took and carried away the branches whereby the said John has . . . suffered damage to the value of 10*s*. [This evidently refers to pollarding.]
>
> *Court roll, Hatfield Broad-oak (Essex), 1443*[274]

> John Petye cut down 1 poplar without permission . . . [fined 2*s*.] Will Gunnild cut down 1 abel and sold it without permission . . . worth 2*s*. 6*d*. [The trees were the lord of the manor's; Gunnild was apparently acquitted.]
>
> *Court roll, Nowton (Suffolk), 1310*[330]

> The Lady Countess has one ancient and decayed poplar growing too far over the King's highway [and agrees to let the parish have it for a bonfire].
>
> *Court roll, Great Canfield (Essex), 1422*[288]

> [A tenant] damaged the common highway and made a nuisance by cutting down trees.
>
> *Court roll, East Donyland (Essex), 1385*[95]

> John Gru . . . cut off the branches of an ancient oak without permission, amounting to 1200 billets worth 6*s*. [Another gigantic tree: there were about 500 billets to the ton of firewood.]
>
> *Court roll, West Donyland, 1392*[95]

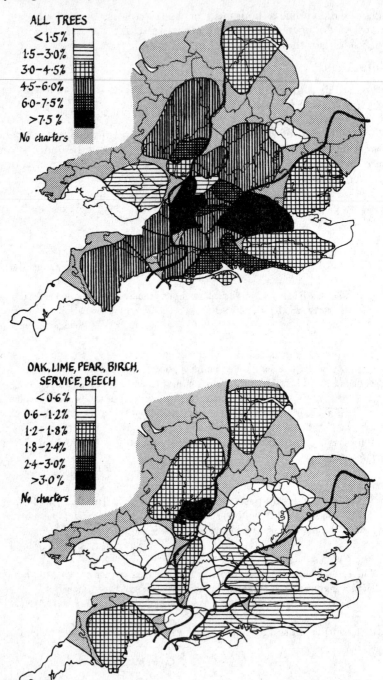

Fig. 10.1 Distribution of trees in Anglo-Saxon and Welsh charters, as a percentage of all boundary features.

HAWTHORN, BLACKTHORN,
APPLE, ELDER, LUSPURN
Key us for Oak etc.

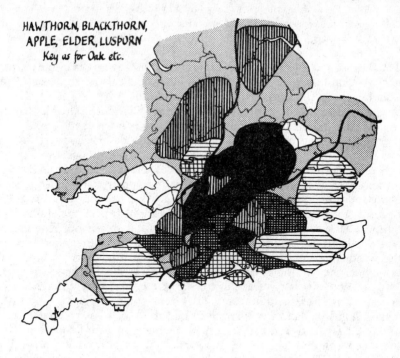

WILLOW, WITHY, SALLOW.
ASH, ALDER, MAPLE,
ELM, HAZEL, NUT,
HOLLY, ASPEN,
BOX, YEW
Key as for Oak etc.

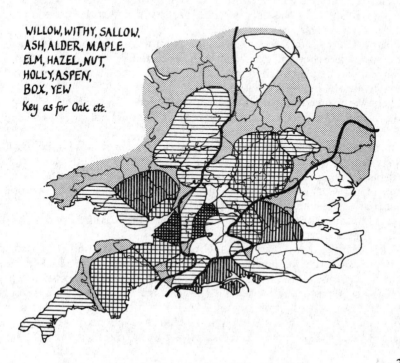

215

> John . . . Gybbe cut down one willow in which was a swarm of bees (*unum swarm apum*) and destroyed the said swarm and took the wax and honey. [Fined 40*d*.]
>
> *Court roll, West Donyland, 1391*[95]

The Suffolk and Essex examples are from well-hedged parts of the country, but non-woodland trees existed even in open-field districts, as at Gamlingay (Cambs). They comprised both pollards and timber trees. The latter, as in two instances just quoted, were often much larger and more valuable than trees in woods. At Hindolveston, which had rather few non-woodland trees, I find that the average income between 1255 and 1327 from trees on 2200 acres of farmland was £0.53 a year, equivalent to that from 12 acres of the local woodland.

Some records of species are given in Table 10.2. At Hindolveston, for instance, ash is often mentioned, willow occasionally, and alder once; in the Donylands there are six references to oak, one to elm, and one to willow. Records are of timber trees or pollards and for this reason do not often mention thorn. The species are independent of the local woodland. The commonest non-woodland tree could be oak, ash, elm, poplar, or willow; there is no trace of the woodland convention of selecting oak as a timber tree. Elm, although commoner than in Anglo-Saxon charters, was probably less abundant than now.

Apart from the lack of exotic trees, the most striking difference from the present scene was the abundance of (black) poplar, probably the fifth commonest non-woodland tree mentioned in Suffolk and Essex. Poplar and abele, among the few native softwood trees, were much used for floorboards etc. in an age when conifers had to be imported.[361] Poplars were felled at Brandon (Suffolk) for flooring the rabbit-warren lodge in 1386–7;[362] they evidently grew in this valley of the then-woodless Breckland much as they still do at nearby Icklingham. They were not all timber trees; at Polstead (Suffolk) we hear of four 'bollyng poplars' (ie. pollards, p.65) in 1407,[333] and at Writtle (Essex) in 1398–9 a wayside poplar was shredded (p.229).[324]

Pollard willows along watercourses are recorded at Cambridge, both in the town fens (where they still exist) and in the open-fields.[241,363] At Oxford in 1301 an inquest was held on a schoolmaster who fell into the Cherwell from a pollard willow while cutting rods with which to beat his boys.[364]

There were some non-woodland trees in Scotland. In the Southern Uplands medieval perambulations, like those of Anglo-Saxon England, often mention thorns and trees marked with crosses.[44]

Timber of non-woodland trees must often survive in medieval buildings but is seldom identifiable, apart from poplar. Pruning branches from roadside trees is often mentioned in court rolls, and it is not uncommon to find the sawn-off stump of a branch embedded by further growth of the tree.[365] Bollings of pollards are occasionally mentioned as felled for timber; in a house at Stebbing (Essex) I have seen an entire small elm pollard used as the lintel of a (post-medieval) great fireplace.

Until recently there survived at Great Livermere (Suffolk) a fourteenth-century church roof of ingenious design: the timbers were crooked and in consequence some of the trusses were asymmetrical and others not in one plane. They had been sawn lengthwise out of large oaks, even offcuts from the outside of the tree being used. Probably only twelve to fifteen trees were used in the whole roof of thirty trusses. Although the church is quite costly the roof shows much evidence of economy and has always been thatched. Livermere is a woodless Breckland parish. I infer that the parishioners ran out of money for the roof and could not transport conventional timber from outside; they secured a few, very large, crooked trees and had a carpenter of unusual skill who could saw around corners and could design special trusses to make use of these particular trees.[154]

Hedgerow trees probably increased in numbers during the Middle Ages in parallel with the increase of hedges.

The Heyday of Hedgerow Trees, 1500–1750

From 1500 to 1750 the earlier kinds of evidence for farmland trees are reinforced by detailed surveys, maps, and landscape paintings. Some of the trees themselves are preserved in pseudo-medieval parks (p.129).

Surveys Soon after 1495 Thomas Waring made a detailed survey of more than 2000 timber trees at Tanworth-in-Arden (Warwickshire).[334] The trees, except for some small groves, were said to be in 'heges'. Oaks were described in terms of the 'joustes', 'purlyns', and other house timbers that might be made from them, and their bark was valued. Ashes were regarded as wheelwright's timber and are measured as so many felloes in length.

This is the earliest and nearly the most detailed survey of hedgerow trees on a farm or estate. A few valuations of confiscated monastic estates numbered the farmland trees, as on a 170-acre farm at Long Melford (Suffolk) in 1546:

> In [a 3-acre grove] and about the scytuacions of the sayde manor & dyverse tenements there & in the lands perteyninge to the same be growynge 200 okes and elmys of 40 and 60 yeres growth parte usually cropped [ie. pollarded) & shredde [p.229] whereof 160 reseruid for tymber to repayre the houses . . . and to mayn-teyn the hedges & fences about the sayde landes & 40 resydue valued at 6d the tree . . .[337]

Such surveys later become more frequent. They may specify the number of trees, species, and whether timber or pollard. The usual convention is to assign trees to particular fields rather than hedges: we are not told how the surveyor decided to which field to assign the trees in a hedge, or how he avoided counting them twice.

In 1605 James I had a survey made of trees and wood on Crown lands, for he intended to raise money by selling superfluous trees. Trees in woods, parks, commons, Forests, and farmland were numbered and valued; they are entered as 'tymber' or 'decaied'.[366] Decayed trees were presumably pollards: they were of small value per tree and apparently absent from woods, and the sixteenth century, with its slowly-rising price of trees, was hardly a time when large numbers of *timber* trees would have been allowed to rot through under-use. In 1608–9 there was a further survey of timber on Crown lands suitable for shipbuilding, in order that the Navy, then still his Majesty's private Navy, might be maintained without having to spend money on buying timber.[367] Only the larger trees were included, classified according to the riders, futtocks, knees, and other special shapes which each might provide. These surveys, though hasty and unfinished, are extensive and enable woodland and non-woodland trees to be compared.

Table 10.2 Species of farmland trees in surveys and other documents

Place	County	Date	Kind of document	Oak	Ash
Hindolveston[331]	Norf.	1255–1327	Accounts	–	+++
Cambridge[241]	Cambs.	*c.* 1360	Survey	–	–
Woodford[332]	S.W. Essex	1364–73	Court roll	++++	–
Donyland[95]	Essex	1398–9	Court "	+++	–
Writtle[324]	Essex	1398–9	Court "	+++	–
Polstead[333]	Suff.	1407	Court "	+	+
Tanworth[334]	Warw.	*c.* 1500	Survey	1215 (66%)	594 (32%)
Culford[335]	Suff.	*c.* 1540	Survey	–	–
Graces (in Little Baddow)[336]	Essex	1545	Survey	215 (66%)	39 (12%)
Long Melford[337]	Suff.	1546	Survey	+++	–
Basildon[338]	Essex	1558	Survey	–	+++
Blickling[339]	Norf.	1576	Survey	84 / 32½ young } 63%	34 / 33½ young } 36%
Barham[340]	Suff.	1560 × 1600	Court roll	3 (9%)	30 (91%)
Earl's Colne[341]	Essex	1597–1609	Diary	+++ poll.	+ poll.
Ickburgh[342]	Norf.	1651	Survey	–	+++ poll.
Langley[343]	Norf.	1676	Survey	19 (70%)	8 (30%)
Buckenham (near Blofield)[344]	Norf.	*c.* 1700	Survey	236 / 19 young } 49%	194 / 33 young } 44%
Copdock[345]	Suff.	1708	Survey	35 (59%)	12 (20%)
Badwell Ash[346]	Suff.	1730	Survey	34 (18%)	133 (68%)
Bardwell[347]	Suff.	1730	Survey	77 (22%)	205 (59%)
Lindsey[348]	Suff.	1733	Map	1 timb. / 65 poll. } 42%	1 timb. / 9 poll. } 6%
Little Coggeshall[349]	Essex	1734	Survey	131 timb. } 21% / 715 poll.	214 timb. } 15% / 376 poll.
Thorndon[350]	Suff.	1742	Survey	67%	16%
Woodham Ferrers[351]	Essex	1771	Survey	822 (89%)	73 (8%)
Coggeshall[352]	Essex	1787	Survey	686 (79%)	165 (19%)
Little Henny[353]	Essex	1799	Survey	34 (25%)	2 (2%)
Aveley[354]	Essex	1799–1801	Survey	18 (7%)	7 (3%)
Ramsden Bellhouse[355]	Essex	1800	Sale	187 (75%)	47 (19%)
Spexhall[356]	Suff.	1801	Survey	211 (7%)	452 (15%)
Brandeston, Cretingham, Monewdon[357]	Suff.	1821	Survey	238 (3.5%)	555 (8.2%)
Coltishall[358]	Norf.	1827	Sale	175 (75%)	38 (16%)
Frostenden, Wrentham, Uggeshall[359]	Suff.	1849	Survey	96 timb. / 99 young } 33% / 34 poll.	83 timb. / 97 young } 27% / 7 poll.
Barking[360]	Suff.	1881	Survey	541 (43%)	99 (7.9%)
Saham Toney[356]	Norf.	1906	Sale	59 (44%)	75 (56%)

Notes:
1. 173 birch (2.6%), 163 fir, 78 alder, 37 sycamore, 24 chestnut, 15 beech, 11 walnut, 8 lime, 3 holly, 2 plane, 1678 unspecified young (25%), 3127 unspecified poll. (46%)

Elm	Willow	Aspen	Maple	Poplar	Others
–	++	–	–	–	Alder +
–	+++	–	–	–	Hawthorn +
–	–	–	–	–	
+	+	–	–	–	
–	++	–	–	+	
++	–	–	–	+++ poll.	
–	26 (1.4%)	16 (0.9%)	–	–	Alder +
+++ poll.	–	–	–	–	
12 (22%)	–	–	–	–	
+++	–	–	–	–	
+++	–	–	–	–	
2 (1%)	–	–	–	2 (1%)	
–	–	–	–	–	
++ poll. & timb.	+	–	–	–	
+++ poll.	–	–	–	–	
–	–	–	–	–	
34 (6.6%)	–	–	–	–	1 abele, 6 unspecified young
12 (20%)	–	–	–	–	
27 (14%)	–	–	–	–	
58 (17%)	2 (1%)	–	–	2 (1%)	5 sycamore, 1 walnut
14 timb. / 37 poll. }32%	32 poll. (20%)	–	–	–	
370 timb. / 1848 poll. }55%	30 poll. (0.7%)	–	58 timb. / 309 poll. }9.0%	–	10 timb. hornbeam (0.2%)
17%	–	–	–	–	
25 (3%)	–	–	–	–	
22 (3%)	–	–	–	–	
100 (74%)	–	–	–	–	
220 (90%)	–	–	–	–	
15 (6%)	–	–	–	–	
–	–	–	–	–	2351 unspec. poll. (78%)
243 (3.6%)	3 (0.04%)	35 (0.5%)	7 (0.1%)	82 (1.2%)	See Note 1
–	–	–	–	–	See Note 2
18 timb. / 72 young / 47 poll. }20%	–	–	3 poll. (0.4%)	2 (0.3%)	See Note 3
221 (18%)	13 (1.0%)	–	3 (0.2%)	51 (4.1%)	See Note 4
–	–	–	–	–	

2. 10 beech (4%), 5 abele, 4 "red poplar", 1 sycamore
3. 33 lime poll., 20 fir, 7 chestnut poll., 3 hornbeam poll., 2 holly poll., 75 unspecified young
4. 32 cherry (2.6%), 11 alder, 6 hornbeam, 272 conifers and other exotics (22%)

Maps The earliest large-scale maps contain ample evidence of non-woodland trees, which are shown in thousands on, for instance, the Havering (Essex) map of *c*.1610.[368] The pre-1720 maps in Suffolk and Essex Record Offices usually depict a multitude of hedgerow trees, often evenly spaced as a conventional indication of which hedges had trees, but sometimes represented as individuals (as at Terling, Essex, in 1597).[369] The sideways spreading of a hedge (eg. by elm suckers) is indicated by two or more rows of trees. Trees in fields are also shown. Trees lining fen watercourses and greens are depicted on Hamond's plan of Cambridge city (1592) and in a sixteenth-century map of the northern Fens.[370]

Other sources Sources continuing from earlier centuries include estate accounts and even perambulations:

> . . . along the said Parke, goeing as neere to the pale as may be, downe to the River-banks, and soe to a greate Poplar-tree standing on the said banke marked with a crosse . . .

> *Bounds of Colchester, 1671*[371]

Court rolls cease to be informative after 1580, but hedgerow trees continued to cause trouble between landlord and tenant. The usual custom was for timber trees and the bollings of pollards to be the landlord's property; the regrowth of pollards was the tenant's. At Copdock (Suffolk) in 1775 the tenant was required to 'keep . . . Pollard Trees under a regular fall of 9 years growth under the Penalty of 10*s*. a tree'.[372] Such a formal arrangement was unusual, but landlords often objected to tenants starting new pollards. In 1611 Roger Harlackenden, lord of Earl's Colne (Essex)

> went to Samuell berners ground & ther we found 60 upright timbertrees at ye least yt had been girt [ie. made into pollards] within the 2 or 3 year all about 20 years growth some a fadem [6ft] about and many as bigg as a mans middle.[341]

In 1615 he dispossessed a tenant 'for cropping & girting 2 or 3 upright timber trees & selling bollingers'.

Table 10.3 Surveys of farmland trees per acre of land

Place	County	Kind of document	Date
Tanworth[334]	Warw.	Survey	*c.* 1500
Long Melford[337]	Suff.	Survey	1546
Coggeshall[373]	Essex	Map	1619
West Thurrock[374]	Essex	Map	1645–6
Ickburgh[342]	Norf.	Survey	1651
Badwell Ash[346]	Suff.	Survey	1730
Bardwell[347]	Suff.	Survey	1730
Lindsey[348]	Suff.	Map	1733
Little Coggeshall[349]	Essex	Survey	1734
Thorndon[350]	Suff.	Survey	1742
Shipdham[375]	Norf.	Survey	*c.* 1763
Woodham Ferrers[351]	Essex	Survey	1771

The earliest pictures of identifiable landscapes, such as Hoefnagel's view of Norwich in 1580, depict hedgerow trees. They appear in vast numbers in almost all the views of English landscapes by the seventeenth-century artists Jan Siberechts, John Kip, and Mathias Read.

Numbers and kinds of trees At the end of the Middle Ages non-woodland trees were most numerous in Ancient Countryside, but were locally abundant even in open-field areas (Fig. 2.2).

Table 10.3 summarizes surveys which tells us how many trees there were per acre of farmland. We expect these, like modern surveys, to underestimate: pollards and trees too young to be timber were often omitted, and areas with exceptionally many trees may not be covered. Allowing for this tendency, much of the Ancient Countryside in the sixteenth and seventeenth centuries had at least as many hedgerow trees as in 1951 and more than twice what it has now. Many were pollards. James I's 1605 survey shows that pollards often outnumbered timber. On Crown-owned farmland in Essex there were 409 timber and 9121 'decaying' trees; in Hertfordshire the figures were 1110 and 4184.

By the mid-eighteenth century there were more hedgerow trees than ever before or since. At Thorndon (Table 10.3) timber trees and pollards were sixty times as many as the average for eastern England now – indeed they were thicker on that farmland than in most woodland. This was probably exceptional: the owner remarked on the 'Pollard Trees which this Estate is very much incumbered with & if a great deal more was cut down it would be much better for the Land'.

Such immense numbers are confirmed by landscape artists, who often show hedges astonishingly packed with trees.

Oak, ash, and elm were far the commonest species (Table 10.2). Any of the three could predominate according to no obvious pattern, except that oak, then as now, was most often in the majority on the less clayey soils. Elm was distinctly commoner than in the Middle Ages, but willow and poplar had declined. Oak, elm, ash, and others were pollarded; where pollards were thick on the ground they usually included much elm.

Hedgerow timber shows signs of being preferred for shipbuilding, even though this industry was still only a small user. The 1608–9 survey, limited to

| Number of trees | | | | Acres of | Trees |
Timber	Pollard	Young	Total	land	per acre
1851			1851	*c.* 640	2.9
			200	170	1.2
			102	*c.* 114	0.9
			442	385	1.1
	100		100	15.8	6.3
			194	217	0.9
			350	288	1.2
16	143		159	34	4.7
3278	783		4061	603	6.7
361	6058	941	7360	187	39.4
112	145		257	16	16
920			920	*c.* 200	4.6

oak on Crown estates, records 1623 suitable oaks in Norfolk, Suffolk, and Essex. Although there was considerable woodland half these trees were on farmland. Hedgerow trees predominated in large sizes (over 45 cubic feet per tree) and in special shapes for parts of ships such as hooks and knees.

Changes After 1750

The latter eighteenth century saw itself as a time of decline in hedges and hedgerow trees, in consequence of agricultural subsidies, Enclosure Acts, and reorganizing of fields. The quotation on p.27 is from a parliamentary inquiry in 1791 into an alleged shortage of timber. Grubbing-out of hedges and trees was reported from eighteen out of thirty-eight counties examined. This source is perhaps prone to exaggeration; but it is supported by John Clare, one of the few literary writers to tell us what the effects of an Enclosure Act looked like at the time. Clare wrote in sorrow and fury at the tidying-up of the medieval landscape of his childhood and the destruction of Langley Bush, Lea Close Oak, and the pollards which had given Helpston its individuality:

> when in round oaks narrow lane as the south got black again
> we sought the hollow ash that was shelter from the rain
> with our pockets full of pease we had stolen from the grain
> ....
> o words are poor reciepts for what time hath stole away
> the ancient pulpit trees and the play
>
> *Remembrances*

The loss of numbers (though not of individuality) was to some extent made up by trees planted in the new hedges of eighteenth-century enclosures; but many later enclosures appear to have had few or no hedgerow trees. Probably for the first time, hedgerow trees became abundant in Scotland.

From 1810 to 1860, when the price of oak was unusually high, hedge trees were a valuable source of income, as shown by the accounts of St John's College, Cambridge.[376] The college sold wood and timber regularly from wooded estates at Thorington (Essex) and Great Bradley (Suffolk), but also, though less frequently, from estates without woodland. In 1838, for example, Thorington produced £219, while timber from two woodless estates realized £370 and £276.

In the late eighteenth century pollarding became unfashionable and new pollards ceased to be formed in most areas, except for willows along watercourses. The reason may have been the growing ascendancy of landlords over tenants. In 1787 St John's College was still complaining that at Headcorn (Kent)

> The generality of tenants . . . strike off the heads of the young oaks . . . and make pollards of them; the heads of the pollards belong to the tenants so that by this means the College Timber and Timber like trees will all be made pollards of . . .[376]

The first edition 6-inch and 25-inch Ordnance Survey, surveyed from 1845 to 1888, attempted to record every non-woodland tree. I have counted hedgerow and field trees on 550 fifty-acre sample plots and estimate that in all England the Survey depicts 23 million individual trees, just under one per acre of farmland. This seems to be rather fewer than we have now, but there was probably some under-recording of small trees, and the size of the symbols prevented trees from being shown that were less than 30 feet apart. Although eastern England then had hardly fewer trees per acre than the rest of the country, there had been a decline from the great numbers of the eighteenth century. Lands in Little Coggeshall which had had 4061 trees in 1734 had only 508 trees mapped in 1875, although the hedges were almost unaltered. (Even this figure is a maximum estimate, for it includes all the trees in the boundary hedges.) Thorndon, with 39 trees to the acre in 1742, had 1.2 per acre in 1885. Woodham Ferrers, with 4.6 trees per acre in 1742, had 1.0 in 1873. Less well-tree'd areas fared better: the 1.2 trees per acre at West Thurrock in the seventeenth century had become 1.3 by the nineteenth, and at Badwell Ash the 0.9 tree per acre of 1730 increased to 1.5.

Records that distinguish species (Table 10.2) show no systematic change in the proportions of oak, ash, and elm. Exotic trees (eg. sycamore and walnut) appear in small numbers from 1730 onwards but did not become abundant until the nineteenth century, and then chiefly in the neighbourhood of houses.

How did the 23 million trees in England *c.* 1870 become the 60 million of 1951? The difference is too great to be explained away as under-recording by the Ordnance Survey: there can be little doubt that hedgerow trees did at least double in those eighty years. The increase was greatest in south-west England: Dorset or Cornwall had surprisingly few trees a century ago. Such an increase would be too slow to be remarked upon, but its cumulative effect is very conspicuous. Many Suffolk and Essex views painted by Constable are now invisible because trees have grown.

Evidence for this increase does not rest on the shaky testimony of the Ordnance Survey alone. The 1951 survey estimated that there were 30 million non-woodland timber trees in England, 17 million 'saplings' (defined as between 12 and 24 inches in girth), and 9 million 'firewood' trees (presumably including pollards). The tree population in 1951 was therefore rapidly expanding. A sapling would usually have been from fifteen to thirty years old, arising between 1921 and 1936. Under normal management, in the twenty years after 1951, at most a fifth of the timber trees would have been felled but almost all the 'saplings' would have grown to timber size. The timber trees alone would have increased to at least 41 million by 1971. That this did not happen is a measure of the effort put into destroying hedges and trees in the 1950s and 1960s.

The period 1750–1870 was, on the whole, an age of agricultural prosperity in which hedgerow trees almost certainly decreased. The period 1870–1951 was, on the whole, an age of agricultural adversity, in which there was less money to spend on either maintaining or destroying hedges. Neglect gave innumerable saplings an opportunity to grow into trees. Moreover there was probably less felling of timber than usual between 1860 and 1914 (cf pp.92–3). Even the great fellings during and between the World Wars, and the Elm Disease epidemic of the 1930s, failed to offset the beneficial effects of neglect.

A definite example of hedgerow trees arising by default are the rows of Scots pines, all of much the same age and all gnarled at the base, which are the characteristic field boundaries of the Breckland. When the open-fields and some of the commons of the Breckland were enclosed in the early nineteenth century, it was the fashion to make new hedges of pine, not indigenous to the area but thought to be suited to its arid climate. A few surviving examples prove that it is possible, with an effort, to keep pines in the form of a hedge. Most of these

223

hedges, however, have passed through periods of neglect, and even a few years' neglect causes pines to grow up irrevocably into trees.

Renewal of Non-woodland Trees

Foresters have long known that planted trees, unless sheltered, are slow to grow and difficult to keep alive; a lesson which modern conservationists insist on learning the hard way, as the fate of the 'Plant a Tree in '73' campaign showed. Despite this most twentieth-century writers assume that farmland trees are all planted: the philosophy that trees are mere artefacts is strong enough to overcome practical considerations.

Like many misapprehensions, this has some truth. Evidence for planting non-woodland trees is stronger and much earlier than for trees in woods. For example:

> In wages of 2 men pulling ashes to plant at Hyndringham and Gateli for 6 days – 2s.
>
> *Account roll, Hindolveston (Norfolk) 1312–3*[329]

> In wages of 1 [man] planting ashes in the manor for 13½ days at 1½d – 20¼d.
>
> *Account roll, Hindringham (Norfolk) 1312–3*[377]

> In pulling plants of thorn and ash to put on 1 ditch from the south of the manor [-house] to the churchyard, 14 works [ie. units of labour service].
>
> *Account roll, Forncett (Norfolk) 1378*[305]

Plants were thus dug up from local woods and hedges, but there was also a nursery trade: in the fourteenth century plants of elm, hazel, willow, and poplar were articles of commerce.[52] Oak is not mentioned, possibly because it is difficult to transplant satisfactorily. There are many examples in later centuries:

> . . . Symon Breakneck . . . shall . . . sett plant and mayntayne to grow . . . for fier woode in . . . every perch in length . . . upon the bankes . . . of all such hedges as shalbee cutt and newe made one younge sale [?sallow] ashe or elme.
>
> *Lease, Writtle (Essex) 1634*[378]

The Little Coggeshall survey of farm trees is accompanied by many records of planting, including walnuts and chestnuts.

Despite all this evidence, confirmed as it is by exotic trees in nineteenth-century records and in the landscape today, the case for planting should not be overstated. Trees of hedges are not a random selection from nurserymen's catalogues. Exotic species, including popular garden trees like hybrid lime, are still a minority, but hedges are full of species which are not planters' trees (eg. maple and many elms). Periods such as the late eighteenth century, when planting was much talked about, cannot – to say the least – be shown to coincide with actual increases in hedgerow trees. Walnuts were much planted in field hedges but are rarely heard of again and may not have survived.

Planted trees, especially oaks, are inevitably at a disadvantage by losing some of their roots in the transplanting. This does not apply to natural saplings and suckers, which grow faster and are not killed by drought. There can be no doubt that, except in new hedges, most hedgerow trees were not planted but promoted from such saplings, which cost nothing and therefore rarely appear in records.

Non-woodland Trees as they are now

Recent decline In the 1960s many influences conspired against non-woodland trees. Unwonted agricultural prosperity coincided with a lack of confidence in free-standing trees as a crop (due, in large part, to the decline of arrangements for selling them). There was money, some of it public, to spend on either destroying hedges or excessively maintaining them, and both operations were mechanized. Established trees were regarded as a nuisance and destroyed for various reasons or pretexts, such as that they supposedly got in the way of maintaining watercourses. Even worse for young trees was the fashion for tidiness. Hedging and trimming formerly done carefully once in five to ten years were now done hastily every year. A man with a tractor, 'brushing' a ditch-bank, could cut off a thousand saplings in an hour without noticing that they were there.

By 1970 conservationists, including many farmers, realized that hedgerow trees were in a bad way, but the cause was disastrously misdiagnosed. The planting mentality had become established and prevailed over the conservation of existing trees. Trees were treated as mere inanimate ornaments with no life or meaning of their own. People were encouraged and financed to plant trees as a matter of routine, without considering whether it was necessary. Species planted were a random mixture of whatever nurserymen wanted to get rid of. When they died this was put down to bad luck with the weather rather than to the planting itself being inadvisable. Official trumpets were blown for the planting of tens of thousands of trees, but no voice was raised against the destruction of hundreds of thousands of natural saplings. Meanwhile Dutch Elm Disease flared up, with results now all too familiar.

Most of these factors have operated from time to time in the past; what is unprecedented is their coming all together. Hedgerow trees have usually declined even more than hedges, and field trees more still. This is still not so everywhere. Where agriculture is less prosperous and less mechanized, farmland trees still flourish. Parts of inland Cornwall, whose erstwhile reputation as a rather bleak land is confirmed by the Ordnance Survey of the 1880s, now have a profusion of hedgerow and even field trees, many of them young and still increasing. The same happens on the poorer lands of Devon, south Essex, and the Weald – indeed anywhere where ancient hedges are a source of saplings and money is not spent on cutting hedges every year. And throughout the country some individual landowners do understand hedgerow trees, mark and protect likely natural saplings, and where they have to plant take the trouble to cherish and water the planted saplings. Some public authorities, such as Essex County Council, have learnt from experience and encourage the promotion of existing young trees.

A dying landscape? It is more diplomatic to blame Nature for the decline of hedgerow trees. The present trees were planted – so a popular argument runs – in an enclosure movement of 150–200 years ago and are now near the end of a supposedly well-defined life-span. Rarely if ever is evidence adduced on the actual age of existing trees or the longevity of particular species. This argument is propped up by two others: that the 'stag-head' phenomenon, common in hedgerow trees, presages their death; and that there ought to be 'six saplings to every mature tree', any population with fewer being deemed to be in a decline.

It is in fact most unusual for a farmland tree (except for birch, hybrid poplar, and other very short-lived species) to reach anywhere near its potential life-span. To diagnose, as is often officially done, a 130-year-old oak as 'dying of old age' is no more reasonable than it would be to speak in the same way of an eighteen-year-old man. Not many farmland oaks are more than 200 years old, and those that are 400 years old are not usually in worse condition than those of half this age.

According to the 1951 survey, a third of the non-woodland trees in England were then 'saplings' which would have originated after 1921. Probably these contained more than their share of elm, and so will have been reduced by disease, but this factor will be offset by many of the bigger trees having been felled for timber. Even if no new trees had arisen since 1951, a third of the survivors would by now (1984) still be less than a mere seventy years old.

Stag-head is the name given to the dying-back of the upper branches of a tree (often oak or ash) leaving a bare skeleton (Fig. 10.2). It is often supposed to be a terminal condition, and Norfolk County Council, among others, bases its tree-renewal policy on that belief. Various 'causes' have been proposed – caterpillars, too much or too little drainage, toxic sprays, deep ploughing, etc. – but none is a convincing general explanation. Stag-head runs by districts (it affects more than half the oaks in east Norfolk) rather than by ownerships or land-uses, which is hard to attribute to any agricultural practice; it began long before toxic sprays were invented.

Most stag-headed oaks have been in that condition for several decades. The bark and sapwood of the dead branches have rotted away and the tree has grown a new and healthy crown. 'Matthew Arnold's Tree', an ordinary hedgerow oak near Oxford, has been much photographed over the last eighty years: its original crown gradually died and was replaced by the growth of new branches into a quite different shape.[379] Many other historic oaks have been through a stag-head phase in the past; for instance the Meavy Oak (Devon) was stagheaded in 1833[380] but is no longer. Birkland in Sherwood Forest (Plate XVIII) contains hundreds of ancient oaks, nearly all of which have been stag-headed for at least 100 years; all of them survived the great drought of 1976.

Stag-head is a normal condition, the means whereby a free-standing oak (or ash, elm, or chestnut) overcomes the problem of having, from the material made by a fixed amount of leafage, to add an annual ring every year to an inexorably rising surface area of trunk, branches, twigs, and roots. By retrenchment it reduces the area to be covered and returns to a balance with the leafage. (I have seen 'self-pollarding' behaviour, doubtless for the same reason, in several American wildwood trees.) Dead branches often admit wood-rotting fungi which spread into the trunk, but this need not shorten the tree's life, for there are mechanisms which prevent the fungi from rotting structurally important parts of the timber. The trees which fall in storms are, on the whole, not old, hollow, or 'dangerous' ones, but middle-aged trees which had shown no previous sign of weakness.

The 'six saplings to every mature tree' myth involves misquotation as well as misunderstanding. The 'Merthyr Committee' on hedgerow and farm timber in 1955 suggested that a population of hedgerow trees ought to contain six saplings 'of 12 to 24in. girth, three timber trees of 24 to 40in. girth, two of 40 to 60in.,

Fig. 10.2. Stag-headed tree.

and one of over 60in. girth'.[381] Successive plagiarists have hardened this conjecture into a principle, have left out the two middle size-classes, and have forgotten that for the Committee a sapling was a tree of between a man's arm and a man's leg in thickness.

The Merthyr Committee's figures were conjured out of thin air; we are not told how they were arrived at. On average a free-standing tree would take about 15 years to become a 'sapling' and might spend 15, 15 and 20 years in each size-class, reaching 60 inches at age eighty and being felled after at least a further seventy years. Presumably it was envisaged (perhaps by false analogy with thinning of plantations) that most of the trees would be felled young. Without such felling the number of trees would double every twenty years or so. Nevertheless the Committee's suggestion was more realistic than the travesty of it which is usually quoted. It amounts to one staddle (pole-sized tree) for every timber tree, a figure which is sometimes reached in historical surveys of trees, although usually timber trees outnumbered staddles, even at times of increase.

Historic Trees

Our heritage of farmland trees has been sadly reduced in the last thirty years, and those that remain are often contaminated by acid rain or by fertilizers and agricultural chemicals and have lost the rich lichen and moss flora that they once had. The best old trees are often preserved in places that are no longer farmland, such as pseudo-medieval parks (Chapter 6), but the countryside at large still has many that mean something. Ancient trees are almost everyday objects in England, as they are in no European country except Greece. We neglect them, having been persuaded that substitution is conservation; but they deserve to be recorded, understood, and maintained.

The field archaeologist should always record significant trees. As well as the species, the record should include the girth and spread of the tree and whether it is a pollard, and any visible annual rings or other evidence of its age. Stumps should also be recorded.

Trees of planting fashions and Enclosure Acts Until the nineteenth century a distinction was made in practice between the trees of formal parks and gardens and those of farmland. Except for sycamore (Chapter 4) and for the sequence of fashions in elms (Chapter 11) the trees of the countryside at large continued to be of traditional species.

Enclosure Act hedges sometimes have their original hedgerow trees, which can be dated (when felled) to a year or two after the Act for the particular parish. More often, the original trees are now reduced to coppice stools and the present timber trees are a second generation.

Later it became the custom to plant exotic trees, not only in gardens and parks, but to some extent in the countryside at large. Occasionally this produced some distinctive local characteristic, such as the Breckland pines. But most Victorian plantings are an assortment of fashionable trees which are the same all over the country, such as horsechestnut, hybrid lime, Turkey and holm-oaks. However, a few of these plantings have some historical significance. I have several times found ancient pollards hidden among them. The church of Silverley near Newmarket, long since ruined, stands in a grove of the usual Victorian trees; they prove that the churchyard continued to be maintained after the church was disused.

Pollards Pollards have a strong and mysterious geographical distribution. They still exist in thousands in Essex and Suffolk. In other Ancient Countryside counties, such as Cornwall, there are few, and in Herefordshire, which is otherwise so like Essex, there are almost no pollards. I cannot suggest why.

Pollards in Planned Countryside are confined to closes around villages and occasional ancient hedges elsewhere. As far as I know, all Enclosure Act hedges are too late for new pollards to have been started in them. Existing pollards in earlier hedges, unless destroyed in the process of enclosure, were maintained. If a hedge has pollards it is therefore almost certainly older than the Enclosure Acts.

Most pollards are antiquities; even a quite small bolling can be 400 years old. Usually they are aged between 200 and 600 years, although some giants are older still, and in a few places with a strong tradition new pollards were started in the nineteenth century. Many pollards have not been cut for several decades, although as fuel rises in price this art of managing trees is happily being revived.

The pollard willows of fens and river-banks appear seldom to be of great age, but continue an ancient tradition and are specially important for the variety of wildlife that lives on them (Mabey 1980). Plants such as briars and even sizeable ash and holly trees, and other willows, live in their crowns; as with other pollards, lichens grow on their old bark, many species of insect are specific to their mouldering interiors, and birds and bats roost inside them. Willows are probably the most active branch of pollarding; around Cambridge many of those previously neglected have been cut in recent years, and even some new pollards have been started. The city fens, with pollard willows along watercourses, are a survival of medieval Cambridge which sets off the later formal landscape of The Backs.

The medieval practice of *shredding* – cropping the side-branches of a tree leaving a tuft at the top – vanished from Britain long ago. Only at Haresfield (Gloucestershire) have I seen a few ancient ashes that may once have been shredded.

Ancient non-woodland trees The biggest assemblages of trees more than 400 years old are in parks and Forests; but, scattered through the countryside, single trees (mainly pollard oaks) of improbable size and bizarre shape invite wonder and speculation. Some are well known and loved: there are long lists in Loudon's *Arboretum* (1838).[174] John Clare wrote a sonnet to Burthorp Oak, and another to an

> old huge ash dotterel [pollard] wasted to a shell
> whose vigorous head still grew and flourished well
> where ten might sit upon the battered floor
> and still look round discovering room for more.

Trees, still extant, celebrated in legend and song include Kett's Oak (Hethersett, Norfolk), associated with the Great Rebellion of 1549, and the Fairy Oak (Haresfield), supposed to commemorate the foul murder of Edward II nearby in 1327. Many ancient trees still remain to be recognized; they turn up in unlikely places, and bring the thrill of discovery even into so unexpected a spot as the middle of Kew Gardens. They all have meaning and tell us of their environment and management when young.

Some ancient trees are in villages and hamlets: for instance the Great Elm of Rosuic, possibly the original tree of one of the variants of *Ulmus stricta* (p.236), a pollard in the remote hamlet of Rosuic in a hollow of the Goonhilly Downs in Cornwall; the Meavy Oak on the edge of Dartmoor; the Eardisley Oak (Herefordshire); the Yeldham Oak, long dead, in Great Yeldham (Essex); the Caermarthen Oak, also dead, in the middle of the town; and the Winfarthing Oak (Norfolk), which disappeared in the nineteenth century.

Churchyard yews have their special lore and books.[382] Famous examples are the immense yews of Crowhurst (Sussex), Woolland (Dorset), and Tandridge (Surrey). Similar yews exist in Wales (eg. at Strata Florida Abbey), Scotland, and Ireland, where on the whole ancient trees are rare.[383] Yews are difficult to date by annual rings. People believe that they are very slow-growing and that the big ones are of fabulous antiquity, 2000 years old or more. They are therefore supposed to have been sacred trees before the churches were built. As far as I know, however, there is nothing to connect yews with pagan religion; indeed the only written evidence for yews as sacred trees comes from the Christian laws of Wales, which require compensation equivalent to sixty sheep for destroying a 'saint's yew'.[90] The theory that churches were built on pagan sacred sites has received disappointingly little support from excavation.[384] If yews were a feature of early churches, why are there no place-names such as Yewchurch? Although some of the great yews have increased little in the last hundred years, the tree can grow quite fast when young, and their ages may be exaggerated. A big yew can well be as old as the present church but is unlikely to be older than its Anglo-Saxon predecessor. Nor do I know of any evidence for the tradition that yews were grown for longbows (p.237). The age and meaning of churchyard yews remain a mystery.

Not all ancient churchyard trees are yews: there are for instance the giant pollard elms (now dead) at Farnham and Waltham Abbey (Essex). The magnificent limes of Lavenham churchyard (Suffolk) are *Tilia cordata* and presumably antedate the fashion for hybrid limes.

Archaeologists record the earthworks and holloways of deserted and shrunken settlements but often fail to appreciate that ancient trees are their last living inhabitants. Lindsey Castle (Suffolk), for instance, a curious inverted castle with concentric earthen ramparts around a low-lying motte in the bottom of a valley, still has pollard oaks, elms, ashes, and maples and ancient lime stools which may well go back to when it was a castle. Many shrunken villages of the east Midlands have rows of ancient elms marking their streets and hedges (Plate XXId).

Most other ancient trees are on boundaries. Certain very select trees define parish boundaries on early (and occasionally current) editions of the larger-scale Ordnance Survey. They are specified as 'Oak Pollard', 'Pollard Elm', 'Ancient Yew' (on the Surrey Downs), etc. Another type of boundary that often has ancient trees is the edge of the strip of meadow that occupies a flat-bottomed valley. This very important and early boundary often has a substantial lynchet (p.159) set with giant pollards. A few other ancient trees are in hedges of apparently no special significance; they survive by chance to remind us that any ordinary mixed hedge can be over 500 years old.

Ancient trees standing in fields are an unlikely survival but a few still exist, for example the giant oak of Thorpe Morieux (Suffolk). The home close near a medieval farmstead may have up to a dozen pollard oaks, like a miniature park, a reminder of centuries of horses resting in their shade; there are good examples at Browick Hall (Wymondham, Norfolk) and at Denston and Great Glemham (Suffolk). A characteristic of the edges of the Breckland, of which several examples survive, is a field full of improbable numbers of pollard oaks (Plate XVI) or less often black poplars. These are not relics of woodland: a sixteenth-century map of Risby (Suffolk) clearly differentiates between the Little Wood and Brome Close (a field with many trees),[385] both of which are still extant. The field-with-trees may have been a Breckland substitute for a lack of woodland.

One of the oldest approximately datable oaks in England is the Queen's Oak, Huntingfield (Suffolk). Although long a field tree it is the last relic of the medieval Huntingfield Park, and is thus one of the very few farmland trees to have an earlier history in wood-pasture or woodland. In the last two centuries it has been much described and pictured, with results which are useful in understanding the physiology of very old trees. It is a pollard and was once one of the biggest oaks in England. From measurements in 1780[386] I estimate it to be now about 1000 years old. Already in 1780 it was stag-headed; it has since been through at least two cycles of dieback and regrowth. It is now much smaller than 200 years ago but is stable.

Ancient hawthorns are now to be found chiefly in a few parks and Forests (especially Hatfield Forest, Essex). Few successors survive of the mere-thorns of Anglo-Saxon charters, though one of the boundary thorns of Downing College stood into the twentieth century beside the present Cambridge Botany

School.[387] The Glastonbury Thorn, the most famous sacred tree in England, was apparently burnt as a suspected Papist, but grafts had been taken from it and its distinctive early-flowering genes live on in cultivation. Ireland still has many sacred thorns.[387] The largest thorn now in England is probably the Hethel Thorn in Norfolk, already a famous ancient tree in 1755.[174]

The great sweet-chestnut of Tortworth (Glos) (Plate I) was already described in 1706 as a tree of legendary antiquity.[388] It has propagated itself by the sprawling and rooting of its lower limbs, which now form seventeen secondary trunks around the parent trunk. This one tree begins to constitute a wood, with dog's-mercury, bluebell, lesser celandine, and wild garlic under it. The original trunk has not changed much in appearance; in 1977 it measured 36 feet 1 inch in girth below the lowest branch, whereas eighteenth-century figures vary from 44 to 57 feet! It confirms the presence of chestnut in England by the early Middle Ages (p.55). It is situated outside the churchyard, quite a common place for an ancient tree, though we cannot tell what this signifies.

CHAPTER 11

Elms

It is certainly strange that the pathology of trees should have been comparatively neglected in this country . . . The elms . . . whether insects or impeded exhalation be the cause, these characteristic ornaments of our parks have a sickly look. It has been predicted by a prophet of dendrology that elms will be extinct in England before another century has elapsed. The bare idea of such a calamity should rouse the Woods and Forests – for the functions of that department have not expired with its name – from their lethargy on the subject.

The Times, 30 January 1862

. . . the perill of συνολεθρισμὸς or one tree perishing with another, as it happeneth ofttimes from the sick *effluviums* or entanglements of the roots, falling foul with each other. Observable in Elmes set in hedges, where if one dieth the neighbouring Tree prospereth not long after.

Sir Thomas Brown, *The garden of Cyrus, 1658**

Elms have a chapter to themselves. They are the most complex and difficult trees in western Europe, and the most intimately linked to human affairs. Oak and hazel have played at least as great a part in shaping civilization, but have not themselves been shaped by civilization as have elms. And elm has the extra historic complication of disease.

Most of us can imagine a typical ash or hawthorn, and can recognize maple and sycamore as species of the same genus. But there is no typical elm, nor is it possible to identify elm species in this definite way. This is connected with elms having largely abandoned sex as a means of reproduction. Most kinds arise not from seed but from suckers out of the roots of previous elms (Fig. 5.1). A parent elm gives rise to a clone of identical elms, each an exact copy of itself. Seedlings do, rarely, arise in the conventional way; every seedling tends to differ from its parents and to add to the number of identifiable elm clones in the world. Without the restraining influence of sex on evolutionary change, elms (like dandelions and brambles) have produced a multitude of different forms. The taxonomist, devising Latin names, cannot keep up with this process.

Elms and Men

Wych-elm, *Ulmus glabra*, is a conventional species and stands apart from the other elms. It is variable, but no more so than maple or hornbeam. It grows from seed in the usual way, and when cut down coppices from the stump. In

---

* I am indebted to Dr Hilary Belcher for drawing my attention to this passage.

other elms seedlings are rare (though I have seen them myself) and are the source of new varieties. Seedlings account for small elm clones in places like railway embankments which they could hardly have reached otherwise.

Elm evolution is linked to human affairs. Elms are ideal trees of farmland and around buildings: they are easily propagated, fast-growing, quite long-lived, elegant, capable of pollarding, resistant to salty winds, and tenacious of life. Every time a suckering elm is cut down or dies of disease, there are a dozen or more suckers waiting to replace it with genetically-identical successors – a fast, automatic process needing no human intervention. Even in a normally highly-farmed landscape, a few years' neglect will produce hedgerow elms in thousands. Of the village of Fleury near Verdun, where a million men killed each other in World War I, not one stone remains upon another; but the village elms have grown again from bits of root that lay near the surface of the cratered earth.

Besides selecting and propagating particular elms, men have made hedges, ditches, small woods, and roadside verges. These are ideal environments in which existing varieties can maintain themselves and survive periods of unpopularity, and in which new varieties and hybrids can arise naturally. In Buff Wood (East Hatley, Cambridgeshire) there are at least 29 elm clones in 40 acres; some of them are the same as other local elms, but other clones are unique. In North America, with its short history of hedges and permanent villages, the variation of elms is simple.

Elms are thought of as non-woodland trees, and even such writers as Tansley and Richens pass over woodland elms. Woodland elms are important, but I have written of them elsewhere (Rackham 1980); here I deal mainly with non-woodland elms.

Elms of fashion, tradition, and evolution Clones of elm appear to perpetuate themselves for ever unless carefully eradicated: hedges and settlements may accumulate all the elms that they have ever had. Some are plantsmen's elms, the result of fashions in tree-planting: the Wheatley Elm of the 1920s and 1930s, the Huntingdon Elm of the 1890s and 1900s, the English Elm of the eighteenth and nineteenth centuries (outside its earlier distribution), and the Dutch Elm of the early eighteenth century. How far back these go is uncertain: nurserymen have been selling elm plants for at least 600 years (p.224). In practice a distinction can be drawn between the *fashion* elms of the last 300 years, the *traditional* elms which go back to the Middle Ages or earlier, and the *evolution* elms which are new clones from chance seedlings.

Fashion elms are of a few common kinds, appearing throughout the country in a time-sequence: I have never seen an ancient Wheatley or Huntingdon Elm. Traditional elms are of many kinds, with definite, often complex, geographical distributions. The elms of Longstowe (Cambridgeshire) differ from those of Toft, and the parish of Bourn, which lies between, has both. They often include pollards and ancient trees. A speciality of Cambridgeshire and Huntingdonshire are the giant pollard elms of fantastic shapes which mark out the boundaries of ancient closes in villages and deserted villages (Plate XXId).

Evolution elms are those, usually small, clones which differ from the local traditional elm but are not of a recognized plantsmen's variety. They are often of remarkable appearance. Individual evolution elms may be up to 300 years old and may be from clones that are older still.

233

The Kinds of Elm (Plate XXI, Figs 11.1, 11.3)

The treatment of trees is the weakest part of most county Floras, and elms are treated worse than other trees. They have many distinguishing characters, but few that can be precisely expressed in words or figures; the trees cannot be preserved in herbaria and are difficult to photograph convincingly; leaf characters vary from one part of the tree to another. Mistakes are common even among scholars.

The two elm specialists, Dr R. Melville and Dr R.H. Richens, disagree on how to classify elms. Melville recognizes seventeen kinds of elm, six of them regarded as species and eleven as hybrids (some of which are claimed to be from three or four parent species).[389] Richens has recognized at least forty different elms, which does better justice to the variety that exist; they are defined in terms of eight leaf measurements, and are named after 'type localities' where they were found.[390] My classification, derived in large part from Richens's work, is a pragmatic one intended for identifying elms; other, more learned men can argue about the status of the names given to them.

Descriptions apply to large, free-standing trees, and to leaves on slow-growing twigs fully exposed to light. Suckers and young elms are difficult to identify.

Wych-elm, *Ulmus glabra* The common elm of the Highland Zone and of Scotland and Wales. A broad-spreading tree, with trunk broadly forking like a Y. Bark thin, long remaining smooth. *No suckers*. Big, broad, very rough leaves with a long point (three points on some leaves) and *almost no stalk*. Twigs fork in a Y.

All specialists agree that this is an ordinary species and is different from other elms.

The 'English Elm' group, known as *Ulmus procera* The traditional elms of the Midlands, Welsh Border, southern England, and south Essex; an older fashion elm of the rest of England and of Edinburgh and Dublin.

Usually dead: the common southern and Midland form is extremely susceptible to the present Dutch Elm Disease, and is now totally reduced to suckers except in the Brighton area. Strongly suckering. Massive, straight or slightly sinuous, upright trunk with short, stout, near-horizontal branches bearing heavy masses of dark foliage. Bark cracking horizontally as well as vertically into small plates. *Leaves broad* (at least two-thirds as wide as long), usually *all rough*, appearing early in the year and staying into December.

These are the most widespread and familiar elms, and now the most regretted. They are not very variable: only a few unusual kinds, such as the 'Coritanian Elm' with smooth leaves, can easily be distinguished. Elms of this group are more varied on the Continent. The 'English Elm' introduced to New England resembles the northern and Irish form more than the common elm of southern England.

The East Anglian or 'smooth-leaved' elms, known as *Ulmus minor* (= *U. carpinifolia*) The traditional elms of East Anglia, the north-east Midlands, and

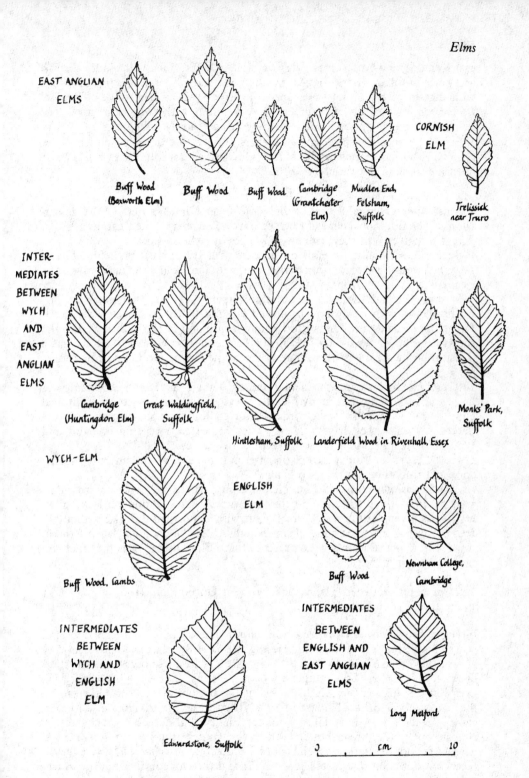

Fig. 11.1. Typical leaves from sixteen different elms.

east Kent. Strongly suckering. Very variable in habit, often with sinuous trunk and graceful foliage. Bark rugged, cracking vertically. Trunk and boughs often with masses of epicormic twigs sprouting from two or four rows of bosses. *Leaves narrow*, usually pale green, *smooth*, often with *long stalks* and very asymmetric bases, appearing late in the year and mostly falling early.

East Anglian elms come in bewildering variety. A traditional elm may be peculiar to a single parish, and evolution elms more local still. Plates XXI c, d, e illustrate some of the variety of forms.

Cornish and Channel Island elms, known as *Ulmus stricta* (= *U. angustifolia*) The traditional elms of Cornwall, west Devon, and the Channel Islands. The distinctive 'Wheatley' clone was a modern fashion elm.

Suckering. Variable in habit but mostly with stiffly erect branches. *Leaves very small, tough, smooth*, rather dark green, with long stalks and nearly symmetrical bases.

Within England these are less variable than the East Anglian elms. The Cornish Elm, with its upright habit and late leaf-fall, is the most widespread. Other, more spreading kinds grow round Truro and in the Lizard Peninsula; the Great Elm of Rosuic (p.229) is one of these. The Wheatley variety has a 'Chianti-bottle' profile with rounded base to the crown and tall narrow top.

Intermediates between *glabra* and *minor*, known as *Ulmus hollandica* A large and variable group; many may be hybrids. They are common traditional elms along the Suffolk–Essex border. They combine various characters of the parents. Usually they have suckers. They are often spreading in habit and typically have pendulous or even weeping twigs, occasionally to a spectacular degree. Leaves are sometimes of the size and shape of wych-elm but with the stalk and smoothness of East Anglian.

Among fashion elms, the Dutch is strongly suckering with an irregular, spreading habit and forking branches and twigs. The Huntingdon lacks suckers; it has a very distinctive, formal habit with a short trunk forking about 12 feet up into an inverted cone of big boughs. It is the common late-Victorian town elm; being resistant to the present Dutch Elm Disease, it is the chief elm now surviving in cities.

Intermediates between *glabra* and *procera* Uncommon, and as far as I know always evolution elms.

Intermediates between *procera* and *minor* These have occasionally appeared on the borders of *minor* and *procera* territory. But the most famous of this group, the Long Melford (Suffolk) elms, are not in a frontier situation; they illustrate the mystery and complexity of elm history. Three mighty elms, well over 100 feet high (Plate XXIh), stood at the bottom of Melford Green until they succumbed to Elm Disease in 1978. They were the survivors of a former clone of at least nine elms. They combined English and East Anglian characters almost equally (eg. broad but smooth leaves, straight but not upright trunk). These were not the traditional elms of Melford, which are *minor*, nor were they a recent introduction: one dated from 1757, and the clone itself could be much older. They were apparently unique and were presumably evolution elms.

Prehistory and History

Wildwood and the Elm Decline In wildwood days some kind of elm grew almost throughout the British Isles. In much of Ireland, and probably of Wales, elm was the commonest tree or was second to hazel. Elsewhere it was the third, fourth, or fifth commonest tree. The pollen evidence suggests patches of elmwood, and also perhaps scattered elms among wildwood of other trees.

In about 4000 BC half the elm suddenly vanished from Europe. This *Elm Decline* was so universal and so rapid that pollen analysts use it for dating their deposits. It is somehow connected with the appearance of Neolithic agriculture. The Decline was highly specific to elm, was much more sudden than other changes in the abundance of trees, and did not affect elms in America.

The archaeology of elm begins soon after. In the early Neolithic of the Somerset Levels, elm is the fifth commonest tree among the poles and timber used in the Sweet Track (p.382); it comes after hazel, oak, ash, and holly. More elm underwood was used than timber; there is no sign that elm was selected for use in particular parts of the structure.

The written record Old English has two words, *wice* and *elm*. Both are common in place-names (eg. *Witch*ford and *Elm* in the Isle of Ely). In charters, *elm* is unknown and there are only thirteen mentions of *wice*, half of them in the Mendips. This does not prove that elms were rare: since they grow in groups, individual elms would not make good landmarks.

It would be pleasant to think that *wice* meant wych-elm and *elm* meant the suckering elms. Alas, this distinction was not properly drawn, even by professional botanists, until the eighteenth century, and there is no evidence of what the Anglo-Saxons meant. Dr Richens claims that the words are regional, *elm* being used in the Midlands and most of southern England (Richens 1983).

From the fourteenth century onwards, references to elms – usually as hedgerow trees – come thick and fast. For example, in Essex there were elms round the garden of Sir Henry de Hadham at Witham, *c.*1320,[391] and at West Donyland in 1397 one John Shepherd was fined 4*d.* for cutting off a branch of a certain elm at a place called Ffayrelmes.[95] Dr Richens has collected similar examples from most English counties. By the end of the Middle Ages, elm was one of the four common hedgerow trees, but only locally the commonest. The traveller Leland in 1542 noted the 'elme wood, wherwith most part of al Somersetshire ys yn hegge rowys enclosid.'[392]

The archaeological record Until the Middle Ages elm timber is not very common among excavated artefacts. From the twelfth century onwards, it becomes second in importance to oak. Some of its uses involved specific properties; in others it was merely another timber tree, cheaper than oak (especially in large sizes) but more difficult to work.

Elm was supposed not to rot in a wet environment; it was used for piles (eg. of London and Rochester bridges and some medieval waterfronts), coffins, and water-mains (Richens 1983). Being strong in tension across the grain, it was (and is) used for the naves of wheels (with their mortices in all directions), the seats of chairs, and the heads of mallets. Only in modern times does elm appear to be used for platters and bowls. Elm poles made the second-best bows (the best being of Spanish or Venetian yew).[393]

As an ordinary timber, elm forms about 6 per cent of the medieval buildings that I have seen. Sometimes it appears as exceptionally long or thick timbers or wide floorboards, which would have been difficult to get in oak, but much medieval elm consists of small trees. Many small and humble houses are partly, and a few wholly, of elm: at Nayland (Suffolk) there is an elm miniature aisled hall probably of the thirteenth century. Elm could rise higher in the social scale, even to such a grand edifice as the great barn of Frocester (Gloucestershire). Apart from the headstocks of bells (Richens 1983), I have never found it in a medieval church, even where there was economy in the use of oak. Elm is commoner in post-medieval timber buildings, including great barns.

Elm also appears as underwood, but much less commonly than hazel and sallow.

Recent history The earliest identifiable fashion elm is the self-perpetuating Dutch Elm. It is a widespread hedgerow tree, especially in the Breckland, Cornwall, and Irish Midlands. It is traditionally linked with King William of Orange, and supposedly brought from Holland at his accession in 1689. This story, though plausible, is first heard of half a century later and carries little conviction, since people could not reliably distinguish elms at the time. The similar tradition about white poplar is certainly false (p.208). The Dutch Elm is reported to be rare in Holland but to occur in Picardy (Richens 1983); it could easily have originated in England.

Later landscapes display a succession of fashionable elms, but this is not the whole story. The park of Wimpole (Cambridgeshire) was begun about 1700 and was worked on by most of the great names in landscape design (p.000): Bridgeman, Robert Greening, Brown, and Repton. Mr John Phibbs has found trees of the appropriate dates and others which are both earlier and later. He has drawn my attention to a group of distinctive, exceptionally tall East Anglian elms right in front of the house. These have annual rings going back to the 1630s and are thus older than the park; they were preserved through all the successive re-landscapings. These, and several other clones of elm scattered through the park, are the traditional elms of the lost village of Old Wimpole which lay on the site. All of them correspond to groups of trees on a map of Wimpole in 1638.[394] The clones are similar but not identical, and evidently underwent some evolution before the park was made. Occasionally these elms were planted by the landscapers instead of fashionable kinds. The great south avenue, planted about 1718, comprised about two-thirds English and one-third Old Wimpole elms (Plate XIX).

Where Did Our Elms Come From?

The present distribution of traditional elms was reached at latest by 1500. Written sources do not distinguish the species, but I have been able to identify, to some extent, particular elms from ancient timbers. The results are consistent with the traditional elm species still in the locality: for instance East Anglian elms – small, crooked, burry, and slow-growing – in Suffolk and Cambridgeshire, and English Elm at Gloucester.[210] In the last five centuries elms have increased and their pattern has been complicated by evolution and the addition of fashion elms, but the main distributions of traditional elms have not changed much.

At first sight it would seem that elms were much less common before 1200. Possibly this was not really so: elms may have been reduced by management (or disease) to the state of underwood and may thus be poorly recorded.

How do we extrapolate this into prehistory? Prehistorians suppose that only wych-elm is native and all the others were introduced by human agency. This is a conjecture based on no direct evidence – for it is usually held to be impossible to identify the species of elm from pollen or other remains – but has come to be widely accepted.

Dr Richens (1983) proposes that from the Bronze Age onwards people have sent for favourite kinds of elm from different parts of the Continent, and have planted them around their homes; that these introductions went on down to the Middle Ages and have given rise to the traditional elms; and that the more widespread kinds of elm are those that were earlier introduced. His remarkable theory would back-date the nurseryman's practice by two millennia, and would have wide repercussions in landscape history. Is it true?

Dr Richens's argument depends on the claim that each kind of traditional elm in England so closely resembles a continental elm that it has to be derived therefrom. Unfortunately these resemblances have never been fully published with adequate drawings or photographs, and I am not convinced of their cogency. Nor do the archaeological connexions, which Dr Richens has claimed with the places from which he derives our elms, carry compelling support for his theory. And even if a particular elm in England is really the same as – and does not merely happen to resemble – a continental elm, why should not both be the shrunken remnants of a formerly continuous population? Dozens of other species, eg. oxlip, pasque-flower, strawberry tree, have just such a disjunction, but nobody suggests that it is artificial.

The very basis of Dr Richens's thesis, that elms (other than wych) are not native, is inferred from the beliefs that they do not grow from seed and do not enter into native woodland. Neither is a true observation, but even if they were, elms would not be proved to be exotic. Two species of lime are certainly indigenous, as prehistoric remains prove, even though they now rarely grow into trees from seed. And with so little native woodland left, we can hardly expect all the kinds that once existed to survive. Dr K.D. Bennett appears recently to have solved the problem of distinguishing elm pollens; he has definite evidence that there was East Anglian as well as wych-elm in Norfolk before the Elm Decline.[395]

I propose that England before the Neolithic had wych-elm and probably many kinds of East Anglian elm. It may also have had English and Cornish elms, but the case for these being native is weaker.[396] Elms, like black poplar, grew chiefly on flood-plains and other very valuable land, and were so diminished by prehistoric agriculture that many kinds no longer have a natural habitat. Before they disappeared, some kinds were adopted as farmland trees by prehistoric men. This would naturally favour the more strongly-suckering kinds. Elms were doubtless propagated between townships, but there is no need to invoke long-distance introductions. English and continental farmers may independently have chosen similar elms. Different elms have been brought together and allowed to form hybrids, which they might not have done in nature. Strongly-suckering elms have been given the chance to invade ancient woods, where they now grow alongside remnants of the original woodland elms. Many clones have expanded; others have shrunk through destruction of hedges at various times, disease, or competition.

Elm Disease

Elms are subject to many diseases. They have the famous and mysterious property of unexpectedly dropping big boughs. Of this I have many times been a near-witness, with English and East Anglian elms and also in America. It happens, not under the stress of gales or heavy rain, but on calm hot days. The boughs do not, therefore, drop through weakness, but are actively severed. I suspect some connection with the bacterial wetwood that infects nearly all elms (Rackham 1975); the wetwood bacteria generate methane gas under pressure which is capable of rending the wood apart.

Elm Disease *par excellence* is the work of a microscopic fungus, *Ceratocystis ulmi*, which lives within the outer wood. It damages the tree by blocking the water-conducting vessels and by interfering with the tree's hormones. An affected tree wilts, as if by drought, and its twigs grow into curves as if poisoned by weedkiller; the poison is powerful enough to bend limbs as thick as a man's leg.

The fungus gets from tree to tree mainly by the two elm bark beetles, *Scolytus scolytus* and *S. multistriatus*. The female beetle makes a tunnel under the bark of a recently-dead elm and lays eggs in it. The eggs hatch into grubs which make tunnels of their own, gradually increasing in size, at the ends of which they pupate; these form the familiar pattern of superficial grooves incised under the bark of dead elms. The fungus produces spores inside the tunnels; these rub off on to the adult beetle when they emerge from the pupae (chiefly in late May). The new beetles fly off to living elms and feed by nibbling the bark and wood of the crotches of twigs. In so doing they are liable to inject spores into the tree. The fungus may then spread downwards and upwards to involve the branch and eventually the whole tree. Sometimes it is sucked into a neighbouring tree via the roots – hence the death of rows of elms in hedges remarked upon over 300 years ago by Sir Thomas Brown.

Elm bark beetles can exist independently of the disease; with very rare exceptions, they attack only dead elms and do no damage. Related beetles live on ash and other trees but do not carry diseases.

The present epidemic (Fig. 11.2) After many years of quiescence Elm Disease flared up in the late 1960s. The first outbreak began at Tewkesbury in about 1965, and was followed by others from near Bristol, Southampton, London, Plymouth and Ipswich. Inland outbreaks appeared in north-east Hampshire, the Breckland, and north Buckinghamshire.

From six of these nine points of origin the disease radiated outwards at some 8 miles a year, rain or shine, as inexorably as a culture of the fungus spreading across a petri-dish. By 1972 the Tewkesbury and Bristol outbreaks had joined, and by 1977 almost every large elm within a 40-mile radius was dead. Elsewhere events took a different course. Neither the Ipswich, Breckland nor the Plymouth foci made much progress; and the advancing front from the Midlands slowed and broke up on reaching Cambridgeshire and Essex. The steady advance gave way to skirmishes and rearguard actions, in which some elm clones have succumbed and others are still alive. Every part of East Anglia now (1984) has the disease, but beleaguered survivors of elms still hold out even near the points of origin. There are similar inconclusive battles in Cornwall, east Kent, northern England, and Ireland.

The present epidemic is more virulent than previous ones. It spreads more easily via the roots. If it fails to kill a tree in one year, it has the evil characteristic of being able to continue the next year without re-infection. But elm clones are seldom killed completely; suckers or coppice shoots remain alive. Elms in woods more often escape.

Some elms are much more susceptible than others.* By ill luck the most susceptible elm to this epidemic was also the most widespread, the southern variety of the English Elm, whose vast traditional territory happened to include six of the points of origin. Probably every single large English elm between Manchester, Chichester, and Exeter has succumbed (though suckers remain alive). Only near Brighton, where the local authority has made a serious effort to protect the elms by burning dead trees promptly, before the beetles have emerged, do many large southern English Elms survive.

In the territories of East Anglian, Cornish, and wych-elms (and of the northern and Irish varieties of English Elm) the disease has spread slowly and unevenly. It has often started by attacking English Elm planted as a fashion tree, which has been sought out and killed and has infected its more resistant traditional neighbours. Varieties with most resistance include Huntingdon Elm and, among the *minor* group, the elms of Boxworth (Cambridgeshire) and Dengie (Essex).

Just as English Elms are killed even where they are not the common elm, so other elms sometimes stay alive even when surrounded by dead English Elms. In Wimpole South Avenue (p.29), the last English Elm died in 1976, but two out of three of the intermingled East Anglian elms were still healthy. (The avenue was then destroyed.) At Flatford (Suffolk) the *procera* elms, introduced soon after the time of Constable, the artist, all died about 1974, but the ancient *minor* pollards are still alive. It takes many beetle bites to be sure of killing a *minor* elm. Large elms surviving in the Manchester-Chichester-Exeter triangle are rare examples of wych, Huntingdon, or East Anglian elms.

There are at least four similar epidemics in Europe. One has been spreading outwards from Paris, where I estimate that it began *c*.1964; it reached Calais in 1979. There are others around Geneva and Innsbruck. A fourth, centred on Reggio (Emilia) has devastated the pollard elms on which the Italians, as in the days of Columella and Vergil, train their vines.

Recent history The disease was first noticed in France in 1918 and in the ensuing years almost throughout Europe. It is called Dutch Elm Disease because it was studied in detail in Holland, where there was a severe epidemic.

In England the disease was first noticed in 1927, and became an epidemic which defied attempts at control. The disease reached a peak about 1936 and then mysteriously declined, but not because it had run out of susceptible trees. New infections became less common and trees more often recovered. Between 10 per cent and 20 per cent of the full-grown elms in Britain were killed; but by 1960 they had been replaced by suckering and the epidemic had been forgotten.[398] It has sometimes left a dated record: when a tree recovers, a permanent stain remains in the wood of the annual ring that was infected. In this epidemic the English Elm was not specially susceptible.

---

* Susceptibility and resistance are complex matters. A resistant tree may be unattractive to beetles, or not easily infected by them, or may not easily succumb once infected.[397]

The Dutch epidemic ran a similar course, as did others at different times in Poland, Austria, and south-west Asia:[399] the disease raged for twenty to thirty years and then declined for no apparent reason.

The disease, and at least one of the bark-beetles, was introduced to America on logs imported with bark attached. It was first noticed in the eastern United States in 1930. It has progressed widely, having reached Minnesota and Colorado, but rather slowly and unevenly: there is little disease in eastern Massachusetts. The American Elm, which resembles our wych-elm, is very susceptible.

Earlier history There is evidence, mainly from documents but also from annual rings, that Elm Disease has a much longer history in Europe than is generally realized. Here I summarize details published more critically elsewhere (Rackham 1980).

From 1819 onwards a mysterious death of elms was noticed in Cambridge and London. The condition spread and ravaged the elms of France, Belgium, and Holland in the 1830s and 1840s. For example:

> In spring we see the leaves sprout forth from the venerable trunks in all the luxuriance of vegetation, when of a sudden they are blasted as if by lightning, the bark falls from the stem, and long ere winter the finest tree perhaps in the park is only fit for fire-wood . . . Now every elm is in some degree infected, and every week we may observe that a tree has perished.
>
> *St James's Park, 1823*[400]

> In an elm a great limb dies all at once from the point right into the trunk, while all the rest keeps green; then another limb goes, and so on until the whole tree is dead within a few weeks . . .
>
> *Windsor Great Park, c.1860*[220]

The epidemic attracted exactly the same attention as did Dutch Elm Disease in the 1930s and 1970s. Correspondents deplored the death of favourite trees, and urged public authorities to fell or lop infected elms. The connexion with bark-beetles was noticed, and attention was drawn to the danger of leaving felled logs lying near living elms. Quack 'remedies', such as removing the lower bark of threatened trees, flourished. The epidemic finally achieved the distinction of an editorial in *The Times*, quoted at the head of this chapter. But this was almost the last that was heard of it. After 1864 no more dead elms were noticed, and by the time that Dutch Elm Disease was discovered the earlier epidemic had been forgotten.

Innumerable 'causes' were proposed at the time: bark-beetles, wetwood, too little drainage, too much drainage, excavations for gas-mains, escapes of gas, vandalism, and the inevitable 'old age and the want of nourishment'. Nearly all of these can be discounted, for they would have killed other trees as well as elm and would not have ceased in the 1860s. Only bark-beetles are specific to elm. These can indeed occasionally lay their eggs in living trees and damage or even kill them, but this behaviour happens only when an exceptional drought coincides with an abnormal supply of beetles emerging from previously-killed elms. This occurred in 1976, but in the nineteenth century only 1826 and 1846 are possible years: bark-beetles cannot thus be a general explanation of the earlier epidemic.

Attack by a fungus was not considered at the time. This is not surprising, for the cause of Dutch Elm Disease is not obvious. *Ceratocystis* is inconspicuous, and nineteenth-century mycology could hardly have detected it. The 1819–64 epidemic had all the then observable marks of Dutch Elm Disease: the symptoms as described, the rate of spread, the continuance year after year regardless of weather, and the eventual mysterious decline. The theory that *Ceratocystis* was responsible covers all the facts, which no other known explanation does, and is not inherently unlikely.

Were there earlier epidemics? There are some definite indications, such as Sir Thomas Brown's observation. The name *Scolytus destructor* was given to the great bark-beetle on evidence, dating from c.1780, that it was destroying elms around Oxford.[401] I have indications from annual rings that *Ceratocystis* was certainly present in 1867 and may have been damaging elms in the fifteenth century.* And for many centuries elm has been the tree of death – not merely as a hackneyed symbol like coffin-boards or funerary cypresses. Dead trees in literature are surprisingly often elms. The other diseases of elm rarely kill it; indeed from 1300 to 1850, when trees were more systematically used than they are now and there were few road-works and no agricultural chemicals, any dead tree would have been unusual. Why did St Martin and St Zenobius work the miracles of bringing dead elms back to life?[402] Why was Falstaff addressed as 'thou dead Elme'?[403] The young dead trees common in Italian paintings and drawings from 1450 to 1530 – what are they if not elms blasted with Elm Disease? Why was it possible in the eighteenth century to insure one's elms against death? Elm was evidently well known to be the tree that specially shared man's fragile tenure of life, and it is difficult to suggest any other explanation than Elm Disease.

The Elm Decline Disease is customarily rejected as the cause of the prehistoric Elm Decline, on the grounds that Dutch Elm Disease was a twentieth-century introduction from Central Asia. This theory is based on no stronger evidence than the supposed failure to observe it earlier, which has now been disproved. If elms were ravaged, apparently by Dutch Elm Disease, in the nineteenth or the fifteenth century, they could have been ravaged in the Neolithic.

What else could have caused the Elm Decline? It is often guessed that the climate or soils were becoming less suitable. Neither change would account for so sudden and universal a disaster, affecting only elms and only in the Old World. For instance, if the climate deteriorated, it would not have caused a general decline: elm would have been wiped out in areas where the climate had already been marginal, but would not have been affected in the middle of its climatic range. A change in climate (or soil) so drastic as to cause an elm decline throughout Europe would inevitably have affected other trees, and would also have been noticed by American species of elm.

Because the Elm Decline appeared at the same time as early agriculture, it has often been attributed to Neolithic exploitation. The first farmers in northern Europe, so the argument runs, brought livestock for which there was at first no pasture because of the abundance of trees. Instead of grass, they fed their animals on tree leaves, of which elm was the favourite. Elms were pollarded for

---

* Bark-beetle galleries are not uncommon on the surface of ancient elm timbers. Their orientation occasionally suggests that the tree died on its feet; my earliest example is dated c.1300.

Elms

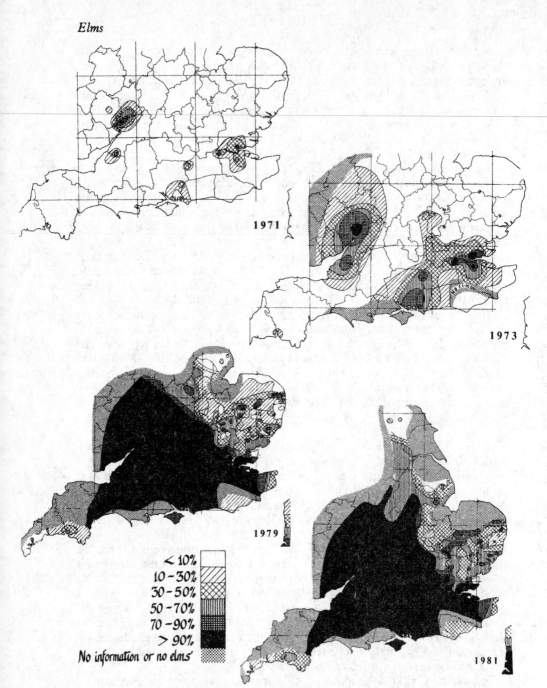

1971

1973

1979

< 10%
10 - 30%
30 - 50%
50 - 70%
70 - 90%
> 90%
No information or no elms

1981

Fig. 11.2. Progress of the present epidemic of Dutch Elm Disease. What is mapped is the proportion of elms killed or severely diseased at the end of each year, as a proportion of all elms more than 20 feet high at the start of the epidemic. No account is taken of recovery or of new elms growing in areas already ravaged. From my own observations, supplemented by the Forestry Commission survey of 1971[623] and subsequent surveys, and by reports from many other observers.

244

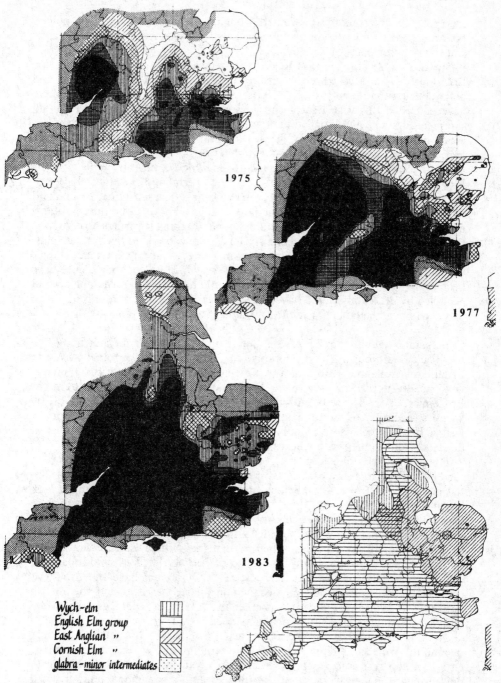

1975

1977

1983

Wych-elm
English Elm group
East Anglian "
Cornish Elm "
glabra - minor intermediates

Fig. 11.3 (bottom right). Distribution of elms. The hatching shows to what group (or groups) the common traditional elms of an area belong. No account is taken of woodland elms, fashion elms, or small outlying populations. From my own observations supplemented from Richens (1983).

this purpose and thereby prevented from producing a full crop of pollen. Pollarding trees for cattle fodder is indeed a standard practice in the Himalayas and the remoter parts of the Alps.

But this explanation is insufficient. Elms covered about one-eighth of the British Isles – at least three times the total area of all trees coppiced and pollarded at any time in history.[404] There were not enough Neolithic people to have pollarded this vast area of elms, even if they had nothing else to do all summer. Elm was not equally abundant everywhere; where it was scarce, ash, hazel, holly, etc. would have been used instead. But the Decline affected only elm, regardless of whether it was common or rare.

Elm Disease is the only known explanation which covers all the facts of the Elm Decline: it is the only cause sufficiently powerful and specific to have had such an effect on elms alone, and which could have reached Great Britain and Ireland but not America. Neolithic activity could well have set up the conditions in which an epidemic could get out of hand. Making clearings would have created wood-margin and free-standing elms, more exposed to beetles than elms in wildwood. Elms which grow fast after pollarding, as recent experience shows, are more liable to develop Dutch Elm Disease. Once killed, they would have been replaced by pollarding others, which would have died in turn. The ground occupied by dead elms would have been used as pasture or arable. Elm Disease may well have helped civilization, as well as civilization helping the disease.

Conclusions Dutch Elm Disease is not an unheard-of calamity, striking like the Black Death out of the mysterious East. The fungus has probably lived in Britain for millennia. Most of the time it does minor, unnoticed damage. Occasionally it turns into virulent forms, kills trees, and attracts attention. Epidemics, as far as can be judged from those now in progress, are set off by 'aggressive strains' of the fungus, which can be recognized in the laboratory as well as by their behaviour. Similar virulent mutations appear in all manner of diseases, from influenza to wheat rust.

The aggressive strains at present loose in Europe are of two kinds, of which the one in Britain is supposed to have come from America.[405] The circumstantial evidence is strong. The British and American forms of the fungus look identical in the laboratory. Most of the points of origin were near ports. Elm logs with bark attached have been imported from infected areas of Canada, and infected beetles have been seen to emerge from them. But the matter is not quite so simple. Americans universally believe that their Elm Disease is not native, but was similarly introduced on elm logs from Europe. The Paris and Innsbruck outbreaks are also of the American type,[406] but do not have the American connexion, and both (from my observation) started earlier than the British outbreak. It is an open question whether the American-type aggressive strain mutated in America or Europe or independently in both.

The greatest unsolved problem of Elm Disease is why its epidemics should decline in virulence. Plants, having no immunological system, cannot apparently develop resistance to diseases as men do to influenza. A new form of non-virulence evidently arises in the fungus, and is somehow communicated throughout the virulent strain so as to cause its extinction. A parallel is known in the chestnut-blight disease of sweet-chestnut. This disease (it has never reached Britain) was introduced to New York about 1900, and devastated the American chestnut, a very important tree, even more thoroughly than our elms have been.

It has also ravaged the chestnuts of Italy and France. But both in Europe and America it has at last been checked by the appearance of a virus that parasitizes the fungus and prevents it from killing the tree. In Italy the epidemic is well into its decline.[407] The disease still exists but kills only twigs and branches.

Nobody knows whether there is a similar virus of Dutch Elm Disease. But some such interaction, with the fungus mutating and releasing itself from the restraint of the virus, and the virus in turn mutating and catching up with the fungus, would cover all the facts of *Ceratocystis* epidemics as no other explanation appears to do. On the experience of previous epidemics, the present one should soon be passing its peak. There are some encouraging signs – infected trees recover less rarely than ten years ago – but these are difficult to distinguish from the disease having run into more resistant elms.*

Elms are by no means a lost cause. Suckers should be cherished to restore the magnificent variety of elms to our successors. Here, as often, conservation's chief enemy is tidiness.

Elm Disease epidemics have been more frequent and more destructive in the twentieth century: international trade – often unnecessary – disperses virulent strains. The dead elms of England and New England are both monuments to the unwisdom of carrying coals to Newcastle.

A lesson yet to be learnt from the Dutch Elm Disease experience is to put no trust in supertrees. There is a fashion, thoughtlessly written into Common Market legislation, for planting only trees of officially approved strains selected for supposed commercial qualities. This should be resisted by conservationists. It may or may not work: the Forest of Dean was ruined last century by replacing its local oaks by what were thought to be super-oaks (p.147). A world in which all oaks and ashes are genetically selected will have lost much of the meaning and beauty of oak and ash. And trees without genetic variety are specially liable to succumb to new epidemics. Dutch Elm Disease would now be controllable had not our ancestors unwittingly prepared the ground for it by promoting the English Elm, a super-elm which combined all the desirable qualities of elm but was to be disastrously vulnerable to a future disease.

---

* The Reggio (Emilia) epidemic, which was a few years earlier than the English one, killed at least 80 per cent of the elms in the 1970s. I now find (1984) that the survivors, though few, are healthy and there is little disease. Surviving elms appear to be of the same clones as those that died.

CHAPTER 12

Highways

Along the river to Stretford beyond Tothele; from there straight along the public road which was called by the ancients 'stret' and is now 'fos'; to the other Stretford under Bubbethorne, to the water which is called Ingelbourne . . .

The Foss Way in the Latin bounds of Brokenborough (Wiltshire), 956[408]

By far the greater part of modern roads go back at least to the Saxon age, and many thousands of miles of them, the ridgeways, have had a continuous existence going back into times long before history began.

G.B. Grundy, 1933[18]

Roads, bridleways, and footpaths tell the traveller how to get to his destination by a route which avoids some natural obstacles; they provide a surface for wheels or feet, and bridges, fords, etc. to overcome other natural obstacles; and they have boundaries within which to confine the traveller and his animals and thus to prevent conflict between travellers and residents.

In modern Britain these three functions are usually combined, but this need not be so. In the less mountainous parts of modern Greece the climate does not require ordinary roads to have special surfaces, the customs of land tenure do not require them to be fenced, and it is thus very easy to make new roads. The stranger is confronted with a plethora of minor roads not marked on the map; it is embarrassingly difficult to distinguish roads in use from disused or unfinished roads, the public highway from private tracks, and even between roads and the rest of the landscape. The much more stable road system of Britain is partly the consequence of our climate and multitude of rivers, which require paths and roads to be structures and not mere routes; it also reflects English and Welsh, rather than Scottish or continental, attitudes to rights of way. The idea that ownership of land includes rights to keep the public off it and to be rude to well-behaved trespassers is partly due to the general increase in landowners' rights in the last 200 years; but traces of this idea can be found in documents from earlier periods and in the landscape itself.

A well-developed road system is often supposed to be comparatively modern, a product of what we like to think of as an industrial society. Previously, we are told, there had been a 'pre-industrial society' of self-sufficient peasants; they usually stayed at home, and when they did go in for long-distance transport they used waterways. I have seen a learned article on medieval roads based on the fourteenth-century Gough Map, our earliest road-map, as if the main roads which it shows were the total road-system in existence. This thesis is based partly on general notions of progress and partly on complaints of the state of the roads: if roads were as bad in the sixteenth century as people then said they were, they must have been worse in the fourteenth century and non-existent in the twelfth.

Archaeological and documentary evidence of roads and transport tell a very different story. Complaints are poor evidence: as our own times show, the public is never content with roads, however good, as long as there is a prospect of getting someone else's money spent on bettering them. Transport has had its ups and downs, but its primitive age passed away long before the earliest records. The pre-industrial society, if it ever existed, must be set far back into prehistory. Even in the Mesolithic period, tools of chert were transported well over 100 miles from the source of this rock in the Isle of Portland (Taylor 1979, p.7). From the Neolithic onwards Britain has had a fully-developed network of major and minor communications. The known Roman roads are but a small part of a system that penetrated to every part of England; they are no more representative of all roads in the Roman period than motorways are representative of all twentieth-century roads. By late Anglo-Saxon times it was possible to transport almost anything by land that could be transported before the eighteenth century; the problem of organizing the upkeep of main highways used for long-distance as well as local transport had partly been solved. Inland waterways were rudimentary at this time and for many centuries after.

Highways include not only main and minor roads joining settlements, but also lanes and ways leading to fields and woods. Their history is not merely of pedlars and pack-horses – important though the latter have been at certain times and in certain places.[409] The design of roads, bridges, and town streets stems from the invention of the iron-tyred wheel in the Iron Age. No pack-horse can move heavy timber or large building stones. At least since the Anglo-Saxon period, carts have been part of ordinary farm equipment. Where narrow 'pack-horse' bridges survive, these are usually meant to carry pedestrians and animals dryshod while carts go through the adjoining ford. Anyone who has been to Genoa, the lesser Greek islands or the Near East will know the difference between our landscapes and townscapes, shaped by two thousand years of wheels, and those designed for mules and camels.

I shall use the word 'highway' to include roads, bridleways, and footpaths. The verges as well as the metalling form part of the highway and are included in its width, unless otherwise stated. 'Lane' will mean a road (less often a path) confined between hedges, fences, or ditches; 'track' will mean a road not so delimited.

Prehistoric Highways

One function of highways, that of preventing the traveller from getting lost, is older than mankind; deer and badgers make paths as well as men. Evidence of specific highways is as old as civilization, and is of two kinds. We have the boundaries or structures of particular lanes or tracks, generally disused but revealed by excavation or aerial photography. We also have long-distance routes, conventionally called 'tracks' although some of them were probably lanes, many of which can be identified with existing highways; these rarely involve actual prehistoric remains and the evidence for the identification is mainly circumstantial. It is not often possible to bring together these two kinds of evidence, but they are not contradictory. The second kind relates to the trunk roads of prehistory and the first kind to the minor roads and footpaths; as yet we can seldom see the system as a whole.

Prehistoric tracks and lanes The actual fabric of prehistoric highways is beautifully preserved in the wooden 'trackways', of Neolithic to Iron Age date, across the peat of the Somerset Levels (Chapter 17). These were a specialized and sometimes very elaborate kind of highway. The technology died out before the historic period, and they have left no mark on the visible landscape.

The banks or cropmarks of disused 'Celtic' or other prehistoric field systems often reveal lanes as well as fields (Fig. 12.1). Most settlements and farmsteads were reached by at least one lane. Many of them had other lanes ending among fields; but, in prehistory as later, not every field adjoined a lane, and many could be reached only across other fields.

Where prehistoric field systems are still in use it is likely that the lanes that go with them are prehistoric too. This almost certainly true of many of the lanes of Cornwall. Indeed it is very possible, though difficult to prove, that much of our minor road system, at least in Ancient Countryside, is really prehistoric. Many lanes in Hampshire, Essex, or north-west Dorset are certainly of Anglo-Saxon antiquity, but as yet we have little evidence of how much older they may be. Students of disused field systems should look for instances (C.C. Taylor gives a Dorset example) where a lane between former prehistoric fields on downland is continued below the edge of the downland by an existing lane between fields still in use.

Prehistoric long-distance highways The Neolithic was already an age of industry. Stone tools were factory-made articles originating from particular sources of hard stone. The biggest industry was based on the flint mined at

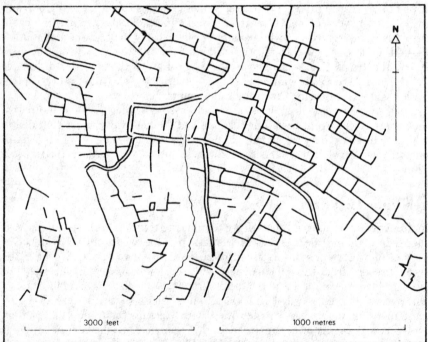

3000 feet   1000 metres

Fig. 12.1. Prehistoric lanes in a downland 'Celtic Field' system. Dole's Hill in Puddletown, Dorset. After Taylor (1979) by permission.

Grime's Graves in Norfolk (Chapter 16). Yet Norfolk is full of stone tools from the Lake District, Cornwall, and Wales. The facts of geology, with which there is no arguing, prove not only that Neolithic people had regular long-distance transport but that they had already developed the light-hearted 'coals to Newcastle' attitude to it with which we are familiar today. Transport increased with the invention of metals; and for every enterprise ,sending out stone or bronze articles which have survived there were probably ten others sending out perishable goods.

Long-distance roads such as the Icknield Way, the various Ridgeways, and the Pilgrims' Way in Surrey are usually regarded as prehistoric main highways. This is based partly on tradition, but there is an argument which runs as follows. Neolithic, Bronze and Iron Age people lived on high ground where their settlements, barrows, and field systems are still obvious on what is now downland or moorland. These habitable areas were islands in a sea of uncultivable and impassable wildwood on heavy lowland soils. Main routes followed the populated ridges and crossed the inhospitable lowlands, if at all, by the shortest possible way.

This argument was convincing up to thirty years ago but has been weakened by new discovery. We now know that settlements were not specially concentrated on the high ground; the evidence is better preserved there because of less ploughing in more recent times. On low ground the evidence is at least as abundant but is more difficult to find. The 'Jurassic Way' from Stamford to Banbury was claimed in 1940 as prehistoric on the grounds that most of the sites then known lay close to it; vastly more sites have been found since then, and the Jurassic Way is now seen to *avoid* the more populous parts of Northamptonshire (Taylor 1979). Moreover, the argument that highways with settlements along their length were necessarily important is unsound. Roman, Anglo-Saxon, and medieval minor settlements often avoided contemporary main roads (Fig. 12.2), for very good reason. A trunk road is a highway for armies. At least two armies out of three will be either hostile or unfed; main roads are dangerous neighbours.

The traditional 'prehistoric tracks' are probably genuine, at least in their general direction. Indeed their exact courses, if not their boundaries, are sometimes proved by Anglo-Saxon records and parish boundaries to be well over a thousand years old. Many are ridgeways, minimizing the need for river crossings – although, knowing little of what prehistoric people could accomplish in making bridges and fords, we cannot say how advantageous this was. Sometimes, as with the Icknield Way in Cambridgeshire, they avoid heavy soils on which paving would be needed. Often they provide alternative routes. The traveller along the Chilterns, for instance, could choose between the 'Upper Icknield Way', following the chalk escarpment above the spring-line, and the 'Lower Icknield Way' over the claylands at the foot of the scarp. The upper would have been an all-weather road but had steep hills and many diversions round valleys; the lower saved time and effort but its many fords and sloughs would have made it a summer and autumn route (see also Figs. 2.3, 12.3)

It can no longer be asserted that the recognized prehistoric tracks are the whole, or even the most important, of those that existed. There were presumably others, at least as important, on low ground, which can now rarely be distinguished from other roads. And the distinction between prehistoric and Roman roads turns out to be less definite than we should expect.

Roman Roads

The most obvious legacy of the Romans to modern England is the roads whose uncompromising red lines stare out of almost every page of the motoring atlas. According to tradition, these roads were laid out by military engineers to link towns and fortresses across the intervening miles of trackless and houseless wildwood. On this principle the system is simple and we understand it already; it is fun to discover unknown Roman roads or to fill in gaps in partially preserved ones, but there is nothing fundamentally new to be found out.

The first flaw in this interpretation is that the majority of Romano-British villages, villas, etc. are not on known Roman roads. A roadless settlement was no more reasonable then than it is now. The roads that we recognize as Roman are merely the trunk roads among a network of lesser roads which, over much of England, can scarcely have been less dense than it is today. The trunk roads were not a pioneering enterprise: they were added to an existing Iron Age network, and they involved expropriating the lands of people who happened to be in the way. The system was maintained, and presumably adapted, during four centuries of great changes in population and commerce. The problems dealt with by the Roman highway authorities were not, perhaps, so very different from those of their twentieth-century successors.

How Roman roads were organized The Latin language is rich in words for different kinds of road. In other provinces of the Empire, the Romans had much the same classification of major and minor roads as we have in Britain today. At about the time the Romans were conquering Britain, Siculus Flaccus wrote in his textbook of surveying:

> There are state roads (*uiae publicae*), which are maintained at state expense and bear the names of their originators. These are in the charge of superintendents and are repaired by contractors. For the upkeep of some of them a fixed sum is charged to the [local] landowners from time to time.
>
> There are also local roads (*uicinales*) which branch off the state roads into the country and often run through to other state roads. These are maintained in a different way, by the counties (*pagi*), that is by the head-men of the counties, who normally charge the work of keeping them up to the landowners. Sometimes, we understand, they assign to each landowner certain sections across his own land, which are kept up at his expense. At the ends of the sections they put up notices to show which landlord has to keep up which section over whose land.
>
> There is a [private] right of way to all [pieces of] land. Sometimes, if there is no local road, the way goes over someone else's land . . . this does not provide a right of way for the general public, but [only] for those who have to get to their [own] fields on these roads. There are also shared roads which branch off local roads; these sometimes form a right of way between the two landowners at their further ends, who share the cost equally at their joint expense.[410]

Other Roman authors confirm that there was a great variety of highway authorities responsible for the upkeep of particular roads and classes of roads. Major repairs or making a new main road were the work of emperors, consuls, or benefactors, whose deeds are inscribed on milestones. On the whole this was a civilian matter, but the army took some part in making new roads, especially in the more distant provinces.[411]

Britain became one such a distant province in AD 43, and its first twenty years were bloody and precarious. Boadicea's revolt in 61 horrified even the Roman world; two of her three massacres would have been averted had the legions got there in time. We should therefore expect to find more evidence of the army and of military roads than in most other provinces of the Empire.

The Roman era in Britain was as long and as eventful as the interval between the Reformation and the motor-car. After the first century the military front moved away north and west, leaving Lowland England as an ordinary civilian region. It had inherited an Iron Age road system and a Roman military road system, neither of them intended for the purposes of the second century. Alterations to road systems during the Roman period should be looked for. The fate of 'General Wade's' roads in Scotland (p.272) is a parallel for what happens to military roads when civilians do not use them. Many substantially-built Roman roads have disappeared so completely that they can only be found by excavation; did they already fall into disuse in Roman times?

Structure and boundaries A Roman road typically had two side-ditches, between which was a raised embankment (Latin *agger*) bearing a surface metalled with gravel, stone, or ironworks slag.[411] The ditches might be 80 feet apart, the agger 40 feet wide and 3 feet high, and the metalling 20 feet wide. Not all main roads had ditches and agger; and the dimensions varied widely, even between different parts of the same road, for reasons which are little known.

Roads had bridges and paved fords. In difficult terrain there were causeways and cuttings; elsewhere in the Empire there were massive timber substructures on soft ground and tunnels through mountains.

Kinds of Roman main road What we notice about Roman roads is their straightness on the map. They do not have quite the same mindless geometry as in the American Mid-West, where a nineteenth-century road will go through a swamp, or bridge a bend in a river twice, rather than mar its straight course by going round. But the Roman surveyors evidently did not look around for the easiest or quickest or most easily defended way between two points. The route chosen was instead the most direct way, and was influenced only by the more formidable natural obstacles. Gradients, fens, wet hilltops, perils of ambush, and any protests of people whose land lay in the way were usually ignored.

The Romans were masters of surveying (Taylor 1979). Whoever set out the Foss Way evidently knew in which direction Lincoln lay from Exeter, to within a fraction of a degree, and also knew that the Somerset Levels and multiple river-crossings in Nottinghamshire were insuperable obstacles to going there direct. Between the two deviations round these obstacles, the middle 150 miles of the Foss Way never depart by more than 6½ miles from the direct line. The departures are not accidental; they are due to the method of setting out the road on the ground in detail after its general alignment had been determined. This was evidently done by sighting from hilltop to hilltop; the road therefore changes direction slightly every few miles, nearly always on high ground (Fig. 12.2).

The surveyor of Peddar's Way, starting at the north-west corner of Norfolk, knew to within ½ degree which way to go to reach a certain ford of the Little Ouse, 42 miles away. The road twice deviates very slightly, each time on a hilltop, but returns to the original line on reaching the ford (Fig. 12.3).

253

Roman roads vary in the character of their minor realignments. On Peddar's Way there is one absolutely straight stretch of 19 miles between hilltops; further south, what is probably the same road went for 22 miles ruler-straight into Essex. In contrast, Stane Street, the road west from Colchester, looks amateurish with its very frequent changes of direction, rarely more than two miles straight at a stretch and often much less. These are extreme examples of two kinds of Roman road. Peddar's Way and the Foss Way have rare, sometimes rather abrupt, realignments; Stane Street, and the road from London to Colchester and on towards Norwich, have frequent slight changes of direction.

The reason for the two types of Roman main road has not yet been found (if indeed it has been sought) but I shall risk some guesses. The Foss Way was

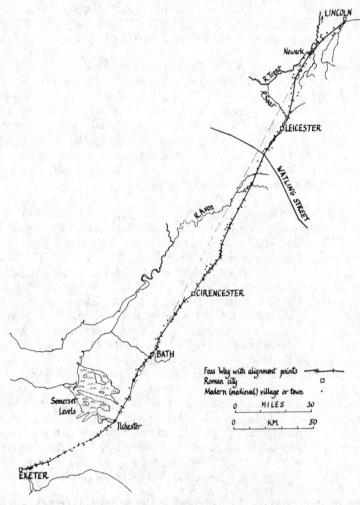

Fig. 12.2. The Foss Way, showing changes of alignment and river crossings incurred or avoided. The straight line betwen the major alignment points at Ilchester and Newark is shown. Many medieval and present villages lie within two miles of the road, but very few indeed are actually on it. The two crossings of the River Soar seem unnecessary.

probably made in the heat of war, to join the military bases of Exeter and Lincoln and to support the front line which lay for a time not far to the west. It was surveyed in a hurry through potentially hostile territory; its planners, having all the manpower of the Roman army to do the hard work, had no need to search for ways round minor obstacles; they could reduce the aligning of the road to a mere problem in navigation. Peddar's Way also appears to be a military road. It has led nowhere in historic times – much ink has flowed in vain attempts to invent a destination for it – but it makes sense as one of a grid of roads built to hold down the territory of the Iceni, Boadicea's tribe. Similar roads were made in all directions from London, even into friendly Sussex, to ensure that there should never be another Boadicea.

Roads of the Stane Street type generally have an evident civilian function. Stane Street itself linked Colchester with lesser towns at Braintree and Braughing. Another road of the same kind went north to the capital of the Iceni at Caistor-by-Norwich and a third went south-west to the London area. Such roads are met by the straighter type of road in such a way as often to suggest that the straighter roads are later. Sometimes they conform to field patterns and

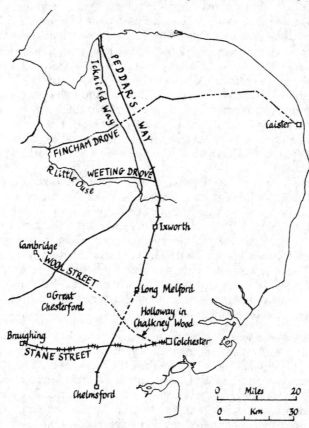

Fig. 12.3. A few of the ancient roads of eastern England. Peddar's Way and Fincham Drove are Roman; Wool Street and Stane Street are probably Iron Age; Icknield Way and Weeting Drove are usually regarded as prehistoric. The alignment points of Peddar's Way and Stane Street are shown.

sometimes not: Stane Street itself cuts across the earlier hedgerow pattern around Braintree as does the Roman road in Fig.8.4, but in The Saints, Suffolk (Fig. 8.2) a field system which we have conjectured to be of the Bronze Age has a 'Roman road' conforming to it.

The matter is illuminated by P.C. Dewhurst's study of what is now the green lane called by Cambridge people The Roman Road, *alias* Wool Street.[412] It begins 4 miles south-east of Cambridge and runs for some 11 miles in the direction of Colchester (Fig. 12.4). In 1959 a pipe-trench was dug along the whole 11 miles and revealed its construction. The part nearest Cambridge looks like a Roman road of the Peddar's Way type and follows the canons of Roman road-building: it had two boundary ditches 42 feet apart, the chalk from which was used to form a raised agger which was metalled with gravel. Where this road crossed the pre-existing Icknield Way the agger was lessened in height to form a level crossing. Wool Street next intersects another Roman road of the Peddar's Way type, leading from the military town at Great Chesterford, in such a way as to establish that Wool Street came first. After this crossing, Wool Street changes its character. Its agger peters out and its straight course disappears. It is still recognizable as a 'Roman road', but becomes a wandering one of the Stane Street type, and in section it is no longer raised but a holloway. The difference is clear even on the 1-inch map but until the excavation nobody noticed it.

Wool Street evidently began as a prehistoric road from Colchester to the small Iron Age town of Cambridge. The rest of it has disappeared but for a length, also a holloway, in and near Chalkney Wood, Essex (p.276).[413] Early in the Roman period it was modernized, straightened and given an agger. (A certain cart, jolting over the roadworks, spilt a load of Nottinghamshire coal, which is still there buried under the Roman gravel.) The work began at the Cambridge end and was abandoned 9 miles out, leaving the rest of Wool Street in the Iron Age state in which it still remains. The Great Chesterford road was added later in the Roman era.

Even among main roads, the distinction between Roman and prehistoric is thus not very clear. The original planning of Wool Street has to be set back at least to the Iron Age. The same is almost certainly true of Stane Street and may be of the less straight 'Roman roads' in general. In the century before the Roman conquest, Britons could have learnt about Roman road surveying and have tried their hands at copying it. The very straight Roman roads appear, on the whole, to be the work of the Roman army, although Wool Street proves that some even of these are adaptations of earlier roads. Further research may discover among Roman main roads all the changes and complexities that we should expect of a 400-year-old network.

Minor roads Roads with aggers and other obvious Roman features were the class-A and class-B roads of the Romano-British period. The innumerable minor roads were much more diverse than the main roads. The Roman or late Iron Age grids of fields in south Essex (Plate XIII) were served by grids of lanes; in recent decades these lanes have come up in the world, and juggernaut lorries ceaselessly negotiate their right-angle bends on the way to Tilbury Docks. In the unplanned Roman landscape of the Fens the roads – now revealed only as cropmarks – show the same kind of irregularity as prehistoric minor road systems (p.383). Presumably some pre-existing main roads, such as the Icknield Way in Norfolk (Fig. 12.3), which were duplicated by Roman roads, survived

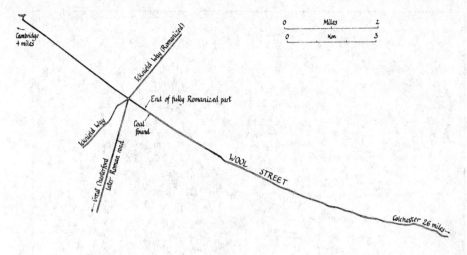

Fig. 12.4. Wool Street near Cambridge, an Iron Age road partly converted into a Roman Road.

unmodernized as minor roads. We can rarely be sure of distinguishing minor Roman from prehistoric roads; who can say how many existing country lanes date from either period?

Anglo-Saxon Highways

It is sometimes supposed that the Roman road system went out of use and was later partly restored. This is unrealistic. Roads are highly artificial and survive only through continuous use. A gravel road neglected for five years gets overgrown with bushes; after ten years it becomes a thicket more impenetrable than if it had never been a road. Blackthorn has a nasty habit of growing on disused highways and powerfully induces passers-by to go round some other way.

The survival of so many Roman roads is a strong argument for continuity of communication and settlement from the Roman to the Anglo-Saxon period. Roman roads that survive in bits and pieces are more eloquent than those that are still through routes. The men of London and Colchester might have kept open a way between those towns, even if all the intervening country had become a wilderness. But what of the road between Braughing and Great Chesterford? Both places ceased to be towns; the Roman road between them was not kept up as a through route, and Rockell's Wood has for centuries blocked its course (Fig. 12.5). But there were still people in these Essex–Hertfordshire backwoods for whom bits of it were of use as local roads. Every few years, through the darkest of the Dark Ages, there has been somebody from Duddenhoe End and Brent Pelham to take a billhook to the blackthorn on two short stretches of Roman road, which stand out by their straightness amid the maze of lanes.

By the later Anglo-Saxon period big heavy things like millstones, timber, salt, iron, and bells and fragile things like pots were being transported to and from the remotest parts of England. Building stone was not necessarily local: stone

Fig. 12.5. A Roman road in Hertfordshire, once a through road but now surviving only as fragments of muddy lane and as an *agger* through Rockell's Wood. At A the *agger* has been converted into a woodbank. The road has acquired many minor wobbles over the centuries. The dead-straight road B, which looks like a continuation, is in fact quite modern. Ordnance Survey 1886.

258

from Barnack (Peterborough) and Box (near Bath) is found in many places up to 80 miles from the quarry.[414] People thought little of going overland to Italy.

The supreme test of Anglo-Saxon communications came in the last weeks of the period. On 20 September 1066 King Harold was told in London that Hardrada had invaded the north. The king covered the 200 miles to York probably in 4½ days. He gathered an army and smote the Danes at Stamford Bridge (note the place-name). Duke William landed at Pevensey, 250 miles from York, on 28 September. Within three days Harold had heard of this second invasion. It took him just four days to get back to London, this time taking his army, which, as we all know, was nearly sufficient to win the Battle of Hastings on 13 October. Few campaigns until the age of helicopters have packed more action into three weeks; it is a tribute not only to Harold's generalship and the endurance of his men but to the effort that his predecessors had put into organizing roads for just such a contingency.

Highways in the Anglo-Saxon charters One in six of the features in English charter boundaries has to do with communications. A total of 1654 roads, ways, and paths are mentioned, 11.6 per cent of all English boundary features; they outnumber every other class of artificial object. Fords and bridges make a further 4.6 per cent of features. In Welsh boundaries, roads etc. form only 4.4 per cent of features and fords a further 2.8 per cent.

Highways are distributed almost evenly throughout England, except in the Fens (Fig. 12.6). Charters from Ancient Countryside mention them rather less often (10.4 per cent) than those from future Planned Countryside (12.8 per cent). Highways were probably at least as numerous in the former but less often selected because there were plenty of woods, hedges, and trees which could be used as landmarks instead.

The many Old English words for highway indicate some thought of classification. The most important highways were called *stræt*, 'street'. These were evidently vehicle roads, often Roman; many of them are still main roads today. Some had names: there are frequent references to Watling Street (already so called throughout its length), the Berkshire Icknield Street, Ermine Street, and 'Buggilde stræt' (now called Ryknild Street, a Roman road in Worcestershire). The Foss Way is often mentioned (see quotation at the head of this chapter).

The term *herepað* occurs 221 times. It literally means 'army path' and is commonly taken to signify a road made for military purposes. When identified on the map, however, herepaðs usually turn out to be ordinary roads without apparent military importance; for instance there is one on the Lizard Peninsula (Cornwall). In Latin charters the phrase used is never the expected *via militaris* but is instead *via publica*, a phrase reminiscent of Siculus Flaccus and possibly meaning a road maintained at public expense. This suggests that the idea behind *herepað* (and the occasional *herestræt*) is that of a highway wide enough for an army; and that in practice it means a B-class road in contrast to the *stræt* which is an A-class road. Herepaðs rarely have proper names.

There is also a regional difference. In the Midlands, north-east England, and Kent *stræt* is the commoner term and is used for almost all main roads. In Wessex and Devon most main roads were called *herepað*, the word *stræt* being reserved for a few very important ones.

Nearly half the highways in the charters are called *weg*, 'way'. This term probably means something less important than a herepað, but it may also have been vague as in later centuries; the same road in Berkshire is called *Icenhilda stræt* and *Icenhilda weg*. Most wegs are now minor roads, but whether they were all vehicular in Anglo-Saxon times is uncertain; once a 'wheel-way' is specified. Ways are fairly evenly distributed, except that few are designated in the London Basin, Weald, or Essex.

The terms *pað* 'path' and *stig* (Modern German *Steig*, 'path') are the bottom rank of highways, corresponding presumably to modern bridleways and foot-paths (occasionally a 'horsepath' is specified). They are less often mentioned than the others; *pað* is commonest in the Dorset Chalklands and *stig* in the Woodless Cotswolds, but little can be made of their distribution.

The word 'road' itself is unknown in Anglo-Saxon literature – it is curiously rare before the seventeenth century – but it does occur, as Old English *rōd*, some fifty times in charters. (The exact frequency is uncertain because of confusion with *rōd*, 'rood', ie. crucifix.) The context implies some kind of highway but the exact meaning cannot be inferred; there is nothing to support the conjecture of some commentators that a track through a wood, the original of the modern 'ride', is meant. *Rōd* is scattered over most of England.

'Lane' (*lane*) occurs eighteen times; it is thinly scattered but is absent from areas with a strong open-field tradition. It may well mean, as in the Middle Ages and later, a minor road between hedges, but this cannot be proved.

Many highways are described as greenways, stone-streets, broadways, small-ways, sandy-ways, roughways, etc. The commonest term of usage is *sealtstræt*,

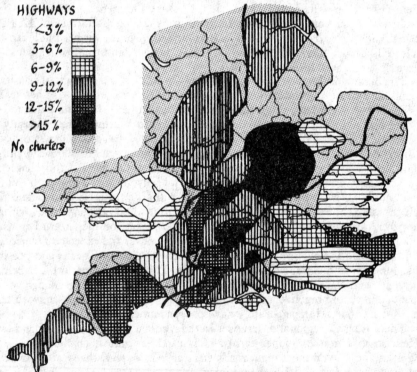

HIGHWAYS

- <3%
- 3-6%
- 6-9%
- 9-12%
- 12-15%
- >15%
- No charters

Fig. 12.6. Distribution of roads, ways, and paths in Anglo-Saxon and Welsh charters, as a percentage of all boundary features.

which (with *sealtrōd*, *sealtpaδ*, etc.) occurs eighteen times, mainly to the south of the great inland salt-deposits of Worcestershire. Other terms are *portstræt*, meaning a road to a market town, and *cyricpaδ* or *cyricstig* 'church-path' (Fig. 9.5). About one way in fifteen was a 'ridgeway' (*hrycgweg*), a term found all over England but especially in south Berkshire where there are still many named Ridgeways (eg. Fig. 2.3).

All classes of highway are quite often described as 'old'. Many ways, paths, etc. were already worn down by centuries of usage: the terms 'holloway' (*hola weg*), 'hollow path', etc. occur thirty-eight times.

River and stream crossings These are mentioned 666 times in English charters, one-sixth being bridges and the rest fords. Their distribution depends mainly on the character of the rivers – Devon, with its countless small streams, has the highest proportion of fords and very few bridges. Bridges are also rare in chalkland regions with their shallow streams. At the other extreme, in the Fens with their presumably deep and muddy watercourses, half the crossings are bridges. Bridges were also common in North-East England, the Thames valley, Kent, Essex, and the Hampshire Basin.

Place-names give us a different insight into Anglo-Saxon river crossings. About 520 settlements in Domesday Book are named after crossings; of these only some forty mention bridges, the rest being fords or wades. The smaller proportion of bridges is very significant, especially as the crossings generating place-names are likely to be more important than those merely chosen as landmarks. Evidently the place-names date on average from a time when bridges were much less common than in the period of the charters. Towns named after bridges (eg. Boroughbridge, Bridgnorth) have a habit of not being mentioned in Domesday: either they did not exist in 1086 or they were then too recent to have administrative status.

Ford and bridge names have a curious geographical distribution. They are, of course, commonest in Devon, where 8 per cent of places in Domesday Book are named after river-crossings; but why should Huntingdonshire, Oxfordshire, and Berkshire have only slightly fewer? And at the other extreme, why should Lancashire, East Yorkshire, and Sussex each have fewer than 1 place in 100 named after a ford or bridge?

We know nothing of how major fords were arranged. The mind boggles at the thought of main roads crossing the unbridged Thames at Ox*ford* or Walling*ford*. The frequent place-name Stanford suggests a constructed ford of stone like those which still exist on minor roads, but the evidence has usually been dredged away. Occasional mentions of 'earth-bridge' in the charters remind us that in literary Old English *brycg* is said to mean 'causeway' as well as 'bridge', but this meaning seems to be rare in topography; a causeway is of no use in crossing a river unless it has a bridge in the middle.

Bridge-repair was neglected in the disorganized centuries after the twilight of Rome. Each of the dozen or more Stratford place-names in England tells of a Roman bridge allowed to rot away. I have, however, found thirteen instances in the charters of *stanbrycg* 'stone bridge', one of them an 'old stone bridge'. Some of these were probably Roman bridges still in use; there are several Roman bridges still in use today in southern Europe, albeit mainly in climates where wet masonry is not attacked by frost as it is here. During the Anglo-Saxon period most of the important bridges were reinstated, and a number of unimportant crossings were bridged. By 1086 place-names such as Bridgeford had become frequent, although *Forde* (Hants) did not get its name of Fordingbridge until later.

Bridge-work was probably organized by the state. From at least the eighth century it was one of the 'three common dues' (the others being military service and work on fortifications), obligations imposed by the Crown on all land-owners. However generous the king might otherwise be, he almost never remitted these duties. The detailed pre-Conquest specification of Rochester bridge happens to survive.[415] Anglo-Saxon engineers had somehow contrived to build a timber-framed bridge of ten spans across the deep and fiercely tidal Medway. The landowners of dozens of named places were made responsible for the upkeep of individual piers and spans. This principle of *pontage* – spreading the repair cost of a bridge among the townships at some distance on either side of it – was to become a normal method of maintaining bridges in the Middle Ages; as late as *c.*1720 my college refused to pay towards Magdalene Bridge, Cambridge, as we should have done on account of owning lands beyond it.

A greater achievement still was the bridging implied by North and South Fambridge in south-east Essex (Fig. 12.7). The road and field grids of the Rochford and Dengie peninsulas line up across the Crouch estuary that divides them. A principal Roman road would have crossed between the two Fam-bridges, both so named (*Fanbruge*, 'fen-bridge') in Domesday Book. But there has been no bridge since the Middle Ages; the tides of the Crouch sweep ¼ mile wide between the bridgeheads, though the Ordnance Survey remembers a ferry.

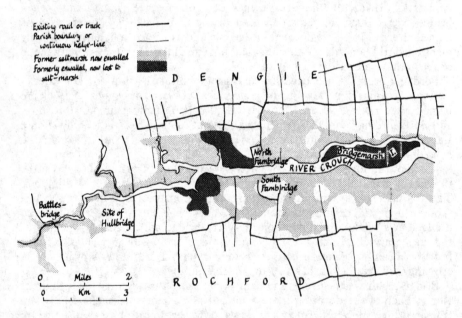

Fig. 12.7. Former bridging-points of the River Crouch estuary, south-east Essex. Also shown are parts of the semi-regular, probably Iron Age, road and field grids of the Dengie and Rochford Peninsulas that align across the estuary. Only the main axes are shown as they survive in extant roads and hedges; Plate XIII is an aerial photograph which includes the north-east corner of this map.

Unless we care to swim our horse, like a gallant lover and his lass in 1598,[416] we must try 3 miles upstream at Hullbridge. Here we find that the medieval bridge fell down in the seventeenth century and has not been replaced, though the map, optimistic as ever, claims a ford. The lowest twentieth-century bridge, Battlesbridge, is 5 miles above the Anglo-Saxon bridge.

Medieval Roads

In the Middle Ages the road system of England was rather denser than it is now. The remote dispersed parish of Wimbish (Essex) had at least twenty-five roads known by name;[417] this not particularly well documented place is typical of Ancient Countryside, in which almost all the modern lanes existed, together with others that have disappeared. Every wood, meadow, house, and barn and most fields and furlongs had vehicle access, and there were also footpath rights-of-way across fields. Moors and heaths were criss-crossed with tracks linking hamlets and farms (p.279). In open-field areas only the through roads have survived to the present; the countless ways leading to the strips have mostly been swept away by enclosure.

Much less has been written on medieval than on Roman roads, but there can be no doubt of their importance: what of the Canterbury Tales or the ceaseless journeys of King John? Monasteries depended on pilgrims and on the commercial running of distant estates. In the seaward Fens, every particle of the stone, timber, lime, iron and lead used to build the great twelfth and thirteenth-century churches had to be brought from a distance and to be paid for out of the sale of produce at a distance. The East Anglian cloth industry was not located near its raw material or its markets. Any town presupposes arrangements for moving thousands of tons of various materials. Detailed illustration may be

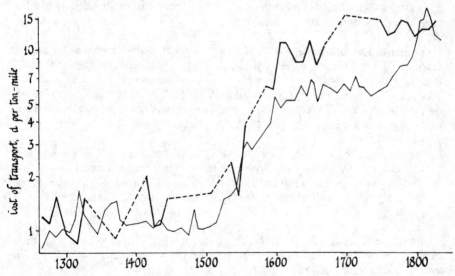

Fig. 12.8. Cost of general-purpose road transport, 1260–1840, in relation to the value of money. Thick line: average cost per ton-mile. Thin line: cost-of-living index. Transport costs mainly from Rogers[52] up to 1680 and Albert[624] thereafter; price index from Brown and Hopkins.[89]

sought in M.K. James's study of the wine trade,[418] or in L.F. Salzman's chapter on the gongfarmers whose duty was to transport tons of 'dounge' out of urban cesspits into the country.[361]

The cost of road transport in the period 1250–1450, when the value of money was relatively stable, averaged about 1·3*d.* per ton-mile for goods that were not fragile or perishable (Fig. 12.8). This seems expensive to us; for instance the cost of moving ordinary oak timber 50 miles was roughly equal to the original cost of the tree.[154] Water transport, where available, cost about a fifth as much. But there was little economizing in transport, and the documents refuse to support the theory that heavy materials were always of local origin or else were moved by water. When the twelfth-century monks of Abingdon (Berks) wanted timber, they sent twelve-ox wains 120 miles to North Wales,[361] passing by on the way the third and fourth largest concentrations of woodland in England at the time.

The medievals were not great builders of new roads. They planned many new towns (eg. Bury St Edmund's) and sometimes made short stretches of new main road in consequence. Parts of the Fens (p.389) seem to have medieval planned rural road systems. New roads presumably also arose from casual short-cuts hardening into highways. But written records of the conscious making of even minor roads are rare:

> The Abbot and Convent shall, at their own expense, cause a hedge to be planted lengthwise from the first gate [on 'Magdeleyn lane'] up to the second, so that the place may become a lane (*venella*) between the two gates . . . taking branches from the trees growing in the said hedge to maintain the hedge.
>
> *Colchester Cartulary, 1272*[419]

This establishes what was meant at the time by 'lane' and by its Latin equivalent *venella* (cf. Modern Scots *vennel*).

Documentation of roads Roads and paths appear in documents as permanent features of the landscape. Any through road, even between two villages, is dignified as 'the king's way' (*regia via*); lesser highways are called 'common way', 'lane', 'church-way' (*via ecclesiastica*), etc. Surveyors used highways to define the location of pieces of land; manorial courts fined people for misusing or failing to maintain the highway. A typical survey entry is:

> A croft [ie. hedged field] called Woodwardescroft between the Lord's wood called Walramswoode [now Lord's Wood] on the west and the croft called Mellerscroft on the east; one end abuts on the way from Ledenrothyng to Goodleste' [Good Easter] on the north, the other on the Abbess of Berkyng's land.
>
> *Leaden Roding (Essex) 1439*[292]

Medieval petty courts were as much concerned with road offences as their modern successors. The commonest transgression was allowing ditches (or worse) to flood the highway:

> John Unwyne does not clean his ditch towards Sowenewode [Soane Wood, Chapter 7] on the King's way, to the public nuisance.
>
> *Court roll, Colchester, 1312*[420]

Nicholas Ravensby . . . has a slowe [slough, a soft place in a lane] and 2 perches of ditch making a nuisance in Hawkeley lane . . .

Court roll, Great Canfield (Essex) 1507[288]

William Barbor junior built a latrine on his holding which runs into the King's way to the nuisance of passers-by.

Court roll, Hatfield Broad-oak (Essex) 1443[274]

Every court had such cases by the score; at Little Bentley (Essex) in the 1480s the going rate for fines was 1*d*. per perch (5½ yards) of offending ditch.[421] Barbor did nothing about his latrine and was fined for it at every subsequent court for at least four years.

Almost as common were fines for leaving timber, wood, earth, muckheaps, dead horses, etc. on the highway or for digging pits in it. The highway could be obstructed by allowing hedges and trees to overgrow it (p.187).

A general duty to help with the upkeep of local highways and bridges was often an obligation of land tenure. Farmers were also expected to maintain particular bridges and culverts where water from their land ran on to the highway:

John Dowe ought to make a bridge, called a fotebregge, in the King's way leading from Dunmowe to Hatfeld brodok . . . on pain of losing 4*s*.

Great Canfield 1510[288]

Little positive attention seems to have been given to surfacing roads, but this mattered less than it would now: wheels were designed for soft ground and many roads were wide enough to pick a way round sloughs. A big consignment of timber was once sent in 1309 from Gamlingay to Grantchester (Cambs) 'at Christmas in hard Frost'.[422]

Ownership of highways; purprestures Minor lanes were occasionally private property:

Lane. Item, pasture in the lane (*venella*) leading from Rothyng Tye to Albosdonn 1 acre 2¾ roods 0 perches

Leaden Roding survey, 1439[292]

With this exception, and except also for unfenced footpaths across fields, highways were part of the common-land of the manor. They had definite boundaries (hedges or ditches) and did not belong to the adjacent farmers (cf. p.281). Much business in manorial courts was concerned with encroachments on common-land, called *purprestures*.

Purprestures could occur on any common-land, but they most often took the form of narrowing a road, either by a neighbouring farmer pushing out his frontage or by a third party setting up a smallholding within the road itself (Fig. 12.9). Manorial courts often condoned purprestures on payment of an annual fine to the lord of the manor:

Robert Cok made a purpresture in the common way, 10 ft long and 1 ft wide . . . 3*d*.

Court roll, Redlingfield, Suffolk, 1276[423]

Highways

A purpresture near the Pillory, 54 ft long, 4 ft wide at one end and 1 ft wide at the other end.

Court roll, Earl's Colne, Essex, 1428–9[424]

A purpresture . . . established by Richard Gyva, turner, of Takeleghe . . . [bounded] by the ditch of the close of the tenant of the said Richard . . . on the north, and the king's way called Stanstret [the Roman road, p.255] on the south; 65 ft long by the said ditch [measured] by a ruler, and in width at both ends and in the middle 3 ft by a ruler. [Gyva paid 1*d.* a year for it.]

Hatfield Broad-oak 1448[274]

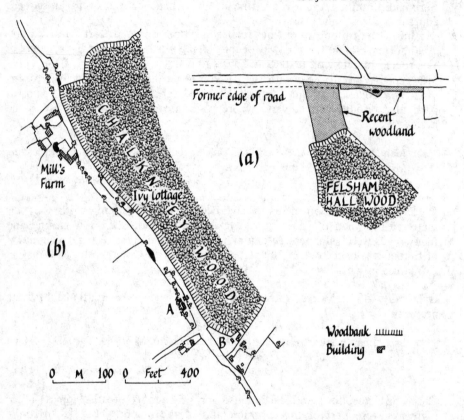

Fig. 12.9. Purprestures on highways.
(a) By a farmer extending his fields on to the road: outside the Bradfield Woods, Suffolk. The Ordnance Survey of 1836 shows a wide road, reduced to its present width soon after. The hedges show that the south side has been narrowed; traces of the original edge still exist in woodland which has grown up since.
(b) By people living in the road and building houses and planting gardens on it: outside Chalkney Wood, Essex. The road now threads its way past four encroachments, three of which were already there in 1598 (Fig. 2.2) and may be much older; they are mapped as in 1876. Ivy Cottage is still a small house as in 1598. Cottage A has disappeared since 1876 and its site has been taken over by the field adjacent. Mill's, already so called in 1598, has grown into a substantial farm and its origin as a purpresture is no longer evident. Cottage B, though it began off the road, has long ago encroached on to it.

266

Also at Hatfield, rents were collected in 1328 for 'a certain place of purpresture for a muckheap' and '1 pit of purpresture outside the gate';[425] in 1446–7 John Nedeman was fined for appropriating 14 feet by 8 feet of the King's way for 'a lay-by (*diuersorium*) to put his cart in'.[274]

A more complicated affair came before the royal courts in 1412. Sir Thomas Hengrave and three others had been granted a licence to divert the road from Mutford to Carlton Colville (north-east Suffolk) where it passed through Mutford Wood; they had stopped up the old road but had not made a new one, and did not own the land on which to do so. The gang were also in trouble for narrowing another road and throwing mud from their ditches on to it, as well as on poaching charges.[426] (The diverted road exists to this day around what remains of the wood.)

Main roads Which were the main roads? The Gough Map, made *c*.1360, shows main roads throughout Great Britain.[427] It is also possible to analyze which roads were used on their daily movements by restless kings such as John and Edward I.[428]

Many medieval main roads are still trunk roads, but there are important differences of detail. The main road into Cornwall did not march across Bodmin Moor and Gossmoor as does the present A30 but went by devious ways round to the north. At the time of the Peasants' Revolt (1381) the main road from London to Norwich crossed the River Lark at Temple Bridge (Icklingham, Suffolk) where there is now but a Breckland cart-track. The present A1 – the Roman road known from Anglo-Saxon times as Ermine Street – was not the only medieval main road from London through Huntingdonshire; there was a choice of three parallel routes, of which Ermine Street is the only one still a main road (Taylor 1979). Similar alternative routes existed in many other places; the state of the road surface and bridges doubtless determined which would be used at any one time. This is why many an obscure lane is now called Old London Road.

Bridges When going to Cornwall by road, the discerning traveller leaves England by one of three great bridges within 7 miles of each other. Greyston Bridge, Horsebridge, and Gunnislake New Bridge are all of the fifteenth century and are still perfect; they cross the Tamar in the deep wooded meanders of its gorge. These are remarkable in their survival, but such a proliferation of noble stone bridges was typical of the later Middle Ages. London Bridge, alas, is no more; but we still have the great tidal bridges of Bideford and Barnstaple (Devon) and Wadebridge (Cornwall); the town bridges of Durham (two), Wakefield, Monmouth, Abergavenny, and Stratford-on-Avon; the east Midland bridges of St Ives, Bromham, and Great Barford; the two bridges in the bend of the Dart gorge at Holne Chase (Devon); the Auld Brig o'Ayr, the Auld Brig o'Balgownie (Aberdeen) and the bridge of Carrick-on-Suir (Ireland); the list could be extended to more than a page.

Timber-framed bridges in the Rochester manner have disappeared leaving no mark on the landscape – although the last main-road bridge in this tradition, at Selby (Yorkshire), was demolished only in the 1970s, and one still survives on the Wye below Hay. Something is known of the carpentry of the lesser bridges, whose timbers come to light when moats are drained.[429]

Exeter West Bridge was one of the earliest of the long stone bridges; six-and-a-half of its original round Norman arches are still extant. It was followed in the thirteenth century by the bridge between Huntingdon and Godmanchester. The masons of these towns could not agree on the architectural details, which change halfway across; but they knew their business, for their bridge now withstands the hourly assault of Juggernaut at fifteen times the load that they would have anticipated.

The chronology of bridge-building is best studied in Cornwall. In the 1920s Charles Henderson recorded thirty-two medieval bridges then extant and written evidence of a further thirty-five. He found also fifty place-names involving the Cornish word *pons* 'bridge'.[430] Five out of six of the bridges themselves were in the *eastern* half of Cornwall, where the big rivers are; but five out of six *pons* place-names are in the *western* half of the county (Fig. 12.10). (Cornish-language names of settlements are equally common in both halves.)

I interpret this as meaning that *pons* could be used of even a small bridge or culvert. Bridges began in Cornwall before 930 – the earliest instance of *pons* – but were still rather few by the twelfth century, when Cornish ceased to be an active language in east Cornwall. Most bridges were built after 1200 and were therefore named in Cornish in west Cornwall, where the language still lived, but in English in the east. Cornwall was a rather poor and backward region, in which bridging probably came later than in England; but for the same reason many ancient bridges survive in the county.

Ordinary bridges were usually maintained by individuals as a manorial custom:

> At Churche Ende, Dunmowe, there is a bridge whiche is daungerous, and so evill that neither horse, nor cart may well pass without danger, neither can men convenientlie parse therebi being the Church path without great annoyaunce. The which bridge is to be repaired by the landeholders of the Parsonage.
>
> We find another bridge broke and gone . . . call Stebbeyng Ford Bryge, but who shall make them, we do not know.
>
> *Great Dunmow (Essex), Quarter Sessions, 1562*[431]

Henderson drew attention to the variety of ways in which lords, corporations, and local authorities maintained major bridges, sometimes out of philanthropy, sometimes for the income from tolls. The great bridges had a spiritual and not merely a utilitarian significance: they were works of charity and piety, the gift of benefactors or subscribed by the public through indulgences. Many of them had chapels or even resident hermits.

Trenches

> In the wood of the Prior at Brunne there was a certain carpenter named Peter de Burgo, a good and trusty man. He was cutting down the wood and selling it, and had taken two other carpenters to cut up the timber. He had made himself a shanty in the wood, in which he ate and drank and spent the night with his mates . . .
>
> Two wealthy and well-known merchants from near Stamford and three strangers . . . were travelling together on the way which is called Arningstrete. They came under the wood of the said Prior after sunset . . . and there the strangers made an attack on the merchants, wounded them, and pulled them from their horses and killed them. The cries of the merchants were heard in the church of

[Long] Stowe . . . The inquest decided that the said Peter was not guilty of the death of the merchants, because . . . when they were killed he was in church at Brunne . . .

The news later came to the ears of King E[dward I] of the death of the merchants and of the place where they had been slain. And an edict went out through all the counties of England that all woods through which there was a common right of way should be cut down to a width of sixty feet on either side of the king's road. And the landowners were set a time-limit under heavy penalty. When he heard this, the prior had the trees standing on the woodbank cut down, and the ditch levelled and filled in, and all the bushes rooted up to a depth of 60 feet . . . William Baldewyn [of Longstowe] did the same with his wood on the other side of the king's road, and so passers-by go in greater security than before.

Liber memorandorum ecclesie de Bernewelle, written 1295–6[432]

Medieval England, like modern Detroit, was dangerous: the traveller could expect to be mugged. Although heathland was the preferred habitat of the top highwaymen from Robin Hood to Dick Turpin, travellers had a strong and

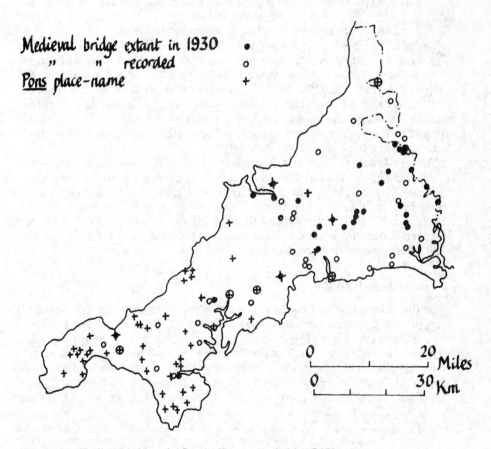

Fig. 12.10. Medieval bridges in Cornwall, as recorded by C. Henderson.

persistent fear of woods and wood-pastures.* Main roads avoided the vicinity of woods where possible, but where woodland was unavoidable it was the practice to make *trenches*, linear clearings each side of the road, to give travellers the appearance of security (Fig. 6.13, Plate III). This was begun before the Conquest in the Chilterns by the piety of Leofstan, Abbot of St Alban's.[433] Many trenches were cut in the thirteenth century, and in 1285 they were made compulsory by a statute to which the Barnwell Chronicle, quoted above, was referring:

> Commanded . . . that the high roads from merchant towns . . . be widened, where there are woods, or hedges, or ditches, so that there be no ditch, underwood (*suthboys*), or bushes, where a man may lurk to do evil near the road, for two hundred feet on one side and for two hundred feet on the other side. Provided that this statute does not apply to oaks, nor to great trees, if they are clear underneath. And if by default of the Lord, who may not want to remove ditch, underwood, or bushes as provided above, robberies are done . . . and murder, the Lord is to be fined at the will of the King. And if the Lord cannot cut down the underwood the country shall help him to do it. And the King wishes that in his demesne lands and woods within Forests or outside, the roads shall be widened as aforesaid.[434]

As far as I am aware no new trenches were made after 1300.†

The place of the Barnwell Chronicle murder is still instantly recognizable (Fig. 12.11). Arningstrete – Ermine Street, now the A14 – runs dark and narrow between Bourn Wood and Longstowe Wood, then as now the only woods on the long stretch from Huntingdon to Royston. The woods have been allowed to grow up to the road again and the scene is once more as it was on that spring evening 700 years ago. Longstowe church stands within earshot. Set back from the road and now within the woods are the thirteenth-century woodbanks (p.98) made to define the edges of the trenches.

Medieval statutes were not obeyed to the letter. The Bourn-Longstowe trenches are in fact 130 feet wide to the middle of the road. Trenches were made haphazardly: along Stane Street, Hatfield Forest has a trench, but I can find no trace of one in Dunmow High Wood. They were not confined to main roads: the village of Leafield, in the middle of the ring-shaped wooded Wychwood Forest, had several trenches leading to it, of which traces remain. As far as I know the statute was ignored in respect of hedges and parks.

Post-medieval Roads

The dissolution of the monasteries in the 1530s destroyed the most powerful corporate bodies with responsibilities and interests in long-distance transport. The medieval principle of road and bridge maintenance as an obligation of land tenure was crumbling; much of the kingdom changed hands, and new owners took up the rights more often than the duties of land ownership. There apparently began a steady increase in traffic. Next came the development of specifically passenger-carrying vehicles, of public transport for persons and

---

* Mr Paul Moxey tells me that even now some east Londoners are afraid to go into Epping Forest.
† The French have similar trenches which they attribute to a road improvement programme of the seventeenth century.

goods, and of the habit of thought that regards time spent in travelling as wasted. From the mid-sixteenth century belated attempts were made to reconstitute arrangements for maintaining roads. Successive statutes empowered parish authorities to conscript labour for the purpose. From the late seventeenth century turnpike trusts were set up to maintain particular roads.

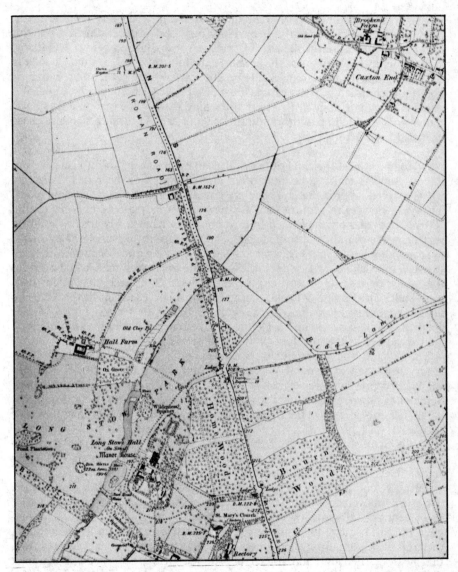

Fig. 12.11. The A14 road between Longstowe and Bourn (Cambs), scene of a dark deed in the 1280s, in consequence of which a trench was made on both sides of the road whose remains still exist in Home Wood and Bourn Wood.
Ermine Street, like most genuine Roman roads, is now by no means straight on the small scale. Ordnance Survey 1886.

An indicator of the physical decline of roads in the sixteenth and seventeenth centuries is the rarity of bridges built in this period and still extant. I have mentioned a few of the great medieval bridges; I am at a loss to provide a comparable list of bridges built between 1540 and 1740, even though these have had 200 fewer years in which to fall down. Elizabethan and Stuart bridges are as rare as Elizabethan and Stuart churches: piety found its expression in other directions.

The cost of road transport went up from about 1·3*d*. per ton-mile in the Middle Ages to 15*d*. per ton-mile by 1700 (Fig. 12.8). Not all this rise was due to inflation: in real terms the cost of transport rose 2½-fold between 1540 and 1690. This increase is probably greater than for any other common goods or services, and is the more remarkable because carters' wages are unlikely to have kept up with inflation.[89] Its causes must await specialist study, but a plausible guess is that the rise in cost reflects worsening roads. The turnpike trusts had much work to catch up with; not until 1800 did haulage again become as cheap as it had been before 1550.

New roads One of the chief duties of Parliament in the eighteenth century was to pass Acts for making, or more often improving, particular roads. Turnpike trusts covered, approximately, what are now the more important A-class roads. They had powers to acquire land for new roads and to levy tolls on traffic. 'Turnpiking' and other planned improvements to main roads usually involved surfacing, the rounding of some bends, and making cuttings and embankments to spare horses and brakes on steep hills. The turnpike into Cornwall continued to use Gunnislake New Bridge but lessened the breakneck medieval descent to the bridge by inserting four hairpin bends. Some completely new main roads were built. The Epping & Ongar Turnpike Trust in *c*.1830 ruined the seclusion of Epping Forest by making the present A11 along its length (Fig. 6.13). At about the same time Great Yarmouth was made less isolated by building Acle New Road across the marshes.

The Old and Young Pretenders, like Boadicea, generated new roads. Military roads, attributed to General Wade, were built across Scotland and northern England to prevent a repetition of the Jacobite rebellions of 1715 and 1745. Some of them were taken over for civilian use and are still main roads; many others fell into decay. On the whole the bridges have lasted better than the roads themselves (Taylor 1979).

In the Scottish Highlands, road systems were often reorganized to follow valleys. Many of the older roads still survive in their pre-turnpike state as tracks across moorland; they often pass unnecessarily high over the mountains.

Turnpike and military roads are outnumbered by the new roads made by the enclosure movement. An early example is the curiously ramshackle seventeenth-century road system of the inland Fens (Fig. 12.12). Each allotment of 2 or 3 square miles was given its own geometrical grid in ignorance of the grids of neighbouring allotments. The main roads, where not inherited from the medieval Fenland, have been improvised, with many sudden bends at different angles, out of this chaotic geometry.

At the parliamentary enclosure of open-fields it was usual to abolish the many ways leading to furlongs, and to set up a planned and greatly reduced set of parish roads. Some of these were old roads unaltered or narrowed (p.199) or slightly realigned; others were wholly new. Through roads, roads past

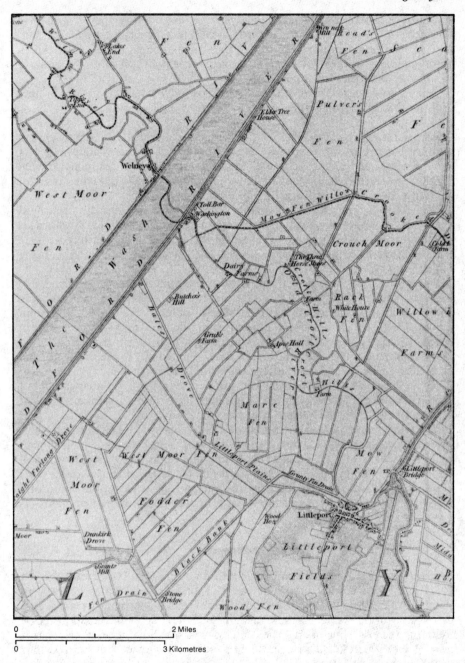

Fig. 12.12. The Fens at Littleport (Cambs), showing how the surveyors who laid out the roads at the Third Draining omitted to make the roads of each allotment join up with those of the next. The diagonal lines define the Ouse Washes. The sinuous meanders are the great roddon which is a relic of the pre-Roman River Cam (Chapter 17). Ordnance Survey 1824.

273

anciently-enclosed crofts, and holloways were less often tampered with than other roads. The new roads run in the straight lines fashionable at the time, but, as C.C. Taylor points out, the Enclosure Commissioners of one parish often forgot to join their minor roads to those of the next parish, resulting in kinks or double-bends at parish boundaries.

Among piecemeal changes in roads the most obvious are diversions around eighteenth-century parks (Fig. 6.4).

Disappearing highways The building of new main roads in the twentieth century is more than balanced by the disappearance of lesser highways. Not only footpaths and minor roads slip out of existence without ceremony: the old Cambridge–Oxford main road via Croydon (Cambs) is now ploughed over for long stretches, though still legally a bridleway.

The turnpike movement, as well as the enclosure movement, destroyed highways: by improving some roads it caused many parallel unimproved roads to fall into disuse. Of the three Great North Roads in Huntingdonshire, two are now reduced to bridleways and in part lost altogether, their traffic being concentrated on the A1.

The process was hastened in the 1930s when minor roads were tarred. No county council could afford to tar all its minor roads; the proportion is probably least in Wiltshire, which still has thousands of miles of chalk road. Roads not favoured with tar often became disused. Long detours are often necessary in Ancient Countryside because the Council forgot to maintain some link in the network of lanes. The late Mr W.H. Palmer pointed out to me the road from Cavendish to Fenstead End, Suffolk, shown on the Bartholomew ½-inch map 1905 (on the advice of the Cyclists' Touring Club) as a 'good secondary road' but now ploughed out. Nearby, three of the four roads to the deserted hamlet of Purton Green, Stansfield, have gone the same way; one of them has a ford beside which, now hidden in the bushes, is a County Council concrete foot-bridge. The lane beside Hayley Wood (Cambridgeshire) was once quite a main road; the village of East Hatley was strung out along it. In 1862 it was still important enough to be given a full-sized railway level-crossing with keeper's cottage. It has now been reduced by the encroaching wood to the width of a single horse, and after passing the wood it dissolves into unmarked rights-of-way across fields.

Ancient Highways As They Are Now

The survival of an ancient road can mean many things. At one extreme, on Wheeldale Moor near Whitby, one can walk on what are said to be the very flagstones of a Roman road. At the other extreme, the motorist on a dual carriageway or the walker threading featureless miles of ploughland may each be following the exact line of an ancient highway of which no material evidence is now visible. Where the course and the boundaries of a road both survive, they may be of very different dates.

Ancient highways are most often preserved on plateaux or at right angles to the contours on slopes. On cross-slopes they require more effort to maintain against the continual creep of soil from above, and tend to disappear when such efforts are not made. In the Dolomites military roads of World War I are already difficult to find on cross-slopes, being at high altitudes where soil creep is fast. Roads get displaced at river-crossings: where a Roman bridge fell down, the road has often been diverted to a ford a mile away, and diverted to a third site when a medieval bridge was built.

Most well-known ancient roads are either ridgeways or run across country regardless of topography. Roads following valleys – and in mountain country generally – are less likely to be preserved, and where preserved are difficult to distinguish from later roads also constrained to follow the same valleys.

Alignments Ancient roads should first be looked for on the map – preferably the last edition of the 1-inch Ordnance Survey, which records both parish boundaries and public footpaths. Maps display alignments – straight or curving – that are not easily visible on the ground. Ordnance Survey identifications of Roman and prehistoric roads are useful and scholarly, though by no means complete. Besides these, almost any rural road with its own proper name will be of at least medieval antiquity.

Alignments are rarely optically straight, and to identify them calls on the human brain's mysterious capacity for recognizing patterns. The Roman layout of south-east Essex is still visible in the pattern of north-south and east-west roads on the 1-inch map, though more complete and obvious on the 2½-inch map. More difficult to spot are those long-distance minor roads that run across country in great sweeping curves (Fig. 12.13). Their names – Drove Road, Bullock Road, etc. – often recall their use in the eighteenth and nineteenth centuries for driving cattle on the hoof from pastures in Ireland, Scotland, and Wales to markets in England. This trade, however, probably came too late to have had much influence on the making of roads, and most drove roads are much older in origin: in Norfolk, for instance, the Weeting Drove is probably prehistoric[435] and the Fincham Drove is the Roman trunk road that supplied the port of Caister-by-Yarmouth.

Alignments alone are dangerous evidence. The amateur – and occasionally the Ordnance Survey – forgets that Enclosure-Act as well as Roman roads are straight; a straight stretch of road in a medieval landscape often results from the enclosure of a tye or small common. In a famous book, *The Old Straight Track*, Alfred Watkins drew attention to the fact that certain ancient sites and other objects lie in approximately straight lines across country. Out of this observation has grown the pseudo-science of 'ley-lines' and their magic properties. Watkins's followers have sometimes allowed enthusiasm to prevail over a sober consideration of whether alignments can have arisen by chance, of the distortions introduced by map-projection, of the chronology of the things aligned, or even of whether anything exists along the course of the alignment.[384]

Alignments need corroborative evidence. A genuine ancient long-distance road is nearly always a parish boundary at least in places. Where there is an apparent gap the road often continues as a public footpath, hedge, or earthwork (Plate III). Where the alignment is known or suspected but the road itself is missing, traces of the road structure should be sought in aerial photographs (as soil-marks or crop-marks) and on the ground. Often this is a task for the excavator, but sections of road-metal are sometimes revealed by chance in newly-dug ditches. Ancient woods across an alignment should be searched, as they preserve features elsewhere destroyed by ploughing. When Ongar Great Park (south-west Essex), which for 900 years had interrupted the Roman road from London to Great Dunmow (Fig. 6.2) was grubbed out, the road came to light as a conspicuous band of flints across ploughland.

Near Earl's Colne (Essex) an alignment of field and parish boundaries, a lane, and the edge of a wood (Fig. 12.14) raises suspicions of an ancient highway. This can be tested nearby in Chalkney Wood, which is crossed by a massive holloway with traces of boundary-banks. Almost certainly this is part of the long-lost course of the Iron Age Cambridge-Colchester road (p.256). The disappearance of the rest of the road is easily explained. The surviving part is on a

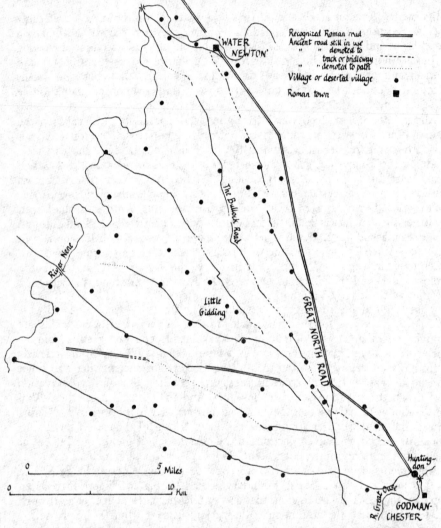

Fig. 12.13. The roads that made for Huntingdon (or was it for Roman Godmanchester?). Most of them are old enough to be parish boundaries; most are ridgeways; and most are through-roads which no longer have destinations. (Two have at times served as alternatives to the Great North Road (Taylor 1979).) The regular arrangement -- some of the irregularities were introduced by Enclosure Acts -- suggests deliberate planning, but for what purpose? This is Little Gidding country, full of shrunken medieval villages; but even taking deserted villages into account, it is hard to make the villages explain the road system or *vice versa*.

276

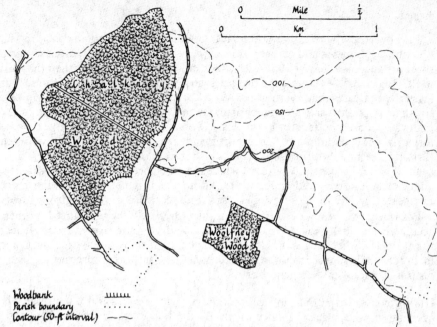

Woodbank · ⊥⊥⊥⊥⊥⊥
Parish boundary · ......
Contour (50-ft interval) · ——

Fig. 12.14. The ancient road of Chalkney Wood, Essex. It survives as:
(i)   a straightish piece of road (in a land of winding lanes) which is also a parish boundary;
(ii) the straight edge of an ancient wood;
(iii) a parish boundary across fields;
(iv) a holloway between slight banks through another ancient wood, overlain by the medieval woodbanks and by later rides and property divisions.
This is an example of the kind of road here regarded as Iron Age. It survives only on plateaux or in woodland. There was no more evidence of it in the sixteenth century (Fig. 2.2).

plateau. Nearly all the missing course would have lain over cross-slopes on which, on these soils, a disused holloway can survive only in woodland. As soon as the road leaves Chalkney Wood it is destroyed by soil-creep leaving only a faint trace.

Road structures and boundaries The straight course of most Roman roads is more obvious on the map than on the ground. Ancient roads, of whatever origin, usually have a course which on the small scale consists of a series of wobbles (Figs. 12.5, 12.11, Plate III). Over the centuries, travellers have had to go round fallen trees, sloughs, holes, muckheaps, purprestures, dead horses, and all the things that people put or allow to remain on the highway; and they have often continued to go round after the obstruction has disappeared. The resulting small diversions come to look as if indeed 'the rolling English drunkard made the rolling English road'. Occasionally a road has a strong enough structure, like the great agger of Ermine Street in Lincolnshire, to resist these diversions and to preserve the straight line. Sometimes, on major roads, the alignment has been approximately restored by modern roadworks. With these exceptions, Roman roads rarely have the long views ahead which the 1-inch map, on which widths are exaggerated, indicates that they ought to have. An exactly straight road is more likely to be an Enclosure Act road.

I do not know whether the original boundaries of any Roman road are still functional. Medieval and earlier roads are very variable in width, often within a short distance, and have boundaries which are even more sinuous than the road itself (Fig. 12.5). Where one hedge is straight and the other sinuous this generally indicates that a farmer has seized part of the highway to his own use. In Ancient Countryside a characteristic feature is the sudden narrowing of the highway where a cottage in a long narrow garden has been built in it. Some formerly wide main roads – eg. north and south of Braintree, or between Birmingham and Stratford-on-Avon, or south of Sherborne (Dorset) – have such 'squatter' houses and gardens, which may themselves be of some antiquity, going on one after another for miles within the original width of the road. Dating the hedges often helps to establish the sequence of these purprestures.

Post-medieval roads, even if not straight, can usually be recognized by their accurately parallel hedges. In the east Midlands, minor roads, often 60 feet wide, made by the earlier Enclosure Acts, contrast with the usually narrower main roads taken over from the Middle Ages. In Cambridgeshire the enclosure commissioners were less generous.

Holloways An expatriate in a new country, where roads roll out prosaically over the ground surface, misses especially the holloways of the English landscape – the lanes mysteriously sunk in deep ravines which protect them from sun and the blasts of winter, lined with great trees whose roots overhang far above, their cavernous shade the home of delicate plants like hart's-tongue fern, shining cranesbill, and moschatel. Holloways are specially typical of parts of England, and have been for more than a thousand years (p.261).

A very few holloways have been made by putting a road into an existing natural ravine – a combination called a 'grundle' in East Anglia. Others, on main roads, are cuttings deliberately excavated to reduce gradients. But most holloways are the result of centuries of erosion on unpaved roads. Traffic loosens the surface and prevents vegetation from holding it, and rain washes away the debris. Usually this requires vehicles, but there are a few foot holloways (eg. the man-wide holloway on the coast path north of Cadgwith, Cornwall).

Holloways are widespread, and to select examples can be little more than to give a list of favourite landscapes. They are abundant in the Lizard Peninsula (Cornwall), south-west Wiltshire (especially the Semley country), and the area south and east of Sudbury (Suffolk). Such landscapes of holloways are typical of Ancient Countryside. Well-developed holloways take at least 300 years to form (I have seen an incipient holloway of some 200 years' wear in Massachusetts) and are therefore less usual in Enclosure Act country, although there are many single holloways inherited from earlier periods that enclosure commissioners failed to destroy.

Development of holloways depends partly on topography – they form most easily on slopes – and partly on geology. The grandest I have seen are in the loess of the Kaiserstuhl in Germany, canyon-like lanes up to 80 feet deep with vertical sides and trees meeting over the top. We do not have loess on this scale, but many readers will know the splendid holloways down to Flatford Mill (East Bergholt, Suffolk), formed in an accumulation of loess washed down from elsewhere in prehistory. Upper Greensand forms the dark and intricate rock-sided holloways around Midhurst in the Sussex Weald. Lower Greensand forms many in Wiltshire (eg. around Urchfont) and Dorset.

Holloways usually have the sinuous outlines of other ancient roads, especially on Lower Greensand where the sides may collapse after heavy rain. Where a holloway has been widened to serve as a main road, one side is usually straightened and the other left sinuous; examples may be seen at Hitchin and Truro.

Unfenced highways A highway, being part of the common-land of the manor, is not usually demarcated from any commons which it may happen to cross. Many roads gradually widen into funnels (in Dorset called 'horns') as they pass into greens, heaths, or wood-pasture (Fig. 6.9). A constant feature of the Lizard Peninsula and other parts of Cornwall is the lane from each farmstead funnelling out between fields on to the moorland.

People crossing unfenced land often find existing tracks too rutted or wet for convenience and make new tracks alongside. Bundles of parallel tracks are typical of ancient routes across heath or moorland and can often be seen, at least from the air, centuries afterwards.

Trenches Although the Ermine Street trenches are now overgrown, many others survived to be recorded on the first edition or even the modern Ordnance Survey. Any parallel-sided gap between a road and a wood (Plate III) should be investigated: there are good examples along the roads through the ancient woods that ring Canterbury and in many places on the A1. Other trenches, now partly overgrown but still detectable through their lack of pollards, line the main roads – other than Epping New Road – through the wood-pasture of Epping Forest (Fig. 6.12). The presence of a trench proves that both the wood and the road are earlier than 1300; however, its absence does not disprove antiquity. Evidence for trenches has often been destroyed or hidden by recent road-widening, grubbing or replanting of woods, ribbon development, and the fashion for 'planting up odd corners'.

Bridges These are a neglected aspect of medieval architecture; even the long bridges are seldom appreciated for the first-rank monuments which they are. Within my lifetime two major medieval bridges in Eastern England – Brandon and St Neot's – have been demolished.

The study of minor ancient bridges is still full of the thrills of discovery. It is not a task for the motorist or even for his passenger; it requires cycling remote lanes and wading under culverts. Medieval bridges tend to have pointed arches, parallel stone ribs under the main arch, and parapets with triangular 'refuges' for pedestrians projecting over the piers, but these features were not always present and the parapets may not survive. Southgate Bridge, Bury St Edmund's, was recently rediscovered buried beneath successive road-widenings. In Cornwall the arch is sometimes replaced by a massive natural flat boulder used as a 'clapper' lintel (but beware of quarried granite slabs used, even in non-granite areas, in more recent times).

Vegetation The verges of highways are old grassland of a peculiar and often rather unstable kind, traditionally grazed and fertilized by the dung of passing beasts and by washings from the road surface. They are not usually among the richest kinds of grassland, but they are important especially in those regions where old grassland of any kind is now rare. In much of England road and railway verges are now the chief home of such general grassland plants as cowslip, knapweed, rock-rose, and hay-rattle (*Rhinanthus minor*). Few species are confined to verges, but many are commoner there than in other habitats; these include oat-grass (*Arrhenatherum elatius* – the characteristic roadside grass which farmers occasionally mistake for wild oats), kex or cow-parsley (*Anthriscus sylvestris* – the well-known spring umbellifer, typical of roadsides rather than of hedges between fields) hedge-garlic (*Alliaria petiolata*), and black horehound (*Ballota nigra*). Chalkland verges have great knapweed and its broomrape parasite (*Centaurea scabiosa* and *Orobanche elatior*). A few national rarities, such as the native grape-hyacinth (*Muscari atlanticum*), are mainly on roadsides.

Most of these plants are not confined to ancient roads. Some, indeed, depend on recent disturbance, such as the (Socratic) hemlock (*Conium maculatum*) now profuse along motorways and the rare mullein *Verbascum pulverulentum* sometimes found on road-widenings in Norfolk. A specially rich kind of verge, related to woodland grassland (p.109), is often to be found where an ancient road approaches an ancient wood.

Tracks and earthen road surfaces themselves support certain plants that withstand being stood on. These include the plantains whose pollen marks the beginning of civilization in the Neolithic. Other plants such as the smaller rushes (*Juncus articulatus* and *J. bufonius*) and creeping buttercup grow in ruts and sloughs.

Little-used tracks and paths and the trodden ground around pasture gates have a specialized flora. Most of these plants require seasonal moisture. Species of muddy tracks are probably the most severely threatened class of the British flora apart from cornfield weeds. Most of them appear to stay in one place rather than to colonize new sites; they are lost partly through the tendency for traffic to be concentrated on fewer tracks and partly through the modern love of drainage. One of the famous Lizard Peninsula rarities, the tiny rush *Juncus mutabilis*, grows in cart-tracks across moorland at places where they cross the edges of loess deposits. This rush, a short-lived annual plant, germinates from buried seed where water seeps into a rut. As D.E. Coombe and L. Frost have shown, this very special habitat depends on a vehicle using a centuries-old track just once or twice a year, and is in danger of being lost through the complete disuse of the tracks. The Lizard has many other cart-rut plants including the curious water-fern *Pilularia globulifera* and several aquatic buttercups. Another threatened plant is mousetail, *Myosurus minimus*, a plant of similar habitats including cattle-trodden gateways on Fenland pastures. The fleabane *Pulicaria vulgaris* was recorded by John Ray in 1660 'in many watery or moist places of the highways' of Cambridgeshire;[436] it has long been extinct in the county and is very severely reduced throughout England. A specialized, and also declining, plant of permanent water trickles in Cornish holloways is the delicate Cornish moneywort, *Sibthorpia europaea*.

Conservation

The loss of specialized plants is but one of many threats to the course, structure, and vegetation of historic highways. Ploughing and obstruction of rights-of-way across fields is a familiar offence which used to be committed with less impunity than it is now:

William atteWater senior ploughed the church-way in a field called Warmelee to
the grave nuisance . . . [fined 1*d.*]

Court roll, Hatfield Broad-oak 1444[274]

As we have seen, even roads and lanes with boundary hedges are seized and
ploughed out by adjoining landowners, though now perhaps less often than
earlier this century.

Purpresture, too, is very much alive. The modern version of the classic
practice begins with a householder mowing the verge outside his garden,
continues with boulders placed to prevent people from driving on the verge, and
ends with the ditch filled in and the verge absorbed into the garden. Some
farmers grub out hedges, fill in ditches, and cultivate the highway up to the edge
of the asphalt. This too is an ancient abuse:

The Abbot of Sibton ploughed up a certain Royal way in Thorington [Suffolk] in
width 3 feet and in length 20 perches.

Hundred Rolls, 1272[437]

Local authorities are curiously reluctant to prevent public land from thus
slipping *gratis* into private hands. They often evade this duty on the pretext that
the soil of highways belongs to the owners of the adjacent lands. This notion
apparently arises from confusing those highways that are mere rights-of-way
across fields with those that are separate parcels of land in their own right. Most
roads, all lanes, and some footpaths are the latter. Highways set out by Enclosure Act or Turnpike Act are expressly vested in the highway authority; and it is
perfectly clear from ancient custom that (with rare exceptions) pre-Enclosure-
Act highways in England, with their verges, are part of the common land of the
manor. In neither case do the highways belong to the adjacent landowners, who
have no more right to annex them or their verges than does anyone else.

The grassland of roads is neglected and abused. Verges are dug up from time
to time. They may be buried by highway engineers who can think of nowhere
better to get rid of excess subsoil (arising through errors in calculating cut-and-
fill). Some county councils in the 1960s (and perhaps even now) sprayed verges
with weedkillers in the childlike belief that this would prevent weeds from
growing on them; weedkillers, alas, kill cowslips more effectively than they kill
weeds. At best, mowing depends on the whims and budgets of highway authorities. Many verges, once mown too often, are now mown too seldom: they turn
into tall tussocky grassland and then into woodland.

It is a pity that so much effort and research should have been put into the new
vegetation of motorway verges (which, to judge by the precedent of the railways, hardly need special treatment) and so little into the deteriorating plant
cover of existing highways. But the latter is not entirely neglected. The work of
the Ramblers' Association in upholding rights-of-way is well known. Less
publicized is the activity of the county Naturalists' Trusts in identifying and
protecting specially important lanes and verges: for example the work of Mrs J.
Mummery for Essex Naturalists' Trust.[438] This is done in collaboration with
highway authorities, but usually no special action is asked for. The selected
verges are given normal management, but are marked by posts so that any
destructive treatment can be avoided.

CHAPTER 13

Heathland

Though (by statute 4 and 5 W. and Mary c.23*) "to burn on any waste, between Candlemas and Midsummer, any grig,† ling, heath and furze, goss or fern, is punishable with whipping and confinement in the house of correction"; yet, in this forest,‡ about March or April, according to the dryness of the season, such vast heath-fires are lighted up, that they often get to a masterless head . . . The plea for these burnings is, that, when the old coat of heath, etc. is consumed, young will sprout up, and afford much tender brouze for cattle; but, where there is large old furze, the fire, following the roots, consumes the very ground; so that for hundreds of acres nothing is to be seen but smother and desolation, the whole circuit around looking like the cinders of a volcano; and, the soil being quite exhausted, no traces of vegetation are to be found for years.

Gilbert White, *The natural history & antiquities of Selborne, 1789*

* 1692–3.
† A Celtic word for ling: Welsh *grug*, Cornish *grük*.
‡ Wolmer Forest, Hants.

Heath is a word that has altered little in meaning since Anglo-Saxon times: it means certain undershrub plants, the heaths and heathers, or vegetation composed of them. The commonest heath undershrub is *Calluna vulgaris*, which Scots and Northumbrians distinguish as *heather* and we in East Anglia call by its Norse name of *ling*. Other related heaths are bell heather *Erica cinerea*, cross-leaved heath *E. tetralix*, Dorset heath *E. ciliaris*, and Cornish heath *E. vagans*. 'Heathland' is also used for tracts of furze (*alias* gorse or whin) although this is not related to the heathers, and is further extended to include bracken-heaths, grass-heaths (in which heather and grassland form a patchwork), and lichen-heaths.

Ling is the characteristic plant of moorland as well as heath. Learned writers frown upon the word *moor* and prefer to write of 'upland heath'. In this book I shall follow a thousand years of English usage in separating the *heaths* of Lowland England and the Scots Lowlands from the *moors* of the Highland Zone, Wales, Scottish Highlands, and Ireland. There is a real distinction between heath and moor, although authorities may disagree on where to draw the line; for instance, the 'downs' of the Lizard Peninsula are often described as heaths, but I shall include them with moorland on the grounds that they have, or have had, a cover of peat.

Heaths are in dry parts of the country, are subject to periodic droughts, and have mineral soils. Moors are in high-rainfall areas and have more or less peat covering the soil. Heaths are clearly the product of human activities and need to

282

be managed as heathland; if neglected they turn into woodland. Moorland is not so evidently an artefact and is more stable.

Heathland Plants and Soils

Ling, heaths, furze, and broom are *undershrubs*, a fundamental and distinctive category of plants recognized by Theophrastus in the fourth century BC[4]. They are woody, but differ from shrubs in that they are permanently low-growing and cannot, even given favourable treatment, grow into trees. Unlike shrubs, they have a definite and short life-span of about thirty years. In old age they are easily killed by frost or drought, and what replaces them may not be of the same species. They cannot survive under much shade. Undershrubs, unlike most trees and shrubs, will burn standing. If burnt or cut in their youth or middle age, they sprout from the base like coppicing trees and are rejuvenated.

Heathland soils Most heaths are on acid soils. Heathland plants, especially ling, alter the soil to produce a distinctive soil type known by its Russian name of *podzol*. The surface is covered by plant debris rotting down to form leaf-mould. Beneath this the top of the mineral soil is bleached to a characteristic whitish or pale grey colour. At a depth usually of 6 inches to 1 foot the soil suddenly changes to a hard black layer called a humus pan, below which is a yet harder, concrete-like, rust-coloured layer called an iron pan. Percolating rainwater has dissolved organic acids out of the leaf-mould and has leached the humus and iron compounds out of the topsoil, leaving it light in colour. These substances have been redeposited lower in the profile, where they have cemented the soil particles together to form pans. Whether or not a podzol forms depends partly on the nature of the soil – in particular on its being acid enough – but also on the chemicals formed in the decaying leaf-mould.

Ling is a plant whose chemistry specially favours podzolization. Podzols are therefore characteristic of heaths and the less peaty moors. Once formed they persist for millennia, even if the vegetation ceases to favour their formation. They are not absolutely diagnostic, for oak and beech on very acid soils (and some kinds of conifer plantation) may form them. But if the excavation of, say, a Bronze Age barrow reveals a podzol profile buried beneath it, this is evidence that the barrow was built in what was then heathland. The researches of Professor G.W. Dimbleby have made much use of buried soils and the pollen preserved in them.

Chalk-heath Heaths are not limited to parts of the country having acid rocks. Some heaths are excellent dispellers of the myth that soils are necessarily formed by the weathering of the underlying rock. Much heathland is over solid geology of chalk or limestones; it depends on superficial layers of sand or loess, which sometimes are so thin that even the drift geological map fails to show them. A mere few inches of acid soil are sufficient for ling and many other heath plants, though not for a fully-developed podzol. The resulting mixture of chalk-grassland species with those of acid soils has long fascinated naturalists.[439]

The famous racecourse of Newmarket lies on, and preserves, an area of chalk grassland with the seemingly incongruous name of Newmarket Heath. Careful search reveals that there really is a heath, with ling and other heath plants on patches of acidic surface deposits. The close mowing of the turf prevents the undershrubs in it from flowering, but probably immortalizes them by resetting the ageing process. Arable fields outside the Heath now have typical thin chalk soils, but this was not always so. The great earthwork called the Devil's Ditch, sectioned by the making of the Newmarket bypass, was found to have beneath it a deep, originally non-chalky soil overlying the chalk. When the Ditch was made, in the late Roman or early Anglo-Saxon period, the area was evidently chalk-heath, a memory of which remains in the names Burwell Heath and Swaffham Heath for the adjacent fields.

Chalk-heath was formerly widespread but is now mostly destroyed by cultivation. Ploughing effaces the acid soil and removes all evidence that there had ever been a heath. Surviving examples are widely scattered on chalk and limestone; the *locus classicus* is Lullington Heath National Nature Reserve near Beachy Head.

Stripes and polygons This wonderful phenomenon is most easily seen in heathland, though by no means confined to it. It was first described in the Breckland, but is widespread in eastern England, especially where sand overlies chalk.[440]

Stripes and polygons are a regular alternation – not a mixture – of two quite different types of vegetation, for instance ling *versus* chalk grassland. On a gentle slope there is a pattern of alternating stripes, usually of 10 to 15 yards between repetitions, running up and down hill. On a level plateau the pattern reorganizes itself (via a transition zone at the top of the slope) into a regular network of meshes of heath enclosing polygons of chalk grassland (Plate XX).

Excavation of stripes reveals a buried system of ridges and troughs (Fig. 13.1). The ridges are of chalky material and almost reach the surface. The troughs are 6 feet or more deep and are completely filled with sand producing a quite even surface. Typical heathland grows on the sand; the chalk produces chalk grassland if it reaches the surface, or chalk-heath if it is lightly covered with sand. Polygons are similar except that the ridges are replaced by domes.

Stripes and polygons are often so regular that at first it is difficult to believe that they are wholly natural. They are a relic of the last Ice Age. When Breckland was tundra it was covered with several feet of a water-sodden slurry of frost-shattered chalk overlying a permanently-frozen subsoil. Every winter the slurry expanded as it froze, and every summer it contracted as it thawed. The resulting pressures squeezed the slurry in such a way as to produce polygonal swellings, which have been fossilized and covered with sand in the state which they had reached when the tundra finally thawed. Stripes are polygons which have been drawn out by the tendency of the whole mass to creep down a slope. Stripes and polygons of various kinds are active in the Arctic tundra at present, and occasionally at high altitudes in the Alps and in Scotland.

Stripes and polygons are visible in arable and forestry crops as well as natural vegetation; they are conspicuous in barley just before harvest because of the different effects of drought on chalk and sand. They are too deep to be effaced by ploughing; one of the classic sites was a field allowed to revert to heath after cultivation. Faint stripes can be confused with demolished medieval ridge-and-furrow. Their spacing is similar, but ridge-and-furrow has headlands, and does not adjust its pattern to slight changes in the shape of the slope as do stripes.

Heaths in other countries Undershrubby vegetation is characteristic of

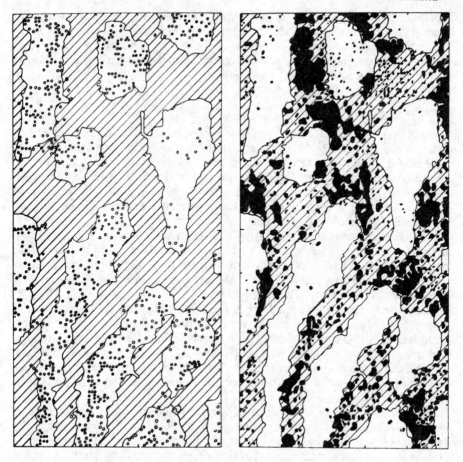

Fig. 13.1. Stripes and polygons in the Breckland: Langmere Hill, Brettenham, Norfolk. The area mapped is 50 × 25 metres. The white areas are chalk grassland; hatching represents acid sands, 1 – 2 metres deep, between the chalk stripes. The area was sown with cocksfoot and white clover in 1958. Three years later, these survive only on the chalk areas; the sands have reverted to heathland with heather. Molehills (left-hand map) are almost confined to chalk; gorse-bushes (right-hand map) to sand. Mapped by J.K. Moore, W.K. Henson, and D.E. Coombe[625] and reproduced by permission.

countries with Mediterranean-type climates; it grows on many types of soil but, as in Britain, often owes its origin and sometimes its continuation to human activities.* Spain, the South of France, Italy, and Greece are full of spiny leguminous undershrubs of which our furze is a northern outlier. Cornish heath is a species whose chief homeland is far to the south; with us it is probably the commonest undershrub of the Lizard, but is almost unknown even in the rest of

---

* The words *bruera*, the Medieval Latin for heathland, and *briar*, the wood of a tobacco-pipe, are both derived from the Old French for the giant Mediterranean heather (*Erica arborea*) from which the best pipes are made.

Cornwall. Some English heaths have many annual plants, another Mediterranean link which distinguishes them from most moorland.

Heaths are an exceptional extension of southern vegetation to a climate in which woodland would be expected. Until recently there were also great heaths in the Netherlands, Denmark, and Sweden.

Heaths in Prehistory

The old belief that heathland is wholly natural, on soils which do not allow trees to grow, has been overtaken by events. In the last 150 years vast areas of heath have ceased to be cut, grazed, or burnt, and have promptly turned into woodland. Many pollen studies – the classic one is from Hockham Mere on the edge of Breckland[441] – make it quite clear that before 6000 BC the traditional heathland areas were covered by trees; heath vegetation existed, if at all, only in very small patches on cliffs and other special habitats.

As a plant community of artificial origin, heathland goes back in a small way before the beginnings of agriculture. The small clearings made by Mesolithic men sometimes lasted long enough to develop into heath. For instance, at Oakhanger (north-east Hants) a buried podzol was found in the excavation of a Mesolithic habitation site (Dimbleby 1962).

Heaths were formed on a much larger scale in the Neolithic and especially the Bronze Age. This is shown by the many barrows and other structures upon them, many of which were sited so as to be seen from a distance. As Dimbleby and others have shown in the heaths of Dorset, the New Forest, and elsewhere in southern England, the buried soils beneath these earthworks prove that heathland podzols had already formed by the Bronze Age. Two such podzols in the Breckland are dated to 900 BC.[442]

How and why were heaths formed? Where ancient woods still exist next to heathland, they are of special types dominated by the trees of infertile soils: oak, beech, or birch, or on slightly less infertile soils hazel or holly. But Dimbleby's pollens from buried soils indicate that the wildwood preceding heathland was a mosaic of lime-woods, hazel-woods, and oak-woods – not very different from the general wildwood of Lowland England, though with rather more oak and birch than usual. Lime could evidently grow on less fertile soils in prehistory than it can now; we shall later see an example where it survived into historic times on a heath. There is nothing to support the common belief among authors that future heaths were 'lightly forested' (whatever that may mean) and thus specially attractive to early farmers.

Evidence for early cultivation of land now heath, in the shape of 'Celtic fields' or other features, is less widespread than for old grassland or moorland. However, many heathland areas were densely populated – the Breckland, with its Neolithic flint-mines, was the first industrialized part of Britain – so we can hardly doubt that some future heathland was ploughed as well as pastured. Some of the more delicate heathland soil structures could probably not have survived a period of cultivation, although Lullington Heath demonstrates that the acidifying properties of chalk-heath plants can, over a period of some centuries without disturbance, restore an acid topsoil to land ploughed in the Roman period.[439]

Even if not used for tillage, heathland would have had many uses to prehistoric farmers and could often have been of more value than trees. As yet there is no evidence of the deliberate destruction of trees to replace them with heather, but such a change would often have been the (not unwelcome) effect of long-continued grazing. Once formed out of wildwood, a heath would have become capable of being burnt, although as we shall see the evidence for historic burning of heath is less than for moorland.

By the Roman period, many heaths already existed, and at least the larger ones appear to have survived the Anglo-Saxon transition; but conversion of wood-pasture to heath was to continue much longer.

Heaths in the Anglo-Saxon Period

Place-names involving 'heath' are many but can be of any date: Haywards Heath, for instance, does not carry the stamp of obvious antiquity. The place-name Heathfield, however, must go back to Anglo-Saxon times, for it involves Old English *feld* meaning 'open space'. There are at least fourteen Heathfields, Hatfields, and Hadfields surviving in England plus several others in charters; the west Yorkshire and Hertfordshire Hatfields are mentioned by Bede so must date from before 730. Similar arguments apply to the ten Hattons (*hæþ* + *tūn*, 'heath-settlement') and the 15 places called Hadley, Headley, Hedley, etc. (*hæþ* + *lēah* heath-clearing). There are also many Hattons in Scotland.

Among heathland plants, broom is much the commonest in place-names: a quick search of the works of Ekwall and Smith produces 103 instances that are known or likely to be pre-Conquest (eg. 25 *Bram*ptons and 12 *Brom*leys or *Bram*leys). Broom is commoner in place-names than any tree except thorn, ash, and willow. 'Bracken' or 'brake' is of Norse derivation and is less common than its Anglo-Saxon equivalent *fearn*; together they appear in at least 74 place-names (eg. *Bracken*thwaite, *Farn*ham, *Far*leigh, *Farn*borough). Place-names involving *fyrs*, *gorst*, or *whin* occur only 26 times – surprisingly since furze is now more widespread than broom. 'Ling' is even rarer (eg. *Lyng* and *Ling*wood, Norfolk).

(The amateur of place-names is warned of three common confusions. 'Furze' is often spelt *fyrs*, *firres*, etc., and is then misinterpreted as 'pine'. 'Fern' in Gaelic place-names is from *fearn*, 'alder'; 'bracken' is *raineach*. Place-names such as *Hatherleigh* usually imply hawthorn (*hageþorn*) not heather.)

Anglo-Saxon charters mention 21 heaths and a further 26 places named after heaths, together making up about 3 in every 1000 features on the boundaries of estates.

Place-names (Fig. 13.2) and charters tell a consistent story. Heathland was widespread in Anglo-Saxon England from Northumberland to Somerset and Kent, though probably not as abundant as woodland. But there are several peculiarities. Evidence of heath and heath plants is much more common in Ancient Countryside: 'heath' itself is very uncommon in areas which had a strong open-field tradition, and the same is discernible with 'fern' place-names and to a lesser extent with 'broom'. There is curiously little evidence of heathland in Devon. And most of the areas where there was later *extensive* heathland have little Anglo-Saxon evidence for it. For instance, the Breckland and west Norfolk were strongholds of heath, and there is every reason to suppose that they have been so since prehistory; yet there are almost no appropriate place-names other than Laken*heath*. The heaths of Dorset and the New Forest certainly existed in Anglo-Saxon times, yet neither charters nor place-names allude to them. This reminds us that features can escape record through being too commonplace.

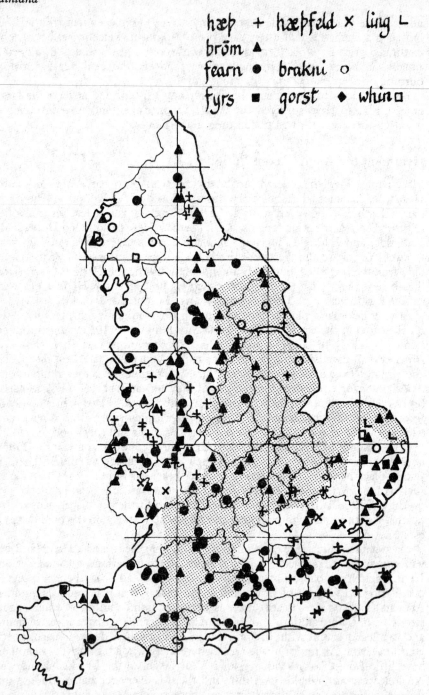

Fig. 13.2. English and Norse place-names alluding to heath, broom, bracken, and furze. The area with a strong open-field tradition is shaded. The names are of towns, villages, and hamlets, and are taken from Smith (1956) and Ekwall (1960).

Heath and wood-pasture The small and moderate-sized areas of heath which gave rise to place-names and allusions in charters were associated in some way with woodland. They are specially common among the great woods of the Weald, and show that the beginnings of Wealden heathland (eg. Ashdown Forest) can be traced back before the Conquest. They are numerous in other well-wooded areas, eg. north-west Warwickshire, south-east Staffordshire, and parts of west Yorkshire. Open-field counties had few heathland place-names except where there was some woodland (eg. north Hampshire). The Cambridgeshire Hatleys were on the edge of one of the few concentrations of woodland in an open-field region; Bedfordshire, comparatively well-wooded for an open-field county, has a number of heathland place-names; whereas such are few in Devon, the least wooded of non-open-field counties.

The juxtaposition of heath and tree-land was common in Anglo-Saxon England, though not necessarily universal as those historians appear to mean who speak in the same breath of 'woodland and waste'. It is inherent in many of the place-names themselves. The -*lēah*, 'clearing', of *Hoath*ley, *Fern*ley, etc. implies woodland surrounding the clearing. *Broom*field, *Fers*field, etc. involve *feld* as an open space in sight of woodland (p.82). Something of the association survived into the Middle Ages and was remembered by Chaucer, though as a mere proverb, in his phrase 'every holt [= wood] and heeth'. The exact nature of the relation invites more detailed study. Here I give two contrasting examples from the charters. The boundary of Ditchampton (Wilts) in 1045 ran

> . . . along the Woodway to the green path; from the path to the great thorn that stands with Grimesdic; along the path to the hoar thorn; from the thorn three acres'-width [12 perches, about 60–70 yards] west of the great *beorh* [hillfort], and three acres'-width to the north; from the *beorh* straight over the heathfield to the stone wall; along the wall to the Portway . . .[443]

This is one of a great group of charters that cover the Grovely Ridge west of Salisbury in minute detail. Ditchampton in 1045 unquestionably had a non-woodland boundary, with its heathfield and stone wall and the clumsy use of thorns and measurements to define a complicated part of the perimeter. The place can be precisely identified (Fig. 13.3), for Grim's Ditch (a Bronze Age linear earthwork) and the hillfort are still there. It is now Heath Wood, and a sixteenth-century map proves that it has been woodland for over four centuries.

Grovely Ridge had many Iron Age hillforts and Romano-British villages. By the end of the Anglo-Saxon period it was uninhabited and had some woodland, as place-names such as *Wood*way and *Grovely* show, and as Domesday confirms. In the Middle Ages the woods rapidly expanded to cover the Anglo-Saxon heathfields. They are still slowly expanding; the last remnants of heath disappeared only recently.

King Harold's foundation charter of Waltham Abbey in 1062 contains several short perambulations, of which this is of Debden in Loughton, south-west Essex:

> First at Tippaburne; from the burn [ie. stream] up to the heath; and from the heath to the boundary of Þecdene [Theydon Bois] with Æffan hecce [probably Abridge] . . .[444]

This is the earliest written record of what in the twelfth century became Epping Forest. Domesday Book, corroborated by a pollen analysis (p.140), leaves no doubt that the Forest-to-be was almost as wooded as it is today; yet here in the charter we find a heath. It was one of those that still existed in the middle of the Forest until very recent decades (Fig. 6.13), all of which are now sadly encroached upon by trees.

The Epping Forest example, which as we shall see has many parallels elsewhere, suggests that much of the tree-land adjacent to heath was not woodland

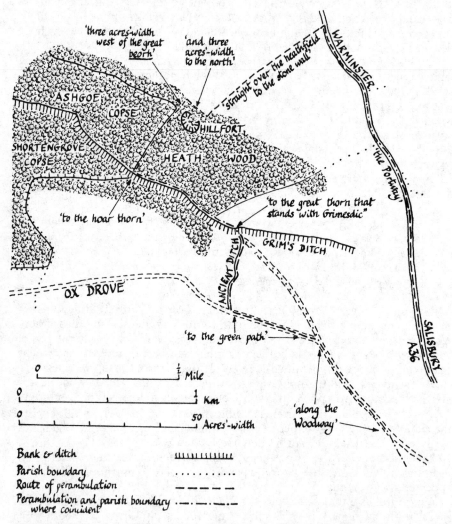

Fig. 13.3. Part of the Ditchampton perambulation (Wiltshire). The map shows the modern features and identifies the bounds of 1045. The woods (partly belonging to the medieval Grovely Forest) are much more extensive than in 1045; they have continued to expand at the expense of the heath even after they were delimited by woodbanks. (Much of the detail has now been destroyed by replanting.) The Anglo-Saxon 'green path' has been renamed Ox Drove (p.275).

in the strict sense but wood-pasture, maintained along with the heath under a single grazing regime. Tree-land and heath were uses of land too infertile for tillage; the balance between them would be determined in the long run by local variations of grazing.

How had Anglo-Saxon heaths come to be in the vicinity of wood-pasture? Analogy with the modern history of southern heaths would suggest that they were remnants of Roman heath or pasture: the successors to the Romans could muster livestock enough to maintain only parts of the heaths as such, the remainder reverting to woodland. This reversion happened at Grovely, where it (unusually) was to continue beyond the Norman Conquest. In the Middle Ages we shall see contrary examples of heath increasing at the expense of the trees of wood-pasture through excessive grazing. This change, too, probably happened locally in the Anglo-Saxon period. It was often deliberately prevented by making woodbanks and keeping livestock out of the remaining woodland.

Medieval Heathland

Domesday Book Heath is not recorded as such in Domesday but is subsumed under pasture, which itself is systematically recorded only in south-west England. Only in Dorset is heath likely to have been extensive enough to be detectable in Domesday pasture records, which I analyze in Chapter 15. The biggest concentration of pasture was in the south-east of the county, where it covered more than half the land area (Fig. 15.1). This corresponds in part to the Dorset heaths of later centuries, on infertile soils overlying the Eocene sands and gravels that extend westward from the New Forest.

Medieval changes The increasing population of the twelfth and thirteenth centuries probably had some effect on heathland, though this can rarely be proved. 'Assarts' of that period are usually assumed to have been from woodland or fen, but the word could equally mean the conversion of heath to farmland, and occasionally this is specified. Piecemeal encroachment has left its mark in the ragged concave outlines of many heathland commons (Fig.13.5).

Heath was a valued resource; the sentiment that regards it as useless land had yet to develop. Most heathland was legally protected as common-land, although manorial courts were not always successful in preventing encroachments, as witness the enclaves of private land which now exist within many commons (Fig. 6.9). Even to the private owner, heath was worth not much less than arable, and references to private heaths are not uncommon. In the twelfth century, the *Colchester Cartulary* mentions at Sandy (Beds) 'all the heath which was anciently fenced (*defensa*) and a warren';[419] this is Sandy Warren, now the home of the Royal Society for the Protection of Birds, where scraps of heath still linger among Victorian plantations.

At the same time, the age-old turning of wood-pasture into heath, probably by too much grazing, reappears. Mousehold Heath will be described later. Another example is at Dedham (Essex), which in the fourteenth century had a large common, part of which was wooded and called *Birchetum*, Wood [composed] of Birches. In the sixteenth century the manorial byelaws included special clauses protecting the 'Lynde Trees upon Deham heath', which might be pollarded 'so that they kille not', but which might not be felled 'by the grounde' on pain of the quite large fine of 3*s*. 4*d*.[539] Lime trees cannot possibly have invaded heathland (p.67) and could only be relics of a former wood. (Conservation has been successful, for the limes have survived even the destruction of the heath, and Mr D. Chesterfield tells me that they are still there in hedges on the site.)

Change from wood to heath is not always noticed in the documents. Wood-cutting rights originally attached to trees may easily be transferred to furze or ling. Heaths are often named after vanished woods (eg. Outwood Common). Although we may not know whether the wood was on the site of the heath or adjacent, the circumstantial evidence for such changes is strong. Middlesex appears in Domesday Book as a very wooded county. By 1754, the date of the first reliable map of the county,[445] it was noted for its heaths; most of the woods had disappeared, and (in contrast to Hertfordshire) had left singularly little record of their existence in the place-names. It is hard to avoid inferring that the woods gradually turned into heaths and thus disappeared without generating place-names. Possibly the Surrey heaths arose in a similar way. The Wealden heaths, which existed in a small way in Anglo-Saxon times, presumably increased in the early Middle Ages and might even have become more extensive than in later centuries. If many of the Wealden woods have not always existed, this would go far to explaining why native lime is so rare south of the Thames.[446]

We might expect woodland to have encroached again on heath when agriculture declined after the Black Death. Such a change, though not easy to detect in written records, would be worth looking for. Unfortunately in the east Midlands, where the effects of the decline are now most evident, there is little heathland.

Rabbits A momentous change in the early Middle Ages was the introduction of the rabbit (Chapter 4). Rabbits added to the motives for maintaining heathland. In the Middle Ages it was evidently held that a landowner had the right to put rabbits on a common without infringing the grazing rights of the commoners. They shared the grazing with the commoners' sheep and cattle and enabled the landowner – often a religious house – to get a good return from land on which he often had few other rights.

Heathland warrens existed all over England and the Scots Lowlands. The biggest concentration was in the Breckland, where a dozen or more adjoined each other for mile after mile (Fig. 13.4). Lakenheath Warren is now one of the largest remaining heaths and is the subject of a study by Mrs G. Crompton and Dr J. Sheail.[447]

The Bishop of Ely, lord of Lakenheath, set up the warren probably in the twelfth century. It was maintained by the Bishop and his private successors for the commercial production of rabbits until World War II. The warren comprised nearly all the common heath of Lakenheath, 2226 acres. The rabbits were confined (after a fashion) by a great bank and ditch, over 10 miles long, topped with furze and regularly patrolled. The warren was crossed by a main road, and to avoid the trouble of rabbit-proof gates the bank was returned along each side of the road for about ¼ mile. Since Lakenheath adjoined other warrens on both sides, leakage of rabbits probably did not matter much. Most of the perimeter bank still stands – on the north side it is double or even triple, for Wangford Warren adjacent had its own bank – but the roadside 'funnels' have, alas, been levelled beneath Lakenheath air-base. The warren lodge has been replaced by a

Victorian building; but its fellow on Thetford Warren, 6 miles away, still stands as a mighty ruin, almost a castle, to remind us of the importance of rabbits in the ecclesiastical economy and the security risks of storing quantities of valuable rabbit-skins and salt rabbits. The building accounts of another warren lodge, at Brandon in the 1380s, show that no expense was spared in hiring masons and carpenters and bringing stone from Northamptonshire and timber from Norfolk.[362]

Common-rights on Lakenheath Warren included grazing for up to 2200 sheep and cutting bracken. Rabbit management was highly organized and included growing hay in Lakenheath Fen to keep the coneys alive in winter.

Heathland Forests I fear that the popular confusion between Forests and woodland is by now ineradicable. I have no more chance of persuading the public that Sherwood Forest was not a wood than Professor J.C. Holt has of getting people to believe that Robin Hood really lived in Barnsdale (west Yorkshire).[448] But I must try.

Sherwood is first heard of as a Forest in 1154. The earliest map, surveyed 1774,[449] shows it as a vast heath encompassing a number of woods, including the famous Birkland and Bilhagh, and the great parks of the 'Dukeries' – Welbeck, Clumber, Thoresby, Rufford, Clipstone, and Newstead. The total area was about 65,000 acres. The *Sherwood Forest Book* of 1251 lists about fifteen woods and groves, including 'Bilhagh et Birkelounde' and others still identifiable in 1774.[450] It has much to say about the management of heath in relation to Forest Law. The woods often appear in Henry III's correspondence as a source of big oaks, but there is no reason to suppose that any of them was of more than a few hundred acres. The charters of Rufford Abbey, of a little earlier, give a similar impression of a number of named and delimited woods.[613]

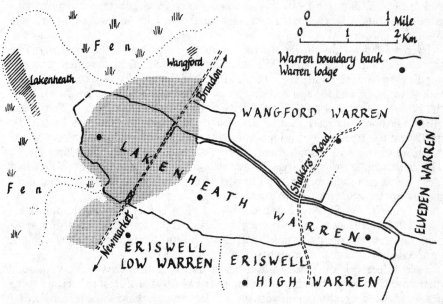

Fig. 13.4. Lakenheath Warren (Suffolk) and its neighbours. The shaded area is now occupied by Lakenheath airfield.

In Domesday Book the area is not an unusual concentration of woodland: the woods recorded for places later having shares in Sherwood Forest add up to 22,500 acres, not all of which was necessarily within the future Forest.

I infer that at least from Anglo-Saxon times Sherwood has consisted of heaths and woods. One of the woods presumably gave its name to the Forest but we cannot tell which wood or what happened to it. In the Viking period another wood was given a Norse name, Birkland (*birki* + *lúndr*, Birch Grove); it has remained distinct for a thousand years and still exists now (Plate XVIII). By 1086 at most a third of the future Forest was woodland. In the thirteenth century the proportion was at most a quarter and could have been much less. The woods may have increased slightly in the later Middle Ages, for Leland is reported going through about 3 miles of woodland on the road past Newstead.[451] By the eighteenth century they were reduced to about a tenth of the total area.

The New Forest has also a history of predominant heathland. As we have seen, several of these heaths are known to go back to the Bronze Age. In recent centuries, native woodland has covered about a quarter of the Forest; the pattern of heath and woodland has been nearly stable; and the place-names indicate that many of the isolated woods have been isolated at least since the Middle Ages (Tubbs 1968). It is controversial how much of William the Conqueror's New Forest was heathland, but the proportion is unlikely to have been less than half.

The Forest of Wolmer (Hants) in Gilbert White's day consisted 'entirely of sand covered with heath and fern . . . without having one standing tree in the whole extent'.[452] This was probably nearly so in the thirteenth century, when Henry III's letters often refer to deer from Wolmer and timber from the twin Forest of Alice-Holt. Other heathland Forests included Rudheath (Cheshire) and most of Windsor Forest. In Ashdown Forest (Sussex) three warrens, with pillow-mounds, suggest that the present heaths go back at least to the Middle Ages.[157]

Even among wooded Forests, which were mostly on acid soils, there were few that entirely lacked heathland. We have seen that the earliest document describing Epping Forest mentions a heath. In 1199 the monks of Stratford Langthorne were allowed to send 960 sheep into a *bruerium* which can be identified as the present Wanstead and Leyton Flats in the south of the Forest. These and other references indicate that nearly a sixth of Epping Forest was heath; the heath and the tree-land, although not demarcated in any way, were very stable until the changes in management of the last hundred years (Rackham 1978). The most wooded of the large Forests was probably Dean, but even this had some pasture in the form of small heathy 'greens'; some of these survived until the era of the Forestry Commission.

A peculiarity of Sherwood and the New Forest is that their legal boundaries extended little, if at all, outside the physical limits of the heath. Possibly, with plenty of pasture, the deer stayed within the physical Forest and it was thought unnecessary to protect them when feeding outside it.

Fallow deer evidently did well in heathland: most heathy Forests produced them, though not as abundantly for their area as wooded Forests.[453] Heaths also produced red deer, though on a smaller scale than moorland. Heathland Forests afforded the local inhabitants the usual opportunities of contributing to the Exchequer through fines for being caught breaking the Forest Law.

Uses and Management of Heathland

Most heathland plants can be grazed, although bracken is unpalatable and somewhat poisonous; they were the staple diet of countless thousands of commoners' livestock, as well as commercial animals such as sheep.

Our sources for other uses of heath tell us mainly about its commercial aspects, although these were probably of less importance than private and communal uses.

Furze and ling Furze is an important and widely-used fuel; it produces a quick hot blaze suitable for heating ovens, getting up a fire in the morning, or burning heretics. In the Hindolveston (Norfolk) accounts of the thirteenth and fourteenth centuries there are frequent small sales of 'Whynnes' from what was evidently a private heath.[331] Also in Norfolk, ¾ acre of whins sold for 4s.[454] Furze as fuel was common down to the nineteenth century and may still be used.

Ling was used as fuel and as low-grade thatch. I have several records of sales; much the largest amount was £2 12s. worth sold at Staverton (Suffolk) in 1305–6.[455]

Not all uses of heath were compatible. Furze and ling that are bitten down by sheep cannot also be cut for fuel. There is some indication that commons tended to be used more for grazing and private heaths for other purposes. In north Norfolk ling was cut regularly like a coppice-wood, for instance:

> a certain piece of heath which every seventh year is worth 5s – that is 8½d per annum.
>
> *Walsingham, early fifteenth century*[456]

Bracken Bracken is a most useful plant. Its general purposes included fuel, litter for livestock, and thatch. The Roman settlers of Vindolanda (Northumberland), who lived like pigs, used bracken as litter for men as well as beasts.[457] I find sales of bracken (*fugerium*) to be commonplace in estate accounts from the Middle Ages onwards. It sold usually for small sums, but at Staverton in 1274–5 14s. worth was sold (plus 5d. worth winkled out of the lord's corn).[458] All three heathland fuels are mentioned in a lease at Hevingham (Norfolk) in 1609: the tenant of the park might not use wood as fuel but was required to 'brewe and bake with furres lyinge and brakes [ie. furze, ling, and bracken]'.[459] At Petworth (Sussex) in 1349–50 men were paid 2s. 6d., about three weeks' wages, to cut bracken 'for composting the lord's land'.[88] In many places byelaws forbade bracken to be cut before the late summer (29 August at Lakenheath),[447] presumably to avoid weakening the plant.

Dr L. Rymer has studied the history of bracken in detail.[460] Burning bracken for potash was a large industry in the eighteenth and nineteenth centuries; the ashes were used in glassmaking,[461] soapmaking, and as a detergent. Bracken was an important brickmaking as well as domestic fuel. Attempts were made to use it as fodder for beasts. The Japanese eat bracken (although it is carcinogenic), but with us it has been only an experimental human food. Rymer has found a host of minor uses in Britain, from rainmaking to contraception.

Burning It is often claimed that periodic burning is a normal, indeed necessary,

part of heathland management. Down the centuries there are occasional records
of heath fires; and legislation against burning indicates that it sometimes happened. For instance:

> Item, to inquire who may have caused waste or destruction of the ling or fern in the
> Forest or may have burnt them to get better pasture for his animals, because they
> are the chief refuge for the Lord King's beasts.
>
> *Sherwood Forest, 1251*[449]

In 1372 there was a fire on 40 acres of heath in Hainault Forest (Essex)
(Rackham 1978). There was a great heath fire in Sherwood Forest in 1624.[462]
(See also the next chapter.)

As Gilbert White appreciated, legislation, however ferocious, could not prevent improper burning. But we must not suppose that all heaths were burnt.
People rarely set fire to their own or each other's crops. Many heaths were so
closely grazed as to be difficult to burn, and those that were not grazed were
being kept up to be cut for other purposes. Fire in a heath, as in a wheatfield,
was a rare accident which most people did their best to prevent. As we shall see,
many heathland plants and animals are now endangered by fires, and could not
have survived to the present had heath fires been a regular event in the past.

Decline of Heaths

From the end of the seventeenth century the technology and philosophy of the
Agricultural Revolution worked against heathland. Innovations in farming practice made it possible to cultivate all but the most difficult soils by crop rotation,
fertilizing, and methods of dispersing podzols; this put an end to much private
heathland. Bracken and ling were no longer regarded as crops, and rabbits
began to be disapproved of. Multiple land-uses were despised; land ownership
was coming to be regarded as conferring an absolute right to do what one pleases
with one's property; and the common-land status of the larger heaths was
attacked by agricultural writers. Heaths were described as 'dreary and desolate
wastes' – maybe they were to those who saw more of them than we can – and as
'useless' and 'barren deserts'. They were seen as the resort of highwaymen. As
we have seen, Forests were supposed to encourage immorality; and heathland
Forests were more immoral than other kinds. Did not trouble over poaching in
Windsor Forest lead to the Black Act in 1723, which created fifty new capital
crimes?[463]

Enclosure Acts were a legal technique for suppressing commons as well as for
amalgamating open-fields. But they were applied more slowly, and most commons survived late enough in England to be recorded in large-scale county
maps. Norfolk was the supreme county for agricultural improvement, and it is
instructive and melancholy to compare Faden's map of 1792–4 with the Ordnance Survey of 1838. By 1793 most of the open-fields (and of the medieval
woods) had gone, but the county was still pervaded with a spider's web of
ramifying heaths and commons, which covered more than half of Breckland.
Only here and there do we see a note such as 'Banham Heath lately Inclos'd'.
Heaths may have been spared through technical difficulties in cultivating them,
or through legal difficulties in securing the agreement of interested parties. Or
landowners may have had scruples against usurping rights of the poor for which

it was difficult to devise a just compensation: Arthur Young in 1800 quotes several instances of Enclosure Commissioners preserving part or the whole of a common, and even an attempt at sowing furze for commoners' fuel.[464] In a few years, however, the difficulties and scruples were overcome and the heaths vanished as if by magic; by 1838 there were almost no commons of more than 100 acres left outside the Breckland.

The same happened at different times elsewhere. The heaths of Essex, once quite extensive, almost disappeared outside Epping Forest. Those of Sherwood Forest were swept away mainly in the 1790s and of Windsor Forest in 1857.

In southern England heaths met a different fate. For centuries trees and bushes had grown intermittently on commons and had been included among their fuel resources. From the early nineteenth century onwards, on many hundreds of commons from Hertfordshire southwards, grazing and cutting declined below the minimum necessary to keep trees from invading. Nearly a sixth of the whole of Surrey turned spontaneously into woodland, mainly in the mid-nineteenth century. In the 1790s Surrey had been about 20 per cent heath and 4 per cent woodland; it is now, according to the Ordnance Survey, 3.2 per cent heath and 15.6 per cent trees. Urbanization began to be a threat in the later nineteenth century: Poole Heath, the biggest in Dorset, was eaten up by the new town of Bournemouth.

. Destruction of heath slackened in the late nineteenth century but was resumed in the twentieth. Agricultural 'reclamation' was resumed in World War II, and little of the heath sacrificed to the war effort has been regained in peacetime. More important than urbanization or even agriculture was tree-planting. Trees had been planted on heaths in the nineteenth century, and self-sown descendants of introduced Scots pines had hastened the decline of the Surrey heaths; but large-scale afforestation of heath became an official policy when the Forestry Commission was founded in 1919. In this way about half of the three largest remaining heathland areas – the Breckland, Sandlings, and Dorset heaths – disappeared, and large areas in Berkshire, Hampshire, and elsewhere. Natural growth of trees destroyed the heaths of Epping Forest and Burnham Beeches, the remaining scraps in Essex, and countless small heaths up and down the kingdom.

Heaths As They Are Now

Rarely does a large heath survive in full use: the best examples are probably in the New Forest. Most remaining heaths are small ones or fragments of large ones. Grazing is seldom, and fuel-cutting very rarely, kept up; the rabbits which perpetuated the grazing have diminished; and even where woodland has not developed the original short and varied vegetation has often been replaced by monotonous bracken, tussocky grasses, or tall furze or ling.

Most surviving heaths are commons and have the characteristic shape of commons, with concave outlines, crossed by roads which enter the common by funnels. The funnels once had gates, usually replaced by cattle-grids where grazing continues. The boundary is lined with houses, which are usually fewer than with other types of common. Suffolk is a good county for heaths, and Wortham Ling (Fig. 13.5), which survives intact, illustrates these features. (Tree encroachment often begins at the edges of a common and may make the boundaries difficult to follow.)

Straight edges to heaths are usually the result of partial destruction. A vanished heath may leave a 'ghost' in the form of boundary-houses now stranded among fields.

Most heaths appear to have had a more stable history than the edges of moorland and less often show evidence of prehistoric land-use. Lullington Heath (Sussex) is an example of Celtic fields in a chalk-heath.[439]

Vegetation and historic land-use in the Breckland Patterns in heathland vegetation may result from natural soil-forming processes, the intrinsic behaviour of plants, and a variety of human activities. The Breckland is the scene

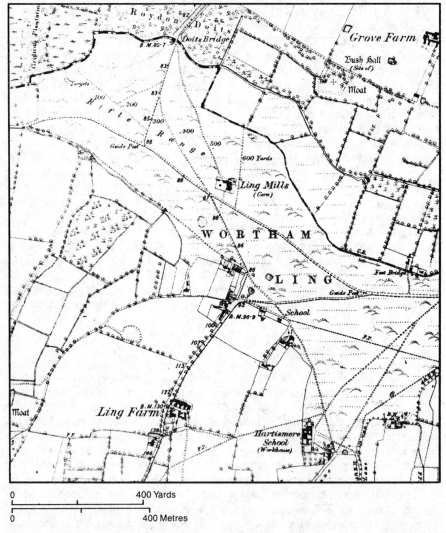

Fig. 13.5. Wortham Ling (Suffolk), a heathland common with the typical shape of commons. The 'Mills' are doubtless the successor of a manorial windmill. Ordnance Survey 1884.

of the classic studies of E.P. Farrow on the effect of rabbits[465] and of A.S. Watt on the relation between soils and vegetation and on the behaviour of bracken,[466] as well as of the more recent work of D.E. Coombe, G. Crompton, and many others. Lakenheath Warren, to which much of the work relates, is a private place, but many of the patterns can be seen by the public in places such as Thetford Heath, Cavenham Heath, and Grime's Graves.

Breckland 'heaths' vary from almost typical chalk grassland, bright with summer flowers where enough rabbits have returned to keep down the tall grasses, to the most acid soils with either pure ling or a bizarre and colourful mixture of different lichens. Often these are closely juxtaposed in patterns created by the stripes and polygons of periglacial prehistory. Superimposed on the latter are the inland sand-dunes which are a curious feature of Breckland and which become active from time to time. In about 1570 the dunes on Lakenheath Warren 'broke prison' and loose sand slowly crept north-east, blown by the wind, burying farmland and buildings, and by the 1660s partly filling up the Little Ouse river 5 miles away.[467] Soon after, the sand went to sleep as mysteriously as it had awoken; but there is still a small blowout on Lakenheath Warren, and despite the growth of trees there are active dunes on Wangford Warren Nature Reserve.*

Overlying the stripes and polygons are patterns produced by the intrinsic behaviour of plants. Bracken grows in ever-widening circles up to hundreds of yards across. It has a creeping, branching underground stem from which fronds arise year by year. New plants very rarely begin from spores (except on decaying buildings) but once started they spread to cover many acres. There is no reason why Breckland bracken plants, like some of those in Finland, should not be six centuries old.[468] Bracken advances at the edge and dies away in the middle, forming a circle with a hollow centre: the older parts of the plant are more susceptible to the severe frosts of this part of England. In sandy parts of Breckland the sedge *Carex arenaria* grows in circular patches for a similar reason. Puffballs and many other fungi likewise grow in circular 'fairy-rings' (p.343) and sometimes affect the growth of the grass so as to be conspicuous from the air.

Other patterns result from millennia of heathland activities. At Grime's Graves hundreds of hills and holes, having most complex plant communities, mark the shafts of Neolithic flint-mines (p.369). On Wangford Warren a round barrow has been re-used as a medieval windmill mound. On Lakenheath Warren, besides the medieval perimeter banks, there are lengths of bank probably made to encourage rabbits to burrow; marl-pits (p.370) dug to improve the pasture for the rabbits; and four squarish embanked enclosures containing faint ridge-and-furrow indicating ancient ploughing. The two World Wars added many other features, including chalk-figures cut as targets for bombing practice and craters from letting off unwanted ammunition.[447, 469]

The Story of Mousehold Heath

This is the rise and decline of one of the great Norfolk heaths, originally covering some 6,000 acres, extending from within the city bounds of Norwich north-eastwards into eight rural parishes (Fig. 13.6).

---

* Suffolk Trust for Nature Conservation.

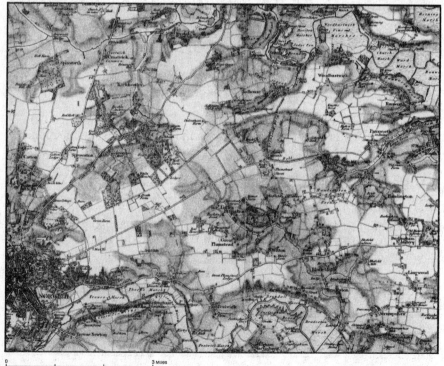

How the Heath began is not known. The area is curiously barren of known prehistoric archaeology, and it is just possible that it remained wildwood until the Anglo-Saxon period. Of the surrounding place-names, two (*Wood*bastwick and Blo*field*) imply woodland. The name *Mushold* is usually interpreted as *mūs* 'mouse' + *holt* 'wood', though it is never recorded as the name of an actual wood.

By 1086 the area was wooded only at the Norwich end, where Thorpe had 'wood for 1200 swine', one of the largest assessments in Norfolk. Thorpe Wood was bestowed on the bishopric of Norwich by Henry I in 1101; being a large wood next to a city, it was a rare and kingly gift. Herbert de Losinga, the first bishop, wrote thus to his woodward:

> As to making a present of Thorpe Wood to the sick or anyone else, I gave you no orders . . . for I appointed you the custodian of the Wood, not the rooter up of it. To the sick, when I come to Norwich, I will give as I did last year, not logs of wood, but money . . . Guard the wood of the Holy Trinity, as you wish to be guarded by the Holy Trinity, and to continue in my favour.[470]

The Bishop is the first individual to have left a record of an interest in woodland conservation. Probably he had no control over grazing rights on the heath, and anticipated that the wood would be eaten away. Like many wood-pasture owners since, he sought in vain to preserve it by not cutting it down.

Thorpe Wood acquired a sinister notoriety in 1144 through the finding there of the body of the boy 'St William of Norwich'. From allusions in the argument over the murder we learn that Thorpe Wood still extended over the present plateau of Mousehold Heath.[471] But it was losing ground: in 1156 Pope Adrian IV referred to 'the Heath with all its wood', and in 1236 'the part of Thorpe Wood which was covered with oaks' is distinguished from the heath part of the wood.[470]

By the sixteenth century, according to a number of maps and views, the Heath had extended all over the plateau; woodland was confined to steep slopes round the edges (where scraps of wood-pasture remain to this day). A map of 1585 shows a 'Warren house' and some 'Stone Mynes Pitts',[472] the earliest of those now abundant on the remaining heath. Until the Reformation there had been a curious sacred grove. Perambulations of Norwich City boundary mention a 'Sayncte Williams Wood', evidently a small one. The site of St William's chapel is still identifiable near the boundary, and is surrounded by a strong double bank and ditch. Appearances indicate that the Cathedral monks had deliberately maintained a fragment of Thorpe Wood, complete with wood-banks, around the place where the body was found, in order to substantiate the dedication to 'St William in the Wood'.

The Heath survived almost unaltered to the end of the eighteenth century. Faden's map shows two 'New Farms' in Woodbastwick, indicating local encroachment before the 1790s. In 1800–1 this era of stability was abruptly ended by a series of Enclosure Acts for the various parishes. By 1838 not a vestige of

Fig. 13.6. Mousehold Heath, Norfolk: (a) on Faden's map of 1793; (b) on the Ordnance Survey of 1838. All the lesser heaths and commons had shared the fate of the great heath by 1838. In the north-east of the map some of the shallower Norfolk Broads appear to have become overgrown.

the Heath remained except for about half the Norwich City portion, some 180 acres. This was acquired by Norwich Corporation in the 1880s as a place of public resort.

This surviving fragment was then still a wild and glorious place, a theme of the Norwich School of artists and of the writer George Borrow. Municipalization has brought roads, playing-fields, and tree-planting. But the Heath now suffers most from lack of grazing. The common-rights were last exercised about a century ago, and trees began to encroach soon after. The municipal horsechestnuts and pines, though incongruous, have not multiplied, but the native oak and birch have spread only too well. Myxomatosis carried off the rabbits which were the last restraint on them. In my lifetime Mousehold has lost most of its remaining character as a heath without acquiring distinction as a wood. Some furze and a little ling remain, and patches even of such less common heath plants as bell heather and dwarf furze – but for how much longer? Young birches are scattered all over the remaining open spaces, and neither cutting nor fire kills them. The future of this ancient heath has contracted to the few years which it will take for these trees to grow to full size.

Conservation

The decline of the heaths of Dorset has often been quoted; Table 13.1 needs no comment. But Dorset is fortunate in that a fifth of its original heathland still exists. More has been lost of the Breckland and Surrey heaths, and much more of the Suffolk Sandlings. Heaths have almost vanished from non-Breckland Norfolk, Leicestershire, Lincolnshire, and Middlesex, and I doubt whether there are 20 acres left in the whole of Essex. Only in the New Forest, Ashdown Forest and east Devon has even a medium-sized heathland area not been substantially reduced. England now has at most a tenth – it may be much less – of the heath of two centuries ago.

Table 13.1 Losses of Dorset* heathland

Date	Area of heath	Average rate of destruction
1086	c.60,000 acres	
1811[473]	75,500 "	0.6 acre per day
1896[473]	56,000 "	0.8 acre per day
1934[473]	45,000 "	2.1 acre per day
1960[473]	25,000 "	1.5 acre per day
1977[474]	15,500 "	

*Including Hampshire west of the river Avon.

Heathland is an ancient and beautiful part of our heritage. It is a symbol of liberty: most heaths are *de facto* open to the public, and their destruction has curtailed the Englishman's already meagre right to explore his own country. It is the habitat of the nightjar, stone-curlew, Dartford warbler, smooth snake, and many other celebrated animals and plants; it is full of antiquities and of complex and fascinating soil and vegetation patterns. It is a special responsibility of England: the Dutch, Danes, and Swedes have been even more single-minded in destroying their heaths, and most of what is left in Europe is ours.

In the darkest days of ericophobia the voices of Gilbert White, John Clare, George Borrow, and Thomas Hardy reminded us of the glory and mystery and freedom of the heath. But few listened: heathland is something that people do not value until they have lost nine-tenths of it. As late as 1937 W.G. Clarke, the great Breckland scholar, wrote of the passing of the heaths with only lukewarm disapproval.[435]

Was the destruction of the heaths necessary? The extra farmland did make an appreciable difference to the nation's resources; and we would now have the greatest difficulty in maintaining all the heath that there was in the eighteenth century. It is no longer useful to speculate on what might have happened had thought been given to using heathland more efficiently instead of turning it into ordinary farmland. Heathland has now shrunk to an insignificant part of the land area, and there is no good reason for destroying any more of it.

Although farmers and foresters show some signs of having reached the limit of their heathland ambitions, the threat of direct destruction has hardly receded. In the 1960s and 1970s the last third of the Dorset heaths was still being eaten up at 1½ acres a day. Heaths are not yet appreciated everywhere: they still enter the minds of civil servants wondering where to put things like nuclear power stations, despite the fact that many remaining heaths have some kind of protection as nature reserves, public places, or military ranges. (Soldiers have a good record as guardians of native vegetation: what would have happened to the heaths around Aldershot or in the northern Breckland had the Army not occupied them?)

The survival of heathland is precarious for other reasons. On most heaths (except in the New Forest) there is not enough grazing to keep down oak and birch. Once a heath has got into the state of Mousehold (or of Hampstead Heath) its conservation becomes an endless struggle against trees. And yet 'amenity' trees have been *planted* on one of the few patches of Mousehold not invaded by wild trees!

Many heaths are precarious because fragmented. A collection of small heaths has a longer edge, from which trees can encroach, than one big heath, and is also less attractive to birds like the Dartford warbler. Pines planted on part of a heath may produce seedlings which destroy the remainder.

Other changes follow myxomatosis. In the Breckland, when rabbits disappeared, many of their favourite plants, such as the catchfly *Silene otites* and the curious fern *Botrychium lunaria*, which had survived for centuries in a bitten-down state, suddenly flourished, only to be smothered later by the competition of taller tussocky grasses. The grass *Deschampsia flexuosa*, hardly known in Breckland before 1954, now covers hundreds of acres. Ling and furze, not rejuvenated by browsing, grow up tall and even-aged; when a drought or frost carries them off, they are replaced by grass or bracken.

Why so much ling should have been replaced by grass is uncertain. In some places (eg. locally in Dorset), its disappearance is attributed to too much grazing. In Epping Forest and on many small heaths its disappearance goes with lack of grazing. Probably ling needs to be maintained by a particular degree of grazing, or by cutting or burning, before it gets too old to rejuvenate.

Most heathland conservationists deplore the increase of bracken. This increase is doubtless partly due to mere lapse of time: bracken plants inevitably get bigger as the years go by. Neglect of the uses of bracken may encourage growth. Cattle (but not sheep) eat it when young and trample the young fronds.

Harvesting was planned to avoid obvious damage to the plant, but the removal even of dead fronds would have exposed the shallow underground stems and young fronds to frost.

Heath fires have increased. This is usually attributed to ever-increasing public carelessness with matches, but is more plausibly yet another result of lack of management. The longer old furze, dead bracken, etc. are allowed to go uncut, the more combustible they become and the hotter the resulting fire. Many heathland animals cannot run away, and some plants are killed by a single burning. Fires are regarded as a serious threat to the smooth snake, sand lizard, natterjack toad, and silver-studded blue butterfly, as well as to commoner creatures like the adder and to ground-nesting birds. Fires have probably eliminated juniper, the broom-like *Genista pilosa*, and the clubmoss *Lycopodium selago* from heaths, except that they survive precariously in fire-sheltered spots among the heaths and moors of the Lizard Peninsula.

It used to be thought that fires would prevent trees from invading – I have said so myself – but recent events disprove this. An oak or birch only a few years old survives most fires: it is killed to ground level but promptly coppices. Burnt areas are specially attractive to birch seedlings, which come up in abundance and prevent heath vegetation from returning. Fires, if anything, favour the formation of woodland.

Few of the recent changes in heath in any way compensate for the loss of its *genius loci*. Wiser men than I have spent many years on the problems without finding an easy answer. The only adequate solution is probably a revival or modification of traditional management. Much might be done with cattle and sheep; two Breckland heaths have been restored to rabbit-warrens. But grazing is unlikely to be enough, and on many heaths the necessary fencing is difficult or illegal. Heaths are an excellent renewable source of fuel, but this involves the familiar problem of harvesting and transporting a loose and bulky material. The world is sadly in need of a cheap and portable machine that collects ling or bracken (or straw, twigs, waste paper, etc.) and crushes them into dense, transportable briquettes.

CHAPTER 14

Moorland

There are trunks of trees found at a considerable depth under ground, in hills and meadows, where there is no vestige of any kind of wood remaining; many of them have visibly suffered from fire, which the traditional history of the country reports to have been occasioned by the Danes burning the forests.

J. Sinclair, Applecross, Wester Ross, 1791.[9]

If heathland reminds us of the sunny *gariga* of Italy, moorland recalls the tundra of the Arctic, extending exceptionally far south into latitudes in which woodland would be expected. Moorland is by far our most extensive natural vegetation, running throughout Highland regions (though not necessarily at high altitudes) from Land's End to Cape Wrath and the Shetlands. Moorland, along with heath, is to foreigners the most distinctively British kind of vegetation. Similar plant communities occur in other countries, mainly at high altitudes; but Scotland is the only accessible country that is more than half moorland, and visitors come from all over the world to see it.

The 'muirs' of Scots legend and song are heather moors, the most widespread kind; but there are moors dominated by other undershrubs such as bog-myrtle and crowberry, by cotton-grass, by grasses (especially on the high tops), or even by mosses and lichens. The wetter moorlands have more or less *Sphagnum* moss along with these other plants. Drier moors often have bracken and merge into heathland; wetter moors merge into valley bogs.

We now use the word 'moor' to mean uncultivated hill-land, as in Dartmoor, Ilkley Moor, and the Lammermuirs. This meaning was familiar to the Anglo-Saxons; in their literature they used *mōr* to translate Latin *mons*, 'mountain'. But Anglo-Saxon place-names, while not ignorant of this use of 'moor', normally use *mōr* in an almost opposite sense, of a low-lying wet place such as Sedgemoor (Somerset) or Sawston Moor (Cambs). Etymologists have wasted much ink in trying to invent a connexion between these meanings, but it is better to accept that these are two separate words whose resemblance is coincidental. Moors of the lowland type are discussed in Chapter 17.

The drier, more eastern moorlands have podzolic soils little different from those of heaths; but typical moors are characterized by *peat*, varying from an inch or two to many feet thick. Peat is the accumulated remains of centuries of dead plants. Where the ground is permanently wet, these do not rot but pile up on the surface to form a black or dark brown layer sharply distinct from the mineral soil underneath. Peat should be distinguished from the rotted leaf-mould which accumulates in dry conditions in acid woods and heathland.

On many western moors, perpetually running with water, peat many feet thick may cover even steep slopes; ecological textbooks call this 'blanket bog'.

One of the natural wonders of Europe is the mighty tract of blanket bog, 150 miles long, extending over hill and strath up to the north Caithness coast. Blanket peat is often cut into by gullies known as *hags*; their vertical sides reveal sections of the peat and expose the remains of plants preserved in the millennia of its formation.

Origins and Prehistory

How far is moorland natural? The origin of moorland is less simple and certain than that of heath. Literary writers traditionally suppose that moorland is primaeval wilderness – while often subscribing also to legends of the Great Caledonian Wood and of Irish bog oak which are inconsistent with that view. In recent decades the opposite theory has gained ground, that all moorland is an artefact made by the destruction of wildwood. Propagandists for modern forestry try to persuade us that moors are 'wet deserts' whose natural vegetation would be wildwood and whose proper land-use is plantation.

For centuries people have dug trunks and stumps of trees out of moorland peat and have used them for fuel, lighting, and timber. They have rightly inferred that the hills were once wooded. M.L. Anderson published a great body of lore about bog-trees.[44] Many of the reports refer to the excellent preservation of the trees and mention the appearance of charring or of axemarks. Hence, no doubt, many of the 'legends' of the Great Caledonian Wood, and of its having been burnt down or felled in the Middle Ages or later and not grown again. Unfortunately, the reports are mostly from the last century, are often not at first hand, and cannot be accepted uncritically. We now know that most, if not all, of the trees are thousands of years older and fell down through natural agency. Some felling by prehistoric men cannot be ruled out; but reports of burning – which, suspiciously, are not limited to pine – are probably due to misunderstanding of the blackening and cracking of bog timber as it dries out.

There is something to be said for both theories of moorland. At one extreme, recent pollen analysis shows that much of the moors of Shetland, Orkney, the Caithness plateau, and the Outer Hebrides is natural tundra which has never had trees.[475] Conversely, Dr Judith Turner has shown that in Mesolithic times wildwood covered the present moors of northern England right up to the highest summits of the Pennines.[476]

Dr Margaret Atherden and I have excavated some remains of trees that preceded the peat of the North York Moors. The site is east of Bilsdale at 1150 feet, well above the highest surviving native wood in the area. We found oaks, birches, and pines. All of them were quite small and had probably felt the effects of altitude. The oaks were the best preserved; the biggest trunk was 20½ feet long and 17 inches in diameter, and came from a tree about 30 feet high.

In the eastern Highlands of Scotland trees may have grown up to an altitude of 3000 feet; but parts of Dartmoor at no more than 2000 feet have apparently always been treeless.[477] In Skye the tree-limit may have been as low as 800 feet,[478] and in the far north it descended to sea-level. Pine stumps have been found in the peat of the Outer Hebrides,[479] and there are nineteenth-century reports of birch, hazel, etc. from Orkney and Shetland. Together with the pollen evidence, this suggests that the tundra boundary in prehistoric Scotland, as in the modern Arctic, was irregular, with groves in favoured spots beyond the edge of continuous wildwood.

The fact that trees grew on what is now moorland before significant human activity does not prove that all moorland would still be wildwood if that activity had never occurred. Moors, especially of the more peaty kind, are not easily colonized by trees. The Forestry Commission induces trees to grow on blanket-peat by dint of ploughing, draining, and fertilizing; but these are heroics of technology and have nothing to do with native vegetation. At Achanalt (Ross & Cromarty) there is a small native pinewood on a piece of broken ground, a shoal in the surrounding ocean of blanket-peat, where the peat is thin and knobs of rock project. The wood is of middle-aged trees with very few young ones; these latter are not on the peat itself but on rock or on the upturned bases of their predecessors. This remnant of Caledonian wildwood has gradually been drowning in the rising tide of peat. Yet not all peat is inhospitable to trees: pines and many other species grow perfectly well on lowland peat (p.393). Within a mile of Achanalt itself, where the peat is many feet thick, I find in hags the roots of prehistoric pines that grew not only on the underlying mineral soil before the peat began to form, but also at different times on the peat itself. Dr Hilary Birks has found such stumps all over Scotland, including Sutherland and Galloway where pine no longer survives. The pines vary in date from about 6500 to 1500 BC; they did not grow all the time in any one place, and they grew at different times in different places.[480]

The high rainfall which causes blanket peat to form also washes out the minerals from it; at present it is usually too infertile even for pine to grow. Local conditions evidently changed from time to time, perhaps through the surface drying out, and enabled trees to colonize for a while.

Replacing wildwood by moor, as with heath, introduces the possibility of fire as an influence, for most moorland will burn whenever the weather is dry.

Moorland evidently ranges from wholly natural to artificial in origin. Much of it is the effect of interactions between human activity and natural processes. Leaching and peat formation would by now anyway have turned large areas of wildwood to moorland; human activities have speeded these processes. In high-rainfall areas, as well as at high altitudes and in the far north, the balance of evidence is that moorland is mainly natural. Wildwood has always been precarious, restricted to favourable localities and times. The accumulating blanket-peat would have made tree growth increasingly difficult as time went on. Even here, however, peat has probably grown faster where would-be farmers destroyed the trees. Human intervention in these areas has merely hastened a southward and downward extension of tundra that would have happened more slowly from natural causes. Eastern Britain is less favourable to peat formation and more favourable to trees, and most of the drier, less peaty moorland, like heathland, would still be wildwood but for human intervention.

Early human activity The boundary between wildwood and tundra in Scotland was probably never stable. Quite early in the post-glacial, at least by the seventh millennium BC, wildwood began to retreat in areas of high rainfall as blanket peat began to grow from wholly natural causes.[480]

From the Neolithic onwards human activity began to predominate. Hundreds of stone circles, from Cornwall to Caithness, with their astronomical relationships demanding a clear horizon, are witnesses that wide areas, now moorland, had ceased to be wooded by the middle Bronze Age at latest.[481] Proof is also supplied by the countless barrows and standing-stones carefully set where they can be seen from a distance. But the moors were not used solely for funerals and astrology. The eighteenth-century discovery of Grimspound, the great

Bronze Age village perched on top of Dartmoor, began a long series of studies which have proved that most of what is now moorland was quite densely populated in prehistory. In some areas there was arable cultivation at twice the elevation at which it is now thought possible. Cultivation did not last long: at such altitudes the soils became leached of their soluble minerals, the land became pasture and eventually was overrun by blanket-bog, and the settlements moved downhill.

Archaeology and pollen analysis show that the time-scale of these events varied and there was not always an arable stage. On Dartmoor and Bodmin Moor the heyday of settlement was the Bronze Age and depression had set in by the Iron Age.[482] Elsewhere events seem to have been later. In southern Scotland and Northumberland, although there was some Bronze Age activity, the predominant settlement remains are the 'scooped homesteads' and hillforts attributed to the Iron Age.[483] On the North York Moors, only the highest points had become moorland by the Bronze Age; settlement was extended downwards in the Iron Age and the Roman period.[484] Similar dates have been found elsewhere in northern England and in North Wales.[485] In Ireland many Iron Age raths (farmsteads) are in what is now moorland.[178] In Derbyshire, exceptionally, cultivation persists even now at well over 1000 feet altitude, but the soils here (loess overlying limestone) are unusually fertile and have resisted leaching.

Evidence of Iron Age or earlier settlement preceding present moorland is abundant everywhere except in the northern and western Scottish Highlands. We might not expect many remains to be visible here because the fast-growing peat would have covered them. Peat growth may have been hastened by a wetter climate – the 'Sub-Atlantic Period' – in the late Bronze and Iron Ages. Farming here would probably have depended on livestock and may have taken advantage of the natural recession of trees.

The retreat first of wildwood and later of agriculture allowed the spread of the shade-intolerant plants which are now abundant in moorland – heather, cottongrass, bog-myrtle, etc. – and of juniper and clubmosses which have recently diminished again through burning. Bracken also spread. Ecologists have a curious tradition of regarding bracken as a woodland plant, but this is not typical of it. It did not flourish in wildwood, but has taken advantage of the formation of moorland to become, as it is now, one of the most extensive of wild British plants.

By the end of the Iron Age all our large moors existed, though they were not as extensive as now; much of their edges would still have been farmland with some wildwood. The retreat of agriculture from moorland has been intermittent. The boundary between the cultivable and the uncultivable is often not sharp, especially on the less peaty moors. Whenever farming has prospered, men whose lands abut on moorland have been tempted to add to their acres by intakes, and adventurous folk have set up detached farmsteads on enclaves of cultivable land in the midst of the moor. Often these enterprises have been short-lived. Edges of moors, especially in south-west England, are an archaeological palimpsest of superimposed field systems, a record of centuries of endeavour and failure, in contrast to the generally more stable history of heaths.

History of Moorland

Charters and place-names Early written evidence is scanty compared to that for heath, because comparatively few documents refer to parts of the British Isles that have moorland.

The word *mōr* occurs 174 times in Anglo-Saxon charters, but the context always demands the fen or bog sense, as do many place-names (eg. Moorgate, London). The charters of Wales occasionally mention *mynydd* 'hill' but are too laconic to help in picturing the vegetation.

Moor in the highland sense often appears in place-names. There is no reason to doubt that many date from Anglo-Saxon times, but only occasionally can this be proved. Dartmoor and Exmoor are not written by name before the twelfth century, but both are obliquely referred to in Domesday Book – the name *Moretun* ('Settlement by Moor'), now Moretonhampstead, implies that Dartmoor had been thought of as The Moor long enough to have had a place named after it; and the entry for the Exmoor township of Molland mentions 'the pastures of the moors' (*pascue morarum*).

The general disappointment is relieved by the charters of Devon and Cornwall. The bounds of Meavy in 1031 run into Dartmoor and mention 'Edswith's Tor' (*edswyþe torre*), evidently one of the tors round the present Burrator Reservoir.[486] The '*Peadingtune* Charter', an undated fragment, crosses Dartmoor above Ashburton and mentions a 'long stone' (presumably a standing-stone), another tor (*cofede tor*), and a patch of furze (*fyrspenn*).[487] Cornish charters sometimes use the Cornish words for moor, *hal* or *gun*, as well as the English *hæpfeld* (p.287).

As often, the perfect topographical illustrations are to be found on the Lizard Peninsula, where there are six perambulations having an Old English text but features listed in Old Cornish. For instance, *trefwurabo* [Traboe in St Keverne] in 977:

> First at *pollicerr* [now a farm called Polkerth]; then by the ditch along the way; then from the way; then to the little ditch on the east side of the way; to *poll hæscen* [Sedge Pool]; down by the brook to *ryt cendeurion* [End-of-Two-Rivers Ford]; then by the brook to *carn nið bran* [Raven's Nest Bluff]; to *deumaen coruan* [Two Rocks of the Ridge]; then along the way to *cruc drænoc* [Thorny Barrow]; then to *carrecwynn* [White Outcrop]; & back again to *pollicerr*.[488]

About half the Lizard is cultivated land, a tangle of lanes, dingles, and tiny fields, where we cannot always follow the Anglo-Cornish surveyor, though we can recognize some of his landmarks (Fig. 14.1). For instance, we can identify that lonely spot in St Keverne parish designated in the bounds of *Lesmanaoc* [Higher Lesneague] in 967 as Eselt's Ford (*hryt eselt*);[489] Mr Oliver Padel tells me that this is the first record of that woman's name which, spelt *Yseult* or *Isolde*, was to capture the imagination of medieval (and Wagnerian) Europe. Hardly less romantic a place is *ryt cendeurion*, now Tregidden Mill, at the beautiful heart of the Lizard Peninsula; there is still a ford, with a clapper footbridge beside it (Fig. 14.2). Dr D.E. Coombe, with whom I have walked much of the Traboe boundary, has identified the preceding point, *poll hæscen*, and tells me that it still has great 'hassocks' of the sedge *Carex paniculata*. The main stream above Tregidden Mill runs up in about 2 miles on to the Goonhilly Downs, an undulating moor dotted with small tors or outcrops of serpentine rock and with round barrows. *Carn nið bran* is a rather prominent tor identifiable from the nineteenth-century Tithe Map of St Keverne. *Deumaen coruan* are two little teeth of rock, the projection of a loess-covered tor – the most insignificant of features, but the only natural landmarks in the wide moorland. They are visible on the skyline all the way from the preceding landmark. The 'way' was an ancient road of some importance, named in medieval perambulations, now long disused but visible in aerial photographs. *Cruc drænoc* is a round barrow at the centre of the moor, at which five parishes meet. For centuries it has been called the Dry Tree, perhaps from a gallows. Beside the barrow there is now a great standing-stone of gabbro, brought from a distance by prehistoric men. This, however, is not used as a landmark either by the perambulation or the parish boundaries, and was evidently fallen at the time; it was re-erected some seventy years ago. From the Thorny Barrow we trudge across half a mile of tussocky moor to the *carrecwynn* – the outcrop (of hornblende-schist) has been largely quarried away, but there are still remains of a conspicuous white lichen (*Ochrolechia* species) to show how it got its name. From here the bounds pass Polkerth and are lost in a maze of ditches and ways.

The Lizard perambulations require a landscape in which the moorland and cultivation of a thousand years ago were much the same as they are now; in places the fields have since advanced a little. Some landmarks allude to plants, some of which are still there, and even to lichens; later perambulations mention *Main mellyn*, Yellow Rocks, an allusion to the yellow lichen *Xanthoria*. Although *cruc drænoc* is no longer thorny, other barrows afford a foothold to clumps of thorns. Many of the points would be useless as landmarks except in open country with vegetation no higher than it is now. *Carn nið bran* would be hidden by tall bushes, and *Deumaen coruan* would be lost even in well-grown bracken. The Lizard perambulations therefore explode the 'tradition' that the Downs were wooded until the Middle Ages. The chief obstacle to following them today is the modest growth of trees and bushes at the edges of the Downs in the last hundred years.

Domesday Book In most of England Domesday does not record moors directly, but merely as gaps in the pattern of settlements. (The Lake District and northern Pennines are not recorded at all.)

Recorded settlement in 1066 usually stops abruptly at about 750 feet altitude; in Exmoor it rises to 900 feet and in limestone Derbyshire to 1000 feet, but in the North York Moors few settlements are named above 500 feet. These altitudes are usually some 250 feet lower than the highest modern farmsteads, but probably do not represent the actual upper limit of eleventh-century habitation. Small farms at high altitudes often originated as summer pastures, known in northern England as 'shields', from settlements lower down. Wales has its ancient tradition of the permanently-occupied *hendre* and summer *hafod*. Secondary settlements rarely appear in Domesday Book, since they were regarded (even if by then permanently inhabited) as dependencies of the parent settlements not worthy of separate record. But the Commissioners, on an excursion into Wales, did record a place Hendrebiffa (near Mold, Flintshire); and such a name implies a corresponding *hafod* higher on the Mountains of Clwyd. The upper limit of settlement was probably little if any lower in the eleventh century than it is now.

In Somerset, Devon, and Cornwall Domesday makes the attempt to record moorland along with other pasture. For pasture we are given either the acreage or the dimensions, from which the acreage can be estimated (p.75). In Table 14.1 I present the figures for the Lizard.

The total pasture on the Lizard adds up to 17,000 acres. Almost the whole of it belonged to places within reach of the Goonhilly Downs or the other moors. Places confined to the wholly-cultivated northern half of the Lizard (Fig. 14.1) had fewer than 300 acres. Similar calculations result in a total of 16,000 acres of arable land, 450 acres of meadow, and about 500 acres of woodland – a grand total of nearly 34,000 acres, which is a satisfactory fit to the 38,000 acres that are the actual area of the Lizard. Domesday Book confirms our inference from the charters that the Lizard landscape has altered little in a thousand years. Then as

Fig. 14.1. The Lizard Peninsula, after the Ordnance Survey of 1811. A: location of Fig. 14.2. B: location of Fig. 14.5. C: Loe Pool (Chapter 16).

311

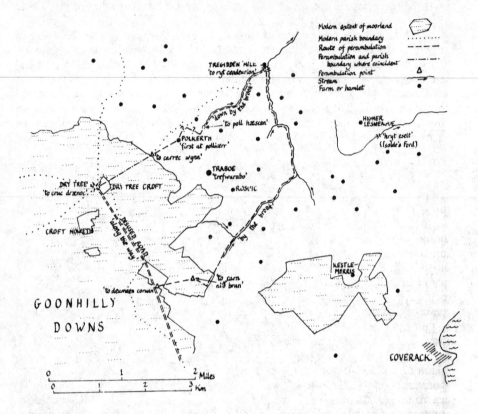

Fig. 14.2. Part of the Lizard Peninsula, including the Traboe perambulation of 967 AD.
All the farms and hamlets shown are known or strongly suspected to date at least from
the Middle Ages. The crofts on the Goonhilly Downs (moorland) are a little later; the
making of a croft at the Dry Tree has diverted the parish boundary. At Rosuic there is
the Great Elm of Rosuic (p.229). For Kestlemerris see Fig. 8.5.

now, the moors were in the south; they were rather more extensive than now,
but Domesday already mentions an outlier of farmland on better soils at Lizard
Town itself on the southern tip. Woodland was confined, as now, to the steep
sheltered valleys of the Helford River in the north. The livestock in 1086
included twenty-two 'untamed mares', which have been interpreted as the
ancestresses of the special ponies for which the Goonhilly Downs, like Dartmoor, were noted in later centuries.

The Lizard is fortunate in its excellent documentation and in that it is a
peninsula, in which the land-uses ought to add up to a definite total area. By a
similar calculation, the pastures assigned to places around Bodmin Moor add up
to 70,000 acres, a reasonable fit to the actual area of the Moor, and there is also
good agreement for the Camborne moors. But the other moorland areas of
Cornwall – St Austell Moor and Land's End – seem to be much underestimated.

For places around Dartmoor, Domesday records only 40,000 acres of pasture,
less than half the area of the Moor as indicated by the map of Domesday
settlements. This discrepancy can be reduced by supposing that the central part

of the Moor (the later Dartmoor Forest) was not divided among settlements but was, as in later centuries, the common pasture for the whole of Devon except Bideford and Totnes.[490] The Domesday Commissioners were not, in general, prepared for such an extra-territorial area and might easily have forgotten to record it. The pasture of Exmoor seems to be fully accounted for, but that of the Mendips is under-recorded.

Table 14.1 Pasture on the Lizard Peninsula in 1086

Places in the cultivated north of the Lizard			
Mawgan	20 acres	20 modern acres	
Boden	½ × ¼ league	130	” ”
Trewarnevas	6 acres	6	” ”
St Keverne	20 acres	20	” ”
Trenance	100 acres	100	” ”
Gear	5 acres	5	” ”
		281	” ”

Places on the edge of moorland			
Winnianton	4 × 2 leagues	8060 modern acres	
Garah	½ × ½ league	250	” ”
Lizard	1½ × ½ league	760	” ”
Trelowarren	1 × ½ league	500	” ”
Bojorrow	½ × ½ league	250	” ”
Trelan[vean]	½ × ½ league	250	” ”
Roscarnon	60 acres	60	” ”
Trelan	3 × 2 leagues	6050	” ”
Trewince	500 acres	500	” ”
		16680	” ”

Medieval changes In the winter of 1069–70 the wrath of William the Conqueror, losing his temper at an insurrection in York, exploded upon the Pennines with the force of many atomic bombs. That is what Domesday Book seems to say: fifteen years later, settlement after settlement (over 300 in all) in dale after dale from Derbyshire to the Tees is described as *Wasta est*, It is waste. But what really happened is uncertain.[491] The *Anglo-Saxon Chronicle* writes briefly of a no more than ordinary reprisal. There is little evidence that moorland and woodland benefited from the tragedy, as we should expect both to have done. With surprisingly few exceptions, the 'waste' places somehow came back to life and their names are still on the map. And why should the Conqueror have been angry with, say, remote Wharfedale and not have wasted places near York where the action had been?

The pressure on land in the twelfth and thirteenth centuries pushed cultivation again up into the moors. An oft-quoted example is Fernacre, a lonely farm at nearly 1000 feet on Bodmin Moor.[492] There are many such little farmsteads high on Dartmoor, and other settlements – some on the scale of villages – appeared in the Pennines (Hoskins 1955). Most of these are first heard of in the thirteenth century and some historians claim that they were then new. Extensions of tillage are more securely dated on Exmoor, because this was a royal Forest whose laws they infringed.[493] Even if only some such settlements are post-Conquest, together they are a substantial extension of farming, sometimes of arable at altitudes where there is now only rough pasture. The total area would have been comparable to that being won at the same time from fen and woodland.

Increased use of the remaining moorland would have accompanied increased cultivation. Both are traditionally associated with the Cistercian Order of monks, who reached Britain in 1128 and founded many great monasteries in the following 150 years. By their Rule Cistercians were required to inhabit solitary places and to be farmers. They were able and energetic men; their buildings are still mighty in dereliction; and scholars have credited them, often on slender evidence, with many transformations in the landscape.

The Cistercians found solitude more difficult to come by in crowded England than in their native France. Their most important houses were close to moorland and had large moorland estates. Examples are the great Yorkshire abbeys of Fountains, Jervaulx, Rievaulx, Byland, and Kirkstall; Newminster (Northumberland); Furness (Lancs); Dieulacress (Staffs); and Abbey Dore (Herefordshire). There was some association with moorland in Wales (eg. Strata Florida (Cardiganshire) and Cwmhir (Radnor)) and Ireland (Vallis Salutis in the Wicklow Mountains). In Scotland the best-known houses were mainly in the southern Uplands (eg. Kelso, Melrose, and Sweetheart Abbeys), but some found solitude in the less remote Highlands (eg. Ardchattan on Loch Etive). The Knights Templars also had moorland interests, for instance Temple on Bodmin Moor.

What effects did the Cistercians have? They took at least a proper interest in farming; often they became agri-businessmen to pay off debts incurred by over-ambitious building. They undoubtedly assarted land from moorland and pushed up the frontier of tillage. The Yorkshire houses, especially, derived much of their wealth from wool, and attached great value to the fells in consequence. They sued one another over moorland boundaries and put up miles of wall to settle disputes (as on Fountains Fell – note the name – in Malham) (Hoskins 1955). It has been claimed that the increase of monkish sheep reduced the red deer (Pearsall 1950). Such changes may have been locally conspicuous, but it would be rash to claim that they were universal. The *Taxatio Ecclesiastica* of 1291 gives statistics of monastic livestock in Wales. The flocks of Cistercian abbeys were numbered only in thousands, rather than the tens of thousands needed to change a whole landscape. Cattle were also important, and at Strata Florida the cattle were valued at slightly more than the sheep.

A study of the settlement history of Weardale, by B.K. Roberts, J. Turner, and P.F. Ward, combines evidence from pollen analysis, field archaeology, and documents.[494] Weardale was predominantly moorland, at least from the Roman period. Trees are well represented in the pollen record because such woodland as existed was close to the bogs from which samples were taken. Ling and grasses occurred but their proportions fluctuate widely; in the Middle Ages there was much less ling than there is now. Whether the Conqueror's vengeance blasted this dale is not known; an apparent decline in pollen of plantains and other farm weeds, at a date within a century of AD 1100, could be attributed to that cause by the imaginative reader. The authors show that by the twelfth century the dale was well provided with villages and farmland. In the thirteenth century the farmland was extended up the dale sides, both by assarts from the moor and by shields becoming all-year homesteads. There is some evidence of a decline in farming in the later Middle Ages, followed by renewed expansion in the sixteenth century and later.

Moorland Forests Weardale was a Forest of the Bishop of Durham, one of the two English prelates who aspired to that princely status symbol. Roberts, Turner, and Ward mention how the deer which lived on the surrounding fells were slaughtered in great drives for the episcopal table.

There were at least thirty-nine Forests in the Pennines and Lake District, almost all of them predominantly moorland: names still well known include the Peak Forest (Derbyshire), Bowland (west Yorkshire), and Rossendale (Lancs). Other moorland Forests included Dartmoor and Exmoor, Stiperstones and Clee (Shropshire), and Pickering (North York Moors). About a third of the 142 royal and private Forests were chiefly moorland, and many of them were large. Dartmoor Forest (50,000 acres) was bigger than any wooded Forest. Almost certainly there was as much moorland as woodland in the physical Forests of medieval England.

Apart from Dartmoor and Exmoor, moorland Forests are relatively little known because few of them were royal. The many private Forests appear to be poorly documented.

In Wales the proliferation of petty marcher princelings and their ill-defined minor Forests cannot properly be analyzed. Many of the moorlands of south and east Wales have been designated Forest at least for a short time. The name survives in Radnor Forest and the Great Forest of Brecknock (Ffores Fawr), both of them mainly at altitudes of 1000 to 2000 feet at which moorland would by then have been the only possible vegetation. Ffores Fawr was not unlike the moorland Forests of England and became royal in the sixteenth century (Linnard 1982). Scotland presents similar difficulties, but some of the best-defined Forests, especially in the Southern Uplands, were mainly moorland: these included the royal Forests of Ettrick, Jedburgh, and the Pentland Hills.[44] The lonely Forest of Ross, on Beinn Eighe, is the earliest known predecessor (*c*.1320)[85] of the post-medieval Forests of the west Highlands.

Some moorland Forests had the peculiarity that their legal boundaries were not greater than, and might be less than, the actual limits of the moorland. There was (and is) a distinction between Dartmoor Forest, the central part of Dartmoor, which covers less than half the Moor and nowhere reaches its edges, and the surrounding 'commons' (Fig. 14.3). In the thirteenth century the Forest jurisdiction, which had applied in theory to the whole of Devon, was reduced to that central part of Dartmoor which was the common-land of almost the whole county. This extra-territorial area became annexed to the parish of Lydford, being the only substantial Crown manor in the surrounding townships, and still forms the greater part of that giant parish. The commons, excluded from the Forest, form part of the territory of 31 adjacent parishes. On Exmoor the legal Forest originally included the whole moor and a narrow belt of surrounding farmland. In the fourteenth century, it was reduced to that central part of the moor, some 20,000 acres, which the Crown owned.[495] In the Pennines, Forests commonly adjoined each other on the moors, just as in the modern Scottish Highlands.

Although wild swine may have spent part of their time on moors in the Forest of Pickering and in Scotland, the only important moorland beast of the chase was the red deer. It is wrong to regard the hart as a specifically woodland animal. He is a beast of tundra and of the great glaciations – a kind of deputy mammoth – who survives through being able to live in woodland during interglacial periods. In woodland red deer grow bigger, and experts claim to be able to tell the habitat of a deer from the bones or antlers. In moorland they eat heather, cotton-grass, lichens, and many other plants. They need shelter in winter, but can travel in search of it, and are content with such meagre cover as old heather or tall bracken.[496]

In the thirteenth century the biggest supplier of red deer to the English king's table was the Forest of Inglewood, a term which seems to have subsumed the four royal Forests in Cumberland. There was some wood-pasture but at least two of the Forests were moorland. Henry III also ordered many harts and hinds from Langthwaite Forest, near the Bishop of Durham's Forest of Weardale. Moderate numbers came from Northumberland, Pickering, Lancashire, the Peak, and the Shropshire Forests, and smaller numbers from Mendip, Exmoor, and rarely Dartmoor. As we have seen, moderate numbers of red deer came from heathland Forests; in wooded Forests they were widespread but mainly in small numbers.[497] Red deer were supplied to the Scots kings from various moorland Forests; Edward I helped himself to them when invading Scotland.[44]

We learn of the operation of moorland Forests from the court records of Exmoor and Dartmoor. Exmoor was a normal Forest; it yielded venison for the king and (by permission) for his friends; it produced revenue from poaching fines, grazing rents, and 'fines' for technically illicit grazing. Deer continued to be caught, even after the legal Forest had been reduced to an inhospitable part of the whole moor. As a later memorandum complained, the deer spent much of their time outside the Forest bounds.[495]

Uses of moorland   Dartmoor provides the best evidence of the medieval use of moorland in an area little affected by the Cistercians.[490] It was only nominally a Forest: hart and hind rarely came before its courts. It would have been even more difficult to keep the royal deer within Dartmoor Forest than in Exmoor. Instead the Forest administration had the complex task of administering the common-land grazing of the Forest, levying small 'fines' on adjacent parishes whose livestock strayed into the Forest from the commons, and collecting somewhat larger fees for animals sent into the Forest from non-adjacent parishes. In 1403–4, a good year, the Duchy of Cornwall (successor to the Crown) derived £66 gross, equivalent to the revenue from a biggish manor. This came from some 6400 cattle, 95 horses, and an unrecorded number of sheep. Licences were also issued to sixty *carbonarii*, 'coal-men', presumably makers of peat charcoal used for smelting tin.[498]

Cattle were important grazers of moorland as well as sheep and deer. There were also goats, important in Wales (Linnard 1982); escaped animals are doubtless the origin of the 'wild goats' now in North Wales and elsewhere, many of which preserve the characteristics of medieval breeds.[59] Moors were important sources of fuel, both peat and furze or ling, and of bracken, although only in the smaller moors (eg. the Lizard) could cutting have had more than a local effect.

Modern history   Exmoor records of the seventeenth and eighteenth centuries tell us of the post-medieval management of a moor.[493] In that period the Forest

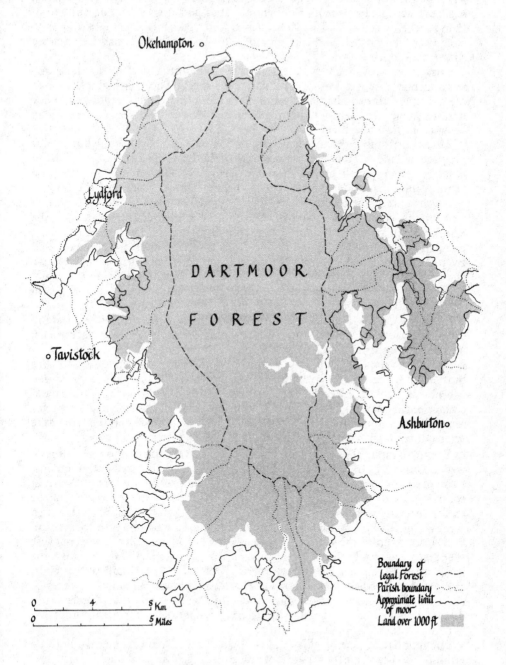

Okehampton ○

Lydford

D A R T M O O R

F O R E S T

○ Tavistock

Ashburton○

Boundary of
legal Forest
Parish boundary
Approximate limit
of moor
Land over 1000 ft

0   4   8 Km
0   5 Miles

Fig. 14.3. The legal boundary of the Forest of Dartmoor in relation to the surrounding parishes and to the actual edge of the moor. The greater part of the moor lying outside the Forest boundary constitutes the commons of the parishes. Adapted from R.H. Worth.[499]

317

– the middle of the moor – was grazed by sheep at the rate of between 1½ and 2 head per acre and by small numbers of cattle and horses. At the altitude of Exmoor this is severe grazing. The surrounding parochial commons appear to have been less grazed, and this may be why there is to this day less heather within the Forest.

Exmoor is probably not typical. Evidence from other moorland areas, though less systematic, suggests more cattle and fewer sheep. The principal cash crop of the old-time Scottish Highlands were black cattle, now almost vanished. They were reared in the Islands, fed in the mainland glens, and driven southwards to be eaten in Edinburgh and London.[496]

After the Middle Ages the rising population seems to have resulted in greater pressure on land in moorland regions than in the Lowland Zone. On the Lizard there are many small crofts, often on islands of loess amid the otherwise uncultivable moors, dated probably to the sixteenth century (p.161). Similar expansions are known from South Wales[170] and Weardale.[494]

With the possible exception of Ireland, the pressure was greatest in the Scottish Highlands and Islands, where a multiplying and fiercely home-loving population wrested a miserable living from a shrinking area of mineral soil. Even the Atlantic rock of North Rona had a population of thirty, who came to a ghastly end in 1685 when shipwrecked rats ate up their stores. Famine was not uncommon even on the mainland, although the introduction of the potato postponed disaster.

Industries had a local effect on moorland through the siting of mines and occasionally of new towns. Surprisingly, peat seems never to have been an important industrial fuel except for tin-working.* A remarkable industrial landscape developed on the west Cornish moors. Here – not uniquely – it was the custom for miners to have little farms as well.[492] The moors, here of granite and not particularly infertile, were almost entirely eaten away by hundreds of cottage enclaves (Fig. 14.4). Little is now left of the mining, but the cottages remain with innumerable lanes, small fields, and little woods on the remaining scraps of common – one of the happiest of post-industrial landscapes.

The topographical effects of the Agricultural Revolution on moorland are not well understood. In Wales and Highland England, large areas of commons, most of them moorland, passed into private control by Enclosure Acts. In contrast to heaths, enclosure was not always followed by the destruction of the native vegetation. Much was said about 'improving' moorland. The celebrated John Knight, with persistence worthy of a better cause, contrived to establish farmsteads even in the heart of Exmoor Forest. Some smaller moors, such as Mendip, were largely eliminated. On Dartmoor, despite its legal protection, the hard labour of convicts created improved grassland on the middle of the moor, and around its edges loopholes in the by-laws allowed adjoining farmers to encroach.[499] Elsewhere, most moorland remained as such, even though subdivided by stone or turf walls. Blanket peat usually defeated agricultural technology.

The moorland scene of today was set by a change from predominantly cattle farming to sheep, partly because of the breeding of Cheviots and Blackfaces

---

* Dartmoor Prison had a peat gasworks.[499]

which were successful on moorland. From the late eighteenth century onwards, sheep-farming on moorland increased almost everywhere from South Wales[170] northward, although not on Exmoor. This change is notoriously associated with the Highland Clearances in Scotland between 1782 and 1854.

The story has often been told of how certain landowners, notably the first Duke of Sutherland, coveted the ancestral lands of their tenants for sheep-ranches, took advantage of the lax tenurial law, and hired unscrupulous agents who evicted the inhabitants by violence, bloodshed, and arson.[500] This undoubtedly happened. It was the most outrageous example of the single-minded pursuit of agricultural profit, which has caused endless lesser mischief before and since; even now the lesson has not everywhere been learnt. As often happens, the profit was short-lived, for the power of sheep to live off blanket-bog had been over-rated. But let us not blame the Duke and his friends, wicked as they were, for emptying all the glens. There are many thousands of deserted settlements in the Highlands, and probably not one in ten tells the melancholy story of eviction.

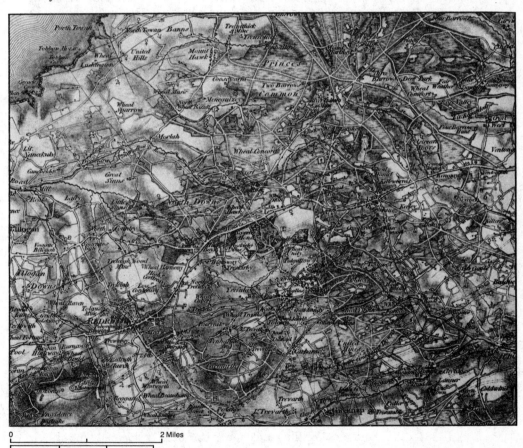

Fig. 14.4. The moors near Redruth, Cornwall, filled with cottages at the time when tin-mining flourished. Ordnance Survey 1811.

The ten-yearly census returns show that the Highlands were dangerously over-populated, and that the population in general rose despite the evictions. The parish of Kildonan (Sutherland), sacked in the 'Year of the Burnings' in 1814, had 1574 inhabitants in 1811 and only 565 in 1821; but this was the most notorious of all the Clearances. The population of all Sutherlandshire was at its highest in the 1850s, when the Clearances ended; it has since fallen by nearly half, most rapidly in the 1910s. Skye had 16,000 inhabitants in 1801; they increased to an alarming 23,000 in 1841, and have since gradually declined to the present figure of 7,000. For half a century the Highlands had lived on the brink of famine. When potato blight arrived in 1845 famine became a reality, though not so catastrophic as in Ireland. It is hardly surprising that from then onwards people should have been drawn away by opportunities for a less poverty-stricken life elsewhere.

After 1850 red deer were revived as beasts of the chase in the Scottish Highlands. The many deer-Forests whose names now sprinkle the map might be dismissed as bogus Highland antiquarianisms, for few of them are known before 1800. But there is a genuine if tenuous link with the medieval eastern Scots tradition of moorland Forests. Forests never declined in Scotland as they did in England; many new ones were declared in the fifteenth, sixteenth, and seventeenth centuries. By the eighteenth century the tradition had spread even to the north-west. A map of 1751 has 'Lord Reay's Forest of Derrymore' in Sutherland, and by 1789 there were a few others including Fainish (now Fannich) Forest in the interior of Ross & Cromarty, and Tarfe Forest far away by Cape Wrath.[501] The moorland deer-Forests of the Highlands are the living representatives of a practice which has continued, though not in the same place, since the reign of Alexander I.

Grouse-gamekeeping is a nineteenth-century development, especially in the Pennines, southern Uplands, and south-eastern Highlands. Grouse are often kept with sheep but are usually separated from deer.

Effects of Burning and Grazing

Burning of moorland has probably always been commoner than of heath. Cutting can seldom have been extensive enough to control the vegetation. Numbers of grazing animals could rarely have been constant, and when they fared badly for a few years the vegetation would accumulate to a point where burning, called 'swaling' or 'swiddening', was possible and desirable to improve the pasture. On Exmoor in 1338

> Richard Gaune of Leucote burnt the moor of the Prior of Taunton near to the Lord King's land of the Forest . . . from which burning the flame of fire leaping out into the heath of the Lord King . . . burnt a hundred acres of heath in the same.[495]

In 1333 a thousand acres of the king's moor had been accidentally burnt.

In 1607 a statute forbade 'raysinge of Fires in moorishe Grounds and mountanous Countries' in the north of England between May and September on pain of a month's imprisonment. It was alleged that there happeneth yerelie a greate distruccion of the Broode of Wildfoule and Mooregame, and by the Multitude of grosse Vapours and Cloudes arrising from those greate Fyers, the Aire is soe distempered and such unseasonable and un-naturall Stormes are ingendred . . . by the violence of those Fires driven wth the Wynd, greate Feildes of Corne growinge have been consumed . . .[502]

Until about 1800 moor-burning was probably casual and sporadic, but with the rise of sheep and grouse management it became a regular practice. Much research has been done on it (Gimingham 1972). Heather is excellent forage for sheep and the staple food of grouse. Red deer, which are favoured in the north-west Scottish Highlands, have a less selective diet. The object of burning is to produce a pure crop of heather, full of soft young shoots; older growth is woody, less palatable, and less nutritious. The favoured age for burning heather is ten to twelve years, about a third of the life-span of the heather plant, at which age it easily regenerates. If left longer the fire is hotter and more destructive and re-vegetation is uncertain.

Moorland management for sheep and grouse is a skilled art; the skills took long to develop, and not everybody now has them. Even a 'well-managed' heather moor, being a monoculture, is liable to be ravaged by pests such as the heather beetle. Sheep are more choosy in their diet than cattle and may encourage unpalatable plants; they may also damage the ground by trampling.

It is almost universally asserted that bracken has increased in recent decades. The extent of the increase is not easy to ascertain, except in those few places where there are early photographs: Sheail (1980) gives a clear example from the North York Moors. In many areas, such as South Wales, much of the spread of bracken has not been on the moors themselves but on the slopes below them, which were once private meadow or pasture but are now disused. F. Fraser Darling, the great authority on the Scottish Highlands, blamed the change from cattle to sheep for encouraging bracken: sheep hardly eat it, and trample it less than cattle.[503] Improper burning, which too often goes with sheep-grazing, is also said to promote bracken at the expense of heather. More important still may be the 'improvements' of the last hundred years. Bracken is a clonal plant (like elms) which inexorably spreads with time up to a limit set by its not tolerating wet ground. Any improvement in drainage allows it to spread further.

Fire and sheep are blamed also for the apparent spread of the tough inedible grass *Nardus stricta*, which now occupies wide areas of the less peaty moorland, and for the starting of gulley-erosion in peat (Pearsall 1950).

In the Peak it has been possible to compare vegetation maps made in 1913 and 1981. About a third of the heather has been replaced by grass, much of it *Nardus*, in sixty-eight years. There have also been losses of bilberry and cotton-grass. Bracken has locally increased. Some of the changes are attributable to sheep, which have increased threefold; at the same time, there has been a decline in grouse-keeping.[504]

Changes of management may be responsible for the wide fluctuations of moorland plants in pollen diagrams. In Weardale, for instance, heather pollen becomes very abundant only in the last 200 years.

Juniper, which indicates lack of burning, has not disappeared from moorland as much as from other habitats; but it is known to have been more abundant in the Southern Uplands, and surviving plants are in protected places such as rock outcrops and islands in lochs.[505]

Moors As They Are Now

Moors, like heaths, show in their vegetation the effects of soil differences, the natural behaviour of plants, and artefacts.

Many moors develop a tussock-and-pan or hummock-and-hollow structure repeated every few yards. A simple instance are the uncomfortable tussocks of the grass *Molinia caerulea* which cause the walker to avoid places where it grows. It is in the nature of this grass to grow in tussocks, but other patterns involve the soil as well as the plant. Peat is sensitive to the accumulation or erosion promoted by different kinds of plant cover. Tussocks and pans on level moorland give way on steep slopes to the regular 'terracets' – about 3 feet wide, much narrower than cultivation terraces – produced by the treading of beasts. In high mountains on mineral soils, freezing and thawing may generate hummocks or stripes and polygons.

In many areas, notably the Pennines, peat is now forming only locally if at all. Changes in management, air pollution, and climate are possible explanations; past hiatuses in peat growth – 'recurrence surfaces' – are well known to pollen analysts. Blanket-peat is often dissected by branching hags; these erosion gullies seem now to be specially active. The process is not always one-way: where peat is still forming I have seen both active hags and the scars of old ones now healed.

Reminders that the climate allows tree growth are occasional rowans perched on big boulders, often miles from woodland, and aspens and birches on cliffs. These are in places where they escape from grazing and peat.

Moorland is thick with the remains of prehistoric settlements and of later periods, both industrial – mine-shafts, engine-houses, etc. – and agricultural. The historic settlements are as yet hardly studied systematically. The Royal Commission on Ancient and Historical Monuments for Scotland has made a beginning in several counties, most completely in Roxburghshire, although dating is difficult.

In the wilds of Ross & Cromarty I have seen ruins wherever an acre or so of mineral soil emerges from the vast blanket of peat, even as high as 1000 feet. In one lonely hollow a well-built kiln proclaims some industrial activity. People could hardly have been driven to wring a living out of this environment by anything but extremest overpopulation. The lowest, least unfavourable settlement has two quite modern little farmsteads, now inhabited only by the few remaining sheep. An iron plough shows that somebody has tried to till the soil, but what crops could have been expected? The place is called Badinluchie, *Bad an Fhliuchaidh*, Place of Wetness, and even in a land where everything is wet it is well named.

Former field-systems are best looked for in aerial photographs, or in places where a recent fire has revealed faint boundary banks or stone-rows. Ridge-and-furrow was often used on former moorland as an aid to drainage. Stripes looking like ridge-and-furrow from the air may be produced by digging off peat to get rid of it, or by the parallel tracks of undefined roads (p.279).

Burning produces a large-scale pattern of sharp-edged tracts, usually several acres at a time, of stages of regrowth after successive fires. It may destroy or hide the small-scale natural pattern. Vegetation is also changed by different kinds of grazing and by fertilizing. All these modern activities tend to change abruptly at walls and fences.

Peat-cutting may affect large areas where the peat is thin. Almost everywhere on the Lizard moors aerial photographs reveal a faint striation of curving lines, much smaller in scale than ridge-and-furrow and rarely visible on the ground. These are thought to be the result of paring off blanket-peat for fuel. Peat was a domestic fuel until within living memory, but some of it may have been for industry. Over the Lizard moors there are some hundreds of 'hut-rectangles', shallow trenches in the form of rectangles about 10 × 17 feet, which are filled with *Molinia* and hence show up well in infra-red false-colour photography. J.J. Hopkins has recently re-interpreted them not as habitations but as hearths for making peat charcoal.[506]

An example from the Lizard The moorland of the Lizard Peninsula shows the effects of many historic activities superimposed on a natural soil pattern determined at the last glaciation. The higher parts of the plateau are covered with 'Short Heath', a dwarf plant community dominated by heather and other species of heath (but not Cornish heath), dwarf furze (*Ulex gallii*) and the grasses *Agostis setacea* and (dwarfed) *Molinia*. In shallow valleys this is abruptly replaced by 'Tall Heath', tall vegetation with the bog-rush *Schoenus nigricans*, *Molinia* (in a taller, very tussocky form), and Cornish heath (*Erica vagans*). As D.E. Coombe and L.C. Frost have shown, Short Heath is on loess-derived soils; Tall Heath is where the loess was washed away in prehistory, exposing soils formed from the underlying serpentine or gabbro rocks. (They also recognize 'Mixed Heath' and 'Rock Heath', relatively dry plant communities more characteristic of coastal cliffs and heaths than of the inland moors.)[507]

Parts of the Short Heath have been taken in for crofts in recent centuries. All the remaining moorland is covered with peat-cutting striations and scattered 'hut-rectangles': the blanket peat which once covered the moors has been entirely consumed, though a few peaty morasses remain in shallow valleys. How the Short and Tall Heaths would have developed had the peat been left we cannot say.

The Predannack Downs Nature Reserve (Cornwall Naturalists' Trust) was surveyed by Cambridge Botany School expeditions in 1970 and 1972. It is a plateau sloping gently to a shallow valley on the east and abruptly to a bigger valley on the south. The plateau and gentle slopes carry the expected Tall Heath and Short Heath. Several variants of these were recognized where there has been past cultivation or where slopes are irrigated by springs. Small patches of Mixed and Rock Heaths occur on outcrops and steep slopes in the south (Fig. 14.5).

From prehistory there are a round barrow and two enclosures marked by faint banks in sweeping curves, one of which is partly replaced by a row of stones. The date of the enclosures is unknown; there is a 'British Village', probably Iron Age, a little way down the main valley.

In historic times the area has belonged to Kynance (now a single farm) and the hamlet of Predannack Wollas (= Lower Predannack). The earliest boundary is a strong stone-built hedge, part of the great outer boundary, 2½ miles long, of the outfield of Kynance, now divided into fields. Later another intake was made from the moor, this time by an earth bank and ditch, and was then subdivided into a row of fields of which we are here concerned with two, called Outer Downs Croft and Homer Downs Croft. The remaining moor was known as Predannack Wollas Common and Goon Vean Kynance (= Little Kynance Down). Faint earthen banks and ditches indicate two successive intakes from the Common; the second left a narrow corridor for access to the still-unenclosed land in the south of the area. Four boundary stones stand in a row across this last piece and evidently demarcate the lands of Kynance and Predannack; the prehistoric stone-row was incorporated into this later boundary. All these enclosures are probably medieval. Their slightly sinuous outlines contrast with the straight-edged but Cornish-named croft of Grochall (perhaps Elizabethan). The two Downs Crofts are shown very accurately on a map in the Lanhydrock Atlas of 1695.[508]

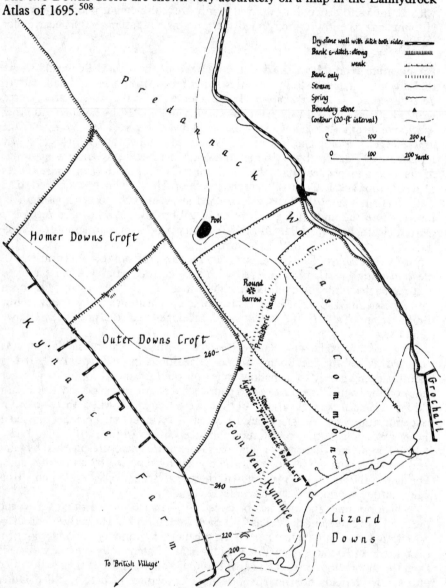

Fig. 14.5. Part of the Predannack Downs on the Lizard Peninsula, Cornwall, showing earthworks and vegetation. Mapped in 1970–2 by D.E. Coombe and the author with the help of students, and also of photographs in Cambridge University Department of Aerial Photography.

Boundary banks run along the streams; it is characteristic of Cornwall that streams between properties are not shared but belong to one side or the other.

Most of the area including old enclosures has been altered by peat-paring but not by cultivation. The prehistoric bank, which ploughing would instantly efface, is unchanged where it is intersected by later banks. Outer and Homer Downs Crofts, however, have been ploughed in the past, and although they have long been moorland their vegetation has become more complex. Variants and intermediates of Tall and Short Heath have been formed, and in places can be seen as stripes corresponding to faint ridge-and-furrow. The loess layer which distinguishes Short from Tall Heath is in places very thin, and once cut through or dispersed by the plough is never restored.

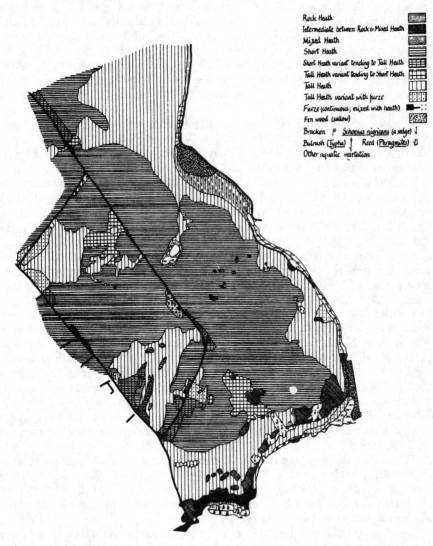

Rock Heath
Intermediate between Rock & Mixed Heath
Mixed Heath
Short Heath
Short Heath variant tending to Tall Heath
Tall Heath variant tending to Short Heath
Tall Heath
Tall Heath variant with furze
Furze (continuous; mixed with heath)
Fen wood (sallow)
Bracken   Schoenus nigricans (a sedge)
Bulrush (Typha)   Reed (Phragmites)
Other aquatic vegetation

Earthworks also affect the vegetation. The barrow, with its increased drainage, is an island of Mixed Heath. Most of the banks have furze, restricted by poor drainage and infertility elsewhere. The corridor leading to Goon Vean Kynance, drained by two ditches, has Mixed Heath and bracken. Some of the streamside banks appear to be the origins from which thickets of sallow and blackthorn are spreading.

Conservation

In general moorland is less threatened than other natural vegetation. It is more extensive than heath, woodland, grassland, and fen put together. About three-quarters of all the moorland that there has ever been still exists. Nor is there a risk that moorland will be lost, as heath and woodland have been, through default and ignorance. Conservationists and the public are well aware of its beauty and interest, and encroachments, if known about, are determinedly and often successfully opposed. The National Parks are concerned with moorland perhaps to the neglect of other, more threatened, wild vegetation. And moorland is inherently more stable than heath or fen; natural changes are less of a problem.

The love of the public for moors and mountains needs no emphasis: I need only mention Loch Lomond, the Pennine Way, the Peak, the Brecon Beacons, Dartmoor. For centuries life in dark Satanic cities has been made liveable by the thought of escape to the freedom and beauty and solitude of the fells.

The British Isles are the world's great moorland countries. Locally there may be some justification for the notion of moorland as 'wet desert' with few plant or animal species. Some moors represent the only kind of native vegetation of which it can be seriously argued that afforestation may increase its biological interest.[509] But this is not true of moorland as a whole, with its varied and complex plant and animal communities, especially in the smaller moorland areas. The importance of the Lizard has at last been officially recognized, after a long period of *laissez-faire*, and several nature reserves and Sites of Scientific Interest have been declared.

Moorland is still being converted to improved grassland and even to arable, sometimes on a large scale. This threatens small and important moorland areas such as the North York Moors. The present public controversy over the ploughing of Exmoor results from the Enclosure Act of 1815, which ended the legal protection of the moor as a Forest and parcelled it out among private owners. The new owners were at liberty to cultivate the moor as soon as they had solved the practical difficulties, which some of them have now done after 170 years. Dartmoor, in contrast, has never had an Enclosure Act and remains mostly intact. Such are the consequences of tampering with the legal status of wild vegetation.

There is a risk that some future technical breakthrough will make it practicable to farm land well outside the bounds of present cultivation. Experience shows that such an 'advance' will rapidly be put to use, regardless of whether the extra produce is needed. There are still people who regard thinly-populated areas as somehow an affront to civilization.

Moorland is still being lost to forestry, though at a diminished rate, and there is a strong possibility that a future Government will resume afforestation. The case for more forestry cannot be dismissed, as can that for more farmland, on the grounds that the Common Market has more than enough already. For

Britain the importing of foreign timber is a genuine economic problem which –
it is often argued – ought to be reduced by growing more timber at home.

No sacrifice of native vegetation can be a complete solution to the problem:
there is not enough land. Not even the most ambitious afforestation proposals
could support the present rate at which we use and waste timber and wood, let
alone any future increase.[509] But moorland, unlike heath and ancient woodland,
is still so extensive that its afforestation might have a measurable, though small
effect on the British timber balance.

It may be argued that to lessen, by a few per cent, the kingdom's dependence
on foreign timber is not a worthy enough cause for sacrificing one of the last
great wildernesses in Europe. It is difficult to make a positive ecological case for
further afforestation: new habitats would indeed be created for plants and
animals, but these are present already in existing plantations, and further
plantations are unlikely to add to them. The area of moorland is so large that the
scientific case against limited and properly planned further inroads is not very
strong. Even the Forestry Commission's most ambitious proposals would still
leave a larger fraction of the original moorland than we now have of woodland
and heath.

The conservationist's attitude to moorland afforestation should be watchful
neutrality. Planting should not be, as often in the past, small-scale, haphazard,
and without attention to what is already there. Small or specialized moorlands
(eg. Exmoor, the Lizard, the flows of Sutherland and Caithness) should not be
planted. I suspect that forestry, ecology, and amenity would be best served by
concentrating plantations in some regions, leaving others wholly unplanted. To
sacrifice almost the whole of some less important region of moorland, in return
for the complete preservation of more important regions, would solve many
problems. A plantation which runs over hill and valley for miles would reduce
the unsightly edges which are unpopular; it would avoid much of the trouble
with deer; and it would satisfy modern foresters, who work best on a large scale.
Let us not chop up the moors into fragments as we have done the heaths. I have
yet to hear a word of objection against the great Kielder Forest (Northumberland).

Natural threats to moorland are not entirely negligible. Trees encroach,
though slowly, even at high altitudes. The famous Wistman's Wood, supposed
to be a relict at 1400 feet on Dartmoor, has nearly doubled its area since 1890.[510]
Trees might be welcomed as adding to the variety and interest of moorland, but
unfortunately the spots most likely to be colonized are rocky patches which
already diversify the scenery and vegetation.

Nor is moorland management always ideal. There are complaints of too little
grazing (as on the North York Moors) and of too much (as on Dartmoor). In
many Scottish Forests the deer are poorly managed and not enough are shot.
Grouse-keeping flourishes, and is no longer quite so destructive as it used to be
of beasts and birds of prey, nor does it generate quite so much ill-will between
landowners and keepers and the public. It cannot be said of the grouse, as it can
of the pheasant and partridge, that gamekeeping maintains an otherwise endangered habitat, but it may well be that the burning of grouse-moors preserves
heather from being replaced by other wild plants. Burning, however, even if
well organized, is a second-best land management: at best it destroys both the
animals and plants that are sensitive to fire, and the creatures that specifically
need *old* heather.

CHAPTER 15

Grassland

> Until recently (within 60 years) most of the chalk district was open and covered
> with a beautiful coating of turf, profusely decorated with *Anemone Pulsatilla*,
> *Astragalus Hypoglottis*, and other interesting plants. It is now converted into arable
> land, and its peculiar plants mostly confined to small waste spots by road-sides,
> pits, and the very few banks which are too steep for the plough. Thus many species
> which were formerly abundant have become rare; so rare as to have caused an
> unjust suspicion of their not really being natives to arise in the minds of some
> modern botanists. Even the tumuli, entrenchments, and other interesting works of
> the ancient inhabitants have seldom escaped the rapacity of the modern agricultur-
> ist, who too frequently looks upon the native plants of the country as weeds, and
> its antiquities as deformities.
>
> C. C. Babington, *Flora of Cambridgeshire, 1860*
> (The plants mentioned are pasque-flower and purple milk-vetch.)

This chapter is about the historic grassland of old pasture and meadow, churchyards and college lawns, clifftops, and wood-pasture launds. Such grasslands are
the classic 'semi-natural' vegetation. They are natural in that the plants are wild
and have not been sown; they are artificial in that they were formed, and are
maintained, by civilization. All sites of old grassland, almost without exception,
were once wildwood and revert to woodland in a few decades if not grazed or
mown.

I am not concerned with the sown grasslands which form the greater part of
those in the British Isles. Most meadow and pasture is sown with varieties of
ryegrass, timothy, clover, etc. bred for the purpose, and is ploughed up and
resown every ten years or so as it gets 'worn out'. It is hardly less an arable crop
than fields of wheat or barley which are annual grasslands.

For an introduction to old grassland I refer the reader to the book *Grassland
ecology and wildlife management* (Duffey 1974). The study of historic grassland
is, alas, mainly English: little is yet known of the history of the old grassland of
Wales, Scotland, or Ireland.

Kinds of Grassland

Meadow is grassland which is mown for hay; *pasture* is grazed by farm animals.
This is a fundamental distinction throughout Europe – for example French *pré*
and *prairie*, German *Wiese* and *Weide*, Latin *pratum* and *pascuum* – and may well
go back to the Iron Age. Before the invention of the scythe, mowing would have
been difficult, and sometimes tree-leaves were dried instead of grass (p.243).
Meadow has been sited, where possible, on land liable to flooding by moving

water. Until recently this was the best land and was reserved for this special purpose. Some limestone grasslands are deliberately burnt, but burning presupposes insufficient grazing and is unlikely to be an ancient practice.

Meadow and pasture are of many kinds; even the sad remnants now left to us are nearly as rich in variation as woodland. Grassland plants, and the communities that they compose, vary according to soil acidity and texture, flooding, slope, aspect, altitude, whether grazed and by what animals, whether mown and at what season, and management history.

A simple example of two types of grassland close together is the pasture, which may be up to 600 years old, on the ridge-and-furrow of medieval arable. In spring the ridges are yellow with buttercups, and the furrows, where water lies, are pink with cuckoo-flower. A more elaborate comparison was made by H. Baker, fifty years ago, among the Oxford flood-meadows. Pixey, Oxey (since destroyed), and Yarnton Meads have a history of centuries of mowing. Port Meadow is similar in all other respects, but (despite its name) has a history of grazing. Their plants are very different. Baker recorded 39 species as growing only on the meads, 26 only on Port Meadow, and 30 species on both. Meadowsweet, sorrel, oxeye, and salad burnet are easily destroyed by grazing but withstand mowing; yarrow, picnic-thistle (*Cirsium acaule*), and some buttercups tolerate grazing but are not found on the hay-meads.[511] Among other reasons, mowing and grazing happen at different times of year, and animals pick and choose what they bite but the scythe does not.

A study of neutral grasslands (those on soils that are neither acid nor basic) has listed three ordinary and twelve distinctive types.[512] A study of Scottish grasslands lists nineteen types.[513] The two lists do not much overlap, and there are doubtless many other kinds still undiscovered or now lost. Grasslands are difficult to study because many of the plants can be recognized only in early summer. A whole book has been written on the grasslands within 20 miles of Sheffield.[514]

Beginnings of Grassland

Trees are the natural vegetation in our latitude round most of the world. Grassland is the commonest alternative in places that are too dry or too high for trees or grazed too much by wild beasts. These influences work together: a given amount of grazing (or of human activity) produces grassland more easily where the climate is marginal for tree growth. In the Alps, most of the high-altitude woodland has for centuries been replaced by meadow and pasture; at middle altitudes woodland is still continuous, with only enclaves of grassland. In North America, the first white men found mainly wildwood in what are now the eastern States, and prairies on the Great Plains. The boundary between the two lay westward of the Mississippi, where the climate becomes too dry for trees, but was not sharp: islands of prairie extended eastward, occasionally right to the east coast. Prairies and woods were determined by a combination of climate, grazing, fire, and Red Indian land management. White men's interference often caused prairie to become invaded by woodland, especially in the eastern outliers.[515] In middle Texas, the prairies were once maintained by great herds of buffalo. The buffalo were exterminated in the last century, and the longhorn cattle which replaced them are now in turn declining; the trees now have only drought to contend with, and I have seen them advancing into what has been prairie for millennia.

Grassland

What natural grassland might there have been in Britain? Our climate is much too wet for grassland without plenty of grazing. We had wild cattle and deer, but (in this interglacial period) no beasts on the majestic scale of the American buffalo herds. Our pre-Neolithic folk had not the advantage of inflammable trees and grasses, which enabled Red Indians to create and maintain grassland by burning. Natural grassland would have been confined to high altitudes, to such areas as were not peat-blanketed in the far north, and to occasional spots (perhaps in dry areas such as the Breckland, or on very infertile soils as in Teesdale[516]) where wild animals congregated. Very windswept coastal clifftops are another possibility: wind-exposure would not prevent trees from growing, but might stunt them so that animals could browse their tops.

Prehistoric pollen and plant remains confirm that grassland was rare before civilization. We know little of the grasses themselves, for all grass pollen looks alike, and when found in a lake deposit it may be that of surrounding reed-beds rather than of grasses in grassland. More can be said of the herbaceous plants of grassland. Most produce only small amounts of pollen, but enough pollen grains, as well as fossil fruits, etc., have been identified for the prehistory of many grassland herbs to be quite well known.

At an earlier period, towards the end of the last glaciation, much of the country had been covered with semi-arctic grassland. When the trees moved in, grassland became very rare from about 10,000 to 4000 BC. In the mountains trees went much higher than now (p.306); wildwood evidently extended nearly to the limit set by climate, unlike what happens in the Alps today. When Neolithic men came, the pollen record shows the sudden reappearance of grasses (as well as cereals) and grassland herbs. Grassland, more completely than moorland, is a product of the transformation of the landscape which began in 4000 BC and continued into Roman times. The only wholly natural grassland is small areas on high mountains.

Where did grassland plants come from? Surprisingly few were introduced by Neolithic men. Some, such as white clover, may be new species (p.60); others, such as meadowsweet, grow in woodland as well as grassland. The majority came from surviving fragments of the late-glacial grassland (Table 15.1) Species after species, both of meadow and pasture, has abundant remains dating from late in the last glaciation, followed by a gap in the record, and then by a sudden reappearance. This is true even of plants that are now relatively southern: salad-burnet (*Poterium sanguisorba*) and the rock-rose *Helianthemum canum* both grew in the semi-arctic grassland. Meadows and pastures, although now well-defined plant communities, have put themselves together mainly from a selection of plants that once grew in places too high or too far north for wildwood.

A few grassland plants did survive at low altitudes. Occasional pollen grains or fruits show that ragged robin, self-heal, and others persisted as rarities through the wildwood period. Significantly, most of these plants now grow in woodland grassland (p.109) as well as in meadow or pasture. The woodland rides and margins of today evidently had some counterpart in wildwood. Whether this was the work of Mesolithic men is controversial: undoubtedly they were less effective in making glades than Red Indians. In earlier interglacials a wider range of grassland plants persisted, and in greater numbers: glades were evidently less rare, as a result of the action of the great beasts that then lived or of Palaeolithic men, than in the very continuous wildwood of the post-glacial period.

Table 15.1 Some grassland plants which are recorded from the Late-Glacial (From H. Godwin, *History of the British flora.*)

Now mainly in meadow	Now mainly in pasture	Now in woodland grassland
Meadow-rue *Thalictrum flavum**	Violet *Viola canina*	Buttercup *Ranunculus repens**
Bird's-foot Trefoil *Lotus corniculatus*	Rock-rose *Helianthemum chamaecistus* and *H. canum*	Cuckoo-flower *Cardamine pratensis**
Burnet *Sanguisorba officinalis*	Pinks *Dianthus* species	Ragged Robin *Lychnis flos-cuculi**
Meadow Saxifrage *Saxifraga granulata*	Lesser Stitchwort *Stellaria graminea*	Self-heal *Prunella vulgaris**
Sorrel *Rumex acetosa**	Purging Flax *Linum catharticum*	Bugle *Ajuga reptans*
Hay-rattle *Rhinanthus minor*	Sainfoin *Onobrychis viciifolia*	Devil's-bit *Succisa pratensis**
Oxeye *Chrysanthemum leucanthemum*	Wild Parsnip *Pastinaca sativa**	
	Sheep's Sorrel *Rumex acetosella*	
	Gentian *Gentianella campestris*	
	Marjoram *Origanum vulgare*	

* Plants for which there is evidence that they survived at low altitudes through the wildwood period.

Prehistoric Grassland

Some prehistoric farmland was grassland and some was arable. Most farmers kept livestock, and often (especially in mountains) pastoral farming predominated. Many of the great traditional grasslands, Highland and Lowland, have barrows and henges which prove that they had lost their trees no later than the Bronze Age. Neolithic long barrows are often sited where they are to be seen from afar, and the astronomical relationships of Stonehenge presuppose an unobstructed horizon. Neolithic and Bronze Age men created much of the downland of the chalk, and also made grassland at previously wooded altitudes in the mountains.

Not all grassland has been stable. 'Celtic fields' and other remains show that vast areas of downland were once under the plough. Grassland has at different times been made out of arable; it has also been lost to heath or moorland (p.308) or bracken. Some chalk grassland was originally chalk-heath (p.283) from which an acid topsoil has eroded away.

We know less of the origin of flood-plain meadows and of the smaller areas of grassland. By the Iron Age, many river terraces were densely populated, and it would be surprising if full use were not made of the flood-lands.

Traditional Management and Uses

Almost any land that is treated as grassland becomes grassland. A wood to which cattle or sheep are admitted loses its woodland plants and quickly turns into grassland with trees (Chapter 6). A stubble-field, if grazed but not ploughed or sown, becomes pasture within a few years, though it may take centuries to gain all the characteristic grassland plants.

Making grassland, although easy, took some years to produce a good pasture, and hence farmers and their landlords traditionally regarded pasture, and especially meadow, as a fixture: they were reluctant to plough it up even if this appeared to be profitable. Sowing of pasture was known in the sixteenth century and was developed, with the growing of clovers and lucerne for seed, in the seventeenth (Kerridge 1967). In the eighteenth century short-term grassland became usual in crop rotations. Nevertheless much meadow and pasture continued to be treated as 'permanent' until World War II.

Some kinds of grassland are manured: the beautiful meadows of Alpine villages are regularly dunged or watered with muck-heap effluent. But large doses of chemical fertilizer have almost the same effect on grassland as weed-killers. Both treatments quickly and permanently convert distinctive meadows and pastures into ordinary ones. Out of the rich mixtures of plants, one or two strong-growing species are favoured, get the upper hand, and suppress the others. The result is the sward of coarse grasses, with clovers and perhaps a few buttercups and thistles, that in Britain is called 'improved' grassland.

The division of grassland into meadow and pasture has to do with feeding animals round the year. Until the tractor was invented every parish, and almost every farm, had both ploughland and livestock. The livestock could feed on pasture for much of the year, but from January to April there was a hungry period when grass was not growing. The horses and oxen that drew ploughs were working hard at this time and had to be fed well, not merely kept alive. Hence the practice of storing hay. Hay had to be cut rapidly and laboriously by hand, and risked spoiling in bad weather. The best grassland, on which the crop grew thickest, was therefore reserved for hay.

In theory every farm should have had access to a minimum of meadow and pasture to keep the beasts of the plough. In practice we find no close correlation between ploughing and meadow. Hay was needed by the horses of towns and monasteries, and many farms grew it for cash. Although root crops, later a staple winter fodder, were not grown before 1650 (Kerridge 1967), there were alternatives to hay. Straw, stubble, and weeds on fallow land might not have been very nutritious, but there was plenty of them: at least a quarter of the arable land of medieval England was fallow, and was used as pasturage, at any one time. There was some sustenance in brambles etc. in wood-pasture. And it was not unknown to feed oxen on corn.

A less obvious function of pasture and meadow was to fertilize arable land. The soil slowly lost fertility – as it now does more rapidly – by minerals leached out by rain, or removed in crops and transferred, via the human body, to middens, gardens, and churchyards. Before fertilizers were imported, these minerals were replaced from the dung of animals that had fed on grassland. Sheep, especially, could be fed on pasture during the day and folded on arable at night, which saved the trouble of handling the dung. Hence the complicated foldcourse customs of medieval East Anglia, and the usual requirement that a tenant should fold his sheep on his lord's land. Later it was often said, at least in books, that the dung of sheep was more valuable than wool or meat.

Anglo-Saxon Meadow and Pasture

The Romans in Britain had scythes and presumably used them on meadow. The first written evidence of grassland management is in a grant by King Hlothere of Kent, dated 679, of an estate in Thanet with meadows (Latin *prata*) and pastures (*pascua*).[517] Many Anglo-Saxon charters mention meadow and pasture as part of the land being conveyed. Meadow is often specially mentioned as an unusual kind of land, sometimes detached from the rest of an estate. At Harwell and Sunningwell (Berkshire) and three other places the meadows have their own little perambulations, like those of detached woods (p.79).

Place-names and charter boundaries have six terms for grassland. 'Meadow', of which 'mead' is a variant representing the nominative case, presents no difficulty: Old English *mǣd* is derived from the verb *māwan*, to mow. The charters contain 101 instances of *mǣd* plus sixteen place-names derived from meads. Meadows, like woods, often had names of their own. Meadows are often mentioned in Essex, South Worcestershire, the Vale of Evesham, and the Mendips, but not at all in North-East England, the Woodless Cotswolds, Hampshire-Sussex Downs, Isle of Wight, Devon, or Cornwall. *Mǣd* is a frequent element in place-names (eg. Runny*mede*) from Lancashire to Suffolk, Kent, and Somerset.

Another word for meadow may be *lēah*, from which are derived 'ley', meaning grassland that has formerly been arable, and 'lea', the poetic habitat of lowing herds. Etymologists usually suppose that this Old English word, of the masculine gender, is the same as the feminine *lēah* meaning 'clearing' or 'wood'. My reading of the charters is that they are distinct words: most instances of *lēah* are feminine and are associated with concentrations of woodland (p.83); a minority are masculine and refer to places on low ground well away from woodland. This kind of *lēah*, where it can be distinguished, is chiefly in areas where *mǣd* is rare or absent. I suggest that this early form of 'ley' is used as an alternative word for 'mead'. If this is correct, meadows were abundant in most of Hampshire, the Reading Basin, and the north-west and east Midlands. Masculine *lēah* is uncommon in place-names, but may be responsible for the few exceptions (eg. Hor*ley*, Oxfordshire) to the rule that -*ley* names went with woodland.

Hamm, which occurs 119 times in charters, is often translated 'water-meadow'; but it really only means a place on a flood-plain, and there is no evidence as to whether it was meadow or pasture. It occurs in place-names, but is difficult to distinguish from the much commoner *ham* 'home'. Examples are East *Ham* (Essex), Crook*ham* (Berkshire), High *Ham* (Somerset). *Hamm* has a south-western tendency and is commonest in Somerset.

Gerstun, 'grass-town', occurs thirteen times in charters and as the place-name Garston. In the Medmeney perambulation it is glossed *pratum* 'meadow';[518] but a 'horse-grass-town' at Wylye (Wiltshire) suggests pasture.

Lǣs is known from Biblical translations to mean 'pasture'. It gives rise to the modern 'leaze', of which 'leasow' is an inflexion as 'meadow' is of 'mead'. It occurs only five times in charters, but is frequent in place-names, especially in East Anglia (eg. *Lez*iate, Bec*cles*). It is often mistaken for the plural of 'ley'.

Edisc is a puzzle. The late-medieval *eddish* meant the after-growth of hay.[519] In the charters *edisc* is a piece of land; literary evidence suggests pasture. The word occurs ten times in charters, and also in East Anglian place-names (eg. Brock*dish*).

By Anglo-Saxon times meadow occurred in most of the area covered by the charters, but there is little evidence for it in Devon, Cornwall, the Fens, or the north. The slight evidence for pasture probably means that it was too common-place to be distinctive. When beating the bounds across a chalk down the thorns, dells, stones, 'heathen burials', etc. were noted; the downland itself was not noteworthy. Meadow and pasture are occasionally mentioned as being communal.

Domesday Book

Meadow Meadow is the best-recorded land-use in Domesday. There are well over 10,000 entries of '*x* acres of meadow'. Nobody has ever added them up, but I have done some approximate sums.*

Meadow was a special kind of land: in all of Domesday England there were only some 300,000 acres, about 1.2 per cent of the land area,† less than arable, pasture, wood, moor, or heath. But it was very well scattered; at least eight settlements out of ten had meadow, compared to only five having wood. Wiltshire was typical: out of 335 settlements, 283 possessed meadows, but usually only 20 acres or less. All the meadows in Wiltshire came to some 8,000 acres, less than 1 per cent of the county.

About one-sixth of the meadow in England was in Lincolnshire. The Lindsey sub-county had some 44,000 acres, 4½ per cent of the land. This was in unexpected contrast to Norfolk and Suffolk. In Suffolk meadow added up to a mere 0.6 per cent of the county, though three places out of four possess a little. There was even less meadow in Devon or Yorkshire (except the Holderness Peninsula), and remarkably little in Cornwall or Cheshire.

In the counties of Cambridge, Bedford, Buckingham, Hertford, and Middlesex the returns are in the form 'meadow for *x* ploughs' or 'for *y* oxen', evidently meaning the amount which would feed so many beasts of the plough. This makes the calculation indefinite, but establishes the important fact that the number of ploughs for which there was meadow was often less than, but very rarely more than, the number of ploughs existing. Elsworth (Cambridgeshire), for instance, had eighteen ploughs but meadow for four ploughs. I estimate that non-Fenland Cambridgeshire and the northern half of Buckinghamshire had nearly as much meadow in proportion as Lindsey.

Meadow was commonest in Lincolnshire and the east Midlands. It was more thinly scattered in areas of ancient enclosure; it was conspicuously rare in the big concentrations of woodland such as the Weald and Chilterns, and also in the Fens.

The Anglo-Saxon and Norman evidence, taken together, shows that the practice of meadow was slow in being fully adopted. England in 1086 had at least as much arable land as in 1500, but much less meadow. Meadow had spread to every part of the country, but countless places had only an acre or two

---

* The records do not cover Shropshire, Lancashire, or the four northern counties.
† I assume that the acre for meadow was the same as the modern acre; it matters little to my conclusions if the acre was bigger.

and many (even in Lincolnshire) managed without it. It was not confined to the most suitable flood-plain land: many places which lacked good meadowland already had meadows. Nor is there a clear relation between ploughing and meadow. Where ploughs were so thick on the ground that it ought to have been difficult to feed the oxen, as in east Norfolk and the Sussex coastal plain, there was at most an average proportion of meadowland.

We have no evidence that meadow began earlier in one type of landscape than another. But it developed more rapidly among the communal enterprise, villages, and open-field farming of the Planned Countryside. In the 'do-it-yourself' landscape of what is now Ancient Countryside, meadow was hardly beyond the experimental stage by 1086. The lack of meadow in the south-west can perhaps be explained by the extensive pasture and the long growing season. But I cannot explain why the men of Lincolnshire should have specialized in meadow, or what they did with so much hay.

Pasture Pasture is mentioned sporadically throughout Domesday England, but only in the five south-western counties and perhaps Oxfordshire is there an attempt at a complete record. Pasture is normally recorded as measuring x furlongs by y; the bigger pastures are measured in leagues. I shall convert the figures, approximately, to modern acres as I did for woodland (p.75). About one place in four – in Somerset one place in two – is given as not having pasture; these include some places that did have sheep. I cannot believe that any settlement really lacked pasture for its livestock, and therefore infer that the record, while giving a general picture of where the pasture was, is less thorough than that of the other land-uses.

For Dorset, pasture adds up to some 177,000 acres, about 28 per cent of the land area. Arable – 2287 ploughlands at 120 acres each – works out at 274,000 acres (44 per cent of Dorset); woodland at 81,000 acres (13 per cent); meadow at 7000 acres (1 per cent). All the land-uses together account for 86 per cent of Dorset, a reasonable fit given the roughness of the data and of the arithmetic. Dorset in the eleventh century was roughly half arable, three-eighths grassland and heath, and one-eighth woodland. One-quarter of the pasture was in the south-east of the county and is to be equated with the Dorset heaths (p.291). Most of the remainder represents the chalk downs (Fig. 15.1); in 1086 nearly half of middle Dorset was chalk grassland. There was a thin scatter of pasture in the more highly cultivated north and west.

Figures for Wiltshire show pasture concentrated in Salisbury Plain and the other chalklands, but very little in the claylands or the Cotswolds. The proportion of pasture, especially on the Marlborough Downs, is less than on the Dorset chalk, which suggests some cultivation of what was downland in later centuries.

Pasture for Cornwall adds up to a third of the county, and for Devon to 9 per cent; both figures relate largely to moorland and are certainly underestimates (p.312). The Somerset entries account mainly for Exmoor and the Mendips, but there was also pasture in the Levels.

Another approach to Domesday pasture is by counting the animals for which it was the main livelihood. England, as covered in 1086, had 81,000 ploughs, theoretically drawn by 648,000 oxen, which with the necessary cows, calves, and bulls implies a million cattle for this purpose alone. There can hardly have been less than 2 million sheep, even if one sheep sufficed to clothe each person. At 5 acres per beast and 1 acre per sheep we have already used up most of the

335

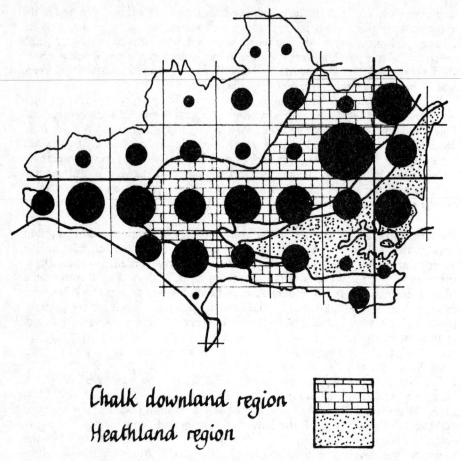

Chalk downland region

Heathland region

Fig. 15.1. Area of pasture in Dorset in 1086, as recorded by Domesday Book. Each black circle represents, at the scale of the map, the total area of pasture possessed by places within its 10-km square.

one-third of England – some 9 million acres – not accounted for by arable, wood, meadow, settlement, and dereliction; and we have yet to provide for dairy cattle or the unnumbered beasts of towns, transport, religion, and war. I can hardly guess how much of the 9 million acres was grassland rather than moor or heath.

The evidence, such as it is, suggests that by 1086 most of the big downlands already existed; there was also pasture scattered in greens, commons, and fields throughout the country. Some places evidently specialized in pasture; others must have had difficulty in feeding even the plough oxen.

Grassland Since 1250

Medieval meadow and pasture Surveys of the thirteenth century and onwards make precise lists of named meadows and pastures, distinguishing those that

336

were private from those that were common. The *Ely Coucher Book* of 1251 says of Little Gransden (Cambridgeshire):

> *Mowing meadow*, viz. In Weldis under Heyle wood thirteen acres.
> *Private* (seperati) *pasture*, viz. What is called Grauis [= Groves], twenty-five acres, where the plough-oxen of the parson of Grantesdene can feed with the Bishop's oxen.
> *Item*, there is a certain pasture which is called Langelund, and it is common to all the village.[19]

On the Bishop of Ely's bigger estate at Barking (Suffolk), the *Coucher Book* mentions meadows called Brademede, Roseburg, and Keneboldsmede. Under private pasture are listed Bromhill, Mersh, Sydbrok, and

> a certain way which is called Hallestrete which is the lord's private pasture, which begins at the white poplar (*abel*) beside Esthach [= East Gate] and continues up to the pasture of Wilfrid Herner for two furlongs.[19]

There was also 'a certain common of pasture which is called Berkingetye', 90 acres.

The England of 1250 was more crowded than in 1086; grassland was scarcer and more fully used. Meadow has increased; much of the country now had something like the 4 per cent of meadow which had been a Lincolnshire speciality in Domesday. The increase was probably at the expense of pasture.

Pasture and especially meadow were very valuable land. Typical land values are given in a survey of Latton (Essex) in 1269–70: 239 acres of arable valued at 6*d.* per acre per annum, 4 acres of wood-pasture at 6*d.*, 6 acres of private pasture at 12*d.*, and 28½ acres of meadow valued at 2*s.*[520] At Bocking (Essex) in 1309, arable (510 acres) was valued at 6*d.* per acre per annum, private pasture (30 acres, including the narrow ways leading to it) at 12*d.*, and meadow (14 acres) at the exeptional figure of 4*s.* per acre per annum; the monks who owned the manor had common-rights for 100 sheep.[521]

Meadow took up all the land suitable for it and some that was unsuitable. The records give the impression that by the thirteenth century most flood-plains, even of small streams, were meadows; this is shown to be so on the earliest maps 300 years later. This is why ancient woods never adjoin rivers unless the banks are too steep for meadow (p.98). At Little Gransden, lacking a flood-plain, the meadow was in 'the Wilds under Hayley Wood'. The place is a hilltop, and although it can flood the water does not flow and would not make a good meadow; yet there seems to have already been a meadow in 1086. Here, as usual, tenants were required to make the lord's hay as a labour service.

Common pastures varied from thousands of acres of downland to the 90 acres of Barking Tye (which still exists) and the acre or so of innumerable hamlet greens such as Pierce Williams Green in Hatfield Broad-oak, Essex (PresWilliamesgrene 1444).[274] A grassland common was legally the same as a wood-pasture common (p.121) and was regulated by the manorial courts in exactly the same way.

There were common as well as private meadows. A few are still extant, such as Port Holme near Huntingdon and the great meads around Oxford and Cricklade. Common meads were divided into strips called *doles*, the lord and each commoner having the hay on one or more doles. After the hay was cut, the meadow was usually grazed as common pasture for the rest of the season. Doles, unlike the curved strips of common arable, were defined by straight lines between stakes. They were often reallocated each year. At Bratton (Wiltshire) the meadow in the 1540s was private one year and common the next.[522] I know a man who owns a 'ball' in Pixey Mead near Oxford – a wooden ball still used in the annual draw for the hay on the doles.

Strip-systems in meadow were more widespread than in arable: for instance, Hatfield Broad-oak had no strip-cultivation but did have a strip-meadow.

Changes in the later Middle Ages After the Black Death in 1340, the shrunken population could not use all the arable land. At Little Gransden in 1356 the Bishop had 400 acres of ploughland

> of which 100 acres have lain derelict (*frisce*) for the past 4 years and are worth nothing a year because they lie in the common for the whole year.[120]

The remaining 300 acres were sown one year and taken into the common the next. Eventually the villagers took over all the Bishop's arable and meadow and added them to their own common pasture and arable. All went well until in 1599 Queen Elizabeth confiscated the manor and sold it to one Richard Skipwith. He, having found 'one old booke called the Byshopps Cowcher', discovered what the demesne lands had been in 1251 and tried to get them back. This involved fifty years of litigation, during which the estate changed hands nine times. The villagers fought both in the courts and on occasion 'with Gunns, pistolls, halberts, pikes, swords, pitchforks, great Clubbs and some of the women with stones in their Aprons'. In 1607 the evidence was called of Christopher Meade, an archaeologist, as to the distribution of ridge-and-furrow, which – it was appreciated – proved where ploughland had been. A small patch of this ridge-and-furrow still exists (Rackham 1975).

Little Gransden is a picturesque example of the change from arable to pasture that happened all over England in the later Middle Ages; it was very conspicuous in the Midlands and perhaps Wiltshire. Not all pasture on Midland ridge-and-furrow is of the 1350s; some – like some deserted villages – may be as late as the eighteenth century. But the change was well advanced by 1500. Sometimes the lord got rid of the tenants and sometimes the tenants got rid of the lord. An important influence (though not at Little Gransden) is the growth of the wool and cloth trades: sheep were more valuable than corn. In Leicestershire and Northamptonshire many lawyers and men of substance bought up estates and ranched sheep where there had been open-fields.

Water-meadows After 1500 there came the growth of that supreme technical achievement of English farming, the irrigated water-meadow.

Irrigated meadows are an ancient and elaborate practice in Italy and the Alps; in the Zermatt Valley, Switzerland, canals have been contrived right up to the glaciers. The earliest known allusion in England is in 1523:

> . . . yf there be any rynning water or lande flode that may be sette or brought to ronne ouer the medowes from the tyme that they be mowen vnto the begynning of

May / and they will be moche the bettr and it shall kylle / drowne / & driue awaye the moldywarpes* / and fyll vp the lowe places with sande & make the grounde euyn and good to mowe. All maner of waters be good / so that they stande nat styll vpon the grounde. But specially that water that cometh out of a towne from euery mannes myddingt or donghyll is best / and will make the medowes moost rankest. And fro the begynning of May tyll ye medowes be mowen and the hay goten in / the waters wolde be set by and ron another way /

        J. Fitzherbert, *The boke of surveying and improvments.*

---

* Moles.
† Midden.

Fitzherbert seems to write from familiarity, but no contemporary account is known of water-meadows in actual operation; they could hardly have gone unrecorded because of the annual cost of maintaining the works. Corroboration comes from an order of the manor court of Affpuddle (Dorset) in 1607 that the waterworks of the common meadow are to be used 'in noe other sorte than in auncient time it hath been used'.[523] This must antedate the claim by one Richard Vaughan to have invented water-meadows in the Golden Valley, Herefordshire, in the 1580s.[524] The practice evidently spread rapidly in Wiltshire and Dorset, where it was widespread by 1620.

A water-meadow is engineered with an elaborate system of channels, levelled to within a fraction of an inch. Water is led off from the river at a weir into channels called *carriages* which distribute it over the meadow. It overflows the carriages and flows over the surface to be caught in channels called *drawns* which return it to a lower point on the river. In the simpler *catchwork* system the water flows from carriage to drawn by the natural slope of the ground. On absolutely level meadows there is a system called *floating*, whereby the water flows down the sides of ridge-and-furrow constructed in order to produce a slope of about 1½°. Meadows need yearly maintenance by a professional *drowner*, especially if cattle have been trampling the little channels.

Floating a meadow increased the crop of hay – the more modest claims were of a fourfold increase. It also advanced the growing season, which was made use of for keeping sheep during the hungry season of early spring. A usual downland practice was to irrigate the meadows in winter; to turn off the water in March and let the sheep (by then near lambing) pasture the young grass; to take the sheep off in late April and let the grass grow up to hay for two months. In summer the meadow might either be used as pasture or be irrigated again for more crops of hay.[525, 526] The main purpose of irrigation was not to prevent drought. The water fertilized the grass with calcium out of chalk springs; it brought nitrate and phosphate from the leachings of arable, the dung of roads and farmyards, and even the sewage of Winchester.[527] And it was supposed to warm the grass, since the river, especially if fed from deep springs, would normally be warmer in winter than the air.

The rewards of floating outweighed the capital cost of the works and the damage done to the meadow in setting them up. Despite its complexity, it was not always the work of private landowners. Many groups of commoners contrived to agree upon, and to pay for, the irrigating of meadows. Thus the men of Wylye (Wiltshire) in 1632 hired John Knight of Stockton, a professional, to float the common meadow.[525]

The Decline of Wild Grassland

By 1700 grass and clover seeds had become articles of commerce, which made it possible to treat pasture as merely another arable crop; but it was to be more than a century until sown grass was fully acceptable as a substitute for old grassland. More important were the Enclosure Acts which abolished many grassland commons and brought the turf under the whim of private ownership.

The remarks of a Cambridge Professor of Botany, quoted at the head of the chapter, are typical of the destruction of chalk grassland in the early nineteenth century. From Royston to Flamborough Head, 170 miles of downland were almost annihilated. The southern downland was less completely destroyed, although Dorset lost more than half its area. Some of the chalkland was a failure as arable and reverted to grass, but never recovered the full grassland flora. Destruction was resumed in the mid-nineteenth century and again, after a lull, more thoroughly than ever since World War II. Dorset now has less than a twelfth of the chalk downland of 1800 — an even smaller proportion than of the heathland. The total for the whole country was estimated at 108,000 acres in 1966 (two-thirds of this in Wiltshire) and is much less now.[528]

Meadows fared even worse, though later. Irrigated meadows are too sophisticated and require too much attention to detail to be successful in the twentieth century; with only one or two exceptions, they have fallen into neglect. Other meadows mostly survived until 1945, but by far the greatest number have been drained and ploughed, planted with poplars, or at best have become pasture. The matter is made worse by the polarization of arable and livestock farming into different parts of the country, so that each no longer uses the other's by-products and unsuitable land.

Even where a meadow or pasture appears to survive, it has usually been improved with fertilizer and weedkiller and is now little different from sown grassland. Not that this mania for improvement is a necessary part of twentieth-century enlightenment. In the Alps improvement is understood differently: from Dauphiné to Slovenia mixed meadows and pastures are the rule and not the exception, brilliant with rampion and oxeye, scabious and cranesbill, and many umbellifers and orchids. These plants are not weeds: Alpine farmers, who are at least as skilled stockmen as we, regard hay containing fewer than a dozen plant species as unfit for bovine consumption.

People still destroy old grassland, and think of clever ways of getting at the last scraps on steep slopes. Unexpected people do it. The pastures of the Wimpole estate – not outstanding, but the most extensive long-established grassland in Cambridgeshire – received less 'improvement' from its last private owner than it has been subjected to since by the National Trust. Roadside verges have suffered in turn from fashions for weedkiller, for too much mowing at the wrong time of year, and for not mowing at all. Railway verges suffer from the lazy practice of heaping waste ballast on one side instead of taking it away. Old grassland in private lawns is hated by gardening writers, who persuade us to despise daisies and to make grass look like plastic grass. The Ministry of Works set a bad example with the surroundings of historic ruins. The fashion for imitating plastic grass has involved the once sacred lawns of colleges and has desecrated churchyards. I have even known people try to destroy fairy-rings, despite the curse on disturbing them.*

---

* An honourable exception are the Salisbury Lawns of Chatsworth, which date from the 1760s and are still treasured for the beauty of their flowers.[614]

Grassland does not disappear by plough and poison alone; it also turns into woodland. In the Mendips, Brockley and Goblin Combes have lost their grassland through tree growth, and the limestone grassland of Cheddar Gorge, with its many rare plants, is about to suffer the same fate. Most of the commons around London are now undistinguished secondary woodland. Detached fragments of grassland are difficult to maintain: some, as on the Devil's Ditch near Newmarket, were kept going for a time by rabbits, but after myxomatosis struck in 1954 hawthorns strode in. Hillsides of grassland have been overrun by bracken. Disused grassland, at best, becomes tussocky and loses its smaller and more precious plants.

Grassland can be spoilt by quite small changes of management, such as mowing instead of grazing or cattle instead of sheep. Altering the time of mowing may change a meadow's character, although slowly as most meadow plants are long-lived and do not have to flower every year. Gang-mowers, as used in municipal parks, are pernicious: the mowings are not used but are left to rot, which in the long term has much the same effect as a dose of fertilizer.

Grasslands As They Are Now

Historic grassland – where the plant community itself is of long standing – survives by the square mile in some Highland areas such as Teesdale, and in three areas protected by the military, namely Salisbury Plain and Porton Down (Wiltshire) and the Stanford Battle Area (Norfolk). Up and down the country there are thousands of fragments, and many more remain to be discovered. Some are on steep or difficult terrain: my native river Waveney has resisted being tamed and, alone among East Anglian rivers, still has the 25 miles of meadow of my childhood. Some are protected – for one lifetime – by an old-fashioned or public-spirited owner. Grassland survives on many commons and greens through being no one person's property. Tracts exist precariously as golf-courses, race-courses, and playing-fields. There are countless scraps, usually ungrazed and threatened by trees, on road and railway verges, cliff edges, prehistoric earthworks, and old quarries. For example, Dr Margaret Atherden's researches in the Tabular Hills, an area of 150 square miles south of the North York Moors, have detected 91 areas of limestone grassland, a third of them on quarries and all but nine of them being less than 12 acres in extent.[529]

Distinctiveness of ancient grassland Can old grassland be re-created? It might be thought so: downland ploughed long ago is often not strikingly different from ancient unploughed areas. An excellent tract of old grassland is the Hills and Holes at Barnack near Peterborough, the quarries from which came the matchless Barnack building stone, exhausted in the late fifteenth century.

I write these words within sight of a beautiful garden glade full of cowslips, woodrush, sorrel, scabious, and (introduced) fritillaries; until 1802 it consisted of arable strips in Cambridge Carm Field (Chapter 8). Many mid-nineteenth-century railway verges are of similar quality. These examples have presumably arisen naturally, but it is now possible (at a price) to buy seed mixtures that imitate such grassland. However, the grasslands of Hatfield Forest (Essex) are still relatively dull after improvement in the 1940s; some areas eluded the improver's tractor, and their orchids and sedges survive but have not spread. The Cambridge city commons still bear the marks of a weedkilling nearly twenty years ago (from which the weeds quickly recovered). Some recent removal of the hawthorns that overran the Cambridgeshire Devil's Ditch has produced thistles and goosegrass, instead of the chalk grassland which it was hoped to regain; these weeds, which require a rich soil, betray the fact that somehow the thorns have permanently added nitrate and phosphate to the chalk.[530] Evidently a meadow or pasture rich in plant life can be made in about 150 years, less time than it takes to make a good wood, but impracticably long in terms of human whims and setbacks.

What of the outstanding grasslands, those that have rare plants? Many typical chalk grassland species are unexpectedly rare or missing on the Porton military ranges. Dr Terry Wells and others attribute many of these absences to the area having been ploughed in the Middle Ages and again in the late eighteenth and nineteenth centuries. They have no difficulty in recognizing grasslands of varying ages up to 130 years since last ploughing. Such plants as horseshoe vetch (*Hippocrepis comosa*), bastard-toadflax (*Thesium humifusum*), the gentian *Gentianella amarella*, and milkwort (*Polygala calcarea* and *P. vulgaris*), which used to be quite common in chalk grassland, are largely restricted to centuries-old turf; if they occur at all at Porton, they are confined to land that escaped the Enclosure Act ploughing.[531] These plants have little power to spread, though they get on to ancient earthworks. The rare sedge *Carex humilis* is found on prehistoric but not medieval earthworks.[532]

The most famous and beautiful rare plant of ancient chalk and limestone grassland is pasque-flower, *Pulsatilla vulgaris*. It is quite robust; it survives picnicking and lack of grazing; but it is instantly destroyed by ploughing and never returns. It has steadily declined as one after another of its sites has been cultivated.[533]

Fritillary, *Fritillaria meleagris*, behaves in the same way in meadows; where it survives it may grow by thousands. It has diminished in the last fifty years more than almost any other British plant (apart from cornfield weeds). Some survivals are in large flood-plain meadows, such as the famous North Meadow at Cricklade and Port Meadow near Huntingdon, which are still dole-meadows. It also occurs in very different, but also ancient, upland meadows in Suffolk (now reduced to three places), where it may grow with anemone, creeping jenny, and other woodland plants.[534] Nothing is known of how or when fritillary or pasque-flower reached old grassland.

Another chalk grassland rarity is juniper. A century ago many chalk downs were dotted with juniper bushes, as they still are in France. Juniper can be the first stage towards woodland: other trees spring up protected by the juniper prickles, and eventually a wood is formed. The junipers cannot survive in a wood, but their dead remains can last for a century as a witness to its origin. Chalkland juniper has thus been the victim of its own way of life, but has been much more reduced by ploughing and by burning, which permanently destroys it. There are now about 80,000 junipers left in Lowland England, half of them in Wiltshire; they diminish yearly.[535] Juniper has a good historical and prehistoric record. It is one of the grassland plants which came out of the tundra. It is still widespread, though diminishing, on moorland. It once grew on heaths in the Lowland Zone. It survives on chalk downs because these are among the few well-drained, unshaded lowland habitats which are not now burnt.

Old grasslands thus have indicator plants in much the same way as old woods. (A few plants are indicators of both: adder's-tongue (*Ophioglossum vulgatum*), pignut, and autumn crocus grow in ancient grassland and ancient woodland but have little power to colonize in either.) Many of them appear not to grow easily from seed; indeed most species that spread in grassland do so by rhizomes or suckers rather than by seed. Plants do have an opportunity to start from seed where the surface is broken by molehills, rabbit-scratchings, and especially anthills, all of which have distinctive floras.

Anthills themselves are characteristic of grasslands of respectable age. Ants are among the animals that go with particular kinds of old grassland. Many species of butterfly require old grassland because their caterpillars feed on specific plants: the most famous is the Large Blue, whose remarkable life-cycle calls for ants and wild thyme.

The dark-green fairy-rings of old grassland are produced by fungi which start at a point and gradually spread outwards. Those generated by *Marasmius oreades* are said to advance at between 5 and 13½ inches a year. Some of the big rings on the Downs are centuries old.[536]

Greens and commons Commons, and their smaller sisters greens and tyes, are a precious survival of old grassland. Most of them are in Ancient Countryside. Typical of East Anglia is the green up to half a mile wide, grazed by horses and cattle, its long grass brilliant with cowslip, meadow saxifrage, hay-rattle, cuckoo-flower, and green-winged orchis; scattered around its edges are ancient houses half-hidden in trees. Such are the Barking Tye of the *Ely Coucher Book* (p.337) and Chippenhall Green, Burgate Great and Little Greens, Mellis Green (Plate XXII), the South Elmham greens in Suffolk, or Morningthorpe Green and Fritton Common in south Norfolk. Most of them are still commons and have escaped chemicals and tree growth. This already ancient type of settlement was taken to America and made the pattern of New England villages.

Commons, whether they be mere triangles where three roads meet or great tracts of heath or wood-pasture, have an irregular concave outline funnelling out into the roads which cross the common (Fig. 6.9, 6.12, 13.5, 15.2 and Plate XXII). A common proclaims itself as the piece of land left over after all the

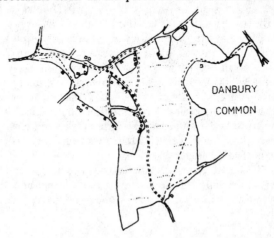

DANBURY
COMMON

Fig. 15.2. Danbury Common, Essex: a medium-sized common with straggling concave outline, crossed by roads and tracks, and with houses around the perimeter and in enclaves. Now much overgrown with trees.

private land has been hedged. Roadside verges are an extension of the common (p.265), although gates or 'hatches' often stood in the mouths of the funnels.

A typical common or tye is bordered by houses which front on to the common and back on to private fields. The perimeter of Epping Forest – technically one of the largest of all commons – has hundreds of such boundary houses. An irregular line of houses sometimes forms the ghostly outline of a common that has been enclosed and destroyed.

Most greens existed in the early Middle Ages. Often they are older than the towns and villages in which they are now embedded. A study of rural greens in mid-Norfolk shows that they came before the houses bordering them: in the twelfth century people forsook the villages where they had been living and moved to the edges of the greens.[537] This cannot be true of all greens: Long Melford, for instance, has a green but is a Roman town. Some big greens were once wood-pastures; Fritton Common still has a few pollard oaks.

Churchyards Churchyards extend into places from which all other wild vegetation has been banished long ago. The tiny beautiful churchyard of Little St Mary's brings wildness (and a rare plant) into the middle of Cambridge; others preserve wildness where there is nothing but fields. Churchyards, alas, are not exempt from the idolatry of tidiness: parochial church councillors who destroy the gravestones of their ancestors, in order to mow the grass more often, can have the same lack of respect for the beauties given them by their Maker. But a small majority of churchyards are still treated as churchyards, loved and appreciated for what they are, and not as municipal gardens.

A churchyard will usually be at least as old as the oldest fragment of the church; many are well over a thousand years old. It will often have been grazed as well as mown – the herbage being the parson's perquisite – and periodically disturbed by gravedigging. A moment's thought will show that the average English country churchyard contains at least 10,000 bodies.

No two churchyards, unless over-tidied, are alike. Each one usually has areas mown several times a year or only once, areas shaded by trees or walls, damp areas on the north side of the church, etc. – at least half-a-dozen kinds of grassland. They have the specialities of old grassland that we noted for greens. A characteristic churchyard plant is meadow saxifrage (*Saxifraga granulata*), which grows on my grandfather's grave and will one day, I hope, adorn mine. (The other lowland saxifrage, *S. tridactylites*, is equally typical of churchyard walls.) Some churchyards tend to a chalk grassland flora, with oxeye, calamint, quaking-grass, and occasional rarities like man orchid. Others imitate woodland, with primroses and anemones. The nettles and cow-parsley are a *memento mori*, for in them is recycled, while awaiting the Last Trump, part of the phosphate of 10,000 skeletons.

Churchyards and churches are crowded with other wildlife: reptiles and amphibians (especially the slow-worm); bats; ferns; and the various lichens on different building-stones and tombstones and even, occasionally, on ancient windows.

CHAPTER 16

Ponds, dells, and pits

The Loe Pool [Fig 14.1], the largest lake in the west of England . . . is formed by several small streams . . . the largest, called the Cober, flowing by the town of Helston, which is situated near the head of the lake . . . The lake is separated from the sea by a belt or bar of small pebbles, which at low-water is perhaps three or four hundred yards wide. Its structure being loose, it allows the water to percolate freely, so that unless the season be very rainy, it does not vary greatly in extent . . . In winter, however, it frequently happens that the quantity of water brought down from the hills exceeds to such a degree that which is strained off through the Bar, that the lake extends into the lower part of the town, floods the road and even some of the houses, and stops the town mills. When this takes place, the parties interested proceed to Penrose, the manor to which the Loe Pool is attached, and delivering to the lord a leathern purse containing three half-pence, request permission to cut through the Bar. This task is frequently much more laborious than one would imagine . . . in a few hours a deep, mighty river is bursting out with inconceivable velocity, and engaging in violent conflict with the waves of the ocean; as the two meet they clash together with terrific uproar, while the sea for twenty, or even thirty miles, is tinged of an ochrous hue . . . If a storm comes in from the west or south-west, the breach in the Bar is soon repaired . . . It is rarely necessary to break the Bar twice in one year, sometimes not even once . . . While the channel remains open, herrings, flounders, and shrimps find their way into the lake and are shut in . . . The Treville family formerly held lands near Helston by the service of providing a boat and nets for the king's use in Loe Pool . . . whenever he should visit Helston.

C. A. Johns, *A Week at the Lizard*, London 1848

A chapter on holes in the ground must have its limits. This is not a book on natural landforms, so I shall not deal with the larger and more obvious lakes formed by the Pleistocene glaciers. Nor can I give a complete history of quarrying and mining, nor deal with pits, ponds, and reservoirs made by industries that are still going on. My purpose is to classify the pits and ponds produced by ancient rural activities, and the smaller natural depressions which are often difficult to distinguish from them. Holes have been little studied, and my classification cannot be exhaustive: no doubt whole categories remain to be discovered.

I shall use *ponds* to mean depressions, natural or artificial, with water in them for most of the year.* Depressions without water will be called *dells* if apparently natural and *pits* if apparently artificial. The word *mere*, originally meaning any

---

* In the United States, 'pond' can mean a natural lake of many square miles.

lake or pond, has become restricted to particular local types of lake: the Lake District, Cheshire and Shropshire, and East Anglia all have their own kind of mere.

How Many Ponds?

This question defies an exact answer: there can be no exact definition of what is or is not a pond, especially at the bottom of the scale. How can we decide objectively whether a hollow is too small, or too infrequently has water in it, to count as a pond, or whether a dumb-bell-shaped pond counts as one pond or two? To define a dell or pit is even more difficult.

Ponds larger than about 20 feet across are shown in blue on some editions of the Ordnance Survey. I have counted such ponds on seventy-five sample sheets of the 2½-inch map, based mainly on surveys of the 1920s. This count, multiplied up, gives a total of 340,000 ponds, lakes, and wet pits in England and Wales. Sheets of the first edition 6-inch map, surveyed in the 1870s and 1880s, show on average twice as many ponds as those on the 2½-inch; the difference is probably due mainly to better cartography rather than to an actual change. If we take the earlier survey and add something for ponds too small or too well hidden to have been mapped, or which had no water at the time the surveyors came, the number of ponds in England and Wales in 1880 was about 800,000, or 14 ponds to the square mile. Including pits and dells the total comes to well over a million. This was when the accumulation of natural and man-made depressions had reached its climax; there are unlikely to be so many now.

Numbers of ponds vary enormously: some of the 10-km squares of the 2½-inch map have more than a hundred times as many ponds as others. Ponds are fewest in mountainous areas (Table 16.1 and Fig. 16.1). In the Highland Zone of England there are usually fewer than 2 ponds per square mile (as shown on the 2½-inch map); the average is increased by local concentrations of

Table 16.1 Abundance of Ponds in England and Wales

	Area surveyed	Ponds per square mile
Wolve's Wood, Hadleigh, Suffolk (ancient wood)	92 acres	298
Fritton Common, Norfolk*	1 sq.km	101
Environs of Stow Bedon, Norfolk*	100 sq.km	32
Environs of Ridley, Cheshire*	100 sq.km	31
Environs of St Austell, Cornwall (industrial)*	88 sq.km	15
Average for Ancient Countryside*		11.7
Average for all England and Wales*		5.8
Average for Planned Countryside*		5.0
Average for Wales*		2.9
Average for Highland England*		2.4
Environs of Hildersham, Cambs*	100 sq.km	1.3
Environs of Narborough, Norfolk in 1883	6 sq.miles	0.5
Environs of Fawcett Forest, Westmorland (mountain)*	100 sq.km	0.3

* Ponds are as shown on 2½-inch maps.

346

industrial pits, especially in Cornwall. Wales has slightly more abundant ponds, especially in Anglesey. In the Planned Countryside of Lowland England, pools are more than twice as many, 5 per square mile; they are locally infrequent on sand and chalk. In Ancient Countryside they are more than twice as abundant again, on average 12 to the square mile. The biggest concentrations of ponds in the agricultural landscape are in south and mid Norfolk and north-east Suffolk, and in a smaller area in Cheshire, with some 30 ponds per square mile, five times the national average. Even this is vastly exceeded by the ponds in some ancient woods.

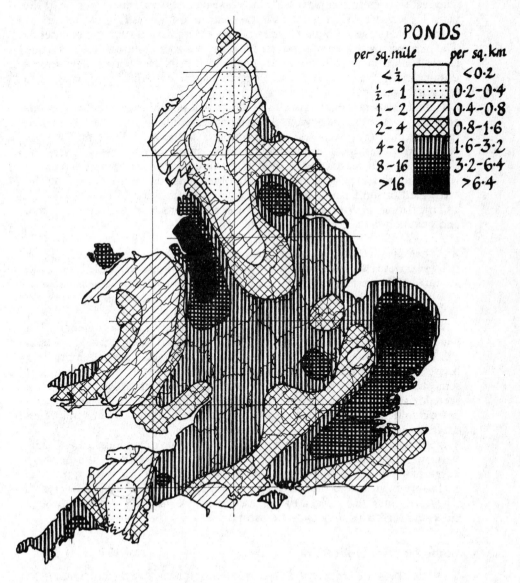

Fig. 16.1. Distribution of ponds in the 1920s.

The detailed as well as the broad distribution of hollows calls for explanation. Usually there are more ponds on commons, in woods, and around villages than in the same area of surrounding land. Did the activities of village, common, and wood make (or preserve) the ponds, or *vice versa*?

Natural and Artificial Depressions

Countrymen love to theorize about holes in the ground and to attribute them to human or supernatural agency, calling them 'marlpits' or 'Devil's Punchbowls'. The reality is more complex, and down-to-earth explanations rarely cover the facts. If ponds were largely dug for cattle to drink from, how is it that very many pasture-fields have no pond or stream, and others have more than one pond? The purpose that a hole was last used for may tell us nothing about its making. Cattle drink from pingos and moats, people sail the Norfolk Broads, and even a genuine marlpit may be an enlargement of a natural dell which made it easier to reach the underlying marl.

I cannot hope to enumerate all the things that people have done with ponds and pits. Apart from the obvious drinking-water and fish, ponds have been used for many industrial purposes. In the countryside, perhaps the commonest are connected with textiles: retting flax and hemp, and beavering woad (a fermentation process that produced the dye).[538] Retting involved steeping the plant in water to rot the soft tissues and leave the fibre: hence the hemp-pits of England – the mud of some ponds contains prodigious quantities of *Cannabis* pollen – and the flaxpits of Northern Ireland. These messy processes were the subject of anti-pollution laws:

> Item if any maner of persons within the Towne of Dedham haue any beauer pitts at their woade howses against the Comon brooke, they shall always be kept cast, so yt the thicke paaste be kept out of the saide brooke, for noying of the common water.
> *By-laws of Dedham (Essex), sixteenth century*[539]

We should first ask of a depression 'What has happened to the contents?'. If a pond or pit was deliberately dug because it was wanted, the excavated material will usually be found close at hand as a bank or mound, unless attempts have been made to hide this by spreading it. Where the pit results from digging out some mineral, we have to ask what the mineral was, how the digger knew it was there, and how he took it away; usually a track led up to the pit and a ramp down into it. Not all the contents of a pit are necessarily usable mineral; often there is a bank or mound of overburden or spoil.

Natural depressions, except pingos, do not have corresponding banks – there never were any contents – and their rounded contours contrast with the sharp edges of all but the oldest pits. Most natural depressions were formed in prehistory by processes that are very slow in historic terms or have now ceased. They are older than any artificial earthwork. A pond which cuts through ridge-and-furrow is unlikely to be natural.

Some Natural Hollows

To what extent are ordinary field-ponds the result of people digging them in an originally smooth land surface? Or was the surface originally pock-marked with

348

dells (as Massachusetts still is), of which all but a few have been ploughed down or filled in? Various kinds of small natural depression may be more abundant than we used to think.

Kettleholes These were formed in glacial times by the melting of blocks of ice which had been embedded in moraines. Classic examples are the Cheshire and Shropshire meres. There is no reason why many smaller ponds in glacial deposits should not have been formed in a similar way. We should expect them to be best preserved in deposits from the last glaciation. The big concentration of ponds in East Anglia is in boulder-clay from an earlier glaciation, so any ice-hollows would have had to survive an interglacial period.

Swallow-holes and sinkholes In Sherrard's Park Wood, Welwyn Garden City, there is a deep funnel-shaped hole, about 80 yards across, containing a pond which varies in depth. Into it flows a stream draining some 25 acres of land. The stream is absorbed and nothing visible comes out.

Such swallow-holes and sinkholes are a feature, perhaps commoner than we think, of chalk and limestone country. Sherrard's Park Wood has acid gravelly soils, but chalk lies not far beneath. Depressions from a foot or two to a mile across, sometimes of rugged contours, sometimes smooth, occur in suitable terrain in many parts of the British Isles. Usually they are round in shape. The smaller ones are often funnel-shaped, but the larger (sinkholes) are flat-bottomed.

Chalk and limestone are slowly dissolved even by ordinary rainwater, and especially by weak acids coming from vegetation and acid rocks. Dissolution tends to be concentrated in particular places. Depressions can form by gradual solution, by the enlargement of fissures, or by caves collapsing.

Swallows and sinkholes have to start in chalk or limestone, but this need not be visible on the surface. Cavities form just as easily – indeed they may be stimulated to form – where some other material lies on top of the limestone. The overlying rock tumbles into them. Probably the biggest flock of swallows in the British Isles, many thousands of them, is in the Millstone Grit mountains of South Wales. The Grit has collapsed into cavities formed in limestone under-neath it.[540] Many of the ponds in East Anglia, although in boulder-clay or Crag, may result from sinkholes in the underlying chalk (Prince 1964).

Depressions occur wherever there is limestone, and are best known from Yugoslavia. The father of all sinkholes was Lake Copais of Ancient Greece, a flat-bottomed depression which contained a fluctuating mere nine miles across.[4]

Landslips When a slope of earth or soft rock gives way, it usually tilts and does not merely slide (Fig. 16.2). The breakaway part comes to rest as a terrace, often crescent-shaped and sloping back into the hillside to form a dell. Terraces persist for centuries and cannot usually be dated, except by the development of vegetation on the scarp at the back.

Landslips happen, often one after another, where a slope is unstable: usually clay alternates with other strata and is lubricated by springs. They are familiar on coastal cliffs, especially in Dorset and the Isle of Wight, and in motorway cuttings; but they can break out on long-established slopes even of only a few degrees.

Landslip terraces have irregular, concave shapes which distinguish them from cultivation lynchets (p.159). They are most likely to be found in woods: I have seen them in valley woods in Essex, Somerset, and south-east Wales.

Pingos The eastern margins of the Fens and the Breckland valleys swarm with ponds of a peculiar type. They are very gregarious (sometimes a hundred ponds to the square mile), round or lobed in shape, and surrounded by banks (Plate XXV). The finest example is the former East Walton Common, Norfolk, with a shoal of deep hollows up to 120 yards across surrounded by steep high chalky banks. It is a world where opposites of wet and dry, acid and alkaline, meet: chalk grassland, *Sphagnum* and cotton-grass bog, heather, and sedge fen all occur within a few yards and overlap in unexpected ways. East Walton is private, but pingos can be seen by the public at Foulden Common nearby; there are other good examples at Thomson Common (Norfolk Naturalists' Trust) and Chippenham Fen, Cambridgeshire (Nature Conservancy Council). Less well-preserved pingos attract our notice as groups of summer-dry field ponds (as in the Cam valley south of Cambridge), mysterious dips in the road (as in the Weeting area of the Breckland), and irregularities in the better-surveyed contours of Ordnance maps. Others are reduced to soil marks: German air photographs of World War II show pingos by the square mile around Lakenheath and Mildenhall.

Well-preserved pingos have a convincingly artificial look, as though somebody had dug a pit and banked the earth around it. But they are certainly natural: there can be no arguing with the dwarf birch, purple saxifrage and other arctic plants from glacial times whose remains have been found in the East Walton pingos.[541] They were evidently formed by ice action before the end of the last Ice Age. The details probably have no exact parallel in the world today,

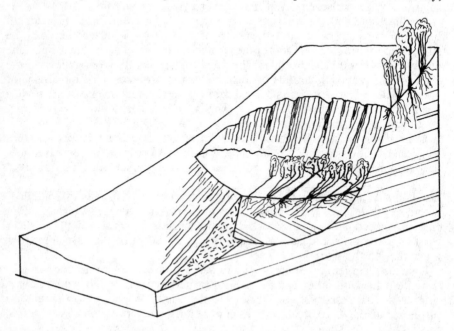

Fig. 16.2. The terrace produced by a rotational landslip.

but similar structures are now being formed in the Mackenzie delta of Arctic Canada; this is how the Eskimo word *pingo* comes to be used of East Anglia ponds.[440]

Pingos are in wet places where, if the surface were permanently frozen, water would be trapped beneath the permafrost layer under artesian pressure from surrounding hills. It is supposed that the permafrost was forced up by this pressure, perhaps over fissures in the underlying chalk, to form mounds of ice, covered with frozen soil, similar to those which the Eskimos are said to call pingos today. The soil, melting in summer, would tend to slip off sideways (Fig. 16.3). When the whole structure finally melted it would thus leave a pond with a bank round it.

Lagoons Where a river debouches on to a soft coast, its mouth is liable to be deflected by the movement of beach material, forming a bar. A small river may be completely blocked to form a lagoon, whose functioning is admirably described in the quotation at the head of the chapter.

The best-known lagoons in Britain are the Fleet behind Chesil Beach, Dorset, and Slapton Ley, Devon. There are many others. The lagoons at the mouths of the small Suffolk rivers (Fig. 17.1) are called broads, but have nothing to do with the Norfolk Broads.

Ponds in Prehistory

The earliest known artificial excavations in Britain are Neolithic mine-shafts (p.369). The oldest made pond known to me is Point Pond in the medieval secondary wood called Great Ridge, west of Salisbury. The pond is a water-hole,

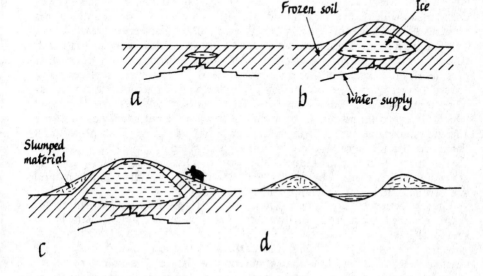

Fig. 16.3. Cross-section of a pingo: (d) as it is now; (a) to (c) as it is supposed to have formed in permafrost. For further details see Sparks and West.[440]

apparently dug into the bottom of an existing dell. It is certainly older than Grim's Ditch, a linear earthwork attributed to the Bronze Age, which makes a detour in order to bisect it. The water-hole would have served pastures which then lay around it: neatly spaced nearby are four embanked enclosures which are supposed to be Iron Age pens for livestock.

H. S. Toms, the pioneer student of ponds, showed by excavation that some embanked ponds near Cissbury (Sussex) had been constructed earlier than the Romans and had been filled by the drainage from prehistoric roads.[542]

Ponds and Dells in Anglo-Saxon England

O. G. S. Crawford, in one of the few learned works that have been written about ponds, drew attention to the many known to have existed in Anglo-Saxon times. They have their own Old English names, or villages are named after them, or they are mentioned in pre-Conquest documents (Crawford 1953). He listed 57 such ponds in Hampshire and adjoining counties; the list could be multiplied many times.

The word 'pond' seems not to appear until the Middle Ages, and then in the specific sense of *dammed* ponds. Nor does 'lake'; the Old English *lace* was a linear feature, apparently a backwater of a river. The normal Anglo-Saxon word is *mere*, which can mean anything from Winder*mere* down to the humblest field-pond. (In the modern spelling of place-names it is often corrupted to 'moor'.) *Pōl*, 'pool', was often, if not always, used by the Anglo-Saxons in the sense of a wide or deep place in a river. The word *seap*, known only from the charters, might be thought to mean a pit or quarry, for we find sand-seaths, loam-seaths, and a chalk-seath; but Crawford, having visited some of the spots, concluded that it meant a 'spring-pond', a water-hole dug in an otherwise dry valley.

Crawford was fascinated by the mysterious hilltop ponds of the Wessex chalklands, which have determined the sites of villages from Roman times onwards. The villages of Ash*more* (north-east Dorset), Butter*mere* (east Wilts), and Dum*mer* (north Hants) each surrounds, and is named after, such a pond. Another hilltop pond, Rock*moor* Pond, at which Buttermere and three other parishes meet, is named in charters of 863 and 961.[543] I know of six places called Liverpool or Livermere (Old English for 'sedge pool'); among these is a Laver-mere (*alias* Wermere, 'Man Mere') in Alvediston (south Wilts), a hilltop pond which Crawford found not to be a natural depression but constructed. Other ancient pond-names are Fowlmere (either 'Fowl Mere' or 'Foul Mere') and Wigmore ('Battle Mere') – there is a little pond called Wigmore on a hilltop in Castle-Camps (south-east Cambs). The town of Diss (Norfolk) has grown up around a natural mere. The Anglo-Saxon landscape was full of ponds natural and artificial, many of which are still there.

The charters refer 246 times to *mere*, which forms 1.72 per cent of all the features named; there are 18 further mentions of places and objects named after meres. (I have excluded a few linear features in which *mere* is a corruption of *gemære*, 'boundary'.) Adding some of the 22 instances of *seap* and the 70 occurrences of *pōl*, we find that about one in fifty of the points by which boundaries were designated was a pond. By far the greatest concentration of meres appears in the Fens, where Whittlesey Mere and its neighbours, great natural lakes all destroyed in the nineteenth century, were important landmarks. Many ponds are mentioned especially in the Vale of Evesham, but also in the Reading Basin, West Hampshire, Wiltshire Claylands, and Hampshire-Sussex Downs. Few are recorded in the Weald, Devon, East Midlands, and the south Wiltshire chalklands. This distribution is not easily related to numbers of ponds as they are now – but the charters do not cover areas where ponds are now specially few or many.

Dry depressions appear in the charters under three names. There are 140 mentions of *pytt* 'pit', 80 of *crundel*, and 40 of *del* 'dell'. Pits included loam-pits (possibly marlpits, see p.370), coal-pits (p.357), and an iron-pit (at Headbourne Worthy, Hants). There are 11 mentions of 'wolf-pit' (and another in the place-name Woolpit, p.35); these are often interpreted as pits to trap wolves, but they are not necessarily in the remote areas where we would expect wolves to have lived, so possibly they allude to one or other of the metaphorical sorts of wolf which haunted the Anglo-Saxon mind. A 'beaver-pit' (*beferpytt*) in Pucklechurch (Gloucestershire) may refer to the beavering of woad (p.348). *Del* was a dry pit, often on chalk downland; etymologists derive the word from *delfan*, to dig, but there is nothing to suggest that it was confined to artificial quarries. *Crundel* was also a dry pit, and may be a dialect alternative to *del*, for the two words tend not to occur together.*

Dells and crundels were concentrated in some chalk and limestone areas: the Marlborough Downs, Dorset Chalklands, Mid Hampshire, Uffington Scarp, and Wooded Cotswolds. Occasional ones are recorded elsewhere. Pits appear almost everywhere, but in large numbers in the Vale of Evesham and the Uffington Scarp.

East Anglian Meres and Irish Turloughs

On East Wretham Heath in the Breckland (Norfolk Naturalists' Trust) is a curious group of ponds (Fig. 16.4). Ringmere lies in a deep depression with a sandy floor. It is famous for its changes of extent and depth. It can rise and fall by at least 15 feet; it can be full in a drought (as in 1724) and nearly dry in a wet summer (as in 1968). Langmere changes usually in step with Ringmere: when full it appears as a lake with an island, when low as a group of three ponds. A third, similarly fluctuating depression has been surrounded by two concentric ring-ditches for an unknown purpose. Between Langmere and Ringmere, and higher than either, is a patch of clay on which are two more ponds: one, called Fenmere, fills or dries up according to the weather; the other, nameless, is deep and never varies by more than a few inches.

Langmere and Ringmere are examples of the Breckland meres, depressions in the chalk whose water-levels are connected to a deep water-table which gradually empties and recharges itself in accordance with variations in rainfall over a period of many months. The most easily examined of such meres is the Devil's Punchbowl nearby. Several are inaccessible in the Stanford Battle Area. Like other fluctuating ponds, these meres are rich in animal and plant life. They produce a surprising range of successive plant communities.[544] Their edges get overgrown with trees which are drowned and killed every few years. In most years the meres swarm with little frogs, and they are well known for wildfowl.

---

* The word may survive in Suffolk as 'grundle', a ravine with a track in it, but in the charters it is a point, not a linear feature.

Recently they have been studied in detail by the Anglian Water Authority in order to protect their distinctive fluctuations against changes which would result from using the chalk for storing the public water supply.

Fluctuating meres are part of the larger story of East Anglian meres in general, those deep round holes which run north from the Breckland to Sham-mer in North Creake and south, via the meres of Diss and Semer, to Wormingford Mere in Essex (Fig. 16.10). They are less documented than the hilltop meres of Wessex. Ringmere gets into the Heimskringla Saga through a battle fought in 1010: St Olave smote the men of Ulfketel Snilling and 'Hringmara heath' ran red with blood.

Meres outside the Breckland do not fluctuate; some of them are connected to streams. All (except perhaps Campsey Ash Mere) overlie chalk, at least indirectly. They are usually circles or ellipses, though several are irregular and Scoulton Mere is ring-shaped, perhaps by the joining of adjacent depressions. They have no corresponding mounds. An artificial origin, unlikely for such

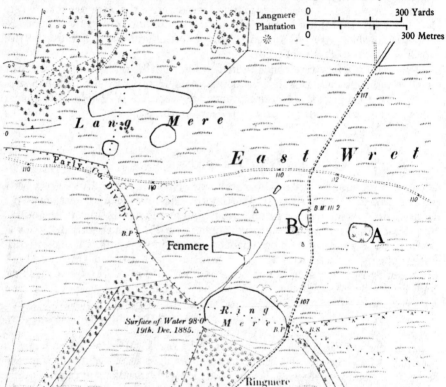

Fig. 16.4. The meres on East Wretham Heath in the Norfolk Breckland. Langmere, Ringmere, and Mere A are fluctuating meres; Fenmere responds directly to the weather; Mere B, the highest, does not fluctuate at all. Depressions in the north are marlpits. Five parishes share in Ringmere. From the Ordnance Survey of 1903–4, which shows an impossible state of the meres. The original survey was done in 1882, when the meres were very full and the three depressions of Langmere had coalesced. In 1903–4 the meres were nearly empty; the revisers noted that Langmere had shrunk to three pools, but neglected to survey the changes in Ringmere and Mere A.

large depressions with Anglo-Saxon names, is ruled out by the deep sediments in many of them, which gives a record of East Anglian vegetation since long before civilization.[545] They are evidently natural sinkholes.

Meres are gregarious. Near Stowmarket, on low ground, is another group. Bosmere, a deep round alder-fringed pool through which the River Gipping used to run, was well known in Anglo-Saxon times, for Bosmere Hundred is named after it.

> Item, there is a certain mere (*mara*) which is called bosemer' and it is wholly the private fishery of the Lord Bishop of Ely.
>
> *Ely Coucher Book, 1251* [an exaggeration: only a small part of Bosmere was the Bishop's property]

Nearby is a larger, shallow depression now prosaically called Baylham Fishpond, but whose real name is Livermere, Sedge Mere. There are at least three smaller ones in the group.

Meres are known for their convergences of parish boundaries. Six parishes meet at Ringmere. At Rymer Point, anciently also called Ringmere, between Thetford and Bury St Edmund's, nine parishes converge (Fig. 16.5). It has been supposed that Rymer is the site of a large vanished mere, but there is no trace of one; instead there are seven well-defined ponds and hollows, the survivors of a shoal of small meres. Doubtless the parishes concerned in Rymer and Ringmere all claimed access to water for their flocks, though the division is untidy; in neither place do the boundaries meet exactly at a point, nor do they share the waterholes equally.[546]

Fluctuating meres are sometimes compared to the *turloughs* of western Ireland, flat-bottomed sinkholes in limestone which fill and empty more regularly than the meres. Occasionally they are connected to the tides. Some turloughs have been cultivated when dry – 'Turlough' is one of the categories of land-use in the Civil Survey of Galway in the 1650s.[10] The short, regular flooding produces more permanent vegetation zones than the slow and unpredictable changes of the Breckland meres; these include shrubs which withstand short immersions.[547]

Ponds and Dells in Woods

Some of the depressions in woods are there by chance, or because woodland has grown up on land spoilt by quarrying or mining. A few are related to woodland as such. There is a large remainder for which human activity is not a sufficient explanation.

Sawpits Pit-sawing is the sawing of a log lengthwise with a two-man saw, one man standing on the log and the other in a pit beneath it. The practice appeared in the fourteenth century – previously one end of the log had been propped on a trestle – and continued into living memory.* Sawpits were sometimes dug in woods; usually they were filled in, but sometimes they were permanent and give rise to place-names. I have yet to see a convincing one, but would expect to find the weathered remains of a pit originally of the size and shape of a churchyard grave.

---

* It produces a characteristic pattern of saw-scratches, not exactly at right angles to the length of the timber, which change direction every few feet.

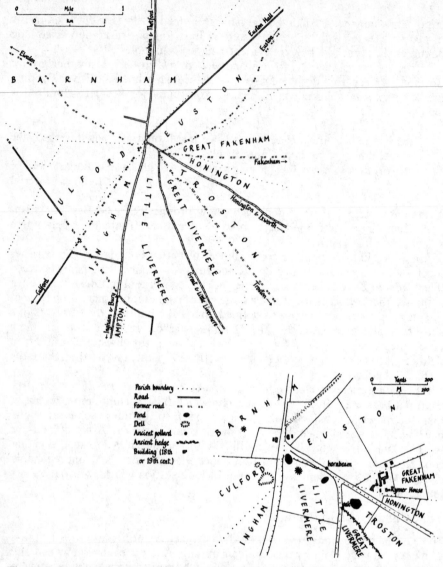

Fig. 16.5. Rymer Point, between Bury St Edmund's and Thetford. From the Ordnance Survey of 1882 and fieldwork.

(a) Eleven parishes and ten roads once converged at this group of small meres on a Breckland heath. The villages are 2–3 miles away. The parishes are now reduced to nine (by the merging of the two Barnhams and the swallowing-up of Little Fakenham either by Euston or by Great Fakenham).

(b) The central area. The seven surviving depressions are shared between Barnham, Euston, Troston, Little Livermere, and Culford. Those of Honington and Great Fakenham could have disappeared in the eighteenth century when Rymer House was built. It is not known whether Great Livermere and Ingham had meres of their own. The heaths were abolished by Enclosure Acts and the present hedges (hawthorn, ash, elm) planted. Previously there had been a few pollard trees on the open heath, and one hedge (of five species) on the Troston-Great Livermere boundary.

Charcoal-pits Charcoal was first made by setting fire to wood buried in a pit, later replaced by the familiar earth-covered stack or iron kiln. The Anglo-Saxon charters mention 'coal-pits' (p.81), none of them where coal-mining would be possible. Charking in pits went on at least into the sixteenth century. Often the pits were filled in afterwards, but survivals might be looked for. I would expect a crater-like dry pit with surrounding bank, thickly strewn with charcoal fragments.

Natural ponds and dells Ancient woods, as we have seen, may have vastly more ponds and dells than the same area of non-woodland. The largest numbers are perhaps characteristic of East Anglia as a glaciated region; there are not so many in Wiltshire or South Wales.

These depressions sink directly into the flat ground, with no trace of a corresponding mound or of a track by which earth might have been carried away. They are usually rounded in shape; sometimes they are mysteriously arranged in pairs (one long pond and one round) or chains (Fig. 16.6). They cut deeply into the subsoil and may have zones of vegetation on their sides. Whether

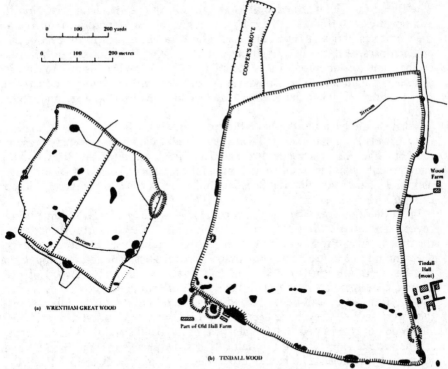

Fig. 16.6. Pairs and chains of ponds in ancient woods.
(a) Wrentham Great Wood, Suffolk. Fifteen depressions (including four pairs) in a 35-acre wood. Some of the ponds have been incorporated in a rudimentary drainage system.
(b) Tindall Wood, Ditchingham (Norfolk). A chain of sixteen ponds crosses the wood. Both woods are on almost perfectly level ground with no known geological discontinuities. The ponds and dells are depressions in the flat surface and have none of the characteristics of artificial excavations.

357

or not they are wet is by chance; some dells 20 feet deep are always dry. Often they have ancient coppice stools within them. Some have been incorporated into woodbanks or used as sumps for drainage grips.

Ancient woods, outside mining areas, have escaped most of the processes by which ponds and pits have been made or effaced. They indicate that the natural land surface was not smooth but full of holes (and also of humps, namely sand-lenses, p.100). Possible explanations include kettle-holes of the last glaciation but one and sinkholes in the underlying chalk; but there may well have been other pond-forming processes not yet identified.

These holes, being obstacles to cultivation, were doubtless commoner on sites that were to be left as ancient woodland; but it would be surprising if they were confined to such places. Probably many field and village ponds, especially those in clusters, are of the same natural origin; but it is difficult to prove this of any particular pond.

Broads

The Broads are familiar and well-loved lakes in the peatlands of East Norfolk and north-east Suffolk. Until 1951 we thought they were natural, remnants of the former estuaries of rivers that had otherwise been filled in by peat or silt, and comparable to the destroyed meres of the Fens. It is a classic of historical ecology how an attempt to give detail to that theory led instead to a quite different conclusion. The Broads are the holes left by a huge industry of peat-digging, of which no memory or legend remains (Lambert and others 1960).

What should have cast doubt on the old theory is the fact that not one of some forty Broads has a name of its own: they are all called after parishes, persons, fens, etc. East Anglian woods, Breckland and Fenland meres, and Breydon (the one certainly natural basin in the Broads area) have Anglo-Saxon or Norse names. This indicates that the Broads, unlike the woods and the meres, did not exist in Viking times.

Proof that the Broads are artificial came from a study of their sediments. Dr Joyce Lambert and Mr J.N. Jennings took some 2,000 cores in rows across all the Broads. Each Broad was found to have been originally a vast pit some 10 feet deep and up to a mile across, with almost vertical sides penetrating through the surface layers into 'brushwood peat' laid down by the fen wildwood of prehistory. The pits had irregular outlines and were subdivided by straight, narrow, vertical-sided, wall-like baulks of the same peat as the surroundings. Since they were formed they have been partly filled in with mud and newer peat, which do not correspond to the older peat of the baulks and the surroundings.

The vertical sides, slicing through earlier strata, prove that the Broads are at least partly artificial. The baulks prove that they are wholly artificial and that the older peat once extended right across them. Many of the larger Broads are divided into strips by a multitude of parallel baulks still discernible as chains of islets (Plate XXIII). The baulks were used as footpaths by the workmen, and remains of gravel surfacing have occasionally been found.

How were these huge excavations made, of which the present Broads are a shrunken remnant? (Fritton Lake is 2 miles long, 200 yards wide, and 15 feet deep – a respectable hole even by twentieth-century standards.) Mr C.T. Smith found abundant records of peat-digging in the archives of Norwich Cathedral Priory and other institutions.

In the thirteenth century east Norfolk and east Suffolk were the most populous part of the British Isles, the most urbanized (with the cities of Norwich and Great Yarmouth), and among the most prosperous. But they had very little woodland. Peat, or 'turf' (Latin *turba*) was the chief fuel. It was dug from small deposits all over East Anglia, even from such unlikely places as North Elmham and Hindolveston (mid Norfolk) and Staverton (east Suffolk), but the biggest amounts were from places such as South Walsham which later possessed Broads. In the 1270s South Walsham earned not much less from sales of peat than from farming. Besides selling peat from their estates, monks used it for their own heating and cooking and even bought it from outside.

The surviving records tell us only of the last few decades of an industry that had probably been going for some time before the records begin. The making of the Broads required the taking away of some 900,000,000 cubic feet of peat; spread over, say, 300 years, this would imply that 12 million turves were consumed a year. Sales from the one estate of South Walsham alone sometimes amounted to ½ million turves a year, and just the kitchens of Norwich Cathedral ate up at least 400,000.

The monks, citizens, and countryfolk of the hinterland were quite capable of digging and burning enough peat to make the Broads. In earlier centuries peat may also have fired the saltpans mentioned in Domesday Book.

If peat were to be dug in Broadland now the workings would fill with water. This would have been less of a difficulty in the thirteenth century. Mr Charles Green showed by excavations in Great Yarmouth that the sea was then (in this area) about 13 feet lower relative to the land than it is now. The tides would not have reached up the rivers as far as the Broads, as they do now. Most of the Broads originally had baulks, through which water would not easily have seeped, isolating them from the rivers. Peat-diggers would have had to cope only with rainfall and the flow of springs, which might have been dealt with by simple baling-out. Subdividing the Broads by baulks may have helped to keep the working faces above water. The details are still unsolved: I cannot conjecture how the makers of, say, Barton Broad or Fritton Lake dealt with the considerable streams that flow through them.

The peat industry suddenly declined in the late thirteenth century, not because it had run out of peat. The cause may have been a cataclysmic surge in the North Sea in December 1287 (p.389). This was much greater than the disastrous surge of February 1953. Despite the higher land level, it may well have reached and drowned all the workings. Such pits as were recovered later succumbed to repeated surges and to a gradual rise in relative sea-level.

When brushwood peat became inaccessible, the users apparently turned to wood or coal brought from a distance. Upland peat-beds, unaffected by the flooding, were still worked; and in Broadland peat of poorer quality was dug from the surface layers. Attempts were made to excavate peat under water by a tool called a dydle, apparently by scraping it off the bottom and making it into briquettes. But Norwich ceased to be a peat-burning city, and by the end of the Middle Ages the 'turbaries' of the Broads had been replaced by fens and waters. Sir Thomas Brown, the seventeenth-century collector of curious information, was unaware that the Broads were artificial. They have since been altered by further submergence, silting, erosion, and the cutting of navigation channels through the baulks.

The Broads have changed more rapidly in the last 150 years. Their surroundings have not escaped the general decline of fenland (Chapter 17). About two-thirds of the water area has already filled itself in, and much of the remainder is very shallow. This is partly a natural change: the Broads have exceeded the half-life of excavations of this depth in this environment. But silting now goes on at least five times as fast as in the nineteenth century.[548] Since 1965 most of the plant and animal life has disappeared. The Broads are no longer the Paradise of my childhood: plants such as water-soldier are nearly extinct, and even frogbit and hornwort (*Ceratophyllum*) are rarities. Fish, insects, and birds have similarly declined. The disappearances are attributed to pollution by the sewage of upstream towns and of boats, and by fertilizers washed out of agricultural land, which not only destroy the plants but indirectly affect the animals and increase the silting. Motor-boats make matters worse by stirring up the mud and by eroding river-banks, which adds to the silting. Many Broads have no motor-boats or no sewage, but significantly the only one still in reasonable health is Upton Broad, which is both private and isolated from field-drains. Part of the sewage pollution has now been remedied, but this by itself is not enough: such vested interests are concerned that there is little immediate hope of reversing the causes of the decline of the Broads, still less of undoing the decline itself.

Moats

A moat is an enclosure, surrounding a building or garden, with substantial wet or dry ditches. I am not concerned with the moats of castles but with those of private houses, often now deserted. (There are also moated churches, monastic sites, and haystacks.[549] Moats around windmill sites, as on the former Alwood Green in Gislingham, Suffolk, are incidental to the making of a mound on which to raise the mill into the wind.)

More than 5,000 moats are known in England (Aberg 1978); they are unevenly distributed (Fig. 16.7). Usually they are on their own or in pairs, but occasionally we find whole villages of moats. East Hatley (Cambridgeshire) now has a moated church, moated tennis-court, moated scrapyard, and others, at least twelve moats in all, and there are eight moats in the deserted village of Bottisham Park (Cambridgeshire).[550] In Ireland about 750 moats are known, chiefly in the southern half; in Wales there are about 140, mainly along the English border; and there are a mere 31 in Scotland. They also occur in Flanders and elsewhere in Europe.

Moats are usually four-sided – squares, rectangles, or irregular – but may be circular or shapeless. The area enclosed varies from 4 acres to ⅛ acre. The ditch is typically about 30 feet wide; the material from it may form a bank either on the outside or the inside or may be spread out to raise the level of the interior. Rarely are there any ruins of a house. Houses in moats were wooden: either they still stand, or they have rotted away leaving at best a scatter of roof-tiles. Most deserted moat interiors are flat, sometimes with small ponds, but nothing to show directly where the house was.

Some moats, especially the grander ones, were crossed by bridges; surprisingly often, when the water is pumped out, the timber trestles of a medieval bridge come to light.[429] Other moats have one or more gaps left for access, which appear to be original. Many have only three sides; this happens too often to be convincingly due to the moat being unfinished or damaged, and when a medieval house still stands where the fourth side would have been we have to suppose that the moat was never meant to be a complete circuit. Moats are often deliberately fed with water: the Bottisham Park moats have an elaborate diversion of a stream to supply each in turn.[550]

Moats used to be thought to go back to a rude antiquity of wolves and bears and clearings in wildwood; writers still cite them as evidence of medieval expansion into wildwood. Their distribution does not bear this out. Moats are very thick on the ground in west Suffolk and west Cambridgeshire, where there

Fig. 16.7. Moated sites, after Aberg (1978) by his kind permission.

361

was less than average woodland. They are numerous in some areas, eg. north-west Warwickshire and north-west Essex, where Domesday Book has extensive woodland, but are quite sparse in the two biggest wooded areas, the High Weald and the Chilterns. In Oxfordshire moats are not specially associated with the wooded Wychwood district. In Hertfordshire they are mainly in the moderately wooded north-east, not in the very wooded south-west. North-east Cambridgeshire, which was almost woodless in the Middle Ages, has plenty of moats.

If moats originated very early, we ought to find this recorded in documents and place-names. Not so: as far as I know, nothing that might be a moat is mentioned in any Anglo-Saxon charter or place-name or in Domesday. (Moats, surprisingly often, are bisected by parish boundaries and ought to appear in charters if they existed.) Medieval references are quite rare. A survey of Offton (Suffolk) in the late thirteenth century mentions a *mota* at the manor-house:[551] this is presumably the moat later dignified with the name of Offton Castle. At Leaden Roding (Essex) in 1439 there was 'the site of the manor [-house] . . . with divers buildings both inside and outside the moat'.[292]

What of archaeology? The great and mysterious moat of the ruined South Elmham Minster, Suffolk, has some claim to be a Roman earthwork, but this is unique. More than a hundred, mostly deserted, moats have been excavated sufficiently to give some evidence of their earliest occupation. The results show that moats began not earlier than 1150, reached the height of fashion in the mid-thirteenth century, and were *démodé* by 1325. A few new moats were dug in the late Middle Ages, and there was a revival in Elizabethan times.[552] There is some evidence for moats being added to existing buildings, as at Quinton, Northants;[553] but where a moat has an internal platform with a medieval house on it, it can hardly be younger than the house. Examples are Tiptofts in Wimbish (Essex), where the oldest part of the timber-framed house may well be of the twelfth century, and Warish Hall in Takeley (Essex), where the house is the thirteenth-century timber Priory of St Valery.

Archaeology and documentation both indicate that moats are of the twelfth or thirteenth centuries. Some may go back a little earlier, but not before the Conquest; and the fashion may well have continued later.

Anyone who has dug so much as a post-hole in boulder-clay, where moats are most numerous, will appreciate that they represent an immense investment of labour. Were they defensive? If so, why are many moats three-sided or interrupted, or provided with external banks from which the interior can be overlooked?* Were they for drainage? If so, why are they so big, why are many of them provided with internal banks which would prevent the drainage of the interior, and why are some deliberately fed with water?

The answer, as Christopher Taylor persuasively argues, is that moats were status symbols.[554] The Middle Ages were full of symbols, from Forests downwards (p.131), that went with particular classes of people. Moats were introduced to defend royal and noble castles; they descended to the manor-houses of the gentry and the houses of ordinary farmers. The common yeoman could not aspire to battlements or his own gallows or dovecote, nor could he afford a park,

---

* A minor protective function cannot entirely be discounted, especially in Ireland. As readers of the *Paston Letters* will know, even in the fifteenth century there was much to be said for inviting passing hoodlums to rob someone else.

but he could have a moat. Just as battlements were to descend the social scale right down to my own Victorian terrace house, so even the villagers of East (*alias* Hungry) Hatley had each his moat. This interpretation explains three-sided moats: status mattered less at the back.

If moats were status symbols which many of their possessors could ill afford, we might expect them where status needed specially to be asserted. Moats are indeed few where the manorial system was strong: each village has, at most, only one or two moats, which are those of manor-houses and stand a little aloof from the village. Where there was a single institutional or absentee landowner a village often needed no moat: the Bishop of Ely had none at his villages of Little Gransden and Balsham (Cambridgeshire), Glemsford (Suffolk), or Hadstock (Essex). Even in village country, there are occasional moats in remote places outside the manorial jurisdiction: for example the moat in Kingston Wood (Cambridgeshire), the seat of a small independent estate. Moats are abundant where the traditions of village communities and open-field agriculture were weak, where there was a multitude of small freeholders or weakly-bound tenants with independence to be asserted. An extreme example is Felsham (Suffolk), with at least twelve moats scattered over the parish; in Domesday Book it had 33 freemen.

A special type of moat does go with woodland. The 'moat-in-a-wood' is a type of settlement frequent all over eastern England. Kingston Wood Manor has been mentioned; in Eversden Wood nearby there is a small, undocumented, double moat. Within 5 miles of Saffron Walden there are at least seven medieval settlements within or abutting on ancient woods, always on the south or west sides. Moats in woods often cut straight through the woodbank, but may be separated by a more or less complex outer enclosure, as with the two moats in Gawdy Hall Wood (Redenhall, Norfolk). A few moats in woods are humble enough to have been the homes of woodwards: there is a tiny one in Bonny Wood (Barking, Suffolk). Most of them suggest that moat-makers deliberately chose to live next to woods: doubtless they appreciated the shelter and perhaps the concealment.

Moats were ornamental as well as symbolic. They give pleasure, as anyone still living within a moat knows. They are useful for sewage and fish. In the later Middle Ages and afterwards moats were used as garden features and adapted, or even dug for the purpose. With many double moats we suspect that the second moat is for a garden. There is a particular type of sixteenth-century landscape-garden surrounded by a quadrilateral moat with mounds, perhaps for summer-houses, at each corner. The best known, at Childerley Hall (Cambridgeshire), was made for the purpose probably as late as 1600.[273] I have found another, cutting into Moorend Wood (Great Raveley, Hunts) which still has its original pollard elms and other trees on the mounds (Fig. 16.8).

Moats are still rather a mystery. They are a warning against trying to write history from documents alone. They belonged to middle-class people who kept few records: they reveal an area of human endeavour which we would hardly know existed had the moats themselves not survived. Readers will have many opportunities to discover unknown moats – they should look first in groves and woods – and to record those already known. Where a medieval house still stands in a moat, they should consider whether it is the original. In a deserted moat they should look for pottery excavated by moles and badgers. The vegetation of moats is too often ignored by archaeologists. Pollards and ancient trees may be a living link with the folk who lived in the moat; so are stinging-nettles (p.108), which may tell us for how long the moat was inhabited and where people put their rubbish.

Dams

The Romans built many dams elsewhere in the Empire – some still function – but I know of none in Britain. Our earthen dams derive from the water-mill technology of the Anglo-Saxons. The perambulations often mention weirs across rivers, but there were also reservoirs behind dams. Crawford found one such when looking for *styrian pol*, said to mean 'pool of the sturgeon', in the Besselsleigh (Berks) bounds of 959. The bounds of South Newnton (Wilts), dated 943, mention a *pynding mersc*, probably meaning 'dam marsh' (Crawford 1953).

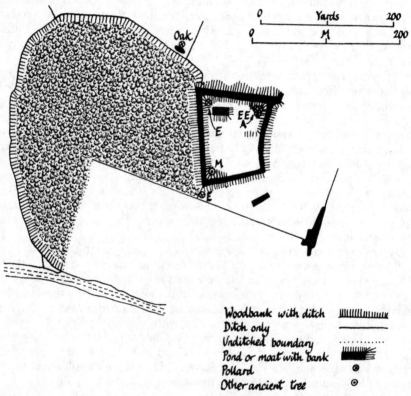

Fig. 16.8. The moat attached to Moor-End or Raveley Wood, Great Raveley, Huntingdonshire. The wood has a mighty medieval woodbank. The moat, perhaps medieval in origin, cuts into this earlier bank; in its present form it appears to be a sixteenth-century garden moat with three corner mounds. On the mounds are ancient pollards and other trees (A ash, E East Anglian elm, M maple) which may be part of the garden. To the east and north are humps and bumps, ponds, and scattered elms suggesting the site of a larger settlement. The straight-edged field to the south is a later intrusion into both the settlement remains and the wood, dated probably between 1766 and 1834. Mapped in 1978.

From the Middle Ages onwards there were many dams for fishponds or to drive mills. They are mentioned in the context of maintenance or of prosecution for wilful damage. The five dams which still hold water in Sutton Coldfield Park, Birmingham, were made about 1420, probably for fulling-mills; they later drove a sword-mill, a button-mill, and other industries.[218] Better known are the many hammer-ponds for driving trip-hammers in the Sussex Weald and other ironworking areas.

A characteristic eighteenth-century dam is that creating the sinuous sheet of water which landscape parks inevitably have. This was not just ornamental: it produced ice, which was stored for the summer in an ice-house, a heavily insulated brick vault often buried in a mound. An ice-house implies a pond close by, even though (as at Ickworth) the dam may long ago have been breached.

Ancient dams are quite common, especially in woods, even where there is no obvious industrial purpose. I have found four in the steep little valleys of the

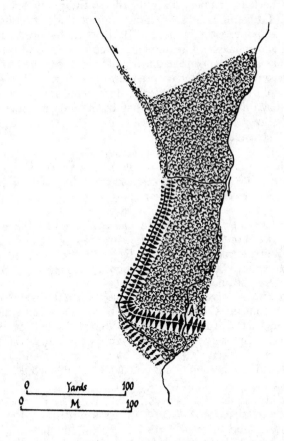

Fig. 16.9. Ancient dam at Hobbs Hole, north-east of Upminster, Essex. The east side of the valley is steeper than the west. The L-shaped earthen dam appears to have created a pond and to have allowed both streams to bypass the pond when required. This would be typical of early fishponds. The dam is now breached at A and the whole site has become a wood.

woods around Southend. There are others in Monks' Wood (Hunts) and its neighbours. Without documents they can seldom be dated. Fig. 16.9 shows a typical small dam in south Essex, over which a grove has grown up. It has a bypass, which suggests a fishpond, despite its remote location.

Fishponds

The Middle Ages were a golden age of fish. With no fertilizers to pollute them, almost all ponds were fishponds. In remote Hindolveston (Norfolk) in 1263–4 a net was bought for eels, and in 1273–4 a pond was 'made' in the manor yard for 10s. and 171 'pikerell' – young pike – were bought for 6s. (from where?) to put in it.[555] Stolen trout pervade manorial court rolls. The archaeologist may be less interested in pike eating each other in field and woodland ponds than in ponds specially made or adapted for fish-farming.

Fish-farming goes back to remote antiquity; it was fully developed by the twelfth century.[556] In La Dombes (France) there is a landscape of thousands of medieval and later fishponds still in use.[557] In Britain the most elaborate fishponds were royal and monastic, but the nobility and gentry had them also. Kings were fond of pike and bream and had many fishponds attached to palaces and royal manors; carpenters were often ordered to work on them. Fish-farming declined after the dissolution of the monasteries. It was still taken seriously in the seventeenth century, although the little that Izaak Walton knew of fish-ponds came from France. At Thorndon (Essex) in 1641 it was alleged that 'malitious and wicked' trustees

> pulled up the Sluce in the Ward's Pond within the . . . Parke and drayned the same and took out of the same pond and carryed away at least 500 Carpes and all other the ffish . . . wch were worth at least xx li.[558]

At Writtle nearby, as late as 1703, a lease of the park enumerated fish as well as deer: 520 store carp, 122 about four inches long, 460 store perch and tench, 26 full-grown tench.[378] Being attractive to thieves, fishponds were usually attached to the house: I am reluctant to believe in any supposed fishpond not sited where an eye could have been kept upon it.

Fishponds belonged to a way of life now vanished from Britain (though recently reintroduced from the Continent). They involved wooden sluices and fixtures and thus cannot survive in disuse. Most often they are seen as earth-works in pasture. The best-preserved are those of abbey ruins and others where the house has disappeared. Those attached to country houses still inhabited have at best been adapted into garden ponds and at worst drowned under a lake *à la* Capability Brown.

The simplest fishpond is merely a dam with a bypass to divert flood-waters around the pond. Others have a row of compartments for different species or ages of fish. The most elaborate have leats for controlling the water in the compartments independently. Ponds may be dammed or excavated or both; they are flat-bottomed and often no more than 3 feet deep. J.M. Steane has described many fine examples in Northamptonshire, such as those of the Knights Hospitallers at Harrington.[556] There are other elaborate ponds at Denny and Anglesey Abbeys, Cambridgeshire; those at Anglesey have many compartments apparently improvised out of two pre-existing moats.[550]

Decoys

A decoy is a device for catching wild ducks *en masse* by making use of their companionable habits. A lake is provided with arms called *pipes*, each about 80 yards long, curved in shape and tapering from their mouths to a point (Fig. 16.10). There should be at least four pipes for use in different directions of wind. In use they are roofed over with netting on hoops and surrounded by

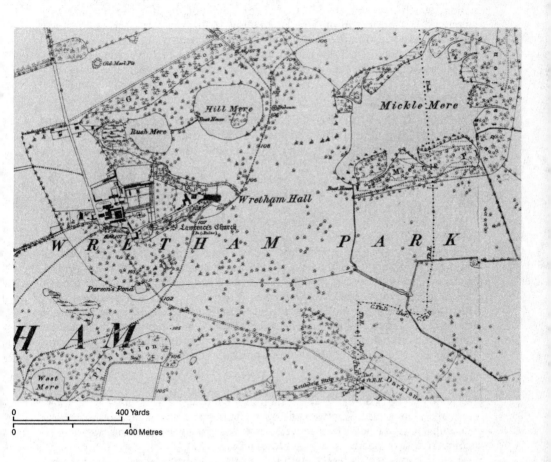

Fig. 16.10. Four non-fluctuating Breckland meres at East Wretham, Norfolk. Mickle Mere has been made into a duck decoy with ten curving pipes. Ordnance Survey 1882.

screens of reeds with peep-holes for observation. A flock of wild ducks alights on the lake and is decoyed into the mouth of one of the pipes: they will follow either tame ducks trained for the purpose or a trained dog looking like (or dressed up as) a fox. Once they are safe inside the pipe the decoy-man waves a red spotted handkerchief behind them. In panic they crowd into the little end of the pipe, where he wrings their necks and puts them on the train for Leadenhall Market.

Decoys (and their name) are alleged to come from Holland. There are said to be medieval records of them, but this I cannot confirm. By the seventeenth century they were established in English practice and metaphor. In their heyday there were over a hundred decoys which slew half a million ducks a year; in those happy days, it seems, there were infinite ducks in the world.[559] Most decoys were within 30 miles of the east coast, but a few were inland. The last decoy still worked may be that at Abbotsbury, Dorset, where ducks are caught to be ringed.

Disused decoys, with their curving arms, can be confused only with armed ponds, which are smaller. Most of them were not dug for the purpose but adapted. Mickle Mere in the Breckland (Fig. 16.10) is a natural mere to which ten arms were added in the 1830s. At least three Broads were made into decoys, including Fritton Lake, the largest Broad, already called 'Fritton Decoy' in 1783;[560] it was a giant decoy with at least twenty-three pipes.

Dewponds

This name is given to a class of ponds on chalklands from east Yorkshire to Dorset and Sussex, with others on the Derbyshire limestone. Unlike the hilltop meres already described, which are on clays and other impermeable materials overlying the chalk, dewponds lie on the chalk itself. Being located on high and seemingly arid hilltops, they are wonderful and have caused extravagant speculation. There is a large and controversial literature summarized in a book by A.J. Pugsley (1939).

Pugsley showed that dewponds are careful constructions, though set in natural dells. They were not made in prehistory by a lost process which causes them to be filled by dew. On the contrary, there is no evidence that the ponds, or the word for them, are older than the nineteenth century. There were still professional makers of dewponds in 1939. A dewpond is, in effect, a miniature copy of the natural hilltop meres: a hollow some 3 feet deep lined with puddled clay, filled by rainfall and runoff from the surrounding slopes with some assistance from mist. It requires skilled attention to detail in choosing the site to make the most of the rainfall and reduce evaporation, in waterproofing, and in protecting the clay layer to prevent animals from putting their hooves through it.

Armed Ponds

In Hayley Wood, Cambridgeshire, there is a pond with four arms, having steep sides and a constructed bottom of glacial boulders. There is no mound corresponding. It is one of the few well-preserved survivors of what was once a common class of ponds in the east Midlands.

Armed ponds were chiefly abundant where Cambridgeshire, Bedfordshire, and Huntingdonshire join. Maps of 1750 and 1820 between them record all the ponds on 5,400 acres, mostly of clayland, near Hayley Wood. There were 151 ponds (18 per sq. mile), of which 55 were armed (32 with three arms, 17 with four, 3 with five, 3 with six).[561] Armed ponds existed elsewhere; for instance, there were seven on a map of Penarth near Cardiff in 1766.[562] They are associated with hedged fields, rare in ancient woodland, and never in open-fields. When they were made is unknown. There are possible armed ponds on a sixteenth-century map of Haveringland (Norfolk).[563] In Aversley Wood (Hunts) there still exists one dug into earlier ridge-and-furrow, now under ancient secondary woodland.

Armed ponds probably had some agricultural purpose such as watering cattle. Statistics of the 151 ponds above mentioned show that ponds with more than three arms were specially likely to be shared between two or more fields, with arms projecting into each field.

Pits, Quarries, and Mines

Pits have been dug in all manner of places and for all kinds of materials. A favourite place was in the middle of the road, as we learn from court rolls. At Gamlingay in 1612 someone was fined 1s. 10d. 'for Diging in the kinges hiewaye';[564] and the Dedham by-laws require the 'water-pits before men's gates' to be fenced to save men and beasts from falling in.[539] People often dug pits on commons, although only the owner of the soil was supposed to. Alongside roads, especially on common-land, we often find small pits for gravel, chalk, or stone with which to repair the road surface. Unusual types of pit include the ochre-pits (for an iron-stained clay used as a pigment) of the Mendip Hills. In areas without limestone, various alternatives to lime mortar were used in building: the growan-pits of Cornwall are where rotten granite and serpentine were dug for this purpose.

Many stone-quarries were for local use – sometimes very local, as with the little quarries in fields on the Derbyshire limestone, where the stone was raised with which to make the field-walls. But by no means all building-stone was used close at hand. The limestones of Barnack (Northants) and Chilmark (Wilts) were transported far and wide in the Middle Ages; the tilestones of Collyweston (Northants) and Stonesfield (Oxford), and Cornish and Welsh slate, were also large commercial enterprises.

Flint-mines Flint has been used for making flint implements; as a building stone; and as flint-and-steel for striking lights and firing guns. It consists of nodules of silica formed in chalk and soft limestone. It is too hard to cut and has to be shaped by breaking, chipping, and flaking. For some purposes any flint, picked off a field, will do, but ambitious flint-knapping requires particular kinds. The best Neolithic tools, architectural flintwork (especially the medieval and Victorian 'flush-work' of shaped flints set in a stone surround), and gun-flints are made from *floorstone*, a black shiny flint that usually occurs in a thin seam deep in the chalk. The relatively small amount of flint used must be multiplied many times to allow for flint wasted in the shaping, and again for the chalk which had to be shifted to get at the floorstone.[565]

At Grime's Graves, in the Norfolk Breckland, some 90 acres of heath are covered with hummocks and funnel-shaped hollows, the remains of 600 mine-shafts sunk by Neolithic men. They dug broad round shafts, up to 40 feet deep, passing through two seams of poor-quality flint to reach the floorstone; from the bottom of each shaft horizontal galleries were made to pick out the flint nodules.[61] The mines were most active around 2700 BC. They were very efficient and removed about 70 per cent of the floorstone, leaving only 30 per cent to hold up the roof. Some of them have been excavated in the last 130 years: I have myself wriggled, pushing a candle, through the galleries made by the hart's-horn picks of Neolithic miners. There are similar flint-mines around Findon (Sussex) and in other chalk districts.

Not all flint-mines in the Breckland are Neolithic. In a few places are to be seen the hills-and-holes produced by less elaborate mines in the last century. Floorstone is still used on a small scale for gunflints and architectural work.[565]

How the medievals got flint is less well known. The chalk beneath Norwich is said to be honeycombed with 'old workings', which from time to time remind the citizens of their existence by enlarging through solution and devouring cars and the occasional house.

Bell-pits and drifts Coal, lead, and other minerals have been won from mines, as well as from quarries and stream-beds, at least since the Roman period. Most of the outcropping coalfields were in production by the late Middle Ages, sometimes by deep mining.[566] But kinds of mine more primitive than the Neolithic flint-mines continued in use down the centuries, and are occasionally used today.

A bell-pit (or 'day-hole') is a shaft sunk vertically down to the mineral-bearing rock. The coal or ore is won by undercutting the base of the shaft. When the miner dares undercut no further he sinks another shaft. Bell-pits are therefore gregarious. When disused they fill themselves in to leave funnel-shaped depressions, typically 20 feet across, surrounded by mounds of spoil.

A drift is produced by tunnelling into a mineral seam from an outcrop on a hillside. Drifts also are gregarious: they now appear as rows of pits following the seam. Often there are remains of a track passing the mouths of the drifts for carting away the mineral.

Clusters of bell-pits are common in mining areas, such as the Durham, Forest of Dean, and South Wales coalfields. Often they are in woodland, including ancient woods. It is rarely possible to date them. Many of the sides of the Welsh coal valleys are pockmarked with the rows of drifts of early miners attacking small seams. Other examples are the 'lead-rakes', rows of pits in the Derbyshire lead country, and the drifts for jet (a hard coal treated as a gem) in north-east Yorkshire.

Flashes The word *flash* can mean any shallow pond, but is most often used of those produced by subsidence when disused mines collapse. Among the best known are those above old coal-mines around Wigan. The flashes of Cheshire result from the collapse of caverns formed when rock-salt was pumped out in the form of brine.

Marlpits Many English soils are not formed by the weathering of the under-lying rocks, but come from thin surface layers of quite different material. It often happens that the subsoil, if dug up and added to the soil, produces a mixture more fertile than either would be by itself: for instance where chalk or chalky clay is overlain by acid soils formed from sand or loess. The word *marl* means clayey chalk or chalky clay, as dug up and applied to acid topsoils; but *marling* can mean the practice of using any subsoil, different from the topsoil, as a fertilizer.

Marling may well go back to Roman times. In the Anglo-Saxon charters the word *lampytt*, 'loam-pit', is the commonest specific kind of pit (12 mentions). I do not know what exactly 'loam' was, but suspect that these may have been marlpits.

Marling and disused marlpits are frequently documented from the thirteenth century onwards: for instance in 1276 a madman jumped into a flooded marlpit in Norfolk (Prince 1964). The practice of marling was already long-established when it became fashionable in the eighteenth century. It is still perfectly valid, but went out of fashion a century ago – farmers now buy chalk and other fertilizers from a distance.

Marlpits are over-recorded. To be genuine, a marlpit has to be geologically plausible: nobody digs for 'marl' where the bedrock is too hard, or water-laden, or not different enough from the topsoil. It should be steep-sided, but with one or more ramps for access by carts. Typical marlpits are in the middle of fields, one pit per field: pits in the corners of fields would double the labour of cartage.

H.C. Prince (1964), in a detailed study of depressions in Norfolk, has been able to account for many of the numerous pits in the north-west of the country as marlpits. There are records of marling, often in connexion with eighteenth-century enclosures; pits in some parishes can be shown to have arisen at that time and to cut through earlier land boundaries. But depressions are even more numerous in the anciently-enclosed middle and south of Norfolk, where marling is little known from documents and would often be unnecessary or impossible. The shapes and locations of the hollows themselves often do not satisfy the conditions. Marling is not a sufficient explanation for the very large numbers of ponds in East Anglia.

Claypits Clay is a raw material for earthworks as well as pottery. Several large pits in the Fens provided the clay used as a thin core to seal banks and river-walls made of permeable materials. Medieval archives record the use of clay for sealing dams, setting millposts, etc.

Clay was an almost universal building material, which has been held to account for the profusion of ponds around clayland villages. How far this is true is difficult to tell. The daub between the timbers of even a large medieval house amounts to only about 40 cubic yards of clay: the contents of one good-sized pond would have made a whole village. But there have usually been generations of earlier buildings – we cannot tell how many – which were flimsy and short-lived; and often there have been buildings with walls entirely of clay. Surviving houses of clay-lump and cob (rammed earth) are rarely older than 1700, but there is archaeological evidence for such earthen houses in earlier centuries. They would have used much more clay than those in which it was merely an infill.

Brickpits The making of bricks and roof-tiles is an under-researched subject, both as regards materials and fuel. Bricks can be made from many kinds of mud, clay, or 'brickearth', that is accumulations of loess. They seem normally to have been burnt close to where the material was dug.

There is usually said to have been no brickmaking in England between the Romans and the thirteenth century. This is supported by archaeological evidence, but the written record is not so clear. The Anglo-Saxons wrote about tiles, and in the bounds of Upminster (Essex), dated 1062, there is a *tigelhyrst*, 'Tilehurst', now Tylers Wood.

Brickpits are of many kinds. Sometimes they are deep rectangular holes reaching a favourite stratum of clay. At Woolpit (Suffolk), with a long-established industry making several kinds of brick, there is a wide area of irregular holes and hills. Brickworks using loess scraped it up from wide shallow excavations which may now be difficult to detect. The site of a works often becomes a 'Kiln Grove' full of rejected bricks and tile-sherds.

Coprolite-pits Coprolites – 'dung-stones' – are lumps of phosphatic rock, so called by savants who thought them the dung of dinosaurs. In the 1860s and 1870s fortunes were made in a 'coprolite rush' for the phosphate in the lowest stratum of the chalk and the underlying gault between Soham (Cambridgeshire) and Royston.[567]

Most of the coprolite was extracted from strip-workings which were filled in and have left nothing but soil- and crop-marks. There are occasional deep water-filled pits with mounds, as on Quy Fen. On Coldham's Common, Cambridge, an avaricious Corporation cashed in early on the phosphate by a method which has left what looks deceptively like ridge-and-furrow.

Craters A crater is a hole in the ground made by violence. This can be natural – volcanic explosions or the impact of meteorites – but more often is by shells and bombs. In north-east France the First World War covered the countryside in craters upon craters for mile after mile, erasing all trace of the previous landscape except for elms (p.233). Square miles of craters large and small, often now in secondary woodland, testify to the slaughter.

In Britain a few craters remain from World War II and possibly from World War I. Occasional bombs and sticks of bombs were dropped by chance on woods, fens, etc., often remote from military targets, where their craters escaped notice and were never filled in.

A crater is a conical hole, typically a few yards across, surrounded by a bank of displaced earth. Craters can usually be distinguished from bell-pits and pingos by their perfectly circular shape and steep fresh contours. The age of trees growing in the pit or on the bank is a useful diagnostic: it is most unlikely that any craters in Britain date from before 1915.

Conservation

Every reader, I suppose, will appreciate the beauty, the aquatic plants and animals, and the historic meaning of ponds and moats. Many will have a similar affection for pits and dells. Even the humble sandpit or chalkpit stands for wildness among endless houses or fields. Where else do inland children first see cliffs, fossils, sand-martins, or woody lianes? How else can geologists see in bulk materials otherwise accessible only in borehole samples?

Little is known of how fast depressions are disappearing or new ones are being created. I need hardly mention the obvious threats from people who fill in ponds because they think they need the land, or from the strange and noisome English habit of putting rubbish in holes.

Ponds also disappear from natural causes: they fill themselves with silt, dead leaves, etc. as part of a well-known process of ecological succession. When the water gets shallower than about 2 feet, reeds and bulrushes root in the bottom and their remains quickly fill up the pond. It is difficult to generalize as to how long this takes. In south-west Cambridgeshire, the Downing Estate Map of 1750 depicts 142 ponds.[568] The Ordnance Survey of 1886 shows only 41 of these as remaining, plus 42 which were not shown in 1750. Some of the difference may be due to differing standards of cartography, and some losses may have been deliberate filling-in; but the half-life of these field-ponds can hardly have been longer than a century. The deeper basins of the Norfolk Broads, where plant growth was rapid, lasted on average about 600 years. But many Anglo-Saxon ponds are still there after a thousand years, and a number of pingos still have water in them after at least 14,000 years.

Ponds are threatened by human activity in subtle ways. They are polluted by the fertilizers and weedkillers which get into almost all farmland drainage. The mania for land drainage often dries up ponds at a distance. Some unknown curse has banished frogs and toads to remote places and suburban gardens. Ponds are rarely wanted for drinking or their other traditional uses and are neglected. Neglect usually includes allowing trees to grow and shade out the aquatic plants. Too much tree growth also threatens dells and pits.

Ponds and pits, more than other habitats, justify the complacent argument that the loss or spoiling of existing sites does not matter if they are replaced by new ones. Aquatic plants and animals move from place to place more quickly than terrestrial, as can be seen in any newly-abandoned gravel-pit. But no new excavation can re-create the meaning of an ancient pit or the primaeval landform of a dell. In practice the best depressions – those that are nature reserves or Sites of Special Scientific Interest – are usually long-established. We cannot see our way to re-creating the habitats of specialized creatures, such as the rare mosses on weathered cliffs in Cambridgeshire chalkpits, or the curious lichens of the Mendip lead-mines. As with the plant-life of roads, the most threatened plants are those that specialize in the alternation of wet and dry. Examples are the buttercup *Ranunculus ophioglossifolius*, a star turn of Gloucestershire Trust for Nature Conservation, which grows in two otherwise ordinary ponds; *Lythrum hyssopifolia*, a rare plant of pingos; and the rare violet *Viola persicifolia* in turloughs.

Much interest still remains from the *Save the Village Pond* campaign of 1974, and there is a handbook on maintaining ponds and wet places.[569] With hundreds of thousands of ponds in existence, there is usually more to be said for conserving them than for making new ones. We can hardly hope to do more than identify and maintain a small proportion of the more important ponds and to oppose the destruction of ponds in general where frivolous or unnecessary. Conservation schemes for ponds can sometimes be overdone. People automatically include tree-planting, forgetting that ponds all too easily acquire their own trees. Digging out sediments is proper for ponds that have been periodically cleaned out, but with others (especially in woods) the mud contains part of the meaning of the pond, and to remove it is to destroy an unread document.

It is time for a similar interest to be taken in pits and dells, on whose conservation very little has been done – although much study has been given to hastening the growth of vegetation on newly-abandoned pits.[570]

CHAPTER 17

Marshes, fens, rivers, and the sea

> There is in the midland regions of Britain a most terrible fen of immense size, which begins at the banks of the river Gronta [now the Cam] not far from the little fort which is called Gronte [Cambridge]; now in fens, now in flashes, sometimes in black oozes swirling with mist, but also with many islands and groves, and interrupted by the braiding of meandering streams . . . up to the sea . . .
>
> . . . When [Guthlac] was questioning the nearest inhabitants as to their experience of this solitude . . . a certain . . . Tatwine declared that he knew another island in the more remote and hidden parts of this desert (*heremi*); many had tried to live there but had rejected it because of the unknown monsters of the desert and the divers kinds of terrors. Guthlac, the man of blessed memory, heard this and besought his informant to show him the place. . . . It is called Crugland ['Barrowland', now Crowland], an island sited in the middle of the fen . . . no settler had been able to dwell there before . . . because of the fantastic demons living there. Here Guthlac, the man of God . . . began to dwell alone among the shady groves of the solitude . . . He loved the remoteness of the place which God had given him. . . .
>
> There was in the said island a barrow . . . which greedy visitors to the solitude had dug and excavated in order to find treasure there; in the side of this there appeared to be a kind of tank; in which Guthlac . . . began to live, building a shanty over it.
>
> *Felix's Life of St Guthlac*
> (Guthlac went to Crowland about AD 699; this was written within 50 years)

Wetlands are a classic example of how historians can be lured into error by paying undue attention to the written word, especially in its more abstract and literary form. Fens have had a bad press ever since the biographer of St Guthlac emphasized the fortitude of his hero by enlarging upon the perils into which his calling led him. Yet these perils, to which Felix devotes several chapters, were mainly spiritual; Crowland had some nasty devils, but was not otherwise a bad place to live in, and others had dwelt there long before the Saint. The material discomforts of fenland were copied and elaborated down the centuries by upland writers who despised a way of life that was not their own. Fen-men were depicted impressionistically as a race apart, fiercely independent, ague-ridden, web-footed, who lived precariously on birds and fish. From this impoverished indolence they were rescued, we are told, against their own unprogressive wishes by the Dutch engineering skills of Sir Cornelius Vermuyden and the capital of the fourth Earl of Bedford. These great men 'drained the Fens' in the seventeenth century, made them into 'rich farmland', and exalted their inhabitants into industrious moneymakers like the rest of us.

This story has been repeated on countless occasions down to our own time. But how is it to be reconciled with the glorious Fenland churches of Walsoken, Whittlesey, March, and many others? Or with the great abbeys of Ely, Peterborough, Ramsey, Thorney, and Crowland? Or with the making of King's Lynn, Wisbech, and Boston, with their magnificent medieval buildings? Or, in other fen districts, with Lydd church or Glastonbury or Selby abbeys? All these show that the real heyday of fenland was in the twelfth and thirteenth centuries, a time when fenmen, remote from political upheavals, enjoyed civilized prosperity and could afford splendid architecture.

There have been three stages in the settlement of fenland. Vermuyden's activities, which I shall call the Third Draining, took place in a very articulate age, and were publicly debated in formal prose, doggerel verse, and distorted maps. We therefore call them *the* draining of the fens, even though little of beauty or architecture has resulted. The preceding Second Draining is recorded in mundane disputes over common-rights and the repair of banks; these workaday documents are rather difficult to read, and were little regarded until scholars such as H.C. Darby, M. Williams, and H.E. Hallam drew attention to them. Most of the capital works already existed by 1250 and are known chiefly from archaeology. The greatest fenland engineering work of any period is not documented at all; from written records we would hardly know of its existence. And until aerial photography we did not know that there had been a First Draining of the fens in Roman times. Possibly a vague memory of these earlier works is responsible for the term 'reclamation' which has long been misapplied to all draining of fens (and recently to all extensions of agriculture), whether on land previously farmed or not.

The history of wetland is very largely the history of its destruction. About a quarter of the British Isles is, or has been, some kind of wetland. Much of our natural vegetation, from alders to primroses, is adapted to differing kinds, degrees, and seasons of waterlogging. Although we have never developed a complete fenland economy like that of China, in the Middle Ages and probably in the Roman period men tried to exploit the distinctive character of fens and to use them in ways complementary to the upland. But almost all our sown crops originated in semi-arid lands, and will not withstand the slightest lack of drainage. From the Third Draining onwards, and especially since World War II, farmers and taxpayers have gone to great trouble and expense to override the natural characteristics of fenland and to reduce it, like the upland, to that imitation of a Turkish steppe in which wheat and barley are at home.

Kinds of Wetland

This chapter is chiefly about 'The Fens', spelt with a capital F, that stretch from Lincoln nearly to Cambridge. Much the same story, though known in less detail, is told by the Yorkshire marshes, from Hull to Doncaster and nearly to Scarborough; the Somerset Levels; Romney Marsh; the Norfolk Broads area; the Wentloog Levels in south-east Wales; Essex and many lesser coastal marshes. All these have responded in similar ways to the natural environment and to human ambition. Inland, there are innumerable smaller wetlands such as Otmoor (Oxfordshire) and Longdon Marsh (Worcestershire).

Saltmarsh, fen, marsh, and bog Wetlands have many causes. Saltmarshes

375

are flooded by the sea at high tide. Tides also cause low-lying rivers to back up and overflow their surroundings with fresh water, as now happens in the Norfolk Broads. Inland wetlands are made by some combination of rainfall, springs, and obstructed rivers. At one extreme are the soggy flat hilltop woods like Hayley Wood, a distinctive feature of England, where there is not enough slope to carry the winter rainfall away. At another are the blanket-bogs on slopes in high-rainfall areas (p.305). A third extreme, in areas of moderate to high rainfall, are the raised bogs – great lenses of *Sphagnum* peat – of, for instance, Cheshire and midland Ireland.

Wetlands are classified by whether they are fresh or salt; whether dead plant remains rot as soon as formed or accumulate to form peat; and by the nature of the peat. Learned writers often use the term *bog* to mean wetlands with acid peat, *fen* for those with neutral or calcareous peat, and *marsh* for those without peat. These are important but not necessarily vernacular distinctions. The word *bog* appears to be Irish-Gaelic, and its use in Great Britain is modern. *Marsh* has been used since Anglo-Saxon times, more often for coastal wetlands, especially saltmarshes. *Fen*, also Old English, is more often used for inland, especially peaty, wetlands. For instance, in The Fens, the seaward, non-peaty, portion is called Marshland, and the inland, peaty part is the Fens proper. But 'marsh' and 'fen' in place-names and early documents do not reliably indicate the nature of a wetland.

Changes in the Coast

Sea-level The history of coastal wetlands is dominated by the relative levels of land and sea. This depends on how much water there is in the ocean, which is in turn determined by how much land-ice there is in the Antarctic and Greenland. But the land also tilts and bends. Although the bigger sea-level changes have happened all round the coast, different areas – even east *versus* west Norfolk – have changed to differing degrees.

Throughout the early post-glacial period, sea-level was much lower than it is now, and all the present coastal wetlands were well inland. The sea rose to about its present relative level in the Neolithic period. For much of the Bronze Age it was higher than now, flooding the coastal wetlands. In the Iron Age the sea again receded. In the late Roman period sea-level suddenly rose again, to recede once more in Anglo-Saxon times. From about 1250 onwards the sea began to rise yet again. At present the whole English coast is still sinking relative to the sea,[571] most rapidly (at nearly a foot a century) in the Thames estuary; Scotland is slowly rising.

When wetlands stand high relative to the sea, they are either freshwater marshes – whose deposits if any are of silt and mud – or are peat-bogs. When they are low, their seaward parts, reached by salt water, consist of salt-marshes and estuaries which deposit marine clays and silts; away from the sea, peat continues to be laid down in tidal freshwater. Most great wetlands therefore consist of a seaward *silt marsh* and a landward *peat fen*. Between these there is a long transition zone, typically with three layers of peat – one Neolithic, one Roman, and one medieval – separated by clays and silts of the Bronze Age and Anglo-Saxon marine transgressions. The thicknesses of peat and silt vary from the Norfolk Broads to The Fens to the Somerset Levels.

Erosion and accretion Coast erosion happens whenever the sea is high enough to reach the bases of cliffs, and either to attack them directly or to wash away the debris of landslips and thus expose them to further collapse from within. Some of the material from the cliffs is transported by wave action or currents along the coast, and is added to beaches, shingle ridges, or saltmarshes elsewhere. The history of accretion in places like Dungeness (Kent), the former port of Rye, the Lancashire dunes, the Culbin Sands (Nairnshire), and Scolt Head Island (Norfolk) is well known. All these matters are dealt with in Professor Steers's book (1969).

On the historical time-scale, accretion and erosion are chiefly important on 'soft' coasts, which have been evened out into straight lines or very gentle curves: examples are the coasts of north-east Norfolk or east Yorkshire. Since Anglo-Saxon times, accretion has added some tens of thousands of acres to the area of Britain, especially in the salt-marshes of Essex and the Wash. These are small areas compared to the amount gained through falling sea-levels, but are often in places where they have important effects: for instance, the medieval port of Harlech has been completely filled in. They include the wonderful shingle ridges of Spurn Point (east Yorkshire) and Dungeness. The greatest curiosity of all, Orford Beach (Suffolk), is 10 miles long and at its neck is less than 100 yards wide; it reached approximately its present shape at least 450 years ago.[572]

Erosion is often thought to be a serious matter: coastal authorities spend public money on defences against cliff erosion vastly greater than the value of the farmland which would otherwise be lost in the lifetime of the works. The biggest losses have been in East Yorkshire, where Domesday Book names 16 places that are now lost to the sea.[491] A strip about 35 miles long and 2/3 mile wide (one-fiftieth of the sub-county) has gone in 900 years. In Norfolk, Happisburgh and Eccles have lost their medieval churches to the sea. In parts of Suffolk at least half a mile has gone, including almost all the town of Dunwich; about half the town had gone by 1587, and the cliff has retreated 1/4 mile since (Fig. 17.1). Erosion is often betrayed by the roads that now run into the sea.

Since at least the Middle Ages, people have tried to prevent erosion and accretion – the latter in order to keep harbours from being silted or masked by shingle-spits. It was soon appreciated that to defend one place usually involves sacrificing another. The history of ports such as Yarmouth and Lowestoft, or Southwold and Dunwich, is full of attempts to direct the forces of nature to the perdition of a rival port. Southwold once lay by a shallow bay called Sole Bay, where the English and Dutch fleets fought in 1672. The town has been able to harden its seafront, which Dunwich, having early lost its harbour, could not afford to do. Centuries later, Dunwich to the south and Easton Bavents to the north have been devoured, so that Southwold now occupies a distinct cape (which the map still calls Sole Bay).

At present, accretion in England is diminished because of rising sea-level and the growth of sea-defences which cut off the supply of new material. Undefended coasts are probably being eroded faster than in previous centuries.

How Fens and Marshes Work

Most large coastal fen systems, including The Fens, consist of a salt-marsh

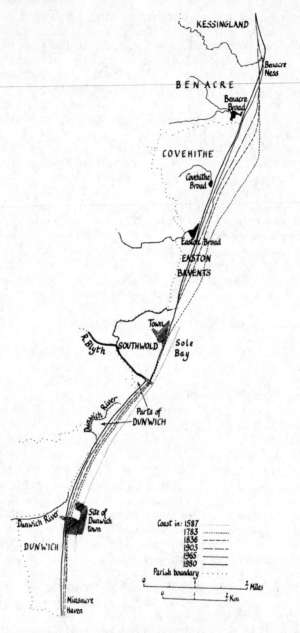

Fig. 17.1. Retreat of the Suffolk coast. The parishes of Dunwich and Easton Bavents have been reduced to slivers; the church of Easton and all but one of those in Dunwich had fallen over the cliffs by 1700. Southwold has lost little. The seventeenth-century Easton Ness has migrated to become Covehithe Ness and then Benacre Ness. 'Sole Bay' and 'Minsmere Haven' still remain on the map as reminders of a vanished topography. The three 'Broads' are not excavations like the Norfolk Broads but lagoons like Loe Pool (Chapter 16); they have migrated inland as the coast has retreated.

fringe, a seaward silt fen or marsh, and a landward peat fen. The silt is usually slightly higher than the others and, in a natural state, would only rarely be flooded. Silt and peat fens are interspersed with islands of upland, and formerly with permanent lakes.

Salt-marshes are dissected by branching, meandering creeks which fill at high tide and empty at low. These are relatively permanent, and are usually preserved as meandering dykes if the salt-marsh is made into farmland (Fig. 17.2).

Fens have rivers flowing into them from the upland; the drainage of about an eighth of England passes through The Fens on its way to the sea. Fen rivers, in their natural state, had broad, definite channels meandering through both peat and silt. The channels were lined with silt deposited by the rivers; they had natural embankments of silt, called *levées*, which confined the rivers during all but exceptional floods. Modern courses of fenland rivers are narrower and have artificial banks. Often they have sluices or hatches ('clyses' in Somerset) which allow the river to discharge at low tide but keep the sea out at high tide.

It is in the nature of fenland to be flooded, and of artificial embanking to make floods rare and catastrophic. They may come from surges of the sea, when storms pile the water against the coast. Historic surges have come nearly always between November and February (despite the belief in equinoctial gales).[573] They do not necessarily coincide with high spring tides; the great surge of 31 January 1953 would have been much worse if it had done so. Flooding can also come from inland, from spates on the rivers, especially if a surge keeps the sluices closed. To guard against this danger, lands called *washes* are set aside to be flooded when necessary; they are most easily made by setting the river-walls back from the river, as on the river Cam below Cambridge.

Flood risks get worse with time, for two reasons. A fenland river deposits silt in its bed and rises above the surrounding land. Eventually it may become unstable, breach a levée, and make off across country in a new course. The Hwang-ho in China is notorious for this instability. Our fen rivers, in their natural state, were surprisingly stable, being little changed even by marine transgressions. There have been many diversions, to such an extent that hardly any natural rivers now survive; but these changes are of Roman date or later, when silting has been aggravated by cultivation upstream, and most of them appear to be artificial. Strips of silt, left by the beds and levées of extinct rivers, are called *roddons*, and are a permanent record of all the fen rivers and canals that there have ever been. Their snaking shapes are familiar in air photographs (Plate XXIV).

When peatland is drained and cultivated, the peat shrinks, partly through compression and partly through oxidation. The land surface is lowered and drainage becomes more difficult. In The Fens, more than half the original area of peat has disappeared altogether; houses, bridges, and railways subside and lean; and many rivers are now perched 14 feet or more above the surrounding farmland. A famous illustration of peat wastage is the Holme Fen Post, an iron column, 22 feet long, buried upright in the peat of Holme Fen (Huntingdonshire) when it was drained, apparently for the first time, in 1848. The peat shrank 6 feet in the first twelve years of drainage. By 1890, 10 feet of the Post was exposed. The drainage of Holme Fen was then abandoned, and shrinkage stopped for thirty-five years. Since 1925 the peat has continued to shrink slowly, being affected by the resumed drainage of other fens nearby. By 1978 the total shrinkage was 12 feet 8½ inches.[574]

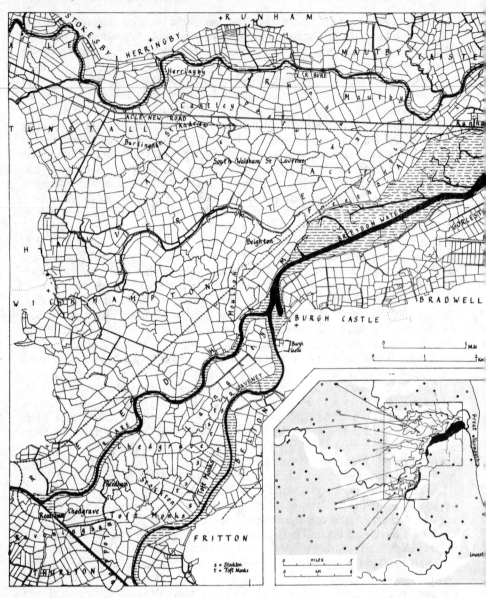

Fen vegetation I shall not try to summarize the immense range of plant communities in wet grassland, fen, bog, and salt-marsh. Historians of wetlands rarely say much about what the vegetation was, and surviving remnants may not be representative.

All native trees are very sensitive to salt in the soil, but many species tolerate some freshwater flooding. Fens quickly turn into woodland when not continuously wet. Most of Wicken Fen has thus become a wood in the last fifty years.[575] Many fens have been wooded in prehistory, but seldom in the last thousand years; most if not all fen woods are modern. Why this should be so is not clear, but it is an argument against the notion that fenland before Vermuyden was under-used.

Much fenland was grassland of some kind, like the Ouse Washes in The Fens now. Medieval records mention several useful plants, *juncus, scirpus, star*, etc., which translators carelessly render 'rush', 'flag', and so on, but which probably had definite meanings. There can be no doubt about *arundo* 'reed' and *carex* 'sedge', both still used for thatching and formerly also for fuel.

Reed is the giant grass *Phragmites australis*. It was (and is) cut annually in shallow water; it was sometimes transported many miles from fenland. For many centuries the reed thatcher (Medieval Latin *arundinator*) has been a different profession from the straw thatcher (*coopertor*). Sedge is properly *Cladium mariscus*, a much less common plant;* it has to be cut every fourth year.

---

* One of the few British plants also native in America, where it is called 'sawgrass'.

Fig. 17.2. Ditches and creeks in the east Norfolk marshes. Dotted lines: parish boundaries. Names in capitals: parishes with their marshes. Lower-case names: marshes belonging to parishes from which they are separated. Blank areas: upland.

In late Roman times this was a great estuary; there was a naval base below the clifftop fort of Burgh Castle. When sea-level fell in Anglo-Saxon times, the salt-marsh became valuable grazing land and was parcelled out among adjacent, and some distant, communities. When sea-level rose again, the marshes were retained by building and heightening banks along the rivers. The land is now well below ordinary high tide level. Each river is bordered by washland flooded at high water.

The map shows the state of *c.*1900. Until 1970 the marshes changed little, and many even of the nineteenth-century drainage windmills still stand. The original salt-marsh creeks (which in The Fens survive mainly as roddons) still function as drainage ditches. The parish boundaries usually follow such creeks. Some of the bigger creeks have turned into lanes which follow the course of their levées. There has been some local tidying-up; but the chief monuments to the Age of Straight Lines are the Acle New Road (1835), New Cut (1833 – the beginning of a Norwich Ship Canal), and railways (1843, 1845, 1882). These all overlie the earlier topography without disturbing it.

After many centuries of sensible use for grazing, this landscape and its famous wildlife are threatened by the cereal craze. The 'Halvergate Marshes' controversy was unresolved at the time of writing.

Inset: detached marshes and their parent settlements. Black points are parishes with contiguous marshland. White points are places with only detached marshland or none. Upland is shaded. There is some degree of forethought in the system, in that several all-upland parishes have acquired shares in the marshland, but there are many anomalies and no attempt at an equal distribution.

Sedge has wicked hacksaw-like leaves; the Anglo-Saxons remembered it because it hurts, and named the rune *eolh*, representing *x*, after it:

> Sedge hath its home   oftest in fen,
> groweth in water   woundeth grimly,
> blood draweth   from any man
> that maketh any   grasp at it.

The Runic Poem

Sedge makes even better thatch than reed, but is less used because it is so bloody to handle.

Fens in Prehistory

Coastal fen systems are largely the creation of rising sea-level. Before the Neolithic they were upland, level and rather ill-drained, but with only small areas of peat. They were covered with wildwood typical, except perhaps in the unusual stature of the trees, of the Lime Province (Fig. 5.2). Some of the 'submerged forests' of our west coasts are the stumps of such trees, killed by rising sea-level. Better known are the 'bog oaks' of the southern Fens. These huge logs – 80 feet to the first branch is not uncommon – represent the last generation of trees to grow on the mineral soil; they were killed by rising water-level, crashed down in storms, and were entombed in the newly-forming peat. Pines and yews are found in places as well as oaks. Pollen and other fossils show that lime, hazel, and alder were more abundant than oak,[576] but these rot easily and were killed in a way that did not preserve them.

Civilization came to fenland at about the same time as the sea began to influence it. To judge by the number of settlements round their edges, fens were some of the earliest land to be used, although we do not know exactly how. The best evidence comes from the Somerset Levels. People lived here on islands and peninsulas. They are chiefly known from their wooden trackways, built to give footing across the soft fen from island to island, and preserved by the ever-growing peat. Scores of trackways have been found; they are the earliest evidence both of woodmanship and of highways. Details are published in a special journal, *Somerset Levels Papers*.

The trackways are of many kinds, doubtless intended for different kinds of traffic or to use particular sizes of wood. The earliest, the Sweet Track, dated 4000 BC, although a mere footway, is the most sophisticated; it involves both underwood and timber. A line of oak planks was supported by an elaborate substructure of stakes and rails to prevent it from being sunk into the peat or displaced by floodwater.[577] From about 3000 BC, hurdles, made to be walked on, were laid down to form trackways. These hurdles are made of interwoven underwood rods, grown for the purpose, like a modern wattle hurdle but using stone tools.[578] Other trackways of various dates consisted of twigs and branches of birch (the lop-and-top of trees felled for some other purpose); of small split alder logs; or of planks cleft from biggish oaks. The tradition continued at least into the Iron Age, being linked to the lake villages of Glastonbury and Meare, but never recovered its Neolithic elaboration. Similar trackways existed in The Fens, though much less evidence has survived modern drainage. In the Bronze Age one apparently crossed a big river (Godwin 1978).

Peat reached something like its present extent in the Neolithic. In the Bronze Age, with rising sea-level, much of the present silt Fens was submerged and covered with marine clay.[579] Peat continued to form in more inland areas; with the passing of time, it grew above the general water-level and became more acid, forming raised bogs.[575]

The natural vegetation of fenland was probably a complexity of pools, reedbeds, grassland, bog-myrtle thickets, and woods, full of wonderful birds and fishes, like the Great Okefenokee Swamp in Georgia today. Trees grew on the peat wherever local or general drainage was sufficient. Stumps of alders and birches, like those of modern secondary fen woodland, have been found in and around the Somerset trackways. In The Fens, some of the peat dried out enough for oak, pine, or yew to grow; their remains form at least two upper layers of 'bog oaks' (Godwin 1978).

The First Draining of the Fens

Falling sea-level at the end of the Iron Age coincided with the coming of the Romans. They had the most elaborate fen-engineering technology that Europe has ever seen, the fruit of centuries of Mediterranean experience.[580] For the first time, by nature and art, the surface of the silt fens was made habitable.

Romano-British settlement in The Fens was fully investigated by the Fenland Research Committee when there was much more visible evidence than there is now.[581] The silt Fens, especially the landward part, were fully cultivated; farmsteads were at least as thick on the ground as they are now. The peat Fens were inhabited mainly on islands, levées, and occasional roddons.

The pattern of farms, fields, and lanes was haphazard; it looks like piecemeal native settlement rather than the rural planning which would be expected of a Roman colony (p.159). But it was assisted, and perhaps made possible, by great engineering works such as canals and river diversions. The Car Dyke, the biggest artificial watercourse that The Fens have ever had, skirted their western edge for nearly 90 miles between Lincoln and Cambridge. Its main function was as a cutoff channel, intercepting lesser rivers and avoiding the burden of maintaining their courses across the fen.[580] A main road ran through the middle of The Fens, connecting the Midlands through Norfolk and the Broads fenland to a port at Caister-by-Yarmouth.

The Fens were probably not specially attractive to the Romano-Britons, but were an overflow of population from what was already, by the second century, a rather crowded upland. As in the Middle Ages, livestock may have been important, the peat fens being used for summer and autumn grazing. The Somerset Levels tell a similar story of silt-fen settlement, though there is not yet much evidence for drainage works.[582] Among inland fens, the Romans appear to have dealt fully with Otmoor. A main road went right across the middle of the moor; there were settlements round its edges, and the town of Alchester was built on a satellite fen.[583]

Salt-making was important in most coastal marshes. It began in the Iron Age and has left abundant remains, sometimes mounds, of pottery containers, evaporating equipment, and burnt earth. These are known best in the Essex marshes ('Red Hills'),[584] but also in Somerset, The Fens, and elsewhere. Their location suggests that silt fens were in some way productive of fuel for evaporation, such as reeds or sedge; already very little of the English coast had woodland.

The Roman settlements were short-lived; on archaeological evidence they declined before the end of the Empire. The cause may have been some combination of rising sea-level, the self-destructive tendency that plagues all fen drainage works, and a disintegrating society that could not keep up the engineering. The farms were deserted, though where not covered by later deposits their fields remained visible until our own time. Many of the watercourses are now reduced to roddons, but not all: the River Cam still joins the Little Ouse instead of making its way to Wisbech, and the south-eastern canals – Soham, Wicken, Reach, Swaffham Bulbeck, and Bottisham Lodes – still function. Perhaps the best surviving Roman canal is the Car Dyke along Potterhanworth Wood, Lincolnshire, with its huge bank of spoil, on which great trees grow, now within the wood.

The Second Draining of the Fens

Anglo-Saxon Even in the darkest of the Dark Ages, fenland was not wholly abandoned to wildfowl and devils. St Guthlac could find a local fisherman able to take him to Crowland in the heart of The Fens, where treasure-hunters had preceded him. The very name *Crugland* appears to remember the Celtic word *crug*, a barrow.

The re-settling of The Fens began well back in the Anglo-Saxon period. Place-names such as Skirbeck show that Vikings as well as Angles were involved. By Domesday Book there were fifty villages, regularly spaced every mile or so in a curious arc round the Wash from Skegness to King's Lynn (Fig. 17.3). They lay on the highest belt of the silt Fen, least exposed to flooding; but they would not have been habitable without the protection of two great banks, the seabank in front and the fenbank in the rear. The banks are first heard of in post-Conquest documents, but were then already long-established with alterations, and had formal arrangements for their maintenance.[585]

The inland Fens were thinly populated, and settlements were almost all on islands. But the charters tell us that by the eleventh century if not before (the critical documents are early forgeries and may copy previous topography) even the peat fen was just as much parcelled out into ownerships as was the upland. Natural lakes – Trundle Mere, Draymere, Whittlesey Mere, etc. – were valued as fisheries; there were named rivers, dykes, and bridges. Vegetation is not specified, except that there were a few woods such as Alderlound and Apinholt. Already there are many references to drainage works, such as 'King Cnut's Delf' (after which King's Delph in Whittlesey is named).

By the end of the Anglo-Saxon period civilization had come to most parts of The Fens, but was still rather thinly spread; The Fens in Domesday Book had less population, agriculture, and wealth than the upland. Substantial engineering works had somehow been organized. To construct a seabank and a fenbank, each 50 miles long, is not something which even in the twentieth century we do every year.

The other great fenlands tell a similar story of settlers encouraged at first by falling sea-levels but soon making banks and dykes of their own. Domesday Book finds this process about half-finished in siltlands but still very incomplete in peatlands. Romney Marsh is very well documented in charters;[586] estates within it are recorded as far back as 700, and by 1000 it had a town, New Romney. Lydd has remains of an Anglo-Saxon stone church. The Somerset

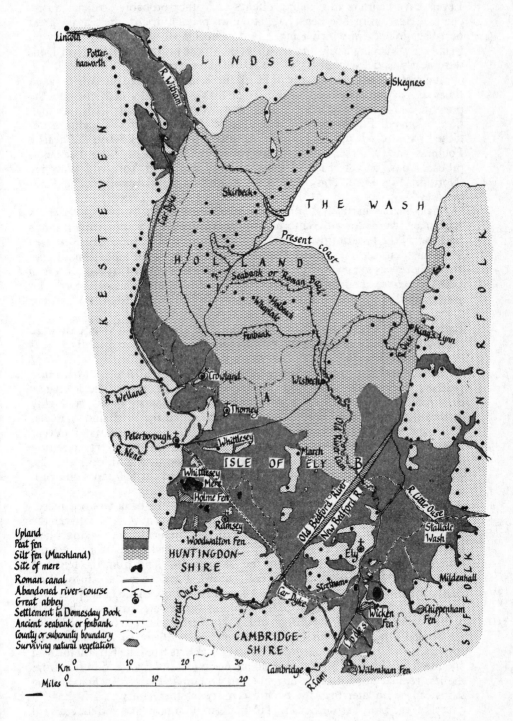

Fig. 17.3. The Fens.

Levels have charters mentioning ditches and other probably artificial water-courses. Here, as in The Fens, habitation was mainly towards the sea; the great peat-bogs inland, in which King Alfred campaigned, were inhabited only on islands. By 1086 the Yorkshire marshes (except the peatlands of the lower Don) were nearly as densely settled as the rest of the county.

Much salt-marsh, particularly in Essex and Kent, was valued in Anglo-Saxon times as pasture for sheep, a use which has occasionally continued to the present. Salt-marsh pastures are often at a distance from the places to which they belonged. For instance, Canvey Island (Essex) consists of eighteen de-tached parts of ten upland parishes, situated up to 7 miles away; the nearby Foulness and Wallasea Islands were so subdivided, as were the marshes – probably now out of reach of the tides – of the lower Yare and Waveney (Norfolk) (Fig. 17.2). This parallels the Anglo-Saxon exclaves of woodland and meadow.

Anglo-Saxon charters often mention inland fens and marshes (cf p.9). They have many words for different kinds of watercourses. *Lace* apparently meant a backwater, the lesser of two or more parallel courses of a river. *Ea* is still used (now misspelt *eau*) of artificial Fenland channels. At South Stoneham (Hampshire) there was a 'new eau' in 1045.[587] The charters tell us that the process of canalizing rivers and making weirs had already begun. This was partly for water-mills, which are often mentioned and are known also from archaeology.

Early Middle Ages Fenland communities after the Norman Conquest were exceptionally lucky in having abundant room for expansion, especially as sea-levels continued to fall.

In The Fens, settlements expanded seaward into salt-marsh and fenward into peatland. New banks were advanced and innings were made. The sea-banks culminated in the making, or re-making, of the 'Roman Bank', a mighty earthwork more than 60 miles long, running all round the Wash and its inlets. This bank was carefully constructed with spurs, acting as breakwaters, every 200 yards on its seaward side; beneath the bank were timber culverts to release drainage water at low tide.[588] These are dated to the thirteenth century. The bank, the greatest of all fen engineering works, stood for 500 years and pro-tected more than a million acres of land.

We can only guess at how the making of the great sea-bank was organized. Collaboration on a smaller scale is recorded in an agreement of 1286 between the parishes of Whaplode and Holbeach and a private landowner for making a new common sea-dyke with a sluice in it. The parishes had funds to pay for the land.[585] There are many records of the 'assarting' of land from the fen. For instance, in the thirteenth century the southward assarts in the Lincolnshire fens met the northward assarts of the Isle of Ely and occasioned a dispute over the county boundary.[589] Some of the intaking was private; some was the work of the Fenland abbeys or the Bishop of Ely. No Vermuyden can be identified for the Second Draining, although the name of Conan Ellison of Holbeach often appears in twelfth-century records.[590] The new assarts from the fen still form an organized landscape of regular straight strips up to 4 miles long, differing from the less regular quadrilaterals of the Third Draining (Fig. 17.4). Some of the strips can be no later than the twelfth century, as they contain Early English churches (eg. Elm, Parson Drove). The pre-Conquest farmland and the seaward intakes are both very irregular, with ditches that preserve the meanders of salt-marsh creeks.

How were the works maintained? The records of manors deal largely with the 'custom of the marsh': particular farmers were responsible for specific banks and channels. The documents were concerned chiefly with negligence and breakdown, and thus give the impression that the system did not work well. From at least the thirteenth century there were regionally-organized Courts of Sewers, with powers to order work to be done; and as the sea-level began to rise again the Crown's authority increased in matters of marsh defence.

From being less prosperous than the upland in 1086, The Fens came to have, by the fourteenth century, much the greatest concentration of agricultural prosperity in England. The Lay Subsidy assessment of 1334 tells us that the seaward Fens contained thirty-one out of the 106 richest places in all England.[591] This amply explains the splendid early medieval Fenland architecture.

Where did the wealth of the Fenmen come from? They were well placed to sell cash crops which could be taken away by barge. Specialities such as eels, and the various wild birds thought to be edible, were important but were hardly wealth. There was some conventional agriculture: some assarts from the fen are stated to have been ploughed. But the riches of The Fens were chiefly in grass, some of which was private and some communal (with grazing rights often including distant parishes). Fenmen had flocks and herds of their own, producing meat, butter, wool, and livestock for sale; they also sold hay and hired grazing to upland farmers. They sold reeds and sedge for thatching, and peat, reeds, and sedge for fuel. This fuel was also used for boiling salt; the edges of the Wash were one of the chief sources of supply to that salt-addicted age.[585,592]

The inland Fens were less fully developed, but here too there were medieval drainage works as well as the remains of Roman works. Arable covered the fen islands and some of the margins of the peat. Churches, as at March and Whittlesey, record the prosperity of those times.

By 1300 The Fens, except for some of the remoter peatlands, were fully used: conflicts often happened between, for instance, reed-cutters and fishermen. The seaward half of Fenland was already much as it is now. For probably the only time in known history we see men working with the distinctive landscape of The Fens, using it to complement the upland, instead of against it. Many Fenland products grew on undrained or partly-drained land. Having The Fens at hand enabled Cambridge and similar places to dispense with pasture, meadow, and woodland.[241]

The Somerset Levels, also, were pastoral and complemented the upland; upland parishes had rights of pasture in them from many miles away. But arable was increasing, both on the siltlands and around islands in the peat moors. All the rivers were diverted into straight courses, apparently for transport as well as flood-control.[593] Much of this was organized by Glastonbury and Muchelney Abbeys. On the Essex coast, Foulness Island – a polder made entirely out of marshland – was mainly enwalled, and a sixth of it ploughed, before 1420.[595] In Romney Marsh sea and river walls were built and sewers and other watercourses were dug; the greatest watercourse, the 'Rhee Wall', was made in the thirteenth century in a vain attempt to rescue the port of Romney from silting.[586] Up and down the country, innumerable sea-banks and straightenings of rivers are to be attributed to this period.

Fenland Forests The importance of fens as farmland is measured by the rarity

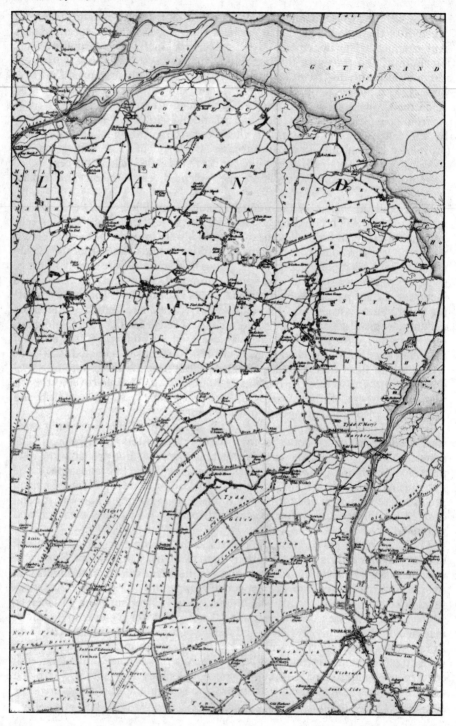

of fenland Forests. The only ones of which I have record are the Forests of Kesteven (Lincolnshire), Hatfield Chase (south-east Yorkshire), and parts of Galtres north-west of York), Malvern Chase (Worcestershire), and Huntingdon.

Roedeer and probably red can be fenland animals: there was a poaching case involving 40 roe at Whittlesey in 1254.[594] But fens, except in a few backward corners, were valuable land, of which the Crown and the great lay lords happened to own little. By the twelfth century, it was difficult to declare a Forest in fenland without infringing some powerful ecclesiastical interest.

Parks in fenland were few, and were mainly on islands.[193]

Later Middle Ages and sixteenth century Fens have always been vulnerable to the occasional big flood, but in the time of their general prosperity the loss of a year's crop now and then seems not to have been much missed. The 'super-surge' of 15 December 1287, which affected especially east Norfolk (p.359) and Romney Marsh, was the first sign of the rising sea-level which has made the fenman's lot more and more difficult. Through the fourteenth century and beyond, there are many records of surges and breaches, and of royal Commissions of Walls and Dykes appointed to enforce responsibilities for upkeep.

The defence of the marshes was largely successful. There were no big losses of enwalled land; there were even a few gains.[595] This is surprising for a time in which much of the Netherlands was permanently lost to the sea, and upland farming in England was faring badly. Ploughland was maintained and even extended in fen and marsh when it was in retreat in the Midlands (p.338).

The upkeep of sea-defences is well documented in Essex.[573] Underwood for this purpose was probably a major use of Essex woodland. Sea-walls were thatched with faggots and mended with hurdles. A breach at Harwich in 1551 was repaired with 967 piles interwoven with 1232 bundles of rods – this method is still used in the Harwich area to trap silt. At West Thurrock the marsh (partly arable as late as 1586) was defended by walls of chalk from nearby Purfleet. Immense monies were somehow found: in 1409 the Abbess of Barking spent £2000 on saving the abbey lands. At precarious Foulness in 1552 the patron of the church 'dydde take awaye the bells . . . to mayntayne ye walls against ye sea'.

Malaria and the fenland way of life From the sixteenth to the nineteenth century the many advantages of fenland were offset by a very high risk of malaria, which was seldom fatal but made life sickly and short. It was most prevalent in coastal marshes, especially those of Essex and Kent, which suggests that it was carried by the brackish-water mosquito *Anopheles maculipennis* subspecies *atroparvus*.[596] It did occur inland in The Fens, the Broads, and near

Fig. 17.4. The seaward Fens, showing stages in the Second Draining. The original, late Anglo-Saxon, landscape is in the middle, around Holbeach and Sutton St Mary's, behind the so-called 'Old Roman Bank'. Its meandering roads are strongly influenced by creeks in the salt-marsh which was then emerging from the sea. The various geometrical landscapes in the south-west half of the map were laid out during the southward expansions of the twelfth and thirteenth centuries. A later expansion northward took in areas such as Holbeach Marsh from the Wash; these areas show the influence of salt-marsh creeks. Ordnance Survey 1824.

the lower Trent, but apparently not in the smaller inland fens nor in the many other places (eg. woods) which harbour mosquitoes.[597]

Malaria gradually declined in the nineteenth century, and is last heard of as a native disease in Kent in 1918.[596] Why it disappeared is a mystery. Nothing was intentionally done against it. Fen drainage is not an explanation: there are still plenty of the right mosquitoes. Various theories (eg. mosquitoes no longer coming indoors) have been suggested.

It is not known whether there was malaria in the Middle Ages. The great churches and fen-banks seem hardly to be the work of a fever-ridden population. Possibly a change in the post-medieval environment, such as the encroachment of salt water, enabled malaria to establish itself where it had not been before.

The Third Draining of the Fens

The medieval fen way of life survived the dissolution of the monasteries. There may have been some decline in the peat fens, but in general the system still worked well in the sixteenth century; The Fens were then still wealthier than the rest of Lincolnshire.[598] The incentive to change it was not local dissatisfaction but the hopes of outside landowners, especially the Crown (as confiscator of monkish lands) and the Earl of Bedford, to make easy money out of arable crops and improved grassland in the peat fens. Under an Act of Parliament in 1600 it became possible for big landowners having shares in a fen to overrule lesser parties and to suppress any common-rights which stood in the way of drainage.

The story of the draining of the 'Bedford Level', that is the peat portion of The Fens, is well known.[599] On the advice of Vermuyden an elaborate system of drains and river-diversions was dug. These included the Old and New Bedford Rivers (1637 and 1651), diversions of the Great Ouse, each 21 miles long – the greatest artificial watercourses since Roman times. The scheme was unpopular: it infringed rights of property; it took away common-rights which could not adequately be compensated; it bestowed lands on the 'Adventurers' who had put up the capital; it made existing inhabitants responsible for maintaining works which they had not asked for; it damaged the natural ecology and reduced the birds and fish; and it grossly underestimated the practical difficulties. Also it was involved with the less scrupulous activities of Charles I, who here (as in the Forests, p.139) failed in his royal duty of protecting the interests of his lesser subjects. The works were much delayed; the important feature of a new Car Dyke, to intercept rivers entering the Fens from the east, was not dug until the 1960s.

Vermuyden's scheme was a short-lived success. It failed to allow for the shrinkage of the peat. Water which should have drained into the rivers by gravity had soon to be pumped by windmills. An ingenious and ramshackle system of drains at different levels had to be constructed and successively adapted. The thinner peats disappeared, and with them the best soils whose cultivation was the original object of the scheme. The lowering of land-level has so far been coped with, though at times with very little margin of safety, by introducing steam, then diesel, and now electric pumps. The present state of The Fens is a somewhat precarious triumph of technology over a deteriorating situation, made possible by vigilance, expensive repairs, and an ever-increasing input of energy.

At times of prosperity almost every little corner of The Fens, and even the meres, has been drained. The destruction of Whittlesey Mere in 1851 was tragic and unreasonable, for Holme Fen nearby was permanently abandoned not long after. Where the Third Draining was not wholly successful, something of the medieval landscape lingered to within living memory, as by the River Lark near Mildenhall; up to World War I this was a place of wonder and delight, with the willow-lined river, full of fish, bordered by commons still in use and meadows with snipe and corncrakes.[600]

Other peat-fens have a similar history. Before working on The Fens, Vermuyden had drained on the Lincolnshire-Yorkshire border. Here he was less successful, and Thorne Waste and its sister moors are still bog to this day. In Somerset, where the Crown had become a large landowner, Charles I and Vermuyden got up a scheme which was defeated by the commoners.[593] Draining, including further canalizing the rivers and destroying the meres, was mainly done between 1780 and 1830. It has made less difference than in The Fens: the land is still pasture, and the peat (with its buried prehistoric trackways) has survived without much shrinkage.

The Enclosure Act movement was very hostile to wetlands. Although we did not, as the French Revolution did, 'abolish' all marshes by statute, agricultural writers treated the existence of even small fens as a scandal; the greedier landowners, not deterred by the poor results from draining the bigger peatlands, repeated the same mistakes on the smaller ones. For instance, in Otmoor, after an Enclosure Act in 1815, great earthworks were dug, and the opposition of the lesser commoners involved legal proceedings, riots, and military intervention. The works were largely defeated by the terrain; all the destruction, ill-feeling, and expense produced only unimproved pasture instead of the arable land which Arthur Young had predicted.[583] The same happened in many other inland fens that had hitherto been protected by common-rights.

Further salt-marshes were enwalled. In the Wash, the coastline was advanced by an average of about 3 miles between 1620 and 1770, and has been set forward by another mile since then; there have been some intakes even in this century. In Essex, Canvey Island was enwalled by Dutch 'adventurers' in the 1620s;[601] down to the nineteenth century additions were made to Foulness Island and the neighbouring coasts. The Traeth Mawr at Portmadoc, once the most beautiful estuary in Wales, was embanked by William Maddocks in the 1800s.

With the general rise in sea-level, it has often become difficult to hold even the ancient innings. At Dagenham (Essex) a surge on 29 October 1707 made a 14-foot breach in the medieval sea-bank. To repair it was almost beyond the power of eighteenth-century technology: companies were formed and bankrupted, and a special Act of Parliament passed, before the gap was stopped in 1720.[602] Many small innings have been lost; for instance, after the 1953 surge Bridgemarsh Island (Essex) was sacrificed in order to use the clay of its walls to repair breaches elsewhere.

Fens and Marshes As They Are Now

In wetlands, more than in most places, the improver has not known when to stop. Since 1945 there has been an onslaught on fen and marsh to make arable land or improved pasture by dint of yet more pumped drainage, and to a lesser extent for industry (as in the Thames Estuary). People have even taken to living on fens and salt-marshes; occasionally, as on Canvey Island in 1953, they pay for it with their lives. Improvement at the public expense still goes on: at the time of writing, Halvergate Marshes in east Norfolk are the subject of a big controversy over ploughing, as if Norfolk did not have enough ploughland already.

Least affected are the salt-marshes. Innings from the land and rising sea-level have squeezed them to a fraction of their former extent, but they are still beautiful, have a wide range of vegetation, and are internationally important for birds. Where they survive they are usually not degraded, except by the aggressive growth of the newly-created cord-grass (p.60). Archaeological features include the Red Hills of ancient salt evaporation, ruined sea-walls, the ridge-and-furrow of brief attempts at cultivation, and the 'farmers' teeth' or lines of stakes, projecting from the mud, marking successive retreats of sea-defences.

Of fens, marshes, and bogs, only small examples survive complete; even in Ireland an intact large bog is a rarity. Surviving fragments of large wetlands are usually degraded in some way: it is rarely possible to preserve a sample and to drain the rest.

About ten pieces of The Fens survive, mostly against the upland or in side-basins where they are partly protected from the general drainage. A wonderful survival of the prehistoric Fens is Dersingham-Wolferton Fen, like a miniature Okefenokee Swamp, in an out-of-the-way corner north of King's Lynn, fed by copious springs of acid water. It has great areas of *Sphagnum*, characteristic plants such as bog-asphodel, cranberry, and sundew, and patches, though not excessive, of birchwood. It is a relict of the raised bogs which once lay along the Fen-upland edge.

The best relict of the medieval silt Fens is the Ouse Washes between the Old and New Bedford Rivers, which survive because they are still used as a flood reservoir every winter. In summer they are dry and are grazed by cattle. The Washes are an internationally important place for migrating birds, and are partly owned by the Royal Society for the Protection of Birds and by Cambridgeshire and Norfolk Naturalists' Trusts. Some common-rights remain. Without grazing the Washes would 'tumble down to woodland' as has Stallode Wash on the Little Ouse. The Ouse Washes preserve many kinds of fen vegetation, and their surface features are a record of millennia. The most prominent is the great roddon of the prehistoric River Cam at Welney, lined with Romano-British settlement earthworks.

Wicken Fen has been a nature reserve for nearly a century. It survived because of complicated landownership: it was divided into strips like a dole-meadow. Most of the strips now belong to the National Trust. It is full of the ridge-and-furrow of nineteenth-century and earlier peat-digging. The Fen now stands about eight feet above its drained and shrunken surroundings. Although isolated except on the west, it is now much too dry, and water has to be pumped on to it. The calcareous peat shows some tendency to turn into a raised bog on drying; the surface of some of the ridges is strongly acid with *Sphagnum*. After 1920 it was allowed to become woodland, with great detriment to its plants and insects. In the last twenty years the National Trust has made much progress in grubbing out trees and in restoring management such as harvesting reed and sedge. In 1982 the fen violet, *Viola persicifolia*, reappeared; it was a Wicken speciality last seen in 1916; it comes with peat-digging and disturbance, and apparently can wait as buried seed, like a coppice-plant (p.108), for at least a century.[603]

Woodwalton Fen is an area of undrained peat between Third Draining ditches. It is much affected by peat-cutting, attempts at cultivation, and shrinkage of its surroundings, but still has some of its acidic vegetation (eg. bog-myrtle).[604] Holme Fen, as we have seen, reverted to fen after a period of cultivation. Chippenham and Great Wilbraham Fens are in side-basins fed by springs. All four are much overgrown with trees.

In other fen districts grassland survives, some of it unimproved and a relict of Second Draining, with ancient dykes and other artefacts. In the Norfolk Broads there is still a dwindling expanse of grazing marsh on the silt; the meandering ditches – relics of saltmarsh creeks – are famous for plant life (now threatened by runoff of fertilizers and chemicals). In the Somerset Levels there are wet grasslands on both the silt and the small area of remaining peat; the latter is being dug away for horticultural peat. In the Broads, where peat-digging might be beneficial, none happens, and the inland peat-fen, once grazed and cut for hay, is now largely woodland of alder, sallow, and even oak. In the Yorkshire fens, some 'ings' – silt-fen grazing marshes – survive, though again threatened by arable farming; and the peat-fens, though relatively small, are largely intact in places like Thorne Waste.

There remain a diminishing number of inland fens and bogs which are either intact or have reverted from attempts at drainage. Like ancient woods, each one is different from every other; I can give only one example. Redgrave and Lopham Fens are on the Norfolk-Suffolk border, in that curious place where the rivers Waveney and Little Ouse flow east and west from the same source. The old peat-diggings here take the form not of furrows but of deep crater-like pits with paths winding between them. These pits are famous as the only home of *Dolomedes plantarius*, the largest British spider. The Suffolk Trust for Nature Conservation here struggles against drying-out, tree growth, and water pollution – the three enemies of fen conservation almost everywhere.

Fenland, even reduced to arable land, preserves some remains of its history. There are industrial monuments, such as the great steam-engine at Stretham (near Ely) and the pumping windmills of the east Norfolk marshes. Old sea-walls are often left behind inland; they are occasionally called back into service to contain flooding which a newer wall fails to hold. Arable fens are a palimpsest of soil-marks: roddons, irregular Roman fields, more regular later fields, and the big pale tracts of shell-marl that mark the sites of meres. These have by now been thoroughly studied in air photographs. Much is still to be done in another area of fenland research – the careful walking of fields, including those of fen islands, looking for scatters of pottery. We still know little of the great buildings, or of the details of the farmsteads, of the First Draining.

Rivers as they are now

The natural habit of most gentle rivers and streams is to meander. Meanders may change of themselves, more often over millennia than over centuries. They most often disappear because people dislike them and cut them off. Sometimes this has a purpose, in that shorter watercourses in fenland delay the problem of silting. Cutting of meanders began in antiquity. Natural watercourses are now quite uncommon, except for some very small ones and those, such as the River Tees, whose meanders were made by a greater river in geological antiquity and are too deep to be tidied away. Lost meanders make ox-bow lakes; even if filled in, a former watercourse may be kept on record in the shape of a parish boundary which still follows the meanders.

The most familiar earthworks that go with rivers are mill-leats, canals which run parallel to a river but at a less gradient so as to gain a difference in height which drives a watermill. The technology goes back to Anglo-Saxon times. Leats often survive the disuse of the mill. In Cambridge city, the river itself has been made into a mill-leat, diverted by massive embankments to follow the edge of a natural gravel terrace.

Fish-weirs are devices of Anglo-Saxon origin consisting of wooden fish-traps placed across the current between an island and one bank. The other side of the island was left open for navigation and for some fish to escape. Fish-weir islands were commonly artificial, placed to take advantage of natural gravel riffles. D.J. Pannett has found remains of forty fish-weirs, some of which still operated in the nineteenth century, on the Shropshire part of the Severn.[605] There was a similar device on the River Calder near Wakefield.[606]

ABBREVIATIONS

AHR	*Agricultural History Review*
BARBS	*British Archaeological Reports, British Series*
BARIS	*British Archaeological Reports, International Series*
BC	*Biological Conservation*
BCS	Birch, W. de. G. *Cartularium Saxonicum* London (1885–93).
BM	British Library
CBA	Council for British Archaeology
CRO	Cambridgeshire Record Office
EHR	*Economic History Review*
EN	*Essex Naturalist*
ERO	Essex Record Office
ESRO	Suffolk Record Office, Ipswich
FS	*Field Studies*
GJ	*Geographical Journal*
GRO	Gwent Record Office
JE	*Journal of Ecology*
JHG	*Journal of Historical Geography*
JLSB	*Journal of the Linnaean Society (Botany)*
K	Kemble, J.M. *Codex diplomaticus aevi Saxonici* London (1839–48).
LH	*Landscape History*
MA	*Medieval Archaeology*
MCR	Merton College (Oxford) Records
NC	*Nature in Cambridgeshire*
NNRO	Norfolk & Norwich Record Office
PCAS	*Proceedings of Cambridge Antiquarian Society*
PhTRS	*Philosophical Transactions of the Royal Society*
PRO	Public Record Office
PSIA	*Proceedings of the Suffolk Institute of Archaeology*
SF	*Scottish Forestry*
SLP	*Somerset Levels Papers*
TDAAS	*Transactions of the Devonshire Association for the Advancement of Science*
USNA	United States National Archives, Washington (Cartographic Branch)
VA	*Vernacular Architecture*
VCH	*Victoria County History*
WSRO	Suffolk Record Office, Bury St Edmund's

BIBLIOGRAPHY

A selection of works of general interest, referred to in the text by author's name and date.

Aberg, F.A. (1978) *Medieval moated sites* CBA Research Report **17**.
Baker, A.R.H. and Butlin, R.A. (eds) (1973) *Studies of field systems in the British Isles* Cambridge.
Beresford, M. (1957, 2nd ed 1971) *History on the ground* Methuen, London.
Body, R. (1982) *Agriculture: the triumph and the shame* Temple Smith, London.
Bowen, H.C. and Fowler, P.J. (eds) (1978) *Early land allotment* BARBS **48**.
Chadwick, L. (1982) *In search of heathland* Dennis Dobson, London.
Crawford, O.G.S. (1953) *Archaeology in the field* Dent, London.
Darby, H.C. (1971) *The Domesday geography of Eastern England* Cambridge. (Parallel volumes for other regions.)
Darby, H.C. (ed) (1973) *A new historical geography of England* Cambridge.
Darby, H.C. and Versey, G.R. (1975) *Domesday gazetteer* Cambridge.
Dimbleby, G.W. (1962) *The development of British heathlands and their soils* Oxford.

Duffey, E. (ed) (1974) *Grassland ecology and wildlife management* Institute of Terrestrial Ecology, London.

Ekwall, E. (1960) *The concise Oxford dictionary of English place-names* Oxford.

Fitzrandolph, H.E. and Hay, M.D. (1926) *The rural industries of England and Wales. I. Timber and underwood industries and some village workshops* Oxford.

Gimingham, C.H. (1972) *Ecology of heathlands* Chapman & Hall, London.

Godwin, H. (1975) *History of the British flora* 2nd ed Cambridge.

Godwin, H. (1978) *Fenland: its ancient past and uncertain future* Cambridge.

Hawksworth, D.L. (ed) (1974) *The changing flora and fauna of Britain* Academic Press, London.

Hooke, D. (1981) *Anglo-Saxon landscapes in the west Midlands: the charter evidence BARBS*.

Hoskins, W.G. (1955) *The making of the English landscape* Hodder & Stoughton, London.

Hoskins, W.G. (1959) *Local history in England* Longmans, London.

Hoskins, W.G. (1967) *Fieldwork in local history* Faber, London.

Lambert, J.M., Jennings, J.N., Smith, C.T., Green, C. and Hutchinson, J.N. (1960) *The making of the Broads: a reconsideration of their origin in the light of new evidence* Royal Geographical Society, London.

Lever, C. (1977) *The naturalized animals of the British Isles* Hutchinson, London.

Linnard, W. (1982) *Welsh woods and forests: history and utilization* Cardiff.

Mabey, R. (1980) *The common ground: a place for nature in Britain's future?* Hutchinson, London.

Margary, I.D. (1973) *Roman roads in Britain* 3rd ed Baker, London.

Pearsall, W.H. (1950) *Mountains and moorlands* Collins, London.

Peterken, G.F. (1981) *Woodland conservation and management* Chapman and Hall, London.

Pollard, E., Hooper M.D. and Moore, N.W. (1974) *Hedges* Collins, London.

Prince, H.C. (1964) 'The origin of pits and depressions in Norfolk' *Geography* **49** 15–32.

Pugsley, A.J. (1939) *Dewponds in fact and fable* Country Life, London.

Rackham, O. (1975) *Hayley Wood: its history and ecology* Cambs & Isle of Ely Naturalists' Trust, Cambridge.

Rackham, O. (1976) *Trees and woodland in the British landscape* Dent, London.

Rackham, O. (1978) 'Archaeology and land-use history' *Epping Forest – the natural aspect?* ed D. Corke *Essex Naturalist* **N.S.2** 16–57.

Rackham, O. (1980) *Ancient woodland: its history, vegetation and uses in England* Edward Arnold, London.

Ratcliffe, D.A. (1977) *A nature conservation review* Cambridge.

Richens, R.H. (1983) *Elm* Cambridge.

Rowley, T. (ed) (1981) *The evolution of marshland landscapes* Department of External Studies, Oxford.

St Joseph, J.K.S. (ed) (1977) *The uses of air photography* 2nd ed Baker, London.

Sheail, J. (1971) *Rabbits and their history* Newton Abbot.

Sheail, J. (1980) *Historical ecology: the documentary evidence* Institute of Terrestrial Ecology, Cambridge.

Shoard, M. (1980) *The theft of the countryside* Bath.

Smith, A.H. (1956) *English place-name elements* Cambridge.

Steers, J.A. (1969) *The sea coast* 2nd ed Collins, London.

Tansley, A.G. (1939) *The British Islands and their vegetation* Cambridge.

Taylor, C. (1974) *Fieldwork in medieval archaeology* Batsford, London.

Taylor, C. (1975) *Fields in the English landscape* Dent, London.

Taylor, C. (1979) *Roads and tracks of Britain* Dent, London.

Timperley, H.W. and Brill, E. (1965) *Ancient trackways of Wessex* Dent, London.

West, R.G. (1977) *Pleistocene geology and biology* 2nd ed Longmans, London.

REFERENCES

1 Rodwell, R. and Rodwell, K. *Historic churches: a wasting asset* CBA Research Report **19** (1977).

2 Maitland, F.W. *Domesday Book and beyond* Cambridge (1897). [Reprinted (Fontana, London) 1960 and later.]

3 Tusser, T. *Five hundred pointes of good husbandrie* (1573) [Ed W. Payne and S.J. Herrtage, Trübner 1878.]

4 Rackham, O. 'Observations on the historical ecology of Boeotia [Greece].' *Annual of the British School of Archaeology at Athens* **78** (1983), 291–351.

5 Evelyn, J. *Sylva, or a discourse of forest-trees* 1st ed London (1664).

6 [Defoe, D.] *A Tour thro' the whole Island of Great Britain* London (1724).

7 Erdtman, G. 'Studies in the micropalaeontology of post-glacial deposits in northern Scotland and the Scotch Isles, with special reference to the history of the woodlands', *JLSB* **46** (1924), 449–504.

8 Davies, W. *An early Welsh microcosm: studies in the Llandaff charters* Royal Historical Society, London (1978).

9 Sinclair, J. *The statistical account of Scotland* 21 vols Edinburgh (1791–9). *The new statistical account for Scotland* Edinburgh (1936).

10 *The Civil Survey AD 1654–1656*, ed R.C. Simington. 10 vols Stationery Office, Dublin (1931–61).

11 Sawyer, P.H. *From Roman Britain to Norman England* Methuen, London (1978).

12 BCS 1048.

13 Taylor, C.C. *Village and farmstead: a history of rural settlement in England* Philip, London [1983].

14 Kemble, J.M. *Codex diplomaticus aevi Saxonici* 6 vols London (1839–48).

15 Birch, W. de G. *Cartularium Saxonicum* 3 vols London (1885–93).

16 Hart, C.R. *The early charters of Eastern England* Leicester (1966). (Parallel volumes for other regions.)

17 Sawyer, P.H. *Anglo-Saxon charters: an annotated list and bibliography* Royal Historical Society, London (1968).

18 Grundy, G.B. *Saxon Oxfordshire: charters and ancient highways* Oxford (1933). (He wrote many books and articles on similar themes.)

19 Unpublished; three medieval copies are BM Cott. Claud. C xi, Gonville & Caius College (Cambridge) MS 489/485, Ely Diocesan Registry (in CUL) G/3/27.

20 Rackham (1980) p. 19.

21 Price, D.J. 'Medieval land surveying and topographical maps.' *GJ* **121** (1955), 1–10.

22 [Edmonds, A.J.] *A history of Great Gransden in the county of Huntingdon* Tomson, St Neot's (1892–3).

23 Jones, B.M. and Griffiths, J.C. *Aerial surveying by rapid methods* Cambridge (1925).

24 Evans, G.E. *Where beards wag all: the relevance of the oral tradition* Faber, London (1971).

25 Thomas, K. *Man and the natural world: changing attitudes in England* Allen Lane, London (1983).

26 Rackham (1976) p.101.

27 Rackham (1980) p.237.

28 Mellanby, K. 'Hedges – habitat or history.' *Natural World* 5 (1982), 27–9.

29 Marquand, E.D. 'In memoriam John Ralfs.' *Report and Transactions of Penzance Natural History Society* NS 3 (1890), 225–40.

30 Martin, P.S. and Wright, H.E. (eds) *Pleistocene extinctions: the search for a cause* New Haven (1967).

31 Grigson, C. 'Cattle in prehistoric Britain.' *The Ark* 9 (1982), 41–9.

32 Whitehead, G.K. *The ancient white cattle of Britain and their descendants* Faber, London (1953).

33 Piggott, S. *The Neolithic cultures of the British Isles* Cambridge (1954).
34 Everitt, A. 'River and wold: reflections on the historical origins of regions and pays.' *JHG* 3 (1977), 1–19.
35 *De spectaculis* VII, 35.
36 *Itinerarium Kambriae* II, iii.
37 Harting, J.E. *British mammals extinct within historic times, with some account of British wild white cattle* London (1880).
38 *Calendar of Patent Rolls.*
39 Elton, G.R. *England 1200–1640* Sources of History, London (1969), p.127.
40 Morgan, F.C. *A short account of the church of Abbey Dore* Abbey Dore (1965).
41 Dent, A. *Lost beasts of Britain* Harrap, London (1974).
42 *Gesta regum anglorum* II, 155.
43 Ritchie, J. *Animal life in Scotland* Cambridge (1920).
44 Anderson, M.L. *A history of Scottish forestry* Nelson, London (1967).
45 Pennant, T. *A tour in Scotland* Chester (1771).
46 Lauder, T.D. *An account of the great floods of August 1829 in the province of Moray* Elgin 1830.
47 *House of Commons Journal.*
48 *Topographia Hiberniae* I, xxiv.
49 *Calendar of Close Rolls.*
50 ERO: survey of Earl's Colne by Israel Amyce (1598).
51 Ailesbury, Marquess of *A history of Savernake Forest* Devizes (1962).
52 Rogers, J.E. Thorold *A history of agriculture and prices in England* 6 vols. Clarendon, Oxford (1866–1902).
53 25 Henry VIII c. 11.
54 Fisher, J. and Lockley, R.M. *Sea-birds* Collins, London (1954).
55 Storer, J. *The wild white cattle of Great Britain* London (1879).
56 *Vita Sancti Thomae Cantuariensis archiepiscopi.*
57 Boethius, H. *Scotorum historia* Parisiis 1574 [written 1527].
   Leslie, J. *The historie of Scotland* [Ed E. G. Cody, Blackwood, Edinburgh 1888.]
   Bannatyne, R. *Memorials of transactions in Scotland, 1569–73* [Ed. R. Pitcairn, Bannatyne Club, Edinburgh 1836.]
58 Bilton, L. 'The Chillingham herd of wild cattle.' *Transactions of the Natural History Society of Northern Durham* 12 (1957), 137–60.
59 Corbet, G.B. and Southern, H.N. *The handbook of British mammals* 2nd ed Blackwell, Oxford (1977).
60 Fraser, F.C. and King, J.E. 'Faunal remains.' *Excavations at Star Carr*, ed J.G.D. Clark, Cambridge (1954).
61 Clarke, R.R. *Grime's Graves, Norfolk* H.M.S.O., London (1963).
62 Rackham (1980) p.183.
63 Langley, P.J.W. and Yalden, D.W. 'The decline of the rarer carnivores in Great Britain during the nineteenth century.' *Mammal Review* 7 (1977) 95–116.
64 NNRO: RQG 252.
65 NNRO: Dean & Chapter Roll 4753.
66 Letts, M. (ed) *The travels of Leo of Rozmital* . . . *1465–1467* Hakluyt Society, Cambridge (1957).
   Sneyd, C.A. (ed) *A relation, or rather a true account, of the Island of England* . . . *about the year 1500* Camden Society, London (1847).
67 Turner, W. *Avium praecipuarum* . . . *brevis & succincta historia* Colonia (1544).
   Nisbet, I.C.T. 'The kites of sixteenth-century London.' *British Birds* 52 (1959), 239–40.
   Bramwell, D. 'Bird remains from medieval London.' *London Naturalist* 54 (1974), 15–20.
68 Brown, L. *British birds of prey* Collins, London (1976).
69 Perring, F.H. 'Changes in our native vascular plant flora.' In Hawksworth (1974), pp 7–26.

References

70 Ellis, W. *The Timber-Tree Improved* London (1744). (I am grateful to Dr D.E. Coombe for giving me this reference.)

71 Large, E.C. *The advance of the fungi* Jonathan Cape, London (1940).

72 Rackham (1980) pp 90–2.

73 Hawksworth, D.L. and Rose, F. *Lichens as pollution monitors* Edward Arnold, London (1976).

74 Holmes, E.M. 'Mosses [and lichens] of Hatfield Forest.' *EN* **4** (1890) 218–25.

75 Rose, F. and Wallace, E.C. 'Changes in the bryophyte flora of Britain.' In Hawksworth (1974), pp 27–46.

76 Pratt, A. *The flowering plants and ferns of Great Britain* S.P.C.K., London (1854).

77 Clapham, A.R., Tutin, T.G. and Warburg, E.F. *Flora of the British Isles* 1st ed Cambridge (1952).

78 Bennett, A. '*Senecio paludosus* and *S. palustris* in East Anglia.' *Transactions of Norfolk & Norwich Naturalists' Society* **6** (1899) 457–62.

79 Walters, S.M. 'The rediscovery of *Senecio paludosus* L. in Britain.' *Watsonia* **10** (1974) 49–54.

80 Laycock, G. *The alien animals: the story of imported wildlife.* Ballantine, New York (1966).

81 Corbet, G.R. 'The distribution of mammals in historic times.' In Hawksworth (1974) pp 179–202.

82 *Gemma ecclesiastica* I, 53; *Itinerarium Kambriae* II, ii.

83 Ziegler, P. *The Black Death* Collins, London (1969).

84 Spencer, H.E.P. 'Rabbit.' *Transactions of the Suffolk Naturalists' Society* **9** (1956) 369.
Veale, E.M. 'The rabbit in England.' *AHR* **5** (1957) 85–90.

85 Gilbert, J.M. *Hunting and hunting reserves in medieval Scotland* John Donald, Edinburgh (1979).

86 Royal Commission on Ancient and Historical Monuments in Wales, *Glamorgan* vol. III part 2 (1982) 313–45.

87 ERO: D/DB L1/6/10.

88 Salzman, L.F. (ed) *Ministers' accounts of the manor of Petworth 1347–53* Lewes (1955).

89 Brown, E.H. and Hopkins, S.V. 'Seven centuries of the prices of consumables, compared with builders' wage-rates.' *Economica* **23** (1956) 296–313.

90 Wade-Evans, A.W. *Welsh medieval law; being a text of the laws of Howel the Good* Oxford (1909).

91 Witherby, H.F. and others. *The handbook of British birds* Witherby, London (1938–41).

92 Lowe, P.R. 'The differential characters in the tarso-metatarsi of *Gallus* and *Phasianus* as they bear on the problem of the introduction of the pheasant into Europe and the British Isles.' *Ibis* **13th ser. 3** (1933) 332–43.

93 Yarrell, W. *A history of British birds* Van Voorst, London (1843).

94 Stubbs, W. *The foundation of Waltham Abbey* Parker, Oxford (1861).

95 ERO: D/DHt M145.

96 Smith, T. 'The birds of Staffordshire.' *Transactions & Annual Report of North Staffordshire Field Club* **81** A 217–48.

97 Matheson, C. *Changes in the fauna of Wales within historic times* National Museum of Wales (1932).

98 Sharrock, J.T.R. *The atlas of breeding birds in Britain and Ireland* Tring (1976).

99 Shorten, M. *Squirrels* Collins, London (1954).

100 Barrett-Hamilton, G.E.H. *A history of British mammals* Gurney & Jackson, London (1910).

101 Pitt E. 'Concerning the *Sorbus pyriformis*.' *PhTRS* **11** (1678) 978–9.
Rackham (1980) p.359.

102 Scannell, M.J.P. '*Juncus planifolius* R.Br. in Ireland.' *Irish Naturalists' Journal* **17** (1973) 309ff.

103 Barrington, D. 'A Letter . . . on the Trees which are supposed to be indigenous in *Great Britain.' PhTRS* **59** (1769) 23–38.

104 Ducarel, A.C., Hasted, E. and Thorpe, J. 'A Letter concerning Chesnut Trees.' *PhTRS* **61** (1772) 136–69.

105 Huntley, B. and Birks, H.J.B. *An atlas of past and present pollen maps for Europe: 0–13000 years ago* Cambridge (1983).

106 Meriana, G. *Il castagno.* Cassa di Risparmio, Genova [c.1979].

107 Henderson, C. *Essays in Cornish history* Clarendon, Oxford (1935), pp 141–4.

108 *Sylva,* 3rd ed.

109 NNRO: Felbrigg muniments, W. Windham's Green Book.

110 WSRO: E3/10/10.5.

111 Cross, J.R. 'Biological Flora of the British Isles: *Rhododendron ponticum* L.' *JE* **63** (1975) 345–64.

112 Merrett, C. *Pinax rerum naturalium Britannicarum* Roycroft, London (1666).

113 De la Marck, J.B.A.P.M. and De Candolle, A.P. *Flore française* 3e éd Paris (1805).

114 Myerscough, P.J. 'Biological Flora of the British Isles: *Epilobium angustifolium* L.' *JE* **68** (1980) 1047–74.

115 Kent, D.H. '*Senecio squalidus* in the British Isles.' *Proceedings of the Botanical Society of the British Isles* **2** (1956) 115–8; **3** (1960) 375–9.

116 Jones, W.E. 'Changes in the seaweed flora of the British Isles.' In Hawkswortrh (1974), pp 97–114.

117 Rackham (1980) p.297.

118 Rosser, E.M. 'A new British species of *Senecio.' Watsonia* **3** (1955) 228–32.

119 Perring, F.H. '*Bromus interruptus* (Hack.) Druce – a botanical dodo?' *NC* **5** (1962) 28–30.
Donald, D. '*Bromus interruptus* (Hack.) Druce – dodo or phoenix?' *NC* **23** (1980) 48–50.

120 PRO: E143/9/2.

121 PRO: E311/37 f.215.

122 Private document kindly communicated by the late Sir George Leeds.

123 *The agricultural state of the kingdom, in February, March and April 1816* London (1816) [Reprinted Bath (1970)].

124 Braun, L.E. *Forests of eastern North America* Blakiston, Philadelphia (1950).

125 Baker, C.A., Moxey, P.A. and Oxford, P.M. 'Woodland continuity and change in Epping Forest.' *FS* **4** (1978) 645–69.

126 Turner, J. and Hodgson, J. 'Studies in the vegetational history of the northern Pennines. II. An atypical pollen diagram from Pow Hill, Co. Durham.' *JE* **69** (1981) 171–88.

127 Mellars, P. 'Fire ecology, animal populations and man: a study of some ecological relationships in prehistory.' *Proceedings of the Prehistoric Society* **42** (1976) 15–45.

128 Coles, J.M. *Archaeology by experiment.* Hutchinson, London (1973).

129 Raup, H.M. and Carlson, R.E. *The history of land use in the Harvard Forest.* Harvard Forest, Petersham, Mass. (1941).

130 Drury, P.J. and Rodwell, W. 'Settlement in the later Iron Age and Roman periods.' *Archaeology in Essex to AD 1500,* ed D.G. Buckley, CBA Research Report **34** (1980) 59–75.

131 Papers by J. Weeks, W.S. Hanson, and H. Chapman in *Woodworking techniques before AD 1500,* ed S. McGrail, BARIS **129** (1982) 157–98.

132 *Husbandry* VI.4.

133 *Res rustica* IV. xxxiii. 4.

134 Cleere, H. 'Some operating parameters for Roman ironworks.' *Bulletin of the Institute of Archaeology* **13** (1976) 233–46.
Rackham (1980) p.108.

135 Brodribb, A.C.C., Hands, A.R. and Walker, D.R. *Excavations at Shakenoak* (1968–73).

136 BCS 123.

References

137 K 765.
138 K 1292.
139 Witney, K.P. *The Jutish forest*. Athlone Press, London (1976).
140 Ford, W.J. 'Some settlement patterns in the central region of the Warwickshire Avon.' *Medieval settlement: continuity and change*, ed P.H. Sawyer, Edward Arnold, London (1976) 274–94.
141 BCS 913.
142 Robertson, A.J. *Anglo-Saxon charters, edited with translation and notes* Cambridge (1939), no. VII.
143 BCS 854.
144 BCS 1229.
145 Whitelock, D. *Anglo-Saxon wills* Cambridge (1930), no. XIII.
146 Robertson (note 142), no. V.
147 Gelling, M. *The place-names of Berkshire* English Place-name Society, Cambridge (1973–6).
148 Lennard, R. 'The destruction of woodland in the eastern counties under William the Conqueror.' *EHR* 15 (1945) 36–43.
149 BCS 62.
150 *De rebus gestis Ælfredi* 55.
151 Rackham, O. 'Knapwell Wood.' *NC* 12 25–31.
152 NNRO: Dean & Chapter Rolls 4750–1.
153 Rackham, O. 'Grundle House: on the quantities of timber in certain East Anglian buildings in relation to local supplies.' *VA* 3 (1972) 3–8.
154 Rackham, O. 'The growing and transport of timber and underwood.' *Woodworking techniques* (note 131) 199–218.
155 Chapman, F.R. *Sacrist rolls of Ely*. Cambridge (1907).
I am indebted to Mrs Beth Davis for showing me the building.
Holton-Krayenbuhl, A.P.B. and others. *The Three Blackbirds: a medieval house in Ely, Cambridgeshire* Ely Preservation Trust (1984).
156 NNRO: Dean & Chapter Roll 4777.
157 Brandon, P. *The Sussex landscape* Hodder & Stoughton, London (1974).
158 Rackham (1980) p.158.
159 Hockey, S.F. *The account-book of Beaulieu Abbey* Royal Historical Society, London (1975).
160 Flinn, M.W. 'Timber and the advance of technology: a reconsideration.' *Annals of Science* 15 (1959) 109–20.
Hammersley, G. 'The charcoal iron industry and its fuel.' *EHR* 2nd ser. 26 (1975) 593–613.
161 Lindsay, J.M. 'Charcoal iron smelting and its fuel supply: the example of Lorn furnace, Argyllshire, 1753–1876.' *JHG* 1 (1975) 283–98.
162 Yarranton, A. *England's improvement by sea and land* London (1677).
163 Cornforth, J. *Country houses in Britain – can they survive?* Country Life, London (1974).
164 Grove, R. *The future for forestry* British Association of Nature Conservationists (1983).
165 Rackham (1980) p.250.
166 Peterken, G.F. (1974). 'A method for assessing woodland flora for conservation using indicator species.' *BC* 6 (1974) 239–45.
167 *Speculum Ecclesiae* III. 12.
168 Rees, W. *The historical map of South Wales and the Border in the fourteenth century* Cardiff (1933).
169 Linnard (1982) p.70.
170 Williams, M. *The making of the South Wales landscape* Hodder & Stoughton, London (1975).
171 Gilbert (ref. 85), p.237.
172 Rackham (1976) p.103, following Anderson (ref.44).

173 Tittensor, R.M. 'History of the Loch Lomond oakwoods.' *SF* 24 (1970) 100–18.
  Rymer, L. 'The exploitation of woodlands in the parish of North Knapdale,
  Argyllshire.' *SF* 31 (1977) 244–50.
174 Loudon, J.C. *Arboretum et fruticetum britannicum* Longmans, London (1838).
175 Birks, H.H. 'Studies in the vegetational history of Scotland. I. A pollen diagram
  from Abernethy Forest, Inverness-shire.' *JE* 58 (1970) 827–36.
176 Kelly, D.L. 'The native forest vegetation of Killarney, south-west Ireland: an
  ecological record.' *JE* 69 (1981) 437–72.
  Watts, W.A. unpublished.
177 Mitchell, G.F. *The Irish landscape* Collins, London (1976).
178 Aalen, F.H.A. *Man and the landscape in Ireland* Academic Press, London (1978.)
179 McCracken, E. *The Irish woods since Tudor times* David & Charles, Newton Abbot
  (1971).
180 McCracken, E. 'The woodlands of Ireland circa 1600.' *Irish Historical Studies* 11
  (1959) 271–96.
181 Wallace, P.F. 'Carpentry in Ireland AD 900–1300 – the Wood Quay evidence.'
  Woodworking techniques (note 131), 263–300.
182 Pigott, C.D. 'Regeneration of oak-birch woodland following exclusion of sheep.' *JE*
  71 (1983) 629–46.
183 Peters, B.C. 'Michigan's oak openings: pioneer perceptions of a vegetative
  landscape.' *Journal of Forest History* (January 1978) 18–23.
184 Lindsay, M.M. and Bratton, S.P. 'Grassy balds of the Great Smoky Mountains:
  their history and flora in relation to potential management.' *Environmental
  Management* 3 (1979) 417–30.
185 Rackham, O. 'Neolithic woodland management in the Somerset Levels: Garvin's,
  Walton Heath, and Rowland's Tracks.' *SLP* 3 (1977) 65–71.
186 Spray, M. 'Holly as fodder in England.' *AHR* 29 (1981) 97–110.
187 BCS 898.
188 Tittensor, A. and Tittensor, R. *Natural history of The Mens, Sussex* Horsham
  Natural History Society (1977).
189 Watson, C.E. 'The Minchinhampton custumal and its place in the story of the
  manor.' *Transactions of the Bristol & Gloucs Archaeological Society* 54 (1932) 203–385.
190 ERO: D/D Ba M27.
191 Grigson, C. 'Porridge and pannage: pig husbandry in Neolithic England.'
  Archaeological aspects of woodland ecology, ed M. Bell and S. Limbrey, BARIS 146
  (1982) 297–314.
192 *Res rustica* IX. i.
193 Cantor, L. *The medieval parks of England: a gazetteer* Loughborough (1983).
194 Munby, L.M. *The Hertfordshire landscape* Hodder & Stoughton, London (1977).
195 Rees (ref. 168); Linnard (1982).
196 *Rotuli Litterarum Clausarum.*
197 PRO: C135/48(2).
198 Shirley, E.P. *Some account of English deer parks* Murray, London (1867).
199 Parker, W. *The history of Long Melford* London (1873).
200 Dickens, A.G. *The register or chronicle of Butley Priory, Suffolk, 1510–1535*
  Wykeham, Winchester (1951).
201 *Ickworth Survey Boocke Ano 1665*, ed J. Hervey.
202 Phibbs, J.L. *Wimpole Park, Cambridgeshire* National Trust (1980).
203 WSRO: 2130/1,2.
204 Liebermann, F. *Die Gesetze der Angelsachsen*, vol 2. Halle (1906).
205 Calendar of Liberate Rolls.
206 Linnard (1982) p.32–3.
207 Rackham (1980) p.179
208 Cox, J.C. and Greswell, W.H.P. 'Forestry.' *VCH Somerset* vol 2 (1911) 547–72.
209 Rackham (1980) p.181.

References

210 Rackham, O., Blair, W.J. and Munby, J.T. 'The thirteenth-century roofs and floor of the Blackfriars Monastery at Gloucester.' *MA* 22 (1978) 105–22.
211 Hammersley, G. 'The Crown woods and their exploitation in the sixteenth and seventeenth centuries.' *Bulletin of the Institute of Historical Research* 30 (1957) 136–61.
212 Addison, W. *Queen Elizabeth's Hunting Lodge and Epping Forest Museum*, with note by C.A. Hewett. City of London Corporation [*c*.1979].
213 Hammersley, G. 'The revival of the forest laws under Charles I.' *History* 45 (1960) 85–102.
214 Vancouver, C. *General view of the agriculture of Hampshire* (1813) p.496.
215 Peterken, G.F. 'Long-term changes in the woodlands of Rockingham Forest and other areas.' *JE* 64 (1976) 123–46.
216 Rackham, O. 'The Avon Gorge and Leigh Woods.' In *Archaeological aspects of woodland ecology* (ref. 191), 171–6.
217 Peterken, G.F. 'Development of vegetation in Staverton Park, Suffolk.' *FS* 3 (1969) 1–39.
       Rackham (1980) p.293–4.
218 Beresford, M. *History on the ground* Methuen, London (1957).
219 Hart, C.E. *The extent and boundaries of the Forest of Dean*. Gloucester (1950). *Royal Forest: a history of Dean's woods as producers of timber* Oxford (1966). *Archaeology in Dean* Gloucester (1967). Also other books.
220 Menzies, W. *The history of Windsor Great Park and Windsor Forest* Longmans, London (1864).
221 Papers by E. Duffey, P.M. Hammond, and A. South in Hawksworth (1974).
       Rose, F. 'The epiphytes of oak.' *The British oak: its history and natural history*, ed M.G. Morris and F.H. Perring, Classey, Faringdon (1974) 274–97.
       Welch, R.C. *Windsor Forest study: wildlife conservation report* Crown Estate Commission and Nature Conservancy (1972).
222 Shakespeare, W. *As You Like It* IV. iii. 105.
223 Plomer, W. (ed) *Kilvert's diary, selections* Jonathan Cape, London (1938–40) and later editions.
224 Rose, F. and James, P.W. 'The corticolous and lignicolous [lichen] species of the New Forest, Hampshire.' *Lichenologist* 6 (1974) 1–72.
225 Sparke, J. *Historiae Anglicanae scriptores*, vol 2 (1723).
226 Ketton-Cremer, R.W. *Felbrigg: the story of a house* Hart-Davis, London (1962).
227 NNRO: 44D1 15451; MR 108 241 × 4; MR 235 242 × 1.
228 *Chertsey cartularies* Surrey Record Society 12 (1933) I pp 281, 318, 322.
229 Rackham (1980) p.290–1.
230 Seebohm, F. *The English village community* London (1883).
231 Edwards, D. 'Air photography and early fields in Norfolk.' Bowen and Fowler (1978) 99–102.
232 Gawne, E. and Cox, J.V.S. 'Parallel reaves on Dartmoor.' *Transactions of the Devonshire Association for the Advancement of Science* 100 277–91.
233 Papers by Bradley & Richards and Riley in Bowen and Fowler (1978).
234 Caulfield, S. 'Neolithic fields: the Irish evidence.' Bowen and Fowler (1978) 137–44.
235 Whittington, G. 'Towards a terminology for strip lynchets.' *AHR* 15 (1967) 103–7.
236 Bradford, J. *Ancient landscapes* Bell, London (1957).
237 Russell, V. *West Penwith survey* Cornwall Archaeological Society, Truro (1971).
238 Royal Institution of Cornwall, Truro: Henderson parochial history MS.
239 BCS 1197.
240 Gascoyne, J. *A map of the county of Cornwall* London [*c*.1690].
241 Hall, C.P. and Ravensdale, J.R. *The West Fields of Cambridge* Cambridge Antiquarian Records Society (1976).
242 ESRO: HA240 2508/1092.
243 Orwin, C.S. and Orwin, C.S: *The open fields* Oxford (1938).

244 Howard, E. 'Essex hedgerows as landmarks of history.' *Essex Review* **20** (1911) 57–74.

245 *Ely Coucher Book* (ref. 19).

246 Greenhill, M. and Dunbar, E. *A book of farmcraft* Longmans, London (1942).

247 Kerridge, E. 'Ridge and furrow and agrarian history.' *EHR* **2nd ser 4** (1951) 14–36. Beresford, M.W. 'Ridge and furrow and the open fields.' *EHR* **2nd ser 1** (1948) 34–45.

248 Bagwell, R. *Ireland under the Stuarts and during the Interregnum* Longmans, London (1909).

249 Taylor, C. *The archaeology of gardens* Prince's Risborough (1983).

250 Hall, D. 'The origins of open-field agriculture: the archaeological fieldwork evidence.' *The origins of open-field agriculture*, ed T. Rowley, Croom Helm, London (1981) 22–38.

251 Harrison, M.J., Mead, W.R., and Pannett, D.J. 'A Midland ridge-and-furrow map.' *GJ* **131** (1965) 365–9.

252 Kain, R. and Mead, W.R. 'Ridge-and-furrow in Cambridgeshire.' *PCAS* **64** (1977) 131–7.

253 Gonner, E.C.K. *Common land and inclosure* Macmillan, London (1912).

254 CUL: MS Plans 550R.

255 Bishop, T.A.M. 'Assarting and the growth of the open fields.' *EHR* **6** (1936) 13–29.

256 Taylor, C.C. 'Archaeology and the origins of open-field agriculture.' *The origins of open-field agriculture* (ref. 250) 13–21.

257 Elliott, G. 'Field systems of northwest England.' Baker and Butlin (1973) 41–92.

258 Powell, S.C. *Puritan village: the formation of a New England town* Middletown, Connecticut [1963].

259 Dymond, D.P. 'The parish of Walsham-le-Willows: two Elizabethan surveys and their medieval background.' *PSIA* **33** (1974) 195–211.

260 Fox, H.S.A. 'Approaches to the adoption of the Midland system.' *The origins of open-field agriculture* (ref. 250) 64–111.

261 Harvey, M. 'The origin of planned field systems in Holderness, Yorkshire.' *Ibid.* 184–201.

262 Harvey, M. 'Regular open-field systems on the Yorkshire Wolds.' *LH* **4** (1982) 29–39.

263 Beresford, M.W. and St Joseph, J.K.S. *Medieval England: an aerial survey* 2nd ed Cambridge (1979).

264 Baker and Butlin (1973) p.624.

265 Hooke, D. *Anglo-Saxon landscapes of the West Midlands: the charter evidence.* *BARBS* **95** (1981).

266 BCS 925.

267 BCS 1120.

268 Bassett, S.R. *Saffron Walden: excavations and research 1972–80.* CBA Research Report **45** (1982).

269 Jones, G.R.J. 'Field systems of North Wales.' Baker and Butlin (1973) 430–79.

270 Davies, M. 'Field systems of South Wales.' Baker and Butlin (1973) 480–529.

271 Whittington, G. 'Field systems of Scotland.' Baker and Butlin (1973) 530–79.

272 Buchanan, R.H. 'Field systems of Ireland.' Baker and Butlin (1973) 580–618.

273 Royal Commission on Historical Monuments. *West Cambridgeshire* H.M.S.O., London (1968).

274 ERO: D/DK M1.

275 ERO: T/M 378.

276 ESRO:HD/323/1.

277 Balchin, W.G.V. *Cornwall: an illustrated essay on the history of the landscape* Hodder & Stoughton, London (1954).

278 *Res rustica* XI. iii. 3–5.

279 I. 34.

280 *De condicionibus agrorum.*

References

281 *De bello Gallico* II. xvii.
282 Robinson, M. 'The problem of hedges enclosing Roman and earlier fields.' Bowen and Fowler (1978) 155–8.
283 BCS 207.
284 BCS 816.
285 BCS 751.
286 BCS 1139.
287 MCR 5382.
288 Eland, G. *At the courts of Great Canfield, Essex* Oxford (1949).
289 Ault, W.O. *Open-field farming in medieval England* Allen & Unwin, London (1972).
290 Rackham (1980) p.353.
291 Menner, R.J. 'The Man in the Moon and hedging.' *Journal of English and Germanic Philology* **48** (1949) 1–14.
292 ERO: D/DHf M19.
293 Cromarty, D. *The fields of Saffron Walden in 1400* Essex County Council (1966).
294 Newton, R. *The Northumberland landscape* Hodder & Stoughton, London (1972).
295 Moorhouse, S.A. 'Documentary evidence for the landscape of the manor of Wakefield during the middle ages.' *LH* **1** (1979) 44–58.
296 Emmison, F.G. *Catalogue of maps in the Essex Record Office, 1566–1855.* Essex County Council (1947). (With supplements.)
297 Raistrick, A. *Old Yorkshire Dales* David & Charles, Newton Abbot (1967).
298 ERO: D/DL M18.
299 PRO: LRRO 5/39.
300 Emmison, F.G. *Elizabethan life: home, work, and land.* Essex County Council (1976).
301 CRO: account-book of Admiral Edward Russell. (Mr J.M. Farrar kindly brought this document to my attention.)
302 ESRO: HA93.
303 Callander, R. *Drystane dyking in Deeside* Aberdeen Peoples Press (1982).
304 *Les bocages: histoire, écologie, économie* Université de Rennes (1976).
305 Davenport, F.G. *The economic development of a Norfolk manor 1086–1565* Cambridge (1906).
306 Richens, R.H. 'Studies on *Ulmus*. VII. Essex elms.' *Forestry* **40** (1967) 184–206.
307 CRO: 152/P11.
308 CRO: P79/26/2.
     Baker, R.G. *New Map of the University and Town of Cambridge* London (1830).
309 Rackham, O. 'The Forest of Neroche and the fuel supply of the Donyatt kilns.' *Excavations at Donyatt, Somerset*, ed R. Coleman Smith and T. Pearson. (Forthcoming.)
310 Straton, C.R. (ed) *Survey of the lands of William, first Earl of Pembroke* Roxburghe Club (1909).
311 Addington, S. 'The hedgerows of Tasburgh.' *Norfolk Archaeology* **37** (1978) 70–83.
312 Willmot, A. 'The woody species of hedges with special reference to age in Church Broughton Parish, Derbyshire.' *JE* **68** (1980) 269–86.
313 Helliwell, D.R. 'The distribution of woodland plant species in some Shropshire hedgerows.' *BC* **7** (1975) 61–72.
314 Pollard, E. 'Hedges. VII. Woodland relic hedges in Huntingdon and Peterborough.' *JE* **61** (1973) 343–52.
315 Laundon, J.R. 'The use of lichens for dating walls in Bradgate Park, Leicestershire.' *Transactions of Leicester Literary & Philosophical Society* **74** (1980) 11–30.
316 Palmer, W.H. and Miller, A.K. 'Botanical evidence for the recession of a glacier.' *Oikos* **12** (1961) 75–86.
317 K624.
318 BCS 801.
319 Forestry Commission. *Census report no. 2. Hedgerow and park timber and woods under five acres* H.M.S.O., London (1951).

320 Forestry Commission *Census of woodland and trees, 1979–82.* vol 1 Edinburgh (1983).
321 Gibbs, J.N. and Howell, R.S. *Dutch Elm Disease survey 1971. Forestry Commission Forest Record* **82** (1972).
322 Westmacott, R. and Worthington, T. *New agricultural landscapes* Countryside Commission, London (1974).
323 Milne-Redhead, E. 'The black poplar survey.' *Botanical Society of the British Isles News* **33** (1983) 6.
324 ERO: D/DP M201.
325 Harris, R. 'Poplar crucks in Worcestershire and Herefordshire.' *VA* **5** (1974) 24–5.
326 Gover, J.E.B., Mawer, A., Stenton, F.M. and Madge, S.J. *The place-names of Middlesex* Cambridge (1942).
327 Meikle, R.D. '*Populus* L.' *Hybridization and the flora of the British Isles*, ed. C.A. Stace, Academic Press, London (1975) 303.
328 NNRO: Dean & Chapter Roll 4742.
329 NNRO: Dean & Chapter Roll 4755.
330 WSRO: E2/9/1.
331 NNRO: Dean & Chapter Rolls *passim.*
332 ERO: D/DCy M1.
333 BM: Add. Roll 27687.
334 Smith, L.D.W. 'A survey of building timber and other trees in the hedgerows of a Warwickshire estate, *c.*1500.' *Transactions of the Birmingham and Warwickshire Archaeological Society* **90** (1981) 65–73.
335 PRO: E318/807.
336 ERO: D/DGe M135.
337 PRO: E318/288.
338 ESRO: HA68:484/751.
339 NNRO: NRS 8582 21C2.
340 ESRO: HA 230/A1/1.
341 ERO: Temp. Access. 897.
342 NNRO: Walsingham XXVI/4 (414 × 6).
343 NNRO: NRS 11126.
344 NNRO: Beauchamp-Proctor 334.
345 NNRO: Walsingham XXXIII/13.
346 WSRO: E3/10/10.8.
347 WSRO: E3/10/10.5.
348 WSRO: E3/5/1.
349 ERO: D/DDc E/15/2–3.
350 WSRO: T1/1/16.
351 ERO: D/Ra E1.
352 ERO: D/DHt E13.
353 WSRO: 613/642/3.
354 ERO: D/DL E12.
355 ERO: D/DBe T18.
356 NNRO: RQG 226.
357 ESRO: HA50/18/14.4.
358 NNRO: Spelman 316 × 1235.
359 NNRO: Dean & Chapter of Norwich Estates 269 726.
360 ESRO: HA1/HB6/4/9.
361 Salzman, L.F. *Building in England down to 1540* Clarendon, Oxford (1952). Rackham (1980) p.151.
362 Iveagh muniments: Suffolk MS 148. [Kindly communicated to me by the late Rev. J.T. Munday.]
363 Lobel, M.D. *Historic towns: Cambridge* Scolar, London (1974).
364 Coulton, G.G. *Life in the Middle Ages* Cambridge (1967) p.74.
365 Rackham (1980) p.157.

References

366 PRO: SP14/42.

367 PRO: E178/4988.

368 Emmison, F.G. (ed) *Catalogue of maps in the Essex Record Office: 1st supplement* Chelmsford (1952), plate I.

369 ERO: T/M 63.

370 Private: no. 29 in exhibition of Old Fenland Maps by the Wisbech Society (1976).

371 Morant, P. *The history and antiquities of the county of Essex* London (1768), I, 92–3.

372 NNRO: Walsingham (Suffolk).

373 PRO: DL44/1034.

374 ERO: D/DU 15.

375 ESRO: HA54 970/360.

376 Howard, H.F. *An account of the finances of the College of St John the Evangelist in the University of Cambridge* Cambridge (1935).

377 NNRO: Dean & Chapter Roll 4899.

378 ERO: D/DP E26.

379 Spriggs, G.M. 'The search for Matthew Arnold's Tree.' *Country Life* **159** (1976) 290–1.

380 Loudon (ref.174) p.1757.

381 *Report of the committee on hedgerow and farm timber* H.M.S.O., London (1955).

382 Cornish, V. *The churchyard yew and immortality* Muller, London (1946).

383 Baillie, M.G.M. *Tree-ring dating and archaeology* Croom Helm, London (1982).

384 Williamson, T. and Bellamy, L. *Ley lines in question* World's Work, Kingswood, Tadworth (1983).

385 WSRO: 449/8/2.

386 Davy, C. *Letters, addressed chiefly to a young gentleman, upon Subjects of Literature* Bury St Edmund's (1787).

387 Cornish, V. *Historic thorn trees in the British Isles* Country Life, London [1941].

388 Evelyn, J. *Sylva*, 4th ed.

389 Melville, R. '*Ulmus* L.' *Hybridization and the flora of the British Isles* (ref.327) 292–9.

390 'Essex elms' (ref.306) and papers on the elms of 5 other counties in *Forestry* **32** to **38**.

391 Fisher, J.L. 'The Leger Book of St John's Abbey, Colchester.' *Transactions of Essex Archaeological Society* **NS 24** (1951) 77ff.

392 Leland, J. *Itinerary* (ed L.T. Smith, London 1907), Part II.

393 Hardy, R. *Longbow* Cambridge (1976).

394 CRO.

395 Bennett, K.D. 'Devensian Late-glacial and Flandrian vegetational history at Hockham Mere, Norfolk, England.' *New Phytologist* **95** (1983) 457–487.

396 Rackham (1980) p.280.

397 Webber, J. 'Flourishing elms.' *The Times*, 26 May 1984.

398 Peace, T.R. *The status and development of elm disease in Britain* Forestry Commission Bulletin **33** (1960).

399 Heybroek, H.M. 'The Dutch elm disease in the Old World.' Referate, *XIV IUFRO Kongress, München* **5** (1967) 447–54.

400 Dendrophilus. 'Discovery of the secret Destroyers of the Trees in St James's Park.' *Philosophical Magazine* **62** (1823) 252–4.

401 Fabricius, J.C. *Species insectorum* Hamburg and Kiel (1781).

402 Richens (1983) p.119.

403 Shakespeare, W. *The Second Part of Henrie the Fourth* II. iv.

404 Rackham (1980) p.266.

405 Brasier, C.M. and Gibbs, J.N. 'Origin of the Dutch elm disease epidemic in Britain.' *Nature* **242** (1973) 607–9.

406 Brasier, C.M. 'The future of Dutch elm disease in Europe.' *Research on Dutch elm disease in Europe*, ed. D.A. Burdekin, H.M.S.O., London (1983), 96–104.

407 Anagnostakis, S.L. *The American chestnut: new hope for a fallen giant* Bulletin of Connecticut Agricultural Experimental Station, New Haven **777** (1978).

408 BCS 922.

409 Hey, D. *Packmen, carriers and packhorse roads: trade and communications in north Derbyshire and south Yorkshire* Leicester (1980).
410 *De conditionibus agrorum.*
411 Chevallier, R. *Les voies romaines* Amand Colin, Paris (1972).
412 Dewhurst, P.C. 'Wool Street, Cambridgeshire.' *PCAS* 56 (1963) 42–60.
413 Rackham (1980) p.249.
414 Jope, E.M. 'The Saxon building-stone industry in southern and midland England.' *MA* 8 (1964) 91–118.
415 BCS 1321.
416 Emmison, F.G. *Elizabethan life: disorder* Essex County Council (1970) p.186.
417 Wiseman, I. *Wimbish through the centuries* Chelmsford (1974).
418 James, M.K. *Studies in the medieval wine trade* Clarendon, Oxford (1971).
419 Moore, S.A. (ed) *Cartularium monasterii Sancti Johannis Baptiste de Colecestria* Chiswick, London (1897).
420 Jeayes, I.H. and Benham, W.G. *Court rolls of the borough of Colchester. I. 1310–52* Colchester (1921).
421 ERO: D/DB M122.
422 MCR 5368.
423 ESRO: 50/3/121.
424 ERO: D/DPr 1/19.
425 ERO: D/DBa M10, 11.
426 *Calendar of Inquisitions Miscellaneous* VII, 435–6.
Calendar of Patent Rolls 1408–13.
427 *Map of Great Britain c.AD 1360 known as the Gough Map* Royal Geographical Society, Oxford (1958).
428 Hindle, B.P. 'Roads and tracks.' *The English medieval landscape*, ed L.M. Cantor, Croom Helm, London (1982), 193–217.
429 Rigold, S.E. 'Structural aspects of medieval timber bridges.' *MA* 19 (1975) 48–91.
430 Henderson, C. and Coates, H. *Old Cornish bridges and streams* Exeter (1928).
431 Dowsett, D.C. *Dunmow through the ages* Letchworth [c.1975].
432 Clarke, J.W. (ed) *Liber memorandorum ecclesiae de Bernewelle* Cambridge (1907).
433 Riley, H.T. (ed) *Gesta abbatum monasterii S. Albani* Longmans, London (1867).
434 *Statutes of the Realm* i.97.
435 Clarke, W.G. *In Breckland Wilds* Robert Scott, London (1925) (2nd edition 1937.)
436 Ray, J. *Catalogus plantarum circa Cantabrigiam nascentium* Cambridge (1660).
437 *Rotuli hundredorum temp. Hen.III & Edw.I in Turr' Lond' et in curia receptae Saccarij Westm. asservati* H.M.S.O., London (1818).
438 *Botanical Soc. of the British Isles News* 36 (1984) 30.
439 Grubb, P.J., Green, H.E., and Merrifield, R.C.J. 'The ecology of chalk heath: its relevance to the calcicole-calcifuge and soil acidification problems.' *JE* 57 (1969) 175–212.
440 Sparks, B.W. and West, R.G. *The ice age in Britain* Methuen, London (1972).
441 Godwin, H. and Tallantire, P.A. 'Studies in the post-glacial history of British vegetation. XII. Hockham Mere, Norfolk.' *JE* 39 (1951) 285–307.
442 Perrin, R.M.S., Willis, E.H., and Hodge, C.A.H. 'Dating of humus podzols by residual radiocarbon activity.' *Nature* 202 (1964) 165–6.
443 K 778.
444 K 813.
445 Rocque, J. *A topographical map of the county of Middlesex.* London [1754].
446 Pigott, D. 'Native lime trees in Surrey.' *Surrey Trust for Nature Conservation: Newsletter* 60 (1982) 6–8.
447 Crompton, G. and Sheail, J. 'The historical ecology of Lakenheath Warren in Suffolk, England: a case study.' *BC* 8 (1975) 299–313.
448 Holt, J.C. *Robin Hood.* Thames & Hudson, London (1982)
449 Chapman, J. *Nottinghamshire, survey'd in 1774* London (1776).

References

450 Boulton, H.E. (ed) *The Sherwood Forest Book* Thoroton Society, Nottingham (1965).
451 *Itinerary* (ref.392) Part I fo.110.
452 *Natural history of Selborne*, letter VI.
453 Rackham (1980) p.182.
454 Rogers (ref.52) II.575.
455 PRO: SC6/1005/21.
456 PRO: SC/11/27.
457 Seaward, M.R.D. 'Observations on the bracken component of the pre-Hadrianic deposits at Vindolanda, Northumberland.' *JLSB* 73 (1976) 177–85.
458 PRO: SC6/1005/8.
459 NNRO: NRS 18248 33A6.
460 Rymer, L. 'The history and ethnobotany of bracken.' *JLSB* 73 (1976) 151–76.
461 Kenyon, G.H. *The glass industry of the Weald* Leicester (1967).
462 *VCH Nottinghamshsire* I. 375.
463 Thompson, E.P. *Whigs and hunters: the origin of the Black Act* Allen Lane, London (1975).
464 Young, A. *General view of the agriculture of the county of Norfolk* London (1804).
465 Farrow, E.P. *Plant life on East Anglian heaths* Cambridge (1925).
466 Watt, A.S. 'The ecological status of bracken.' *JLSB* 73 (1976) 217–39.
467 Wright, T. 'A curious and exact relation of a *Sand-floud*, which hath lately overwhelmed a great tract of Land in the County of *Suffolk*.' *PhTRS* 3 [recte 4] (1668) 722–5.
468 Oinonen, E. 'The correlation between the size of Finnish bracken (*Pteridium aquilinum* . . .) clones and certain periods of site history.' *Acta forestalia Fennica* 83 (1967) 97–144.
469 Crompton, G. and Taylor, C.C. 'Earthwork enclosures on Lakenheath Warren, West Suffolk.' *PSIA* 32 (1972) 113–20.
470 Supple, W.R. *A history of Thorpe-next-Norwich* Norwich (1917).
471 Anderson, M.D. *A saint at stake* Faber, London (1964).
472 Kirkpatrick, J. *The streets and lanes of the city of Norwich* Norwich (1889).
473 Moore, N.W. 'The heaths of Dorset and their conservation.' *JE* 50 (1962) 369–91.
474 Bibby, C.J. 'Conservation of the Dartford warbler.' *BC* 13 (1978) 299–307.
475 Birks, H.J.B. and Madsen, B.J. 'Flandrian vegetational history of Little Loch Roag, Isle of Lewis, Scotland.' *JE* 67 (1979) 825–42.
476 Turner, J. and Hodgson, J. 'Studies in the vegetational history of the northern Pennines. I. Variations in the composition of the Early Flandrian forests.' *JE* 67 (1979) 629–46.
477 Godwin (1975) p.304.
478 Birks, H.J.B. *Past and present vegetation of the Isle of Skye: a palaeoecological study* Cambridge (1973).
479 Wilkins, D.A. 'The Flandrian woods of Lewis (Scotland).' *JE* 72 (1984) 251–8.
480 Birks, H.H. 'Studies in the vegetational history of Scotland. IV. Pine stumps in Scottish blanket peats.' *PhTRS* B270 (1975) 181–226.
481 Burl, A. *The stone circles of the British Isles* New Haven (1976).
482 Axton, E.C. *Bodmin Moor* David & Charles, Newton Abbot (1875).
483 Royal Commission on Ancient and Historical Monuments in Scotland, *Peebles* H.M.S.O., Edinburgh (1967).
484 Atherden, M.A. 'The impact of late prehistoric cultures on the vegetation of the North York Moors.' *Transactions of the Institute of British Geographers* NS 1 (1976) 284–300.
485 Elner, J.K. and Happey-Wood, C.M. 'The history of two linked but contrasting lakes in North Wales from a study of pollen, diatoms and chemistry in sediment cores.' *JE* 68 (1980) 95–122.
486 K 744.

487 BCS 1323.
488 Davidson, J.B. 'On some Anglo-Saxon charters at Exeter.' *Journal of the British Archaeological Association* **39** (1883) 259–303.
489 BCS 1197.
490 Gill, C. (ed) *Dartmoor: a new study* David & Charles, Newton Abbot [1971].
491 Darby, H.C. and Maxwell, I.S. *The Domesday geography of Northern England* Cambridge (1962).
492 Balchin, W.G.V. *Cornwall: an illustrated essay on the history of the landscape* Hodder & Stoughton, London (1954).
493 Hallam, O. 'Vegetation and land use on Exmoor.' *Somerset Archaeology and Natural History* (Oct. 1978) 37–51.
494 Roberts, B.K., Turner, J. and Ward, P.F. 'Recent forest history and land use in Weardale, Northern England.' *Quaternary plant ecology*, ed H.J.B. Birks and R.G. West, Blackwell, Oxford (1973) 207–221.
495 McDermot, E.C. *The history of the Forest of Exmoor* (1911).
496 Darling, F.F. *Natural history in the Highlands and Islands* Collins, London (1947).
497 Rackham (1980) p.183.
498 Woolner, D. 'Peat charcoal.' *Devon & Cornwall Notes & Queries* **30** (1967) 118–20.
499 Spooner, G.M. and Russell, F.S. (eds) [*R.B.*] *Worth's Dartmoor* David & Charles, Newton Abbot (1967).
500 Prebble, J. *The Highland clearances* Secker & Warburg, London (1963).
501 Maps of Scotland by J. Dorret (1751) and by J. Ainslie (1789).
502 7 Jas. I c.17.
503 Darling, F.F. *West Highland survey* Oxford (1955), p.172–3.
504 Anderson, P. and Yalden, D.W. 'Increased sheep numbers and the loss of heather moorland in the Peak District, England.' *BC* **20** (1981) 195–213.
505 Spence, D.H.N. 'Studies on the vegetation of Shetland. III. Scrub in Shetland and on South Uist, Outer Hebrides.' *JE* **48** (1960) 73–95.
506 Hopkins, J.J. 'Turf huts in the Lizard district: an alternative suggestion for their interpretation.' *Journal of the Royal Institution of Cornwall* **8** (1980) 247–9.
507 Coombe, D.E. and Frost, L.C. 'The heaths of the Cornish serpentine.' *JE* **44** (1955) 226–56.
508 At Lanhydrock House, Cornwall; kindly communicated to me by Dr D.E. Coombe.
509 Forestry Commission. *The wood production outlook in Britain: a review* H.M.S.O., London (1977).
510 Proctor, M.C.F., Spooner, G.M., and Spooner, M.F. 'Changes in Wistman's Wood, Dartmoor: photographic and other evidence.' *TDAAS* **112** (1980) 43–79.
511 Baker, H. 'Alluvial meadows: a comparative study of grazed and mown meadows.' *JE* **61** (1937) 408–20.
512 Ratcliffe (1977) p.185–7.
513 Burnett, A.H. *The vegetation of Scotland* Oliver & Boyd, Edinburgh (1964).
514 Grime, J.P. and Lloyd, P.S. *An ecological atlas of grassland plants* Edward Arnold, London (1973).
515 Cronon, W. *Changes in the land: Indians, colonists, and the ecology of New England* Hill & Wang, New York (1983).
516 Jeffrey, D.W. and Pigott, C.D. 'The response of grasslands on sugar-limestone in Teesdale to application of phosphorus and nitrogen.' *JE* **61** (1973) 85–92.
517 BCS 45.
518 BCS 930.
519 Fitzherbert, J. *The boke of surveying and improvments* London (1523).
520 PRO: C132/38(15).
521 ERO: T/A 262/14/1.
522 PRO: E318/986.
523 Bettey, J.H. 'The development of water meadows in Dorset during the seventeenth century.' *AHR* **25** (1977) 37–43.

524 Vaughan, R. *Most approved, and long experienced water-workes* London (1610).

525 Kerridge, E. 'The sheepfold in Wiltshire and the floating of the watermeadows.' *EHR* **2nd ser 6** (1954) 282–90.

526 Moon, H.P. and Green, F.H.W. 'Water meadows in southern England.' *The land of Britain*, ed L.D. Stamp, Geographical Publications, London, part 89 (1940), 373–90.

527 Sheail, J. 'The formation and maintenance of water-meadows in Hampshire, England.' *BC* **3** (1971) 101–6.

528 Blackwood, J.W. and Tubbs, C.R. 'A quantitative study of chalk grassland in England.' *BC* **3** (1971) 1–5.

529 Atherden, M.A. *Limestone grasslands of the North York Moors* (1983).

530 Grubb, P.J. and Key, B.A. 'Clearance of scrub and re-establishment of chalk grassland on the Devil's Dyke' *NC* **18** (1975) 18–22.

531 Wells, T.C.E., Sheail, J., Ball, D.F. and Ward, L.K. 'Ecological studies on the Porton Ranges: relationships between vegetation, soils and land-use history.' *JE* **64** (1976) 589–626.

532 Coombe, D.E. in Pigott, C.D. and Walters, S.M. 'On the interpretation of the discontinuous distributions shown by certain British species of open habitats.' *JE* **42** (1954) 95–116.

533 Wells, T.C.E. and Barling, D.M. 'Biological flora of the British Isles: *Pulsatilla vulgaris* . . .' *JE* **59** (1971) 275–92.

534 Trist, P.J.O. '*Fritillaria meleagris* L. at Mickfield, Suffolk.' *Suffolk Natural History* **17** (1978) 332–4.

535 Ward, L.K. 'The conservation of juniper. I. Present status of juniper in Southern England.' *Journal of Applied Ecology* **10** (1973) 165–88.

536 Ramsbottom, J. *Mushrooms and toadstools* Collins, London (1953).

537 Wade-Martins, P. 'The origins of rural settlement in East Anglia.' *Recent work in rural archaeology*, ed P.J. Fowler, Bradford-on-Avon (1975) 137–57.

538 Hurry, J.B. *The woad plant and its dye* Oxford 1930.

539 ERO: D/DQ 23/3.

540 Thomas, T.M. 'Swallow holes on the millstone grit and Carboniferous limestone of the South Wales Coalfield.' *GJ* **120** (1954) 468–75.

541 F.G. Bell in *The ice age in Britain* (ref.440).

542 Toms, H.S. 'Ancient ponds near Cissbury.' *Sussex County Magazine* **1** (1927) 404–7.

543 BCS 508, 1080.

544 Coombe, D.E., Douse, A.F.G. and Preston, C.D. 'The vegetation of Ringmere in August 1974.' *Transactions of Norfolk and Norwich Naturalists' Society* **25** (1981) 206–17.

545 Hunt, T.G. and Birks, H.J.B. 'Devensian late-glacial vegetational history at Sea Mere, Norfolk.' *Journal of Biogeography* **9** (1982) 517–38.

546 Dymond, D.P. 'The Suffolk landscape.' *East Anglian studies*, ed L.M. Munby, Heffer, Cambridge (1968) 17–47.

547 Praeger, R.L. *Natural history of Ireland* Collins, London (1950).

548 Nature Conservancy Council. *The future of Broadland* (1977).

549 Green, J.P. 'Moated hay stacks.' *LH* **4** (1982) 69.

550 Royal Commission on Historical Monuments. *North-east Cambridgeshire* H.M.S.O., London (1972).

551 PRO: DL43/9/8.

552 Le Patourel, H.E. and Roberts, B.K. 'The significance of moated sites.' Aberg (1978) 46–55.

553 Taylor, R. in Steane, J.M., *The Northamptonshire landscape* Hodder & Stoughton, London (1974) p.118.

554 Taylor, C.C. 'Medieval moats in Cambridgeshire.' *Archaeology and the landscape*, ed P.J. Fowler, John Baker, London (1972) 237–49.

555 NNRO: Dean & Chapter Rolls 4741, 4774.

556 Steane, J.M. 'The medieval fishponds of Northamptonshire.' *Northamptonshire Past & Present* **4** (1971) 299–310.

557 Denis-Huot, M. 'Les étangs de la Dombes.' *Chasseur Français* (février 1982) 62–5.
558 ERO: D/DP L36/26.
559 Payne-Gallwey, R. *The book of duck decoys* Van Voorst, London (1886).
   Kearton, R. *With nature and a camera* Cassell, London (1897).
   Tibbs, R. 'Decoy way to harvest duck in hundreds.' *Cambridge Evening News*, 12 Nov. 1983, 9.
560 Hodskinson, J. *The county of Suffolk surveyed* Faden, London (1783).
561 Rackham, O. 'The armed ponds of Cambridgeshire.' *NC* 11 (1968) 25–7.
562 GRO: D/DP 1.
563 NNRO: NRS 21400 Hav. Box 9.
564 MCR 5493.
565 Forrest, A.J. *Masters of flint* Dalton, Lavenham (1983).
566 Nef, J.U. *The rise of the British coal industry* Routledge, London (1932).
567 Grove, R. *The Cambridgeshire coprolite mining rush* Oleander, Cambridge (1976).
568 Downing College, Cambridge, archives.
569 British Trust for Conservation Volunteers. *Waterways and wetlands: a practical conservation handbook* (1976).
570 Bradshaw, A.D. and Chadwick, M.J. *The restoration of land* Blackwell, Oxford (1980).
571 Dunham, K.C. and Gray, D.A. (eds). 'A discussion of problems associated with the subsidence of southeastern England.' *PhTRS* A272 (1972) 79–274.
572 *Orford Ness: a selection of maps mainly by J. Norden presented to James Alfred Steers* Heffer, Cambridge (1966).
573 Grieve, H. *The great tide: the story of the 1953 flood disaster in Essex* Chelmsford (1959).
574 Hutchinson, J.N. 'The record of peat wastage in the East Anglian fenlands at Holme Post, 1848–1978 AD.' *JE* 68 (1980) 229–49.
575 Godwin, H., Clowes, D.R. and Huntley, B. 'Studies in the ecology of Wicken Fen. V. Development of fen carr.' *JE* 62 (1974) 197–214.
576 Rackham (1980) p.101–3.
577 Coles, J.M., Hibbert, F.A. and Orme, B.J. 'Prehistoric roads and tracks in Somerset. 3. The Sweet Track. *Proceedings of the Prehistoric Society* 39 (1973) 256–93.
578 Coles, J.M. and Orme, B.J. 'Neolithic hurdles from Walton Heath, Somerset.' *SLP* 3 (1977) 6–29.
579 Hall, D. and Wilson, D. 'Elm: a field survey.' *PCAS* 68 (1978) 21–46.
580 Potter, T.W. 'Marshland and drainage in the Classical world.' Rowley (1981) 1–19.
581 Phillips, C.W. (ed) *The Fenland in Roman times* Royal Geographical Society (1970).
582 Leech, R.H. 'The Somerset Levels in the Romano-British period.' Rowley (1981) 20–51.
583 Bond, C.J. 'Otmoor.' Rowley (1981) 113–35.
584 De Brisay, K. 'The excavation of a Red Hill at Peldon, Essex, with notes on some other sites.' *Antiquaries' Journal* 58 (1978) 31–60.
585 Hallam, H.E. *The new lands of Elloe* Leicester 1954.
586 Brooks, N.P. 'Romney Marsh in the early middle ages.' Rowley (1981) 74–94.
587 K 776.
588 Taylor, A. and Hall, D. ' "Roman Bank" – a medieval seawall.' *PCAS* 64 (1977) 63–8.
589 Owen, A.E.B. 'A Fenland frontier: the establishment of the boundary between Cambridgeshire and Lincolnshire.' *LH* 4 (1982) 41–6.
590 Major, K. 'Conan son of Ellis, an early inhabitant of Holbeach.' *Associated Architectural Societies' Reports and Papers* 42 (1934) 1–28.
591 Glasscock, R.E. 'England *circa* 1334.' *A new historical geography of England*, ed H.C. Darby, Cambridge (1973), 136–85.
592 Darby, H.C. *The medieval Fenland* Cambridge (1940).
593 Williams, M. *The draining of the Somerset Levels* Cambridge (1970).

References

594 Turner, G.J. *Select pleas of the forest* Selden Society, London (1901).

595 Smith, J.R. *A history of an Essex island parish [Foulness]* Chelmsford (1970).

596 Dobson, M. ' "Marsh Fever" – the geography of malaria in England.' *JHG* **6** (1980) 357–89.

597 James, S.P. 'The disappearance of malaria from England.' *Proceedings of the Royal Society of Medicine* **23** (1929) 71–87.

598 Thirsk, J. *Fenland farming in the sixteenth century* Leicester (1953).

599 Darby, H.C. *The draining of the Fens* 2nd ed Cambridge (1956).

600 Wells, E. *Fenland boyhood* Mildenhall Museum (1983).

601 Cracknell, B.E. *Canvey Island: the history of a marshland community* Leicester (1959).

602 O'Leary, J.G. *VCH Essex* vol 5 (1966) 285–9.

603 Rowell, T.A. 'The fen violet at Wicken Fen.' *NC* **26** (1983) 62–5.

604 Duffey, E. 'The management of Woodwalton Fen: a multi-disciplinary approach.' *The scientific management of animal and plant communities for conservation* ed E. Duffey and A.S. Watt, Blackwell, Oxford (1971) 581–97.

605 Pannett, D.J. 'Fish weirs of the River Severn.' Rowley (1981) 144–57.

606 Moorhouse, S.A. 'Documentary evidence for the landscape of the manor of Wakefield during the middle ages.' *LH* **1** (1979) 44–58.

607 Rackham, J. '*Rattus rattus*: the introduction of the black rat into Britain.' *Antiquity* **53** (1979) 112–20.
    Armitage, P., West, B. and Steedman, K. 'New evidence of the black rat in Roman London.' *London Archaeology* **4** (1984) 375–83.

608 Schumer, B. *The evolution of Wychwood to 1400: pioneers, frontiers and forests* Leicester (1984).

609 Carr, A.D. *Medieval Anglesey* Llangefni (1982).

610 For a detailed account see Hanson, M.W. 'Lords Bushes: the history and ecology of an Epping Forest woodland.' *EN* **7** (1983) 1–69.

611 For example Rooke, H. *Descriptions and sketches of some remarkable oaks in the park at Welbeck . . .* White & Robson, London (1790).

612 Boyd, W.E. 'Prehistoric hedges: Roman Iron Age hedges from Bar Hill.' *Scottish Archaeological Review* **3** (1984) 32–4.

613 Holdsworth, C.J. (ed) *Rufford Charters* Thoroton Society, Nottingham (1972 and 1974).

614 Gilbert, O.L. and Hopkins, D.H. 'The ancient lawns of Chatsworth.' *The Garden* **108** (1983) 471–4.

615 Sturt, G. *The wheelwright's shop* Cambridge (1923).

616 Wilson, D. R. 'Pit alignments: distribution and function.' Bowen and Fowler (1978) 3–6.

617 MCR 6/17.

618 Seaward, M.R.D. and Hitch, C.J.B. *Atlas of the lichens of the British Isles* vol.1 Institute of Terrestrial Ecology, Cambridge (1982).

619 Huntley, B. and Birks, H.J.B. *An atlas of past and present pollen maps for Europe: 0–13000 years ago* Cambridge (1983).

620 Bowen and Fowler (1978) Fig. 11.6.

621 Hooper, M.D. 'Hedges and local history.' *Hedges and local history* National Council of Social Service (1971) 6–13.

622 CRO.

623 Gibbs, J.N. and Howell, R.S. *Dutch Elm Disease survey 1971* Forestry Commission, London (1972).

624 Albert, W. *The turnpike road system in England, 1663–1840* Cambridge (1972).

625 St Joseph (1977) Fig. 6.

626 USNA, Group No. 373, GX 10019 SD 112.

627 *Ibid.* GX 10407 SG 26.

628 *Ibid.* GX 10358 SD 011.

629 *Ibid.* GX 10019/88.

INDEX AND GLOSSARY

Words here given a definition are printed in **_bold italic_**. Further definitions or explanations are to be found on pages numbered in **_bold italic_**. Page-numbers in **bold** are main references.

Aldershot Ha 303
Alexander the Great 184
Alfred, King 63, 386
algae 43, 59
Alice-Holt Forest Ha 294
alignments 275 and see *straight lines*
Alliaria see *hedge-garlic*
Allium see *garlic*
Alnus see *alder*
Alopecurus see *blackgrass*
Alps 34, 120, 178, 181, 244, 284, 329, 332, 338, 340
altitudinal limits 110–1, 180, 306, 310
Alwood Green Sf 360
America, North 43, 52, 58–60
  South 48, 181
  United States
    chestnut disease 246–7
    commons 343
    dells 349
    elms 233–4, 237, 242–3, 246–7
    fields 75, 156, 170, 178
    hedges 181–2, 204
    introductions to and from 45, 51, 53, 246–7
    perambulations 9
    ponds 345
    prairies 329
    roads 253
    sawgrass 381
    swamps 383
    trees, ancient xiv, 151
    wildwood 64, **68–73**, 226
    woodland 68, 73, 75, 102, 207–8
    wood-pasture 71, 120
Amesbury Wi 13, 50, 77
Ancient Countryside: districts whose fields, woods, roads, etc. date predominantly from before A.D. 1700. **Chapter 1, Fig. 2.2b**, 98, Chapter 8, 197–9, 221, 334–5, 346–7
  in Anglo-Saxon charters 12, 173–6, 185, 205, 212–3, 259, 287
  roads in 250, 263, 274, 278
Anderson M.L. 131–2, 306
anemone *Anemone nemorosa* 63, 108, 120, 203, 342–4
Anglesey 52, 58, 110, 347
Anglesey Ca 366
Anglo-Saxon charters **8–12**, 19, 34, 372
  depressions 352–3, 357, 362, 364, 370
  fens 384, 386
  field-systems 172–6, Fig. 8.9
  grassland 333–4
  heath 287, 289, Fig. 13.3
  hedges 185–6, Fig. 9.1
  Lizard 161, 309–12, Fig. 14.2
  regions *Fig. 2.1*
  rivers 364
  roads etc. 248, 259–62
  trees 209–13, Fig. 10.1, 230, 237

woods 79–84, Figs 5.5, 5.6
wood-pasture 120–1, 130
Anglo-Saxon Chronicle 23, 49, 130, 313
Anglo-Saxon language 8, 9, 12, 36, 63, 185, 305, 333, 352–3, 364
  hedges in 12, 123, 175–6, 185–6
  woods in 79, 97, 102
Anglo-Saxons xiv, xvi
annuals 53, 286
anthills 342
Anthriscus see *cow-parsley*
Antiparos 47
antlers 39, 316, 370
aphids 43
Appalachians 120
apple *Malus domestica* 60, 205, 210–2 and see *crab*
Applecross (Ross & Crom.) 305
Apsley Guise Bd 81
Arbutus see *strawberry-tree*
archaeology, importance of 6–7, 249, 338, 375
Ardchattan (Argyll) 314
Arden Wa 88
Argyll 51
armies 251, 255
arms race 91
Arnold M. 226
Arrhenatherum see *oat-grass*
Artemisia see *mugwort*
Arum see *lords-and-ladies*
ash *Fraxinus excelsior* 29, 63, 65, 71, 73, 86, 140–1, 144, 151
  hedgerow 181–2, 197, 200–3
  non-woodland 5, 205, 209–13, 216–8, 221–6, 229–30
  stools 102, Plates IV, V
  woodland 67, 69, 104–6, 111, 115
Ashdown Forest Sx 289, 294, 302
ashes 109, 295
Ashmore Do 167, 352
Ashwell Ht 60, 209
Asia 242–3
aspen *Populus tremula* 65, 68, 86–7, 105, 140–1, 207–12, 219, 322
assart: private farmland formed out of common-land. 291, 315
Asser 84
Aston pn 209
Aston-by-Clun Sh 207
Aston M. 80
Astragalus see *milk-vetch*
Atherden M. 306, 341
Attingham Park Sh 145
auk, great 38
aurochs 33, 38
Australia 48, 53
Austria 26, 164, 174, 181, 210, 242
autumn crocus *Colchicum autumnale* 342
Aveley Ex 218
avens, water- *Geum rivale* 63
avenues 29, 56, 67, 151, 241, Plate XIX

Aversley Wood (Sawtry Hu) 369
Avon Wi 173
Avon Gorge (Bristol) 141, Fig. 6.10
Ayr 267

Babes-in-the-Wood 79
Babington C.C. 25, 328
badger 249, 363
Badwell Ash Sf 218, 220, 223
Baker H. 329
Balearic Islands 47
Balgownie (Aberdeen) 267
Ballota see *black horehound*
Balsham Ca 85, 363
Baltic 88
Banham Nf 296
Bar Hill (Dunbarton) 184
barberry *Berberis vulgaris* 42–3
Bardwell Sf 57, 218, 220
Barham Kt 33
Barham Sf 218
bark 92, 109–11, 217
bark-beetles 240 and see *elm*
Barking Ex 125, 389
Barking Sf 85, 168, 218, 337, 343, 363
Barnack Pe 259, 341, 369
Barnet pn 84
barns 4, 87, 238, 263
Barnsdale YW 293
Barnstaple Dv 267
Barnwell (Cambridge) 269–70
baronies *19*
barrels 115–6
Barrington D. 54–5
barrows vii, 10, 25, 100, 159, 251, 299, 331, 374, 384
  on moorland 307, 309–10, 325
  soils under 283, 286
Barton Broad Nf 359, Plate XXIII
Basildon Ex 161, 218
bast see *lime*
bastard-toadflax *Thesium humifusum* 342
Bastwick Nf 209
Bath asparagus *Ornithogalum pyrenaicum* 42
bats 151, 228, 344
battlements 362–3
Battlesbridge Ex 263
baulks *165*, **Fig. 8.6**, 167, 174, 176, 189
Baylham Sf 355
beaches 377
Beaconsfield Bu 82
bear 32–4
Beardsley T. 207
Beare wn 97
Beasfield Kt 185
Beaulieu Ha 89
beaver (animal) 34, 58
beaver (verb) 348, 353
Beccles Sf 333
Bede, Saint 8, 287
Bedford, Earl of 374, 390

Bedford Rivers 390, 392, Plate XXIV
Bedfordshire 58, 289, 334, 368
beech *Fagus sylvatica* 52, 56–7, 69, 71, 75, 112, 122, 283, 286
  non-woodland 209–12, 218–9
  woodland 105–6, 109–10, 150
  wood-pasture 140–1, 147, 151–2
bees 216
Beinn Eighe (Ross & Crom.) 315
Belgium 208, 242 and see *Flanders*
Belhus (Aveley Ex) 189
bell-pits 370, 372
bells 238, 257, 389
Benacre Sf Fig. 17.1
Bennett K.D. 239
Benson Ox 79
Bentley Grange YW 172
Berberis see *barberry*
Beresford M.W. 19, 168
Berkhamsted Ht 141
Berkshire 1–2, 10, 19, 20, 123, 212, 261, 297
  Claylands Figs 1.1, *2.1*, 175, 185
  field-systems 156, 176
Bernwood Forest Bu 39
Besselsleigh Br 364
Betula see *birch*
Beverley YE 34
Bible 129
Bickenhall So 202
Bideford Dv 267
bilberry *Vaccinium myrtillus* 321
birch *Betula pendula* and *pubescens* 8, 24, 96, 145, 150, 209, 322
  colonizer 67, 182, 302–4
  dwarf (*B. nana*) 350
  non-woodland 5, 210–2, 218, 226
  place-names 8, 209, 294
  wildwood **68–70**, Fig. 5.2, 286, 306, 382–3
  woodland 63, 69, 71, 87, 104–6, **111–2**, 291, 392
Birch W. de G. 10
Birchet wn 97, 291
bird-cherry *Prunus padus* 105
bird's-foot trefoil *Lotus corniculatus* 331
Birkenhead Ch 59
Birkland (Sherwood Forest Nt) 151, 226, 293, Plate XVIII
Birks H.H. 307
Birks H.J.B. 70
Birmingham 84
Bishop's Cleeve Wo 210
bittern 27, 37
Black Death 23, 46, 88, 98, 109, 170, 292, 338
blackgrass *Alopecurus myosuroides* 54
black horehound *Ballota nigra* 280
blackthorn *Prunus spinosa* 5, 181–2, 184, 200, 203, 211–2, 257, 325 and see *thorn*
Blean Kt 81, 84
Blenheim Ox 145
Blewbury Br 205
Blickling Nf 218

Index and Glossary

Index and Glossary